T0235650

Lecture Notes in Artificial Intelligence   12613

Subseries of Lecture Notes in Computer Science

Series Editors

Randy Goebel
University of Alberta, Edmonton, Canada
Yuzuru Tanaka
Hokkaido University, Sapporo, Japan
Wolfgang Wahlster
DFKI and Saarland University, Saarbrücken, Germany

Founding Editor

Jörg Siekmann
DFKI and Saarland University, Saarbrücken, Germany

Ana Paula Rocha · Luc Steels ·
Jaap van den Herik (Eds.)

Agents and Artificial Intelligence

12th International Conference, ICAART 2020
Valletta, Malta, February 22–24, 2020
Revised Selected Papers

 Springer

Editors
Ana Paula Rocha
LIACC, University of Porto
Porto, Portugal

Luc Steels
ICREA, Institute of Evolutionary Biology
Barcelona, Spain

Jaap van den Herik
Leiden University
Leiden, The Netherlands

ISSN 0302-9743   ISSN 1611-3349 (electronic)
Lecture Notes in Artificial Intelligence
ISBN 978-3-030-71157-3   ISBN 978-3-030-71158-0 (eBook)
https://doi.org/10.1007/978-3-030-71158-0

LNCS Sublibrary: SL7 – Artificial Intelligence

This Springer imprint is published by the registered company Springer Nature Switzerland AG
The registered company address is: Gewerbestrasse 11, 6330 Cham, Switzerland

Preface

The present book includes extended and revised versions of a set of selected papers from the 12th International Conference on Agents and Artificial Intelligence (ICAART 2020), held in Valletta, Malta, from 22 to 24 February, 2020.

ICAART 2020 received 276 paper submissions from 55 countries, of which some 8% were included in this book. The papers were selected by the event chairs and their selection is based on a number of criteria that include the classifications and comments provided by the program committee members, the session chairs' assessment and also the program chairs' global view of all papers included in the technical program. The authors of selected papers were then invited to submit a revised and extended version of their papers having at least 30% innovative material.

The purpose of the International Conference on Agents and Artificial Intelligence was to bring together researchers, engineers and practitioners interested in theory and applications in the areas of Agents and Artificial Intelligence. Two simultaneous related tracks were held, covering both applications and current research work. One track focused on Agents, Multi-Agent Systems and Software Platforms, Distributed Problem Solving and Distributed AI in general (of which 7 contributions are included). The other track focused mainly on Artificial Intelligence, Knowledge Representation, Planning, Learning, Scheduling, Perception, Reactive AI Systems, Evolutionary Computing and other topics related to Intelligent Systems and Computational Intelligence (of which 16 contributions are included).

The papers selected to be included in this book contribute to the understanding of relevant trends of current research on Agents and Artificial Intelligence.

We would like to thank all 71 authors for their contributions (23 in total). Moreover, we are grateful to the reviewers who have helped to ensure the quality of this publication.

February 2020

Ana Paula Rocha
Luc Steels
Jaap van den Herik

Organization

Conference Chair

Jaap van den Herik   Leiden University, The Netherlands

Program Co-chairs

Ana Paula Rocha   LIACC/FEUP, University of Porto, Portugal
Luc Steels   ICREA, Institute of Evolutionary Biology (UPF-CSIC) Barcelona, Spain

Program Committee

Thomas Ågotnes   University of Bergen, Norway
Varol Akman   Bilkent University, Turkey
Isabel Alexandre   Instituto Universitário de Lisboa (ISCTE-IUL) and Instituto de Telecomunicações, Portugal
Vicki Allan   Utah State University, USA
Klaus-Dieter Althoff   German Research Center for Artificial Intelligence/University of Hildesheim, Germany
Frédéric Amblard   IRIT - Université Toulouse 1 Capitole, France
Ilze Andersone   Riga Technical University, Latvia
Alla Anohina-Naumeca   Riga Technical University, Latvia
Jean-Michel Auberlet   IFSTTAR (French Institute of Science and Technology for Transport, Development and Networks), France
Reyhan Aydoğan   Özyeğin University, Turkey
Kerstin Bach   Norwegian University of Science and Technology (NTNU), Norway
Farshad Badie   Aalborg University, Denmark
Irene Barba Rodríguez   Universidad de Sevilla, Spain
Federico Barber   Universidad Politécnica de Valencia, Spain
Suzanne Barber   The University of Texas, USA
Francesco Barile   Free University of Bozen/Bolzano, Italy
Roman Barták   Charles University, Czech Republic
Teresa Basile   Università degli Studi di Bari, Italy
Montserrat Batet   Universitat Rovira i Virgili, Spain
Nabil Belacel   National Research Council of Canada, Canada
Salem Benferhat   CRIL, France
Carole Bernon   University of Toulouse III, France
Carlos Bobed   everis/NTT Data & University of Zaragoza, Spain
Marco Botta   Università degli Studi di Torino, Italy

Bruno Bouchard	LIARA Laboratory, Université du Québec à Chicoutimi, Canada
Lars Braubach	Universität Hamburg, Germany
Jörg Bremer	University of Oldenburg, Germany
Ramon Brena	Tecnológico de Monterrey, Mexico
Paolo Bresciani	Fondazione Bruno Kessler, Italy
Daniela Briola	Università degli Studi di Milano-Bicocca, Italy
Aleksander Byrski	AGH University of Science and Technology, Poland
Giacomo Cabri	Università di Modena e Reggio Emilia, Italy
Patrice Caire	Stanford University, USA
Silvia Calegari	Università degli Studi di Milano-Bicocca, Italy
Valérie Camps	IRIT - Université Paul Sabatier, France
Antonio Camurri	University of Genoa, Italy
Nicola Capodieci	Università di Modena e Reggio Emilia, Italy
Javier Carbó Rubiera	Universidad Carlos III de Madrid, Spain
Amilcar Cardoso	University of Coimbra, Portugal
John Cartlidge	University of Bristol, UK
Cristiano Castelfranchi	Institute of Cognitive Sciences and Technologies - National Research Council, Italy
Wen-Chung Chang	National Taipei University of Technology, Taiwan, Republic of China
Mu-Song Chen	Da-Yeh University, Taiwan, Republic of China
Davide Ciucci	Università degli Studi di Milano-Bicocca, Italy
Flávio Soares Corrêa da Silva	University of São Paulo, Brazil
Paulo Cortez	University of Minho, Portugal
Matteo Cristani	University of Verona, Italy
Fernando da Souza	Centro de Informática - Universidade Federal de Pernambuco, Brazil
Dipankar Das	Jadavpur University, India
Riccardo De Benedictis	CNR - Italian National Research Council, Italy
Daniele De Martini	University of Oxford, UK
Alessandra De Paola	University of Palermo, Italy
Enrico Denti	Alma Mater Studiorum - Università di Bologna, Italy
Bruno Di Stefano	Nuptek Systems Ltd., Canada
Dragan Doder	Utrecht University, The Netherlands
Michel Dojat	Université Grenoble Alpes, France
Francisco Domínguez Mayo	University of Seville, Spain
Ruggero Donida Labati	Università degli Studi di Milano, Italy
Kurt Driessens	Maastricht University, The Netherlands
Thomas Eiter	Technische Universität Wien, Austria
Fabrício Enembreck	Pontifical Catholic University of Paraná, Brazil
Fabrizio Falchi	ISTI-CNR, Italy
Petros Faloutsos	York University, Canada
Christophe Feltus	Luxembourg Institute of Science and Technology, Luxembourg

Stefano Ferilli	University of Bari, Italy
Edilson Ferneda	Catholic University of Brasília, Brazil
Alexander Ferrein	MASCOR Institute, FH Aachen University of Applied Sciences, Germany
Vladimir Filipović	University of Belgrade, Serbia
Klaus Fischer	German Research Center for Artificial Intelligence DFKI GmbH, Germany
Roberto Flores	Christopher Newport University, USA
Agostino Forestiero	ICAR-CNR, Italy
Claude Frasson	University of Montreal, Canada
Katsuhide Fujita	Tokyo University of Agriculture and Technology, Japan
Julián García García	Web Engineering and Early Testing (IWT2, Ingeniería Web y Testing Temprano), Spain
Leonardo Garrido	Tecnológico de Monterrey, Campus Monterrey, Mexico
Alfredo Garro	Università della Calabria, Italy
Serge Gaspers	The University of New South Wales, Australia
Benoit Gaudou	University Toulouse 1 Capitole, France
Andrey Gavrilov	Novosibirsk State Technical University, Russian Federation
Franck Gechter	University of Technology of Belfort-Montbéliard, France
Herman Gomes	Universidade Federal de Campina Grande, Brazil
Francisco Gómez Vela	Pablo de Olavide University, Spain
David Green	Monash University, Australia
Emmanuelle Grislin-Le Strugeon	LAMIH-UMR CNRS 8201, France
Luciano H. Tamargo	Institute for Computer Science and Engineering, Universidad Nacional del Sur, Argentina
James Harland	RMIT University, Australia
Hisashi Hayashi	Advanced Institute of Industrial Technology, Japan
Emma Hayes	University of the Pacific, USA
Samedi Heng	Université de Liège, Belgium
Pedro Henriques	University of Minho, Portugal
Vincent Hilaire	UTBM, France
Hanno Hildmann	TNO, The Netherlands
Koen Hindriks	Vrije Universiteit Amsterdam, The Netherlands
Rolf Hoffmann	Darmstadt University of Technology, Germany
Sviatlana Höhn	University of Luxembourg, Luxembourg
Władysław Homenda	Warsaw University of Technology, Poland
Wei-Chiang Hong	Oriental Institute of Technology, Taiwan, Republic of China
Mark Hoogendoorn	Vrije Universiteit Amsterdam, The Netherlands
Aleš Horák	Masaryk University, Czech Republic
Marc-Philippe Huget	Université Savoie Mont Blanc, France

Dieter Hutter	German Research Centre for Artificial Intelligence, Germany
Hiroyuki Iida	JAIST, Japan
Luis Iribarne	University of Almería, Spain
Agnieszka Jastrzębska	Warsaw University of Technology, Poland
Michael Jenkin	York University, Canada
Luis Jiménez Linares	University of Castilla-La Mancha, Spain
Yasushi Kambayashi	Nippon Institute of Technology, Japan
Norihiro Kamide	Teikyo University, Japan
Geylani Kardaş	Ege University International Computer Institute, Turkey
Petros Kefalas	CITY College, International Faculty of the University of Sheffield, Greece
Gabriele Kern-Isberner	TU Dortmund, Germany
Matthias Klusch	German Research Center for Artificial Intelligence (DFKI) GmbH, Germany
Mare Koit	University of Tartu, Estonia
Martin Kollingbaum	University of Aberdeen, UK
Pavel Král	University of West Bohemia, Czech Republic
Uirá Kulesza	Federal University of Rio Grande do Norte (UFRN), Brazil
Setsuya Kurahashi	University of Tsukuba, Japan
Cat Kutay	University of Technology Sydney, Australia
Daniel Ladley	University of Leicester, UK
Divesh Lala	Kyoto University, Japan
Ramoni Lasisi	Virginia Military Institute, USA
Nuno Lau	Universidade de Aveiro, Portugal
Egons Lavendelis	Riga Technical University, Latvia
Marc Le Goc	Polytech Marseille, France
Agapito Ledezma	Carlos III University of Madrid, Spain
Ladislav Lenc	University of West Bohemia, Czech Republic
Letizia Leonardi	Università di Modena e Reggio Emilia, Italy
Renato Levy	Intelligent Automation, Inc., USA
Churn-Jung Liau	Academia Sinica, Taiwan, Republic of China
Jianyi Lin	Khalifa University, UAE
Francesca Lisi	Università degli Studi di Bari "Aldo Moro", Italy
Jonah Lissner	Technion - Israel Institute of Technology, Israel
Stéphane Loiseau	LERIA, University of Angers, France
António Lopes	ISCTE-Instituto Universitário de Lisboa, Portugal
Noel Lopes	IPG, Portugal
Henrique Lopes Cardoso	Universidade do Porto, Portugal
Daniela Lopéz de Luise	CIIS Lab, Argentina
Audronė Lupeikienė	VU Institute of Data Science and Digital Technologies, Lithuania
Luís Macedo	University of Coimbra, Portugal
Lorenzo Magnani	University of Pavia, Italy

Nadia Magnenat Thalmann	NTU, Singapore and MIRALab, University of Geneva, Switzerland
Letizia Marchegiani	Aalborg University, Denmark
Jerusa Marchi	Universidade Federal de Santa Catarina, Brazil
Mourad Mars	Umm Al-Qura University, Saudi Arabia
Philippe Mathieu	University of Lille, France
Eric Matson	Purdue University, USA
Toshihiro Matsui	Nagoya Institute of Technology, Japan
Fiona McNeill	Heriot-Watt University, UK
Paola Mello	Università di Bologna, Italy
Marjan Mernik	University of Maribor, Slovenia
Tamás Mészáros	Budapest University of Technology and Economics, Hungary
Ambra Molesini	Alma Mater Studiorum - Università di Bologna, Italy
Raúl Monroy	Tecnológico de Monterrey, Mexico
Manuela Montangero	Università di Modena e Reggio Emilia, Italy
Valentin Montmirail	Schneider Electric, France
Monica Mordonini	University of Parma, Italy
José Moreira	Universidade de Aveiro, Portugal
Maxime Morge	Université de Lille, France
Andrea Morichetta	Unicam, Italy
Gildas Morvan	Université d'Artois, France
Bernard Moulin	Université Laval, Canada
Ahmed Moustafa	Nagoya Institute of Technology, Japan
Muhammad Marwan Muhammad Fuad	Coventry University, UK
Santosh Kumar Nanda	Tonkabi India Pvt. Ltd., India
Luis Nardin	National College of Ireland, Ireland
Juan Carlos Nieves	Umeå Universitet, Sweden
Agris Nikitenko	Riga Technical University, Latvia
Antoine Nongaillard	University of Lille, France
Houssem Eddine Nouri	SOIE-COSMOS, École Nationale des Sciences de l'Informatique, Université de la Manouba, Tunisia
Luis Nunes	Instituto Universitário de Lisboa (ISCTE-IUL) and Instituto de Telecomunicações (IT), Portugal
Michel Occello	Université Grenoble Alpes, France
Akihiko Ohsuga	The University of Electro-Communications (UEC), Japan
Haldur Õim	University of Tartu, Estonia
Andrei Olaru	Politehnica University of Bucharest, Romania
Joanna Isabelle Olszewska	University of the West of Scotland, UK
Stanisław Osowski	Warsaw University of Technology, Poland
Takanobu Otsuka	Nagoya Institute of Technology, Japan
Hong-Seok Park	University of Ulsan, Korea, Republic of
Andrew Parkes	University of Nottingham, UK
Krzysztof Patan	University of Zielona Góra, Poland

Manuel G. Penedo	Investigation Center CITIC, University of A Coruña, Spain
Loris Penserini	TTP Technology, Italy
Danilo Pianini	Università di Bologna, Italy
Gauthier Picard	ONERA, France
Sébastien Picault	INRAE, France
Marcin Pietroń	AGH University of Science and Technology, Poland
Anitha Pillai	Hindustan Institute of Technology and Science, India
Agostino Poggi	University of Parma, Italy
Enrico Pontelli	New Mexico State University, USA
Filipe Portela	Centro ALGORITMI, University of Minho, Portugal
Roberto Posenato	Università degli Studi di Verona, Italy
David Pynadath	University of Southern California, USA
Riccardo Rasconi	National Research Council of Italy, Italy
Luís Reis	University of Porto, Portugal
Lluís Ribas-Xirgo	Universitat Autònoma de Barcelona, Spain
Patrizia Ribino	ICAR- CNR, Italy
Alessandro Ricci	Alma Mater Studiorum - Università di Bologna, Italy
Fátima Rodrigues	Instituto Superior de Engenharia do Porto (ISEP/IPP), Portugal
Daniel Rodríguez	University of Alcalá, Spain
Juha Röning	University of Oulu, Finland
Álvaro Rubio-Largo	University of Extremadura, Spain
Rubén Ruiz	Universidad Politécnica de Valencia, Spain
Luca Sabatucci	ICAR-CNR, Italy
Fariba Sadri	Imperial College London, UK
Lorenza Saitta	Università degli Studi del Piemonte Orientale "Amedeo Avogadro", Italy
Francesco Santini	Università di Perugia, Italy
Fabio Sartori	University of Milano-Bicocca, Italy
Jurek Sasiadek	Carleton University, Canada
Domenico Fabio Savo	Università degli Studi di Bergamo, Italy
Vitaly Schetinin	University of Bedfordshire, UK
Stefan Schiffer	RWTH Aachen University, Germany
Christoph Schommer	University of Luxembourg, Luxembourg
Michael Schumacher	University of Applied Sciences and Arts of Western Switzerland (HES-SO), Switzerland
Frank Schweitzer	ETH Zurich, Switzerland
Valeria Seidita	University of Palermo, Italy
Emilio Serrano	Universidad Politécnica de Madrid, Spain
Shital Shah	Microsoft Research, USA
Denis Shikhalev	The State Fire Academy of EMERCOM of Russia, Russian Federation
Jaime Sichman	University of São Paulo, Brazil
Marius Silaghi	Florida Institute of Technology, USA
Giovanni Sileno	University of Amsterdam, The Netherlands

Additional Reviewers

Andrea Campagner	University of Milano-Bicocca, Italy
Meggy Hayotte	Université Côte d'Azur, France
Alessio Langiu	CNR-ICAR, Italy
Apurba Paul	Jadavpur University, India
Pascal Reuss	University of Hildesheim, Germany
Dipanjan Saha	Techno India, India
Jakob Schoenborn	University of Hildesheim and German Research Center for Artificial Intelligence, Germany
Yuichi Sei	University of Electro-Communications, Japan
Joaquin Taverner	Universitat Politècnica de València, Spain

Invited Speakers

Carles Sierra	IIIA-CSIC, Spain
Marie-Christine Rousset	Université Grenoble Alpes and Institut Universitaire de France, France
Bart Selman	Cornell University, USA
Rineke Verbrugge	Bernoulli Institute, University of Groningen, The Netherlands

Contents

Agents

Herd Behavior Is Sufficient to Reproduce Human Evacuation Decisions During the Great East Japan Earthquake

Akira Tsurushima[✉][iD]

SECOM CO., LTD., Intelligent Systems Laboratory, Tokyo, Japan
a-tsurushima@secom.co.jp

Abstract. We previously developed an evacuation decision model to represent the herd behaviors of evacuees during a disaster evacuation and employed it to analyze symmetry breaking in evacuation exit choice, a phenomenon in which people tend to gather at one specific exit during an evacuation. This model had yet to be tested against real disaster data owing to a difficulty in acquiring such data. An analysis of video clips captured during the Great East Japan Earthquake revealed unusual evacuation behaviors of people in a meeting room, namely, the evacuation decision between fleeing and drop, cover, and hold-on actions depending on the distance from the exit. Such behaviors have yet to be reported in the literature. We conducted simulations and reproduced these evacuation behaviors using an evacuation decision model and determined that simple herd behaviors among evacuees are sufficient to reproduce these unusual evacuation behaviors. We also conducted logistic-regression, graph-centrality, and sensitivity analyses to examine the nature of these simulation results.

Keywords: Evacuation behavior · Herd behavior · Decision-making · Video analysis · Response threshold model

1 Introduction

Cognitive biases, i.e., mental inclinations used to derive irrational decisions or erroneous behaviors, during disaster evacuation situations have received the attention of numerous researchers and experts owing to their serious effect on the evacuation results, including a loss of life. Herd behavior is one of the most typical cognitive biases of this type [7, 10]. During herd behavior, people make decisions not by themselves but based on the decisions of other people, and this behavior sometimes incurs unusual phenomena, particularly during crowd evacuations. The symmetry breaking in exit choice has become a well-studied example of unusual phenomena caused by herd behavior during crowd evacuations [1, 27].

When a group of people attempt to evacuate an environment with multiple exits, the exits are often used unevenly, and people tend to gather at one specific exit. This phenomenon of symmetry breaking in exit choice is considered irrational because the expected evacuation time will be the shortest, meaning a safe evacuation will be achieved if these exits are used evenly. We developed and proposed an evacuation decision model [25] to represent human herd behaviors during the evacuation processes,

© Springer Nature Switzerland AG 2021
A. P. Rocha et al. (Eds.): ICAART 2020, LNAI 12613, pp. 3–25, 2021.
https://doi.org/10.1007/978-3-030-71158-0_1

and we employed it to analyze the symmetry breaking in evacuation exit choices. The evacuation decision model revealed that simple herd behaviors are sufficient to reproduce a symmetry breaking in exit choice, and that no intentional or rational decisions are required for this phenomenon to emerge [27].

Research on human behaviors during a disaster evacuation has been primarily conducted through interviews [9, 19], laboratory experiments using human subjects [11,22], and laboratory experiments using nonhuman animals [1,21]. However, these techniques are limited for the following reasons:

1. interviews can only be conducted with survivors,
2. it is difficult to reproduce the mental pressure of real evacuations in laboratory experiments, and
3. animal behaviors are not necessarily identical to human behaviors.

None of the above aspects provide assurance that the data obtained through these methods refer to real human behaviors during a disaster situation.

Like many other phenomena regarding disaster evacuations, the symmetry breaking in exit choice has been studied through these methods because no numerical data are available owing to the difficulty of gathering such data during a real situation. Additionally, data for disaster evacuations are only available for certain global cases such as the evacuation time and the number of evacuees of specific groups. Thus, we reproduced the symmetry breaking phenomenon in a qualitative sense, although these results have yet to be validated against objective data owing to the absence of real data.

In constructive approaches for human behaviors during disaster evacuations, including our studies, model validation is crucial but difficult owing to the limited amount of objective data. Hence, data for human evacuations, which are both objective and numeric, are extremely valuable in this sense. With an increase in the numbers of surveillance cameras and smartphones, video images of human behavior during disasters have been recorded. These videos have recently been analyzed, and human evacuation behaviors have been investigated [8, 12, 15, 30]. However, problems such as accessibility and poor video quality have limited the success of these approaches [23].

A video clip captured in a meeting room in Sendai during the Great East Japan Earthquake of March 11, 2011 (Fig. 1), is exceptionally valuable for the following reasons:

– the earthquake was captured in one continuous scene from beginning to end,
– the initial positions of the people in the room when the shaking began were clearly recorded, and
– the professionalism of the camera crew rendered it relatively easy to examine the behavior of every individual during the earthquake.

By studying this video, real human behaviors during an earthquake can be analyzed.

In a previous study, we analyzed the behavior of individuals in this video and found unusual human evacuation behaviors that had yet to be reported in the literature. We also attempted to reproduce this real human evacuation behavior using the evacuation decision model for validation purposes and revealed that a simple herd behavior is sufficient to reproduce such behavior [28].

This paper extends our previous research in two ways. First, we conducted 500 simulations rather than 150 simulations to obtain more accurate results, and the results in Sect. 5.3 are replaced by new data that had been acquired through these simulations. Second, we conducted two more analyses to examine the nature of the simulation model and its results. A graph centrality analysis is conducted to investigate the influence dynamics among agents during the evacuation processes. The influence between two decisions of the agents produces a complex network, and the relations of the agents within the network are analyzed through graph centralities. Moreover, the sensitivities of the parameters of the evacuation decision model are analyzed. Because the population density and defined vicinity of an agent are two influential factors affecting herd behaviors, we conducted a sensitivity analysis for agent population densities and a variety of agent vicinities. These analyses are given in Sects. 6.2 and 6.3, respectively.

2   Related Studies

Since it was difficult to obtain objective data, research on human behaviors during earthquake evacuations have been conducted primarily through interviews, case studies using surveys, or experiments using animals or humans. The subjects of case studies include the 2004 Mid-Niigata prefecture earthquake [17], 2010 Chile earthquake [9], and Great East Japan Earthquake [20]. Herein, we investigated the behavioral and psychological reconstruction processes for the victims [17], distributions of departure times of tsunami evacuations [19], solidarity behaviors, and pre-/post- earthquake evacuation behaviors [9, 20]. Several studies have been conducted on human and animal evacuation experiments such as [3, 13, 14, 18]. However, most of the experimental studies on such evacuations did not specify the types of disasters owing to the complexity of the environment setting for each disaster, but instead focused on general evacuation behaviors.

In recent years, with the spread of security cameras and smart devices, several video images of evacuations have been accumulated. By analyzing this footage, a new approach has emerged to investigate real-life human evacuation behaviors. This approach led to the discovery of particular evacuation behaviors such as when people prefer a safer place than a place near the door during high intensity tremors, to maintain social attachment during evacuation, to follow the actions of the majority, and to stay in safer and familiar places after an earthquake [8]. The findings of the evacuation behaviors varied among countries [2, 8]. The differences in behaviors between evacuation drills and real-life evacuations [12, 30], and estimations of walking speed during earthquake evacuations [15], were also examined.

In particular, a study of student evacuation behavior analysis in a video by Gu et al. (2016) found that reaction times were linear during evacuation drills but nonlinear in actual evacuation situations. Furthermore, they found that the cumulative curve of the number of evacuees was linear in evacuation drills and nonlinear in actual situations [12].

Although video databases that accumulate such evacuation videos have been created and are being used by researchers [2], many videos only partially record the situation, and few of them can be used for quantitative analysis.

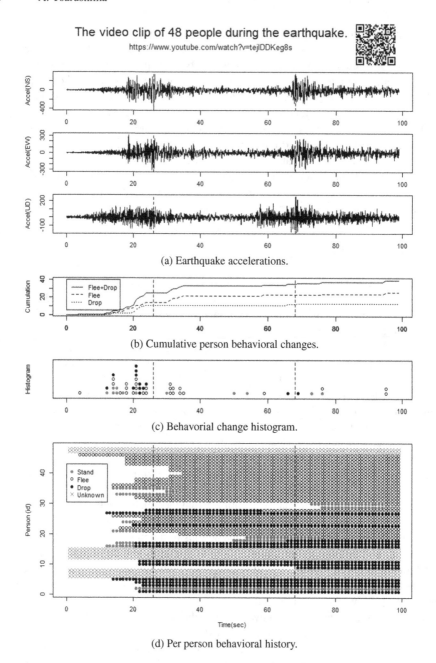

(a) Earthquake accelerations.

(b) Cumulative person behavioral changes.

(c) Behavorial change histogram.

(d) Per person behavioral history.

Fig. 1. Temporal behavioral changes in 99 s, of 48 people in the video [28].

Most studies have focused on fleeing behaviors during evacuations, and only a few studies have mentioned drop, cover, and hold-on actions [2,8]. In this study, by analyzing videos captured during the Great East Japan Earthquake, we investigated the decisions of the evacuees between performing a drop, cover, and hold-on action or fleeing the room.

3   Video Analysis

At 14:46 on March 11, 2011, the Great East Japan Earthquake with a magnitude of 9.0 occurred off the coast of Japan. The video footage in Fig. 1 was taken during an earthquake in a hotel conference room in Miyagino-ku, Sendai City, Miyagi Prefecture. This video records the evacuation behaviors of 48 people during the earthquake. We created quantitative data on the evacuation behaviors of the 48 people by closely tracking each of these behaviors visually. However, the last 40 s were excluded from the analysis owing to a power outage in the video. The following three types of evacuation behavior are recorded in the video:

1. standing and remaining at the current position (Stand),
2. exiting and fleeing from the room (Flee), and
3. hiding under the table, also known as "drop, cover, and hold-on" (Drop)

This data consists of the times when Stand, Flee, and Drop actions were taken for each of the 48 people, and their indoor positions at the time of the earthquake. These data are organized in Fig. 1b–d.

Figure 2 depicts the initial positions of all 48 people when the earthquake started. The room is square-shaped, with only one exit shown in the lower right corner. Initially, all 48 people were sitting at tables in a square, with everyone facing inward.

Figure 1d shows the temporal behavioral changes for each of the 48 people for 99 s after the shaking started. In the chart, the gray, white, and black circles indicate standing, fleeing, and dropping behaviors, respectively, whereas × indicates a behavior that is unidentifiable from the video. For example, the first person to take action (Flee) is No. 46, which shows that it was 4 s after the start of the earthquake. The last person to take action (Stand) was No. 29, indicating that he had been sitting in a chair for 75 s after the start of the earthquake. Figure 1c depicts the number of times that people changed their behaviors. For example, a person changing his/her behavior from sitting to fleeing is indicated by a white circle at the time the behavior changed. Figure 1b shows a cumulative curve of the number of behavioral changes in people. Figure 1c. The dotted, dashed, and solid lines indicate dropping, fleeing, and the sum of both behaviors, respectively. Figure 1a depicts the acceleration generated by the earthquake in the North-South, East-West, and up-down directions[1]. Two vertical dashed lines at 28 and 68 s indicate the two peaks of shaking intensity. As shown in Fig. 1b, in the actual earthquake evacuation, the cumulative curve of the number of people taking part in evacuation behaviors is a convex curve. This is consistent with the results of Gu et al. (2016), in which the cumulative curve in evacuation drills is linear and the cumulative curve in actual evacuations is a convex curve [12].

---

[1] https://www.data.jma.go.jp/svd/eqev/data/kyoshin/jishin/110311_tohokuchiho-taiheiyouoki/index.html
(Observation Point: Sendai-shi, Miyagino-ku, Gorin).

Fig. 2. Initial location of people in video [28].

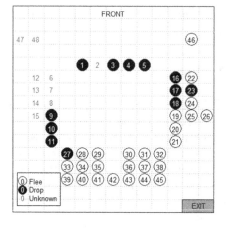

Fig. 3. Selection of drop and flee at end of video [28].

Figure 3 shows the final actions taken by 48 people 99 s after the start of the earthquake at their respective initial positions. A white circle with a black number denotes an evacuee who selected a fleeing behavior, and a black circle with a white number denotes an evacuee who selected a dropping behavior. A gray number is an evacuee whose behavior is unknown. In summary, 26 evacuees fled, and 12 evacuees dropped.

Figure 3 illustrates that most people close to the exit decided to flee, whereas those farther from the exit decided to drop, which is an intriguing behavior that had not been previously reported. The boundary between fleeing and dropping crosses the room diagonally, as if people within a certain distance from the exit decided to flee and the others decided to drop, leading to the following hypothesis.

Hypothesis 1. The evacuation decision between fleeing or dropping is based on the distance from the exit.

However, a different hypothesis can be considered for this phenomenon.

Hypothesis 2. The herd behavior among people causes a diagonal spatial pattern even if all individuals randomly choose to flee or drop.

This means that people are consciously making only random choices, but herd behaviors that work between people automatically produce diagonal spatial patterns. Herd behavior is a behavior possessed by many animals including humans and is frequently observed in evacuation situations. Therefore, it is worthwhile to examine this hypothesis.

It is clear that Hypothesis 1 can generate a diagonal spatial pattern. However, this hypothesis requires higher-level cognitive processes such as rules, scenarios, or procedures to estimate the distance to the exit and to judge whether this distance is above a certain threshold. By contrast, Hypothesis 2 requires only lower-level cognitive processes, i.e., herd behaviors, which are typical in many organisms.

The purpose of this study is to show that Hypothesis 2 holds by multiagent simulation using agents that incorporate only random selection and herd behavior. Since actions other than the herd behaviors implemented in the agents are merely random choices, this simulation model implies that simple herd behavior is a sufficient condition for generating the diagonal spatial patterns from which Flee and Drop decisions emerge.

4   Evacuation Decision Model

The evacuation decision model is inspired by the response threshold model in biology [4,5], which represents the division of labor in eusocial organisms, and represents human herd behavior during evacuation [24,26]. The evacuation decision model has been used to analyze cognitive aggregation during evacuation [24] and symmetry breaking in exit choice [26].

In the evacuation decision model, the environment has an objective risk value r, which refers to the severity of the disaster threat. Agent i in the environment has two mental states: $X_i = 0$ and $X_i = 1$. When $X_i = 1$, the agent decides its own action according to its own intention, but when $X_i = 0$, the agent decides its own action depending on the actions of surrounding agents. The former state is called the leader, and the latter state is called the follower. During evacuation, the value of X_i always changes with a certain probability. As a result, agents sometimes act as leaders and sometimes as followers.

The agent has a parameter θ_i, called a response threshold, that determines the degree to which the agent participates in the evacuation. The values of θ_i vary by agent. The probability that an agent will become a leader per unit time is [28]

$$P(X_i = 0 \rightarrow X_i = 1) = \frac{\hat{s}_i^{\,2}}{\hat{s}_i^{\,2} + \theta_i^2}, \tag{1}$$

where $\hat{s}_i$ is the local estimation in the stimulus of the environment associated with agent i. This probability depends only on the response threshold θ_i and the environmental stimulus $\hat{s}_i$; however, no individual agent can sense the true value of the environmental stimulus s_i. The value used in the calculation is $\hat{s}_i$, a local estimate of the true environmental stimulus.

The probability that an agent will become a follower per unit time is [28]

$$P(X_i = 1 \rightarrow X_i = 0) = \epsilon, \tag{2}$$

where ϵ is a fixed probability common to all agents. This value is given in the simulation parameters. The estimation of the stimulus of agent i per unit time is given by the following difference equation: [28]

$$s_i(t+1) = max\{s_i(t) + \hat{\delta} - \alpha(1 - R)F, \ 0 \ \}, \tag{3}$$

where $\hat{\delta}$ is an increase in the stimulus per unit time [28]

$$\hat{\delta} = \begin{cases} \delta & \text{if } r > 0 \\ 0 & \text{otherwise,} \end{cases} \tag{4}$$

and α is a scale factor of the stimulus. Additionally, R is the risk perception function, which is a function of the objective risk r [28]:

$$R(r) = \frac{1}{1 + exp(-g(r - \mu_i))},$$ (5)

where g is the activation gain determining the shape of the sigmoid function. Additionally, μ_i is the risk perception of agent i, which represents an individual's sensitivity to risk. The evacuation progress function, i.e., the local estimation of the evacuation progress of agent i, is [28]

$$F(n) = \begin{cases} 1 - n/N_{max} & n < N_{max} \\ 0 & \text{otherwise,} \end{cases}$$ (6)

where N is the number of agents in the vicinity that have not yet taken an evacuation action, and N_{max} is the maximum number of agents in the vicinity. In other words, the agents judge that the overall evacuation has not yet progressed if the ratio of agents in the vicinity who have not taken evacuation action is large, or that progress has been made if the ratio is small.

5 Earthquake Evacuation Simulation

The purpose of this study is to show that Hypothesis 2 in Sect. 3 can reproduce the convex curve of the cumulative number of evacuees in Fig. 1b and the diagonal spatial pattern in Fig. 3 using multiagent simulations. This section describes the details of this simulation. This simulation setting represents a situation similar to the video in Fig. 1, but it is not exactly the same. The simulation model was implemented using NetLogo 6.0.2 [29].

5.1 Configuration

A square room of 40×40 units with the lower right as the origin is the environment for this simulation. This room has one exit at the bottom right. Initially, 500 agents $A = \{a_1, a_2, \ldots, a_{500}\}$ are randomly distributed in the region from 3 to 38 units for the X and Y coordinates. Assuming a simulation time of $t = 1, \ldots, T$, an agent $a_i \in A$ has coordinates $x_i(t), y_i(t) \in \mathbb{R}$, a local estimation of stimulus $s_i(t) \in \mathbb{R}$, mental state $X_i(t) \in \{1, 0\}$, and an action $\pi_i(t) \in \{undecided, flee, drop\}$, where $undecided$ indicates that the agent has not yet determined an action, $flee$ indicates that the agent has decided to flee, and $drop$ indicates that the agent has decided to drop. In this simulation, both Flee and Drop are evacuation behaviors; therefore, the value of n in Eq. 6 is $n = |\{a_j \ in V_i \mid \pi_j(t) = undecided\}|$. Furthermore, an agent has two parameters: response threshold θ_i and risk sensitivity μ_i. Let $x_i(1), y_i(1) \sim U(3, 38)$, $s_i(1) = 0$, $X_i(1) = 0$, $\pi_i(1) = undecided$, $\theta_i \sim U(0, 100)$, and $\mu_i \sim U(0, 100)$ be the initial values of the simulation, with the simulation terminated at $T = 270$.

The vicinity of a_i is defined as $V_i = \{a_j \in A \mid \nu(a_j, a_i)\}$, where $\nu : A^2 \to \{true, false\}$, and ν refers to a range of five units $120°$ toward the direction of motion of a_i.

Algorithm 1. Leader's action (Random Selection) [28].

---

if $\pi_i(t) = undecided$ **then**
    $\tau \sim U(0,1)$
    if $\tau \leq 0.5$ **then**
        $\pi_i(t) \Leftarrow drop$
    else
        $\pi_i(t) \Leftarrow flee$
    end if
end if
if $\pi_i(t) = flee$ **then**
    Solve Problem 1 and determine $\Delta x, \Delta y$
    $x_i(t) \Leftarrow x_i(t) + \Delta x; \quad y_i(t) \Leftarrow y_i(t) + \Delta y$
end if

Algorithm 2. Follower's action (Herd Behavior) [28].

$n_d \Leftarrow |\{a_j \in V_i \mid \pi_j(t) = drop\}|$
$n_e \Leftarrow |\{a_j \in V_i \mid \pi_j(t) = flee\}|$
$n_u \Leftarrow |\{a_j \in V_i \mid \pi_j(t) = undecided\}|$
if $n_d > n_e$ **and** $n_d > n_u$ **then**
    $\pi_i(t) \Leftarrow drop$
else if $n_e > n_d$ **and** $n_e > n_u$ **then**
    $\pi_i(t) \Leftarrow flee$
end if
if $\pi_i(t) = flee$ **then**
    Solve Problem 1 and determine $\Delta x, \Delta y$
    $x_i(t) \Leftarrow x_i(t) + \Delta x; \quad y_i(t) \Leftarrow y_i(t) + \Delta y$
end if

At each time step, an agent with $\pi_i(t) = flee$ moves toward the exit (G_x, G_y) by $\Delta x, \Delta y$, as determined by solving Problem 1 [28].

Problem 1

$$min \ (x_i(t) + \Delta x - G_x)^2 + (y_i(t) + \Delta y - G_y)^2 \tag{7}$$
$$s.t. \qquad\qquad \Delta x^2 + \Delta y^2 = 1 \tag{8}$$

An agent with $\pi_i(t) \neq flee$ remains at the same position, i.e., $\Delta x = 0$ and $\Delta y = 0$.

The procedure for the entire simulation is shown in Algorithm 3. Agent a_i executes Algorithm 1 when $X_i = 1$ and Algorithm 2 when $X_i = 0$. Agents decide their behaviors based on their own intentions only when Algorithm 1 is executed; this is a random selection.

The room has an objective risk that starts at $r(1) = 0$ and increases by 1 for each time step up to the maximum value of $r(t) = 100$. The local estimation of the stimulus of a_i starts at $s_i(1) = 0$ and is incremented by δ at each time step as $F \approx 0$ during the initial stages of the simulation. Thus, $P(X_i = 0 \to X_i = 1)$ gradually increases depending on θ_i, resulting in the emergence of leader agents. Subsequently, followers appear, and herding spreads among the agents.

Finally, the overall simulation procedure is shown in Algorithm 3. The following parameters were used: $\alpha = 1.2$, $\delta = 0.5$, $\epsilon = 0.2$, $g = 1.0$, and $N_{max} = 10$.

Algorithm 3. Simulation.

Initialization
for $t = 1$ to T **do**
  $r \Leftarrow min\{r + 1, \ 100\}$
  for all $a_i \in A$ **do**
    Calculate R {Equation 5}
    Calculate F {Equation 6}
    Calculate s_i {Equation 3}
    $\tau \sim U(0, 1)$
    if $X_i = 1 \wedge \tau < P(X_i = 1 \rightarrow X_i = 0)$ **then**
      $X_i \Leftarrow 0$
      Execute Algorithm 2 {Follower's action (Herd Behavior)}
    else if $X_i = 0 \wedge \tau < P(X_i = 0 \rightarrow X_i = 1)$ **then**
      $X_i \Leftarrow 1$
      Execute Algorithm 1 {Leader's action (Random Selection)}
    end if
    if $(x_i(t) - G_x)^2 + (y_i(t) - G_y)^2 < 1$ **then**
      $A \Leftarrow A \setminus a_i$ {Remove a_i from the environment if the exit has been reached.}
    end if
  end for
end for

5.2   Result 1

In this section, the results of the simulation described in Sect. 5.1 are presented.

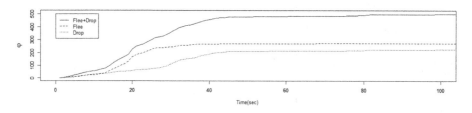

Fig. 4. Cumulative number of evacuees over simulation time [28].

Figure 4 shows the cumulative curves of the evacuees who conducted evacuation actions per simulation time. The solid line in the chart is obtained through the function $\varphi(t)$ [28]:

$$\varphi(t) = \varphi(t - 1) + \sum_{a_i \in A} \gamma_i(t), \qquad (9)$$

where [28]

$$\gamma_i(t) = \begin{cases} 1 & t = min\{z \mid \pi_i(z) \neq undecided\} \\ 0 & \text{otherwise}, \end{cases} \qquad (10)$$

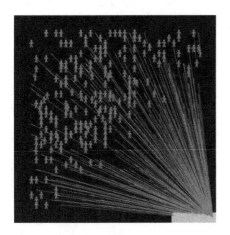

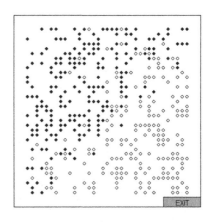

Fig. 5. Distribution of the remaining agents in the room at the end of the simulation. Straight lines towards the exit show the trajectories of fleeing agents.

Fig. 6. Initial locations and decisions between fleeing and dropping. Black circles refer to $\pi_i(T) = drop$, and white circles refer to $\pi_i(T) = flee$.

and $\varphi(0) = 0$. The function $\varphi(t)$ is the time change of the cumulative curve of the evacuees who chose Flee or Drop, and is convex upward as in Fig. 1b. This is consistent with the results of Gu et al. (2016) [12].

Figure 5 shows the coordinates $x_i(T), y_i(T)$ of remaining agents in the room at $t = T$. Straight lines to the exit are the trajectories of the agent who chose Flee. There are 249 agents left in the room, all of whom have chosen Drop. All of these agents remain far from the exit, forming a diagonal spatial pattern similar to Fig. 3.

If we divide the room into two spaces with a diagonal line $y = x$ and let the number of agents in the upper-left space be $N_u = |\{a_i \mid y_i(T) \geq x_i(T)\}|$ and the lower-right space be $N_l = |\{a_i \mid y_i(T) < x_i(T)\}|$, we have $N_u = 221$ and $N_l = 28$, with a difference of $N_d = N_u - N_l = 193$.

Here, we adopted entropy to evaluate the simulation results quantitatively [6]. Figure 6 shows the action of each agent at the end of the simulation at their initial location at $t = 1$. The black and white circles represent $\pi_i(T) = drop$ and $\pi_i(T) = flee$, respectively. As shown in Fig. 6, with a few exceptions, most agents initially located in the upper-left space decided to drop, and those in the lower-right space decided to flee. To evaluate whether the decision between fleeing and dropping is divided by the diagonal line $y = x$, entropy H is introduced as follows [28]:

$$H = -r_g \, log_2(r_g) - r_b \, log_2(r_b), \tag{11}$$

where [28]

$$r_g = L_g/(L_g + L_b) \tag{12}$$
$$r_b = L_b/(L_g + L_b), \tag{13}$$

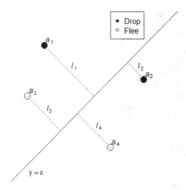

Fig. 7. Calculations of L_g and L_b. In this case, $L_g = l_1 + l_4$ and $L_b = l_2 + l_3$ [28].

and [28]

$$L_g = \sum_{\{a_i | y_i(1) \geq x_i(1) \wedge \pi_i(T) = drop\}} l_i + \sum_{\{a_j | y_j(1) < x_j(1) \wedge \pi_j(T) = flee\}} l_j \qquad (14)$$

$$L_b = \sum_{\{a_i | y_i(1) \leq x_i(1) \wedge \pi_i(T) = drop\}} l_i + \sum_{\{a_j | y_j(1) > x_j(1) \wedge \pi_j(T) = flee\}} l_j, \qquad (15)$$

where [28]

$$l_i = \sqrt{2 \left(\frac{x_i(1) - y_i(1)}{2} \right)^2} \qquad (16)$$

and l_j is the minimum distance between the initial position of a_i and the diagonal $y = x$. Additionally, L_g is the sum l_i of the shortest distances to the diagonal from the initial position of a_i in the upper-left space with $\pi_i(T) = drop$ and an agent in the lower-right space with $\pi_i(T) = flee$. Conversely, L_b is the sum of l_i of the shortest distance to the diagonal from the initial position of agent a_i in the upper-left space with $\pi_i(T) = flee$ and an agent in the lower-right space with $\pi_i(T) = drop$. For example, in the case of Fig. 7, $L_g = l_1 + l_4$ and $L_b = l_2 + l_3$.

With a smaller H, fleeing and dropping behaviors are delineated by the $y = x$ diagonal, whereas the behavior becomes intermingled if H is close to 1.0. The entropy shown in Fig. 6 is $H = 0.18$.

We used the distance from $y = x$ instead of the number of agents in the calculation of entropy because the positions of the remaining agents are also important when evaluating the diagonal spatial pattern.

5.3 Result 2

In order to generalize the results in Sect. 5.2, 500 simulations were conducted, and the results of these simulations are presented in this section. The time evolution of the cumulative number of evacuees in the 500 simulations of $\Phi(t) = \overline{\varphi(t)}$ is shown in Fig. 8. This curve is convex upward and smoother than that of Fig. 4.

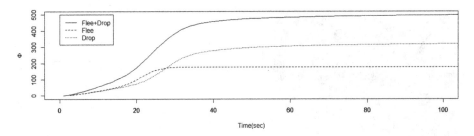

Fig. 8. Mean values of $\varphi(t)$ and $\Phi(t)$, for 500 simulations.

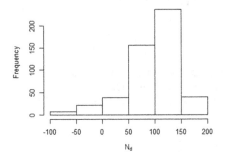

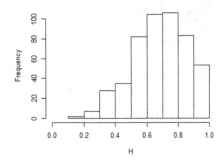

Fig. 9. Histogram of N_d.   **Fig. 10.** Histogram of H.

A histogram of the difference N_d in the number of agents in the space divided by the diagonal line $y = x$, as shown in Fig. 9, and a histogram of the entropy H of decision-making at the time of evacuation are shown in Fig. 10. The mean, standard deviation (σ), and minimum and maximum values of N_d and H are summarized in Table 1.

Table 1. Statistics of N_d and H for 500 simulations.

	min	mean	σ	max
N_d	−89.0	96.83	48.04	192
H	0.15	0.68	0.18	1.00

Figure 11 is the kernel density distribution of the coordinates $x_i(T)$, $y_i(T)$ of the agents remaining in the room at $t = T$. The figure shows a higher kernel density at a farther position and a lower kernel density at a closer position, illustrating a high correlation between the distance from the exit and the agents remaining in the room at the end of the simulation. This shows that simple herd behavior is sufficient to reproduce a diagonal spatial pattern recorded in the video clip during the Great East Japan Earthquake.

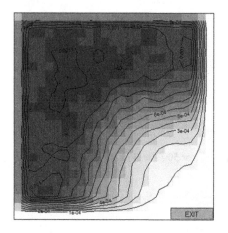

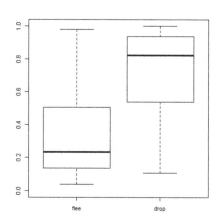

Fig. 11. Kernel density of $x_i(T)$ and $y_i(T)$ throughout room. Dark areas represent high density, and light areas represent low density.

Fig. 12. Logit model discriminating between dropping and fleeing [28].

6 Analysis

We conducted three analyses to examine the results of the simulations. First, we conducted a logistic regression analysis to explore the primal factor that gives rise to the diagonal spatial pattern. Second, a graph centrality analysis was applied to uncover the influence dynamics among agents during the evacuation. Finally, a sensitivity analysis was conducted to investigate the robustness and parameter sensitivities of the results.

6.1 Logistic Analysis

In a previous study [28], we conducted a logistic regression analysis to investigate the effect of each parameter of the agent on the final decision $\pi_i(T)$ by assuming $drop = 1$ and $flee = 0$. The parameters are response threshold θ_i, risk sensitivity μ_i, and distance from the exit [28]

$$L_i = \sqrt{(x_i(1) - G_x)^2 + (y_i(1) - G_y)^2}. \tag{17}$$

A total of 200 and 500 training and test samples, respectively, were randomly selected from 75,000 samples (500 agents × 150 simulations in [28]). Large amounts of training data reduce both the p-value and the reliability of the analysis; therefore, we

Table 2. Results of logistic analysis. Coefficients and P-values [28].

	Intercept	L_i	θ_i	μ_i
coeff	−3.4486	0.0033	0.0115	0.0055
P-values	0.0	0.0	0.0796	0.3532

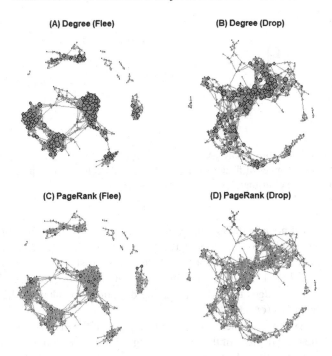

Fig. 13. Influence graphs with centralities. From left, size of nodes shows degree of fleeing, degree of dropping, PageRank of fleeing, and PageRank of dropping agents.

set the number of training data to 200 samples. The results of the logistic regression analysis in terms of the coefficients and p-values are shown in Table 2. From Table 2, the primary factor in the drop or flee decision is the distance between the agent and the exit ($p < 0.01$). This implies that the response threshold θ_i may have certain effects on the decision ($p < 0.1$), whereas the risk sensitivity μ_i may not have any effect ($p > 1$).

We attempted to discriminate 500 test data by using a logit model created by the logistic regression analysis. The results are shown in Fig. 12. The figure shows that the logit model is capable of discriminating between Drop and Flee for unknown data.

6.2   Graph Centrality Analysis

In this section, we focus on the results presented in Sect. 5.2 and investigate how agents influence each other during the evacuation processes using social network analysis techniques. Influences among agents are dynamic and complex because an agent imitates the behaviors of nearby agents that vary from time to time owing to a herd behavior. The decision of one agent affects the behaviors of the other agents that happen to be within the vicinity of the agent, and these behaviors may influence the first agent later. This interconnected system of influence among the evacuees forms a complex network.

Figure 13 shows directed graphs of the influences among agents. A node represents an agent, and an arrow connecting two agents represents the influence of herd behaviors between them; the root node affects the arrowhead node. The size of the node represents

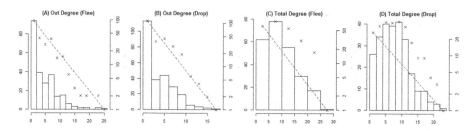

Fig. 14. Graph Centrality Histograms: (A) out-degrees of fleeing agents, (B) out-degrees of dropping agents, (C) total degrees of fleeing agents, and (D) total degrees of dropping agents. Additionally, ×s show value of histograms on logarithmic scale.

the centrality of that node in the graph. In Fig. 13, graph (A)—the degree of centrality of a fleeing agent, graph (B)—a dropping agent, graph (C)—the PageRank centrality of a fleeing agent, and graph (D)—a dropping agent. In the first and second graphs (i.e., graphs A and B in Fig. 13), as we were interested in studying attributes of affecting agents, we limited the edges towards the leaving directions to calculate the degree of centralities of the nodes (out-degrees).

Figure 14 shows the frequencies of the node degrees of the graphs given in Fig. 13. Histograms of the node degrees of the graphs in Fig. 13 are presented in Fig. 14 (the left axes), and the values of these histograms (×s in the charts in Fig. 14) are also plotted on the logarithmic scale (the right axes) over these histograms. The first and second charts in Fig. 14 show histograms of out-degrees, and the third and fourth charts show histograms of the total degrees. In the first and second charts (A and B in Fig. 14), a few nodes have high out-degrees, whereas most of the nodes have low out-degrees; in addition, ×s are on the straight dashed line yielding a scale-freeness of the graphs. However, this does not hold for the third and fourth charts (C and D in Fig. 14), and the scale-freeness is not observed for the total-degree graphs.

In the graphs of the fleeing agents (A and C in Fig. 13), we can see a small number of clusters connected by a few agents, meaning that many agents egress in the form of groups. By contrast, in the graphs of the dropping agents (B and D in Fig. 13), almost all agents are connected and form one large cluster, meaning that the influences of the dropping behaviors propagate over all dropping agents and interconnect them.

In comparison, the degree of centrality graphs (A and B in Fig. 13) have more nodes with high centralities than PageRank centrality graphs (C and D in Fig. 13). Despite scale-freeness, in the degree of centrality graphs, many agents still affect each other. In other words, there is no evidence indicating that more agents are affected by a few specific agents.

PageRank centrality, which is an eigenvector with the highest eigenvalues of the transition matrix representing the influence graph, illustrates important nodes that are affected by many agents and may affect many others. The PageRank centrality graphs in Fig. 13 show that a few nodes are more important than the other nodes, although the sizes of these nodes are relatively small. This implies that the effects of these important nodes might be insignificant. To verify this, we eliminated the top five agents that had the highest PageRank from the original setting presented in Sect. 5.2 and conducted a

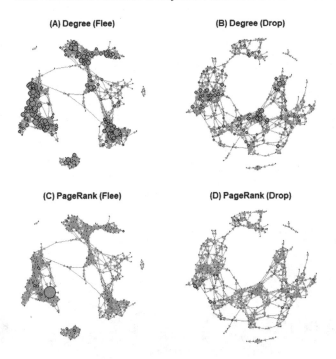

Fig. 15. Influence graphs with centralities when removing top five agents with highest PageRank.

new simulation. Figure 15 shows centrality graphs of the simulation results. Comparing Figs. 13 and 15, the main features of these graphs show only slight changes even though some nodes with a high PageRank were eliminated, indicating that these features presented in the analysis cannot be altered by changing the behaviors of a small number of agents.

6.3 Sensitivity Analysis

Thus far, we have conducted simulations with a vicinity setting of five units for the distance and 120° toward the heading direction of an agent. During a herd behavior, an agent selects the behavior adopted by the highest number of agents within his/her vicinity (Algorithm 2). Thus, the definition of the vicinity of an agent is crucial; subsequently, the final results of the simulations depend on this definition, and the agent considers the decisions of the other agents within this range to make his/her own decision. Therefore, we conducted simulations by varying the definition of the vicinity of the agents to examine the sensitivity of the defined vicinity on the results.

Figure 16 shows the results of the sensitivity analysis. The distance was varied from 0 to 20 units (rows), and the angle was varied from 20 to 360° (columns). Each cell in the figure refers to the result of 100 simulations for the given settings; in addition, dark areas represent the high densities of the dropping agents remaining at the end of the simulation, and light areas represent low densities.

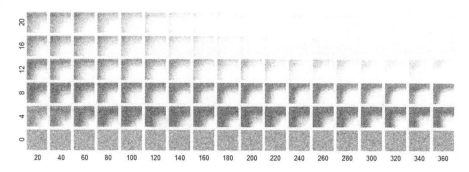

Fig. 16. Final positions of remaining agents with varying distances and angles of agent vicinities.

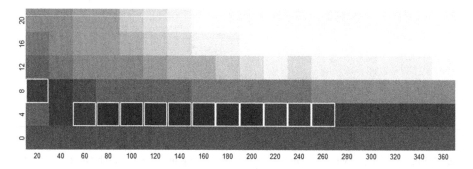

Fig. 17. Total number of remaining agents with varying distances and angles of agent vicinities.

In Fig. 16, the results similar to Fig. 11 can be observed within a broad range in the figure, showing that these results are insensitive to the vicinity definitions. However, a closer look raises a few more interesting insights. Notice that most cells in the upper-right areas of the figure have light colors, which means that a small number of agents remained at the end of the simulations. This area represents vicinities with long distances and wide angles, referring to extensive vicinities. Figure 17 shows a heat map of the mean number of remaining agents (dropping agents) at the end of the simulations; light colors show low populations, and dark colors show high populations. This figure also indicates low populations in the upper-right areas. These two figures also depict high populations in the lower-left areas; however, the highest population area is not located at the lowest and leftmost corner in Fig. 17. The white square frames in Fig. 17 indicate that the mean number of remaining agents is higher than 300. The lowest row refers to settings with a distance of zero, i.e., agents with no vicinity, yielding simulations without herd behaviors. Therefore, the only behavior the agents can take is a random choice between fleeing and dropping. The lowest rows in Fig. 16 show that the remaining agents are distributed throughout the area evenly. In these cells, the mean number of remaining agents is 250 because each agent merely makes an independent random choice. The observation in this section reveals that broad vicinities propagate fleeing behaviors toward a widespread range of the environment, and limited

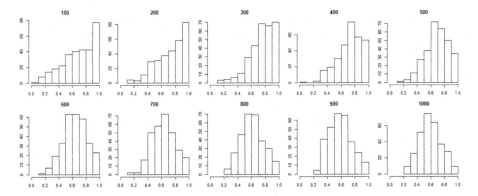

Fig. 18. Histograms of the number of remaining agents with varying populations of agents.

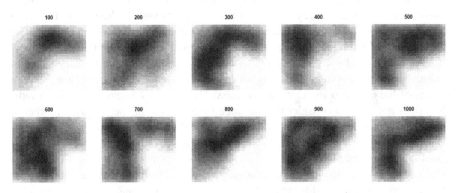

Fig. 19. Final positions of remaining agents with varying populations of agents.

vicinities propagate dropping behaviors. However, if the vicinities are too small, then agent behaviors approach a simple random choice because the effect of the herd behaviors becomes negligible.

Population density is another important factor affecting the simulation results because the number of agents within the vicinity depends on the density of the agents. We conducted experiments by varying the number of agents in the environment from 100 to 1000; each experiment consisted of 300 simulations. Figure 18 shows a histogram of H for each experiment. The values of H are distributed over a broad range of domains; however, the figure shows that population densities affect the peaks of the distributions. The peak is close to 1 when the population is low, whereas it becomes close to 0.5 if the population is high.

Figure 19 depicts heat maps of the final positions of the remaining agents for each experiment; the ranges with dark colors represent the areas with high frequencies of remaining agents, whereas light colors represent the areas with low frequencies. In all diagrams in Fig. 19, the lower-right areas in each heat map have light colors, leading to low densities of the remaining agents, which are in good agreement with Fig. 11. The results of the sensitivity analysis revealed that the unusual evacuation behaviors captured in the video clip are unaffected by the population density of the agents (Fig. 19), and a higher population density will bring about higher frequencies of this phenomenon (Fig. 18).

7 Discussion

Our simulation results in Figs. 5 and 6 show that the decision between dropping and fleeing is determined by the distance from the exit. However, Figs. 9 and 10 indicate that the results from the simulation vary, i.e., the results described in Sect. 5.2 are not always obtained. Contrary to our expectations, some simulations showed $N_d = -89$, signifying that more agents remained in the area closer to the exit, whereas other simulations resulted in $H \approx 1.00$, implying a combination of dropping and fleeing behaviors.

Although we concede that exceptional cases like these do occur, the evacuation decision model is clearly able to produce results similar to our findings from the video analysis of the Great East Japan Earthquake, albeit at a slightly lower frequency. The kernel density of the results in Fig. 11 agrees well with the statement above. Furthermore, the results of the logistic regression analysis revealed that the primary factor in deciding between dropping and fleeing for individual agents was the distance between their initial location and the exit. Nonetheless, Hypothesis 2 suggests that each individual does not have to consider this distance to determine his/her behavior; rather, a simple herd behavior is sufficient to produce a diagonal spatial pattern.

The analysis described in Sect. 6.2 illustrates that the influences among the agents form a complex scale-free network. The experiment removing the top-five highest PageRank agents resulted in another complex network, implying that the nature of the network is unaltered by modifying a small number of agents. Guiding the crowd toward safer evacuations behaviors is useful and desirable. The centrality analysis conducted in our studies suggests that controlling a small number of evacuees is insufficient to control the behaviors of the entire crowd. The sensitivity analysis described in Sect. 6.3 indicates that the diagonal spatial pattern captured in the video clip of the Great East Japan Earthquake can be reproduced within a broad range of population and vicinity parameters. The diagonal spatial pattern is robust and insensitive to the model parameters.

As the most remarkable aspect of this analysis, the results were produced by agents who have no higher-level cognitive processes. The agents in our model performed only either imitations or random selections, both of which are unintelligent behaviors. Neither distance estimations nor thresholds are necessary to reproduce the behaviors in the video. From the discussion thus far, we conclude that Hypothesis 2 holds.

The fact that Figs. 4 and 8 are consistent with Fig. 1b, and that the cumulative curve of the evacuees shows convex and real evacuation situations [12], provides additional support that our simulations using the evacuation decision model can yield realistic results.

Hypothesis 2 and the results of the analyses above indicate that

1. the primal factor of the phenomenon is the distance from the exit,
2. the scale-freeness of the network is robust, and
3. the phenomenon is insensitive to the model parameters.

This may suggest that the diagonal spatial pattern captured in the video clip is induced more by physical factors than by intentional cognitive factors of the agents.

We do not deny Hypothesis 1; rather, we consider it natural for people close to the exit to select a fleeing action intentionally. In reality, we believe that both Hypothesis 1 and Hypothesis 2 hold simultaneously. A real evacuation process is a complex combination of higher-level cognitive processes such as decision-making and lower-level cognitive processes such as herd behavior. Some researchers also pointed out the importance of an individual's emotional responses during crowd evacuation processes [16].

This study demonstrated that an evacuation decision model can reproduce the real human evacuation behaviors that were recorded in a video of the Great East Japan Earthquake and can be used to analyze human herd behaviors during an earthquake. Tsurushima [26,27] demonstrated that a simple herd behavior can reproduce symmetry breaking in exit selection when using the evacuation decision model. Furthermore, the analysis presented herein revealed the significance of herd behavior in collective evacuations. Hence, the evacuation decision model is advantageous for a quantitative analysis of the effects of herd behavior in human evacuations.

Finally, some potential methodological weaknesses should be considered. The video clip analyzed in this study is the only instance in which we can find the specific evacuation behavior discussed in this paper. We do not know the universality of these behaviors under other evacuation scenarios. There is also a possibility of errors occurring in the video analysis phase because this process was controlled manually. The simulation was not configured identically with the actual events captured in the video, for example, the number or initial layout of the agents. It would be interesting to experiment with a more realistic design, and a comparison of these two studies may bring about some new findings of crowd evacuations. However, such experiments are reserved for a future study.

8 Conclusion

By analyzing a video captured during the Great East Japan Earthquake, we discovered that the decision between dropping and fleeing was influenced by the distance to the exit, a finding that was not previously reported. We reproduced this finding, which is the diagonal spatial pattern of the remaining evacuees, using an evacuation decision model, and revealed that simple herd behaviors are sufficient to reproduce this phenomenon. Analyses of the simulation results show that these results are robust and insensitive to the model parameters.

Acknowledgement. The author is grateful to Kei Marukawa for his helpful comments and suggestions. The author would like to thank Editage (www.editage.com) for English language editing.

References

1. Altshuler, E., Ramos, O., Nuñez, Y., Fernańdez, J., Batista-Leyva, A.J., Noda, C.: Symmetry breaking in escaping ants. Am. Nat. **166**(6), 643–649 (2005)

2. Bernardini, G., Lovreglio, R., Quagliarini, E.: Proposing behavior-oriented strategies for earthquake emergency evacuation: a behavioral data analysis from new Zealand, Italy and Japan. Saf. Sci. **116**, 295–309 (2019)
3. Bode, N., Holl, S., Mehner, W., Seyfried, A.: Disentangling the impact of social groups on response times and movement dynamics in evacuations. PloS One **10**, e0121227 (2015)
4. Bonabeau, E., Theraulaz, G., Deneubourg, J.L.: Quantitative study of the fixed threshold model for the regulation of division of labour in insect societies. Proc. R. Soc. B **263**(1376), 1565–1569 (1996)
5. Bonabeau, E., Theraulaz, G., Deneubourg, J.L.: Fixed response thresholds and the regulation of division of labor in insect societies. Bull. Math. Biol. **60**, 753–807 (1998)
6. Crociani, L., Vizzari, G., Yanagisawa, D., Nishinari, K., Bandini, S.: Route choice in pedestrian simulation: design and evaluation of a model based on empirical observations. Intelligenza Artificiale **10**, 163–182 (2016)
7. Cutter, S., Barnes, K.: Evacuation behavior and three mile Island. Disasters **6**(2), 116–124 (1982)
8. D'Orazio, M., Spalazzi, L., Quagliarini, E., Bernardini, G.: Agent-based model for earthquake pedestrians' evacuation in urban outdoor scenarios: behavioural patterns definition and evacuation paths choice. Saf. Sci. **62**, 450–465 (2014)
9. Drury, J., Brown, R., González, R., Miranda, D.: Emergent social identity and observing social support predict social support provided by survivors in a disaster: solidarity in the 2010 Chile earthquake. Eur. J. Soc. Psychol. **46**(2), 209–223 (2015)
10. Elliott, D., Smith, D.: Football stadia disasters in the United Kingdom: learning from tragedy? Ind. Environ. Crisis Q. **7**(3), 205–229 (1993)
11. Garcimartín, A., Zuriguel, I., Pastor, J., Martín-Gómez, C., Parisi, D.: Experimental evidence of the "faster is slower" effect. In: Transportation Research Procedia: The Conference on Pedestrian and Evacuation Dynamics (PED 2014), Delft, The Netherlands, vol. 2, pp. 760–767, 22–24 October 2014
12. Gu, Z., Liu, Z., Shiwakoti, N., Yang, M.: Video-based analysis of school students' emergency evacuation behavior in earthquakes. Int. J. Disaster Risk Reduction **18**, 1–11 (2016)
13. Haghani, M., Sarvi, M.: Following the crowd or avoiding it? empirical investigation of imitative behaviour in emergency escape of human crowds. Anim. Behav. **124**, 47–56 (2017)
14. Haghani, M., Sarvi, M.: 'Herding' in direction choice-making during collective escape of crowds: how likely is it and what moderates it? Saf. Sci. **115**, 362–375 (2019)
15. Hori, M.: Introduction to Computational Earthquake Engineering, 3rd edn. World Scientific (Europe), London (2018)
16. Kefalas, P., Sakellariou, I.: The invalidity of validating emotional multi-agent systems simulations. In: Proceedings of the 8th Balkan Conference in Informatics. BCI 2017, pp. 8:1–8:8. ACM, New York, NY, USA (2017)
17. Kimura, R., Hayashi, H., Tatsuki, S., Tamura, K.: Behavioural and psychological reconstruction process of victims in the 2004 mid-niigata prefecture earthquake. In: Proceedings of the 8th US National Conference on Earthquake Engineering, pp. 1–9 (2006)
18. Lovreglio, R., Borri, D., dell'Olio, L., Ibeas, A.: A discrete choice model based on random utilities for exit choice in emergency evacuations. Saf. Sci. **62**, 418–426 (2014)
19. Mas, E., Suppasri, A., Imamura, F., Koshimura, S.: Agent-based simulation of the 2011 great east japan earthquake/tsunami evacuation: an integrated model of tsunami inundation and evacuation. J. Nat. Disaster Sci. **34**(1), 41–57 (2012)
20. Morita, T., Tsukada, S., Yuzawa, A.: Analysis of evacuation behaviors in different areas before and after the great east Japan earthquake. In: Fifth International Conference on Geotechnique, Construction Materials and Environment (2015)
21. Saloma, C., Perez, G.J., Tapang, G., Lim, M., Palmes-Saloma, C.: Self-organized queuing and scale-free behavior in real escape panic. PNAS **100**(21), 11947–11952 (2003)

22. Schmidt, S., Galea, E. (eds.): Behaviour - Security - Cluture (BeSeCu): Human behaviour in Emergencies and Disasters: A Cross-cultural Investigation. Pabst Science Publishers, Lengerich (2013)

23. Shiwakoti, N., Sarvi, M.: Understanding pedestrian crowd panic: a review on model organisms approach. J. Transp. Geogr. **26**, 12–17 (2013)

24. Tsurushima, A.: Modeling herd behavior caused by evacuation decision making using response threshold. In: Pre-proceedings of the 19th International Workshop on Multi-Agent-Based Simulation (MABS2018) - A FAIM workshop. Stockholm, Sweden (2018)

25. Tsurushima, A.: Modeling herd behavior caused by evacuation decision making using response threshold. In: Davidsson, P., Verhagen, H. (eds.) MABS 2018. LNCS (LNAI), vol. 11463, pp. 138–152. Springer, Cham (2019). https://doi.org/10.1007/978-3-030-22270-3_11

26. Tsurushima, A.: Reproducing symmetry breaking in exit choice under emergency evacuation situation using response threshold model. In: Proceedings of the 11th International Conference on Agents and Artificial Intelligence. ICAART, vol. 1, pp. 31–41. INSTICC, SciTePress (2019)

27. Tsurushima, A.: Symmetry breaking in evacuation exit choice: impacts of cognitive bias and physical factor on evacuation decision. In: van den Herik, J., Rocha, A.P., Steels, L. (eds.) ICAART 2019. LNCS (LNAI), vol. 11978, pp. 293–316. Springer, Cham (2019). https://doi.org/10.1007/978-3-030-37494-5_15

28. Tsurushima, A.: Validation of evacuation decision model: an attempt to reproduce human evacuation behaviors during the great east Japan earthquake. In: Proceedings of the 12th International Conference on Agents and Artificial Intelligence. ICAART, vol. 1, pp. 17–27. INSTICC, SciTePress (2020)

29. Wilensky, U.: NetLogo, Center for Connected Learning and Computer-Based Modeling, Northwestern University, Evanston, IL (1999)

30. Yang, X., Wu, Z., Li, Y.: Difference between real-life escape panic and mimic exercises in simulated situation with implications to the statistical physics models of emergency evacuation: The 2008 Wenchuan earthquake. Physica A: Stat. Mech. Appl. **390**(12), 2375–2380 (2011)

Intelligent Local Energy Communities: A Multiagent System Approach

Roman Denysiuk[1]([envelope]) [iD], Fabio Lilliu[2] [iD], Meritxell Vinyals[1],
and Diego Reforgiato Recupero[2,3] [iD]

[1] CEA, LIST, 91191 Gif-sur-Yvette, France
{roman.denysiuk,meritxell.vinyals}@cea.fr
[2] University of Cagliari, Via Ospedale 72, Cagliari, Italy
{lilliu,diego.reforgiato}@unica.it
[3] R2M Solution s.r.l., Via Fratelli Cuzio 42, Pavia, Italy

Abstract. The electric power grid undergoes a transformation, with many consumers becoming both producers and consumers of electricity. This transformation poses challenges to the existing grid as it was not designed to have reverse power flows. Local energy communities are effective in addressing those issues and engaging grid users to play an active role in the energy transition. Such communities encourage the consumption of the excess of renewable energy locally, which reduces the stress on the grid and the costs for the users. In this paper, we present a multiagent system developed to implement an intelligent local energy community. The multiagent system models the energy grid as a network of computational agents that solve energy flow problems in a coordinated way and use the solutions for controlling flexible loads. The model effectively distributes the tasks among the agents considering the flows of electricity and heat. The Alternative Direction Method of Multipliers determines the agent interaction protocol. The obtained results demonstrate the ability of the multiagent system to automate an intelligent operation of the community while reducing the energy costs and ensuring the grid stability.

Keywords: Multiagent system · Local energy community · Flexibility services · Community energy optimisation · Building energy optimisation · Demand response

1 Introduction

In the last decades renewable energy has become a topic of primary importance. Renewables are viewed as an alternative to traditional fossil fuels with the advantage of being endless natural sources with lower carbon dioxide emissions. However, the benefits of renewable energy come at a price of increasing complexity regarding safe operation of the energy grid [5,6]. Motivated by financial and environmental concerns, many grid users have become both producers

© Springer Nature Switzerland AG 2021
A. P. Rocha et al. (Eds.): ICAART 2020, LNAI 12613, pp. 26–51, 2021.
https://doi.org/10.1007/978-3-030-71158-0_2

and consumers of electricity – the so-called prosumers. The proliferation of distributed energy resources poses several challenges, which include two-directional power flow and overload issues due to intermittent nature of renewables and irregular consumption [10].

Local Energy Communities (LECs) is a promising way to integrate renewable energy sources and engage grid users in the energy transition [16,19]. Communities often include members who know and trust each other as well as share common goals and interests. LECs enable energy exchange at the community level allowing grid users to buy and sell energy locally. Local energy exchange is beneficial as losses due to transmission of electricity over long distances are avoided and funds are kept withing local economy. Communities can also participate in energy markets (e.g. wholesale, balancing, reserve markets ...), since by acting together, community members have stronger negotiation power when interacting with other energy market participants.

During recent years, the focus on LECs has been growing steadily leading to a number of industrial projects and research publications [16]. In this view, one interesting topic is the design of a peer-to-peer (P2P) market in which participants can buy and sell their energy. In [13], this was approached using the concept of virtual currency for governing the exchange of energy between community members, being the effectiveness of the local market highly depending on the definition of functions that determine buying and selling prices [3,11]. While the functions proposed in [13] were designed to encourage balance between energy production and consumption, they ignored other important aspects such as the possibility of peers to adopt a strategic behavior. Usually, these strategic aspects are taken into account by means of game theory. In [14], price-based schemes and a game-theoretical framework have been investigated to coordinate flexible demand. The study described a promising approach but lacked consideration of distributed generation and energy storage systems. In [15], an auction-based market mechanism has been presented in which households submit their consumption bids and generation offers, which are, in turn, being used to determine prices and allocate energy. However, under these auction based schemes, participants need to provide accurate estimates of energy and prices to get profitable results, their final benefits being dependant on the outcome of complex forecasting models. Major advantages of P2P schemes are related to their decentralized nature as no central supervisory entity is needed and privacy concerns are diminished.

On the other hand, there is the possibility of creating a cost sharing mechanism in which the community has a single electricity bill that is shared among its members. This approach assumes a common goal to be pursued instead of individual ones and aims for cooperative behaviour of community members. In [12], a two stage aggregated control is proposed to realize this idea where an energy sharing coordinator controls flexible devices. An interior-point method was used to minimize the energy costs of the community. However, the centralized nature of this method is a major drawback that is also common to many existing approaches based on energy sharing. Centralization limits scalability and rises concerns about privacy as data are stored and processed in a single location. In contrast with centralised approaches, multiagent systems are well established paradigm for implementing decentralize computerized systems. A good survey regarding MAS applications for microgrid control can be found in [8]. Closer to our work, peer-to-peer trading in a local energy community using MAS has been previously addressed by [20,21]. As in this paper, both works uses the Alternating Direction Method of Multipliers (ADMM) as the underlying protocol for agent negotiation. However, [20] is based on a very simplistic and abstract electricity prosumer model that consists on a set of allowed power profiles and a measure of dissatisfaction with respect to each profile. Similarly, [21] only considers electricity and a limited number of flexible devices. In conclusion, existing works often miss a careful outline of multiagent modeling methodology, use simple prosumer models and mostly focus on a single type of energy such as electricity.

Against this background, this paper presents a multiagent system developed for managing a local energy community. The multiagent models the energy network accounting for both electricity and heat. It solves an optimal power flow problem that is formulated as a convex optimization problem. Solutions yield optimal actions for controlling devices. The optimization is performed by decomposing the underlying problem into a number of smaller subproblems that are distributed among different computing agents. This study builds on our previous work presented as a conference paper in [4]. Herein it is consolidated and extended in several important ways: (i) we describe a multiagent system modeling starting from an individual building; (ii) we extend a congestion management approach by adding the model for ensuring flexibility delivery; and (iii) we present new results including fitting model parameters, building optimization, and congestion management.

The remainder of the paper is structured as follows. Section 2 outlines the decentralised optimization approach used to solve the underlying decision making problem. Section 3 presents multiagent system models. Section 4 details, for each type of agent, the local optimisation that allows them to participate in the decentralised negotiation. Section 5 presents and discusses the obtained results. Finally, Sect. 6 concludes the work.

2   Decentralised Optimisation Approach

We develop a multiagent system (MAS) with the aim to enable an autonomous and intelligence functioning of a local energy community. MAS models the energy grid as a network of computational agents that solve individual tasks and interact by exchanging messages. We use the Alternating Direction Method of Multipliers (ADMM) as the protocol for agent interactions, which determines the structure and order of messages. ADMM is a variant of augmented Lagrangian method for solving constrained optimization problems. It offers a powerful framework for distributed problem solving, which is suitable for problems whose structure

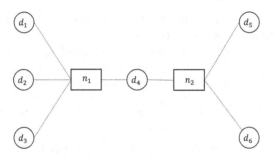

Fig. 1. A bipartite graph represents energy network and describes the structure of MAS. Two types of nodes are devices and nets, respectively depicted by circles and rectangles.

can be represented by a bipartite graph. With this representation, nodes in the graph are assigned with tasks whilst edges show the structure of interactions and coupling between the tasks.

We represent energy networks as bipartite graphs and refer to agents and nodes interchangeably. In graphs, there are two types of nodes such as devices and nets that are depicted by circles and rectangles respectively, as shown in Fig. 1. The MAS manages the community energy network by controlling flexible loads. Flexible loads are those loads whose consumption can be shifted to better meet grid users' needs and goals. The needs are related to satisfying comfort preferences of residents. The goals involve reducing the energy costs and ensuring the grid stability. The first goal is sought by making a better use of locally produced renewable energy through increasing self-consumption. This is because renewable energy is free for a particular household if is produced from its rooftop panels, and is cheaper when it comes from the neighborhood relative to that imported from the grid. The second goal relates to the fact that power flows should be within grid capacity limits. It is achieved by avoiding both excessive consumption of energy from the grid and excessive injection of renewable energy into the grid.

The needs and goals of grid users are addressed by solving power flow problems with appropriately formulated objective and constraint functions. The obtained solutions yield optimal control actions for agents. The structure of MAS described by a bipartite graph allows to formulate an optimization problem in the form

$$\underset{x_i \in \Omega_i, z_i \in \Theta_i}{\text{minimize}} \quad \sum_{i \in D} f_i(x_i) + \sum_{i \in N} g_i(z_i) \tag{1}$$
$$\text{subject to} \quad x_i = z_i, \quad \forall i \in N$$

where f_i is a real valued objective function, defined in the feasible region Ω_i, that is associated with the i-th device, g_i is a real valued objective function, defined in the feasible region Θ_i, that is associated with the i-th net, x_i and z_i are the decision variables associated with the i-th device and net respectively.

The constraints account for the fact that respective device and net agents should agree upon the values of shared variables.

Finding the minimizer to an equality constrained optimization problem is equivalent to identifying the saddle point of the associated Lagrangian function. This gives the following augmented Lagrangian function

$$L(x, z, \lambda) = \sum_{i \in D} f_i(x_i) + \sum_{i \in N} g_i(z_i) + \frac{\rho}{2} \sum_{i \in N} \|x_i - z_i + u_i\|_2^2 \qquad (2)$$

where $u_i = \lambda_i/\rho$ is the scaled dual variable (for Lagrange multipliers λ_i), x_i and z_i are primal variables.

The augmented Lagrangian function (2) is minimized with respect to primal and dual variables. Each iteration involves the following steps.

Step 1. Device agents compute in parallel their optimal variables by solving

$$x_{i \in D}^{(k+1)} = \arg\min_{x_i \in \Omega_i} f_i(x_i) + \frac{\rho}{2} \|x_i - (z_i^k - u_i^k)\|_2^2 \qquad (3)$$

The corresponding values are communicated to neighboring nets.

Step 2. Net agents compute in parallel their optimal variables by solving

$$z_{i \in N}^{(k+1)} = \arg\min_{z_i \in \Theta_i} g_i(z_i) + \frac{\rho}{2} \|z_i - (x_i^{(k+1)} + u_i^k)\|_2^2 \qquad (4)$$

Step 3. Net agents in parallel update their dual variables.

$$u_{i \in N}^{(k+1)} = u_i^k + (x_i^{(k+1)} - z_i^{(k+1)}) \qquad (5)$$

The corresponding primal and dual variables are sent to neighboring devices.

The above steps are repeated until convergence criteria are met. The convergence criteria are checked locally by nets and defined for primal and dual residuals as

$$r^{\text{primal}} < \epsilon^{\text{primal}}$$
$$r^{\text{dual}} < \epsilon^{\text{dual}} \qquad (6)$$

where $\epsilon^{\text{primal}}, \epsilon^{\text{dual}}$ are small positive numbers representing primal and dual tolerances, respectively. The primal and dual residuals are computed as

$$r^{\text{primal}} = \|x_i^k - z_i^k\|_2$$
$$r^{\text{dual}} = \|\rho(z_i^k - z_i^{k-1})\|_2 \qquad (7)$$

If the device and net functions $f(x)$ and $g(z)$ are convex, the constraint residual under ADMM is guaranteed to converge to zero and the objective value to the minimum of the dual problem, see [1].

3   Community and Multiagent Models

In this section we first give a general description of the community under study. Next we present a multiagent model of the energy network in individual building. Then we present a multiagent model of the whole community aggregating the models of different buildings.

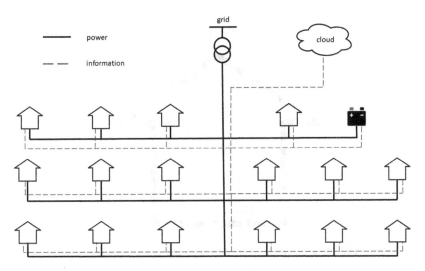

Fig. 2. Architecture of local energy community.

3.1 Local Energy Community

As reported in [4], our study case involves a community of households located in the central Netherlands. Figure 2 depicts a general architecture. The community consists of 16 households and a district battery with the capacity of 220 kWh. Each household has a heat pump of 2 kW combined with a hot water buffer of 200 L. The heat pump is used for heating both domestic hot water and spatial heating. Each house has solar photovoltaics capable of producing up to 7 kW. Additionally, there is one in-home battery with the capacity of 7.8 kWh.

There is also the information and communications technology infrastructure that consists of different communication devices, software applications and protocols. Each house is equipped with a local energy gateway that is connected with flexible devices and it is able to communicate with the backend run on a cloud by means of the Advanced Message Queuing Protocol. Local energy gateways are used to control flexible devices and to communicate sensory data. The MAS runs on the cloud. The cloud also provides means for interaction with other energy market participants.

3.2 Building Energy Network

As a first step we develop multiagent models of building energy networks considering each building individually. Based on the presence of in-home battery we distinguish buildings with and without battery. Figure 3 displays the computation graph describing multiagent system for the building with battery.

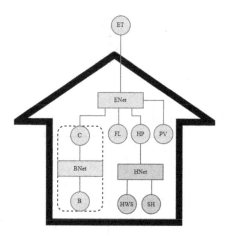

Fig. 3. Multiagent model of building energy network.

The agent types and roles were defined in [4] and are as follows:

- Electrical Net (ENet) models the electrical network in the house energy system ensuring the balance of electrical energy.
- Heating Net (HNet) models the heating network in the house energy system ensuring the balance of heat energy.
- Battery Net (BNet) ensures the energy balance in the decomposed model of battery.
- External Tie (ET) represents a connection to an external source of power.
- Connector (C) connects two nets modelling the transmission of energy. The transmission can be associated with losses. The transmission loss from ENet to BNet models a charging efficiency. The transmission loss from BNet to ENet models a discharging efficiency.
- Battery (B) models an electrical storage that can take in or deliver energy.
- Photovoltaics (PV) represents solar panels that generate electricity from absorbing sunlight.
- Fixed Load (FL) represents an inflexible energy consumption that must be satisfied.
- Heat Pump (HP) models the transformation of electricity to heat with some conversion coefficient.
- Space Heating (SH) models indoor air temperature that must be kept within comfort limits.
- Hot Water Storage (HWS) models the hot water tank and the domestic hot water consumption.

The model includes the electrical and heating networks shown in blue and red respectively. These networks account for the flows of respective types of energy. A heat pump agent (HP) connects two networks serving as a converter of electricity to heat. Net agents ensure the balance of corresponding energies (i.e. the ENet ensures electricity balance, the HNet heating balance and the BNet balance inside the battery model). The battery with losses is represented by connector, net and battery agents. The connector agent (C) that connects to the battery net models losses associated with charging and discharging. Finally, the battery agent (i.e. B) models linear constraints associated with its charge capacity. The models of remaining buildings are obtained by eliminating agents related to the in-home-battery.

3.3   Community Energy Network

In [4], we developed a multiagent model of the community energy network. The model is shown in Fig. 4. It was obtained by aggregating individual models of district assets, such as houses and the battery storage, and connecting them to LEMNet agent. LEMNet represents a local energy market where district actors negotiate their energy exchange. LEMNet is also connected to an external source of power that represents a connection point between the community and the main grid. In this view, the interaction protocol defined by the ADMM algorithm models negotiation of the energy exchange between actors in the community. The actors are the district battery storage, the prosumers and the main grid. Connector agents (i.e. C) that connect houses to the LEMNet serve as interface between the prosumers and the local energy market.

Agents connected to LEMNet negotiate energy exchange at the community level. In each iteration, LEMNet sends messages that can be viewed as requests. These messages contain the amount of energy requested, z_i^k. The sign is used to distinguish between production and consumption. From a recipient perspective, a positive value indicates that the energy flows towards the recipient, a negative value indicates the flow towards the sender. It also includes the price, u_i^k, which not only indicates the current market price, but also is used to distinguish between a situation of overconsumption (in which the price are positive) and a situation of underconsumption (in which the price are negative). Agents coordinate their actions through negotiation until consensus is reached on their energy use. The resulting actions in terms of energy use represent the optimal decisions with respect to the common goal of reducing the energy cost for the community.

Along with the cost effectiveness, the MAS aims to ensure safe operation of the energy grid. The grid has the potential to experience times of intensive injection of renewable energy and excessive pulling of energy due to high consumption. Such conditions increase stress on the grid and could push it into failure. The grid condition when its capacity is insufficient to accommodate the requested power flows is referred to as congestion. Congestion management is performed to avoid overload and to ensure stability of the grid.

We consider congestion management using the Universal Smart Energy Framework (USEF) [7], which focuses on the use of market-based flexibility for congestion management. The aggregator and the Distribution System Operator (DSO) are two major players involved. The aggregator is an energy market participant that aggregates the energy consumption and generation of several

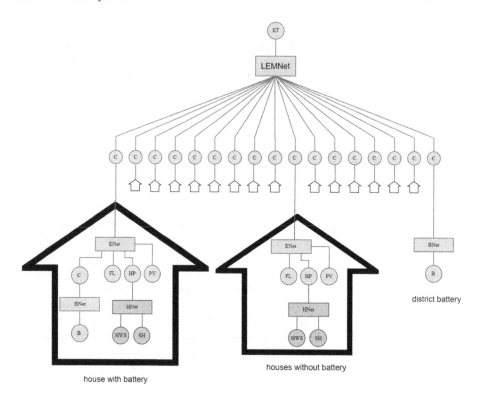

Fig. 4. Multiagent model of the community energy network.

consumers aiming to maximize the value of flexibility. The DSO is responsible for the operation and maintenance of the distribution grid ensuring that
the energy in the system can flow between suppliers and consumers. The DSO
performs grid safety analysis identifying potential congestion points. In case of
congestion, the DSO procures flexibility through market based procedures sending a flexibility request to the aggregator active at the congestion point. This
request indicates the need to reduce load and the available capacity at each
time interval. In response, the aggregator optimizes its portfolio and provides a
flexibility offer in terms of energy profile and price. The DSO analyses the offer
and responds with an updated request or a flexibility order. The former occurs
if the offer is not sufficient to solve the congestion. The latter indicates the offer
is accepted and the aggregator is to be paid for the delivered flexibility. The
flexibility is negotiated for the next day, starting after midday and continuing
until agreement or timeout.

Our multiagent system is a part of the aggregator's infrastructure used to
provide flexibility services to the DSO. For congestion management, the structure
of the MAS remains as is in Fig. 4. Appropriate modifications are only introduced
to the ET agent. Congestion management determines two running regimes for the
MAS. The negotiation phase happens for the day ahead, where the MAS provides

solutions in response to flexibility requests. The DSO requests are transformed into constraints limiting power flows and the constrained optimization problem is solved yielding corresponding flexibility offers. During the course of the operating day, the MAS balances the differences between day-ahead commitments and the actual real-time operation. This is approached by solving optimization problems with objective functions aiming to minimize mismatch between target and actual energy use in the community.

4   Local Agent Optimisation Models

This section presents formulations of agents local subproblems and describes how those are solved.

4.1   Nets

All the net agents are considered to be instances of the Net agent. This agent solves the following subproblem[1] [4]

$$
\text{minimize: } \sum_{\tau=1}^{H} (z_1(\tau) - y_1(\tau))^2 + \ldots + \sum_{\tau=1}^{H} (z_n(\tau) - y_n(\tau))^2
$$
$$
\text{subject to: } \sum_{i=1}^{n} z_i(\tau) = 0, \quad \tau = 1, \ldots, H.
$$
(8)

where n is the number of neighbors. The constraints aim to ensure the energy balance. The problem (8) is solved by projecting the variables received from neighboring devices onto the feasible region. For each time interval $\tau = 1, \ldots, H$ and each neighbor $i = 1, \ldots, n$, the optimal values are computed as

$$
z_i^*(\tau) = x_i - \bar{x}(\tau)
$$
(9)

where $\bar{x}(\tau)$ is the average of neighbors' variables at time interval τ.

4.2   External Tie

External Tie (ET) represents a connection to an external source of power. There are three different operational modes defined as follows.

Minimizing Energy Cost. It is associated with the objective function aiming at minimizing the energy cost. The ET agent solves the following local subproblem

$$
\text{minimize: } \sum_{\tau=1}^{H} -c(\tau)\, x(\tau) + \frac{\rho}{2} \sum_{\tau=1}^{H} (x(\tau) - y(\tau))^2
$$
(10)

---

[1]   For better readability, we use $y(\tau) = x(\tau) + u(\tau)$ for the net agents and $y(\tau) = z(\tau) - u(\tau)$ for the device agents, $\tau = 1, \ldots, H$.

where

$$c(\tau) = \begin{cases} c^{\text{sell}}(\tau) & \text{if } x(\tau) \geq 0 \\ c^{\text{buy}}(\tau) & \text{otherwise} \end{cases} \tag{11}$$

$c^{\text{sell}}(\tau)$ and $c^{\text{buy}}(\tau)$ are the prices of exported and imported energy, respectively. A positive value of $x(\tau)$ indicates the energy is exported to the grid while a negative value of $x(\tau)$ indicates the energy is imported. The function is separable and thus we can consider each of its components separately. The subproblem is solved by finding a critical point for $x(\tau) \geq 0$ as

$$x^+(\tau) = \max\{0, \ c^{\text{sell}}(\tau)/\rho + y(\tau)\} \tag{12}$$

and a critical point for $x(\tau) \leq 0$ as

$$x^-(\tau) = \min\{0, \ c^{\text{buy}}(\tau)/\rho + y(\tau)\} \tag{13}$$

Both $x_+^*(\tau)$ and $x_-^*(\tau)$ are evaluated using (10). The one having the lower value is selected to be the optimal value of $x^*(\tau)$ at time interval τ.

Addressing Flexibility Request. The flexibility request from the DSO is transformed into the set of constraints restricting the flow of energy coming into and out from the community. This is addressed by extending the subproblem of the ET agent as follows

$$\begin{aligned} \text{minimize: } & \sum_{\tau=1}^{H} -c(\tau)\, x(\tau) + \frac{\rho}{2} \sum_{\tau=1}^{H} (x(\tau) - y(\tau))^2 \\ \text{subject to: } & x^{\min}(\tau) \leq x(\tau) \leq x^{\max}(\tau) \ \ \tau = 1, \ldots, H \end{aligned} \tag{14}$$

Notice that in (14) the objective function is the same as in (10) but constraints are added to address the flexibility request. The problem is separable and is solved by finding solutions for individual components. The critical point for $x(\tau) \geq 0$ is

$$x^+(\tau) = \max\{0, \ \min\{x^{\max}(\tau), \ c^{\text{sell}}(\tau)/\rho + y(\tau)\}\} \tag{15}$$

and for $x(\tau) \leq 0$ it is

$$x^-(\tau) = \min\{0, \ \max\{x^{\min}(\tau), \ c^{\text{buy}}(\tau)/\rho + y(\tau)\}\} \tag{16}$$

Both $x_+(\tau)$ and $x_-(\tau)$ are evaluated using (14). The one having the lower value is selected to be the optimal value of $x^*(\tau)$ at time interval τ. The projection ensures that the solution lies within the feasible region and satisfies the constraints.

Ensuring Flexibility Delivery. The community should fulfill its obligations by delivering the energy profile agreed with the DSO during negotiation. Forecasts are imperfect and yield differences between predicted and observed values. Control actions based on inaccurate forecasts have the potential to mismatching the agreed energy use, which in turn leads to economical penalties. The MAS mitigates potential deviations from the target profile by running in a rolling horizon regime with the ET agent solving the following subproblem

$$\text{minimize: } \sum_{\tau=1}^{H} -c(\tau)\, x(\tau) + \sum_{\tau=1}^{H} \frac{w(\tau)}{2}(x(\tau) - t(\tau))^2 + \frac{\rho}{2} \sum_{\tau=1}^{H} (x(\tau) - y(\tau))^2 \quad (17)$$

where $t(\tau)$ is the target energy consumption/production and $w(\tau)$ is the penalty coefficient. The subproblem (17) extends the original subproblem of ET agent in (10) by adding an extra term that penalizes the deviation from the target values. The problem is separable and is solved by finding solutions for individual components. The critical point for $x(\tau) \geq 0$ is

$$x^{+}(\tau) = \max\left\{0, \; \frac{c^{\text{sell}} + \rho\, y(\tau) + w(\tau)\, t(\tau)}{\rho + w(\tau)}\right\} \quad (18)$$

and for $x(\tau) \leq 0$ it is

$$x^{-}(\tau) = \min\left\{0, \; \frac{c^{\text{buy}} + \rho\, y(\tau) + w(\tau)\, t(\tau)}{\rho + w(\tau)}\right\} \quad (19)$$

Both $x_{+}(\tau)$ and $x_{-}(\tau)$ are evaluated using (17). The one having the lower value is selected to be the optimal value of $x^{*}(\tau)$ at time interval τ.

4.3 Connector and Heat Pump

Connector (C) and heat pump (HP) agents connect two nets modelling the transmission of energy between different parts of the energy network. The transmission can be associated with losses. Both C and HP are instances of an agent that solves the following subproblem [4]

$$\begin{aligned}
\text{minimize: } & \frac{\rho}{2} \sum_{\tau=1}^{H} (x_1(\tau) - y_1(\tau))^2 + \frac{\rho}{2} \sum_{\tau=1}^{H} (x_2(\tau) - y_2(\tau))^2 \\
\text{subject to: } & \eta_1\, x_1(\tau) = -x_2(\tau) \quad \text{if } 0 \leq x_1(\tau) \leq x_1^{\max}(\tau) \\
& -x_1(\tau) = \eta_2\, x_2(\tau) \quad \text{if } 0 \leq x_2(\tau) \leq x_2^{\max}(\tau)
\end{aligned} \quad (20)$$

where $\eta_1, \eta_2 \in (0, 1]$ are transmission efficiencies and $x_1^{\max}, x_2^{\max} \geq 0$ are the maximum values restricting the energy flow from the corresponding net. The two constraints correspond to the two possible scenarios: (i) when the energy flows from net 1 to net 2 and (ii) when the energy flows in the opposite direction, from net 2 to net 1. The problem (20) is separable and is solved for each time step τ individually by finding critical points for two cases and selecting the one with a lower value of objective in (20).

4.4 Photovoltaics and Fixed Loads

On one hand, photovoltaics (PV) represent solar panels that generate electricity from absorbing sunlight. On the other hand, a Fixed Load (FL) represents an inflexible energy consumption that must be satisfied. Both PV and FL are instances of an agent that solves the following subproblem [4]

$$\text{minimize: } \frac{\rho}{2} \sum_{\tau=1}^{H} (x(\tau) - y(\tau))^2$$
$$\text{subject to: } x(\tau) = \hat{x}(\tau), \quad \tau = 1, \ldots, H \tag{21}$$

where $\hat{x}$ are forecast values. The solution to (21) is trivial ($x^k = \hat{x}$).

4.5   Battery

Battery (B) represents an electrical storage that can take in or deliver energy. The B agent has a set of constraints aiming to keep its state of charge as well as charging and discharging rates within the allowed range. The B agent solves[2] the following subproblem [4]

$$\text{minimize: } \frac{\rho}{2} \sum_{\tau=1}^{H} (x(\tau) - y(\tau))^2$$
$$\text{subject to: } Q^{\min} \leq Q(\tau) \leq Q^{\max}, \quad \tau = 1, \ldots, H \tag{22}$$
$$x^{\min} \leq x(\tau) \leq x^{\max}, \quad \tau = 1, \ldots, H$$

where $Q^{\min}$ and $Q^{\max}$ are the minimum and maximum allowed charge of the battery, $x^{\min}$ and $x^{\max}$ are the limits of discharging and charging rates. The battery's charge evolves as in [9]

$$Q(\tau) = Q^{\text{init}} + \sum_{\tau=1}^{H} x(\tau) \tag{23}$$

where Q^{init} is the initial charge of the battery.

4.6   Space Heating

Space Heating (SH) represents indoor air temperature that must be kept within limits for comfort. The SH agent solves(see footnote 2) the following subproblem [4]

$$\text{minimize: } \frac{\rho}{2} \sum_{\tau=1}^{H} (x(\tau) - y(\tau))^2$$
$$\text{subject to: } T^{\min} \leq T(\tau) \leq T^{\max}, \quad \tau = 1, \ldots, H \tag{24}$$

where $T^{\min}$ and $T^{\max}$ are the temperature limits. For $\tau = 1, \ldots, H$, the room temperature evolves as in [9]

$$T(\tau) = T(\tau - 1) + \frac{\mu}{c} \cdot \left(T^{\text{amb}}(\tau) - T(\tau - 1) \right) + \frac{\eta}{c} \cdot x(\tau) \tag{25}$$

where $T(0)$ is the initial temperature, T^{amb} is the outdoor temperature, μ is the conduction coefficient, η is the heating efficiency and c is the heat capacity of indoor air.

---

[2] The B, SH and HWS agents solve their subproblems using Dykstra's projection method [2,17] with a starting point $x(\tau) = y(\tau)$ for $\tau = 1, \ldots, H$.

4.7 Hot Water Storage

Hot Water Storage (HWS) represents the tank with hot water and the consumption of domestic hot water. The HWS agent solves(see footnote 2) the following subproblem [4]

$$\text{minimize: } \frac{\varrho}{2} \sum_{\tau=1}^{H} (x(\tau) - y(\tau))^2 \tag{26}$$
$$\text{subject to: } T^{\min} \leq T(\tau) \leq T^{\max}, \ \tau = 1, \ldots, H$$

with $T^{\min}$ and $T^{\max}$ are the temperature limits. For $\tau = 1, \ldots, H$, the water temperature evolves as [18]

$$T(\tau) = T(\tau - 1) + \frac{V_{\text{cold}}(\tau)}{V_{\text{total}}} \cdot \left(T_{\text{cold}} - T(\tau - 1) \right) + \frac{1}{V_{\text{total}} \cdot c} \cdot x(\tau) \tag{27}$$

where $T(0)$ is the initial temperature, V_{cold} is the volume of water with temperature T_{cold} entering the tank to replace the consumed hot water, V_{total} is the tank volume, and c is the specific heat of water. The consumption of hot water is given by forecast.

5 Results and Discussion

This section presents and discusses the results of validation tests. The tests were performed using the data for the winter season. Winter days are characterized by the need to use heat pump for both heating domestic hot water and maintaining room temperature within comfort limits. This represents the most challenging optimization scenario as during other seasons heat pump is only used for reheating domestic hot water. The optimization considers a 24-h time horizon divided into 96 program time units (PTUs), with each one corresponding to 15-min interval.

5.1 Estimating Parameters and Validation of Local Models

The local optimization models of agents formulated in Sect. 4 need parameters for their initialization. Some of these parameters represent physical properties whose values can be readily encountered in the literature, e.g. the heat capacity of air or the specific heat of water. Instead, others are more specific for the application context and should be estimated from the data. This is the case of the conduction and thermal efficiency coefficient parameters of the heat pump, space heating and domestic hot water storage agents. For these parameters, in this section we carried out a study to estimate them from the database of historical records and validate in this way the effectiveness of our agent models. In more detail, the values of these parameters were determined through optimization by minimizing a sum of squares representing differences between temperature values from historical data and those computed by agent models.

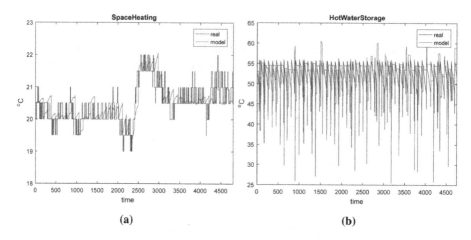

Fig. 5. Temperature profiles given by model and historical data for the (a) space heating and (b) hot water storage agent models.

Figure 5 shows temperature profiles coming from historical data and corresponding models with estimated parameters for the space heating and hot water storage models. The plots refer to the data collected for one house during the first two months of 2019. As expected, there is no perfect fit between the real and estimated values. This can be explained by imperfections in sensors, measurements, noise, as well as the linear nature of models. However, it can be seen that the models can adequately approximate important temperature dynamics regarding both the room air and domestic hot water. Notice that the line representing the values estimated by the model follows the general trend. As to space heating, the model approximates the decrease in room temperature due to weather conditions and its increase as a result of heating as a consequence of the action of the heat pump. Regarding hot water, the model provides adequate temperature estimates for periods of water consumption and reheating. The latter is particularly challenging due to irregular consumption profile and complex thermal dynamics inside the tank.

It is important to note that these plots depict temperature estimates for two months on a daily basis. For each day, the temperature was calculated for each of 96 time slots, corresponding to 15-min intervals during 24 h. The difference between the real and estimated values is smaller in the beginning of each time horizon. This is because the models use real sensor measurements for the previous time slot. When estimating the values for the following time slots, the models rely on estimates from previous slots instead of the real values. This way, errors are accumulated making the discrepancy between the real and estimated values higher in the later time slots. In practice, the above issue can be effectively addressed by a receding (rolling) horizon optimization. This technique involves the MAS updating all the parameters and running the optimization in

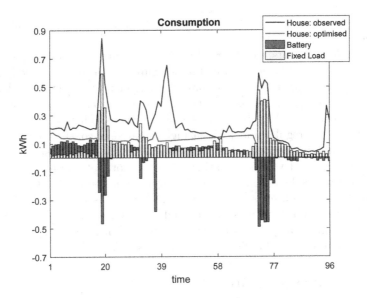

Fig. 6. Energy consumption with shares of different loads.

the beginning of each time slot, i.e. every 15 min. As a result, uncertainties are expected to be cancelled out or minimized.

5.2 Building Optimization

We validated the MAS models of buildings in the community by optimizing each building individually. This represents a valid approach for minimizing the energy costs for community members. Though, in this study, we focus on the collective energy management and use the results of the two approaches for comparison purposes. In the community, the buildings have similar characteristics in terms of devices and consumption patterns. The main source of flexibility in most buildings comes from both the admissible ranges of temperatures for domestic hot water and indoor air. The building with in-home battery has the largest potential in terms of flexibility. The presence of battery allows for storing the energy in time intervals when there is the surplus of PV production. It also enables storing the energy imported from the grid for a later usage (i.e. future domestic needs and/or injecting it back to the grid). Here we limit the presentation of building optimization results to the case of the building with in-home battery.

Figure 6 shows a daily consumption for the building with battery. The effects of optimized battery usage can be observed. The optimization suggests using the battery for storing the energy in off-peak periods and then releasing it to satisfy uncontrollable consumption, which is represented in our models by the flexible load device. The results clearly indicate the benefits of having the battery installed inside the house. The battery provides a significant flexibility in terms of energy usage, which also indicate incentives for investing in electrical storage installation.

From the experiments, we observed that the consumption of heat pumps can be shifted to keep indoor and water temperatures inside the admissible range. Though, the flexibility is relatively limited. This fact can be explained by the power of heat pumps and some characteristics of thermal loads. As for room temperature, heating a building is a very slow process. The use of heat pumps for space heating is regular and without high amounts of consumed energy. This contrast with heating domestic hot water whose consumption is short time and irregular in consumed volume. Heating domestic hot water is a relatively fast process but requires large amounts of energy in short periods of time. Once a large volume of hot water is drawn from the tank, it is replaced by the same volume of cold water that must be heated to ensure the temperature limits with low flexibility. The promise comes from aggregating several heat pumps to increase the amount of flexibility, which is discussed next.

5.3 Community Optimization

Community members participate in community energy management with the common goal of increasing social welfare through collective use of local resources [4]. They coordinate the energy use to reduce the shared cost at the connection point between the community and the main grid. The multiagent system automates the process of coordination by optimizing energy flows and using the solutions for control actions. When running a day ahead optimization, the system attempts to schedule energy consumption for flexible loads to time intervals with available renewable energy. Starting optimization at different time slots during the day changes the perspective as the time horizon moves forward embracing time slots from the next day. The optimization is executed at the beginning of each time interval with updated sensor data. This operational mode is known as rolling horizon optimization. Rolling horizon can mitigate uncertainties in the models, such as forecast errors, and account for the fact that the real time horizon is not limited to a single day.

Figure 7 shows the resulting dairy energy profile of the community as a result of the rolling horizon optimization. For comparison, the graph also shows the results of the day ahead optimization. The day ahead approach yields the results from single optimization run at the beginning of the day. The rolling horizon approach involves the results of 96 optimizations during the day. The data for the first PTU is used for control and is shown in the graphs. The difference can be readily understood. The rolling horizon optimization results in smaller energy exports during times of intense PV generation. This is because the system suggests storing the excess of energy to meet local demand in time slots receding into the future with each optimization run.

The results presented in Fig. 7 refer to the day characterized by a massive energy production from solar panels. The optimized energy profiles yield peaks of energy injection around midday when PV generation is high. This is because no constraints were imposed on possible energy flows. The system solely focuses

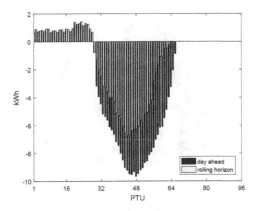

Fig. 7. Energy profile of the community with simple day ahead optimisation and with rolling horizon optimisation, adapted from [4].

on minimizing the energy bill. Although the results indicate that rolling horizon optimization can reduce peaks to some extent, it is not the goal of the community at this step. The issue of dealing with possible grid overload is addressed later as part of congestion management.

The optimal behavior of the community is characterized by shifting consumption of flexible devices to time intervals with electricity available from solar panels. This is because this electricity is cheaper relative to those taken from the main grid. Figure 8 shows the energy use of the heat pumps and the district battery after optimization.

Heat pumps are flexible devices at home level. They are used to provide heat for both domestic hot water and space heating. As expected, the MAS suggests using heat pumps in times with available renewable energy. This is shown in Fig. 8a that depicts a three-dimensional bar chart with the consumption profiles of each heat pump in the community. It can be seen that most of consumption occurs in times of high PV generation. Consumption in other time intervals is dictated by the need to satisfy temperature limits, especially for domestic hot water. The consumption of domestic hot water is irregular with respect to time and amount, especially in the evening.

At the district level, there is a battery storage. When multiagent optimization runs in a rolling horizon mode, at the end of the day, the battery SOC is not at its lower state because it holds some energy to account for the following time horizon. This is shown in Fig. 8b. Figure 8c graphically illustrates the control actions for the battery during the day in terms of the amount of energy charged and discharged in each PTU.

5.4   Comparing Building and Community Optimizations

Community management should ensure its members benefit from collective energy usage. To provide insights about the advantages of community-based

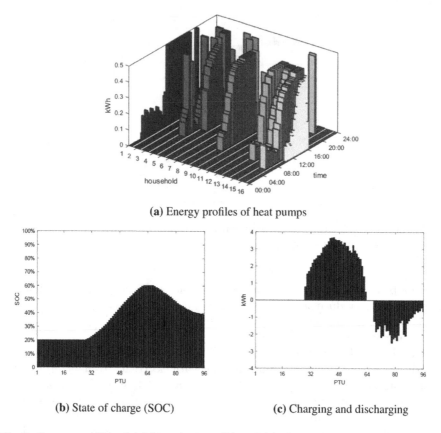

(a) Energy profiles of heat pumps

(b) State of charge (SOC)

(c) Charging and discharging

Fig. 8. Energy profiles of (a) heat pumps, (b) and (c) the district battery as result of the rolling horizon optimization, adapted from [4].

approach we compared the results of in-home and community optimizations [4]. The former optimized community households individually and combined their energy profiles. The latter performed the community optimization. The results indicate the performance of two approaches varies depending on the amount of renewable energy that is locally produced. Community-based approach is better when there is excess of renewable energy. On the other hand, both approaches perform similarly when it is low.

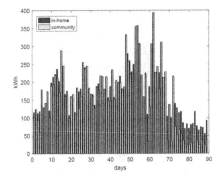

	Optimization	
	In-home	Community
Energy import (kWh)	16072.94	14384.53
Energy export (kWh)	3694.83	1814.42
Self-consumption (%)	59	80

Fig. 9. Comparing individual in-home and community optimizations, adapted from [4].

Figure 9 illustrates the amount of imported energy for the two optimization approaches. It can be seen that for all days community optimization yields less or equal energy import relative to in-home optimization. The two approaches perform similarly only when PV generation is low. The increase in renewable energy generation leads to the decrease in the amount of energy imported from the grid. During the period under consideration, the total renewable energy production was 9047.91 kWh. Similarly to the above daily data, the total energy import and export of the community was reduced.

We also use self-consumption as an indicator for performance comparison. Self-consumption is defined as the ratio between the amount of renewable energy consumed and produced in the community. The results indicate that the community-based optimization approach increases self-consumption. Instead of exporting the produced renewable energy outside the community it is used to meet local demand. These results provide important insights about advantages of collective energy management and the estimates of potential savings. It is also worth noting that economic benefits are accompanied by reduced stress on the main grid.

5.5   Addressing Flexibility Request

When it comes to congestion management, there are two possible scenarios. The first refers to the situation with the excess of injected renewable energy and low local demand. This can readily occur in sunny weather and lead to the increase in voltage that can damage the grid components if proper actions are not taken.

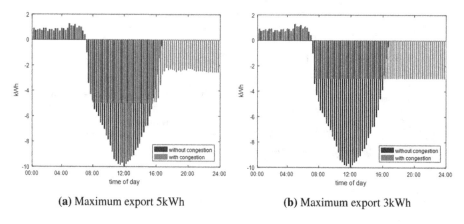

(a) Maximum export 5kWh   (b) Maximum export 3kWh

Fig. 10. Community energy profiles under congestion management scenarios due to overproduction, adapted from [4].

Figure 10 shows a day ahead scenario for the community addressing the over-supply of renewable energy. The energy profiles resulting from unconstrained community optimization are shown in blue. The results obtained when address-ing the flexibility requests are shown in yellow. Two different requests limiting the energy injection are considered, which correspond to the maximum energy injection of 5 kWh and 3 kWh per PTU. It can be seen that both the grid capacity limits are respected by the MAS. The amount of renewable energy injected into the main grid does not exceed the limits requested. This is achieved by shifting the export from peak sunny periods during the day to evening and night hours. This reduces the stress on the distribution grid and provides energy in times of high demand, such as evening hours.

The availability of the storage capacity in the community is critical to exhibit this behavior. The battery enables storing the excess of renewable energy in peak times and later releasing it to meet local demand and for export. Figure 11 shows the behavior of the district battery storage in terms of charging and discharging of energy. The figure illustrates the more grid capacity is limited, the more energy is taken in peak times. It can also be observed that the battery does not take more energy than needed for meeting the flexibility request, which in turn minimizes the losses associated with charging and discharging.

The second scenario aims at avoiding the overload of grid components due to excessive pulling of energy. This situation is common in times when the local production is limited and the consumption is high. Figure 12 shows the results of addressing the flexibility requests to limit consumption to 4 kWh and 3 kWh per PTU. The given day is characterized by the low production from PV panels and the peak in demand around 16:00. The request is addressed by exploiting flexibility from the district battery and heat pumps, as shown in Figure 13. The battery stores the energy imported in off-peak hours and discharges to meet the peak demand. The consumption of heat pumps is shifted closer to midday.

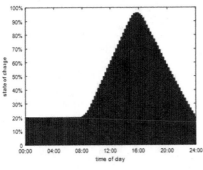

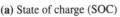

(a) State of charge (SOC)

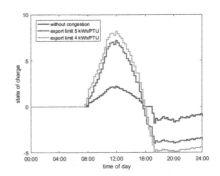

(b) Charging and discharging for different limits of exported energy

Fig. 11. District battery profiles when handling overproduction.

5.6 Ensuring Flexibility Delivery

In the following, we investigate the effectiveness of the mechanism introduced in (17) to deal with the differences between day-ahead commitments and the real-time operation. The differences are expected due to unforeseen changes in behavior of grid users and forecast inaccuracies. We consider the start of the day and the obligation to deliver the profile show in Fig. 10a. This profile results from the negotiation between the DSO and the aggregator and represents the commitment to deliver and consume certain amount of energy at each time interval during the day.

First we examine the effects of both the increase and decrease in energy production from rooftop panels up to 20% relative to the forecast values. Figures 14a and 14b show the updated and the target energy profile of the community. When

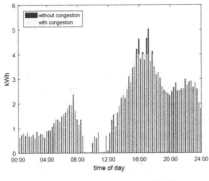

(a) Maximum import 4kWh

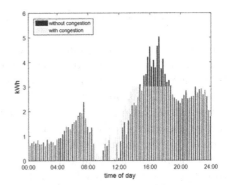

(b) Maximum import 3kWh

Fig. 12. Community energy profiles under congestion management scenarios due to overconsumption, adapted from [4].

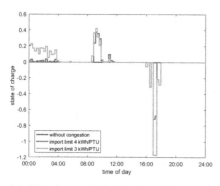
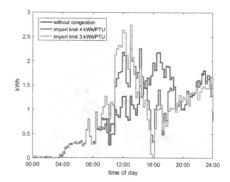

(a) Charging and discharging of community storage with different constraints limiting community import.

(b) Heat pumps consumption in the community with different constraints limiting community import.

Fig. 13. Energy profiles of the district battery and heat pumps when handling over-consumption.

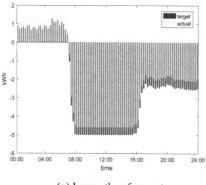
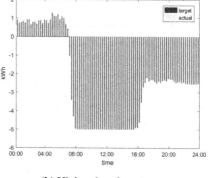

(a) Lower than forecast

(b) Higher than forecast

Fig. 14. Effects of change in PV production during congestion management.

the production is lower than it was expected, the community cannot inject the amount of energy agreed. In terms of injected energy, the actual profile deviates from the target starting from around 8:00 to 24:00. The target and actual profiles also differ before 8:00 when there is no production at all. This is because the quadratic term in (17) penalizes deviations from the target profile in a way so that these are distributed along different time intervals starting from the begging of the time horizon until the actual mismatch happens. On the other hand, when the production is higher than what was expected, the community is able to deliver the target profile. In this case, the excess of energy is injected into batteries. Figure 15 show graphs depicting the state of charge of the district buttery for these two scenarios. The differences between the planned and actual SOC demonstrate a way in which the multiagent system makes use of available flexibility to meet obligations of the energy community.

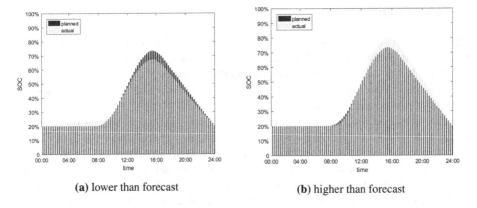

(a) lower than forecast   **(b)** higher than forecast

Fig. 15. SOC of district battery with deviations of PV production in congestion management with a target profile.

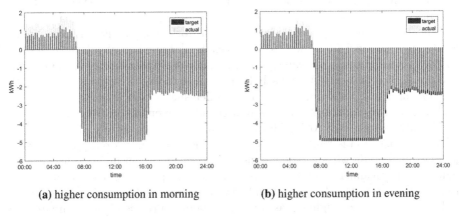

(a) higher consumption in morning   **(b)** higher consumption in evening

Fig. 16. Effects of increased consumption on congestion management with a target profile.

We also study how the increase in consumption affects the ability to deliver the agreed energy profile. Figure 16 depicts the results for the cases of increased energy consumption in both morning and evening. In the former case, the community fails to meet the target only in morning hours while meeting the target during the rest of the day, as shown in Fig. 16a. A different behavior is observed when the consumption is larger than forecast in evening (after 17:00), as shown in Fig. 16. In this case, small deviations from the target profile are experienced throughout the day. This results from optimizing the objective with the quadratic penalty term define in (17). The mismatch is distributed among all time intervals starting from the begging until the last interval with the difference between forecast and actual values. The behaviour is similar to the above discussed case of increased production.

6 Conclusions

This paper presented the multiagent system developed for intelligent and autonomous functioning of the local energy community. The energy grid considering electricity and heat is modelled as the network of computational agents. These agents collaboratively solve energy flow problems and use the solutions to control consumption of flexible loads.

The obtained results showed the ability of the system to reduce the energy costs and to ensure the grid stability while satisfying the needs of the grid users. The optimized energy consumption profiles are meaningful, that is: (i) the energy consumption of flexible loads is scheduled in times when renewable energy is available; and (ii) the export of energy is scheduled so that local demand is met first and only the remaining excess is fed into the main grid. The optimization finds solutions satisfying all the constraints whenever feasible solutions exist. The constraints refer to each time unit and involve allowed levels of batteries' charge, temperature limits, energy flow and energy balance in each node of the network.

The presented study considered the real-world community of households located in a close neighborhood. As observed in [4], these households have similar characteristics in terms of available flexible loads as well as energy consumption and production patterns. All households experience energy surplus and high local demand in same times during the day. Under such circumstances, the energy exchange at the community level is limited and the energy sharing mechanism is not fully appreciated. Although the presence of district battery alleviates this issue, it's operation is costly as it is leased. The community would benefit from joining households without solar panels that are pure consumers. On the one hand, such consumer households would enjoy low prices for locally produced renewable energy. On the other hand, producer households would benefit from selling the energy to neighbors as the corresponding price is higher compared to the one for exporting to the main grid.

As future work, we intend to incorporate uncertainties into optimization as a way to account for forecast inaccuracies and to consider how costs and profits can be fairly distribute between community members.

Acknowledgements. This research has received funding from the European Union's Horizon 2020 research and innovation programme under grant agreement No. 774431 (DRIvE).

References

1. Boyd, S., Parikh, N., Chu, E., Peleato, B., Eckstein, J.: Distributed optimization and statistical learning via the alternating direction method of multipliers. Found. Trends Mach. Learn. **3**(1), 1–122 (2011)
2. Boyle, J.P., Dykstra, R.L.: A method for finding projections onto the intersection of convex sets in Hilbert spaces. In: Dykstra, R., Robertson, T., Wright, F.T. (eds.) Advances in Order Restricted Statistical Inference, vol. 37, pp. 28–47. Springer, New York (1986). https://doi.org/10.1007/978-1-4613-9940-7_3

3. Denysiuk, R., Lilliu, F., Reforgiato Recupero, D., Vinyals, M.: Peer-to-peer energy trading for smart energy communities. In: Proceedings of the 12th International Conference on Agents and Artificial Intelligence, pp. 40–49. ICAART (2020)
4. Denysiuk, R., Lilliu, F., Vinyals, M., Reforgiato Recupero, D.: Multiagent system for community energy management. In: Proceedings of the 12th International Conference on Agents and Artificial Intelligence, pp. 28–39. ICAART (2020)
5. Du, P., Baldick, R., Tuohy, A. (eds.): Integration of Large-Scale Renewable Energy into Bulk Power Systems. PEPS. Springer, Cham (2017). https://doi.org/10.1007/978-3-319-55581-2
6. Hirth, L., Ziegenhagen, I.: Balancing power and variable renewables: three links. Renew. Sustain. Energy Rev. **50**, 1035–1051 (2015)
7. Hodemaekers, J., Bontius, H.: DSO Workstream - market-based congestion management models. Technical report, USEF foundation (2017)
8. Kantamneni, A., Brown, L.E., Parker, G., Weaver, W.W.: Survey of multi-agent systems for microgrid control. Eng. Appl. Artif. Intell. **45**, 192–203 (2015)
9. Kraning, M., Chu, E., Lavaei, J., Boyd, S.: Dynamic network energy management via proximal message passing. Found. Trends Optim. **1**(2), 73–126 (2014)
10. Lilliu, F., Loi, A., Reforgiato Recupero, D., Sisinni, M., Vinyals, M.: An uncertainty-aware optimization approach for flexible loads of smart grid prosumers: a use case on the Cardiff energy grid. Sustain. Energ. Grids Netw. **20**, 100272 (2019). https://doi.org/10.1016/j.segan.2019.100272
11. Lilliu, F., Vinyals, M., Denysiuk, R., Reforgiato Recupero, D.: A novel payment scheme for trading renewable energy in smart grid. In: Proceedings of the Tenth ACM International Conference on Future Energy Systems, pp. 111–115. e-Energy (2019)
12. Long, C., Wu, J., Zhou, Y., Jenkins, N.: Peer-to-peer energy sharing through a two-stage aggregated battery control in a community microgrid. Appl. Energy **226**, 261–276 (2018)
13. Mihaylov, M., Jurado, S., Avellana, N., Van Moffaert, K., de Abril, I.M., Nowé, A.: NRGcoin: virtual currency for trading of renewable energy in smart grids. In: Proceedings of the 11th International Conference on the European Energy Market, pp. 1–6 (2014)
14. Paola, A.D., Angeli, D., Strbac, G.: Price-based schemes for distributed coordination of flexible demand in the electricity market. IEEE Trans. Smart Grid **8**, 3104–3116 (2017)
15. Shamsi, P., Xie, H., Longe, A., Joo, J.: Economic dispatch for an agent-based community microgrid. IEEE Trans. Smart Grid **7**(5), 2317–24 (2016)
16. Sousa, T., Soares, T., Pinson, P., Moret, F., Baroche, T., Sorin, E.: Peer-to-peer and community-based markets: a comprehensive review. Renew. Sustain. Energy Rev. **104**, 367–378 (2019)
17. Tam, M.K.: Alternating projection methods. Ph.D. thesis, University of Newcastle (2012)
18. Tasdighi, M., Ghasemi, H., Rahimi-Kian, A.: Residential microgrid scheduling based on smart meters data and temperature dependent thermal load modeling. IEEE Trans. Smart Grid **5**, 349–357 (2014)
19. Timmerman, W.H.: Facilitating the growth of local energy communities. Ph.D. thesis, University of Groningen, SOM Research School (2017)
20. Verschae, R., Kato, T., Matsuyama, T.: Energy management in prosumer communities: a coordinated approach. Energies **9**(7), 562 (2016)
21. Vinyals, M., Velay, M., Sisinni, M.: A multi-agent system for energy trading between prosumers. DCAI 2017. AISC, vol. 620, pp. 79–86. Springer, Cham (2018). https://doi.org/10.1007/978-3-319-62410-5_10

A Game-Theoretical Incentive Mechanism for Local Energy Communities

Fabio Lilliu[2]([⊠])[iD], Roman Denysiuk[1][iD], Diego Reforgiato Recupero[2,3][iD], and Meritxell Vinyals[1]

[1] CEA, LIST, 91191 Gif-sur-Yvette, France
{roman.denysiuk,meritxell.vinyals}@cea.fr
[2] University of Cagliari, Via Ospedale 72, Cagliari, Italy
{lilliu,diego.reforgiato}@unica.it
[3] R2M Solution s.r.l., Via Fratelli Cuzio 42, 27100 Pavia, Italy

Abstract. Local energy communities (LECs) are structures based on the collaboration of neighbouring prosumers for suiting their energy requests. Prosumers are users participating in the community, which are able to produce energy rather than just consuming it. These communities have the purpose to incentivize usage of renewable energy. Inside them, it is possible to have members that trade energy in a peer-to-peer (P2P) fashion: prosumer can trade their energy surplus with consumers, so that profits remain inside the community and energy is not unnecessarily taken from outside, which avoids strain on the grid and transmission losses. In this work, the goal is to create a game theory model of a P2P market for LECs which takes into account the behavior of prosumers, assuming each of them will aim for their own benefit. The model has the objective to incentivize prosumers to self-consume their own energy, and balance as much as possible production and consumption through the community. The proposed model is described and analyzed with respect to other existing models with similar purposes, both from a theoretical and an empirical point of view. Results show that our model obtains good performances in all the analyzed aspects, outperforming existing ones.

Keywords: Peer-to-peer local energy market · Renewable energy incentive scheme · Local energy community · Smart grid · Game theory

1 Introduction

The energy and climate topics are some of the most debated and important of the last decades, as exhaustible energy sources have problems related to their eventual scarceness and to the environment. In this context, the option of renewable sources (e.g. wind and solar) becomes more and more appealing. As a consequence, there have been many efforts in the direction of creating new policies for encouraging the use of renewable energy sources (RES). These policies act by compensating RES producers (e.g. via direct payment or free energy for off-peak

© Springer Nature Switzerland AG 2021
A. P. Rocha et al. (Eds.): ICAART 2020, LNAI 12613, pp. 52–72, 2021.
https://doi.org/10.1007/978-3-030-71158-0_3

use) for the excess energy they produce. The impact of these policies has been important, as in 2016 energy produced from RES amounted to 30% of the total energy generated in Europe[1]. However, it is not all about opportunities since the intermittent nature of renewable energy has also posed important challenges on grid stability [2,11]. The main problems come from the fact that renewable energy production is irregular, especially through time, and this makes it difficult to match production and consumption through the grid. The inability of current energy policies to deal with such grid issues is currently limiting further penetration of renewables and widespread acceptance.

In the last years, there have been some proposals for creating incentive mechanisms which take these problems into account [1,4,5,10]. The key characteristic of these mechanisms is that they encourage continuous balance between production and consumption by building appropriate payment support functions for both energy producers and energy consumers.

A possibility for these mechanisms is to make use of market-based approaches [4,5]: they are centered around a local market, in which prosumers sell their surplus produced energy and consumers buy the energy they need for themselves. In contrast, the NRG-X-Change mechanism proposed in [10] is not a market-based approach[2] but, unlike traditional support policies, it offers rewards to both prosumers and consumers, proportional to their effort in achieving local energy balance.

The NRG-X-Change mechanism is based around the usage of a virtual currency called *NRGcoin*, which is used for transactions inside the community. However, as analysed in [7], there are some aspects not considered by this mechanism. In particular, it is important to make sure that prosumers will self-consume their own produced energy before either selling their surplus energy, or buying the additional amount they need. Another important aspect is to emphasize energy balance in the grid, by strongly discouraging scenarios where a congestion occurs. The work by [7] analyzed and took care of some of these points; however, they did not study its behavior in a context where agents act selfishly. Therefore, against this background, we advance with this work the state-of-the-art with the following contributions:

- Studying further the original *NRG-X-Change* mechanism and pointing out its main critical points related to its import and export price functions, and the scenarios on which they happen;
- Creating new functions for selling and buying energy which can make the mechanism perform better by a game theoretical point of view, and making use of well-known results about Nash Equilibria in order to do so;
- Proving the effectiveness of our proposals by exploitation of mathematical results, and validating them with simulations carried out on real data from a grid in Cardiff.

---

[1] http://www.eea.europa.eu/data-and-maps/indicators/overview-of-the-electricity-production-2/assessment.

[2] It can not be considered a marked-based approach because energy produced by prosumers is just exported to the grid and then imported by consumers.

This work builds on our previous work presented as a conference paper in [3]. Herein it is significantly consolidated and extended in the following ways: i) we describe more possibilities for building the mechanism in order to address the weak points of NRG-X-Change and at the same time guaranteeing cooperation in an environment where users' behavior is selfish; ii) we provide strong results to measure the efficiency of the newly proposed functions, both by mathematical proof and by simulations; iii) we present new results including a comparison between the previously proposed possibilities and the new ones.

The rest of this work is organized as follows. Section 2 briefly reviews the state-of-the-art literature in related areas. Section 3 reviews the NRG-X-Change mechanism, baseline of our work, highlighting its limitations when achieving the proposed goals. Section 4 presents our game theory formulation of the energy exchange problem. Section 5 presents our game-theoretical incentive mechanism based on novel P2P energy exchange functions. Finally, Sect. 6 describes our experimental results obtained using simulations based on historical data from an existing grid in Cardiff (UK). Section 7 concludes the chapter and outlines some lines of future work.

2   Literature Review

The NRG-X-Change mechanism has yet to be applied to real, existing grids; however, there is some literature which describes its functioning. The most prominent work in this sense is the one from [10], in which the system is described, along with the benefits of exploiting a virtual currency and the interaction between components of the grid. Another work [9] describes a simulation of NRG-X-Change on a local grid, highlighting the performances of the mechanism in a realistic context.

More generally for what the topic of incentive mechanisms is concerned, [11] is a survey which describes the weaknesses of existing mechanisms such as net metering and feed-in tariffs, in particular overconsumption depending on the season, and excessive or not adequate payment for energy producers in different situations. Some new incentive mechanisms are then proposed, in order to overcome those issues. An auction-based incentive system, whose name is Nobel [4], uses an idea similar to stock exchange to regulate energy trading at local level. The work from [5] describes a mechanism named PowerMatcher, that depends on a market design whose agents aim for equilibrium between demand and offer: the agents which operate are named *SD-matchers*. Another incentive system from [1] is based on competition for selling energy between prosumers of the grid and energy generating companies (*Gencos*), and consequent negotiation of price with those who need to buy that energy. This work highlights how the energy cost changes, and the effects of this mechanism when buyers are equipped with a learning strategy. The mechanisms described until now are centered on market mechanisms and on the participation of grid users and prosumers to bidding operations.

Regarding the usage of game theory for issues relative to smart grid, there are many related works in literature. A survey which gives a good overall view of these applications has been published [15], which describes the different approaches and contexts of application. Another survey, [8], addresses mainly works of cooperative game theory, while in our work's context agents operate in a selfish way. Among all of these works, the ones proposed by [13] is conceptually similar to our work for what game theory exploitation is concerned: the difference is that, while they are mostly concerned about the aspects regarding demand response, our work is centered on incentive mechanisms. Our work has also been influenced by [12] and [17], as some of the game theory models we used are very similar to the ones proposed by them.

3   A Base Approach: An Analysis of NRG-X-Change

The starting point for this work is an incentive mechanism for the usage of renewable energy, which is named NRG-X-Change [10]. In what follows we review how this mechanism operates.

Suppose we have a grid with N users, and call them $U_1, \ldots, U_n$. At a fixed unit of time t, there are some users who produce energy and some who consume energy. The former are referred to as *prosumers* and the latter are called *consumers*. Consider the prosumer U_i, and assume that she[3] produces energy and introduces a certain quantity x of it into the grid. In exchange for that, U_i receives a certain quantity of NRGcoins. This quantity is determined by a function named g, which is defined in Eq. 1 of [10] as follows:

$$g(x, t_p, t_c) = x \cdot \frac{q}{e^{\frac{(t_p - t_c)^2}{a}}}. \tag{1}$$

In this function, q and a are two positive real numbers: the former defines the highest possible value of the reward per unit of energy, the latter determines the shape of the function g.

Assume now that another user U_j is a consumer, which takes from the grid a certain quantity of energy which will be denoted by y: this will cost her a certain quantity of NRGcoins. This quantity is defined by another function, which is named h and defined in Eq. 2 of [10] as

$$h(y, t_p, t_c) = y \cdot \frac{r \cdot t_c}{t_c + t_p}. \tag{2}$$

In this definition, r is a positive real number which corresponds to the highest unitary cost that energy can have.

The purpose of the tariffs was to encourage users to shift their loads so that consumption is favored when energy production is locally higher than energy consumption, and disincentivized in the opposite case. Furthermore, the reward for energy production is higher when local energy production and consumption

---

[3] From now on, this is to be read as he/she.

have values close to each other, so that users are incentivized to keep these values as near as possible.

The objective of this work is to create a model for an incentive mechanism for usage of renewable energy, starting from the model of the NRG-X-Change [10] incentive system, which has just been described. However, this mechanism has some crucial weak points: our purpose is to identify and to address them. In particular, as stated in [3] these are the main issues relative to the original mechanism:

1. Guaranteeing that the mechanism does not encourage prosumers to intentionally reduce their own production of energy. The only exception is when excessive production may be harmful for the grid.
2. Considering the eventuality of a congestion, and trying to avoid it.
3. Making sure that self-consumption is always incentivized for prosumers. In particular, making them more willing to consume the energy they produce before either selling their surplus, or buying the extra energy for consumption.
4. Investigating the grid situation assuming users behave selfishly in their load allocation, and making sure that allocations reach a consensus between the grid users.

The issues from 1 to 3 have been solved in [7], where some new cost and reward functions have been designed, which had some useful properties for these purposes. Our objective is to solve the fourth of these issues along with the first three, and we want to do this with the construction of some new appropriate cost and reward functions. In what follows, the functions used in [7] to solve the first three problems will be outlined.

In the following notation, t_p^{-i} and t_c^{-i} are respectively the values for t_p and t_c if the value of x and y is zero. More formally, as reported in Eq. 8 of [3]:

$$
\begin{aligned}
t_p^{-i} &= \sum_{j \neq i} \mathbf{p_j}(t) \\
t_c^{-i} &= \sum_{j \neq i} \mathbf{c_j}(t).
\end{aligned}
\tag{3}
$$

The new reward function g has then been proposed in Eq. 9 of [3] as

$$
g(x, t_p, t_c) = P_{max} \cdot \left(g_1(t(x, t_p^{-i}, t_c^{-i})) - g_1(t(0, t_p^{-i}, t_c^{-i})) \right) - P(x, t_p^{-i}, t_c^{-i}).
\tag{4}
$$

In this formula, $P(x, t_p^{-i}, t_c^{-i})$ is a function which value is greater than zero if the difference between t_p^{-i} and t_c^{-i} is high enough to cause a congestion (that is, if $|t_p^{-i} + x - t_c^{-i}| > B$), and zero otherwise, and P_{max} is a coefficient used to define the amount of the reward. In this definition, g_1 is a function which has been defined in Eq. 5 of [7] as

$$
g_1(t) = \begin{cases} 0 & \text{if } t \leq 0 \\ \dfrac{1}{1+e^{\frac{2t-1}{t^2-t}}} & \text{if } t \in (0,1) \\ 1 & \text{if } t \geq 1 \end{cases}
\tag{5}
$$

this function regulates the behavior of g, and in its definition in Eq. 6 of [7], t is the function

$$t(x, t_p^{-i}, t_c^{-i}) = \frac{t_p^{-i} + x - t_c^{-i}}{2B} + \frac{1}{2}. \quad (6)$$

In this case B is the maximum possible difference between values of t_p^{-i} and t_c^{-i} which would not cause a congestion.

The new cost function h has been defined in Eq. 12 of [3] as follows:

$$h(y, t_c^{-i}, t_p^{-i})$$
$$= Q_{max} \cdot h_1(\frac{t_c^{-i} + y - t_p^{-i}}{B} + 1) \cdot y + P(y, t_c^{-i}, t_p^{-i}). \quad (7)$$

In this definition, Q_{max} is a positive real number which establishes the amount of the tariff: it is is equal to the highest possible unitary cost of the energy. B is another positive real number, which relates to congestion as said in Eq. (6), and $P(x, t_c^{-i}, t_p^{-i})$ is a term which value is zero when $t_c^{-i} + y - t_p^{-i} < B$, and greater than zero if that condition does not hold.

In the definition for h, the function h_1 has been defined in Eq. 8 of [7] as follows.

$$h_1(t) = \begin{cases} 0 & if \ t \leq 0 \\ \sqrt{t} & if \ t \in (0,1] \\ 2 - \sqrt{2-t} & if \ t \in [1,2) \\ 2 & if \ t \geq 2. \end{cases} \quad (8)$$

The functions that have just been described proved to be effective in order to solve the problems detected in the NRG-X-Change mechanism. However, they have not been analyzed yet from the point of view of game theory. In the next section, we will describe a game theory based model for a smart grid, and how can our functions be defined in order to comply to that.

4   A Game Theory Model for Local Energy Communities

This section describes how the main issues treated in this work have been modeled. In particular, following the game theory work done by [12] and [17], a game theory model has been created which describes the grid context and the interactions of the agents within the incentive mechanism: this section outlines the model that has been described in [3].

We start by defining our notation for the problem formulation. As described in Sect. 3.1 of [3], a game $G = (U, S, Q)$ is defined as follows:

- $U = \{U_1, \ldots, U_N\}$ is the set of players.
- $S = \{S_1, \ldots, S_N\}$, where for any $i \in \{1, \ldots, N\}$, S_i is the set of player U_i's strategies.
- $Q = \{q_1, \ldots, q_N\}$, where for any $i \in \{1, \ldots, N\}$, $q_i : \prod_{j=1}^{N} S_j \rightarrow \mathbf{R}$ is the payoff function for player U_i.

From a grid made of N users, it is possible to modelize its behavior as a game in the following way. The set of players is defined by the grid users: we will denote them by U_i, for $i \in \{1, \ldots, N\}$. We now proceed to define the payoff functions and the set of strategies for each player.

Given a grid user U_i, we introduce a vector $\mathbf{c_i}$ defining the energy consumption of U_i, and a vector $\mathbf{p_i}$ which displays the energy production of U_i. These vectors have length equal to the number of time units which make up the considered time horizon; this number will be referred as T. In the case we have considered for our simulations the time horizon has a duration of 24 h, and each time interval is 15 min long: this means that the vectors $\mathbf{c_i}$ and $\mathbf{p_i}$ both have a length of 96. As stated in [3], every component of both vectors $\mathbf{c_i}$ and $\mathbf{p_i}$ is a non-negative real number.

We are also working under the hypothesis that every grid user consumes all the energy she produces, before either selling the surplus produced energy or buying the remaining amount of energy she requires. We are assuming that $\mathbf{c_i}$ and $\mathbf{p_i}$ refer to when self-consumption has already taken place. For this reason, calling $\mathbf{c_i}(t)$ the t−th element of $\mathbf{c_i}$, [3] describes this condition in Eq. 1 as

$$\mathbf{c_i}(t) \cdot \mathbf{p_i}(t) = 0 \ \forall t \in 1, \ldots, T \tag{9}$$

for each $i \in \{1, \ldots, N\}$. Until now, this is a theoretical assumption; however, in later chapters, we will show that all the prosumers in the grid are incentivized to self-consume their energy.

We introduce now the payoff functions, as in [3] with Eq. 2, 3 and 4. For each grid user U_i, we define the corresponding payoff function q_i as the sum of her utility at each time interval. In formal terms:

$$q_i = \sum_{t=1}^{T} q_i(t) \tag{10}$$

where

$$q_i(t) = g(\mathbf{p_i}(t), t_p, t_c) - h(\mathbf{c_i}(t), t_p, t_c). \tag{11}$$

In Eq. 11, the functions g and h are two functions chosen in advance, which determine respectively the reward for U_i for her produced energy and the cost for U_i for her consumed energy. These functions have the property that $g(0, a, b) = h(0, a, b) = 0$ for every $a, b \in \mathbf{R}$. Given a fixed time unit t, the quantities t_p and t_c are determined as defined in [7] and formalized in Eq. 4 of [3]

$$t_p = \sum_{i=1}^{N} \mathbf{p_i}(t)$$

$$t_c = \sum_{i=1}^{N} \mathbf{c_i}(t). \tag{12}$$

These quantities determine respectively the total amount of energy produced and consumed through the grid at the time considered. With the notation we have used until now, at time t, t_p depends on each value $\mathbf{p_i}(t)$ and t_c on each value $\mathbf{c_i}(t)$.

We now highlight how fixed and flexible loads are included in our model: this has already been done by [17]. These are the loads that have been included, defined here as in [3].

- **Production:** We denoted this by $\mathbf{p_i}$. It is the vector which indicates the energy production of the user U_i. In some cases energy production can be altered; however this does not happen in our case, so this is to be considered as a fixed vector.
- **Fixed Consumption:** We call this $\mathbf{f_i}$. It is the vector which indicates the part of the consumption of U_i which does not change depending on choices of the user, and it is a fixed vector by definition. In a real context there is uncertainty about this vector, and precise forecasting is needed to determine it with precision; the work by [6] address this issue by treating it as a vector of probability distributions. However, in this work, we will consider it as known in advance.
- **Shiftable load:** We define it by $\mathbf{h_i}^j$: it is a vector which defines a consumption load of user U_i which can be moved through time. The user can determine the number of time units by which the load - and consequently, the vector - can be shifted; however, it may happen that there are limitations on this number. Expressing a flexible load by $\mathbf{h_i}^j$, we will denote by $r_k(\mathbf{h_i}^j)$ the same vector shifted by k places. In particular, if $k = 0$, we will have $r_0(\mathbf{h_i}^j) = \mathbf{h_i}^j$.

With our notation, suppose that a user has n shiftable loads $\{\mathbf{h_i}^1, \ldots, \mathbf{h_i}^n\}$, and chooses to move each load $\mathbf{h_i}^j$ by an amount k_j of time units. In this case, as stated in Eq. 5 of [3],

$$\mathbf{c_i} = \mathbf{f_i} + \sum_{j=1}^{n} r_{k_j}(\mathbf{h_i}^j). \tag{13}$$

We define the set of strategies of U_i as the set of all the vectors $\mathbf{p_i}$ and $\mathbf{c_i}$ that can be obtained from all the combinations for which loads can be shifted.

Depending on the functions, the defined game changes because its payoff functions q_i change. We now want to see how are they made for the previously defined functions. Regarding the NRG-X-Change mechanism as described in [10], the function $q_i(t)$ is easy to obtain. Recalling its definition from Eq. 11, we can express it like said in Eq. 14 of [3] as

$$q_i(t) = x \cdot \frac{q}{e^{\frac{(t_p - t_c)^2}{a}}} \quad \text{if} \quad y = 0$$

$$q_i(t) = -y \cdot \frac{r \cdot t_c}{t_c + t_p} \quad \text{if} \quad x = 0. \tag{14}$$

It has to be pointed out that at least one between x and y is equal to zero, by the assumption in Eq. 9.

For the model described by [7] it is more difficult to describe the q_i functions, and it may help to treat some different cases separately, as it has been done in [3], from which the following formulas appear as Eq. 15, 16 and 17. We know that either x or y is zero: replacing Eq. (5) and (6) in Eq. (4) and Eq. (8) in Eq. (7):

– **If** $y = 0$, i.e. the user's production is greater than the user's consumption, we have

$$q_i(t) = \frac{P_{max}}{1 + e^{\left(\frac{t_p^{-i}+x-t_c^{-i}}{B}\right)^2 - \frac{1}{4}} \cdot 2^{\frac{t_p^{-i}+x-t_c^{-i}}{B}}} - \frac{P_{max}}{1 + e^{\left(\frac{t_p^{-i}-t_c^{-i}}{B}\right)^2 - \frac{1}{4}} \cdot 2^{\frac{t_p^{-i}-t_c^{-i}}{B}}} \tag{15}$$

– **If** $x = 0$, i.e. the user's consumption is greater than the user's production, we have
  - If $t_p^{-i} > t_c^{-i}$,

$$q_i(t) = -y \cdot Q_{max} \cdot \sqrt{\frac{t_c^{-i}+y-t_p^{-i}}{B}+1} \tag{16}$$

  - If $t_p^{-i} < t_c^{-i}+y$,

$$q_i(t) = -y \cdot Q_{max} \cdot \left(2 - \sqrt{1-\frac{t_c^{-i}+y-t_p^{-i}}{B}}\right) \tag{17}$$

It is significant to point out how a prosumer can adjust her value of x: x is the difference between production and consumption so, even if production curtailment or alteration is discouraged, if she modifies her consumption she can alter this value.

5   Robust P2P Energy Exchange Functions

While the first three issues described in Sect. 3 have already been addressed, the fourth has not been answered yet. To be more precise, our purpose is to verify the presence of a Nash Equilibrium (NE) for the incentive mechanisms described until now and, if the existence of a NE is not guaranteed, to design new cost and reward functions which allow the game to always reach a NE, and which at the same time solve the first three problems described in Sect. 3. In order to do this, we used the procedure described in Sect. 4.3 of [3].

Our approach for evaluating the existing systems in the literature is the following. We started by running tests on the model of the game corresponding to each mechanism in order to observe if the existence of a NE is always guaranteed: in case of positive answer, the aim was to prove mathematically that the system always reaches a NE. In Sect. 6 we show the results of these simulations: neither of those couples of functions ensure that the game reaches a NE.

For this reason, our objective became to design cost and reward functions which make sure that the game outlined in the previous section always reaches a NE. In order to achieve this, we made use of the following result from game theory: if the payoff function of a game is concave, the game always admits a pure

NE [12]. Therefore, the cost function we create has to be convex, and the reward function has to be concave: this way, the payoff function which is obtained like in Eq. 11 will be concave, and exploiting the theorem proven by [14] we can be sure that the game always admits a pure NE.

It is very important that we choose carefully our new functions, so that they fulfill the other requirements in addition to reaching a NE. For ensuring that our new functions g and h always encourage self-consumption for prosumers, we have to make them so that the following inequality, described in Eq. 3 of [7]

$$g(x, t_p, t_c) < h(x, t_p, t_c) \tag{18}$$

is true for every $x > 0$ and for every $t_p, t_c \geq 0$. For making sure that our reward function g does not encourage curtailment, we just need to guarantee that it is a monotonic function with respect to the variable x. Finally, in order to take the possibility of congestion into account actively, it is enough to create penalty terms which further discourage users from creating such a scenario.

In this work, we came up with some proposals for the functions, so that they behave as we just described. We use the notation from Eq. 19 of [3], from which the proposals come from:

$$Z = t_p^{-i} - t_c^{-i} + B. \tag{19}$$

– For the reward function g:
  • **[Logarithm].** One possibility is to use the logarithm function as a baseline for it. This would lead to a function designed in Eq. 20 of [3] as

$$g(x, t_p, t_c) = k_1 \cdot \left(ln \frac{x + Z + a_1}{Z + a_1} \right) \tag{20}$$

  where a_1 and k_1 are parameters, and $a_1 > 0$.
  • **[Square Root].** There is also the possibility to create a function with a behavior similar to the square root function. This can be done with a function like the one from Eq. 21 of [3]

$$g(x, t_p, t_c) = k_1 \cdot \left(\sqrt{x + Z + a_1} - \sqrt{Z + a_1} \right) \tag{21}$$

  where a_1 and k_1 are parameters, and $a_1 > 0$.
– For the cost function h:
  • **[Quadratic].** One idea may be to base our function on the quadratic function. From this, we can create a candidate like the quadratic function from Eq. 22 of [3]

$$h(y, t_p, t_c) = k_2 \cdot \left((y - Z + a_2)^2 - (a_2 - Z)^2 \right) \tag{22}$$

  where a_2 and k_2 are parameters, and $a_2 > 2B$.
  • **[Square Root].** Another idea can be to use the negative square root function. This would lead to the creation of a function like the following, which appears in Eq. 23 of [3]:

$$h(y, t_p, t_c) = k_2 \cdot \left(\sqrt{Z + a_2} - \sqrt{Z + a_2 - y} \right) \tag{23}$$

  where a_2 and k_2 are parameters, and $a_2 > 0$.

We add a term P to every function which has been described above: its purpose is to penalize excess of production and consumption depending on the case, if this may lead to a congestion. For reward functions, P is a function which depends on x, t_p and t_c, and whose value is negative if $t_p - t_c > B$, zero otherwise. For cost functions, P is a function which depends on y, t_p and t_c, and its value is negative if $t_c - t_p > B$, zero otherwise. With the notation we have introduced, a congestion may happen if and only of $Z \notin (0, 2B)$.

It can be seen that the reward functions we have defined are monotonic. This means that a prosumer will always get a higher reward if she produces more energy. As a consequence, she will be incentivized to not curtail her own energy production, as producing less energy will lower her earnings. The only situation where this does not apply is congestion for excess of energy production: in this case, the penalty term of the formula actively disincentivizes further energy production by reducing her income. We have shown that our functions address the first point described at Sect. 4. The second requirement that has to be met is that the cost and reward functions should take actively into account congestion: the functions we are creating respect this requirement, because they have penalty terms for congestion. The third condition holds for every possible couple of functions among the described ones: this will be proven in Sect. 6.1. Lastly, the fourth requirement is fulfilled as a consequence of the theorem proven by [14], which states that a game with concave payoff functions has a pure Nash Equilibrium. The proposed cost functions are convex, the proposed reward functions are concave: for this reason, from Eq. 11, we deduce that the payoff functions are concave, and therefore the game admits a pure Nash Equilibrium.

We created these functions so that they have some useful properties depending on Z. If there is more consumed energy than produced energy at local level, the produced energy has a high value as it is needed to balance the higher consumption: for this reason, the reward functions will have higher values, which means that prosumer will receive a greater compensation for their produced energy. When there is more produced energy than consumed energy at local level, the consumers are less in need for the energy fed into the grid by the prosumers, which means that the reward function will have lower values and consequently prosumers will receive less for their produced energy. For what regards the cost functions, in the case where there is more consumed energy than produced energy at local level, it is important to deter consumers from consuming energy, as it has to be taken from the outside grid; therefore, the cost functions will have higher values, which means that the price for buying energy is higher. In the case where there is more produced energy than consumed energy, however, we would like consumers to increase their energy consumption, as it will be taken from the local grid: consequently, the cost functions will have lower values and the cost of energy for consumers will become lower.

6 Experimental Evaluation

In this section, two main topics are discussed. Section 6.1 proves the self consumption condition for each couple of cost and reward functions obtainable with the new candidate functions, and defines which values of the parameters allow for this condition to be verified. Section 6.2 shows that the baseline functions cannot always ensure the convergence of the game to a NE, while the functions that have been proposed in this work can guarantee that, in accordance with the discussion from the previous chapter.

6.1 Parameterization

In this section, we well make sure that the functions proposed in this work meet the requirement for guaranteeing encouragement of self-consumption of energy. This will be investigated for every one of the four possible couples of cost and reward functions, and then the parameters which allow this condition to hold will be individuated. The first two results have been found in [3], and the proofs are taken from its subsections 5.1.1 and 5.1.2.

Candidate 1: Logarithm Selling, Quadratic Buying. We are considering as the reward function g the one presented in Eq. 20, and as cost function the one presented in Eq. 22.

Our objective is to verify that there is a way to choose the parameters of these two functions, so that Eq. 18 is verified. Substituting the two functions in the self-consumption inequality, as stated in [3], what we want to prove is the existence of parameters k_1, a_1, k_2 and a_2 in such a way that

$$k_1 \cdot \left(\ln \frac{x + Z + a_1}{Z + a_1} \right) < k_2 \cdot \left((x - Z + a_2)^2 - (a_2 - Z)^2 \right)$$

is true for each $x > 0$ and $Z \in (0, 2B)$.

Lemma 1. *For each $x > 0$, $Z > 0$, $a_1 \geq 1$ and $a_2 \geq 2B+1$, and for $k_1 = k_2 > 0$, the inequality*

$$\ln \left(1 + \frac{x}{Z + a_1} \right)^{k_1} < k_2 \cdot x \cdot (x - 2Z + 2a_2) \tag{24}$$

holds [3].

Proof. Taking into account exponents, Eq. 24 becomes

$$\left(1 + \frac{x}{Z + a_1} \right)^{k_1} < e^{k_2 \cdot x \cdot (x - 2Z + 2a_2)}$$

We know that $k_1 = k_2$, so it is possible to cancel out the equal exponents. The inequality that has to be proven can then be written as

$$1 + \frac{x}{Z + a_1} < e^{x \cdot (x - 2Z + 2a_2)}.$$

Now, assigning $a_1 \geq 1$ and $a_2 \geq 2B + 1$, the chain of inequalities

$$1 + \frac{x}{Z + a_1} \leq 1 + \frac{x}{Z + 1} < 1 + x < e^{x^2 + x} \leq e^{x \cdot (x - 2Z + 2a_2)}$$

completes the proof, as it is true for every $x > 0$ and $Z \in (0, 2B)$.

Proposition 1. *The function defined in Eq. 20 with $a_1 = 1$, together with the function defined in Eq. 22 with $a_2 = 2B + 1$, satisfies the self-consumption condition defined in Eq. 18 if $k_1 = k_2 > 0$ [3].*

Proof. By Lemma 1, choosing the parameters as mentioned earlier, the inequality

$$k_1 \cdot \ln \left(\frac{x + Z + a_1}{Z + a_1} \right) = \ln \left(\frac{x + Z + a_1}{Z + a_1} \right)^{k_1}$$
$$= \ln \left(1 + \frac{x}{Z + a_1} \right)^{k_1} < k_2 \cdot x \cdot (x - 2Z + 2a_2)$$
$$= k_2 \cdot \left((x - Z + a_2)^2 - (a_2 - Z)^2 \right).$$

holds for each $x > 0$, $Z \in (0, 2B)$.

Candidate 2: Square Root Selling, Negative Square Root Buying.

In this case, the reward function g is the one presented in Eq. 21, and the cost function is the one presented in Eq. 23.

Proposition 2. *It is possibile to choose the parameters k_1 and a_1 for the reward function defined in Eq. 21, and for the parameters k_2 and a_2 for the cost function defined in Eq. 23, in such a way that those functions respect the inequality in Eq. 18. In particular, this happens if $k_1 = k_2 > 0$ and if $a_1 \geq a_2 + 2B$ [3].*

Proof. The self-consumption condition can be written as

$$k_1 \cdot \left(\sqrt{x + Z + a_1} - \sqrt{Z + a_1} \right) <$$
$$k_2 \cdot \left(\sqrt{Z + a_2} - \sqrt{Z + a_2 - x} \right).$$

Substituting $k_1 = k_2$ and canceling them out, it becomes

$$\sqrt{x + Z + a_1} - \sqrt{Z + a_1} < \sqrt{Z + a_2} - \sqrt{Z + a_2 - x}.$$

Rationalizing the denominators, this holds if and only if

$$\frac{x}{\sqrt{x + Z + a_1} + \sqrt{Z + a_1}} < \frac{x}{\sqrt{Z + a_2} + \sqrt{Z + a_2 - x}}$$

and considering denominators, since we want to prove it for $x > 0$, this is true if and only if

$$\sqrt{x + Z + a_1} + \sqrt{Z + a_1} > \sqrt{Z + a_2} + \sqrt{Z + a_2 - x}.$$

Now, if $a_1 \geq 2B + a_2$, we have the chain of inequalities

$$\sqrt{x + Z + a_1} + \sqrt{Z + a_1} > 2\sqrt{a_1} \geq$$
$$2\sqrt{2B + a_2} > \sqrt{Z + a_2} + \sqrt{Z + a_2 - x}$$

which holds for every $x > 0$, $Z \in (0, 2B)$, and this completes the proof.

Candidate 3: Logarithm Selling, Negative Square Root Buying. This is the case where the selling function g is the one described in Eq. 20, while the proposed buying function h is the one described in Eq. 23.

Lemma 2. *For each $x > 0$, $Z > 0$ and $a_1 = a_2 > 4$, and choosing $k_1 = k_2 > 0$, the inequality*

$$k_1 \cdot \ln\left(1 + \frac{x}{Z + a_1}\right) < k_2 \cdot \left(\frac{x}{2\sqrt{Z + a_2}}\right) \tag{25}$$

holds.

Proof. First, since $k_1 = k_2$, we cancel out the terms. The inequality that has to be proven becomes

$$\ln\left(1 + \frac{x}{Z + a_1}\right) < \frac{x}{2\sqrt{Z + a_2}}.$$

Taking exponential, this becomes

$$1 + \frac{x}{Z + a_1} < e^{\frac{x}{2\sqrt{Z + a_2}}}. \tag{26}$$

However, substituting $a_1 = a_2$, the function

$$e^{\frac{x}{2\sqrt{Z + a_1}}} - 1 - \frac{x}{Z + a_1}$$

is convex, has value zero for $x = 0$, and has a minimum for

$$x = 2\sqrt{Z + a_1} \ln \frac{2}{\sqrt{Z + a_1}}.$$

In particular, since $Z + a_1 > 4$, the minimum is obtained for a negative value of x. This, along with the convexity of the function, implies that Eq. 26 holds for every $x > 0$ and $Z > 0$. Consequently, the lemma is proven.

Proposition 3. *There is a choice for the parameters k_1 and a_1 for the selling function defined in Eq. 20, and for the parameters k_2 and a_2 for the buying function defined in Eq. 23, such that these two functions fulfill the condition defined in Eq. 18. More specifically, this happens if $k_1 = k_2 > 0$ and if $a_1 = a_2 > 4$.*

Proof. The self-consumption condition can be written as

$$k_1 \cdot \left(\ln \frac{x + Z + a_1}{Z + a_1}\right) < k_2 \cdot \left(\sqrt{Z + a_2} - \sqrt{Z + a_2 - x}\right).$$

Substituting $k_1 = k_2$ and canceling them out, it becomes

$$\ln\left(1 + \frac{x}{Z + a_1}\right) < \sqrt{Z + a_2} - \sqrt{Z + a_2 - x}.$$

We can write the right hand side as

$$\sqrt{Z + a_2} - \sqrt{Z + a_2 - x} = \frac{x}{\sqrt{Z + a_2} + \sqrt{Z + a_2 - x}}$$

and this can be estimated by

$$\frac{x}{\sqrt{Z + a_2} + \sqrt{Z + a_2 - x}} > \frac{x}{2\sqrt{Z + a_2}}.$$

Applying Lemma 2, we know that

$$\ln\left(1 + \frac{x}{Z + a_1}\right) < \frac{x}{2\sqrt{Z + a_2}}$$

so, collecting what we have pointed out in this proof, we obtain the chain of inequalities

$$\ln\left(1 + \frac{x}{Z + a_1}\right) < \frac{x}{2\sqrt{Z + a_2}} < \sqrt{Z + a_2} - \sqrt{Z + a_2 - x}$$

which holds for every $x > 0$, $Z > 0$, and this completes the proof.

Candidate 4: Square Root Selling, Quadratic Buying. This is the case where the selling function g is the one described in Eq. 21, while the proposed buying function h is the one described in Eq. 22.

Proposition 4. *There is a choice for the parameters k_1 and a_1 for the selling function defined in Eq. 21, and for the parameters k_2 and a_2 for the buying function defined in Eq. 22, such that these two functions fulfill the condition defined in Eq. 18. More specifically, this happens if $k_1 = k_2 > 0$, $a_1 > 1$ and $a_2 > 2B + 1$.*

Proof. The self-consumption condition can be written as

$$k_1 \cdot \left(\sqrt{x + Z + a_1} - \sqrt{Z + a_1}\right) <$$
$$k_2 \cdot \left((x - Z + a_2)^2 - (a_2 - Z)^2\right).$$

Substituting $k_1 = k_2$ and canceling them out, it becomes

$$\sqrt{x + Z + a_1} - \sqrt{Z + a_1} < x \cdot (x - 2Z + 2a_2).$$

Now, if we choose $a_1 > 1$, $a_2 > 2B + 1$, the left hand side becomes

$$\sqrt{x + Z + a_1} - \sqrt{Z + a_1} < \sqrt{x + 1} - 1$$

and the right hand side becomes

$$x \cdot (x - 2Z + 2a_2) > x \cdot (x + 1).$$

It is also easy to prove that, for every $x > 0$,

$$x \cdot (x + 1) > \sqrt{x + 1} - 1$$

as it is equivalent to

$$x^4 + 2x^3 + 3x^2 + x > 0$$

which is true for every positive value of x.

Putting together the estimations done until now, we have the chain of inequalities

$$\sqrt{x + Z + a_1} - \sqrt{Z + a_1} < \sqrt{x + 1} - 1 <$$
$$x \cdot (x + 1) < x \cdot (x - 2Z + 2a_2)$$

which holds for every $x > 0$, $Z \in (0, 2B)$, and this completes the proof.

6.2   Empirical Results

This section shows the results of our simulations. We recapitulate, that up to this point, two important conclusions have been reached. First, the already existing incentive mechanism described in this work, NRG-X-Change and the improved version theorized by [7], cannot assure the existence of a NE in the game described in Sect. 4. Second, the proposals that we have described in Sect. 3 always guarantee the existence of a NE in that game, in accord with the theoretical results.

For our simulation, we created a script in *Python* language. We have used real data belonging to a grid in Cardiff, which has 184 users: among them, 40 are prosumers. Further information about the grid is described in [16][4].

The game has been simulated in the following way, as described from [3]:

1. We randomly choose a set of N grid users among the 184 from the Cardiff grid, and we denote them by $U_1, \ldots, U_N$. The number N depends on the case we want to simulate, and so it is the number of prosumers among those N users. For each user, their production and consumption at each time unit is known, and each of them has one shiftable load, which initial allocation is randomly determined.
2. This step will be repeated sequentially for each user U_i, starting from U_1, then U_2, and so on until U_N. For each user, we take into account that the values of t_p and t_c can change depending on the choices of other users. After this, the user U_i has the chance to determine where her shiftable load will be allocated. She calculates her payoff function for each possible allocation by considering total production and consumption at each time, and then chooses the allocation which makes the payoff function obtain the highest possible value. Once this step has been performed for all the users, we say that an *iteration* has been run.

---

[4] To obtain the data please send an email to the MAS^{2}TERING coordinator https://www.mas2tering.eu/.

3. For each user, we verify whether their allocation has changed with respect to the previous iteration or not. If no user has changed her allocation, the simulation is over. Otherwise, the simulation continues from step 2 with the updated allocations.
4. If a certain maximum number of iterations has been performed, or if the configuration of the shiftable loads is exactly the same of a configuration which has been reached in a previous iteration, the game ends.

The game will end either at step 3 or at step 4. In the first case, no user has changed their load allocation during the last iteration: this means that the game admits a Nash Equilibrium. In the second case, if the configuration after the last iteration is the same of a previous iteration, the game from then on will repeat itself in the exact same way again and again, which means that it will never reach a Nash Equilibrium. The number of possible configurations for the game is finite: this means that the game will sooner or later reach one of the two states mentioned above, and therefore setting a maximum number of iterations is not necessary. If the simulation requires too much time, however, it may be a good idea to set a limit for their number.

The different configurations (i.e. combination of payoff functions) simulated in order to see whether the algorithm just described converges or not are the following:

- [**Original**]: the original NRG-X-Change buying and selling functions.
- [**Improved**]: buying and selling functions as improved in [7].
- [**Log/Sq**]: buying function as defined in Eq. 22 and selling function as defined in Eq. 20.
- [**SqRts**]: buying function as defined in Eq. 23 and selling function as defined in Eq. 21.
- [**Log/Rt**]: buying function as defined in Eq. 23 and selling function as defined in Eq. 20.
- [**Sq/Sqr**]: buying function as defined in Eq. 22 and selling function as defined in Eq. 21.

The parameters of the functions have been set in such a way that, when local total production and local total consumption are equal, all the selling functions have the same value, and the same is true for all the buying functions. These values have been chosen as close as possible to the tariffs for selling and buying energy in the Cardiff grid. Table 1 details for each configuration of functions and each percentage of prosumers how often the game converges to a NE. For each case and couple of functions, 350 simulations have been performed, and the number of users in the grid varies in a range between 10 and 70 users. In addition to this, Table 2 shows the number of iterations needed on average to reach convergence for the game as well as the average increment in self-consumption among the grid users after the game reaches the equilibrium for each couple of functions.

Table 1. Number of cases in which the game reaches a Nash Equilibrium with respect to the percentage of prosumers in the grid and the couple of functions used. Results from the first four candidate functions have been reported in Table 1 of [3].

Prosumers %	Original	Improved	Log/Sq	SqRts	Log/Rt	Sq/Sqr
10%	15	182	350	350	350	350
30%	164	294	350	350	350	350
50%	342	350	350	350	350	350

Table 2. Average number of iterations for reaching a NE and average increase of self-consumption for every couple of functions. Results relative to the first four candidate functions have been reported in Table 2 of [3].

Functions	Number of iterations to NE	Energy self-consumed
Original	4.7243	15.4634
Improved	4.8542	19.8862
Log/Sq	4.0371	22.8833
SqRts	3.9000	22.8527
Log/Rt	3.9276	22.8906
Sq/Sqr	4.0429	22.8423

We draw the following insights from the results just described.

– The couples of existing functions defined as **Original** and **Improved** does not guarantee that the defined game converges to a NE. However, in coherence with the theoretical results, all the new proposed couples of functions always guarantee the convergence to a NE.
– The results obtained by the **Improved** functions are better than the ones obtained by the **Original** ones. This is true for number of convergence cases at each considered grid size and amount of prosumers, and for the amount of self-consumption; however, the amount of iterations needed on average to reach a NE is a little higher.
– The new proposed couple of functions (**SqRts**, **Log/Sq**, **Sq/Sqr** and **Log/Rt**) outperform the old functions (**Original** and **Improved**) on all the tested aspects. In particular, the newly proposed functions always allow the game to converge to a NE, reach convergence in a lower number of iterations with respect to the baseline functions, and achieve better results in terms of energy self-consumption. Regarding the difference of performance between the couples of new functions that is minimum and not statistical significant.

Finally, we show the effect of the performed game on the amount of net consumption through the community. The graph in Fig. 1, which is reported in [3], Fig. 1, showcases the difference between production and consumption at each time, before and after the game is performed. The figure in particular refers to the situation with 4 prosumers and 36 consumers, even if all cases behave in a very similar way.

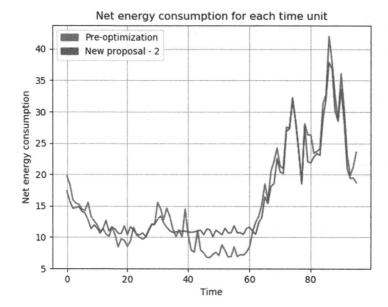

Fig. 1. This graph comes from [3]. Net energy consumption before and after the optimization. The x axis indicates the time units through the day, while the y axis indicates the difference between total consumption and production through the grid. We have depicted the values before the optimization (in red) and after the optimization (in green). It has to be remarked that the shiftable loads were randomly allocated through the day in the initial configuration. (Color figure online)

7   Conclusions and Future Work

The relevance of local energy communities in energy systems is increasing, and the same is true for peer-to-peer energy systems. In this work, mechanisms for local energy trading between grid users have been analyzed, in a context where the users act selfishly for optimizing their own energy profiles. The proposed incentive systems have been tailored so that energy production and self-consumption is encouraged at local level, and balance between produced and consumed energy is promoted.

We have shown through mathematical analysis some important properties of our proposed mechanism, which are not present in previously existing ones. The simulations we have run with data from a real grid show that our proposal gives better results, both in terms of stability in agent decisions and of energy self-consumption through the community. The mechanism encourages consumers to move their loads when there is more local energy production, while prosumers are incentivized to not curtail their own production.

Our directions for future work are aimed at analyzing how these incentive systems can operate with different types of flexibile loads, such as heat pumps and batteries.

Acknowledgements. This research has received funding from the European Union's Horizon 2020 research and innovation program under grant agreement No 774431 (DRIvE).

References

1. Capodieci, N., Pagani, G., Cabri, G., Aiello, M.: Smart meter aware domestic energy trading agents. In: First International E-Energy Market Challenge Workshop (co-located with ICAC 2011). ACM Press (2011), relation. https://www.rug.nl/fmns-research/bernoulli/index. Rights: University of Groningen, Johann Bernoulli Institute for Mathematics and Computer Science

2. Commission, T.E.: European commission guidance for the design of renewables support schemes. In: Delivering the Internal Market in Electricity and Making the Most of Public Intervention. Technical report, The European Commission (2013). https://ec.europa.eu/energy/sites/ener/files/com_2013_public_intervention_swd04_en.pdf

3. Denysiuk, R., Lilliu, F., Recupero, D.R., Vinyals, M.: Peer-to-peer energy trading for smart energy communities. In: Rocha, A.P., Steels, L., van den Herik, H.J. (eds.) Proceedings of the 12th International Conference on Agents and Artificial Intelligence, ICAART 2020, Valletta, Malta, 22–24 February 2020, vol. 1, pp. 40–49. SCITEPRESS (2020)

4. Ilic, D., da Silva, P.G., Karnouskos, S., Griesemer, M.: An energy market for trading electricity in smart grid neighbourhoods. In: 6th IEEE International Conference on Digital Ecosystems and Technologies, DEST 2012, Campione d'Italia, Italy, 18–20 June 2012, pp. 1–6 (2012). https://doi.org/10.1109/DEST.2012.6227918

5. Kok, J.K., Warmer, C.J., Kamphuis, I.G.: PowerMatcher: multiagent control in the electricity infrastructure. In: 4rd International Joint Conference on Autonomous Agents and Multiagent Systems (AAMAS 2005), 25–29 July 2005, Utrecht, The Netherlands - Special Track for Industrial Applications, pp. 75–82 (2005). https://doi.org/10.1145/1082473.1082807

6. Lilliu, F., Loi, A., Reforgiato Recupero, D., Sisinni, M., Vinyals, M.: An uncertainty-aware optimization approach for flexible loads of smart grid prosumers: a use case on the Cardiff energy grid. Sustain. Energy Grids Netw. **20**, 100272 (2019). https://doi.org/10.1016/j.segan.2019.100272

7. Lilliu, F., Vinyals, M., Denysiuk, R., Reforgiato Recupero, D.: A novel payment scheme for trading renewable energy in smartgrid. In: Proceedings of the Tenth International Conf. on Future Energy Systems, e-Energy 2019, Phoenix, United States, 25–28 June 2019 (2019, to appear)

8. Loni, A., Parand, F.: A survey of game theory approach in smart grid with emphasis on cooperative games. In: 2017 IEEE International Conf. on Smart Grid and Smart Cities (ICSGSC), pp. 237–242, July 2017. https://doi.org/10.1109/ICSGSC.2017.8038583

9. Mihaylov, M., et al.: SCANERGY: a scalable and modular system for energy trading between prosumers. In: Proceedings of the International Conference on Autonomous Agents and Multiagent Systems, AAMAS 2015, Istanbul, Turkey, 4–8 May 2015, pp. 1917–1918 (2015). http://dl.acm.org/citation.cfm?id=2773503

10. Mihaylov, M., Jurado, S., Avellana, N., Van Moffaert, K., de Abril, I.M., Nowé, A.: NRGcoin: virtual currency for trading of renewable energy in smart grids. In: 2014 11th International Conference on the European Energy Market (EEM), pp. 1–6. IEEE (2014)

11. Mihaylov, M.: Comparing stakeholder incentives across state-of-the-art renewable support mechanisms. Renew. Energy **131**, 689–699 (2019)

12. Nguyen, H.K., Song, J.B., Han, Z.: Demand side management to reduce peak-to-average ratio using game theory in smart grid. In: 2012 Proceedings IEEE INFO-COM Workshops, Orlando, FL, USA, 25–30 March 2012, pp. 91–96 (2012). https://doi.org/10.1109/INFCOMW.2012.6193526

13. Rad, A.H.M., Wong, V.W.S., Jatskevich, J., Schober, R., Leon-Garcia, A.: Autonomous demand-side management based on game-theoretic energy consumption scheduling for the future smart grid. IEEE Trans. Smart Grid **1**(3), 320–331 (2010). https://doi.org/10.1109/TSG.2010.2089069

14. Rosen, J.B.: Existence and uniqueness of equilibrium points for concave n-person games. Econometrica **33**(3), 520–534 (1965). http://www.jstor.org/stable/1911749

15. Saad, W., Han, Z., Poor, H.V., Basar, T.: Game-theoretic methods for the smart grid: an overview of microgrid systems, demand-side management, and smart grid communications. IEEE Signal Process. Mag. **29**(5), 86–105 (2012). https://doi.org/10.1109/MSP.2012.2186410

16. Sisinni, M., et al.: D2.2 - mas^{2}tering platform design document. MAS^{2}TERING public reports, Febrary 2016. http://www.mas2tering.eu/papers-documents-tools/

17. Soliman, H.M., Leon-Garcia, A.: Game-theoretic demand-side management with storage devices for the future smart grid. IEEE Trans. Smart Grid **5**(3), 1475–1485 (2014). https://doi.org/10.1109/TSG.2014.2302245

On the Combination of Game-Theoretic Learning and Multi Model Adaptive Filters

Michalis Smyrnakis[1]([✉])(iD), Hongyang Qu[2](iD), Dario Bauso[3,4](iD),
and Sandor Veres[2](iD)

[1] Science and Technology Facilities Council, Daresbury, UK
michail.smyrnakis@stfc.ac.uk
[2] Department of Automatic Control and Systems Engineering,
University of Sheffield, Sheffield, UK
{h.qu,s.veres}@sheffield.ac.uk
[3] Jan C. Willems Center for Systems and Control ENTEG,
Faculty of Science and Engineering, University of Groningen Nijenborgh, Groningen,
The Netherlands
[4] Dipartimento di Ingegneria, Università di Palermo,
Viale delle Scienze, Palermo, Italy
d.bauso@rug.nl

Abstract. This paper casts coordination of a team of robots within the framework of game theoretic learning algorithms. In particular a novel variant of fictitious play is proposed, by considering multi-model adaptive filters as a method to estimate other players' strategies. The proposed algorithm can be used as a coordination mechanism between players when they should take decisions under uncertainty. Each player chooses an action after taking into account the actions of the other players and also the uncertainty. Uncertainty can occur either in terms of noisy observations or various types of other players. In addition, in contrast to other game-theoretic and heuristic algorithms for distributed optimisation, it is not necessary to find the optimal parameters a priori. Various parameter values can be used initially as inputs to different models. Therefore, the resulting decisions will be aggregate results of all the parameter values. Simulations are used to test the performance of the proposed methodology against other game-theoretic learning algorithms.

Keywords: Game-theoretic learning · Distributed optimisation · Multi-model adaptive filters · Robot teams coordination · Fictitious play · Bayesian games · Potential games · State based games · Stochastic games

1 Introduction

Teams of robots can be used in many domains such as mine detection [69], medication delivery in medical facilities [16], formation control [45,58] and exploration of unknown environments [31,55]. A common feature shared by these

© Springer Nature Switzerland AG 2021
A. P. Rocha et al. (Eds.): ICAART 2020, LNAI 12613, pp. 73–105, 2021.
https://doi.org/10.1007/978-3-030-71158-0_4

applications is that robots should either minimise a cost function or maximise a utility function in a distributed fashion. Thus, the resulting problem can be formulated as an distributed optimization one. Distributed optimisation arises also in several applications such as in smart grids [2,66], disaster management [25,57], robot team coordination [51,52], sensor networks [23,24,32,68], water distribution system optimisation [2,66] and scheduling problems [61].

In each of the aforementioned applications, the agents need to coordinate to achieve a common goal. If the desired task requires distributed optimisation of a utility or cost function, then the resulting problem turns into a game where each agent optimizes a portion of the common objective function based on local information. In such a scenario, game theory provides formal tools to assess the quality of the solution obtained.

As in [59], in this paper we address two kinds of uncertainty that can be arise in a game theoretic learning process that can be applied in robotic scenarios. The first one is related to uncertainty of measurements. Consider the case where, the robots do not have access to the other robots' states, or if the communication channel is noisy or involves faulty sensors, we say that the game has imperfect information, and the robots have to make a decision under uncertainty. Uncertainty can lead to wrong decision. For example, wrong decisions could be made when the positions of other robots are inferred by noisy odometry or noisy camera input. Another example in which noisy observation can have impact on the coordination process of a robot team is the case of a fleet of Unmaned Aerial Vehicles (UAVs) that need to take images of an area in order to identify the growth of the crops. The images should be taken from various angles. However, it is not always possible for a UAV to know the exact position and bearing of the other UAVs, and therefore, to make correct decisions about when to change photo-shooting angles.

The second form of uncertainty is related with various states or types that the environment or other robots can be. This uncertainty can be in the form of incomplete information. A team of UAVs can know the weather conditions for their tasks, "good" or "bad" weather for example, up to a certain probability. Consider also the case where, each member of a robotic team can be in various possible states regarding its battery life, affecting the possible choices they have. On another setup the choices robots are making in a current snapshot of their mission could affect their future choices.Stochastic, state based and Bayesian games are two categories of games which can be used in order to model distributed optimisation task under those types of uncertainty.

In this paper, we propose a novel game-theoretic learning algorithm, which can be used as a coordination mechanism among robots playing either complete information games with noisy observations or Bayesian games or Markov games. In detail, it is a synchronous algorithm, where Extended Kalman Filters Fictitious Play (EKFFP) [60] is combined with multi-model adaptive filters (MMAFs) [9]. The novelty of our algorithm is that the joint distribution of the uncertainty and the observed actions of other players' action are used to make decisions. Robots use multiple models to solve their optimisation task.

Each model is either a probabilistic representation of the noisy observations model of the other players' states or of the state of the world. Each model of MMAF represents a part of uncertainty and the final decision making is based on a weighted average over all the models.

Note here that a sequence of Bayesian games can also be used to describe partially observable games and decentralised partial observable Markov decision process (dec-POMDPs) [15]. Thus the proposed methodology can be used as a coordination mechanism for each individual Bayesian game (sub-tasks) till a solution to the dec-POMDP is found.

Another advantage of our algorithm, is that in contrast to EKFFP and various heuristic distributed optimisation algorithms, there is no need to tune any parameters. Therefore, there is no need to decide in advance the value of the EKFFP parameters. Instead, random valuations of these parameters can be used simultaneously. Each valuation predicts other robots' strategy from a different angle, which is represented by different models. Therefore, it is easier to adapt to evolution of other robots' strategy.

This article is an extended version of [59]. This version considers more types of uncertainty which are related with two new categories of games, namely stochastic and state based games. In addition, the basic game theoretic definitions and learning algorithms were explained in more detail. Also, additional information is provided regarding the implementation details of the proposed algorithm.

The rest of the paper is organised as follows. Next section contains a brief description of related work. In Sect. 3, a brief description of the game-theoretic notions that will be used in the rest of the paper are presented. In Sect. 4, the learning algorithm EKFFP is presented. Section 5 describes our fictitious play based algorithm, which integrates multi-model adaptive filters and extended Kalman filter. Section 6 discusses some implementation details of our algorithm and game-theoretic learning algorithms in general. In Sect. 7, we evaluate our algorithm in several case studies. In Sect. 8, we summarise our findings and present our future work.

2   Related Work

Distributed learning under noisy observation was considered in [27]. Particle swarm algorithms subjected to intrinsic noise was applied in [42] and [13]. In [21], noisy observations in a different context from this work were investigated, as no directly any knowledge about the noisy observation was used, such as their probability distribution. In [11], the uncertainty was dealt within a game theoretic framework under a simplified assumption that players use the same strategy through the iterations of the game.

Various approaches have been adopted to solve Bayesian games including: Bayesian action graph games [22], Multi-agent influence diagrams [26] and Newton method [19]. The difference between these approaches and the proposed algorithm is that their goal is to find the optimal strategy. However, the search for an optimal solution in cooperative Bayesian games is an NP-hard problem

[65], and thus, is not tractable. On the other hand, in our algorithm players take into account the other players' actions and their possible types when updating their desired action until they reach to a commonly accepted solution, which is usually an equilibrium point to the problem. In [15], an approximate solution was proposed based on an alternating maximisation algorithm, but this is not applicable when robots choose their actions simultaneously. Smooth fictitious play [43] and a variant of fictitious play for Bayesian games with continuous states [44] have been used to solve auctions in a competitive environment, which is not applicable in cooperative games on which this work is focused.

Various reinforcement learning techniques have been proposed as solutions to stochastic games. Examples include minimax Q and Q-learning in [30], decentralized Q-learning, distributed Q-learning, hysteretic Q-learning, and WOLF PHC in [34]. In [54] Classic fictitious play has also been used in order to solve a Markov games that used in order to model robotic arm manipulators. In [33] a log-linear process was proposed to solve state based games. When in [29] a two-memory better reply algorithm was proposed. In contrast, the proposed algorithm since a different model is used for each possible state of the game. Moreover, the model of each state is updated only when the state is active which allows to have a more accurate estimate of opponents' strategies in each state.

3   Game-Theoretic Definitions

This section contains a brief description of some game theoretic definitions that will be used in the rest of the paper.

3.1   Normal Form Games

A game Γ in normal form is defined as a tuple

$$\Gamma = \langle \mathcal{I}, \{A^i\}_{i \in \mathcal{I}}, \{r^i\}_{i \in \mathcal{I}} \rangle,$$

where

- $\mathcal{I}$ is the set of indices of all players;
- A^i is the set of all possible actions of player i and the set product $A = \times_{i \in \mathcal{I}} A^i$ is the set of all joint actions;
- $r^i : A \to \mathbb{R}$ is the utility (reward) function of player i, which computes the reward that the player gains after a joint action is selected.

Joint action a, can be written as $a = (a^i, a^{-i})$, where a^{-i} is the joint action of all players but i. A strategy of player i is a probability distribution over its action space, and let Δ^i denote the set of all the probability distributions over A^i. Each player uses a strategy $\sigma^i \in \Delta^i$ to choose its action. Similarly to actions, a joint strategy $\sigma \in \Delta$ is defined as an element of the set product $\Delta = \times_{i \in \mathcal{I}} \Delta^i$, and σ^{-i} is a joint strategy of all players but i.

In this paper we consider iterative games. In these games, a game is repeatedly played along a discrete sequence of time instances called rounds or iterations when each player chooses their actions based on their strategies, the history of the observed joint actions in the played iterations of the game and the rewardse allocated to them.

A player uses a *pure* strategy when it deterministically chooses actions, therefore it puts all its mass function in a single action $a^i \in A^i$ such that $\sigma^i(a^i) = 1$. When this is not the case, we call such a strategy, *mixed* strategy. The expected reward of player i, given its opponents' strategies σ^{-i}, is denoted by $r^i(\sigma^i, \sigma^{-i})$. If σ^i is a pure strategy with $\sigma^i(a^i) = 1$, the expected reward can be written as $r^i(a^i, \sigma^{-i})$.

The most common deterministic decision rule in game theory is the so-called *best response* (BR) by which players choose the actions which maximise their expected rewards. Formally, the action that a player i will choose, given its opponents strategies σ^{-i}, is

$$BR^i(\sigma^{-i}) = \underset{a^i \in A^i}{\operatorname{argmax}} \quad r^i(a^i, \sigma^{-i}). \tag{1}$$

A normal form game Γ can be either a competitive or a coordination game, depending on its utility function. In competitive games, players have conflicted interests, while in coordination games, they maximise their reward when a common goal is achieved. Table 1 depicts the players' rewards of a zero-sum game, which is an canonical example of competitive games. There are two players in this game: the row player playing actions b^1 and b^2 and the column player playing a^1 and a^2. Each entry in the table represents the reward they receive when the corresponding joint action is played. For example, entry $1, -1$ means that the row player receives 1 and the column player receives -1 when they play joint action (b^1, a^1). Therefore, the reward a player gains is what the other player looses. Similarly, Table 2 presents the rewards of a coordination game where both players receive the same reward.

Table 1. Zero sum game.

	a^1	a^2
b^1	1,−1	−1,1
b^2	−1,1	1,−1

Table 2. Coordination game.

	a^1	a^2
b^1	1,1	0,0
b^2	0,0	2,2

A joint strategy $\tilde{\sigma} = (\tilde{\sigma}^i, \tilde{\sigma}^{-i})$ that satisfies

$$r^i(\tilde{\sigma}^i, \tilde{\sigma}^{-i}) \geq r^i(\sigma^i, \sigma^{-i}) \quad \forall i \in \mathcal{I}, \forall \sigma^i \in \Delta^i$$

is a Nash equilibrium [38]. Nash in [38] showed that every game has at least one equilibrium, i.e., there is at least one strategy $\tilde{\sigma}$ where players do not benefit from deviating from it unilaterally. A Nash equilibrium can be either mixed or pure if the strategy $\tilde{\sigma}$ is a mixed or a pure strategy respectively.

A class of games of particular interest is potential games. In [36], it was shown that distributed optimisation tasks can be cast as potential games. Hence, the search of an optimal solution in a distributed optimisation problem can be seen as searching for a Nash equilibrium in a potential game. A game Γ is a potential game if the rewards of all players can be replaced by a potential function ϕ such that $\forall a = (a^i, a^{-i}) \in A$ and $\forall \bar{a} = (\bar{a}^i, \bar{a}^{-i}) \in A$:

$$r^i(a^i, a^{-i}) - r^i(\bar{a}^i, \bar{a}^{-i}) = \phi(a^i, a^{-i}) - \phi(\bar{a}^i, \bar{a}^{-i}).$$

[36] showed that every potential game has at least one pure Nash equilibrium.

3.2 Bayesian Games

A Bayesian game, or game of incomplete information, is defined as a tuple

$$\mathcal{G} = \langle \mathcal{I}, \{\Theta^i\}_{i \in \mathcal{I}}, \{A^i\}_{i \in \mathcal{I}}, \{p(\theta^i)\}_{\theta^i \in \Theta, i \in \mathcal{I}}, \{r^i\}_{i \in \mathcal{I}} \rangle,$$

where

- $\mathcal{I}$ is the set of player indices;
- Θ^i is the set of types belonging to player i and $\Theta = \times_{i \in \mathcal{I}} \Theta^i$;
- A^i is set of possible actions of player i;
- $r^i : A \to \mathbb{R}$ is the utility function of player i.

Each type of a player represents a possible internal state of the player. At any time, a player can only be in one of its types. The type of a player constitutes its private information, in the sense that each player i knows the type that it is in. In contrast, the other players only know the probability that player i can be in a certain type at that moment. If $\theta^i \in \Theta^i$ is considered as the state of the environment, i.e., the type of a player is the state of the environment (world), then all players have the same types and thus $\Theta^i = \Theta^j, \forall i, j \in \mathcal{I}$. The expected reward of a player in a Bayesian game is then estimated as:

$$r^i(\sigma^i, \theta^i) = \sum_{\theta^{-i} \in \Theta^{-i}} p(\theta^{-i}) r^i(\sigma^i, \theta^i, \sigma^{-i}, \theta^{-i}). \tag{2}$$

A Bayesian Nash equilibrium is defined as

$$\sigma^i \in \operatorname*{argmax}_{a^i \in A} \; p(\theta^i | \theta^{-i}) r^i(\sigma^i, \theta^i, \sigma^{-i}, \theta^{-i})$$

Hence a Bayesian Nash equilibrium is a Nash equilibrium of the expanded game in which each player action space of pure strategies is the set of maps from Θ^i to A^i.

As an example, consider a task allocation scenario: two robots 1 and 2 need to collaborate to finish two tasks: *easy* and *difficult*. The *difficult* task can be performed efficiently only if both robots work together on it. Robot 1 can do both tasks at the same efficiency, and hence it has only one type. Robot 2 has two types A and B. In type A, robot 2 can do the *easy* task with greater efficiency than the difficult task, while in type B, it performs both tasks with the same efficiency. Furthermore, robot 2 always knows its type, while robot 1 only knows that with probability p robot 2 is in type A, and with probability $1 - p$ is in type B. In this game, the world has a unique state and thus does not affect robots' types. Table 3 illustrates an example of the utility function in this Bayesian game.

Table 3. Reward matrices of a two players Bayesian game.

Type A			Type B		
task	difficult	easy	task	difficult	easy
difficult	10,6	5,10	difficult	9,10	5,4
easy	8,5	6,8	easy	8,6	7,5

Each matrix of Table 3 represents the rewards that robots receive. The single type robot is the row player of the game, and the other robot is the column player of the game. If robot 2 is in type A, then both robots receive the rewards in the left matrix, while when it is type B, they receive the reward in the right matrix. For example, the entry 5, 10 of the left matrix means that when robot 1 performs the *difficult* task and robot 2 does the *easy* task and is in type A. In this case, robot 1 receives 5 unit of reward and robot 2 receives 10 units. We reinforce here that at any time of game playing, robot 2 knows exactly which reward matrix is used, while robot 1 makes decisions based on the probability distribution of types of robot 2: p and $1 - p$ for the left and right matrix respectively.

3.3 Stochastic Games

Stochastic games [53] is considering as a multi-agent extension of Markov Decision Processes. In these games the joint actions of the players can change the game that is played. Consider the following case which describes a stochastic game. Two players play repeatedly the zero sum game that is depicted in Table 1, but when the joint actions b^1, a^1 or b^2, a^2 is played then the game that the two players will play will change with probability p to the coordination game that is described in Table 2 and will play this game for the remaining repetitions of the game that should be played.

More formally a stochastic game G is defined as a tuple $G = (Q, \mathcal{I}, A, P, \{r^i\}_{i \in \mathcal{I}})$, where

- Q is a finite set of states
- $\mathcal{I}$ is a finite set of players
- $A = \times_{i \in \mathcal{I}} A^i$ is a finite set of joint actions available for each state in Q.
- P is a $|Q| \times |A| \times |Q|$ transition probabilities matrix with $|Q|$ and $|A|$ denoting the cardinality of Q and A respectively. Thus, $P(q, a, \tilde{q})$ will denote the probability that a state $\tilde{q}$ will be visited from state q when the joint action a will be played.
- $r^i : Q \times A \rightarrow \mathbb{R}$ is the utility function of player i, with $r^i(q, \{a_i\}_{i \in \mathcal{I}})$ denoting the reward that a player will gain if a joint action is played while the game is in state q.

The expected reward that players try to maximise in a stochastic game given a discount factor $\beta \in [0, 1)$ and a mixed strategy σ is defined as:

$$\tilde{r}^i(q, \sigma) = \sum_{t=0}^{\infty} \beta^t \mathbb{E}\left(r^i(q, a) | q_0 = q\right).$$

The Nash equilibrium in the case of the stochastic games is defined as a joint strategy $\tilde{\sigma}^i$ such as:

$$\tilde{r}^i(q, \tilde{\sigma}) \geq \tilde{r}^i(q, (\sigma^i, \tilde{\sigma}^{-i}))\forall \sigma^i \in \Delta^i \forall i \in \mathcal{I}.$$

As an example consider a simple scenario where two UAVs that will have to choose between two areas to monitor, area A and area B. Area A is a narrow and if both robots choose to monitor it there is a chance to crash. Therefore, it is possible that the robots wont be able to monitor any area for the rest of their mission. This problem can be formulated as a stochastic game with the following elements: $Q = x, y$, where state x represents the state that UAVs are functioning and y the state that the UAVs have crashed. The actions that the UAVs have in state x are A and B and they have no action in state y since they have crashed. The rewards of the robots are presented in Tables 4 and 5 for the states x and y respectively.

The transition probabilities when the game is in state x for each possible joint action is given by

$$P_x = \begin{array}{c} \\ (A,A) \\ (A,B) \\ (B,A) \\ (B,B) \end{array} \begin{array}{c} x \quad y \\ \begin{bmatrix} \frac{2}{3} & \frac{1}{3} \\ 1 & 0 \\ 1 & 0 \\ 1 & 0 \end{bmatrix} \end{array}.$$

Table 4. Reward of both players in state x. The left number of each tuple represents the rewards of the first robot (row player), and the second the rewards of the second robot (column player).

	A	B
A	(10,9)	(6,5)
B	(1,7)	(3,8)

Table 5. Reward of both players in state y.

	No action
No action	(0,0)

Each row of P_x represents a joint action and each column represents the possible new state of the game either x or y. When the game is on state y will remain in that state for ever. Under this set up this stochastic game has a pure strategy Markov equilibrium the joint action (A, B) which wouldn't be the equilibrium of the game if the game had only a single state state x.

State-Based Games. State-based games [33] are a simplified version of stochastic games. Similarly to stochastic games are defined as $G = (Q, \mathcal{I}, A, P, \{r^i\}_{i\in\mathcal{I}})$, but the players are myopic and thus they aim to maximise their current expected reward instead of discounted future rewards. Another important difference between stochastic and state-based games is that the in state based games the players are expected to have the same action in all the different states of the game. In these games the notion of recurrent state equilibrium have been proposed [33], which is defined as the tuple of joint action and state (a^*, q^*) such as:

- $q^* \in Q(a^*|q)\forall q \in Q(a^*|q^*)$, where $Q(a^*|q) \subseteq Q$ is the set of reachable states from initial state q when the joint action a is always selected.
- $r^i(q, a^*) \geq r^i(q, a^i a^{*,-i})\forall a^i \in A^i, \forall q \in Q(a^*|q^*), \forall i \in \mathcal{I}$.

Consider the case where they should choose to cooperate or not in order to perform a task. Each time that they choose an action the state of the game can change. An example is the a state-based game presented in [29]. There are three states x, y and z and in each of them corresponds a different game, namely coordination game, prissoners' dielemma and maching pennies. The reward functions of these games are depicted in Tables.

Table 6. Reward of both players for the coordination game. The left number of each tuple represents the rewards of the first robot (row player), and the second the rewards of the second robot (column player).

	Cooperate	Not cooperate
Cooperate	(4,4)	(1,3)
Not cooperate	(3,1)	(2,2)

Table 7. Reward of both players for prisoners' dilemma. The left number of each tuple represents the rewards of the first robot (row player), and the second the rewards of the second robot (column player).

	Cooperate	Not cooperate
Cooperate	(2,2)	(0,3)
Not cooperate	(3,0)	(1,1)

Table 8. Reward of both players for matching pennies game. The left number of each tuple represents the rewards of the first robot (row player), and the second the rewards of the second robot (column player).

	Cooperate	Not cooperate
Cooperate	(−1,1)	(1,−1)
Not cooperate	(1,−1)	(−1,1)

The transition probabilities from each state are given by the following transition matrices:

$$
P_x = \begin{array}{c} \\ (A,A) \\ (A,B) \\ (B,A) \\ (B,B) \end{array}
\begin{array}{ccc} x & y & z \end{array}
\begin{bmatrix} 0 & \frac{1}{3} & \frac{2}{3} \\ 0 & 0 & 1 \\ 0 & \frac{1}{2} & \frac{1}{2} \\ \frac{1}{2} & \frac{1}{2} & 0 \end{bmatrix},\;
P_y = \begin{array}{c} \\ (A,A) \\ (A,B) \\ (B,A) \\ (B,B) \end{array}
\begin{array}{ccc} x & y & z \end{array}
\begin{bmatrix} 0 & 1 & 0 \\ 0 & \frac{1}{4} & \frac{3}{4} \\ 0 & 1 & 0 \\ \frac{3}{5} & \frac{2}{5} & 0 \end{bmatrix},\;
P_z = \begin{array}{c} \\ (A,A) \\ (A,B) \\ (B,A) \\ (B,B) \end{array}
\begin{array}{ccc} x & y & z \end{array}
\begin{bmatrix} 0 & 0 & 1 \\ 0 & 0 & 1 \\ 0 & 1 & 0 \\ 0 & 1 & 0 \end{bmatrix}
\tag{3}
$$

where action A and B correspond to actions cooperate and not cooperate respectively. The recurrent equilibria for this state-based game are the action state pairs (BB, x) and (BB, y)

4   Learning Algorithms

A distributed optimisation task can be cast as a game [67]. However, the formulation of the optimisation task as a game does not directly provide a solution to the game. A coordination mechanism between the robots is needed especially in cases where autonomy is a desirable property of the robot team. Game-theoretic learning algorithms can be used by robots to choose a joint action to solve the

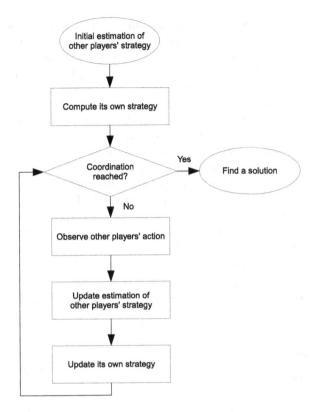

Fig. 1. General procedure of game-theoretic learning algorithms.

game. The canonical example of game-theoretic learning algorithms is fictitious play (FP). Fictitious play is an iterative learning algorithm. Figure 1 illustrates the general procedure of game-theoretic learning algorithms.

In each iteration t, each player estimates other players' strategies, and based on these estimates, chooses an action using the best response decision rule. At the initial iteration, i.e., $t = 0$, every player i maintains some arbitrary, non-negative weights $\kappa_t^{i \to j}$ for each other player j as the estimation of their strategy. In particular, $\kappa_t^{i \to j}(a^j)$ is the weight for action $a^j \in A^j$ of player j. At successive iterations, players update their weight functions based on other players' chosen actions. The update of player i's weight function for player j is computed as follows [18]:

$$\kappa_t^{i \to j}(a^j) = \kappa_{t-1}^{i \to j}(a^j) + \begin{cases} 1 \text{ if } & a^j = a_{t-1}^j \\ 0 \text{ otherwise} \end{cases} \tag{4}$$

where a_{t-1}^j is the action that player j chooses at iteration $t - 1$. Based on these weights, player i then estimates player j's strategy using the following equation:

$$\sigma_t^j(a^j) = \frac{\kappa_t^{i \to j}(a^j)}{\sum_{a^j \in A^j} \kappa_t^{i \to j}(a^j)}. \tag{5}$$

Fictitious play converges to the Nash equilibrium in many classes of games, such as 2×2 games with generic payoffs [35], zero sum games [46], games that can be solved using iterative dominance [37], $2 \times n$ games [4] and potential games [36]. However, this convergence can be very slow [18] because of the implicit assumption that all players use the same strategy throughout the game. In [56] and [60], variants of fictitious play were proposed, which were based on particle filters and extended Kalman filters respectively. These algorithms assume that players adapt their strategies through the iterations of the game. In both variants, the fictitious play process is described as a hidden Markov model (HMM). Each player maintains some unconstrained propensities[1], which are responsible for their strategies. In each iteration of game playing, each player aims to predict other players' propensities, i.e., hidden layer of the HMM, by using the history of other players' actions, i.e., observations layer of the HMM. Figure 2 illustrates the evolution of propensities of player i through the iterations of the game and how they are related to strategies and actions.

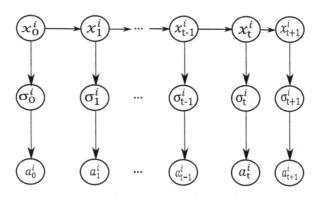

Fig. 2. Propensities propagation throughout the game. The propensity x_t^i at time t depends only on the propensity at time $t - 1$. Moreover, the strategy σ_t^i of player i at time t depends only on the propensity of the same iteration, and the action a_t^i that the player chooses depends only on its strategy at the same iteration as well.

More formally, let $x^i(a^i)$ denote the propensity of player i to play action a^i, and a_t^i the action of player i at the t-th iteration of the fictitious play process. The probability at which each player estimates about the propensity of other players is

$$p(x^j(a^j)|a_0^j, a_1^j, \ldots, a_t^j) \quad \forall j \in \mathcal{I} \setminus \{i\}, \forall a^j \in A^j. \tag{6}$$

This probability was evaluated using particle filters in [56] and extended Kalman filters in [60]. In this paper, we only consider the variant of fictitious

---

[1] The strategies are probability distributions. Thus, when a dynamical model is used to propagate them, new estimates are not necessary to lay in the probability distributions space. For that reason, the intentions of players to choose an action, namely propensities, which are not bounded to probability distribution spaces, are used [56].

play based on extended Kalman filters. But the same methodology can be easily applied to the variant with particle filters. As each player estimates the propensity of every other individual player separately, only inference over a single "opponent" player, say player j, will be presented in the rest of the paper.

4.1 Extended Kalman Filter Fictitious Play (EKFFP)

This variant of fictitious play is based on the assumption that players have no prior knowledge about other players' strategies, and thus, an autoregressive model can be used to propagate the propensities [56]. In addition, inspired from the sigmoid functions that are used in neural networks to connect the weights and the observations, a Boltzman formula is used to relate the propensities with other players' strategies [5]. The following state space model is used to describe EKFFP:

$$x_t^j(a^j) = x_{t-1}^j(a^j) + \xi_{t-1}^j$$
$$I_{a_t^j=a^j}(a^j) = h(x_t^j(a^j)) + \zeta_t^j \tag{7}$$

where $I_{a_t^j=a^j}(a^j)$ is the measurement equation, which relates the propensities to the actions of the players. The noise of the propensity process, $\xi_{t-1}^j \sim N(0, \Xi)$, which comprises the internal states, has zero *mean* and *covariance matrix* Ξ. The error, $\zeta_t \sim N(0, Z)$, of the observations has zero *mean* and *covariance matrix* Z. This error occurs because a discrete 0–1 process, such as the best response in Eq. (1) is represented through the continuous Boltzmann formula $h(\cdot)$ in which τ is a "temperature parameter". The components of the vector h, are evaluated as:

$$h(x^j(a^j)) = \frac{exp(x^j(a^j)/\tau)}{\sum_{a^k \in A^j} exp(x^j(a^k)/\tau)}. \tag{8}$$

The behaviour of the EKFFP algorithm at the t-th iteration of a game can be described as follows. At first, player i uses the EKF process, which is based on the state space in Eq. (7), to predict other players' propensities. Player i then using these estimates, evaluates player j's strategy of choosing an action $a^j \in A^j$, $\sigma_t^j(a^j)$, as follows:

$$\sigma_t^j(a^j) = \frac{exp(\bar{x}_t^j(a^k)/\tau)}{\sum_{a^k \in A^j} exp(\bar{x}_t^j(a^k)/\tau)}, \tag{9}$$

where $\bar{x}_t^j(a^k)$ is player i's prediction of the propensities of player j in order to choose action $a^k \in A^j$ based on the state equations in Eq. (7) and using observations up to time $t-1$. Player i then uses the estimates in Eq. (9) to choose an action using best response in Eq. (1). After all players have chosen an action, they use the EKF update process to correct their estimates about other players' strategies in the light of the recently observed actions. Then, the next iteration of EKFFP starts with $t = t+1$. The EKF estimations can be computed by any standard textbook procedure, such as in [49]. Algorithm 1 summarises the fictitious play algorithm when EKF is to predict other robots' strategies.

Algorithm 1. Extended Kalman filter fictitious play [60].

1: **while** $t < max\ iterations$ **do**
2:     **for all** $j \in \mathcal{I} \setminus \{i\}$ **do**
3:         Predict other players' propensities for the next iteration $t + 1$ using the state equations in Equation (7).
4:         Use the beliefs about other players' strategies in Equation (9) and choose an action using BR in Equation (1).
5:     Observe other players' actions
6:     **for all** $j \in \mathcal{I} \setminus \{i\}$ **do**
7:         Update estimates of player j's propensities using extended Kalman Filtering to obtain $\bar{x}_t^j(a^k)$.
8:     $t = t + 1$

---

5 Multi-model Adaptive Filter EKFFP (Source: [59])

5.1 Multi-model Adaptive Filters

The EKFFP process requires the definition of the covariance matrices Ξ and Z for the random variables ξ and ζ respectively. The performance of the learning algorithm is affected by the values of these covariance matrices. In [60] specific values were proposed for those covariance matrices, although these values are not optimal for all games. In this work, we propose a new approach that uses many models, each of which represents a pair of covariance matrices Ξ and Z. This approach then uses a weighted sum of these models in order to obtain an estimate of other players' propensities, instead of estimating the propensities from a single pair of covariance matrices. For Bayesian games, players can have a propensity estimate for each state of the nature or each type of other players.

The framework that allows many models to be considered under the EKFFP process is multiple model adaptive filters [6,9,10]. Let L be the set of all models that are used. Instead of estimating the propensity in Eq. (6), each player should estimate

$$p(x^j(a^j), l | a_0^j, a_1^j, \ldots, a_t^j), \tag{10}$$

where $l \in L$ is one of the possible models, each of which either refers to a pair of covariance matrices for potential games, or the state of the nature or another player's type Θ^i in Bayesian games.

To simplify notations, we use $\tilde{a}_t^j$ to denote $(a_0^j, a_1^j, \ldots, a_t^j)$. The estimate of other players' propensities in Eq. (10) can be written as:

$$p(x^j(a^j), l | \tilde{a}_t^j) = p(l | \tilde{a}_t^j) p(x^j(a^j) | l, \tilde{a}_t^j), \tag{11}$$

where $p(x^j(a^j) | l, \tilde{a}_t^j)$ for a given l is the standard EKF estimate of other player's propensity and $p(l | \tilde{a}_t^j)$ can be seen as the weight factor of each model.

Using Bayes rule, the probability $p(l|\tilde{a}_t^j)$ can be written as:

$$p(l|\tilde{a}_t^j) = \frac{p(\tilde{a}_t^j|l)p(l)}{\sum_{l \in L} p(\tilde{a}_t^j|l)p(l)}, \tag{12}$$

where $p(l)$ is the prior distribution of the model l. The probability $p(\tilde{a}_t^j|l)$ can be written as

$$
\begin{aligned}
rlp(\tilde{a}_t^j|l) = & \quad p(a_t^j, a_{t-1}^j, \ldots, a_0^j|l) \\
= & \quad p(a_t^j, a_{t-1}^j, \ldots, a_1^j|a_0^j, l)p(a_0^j|l) \\
& \qquad\qquad \vdots \\
= & \ p(a_t^j|\tilde{a}_{t-1}^j, l)p(a_{t-1}^j|\tilde{a}_{t-2}^j, l) \cdots p(a_0^j|l).
\end{aligned}
\tag{13}
$$

The propensities are described by the hidden Markov model, so they are conditionally independent, and thus, Eq. (13) can be written as:

$$p(\tilde{a}_t^j|l) = \prod_{q=0}^{q=t} p(a_q^j|l). \tag{14}$$

5.2   Multi-model Adaptive Filters EKFFP (MMAF-EKFFP)

Let $|L|$ denote the cardinality of set L, and $x_{t,l}^j(a^j)$ the propensity of player j, playing action a^j at the tth iteration under model l. In the multi-model adaptive filters EKFFP process, each player uses $|L|$ models for the propensity of each other player. In particular, each model is a state model:

$$
\begin{aligned}
x_{t,l}^j(a^j) &= x_{t-1,l}^j(a^j) + \xi_{t-1,l}^j \\
I_{a_t^j=a^j}^l(a^j) &= h(x_{t,l}^j(a^j)) + \zeta_{t,l}^j.
\end{aligned}
\tag{15}
$$

For each of these models, player i uses the EKF process to predict player j's propensity, i.e., $\tilde{x}_{t,l}^j(a^k)$, in order to choose an action $a^k \in A^j$ under model l. This prediction is weighted using Eq. (12). The estimate of player j's propensity to choose action $a^k \in A^j$ is then the sum of the weighted estimates of each model:

$$\bar{x}_{t,a^k}^j = \sum_{l \in L} p(l|a^k)\tilde{x}_{t,l}^j(a^k), \tag{16}$$

where $p(l|a^k)$ is evaluated using Eq. (12) and (14). Then Eq. (9) can be applied to evaluate player j's strategy. Each model of the estimates of player j's propensity are updated using the standard EKF process under the light of the new action player j has chosen. Algorithm 2 and Fig. 3 summarise the MMAF-EKFFP algorithm.

Algorithm 2. MMAF-EKFFP, [59].

1: **while** $t < max\ iterations$ **do**
2:     **for all** $j \in \mathcal{I} \setminus \{i\}$ **do**
3:         **for all** $l \in L$ **do**
4:             For each model l predict other players' propensities for the next iteration
                $t + 1$, using Equation (15).
5:             Evaluate $\bar{x}_t^j(a^k)$ using Equation (16)
6:     Compute the beliefs about other players' strategies using Equation (9), and
        choose an action using BR in Equation (1)
7:     Observe other players' actions
8:     **for all** $j \in \mathcal{I} \setminus \{i\}$ **do**
9:         **for all** $l \in L$ **do**
10:            Update each model's estimate of other players' propensities using extended
               Kalman filter to obtain $\bar{x}_t^j(a^k)$
11:     $t = t + 1$

---

6   Implementation Details

In this section, we discuss some implementation details in robotics of the MMAF-
EKFFP algorithm and of game-theoretic learning algorithms in general.

6.1   Utility Functions

Utility functions have been used in robotics as a metric of robots' performance
in various applications such as [8,40,62–64,70]. Utility functions can incorporate
various aspects of a coordination task such as the cost a robot pays to perform
an action, the reward that will be produced if a task is completed successfully,
and the aptness of a robot to perform a specific task. In Sect. 7.1, an example of
a utility function for a task allocation problem [1] is presented.

Methodologies for designing a utility function is out of the scope of this
paper. Nonetheless, we mention here that wonderful life utility (WLU) [67] is
a methodology for constructing a utility function, which allows coordination
tasks to be cast as potential games. An important property of potential games,
especially useful in robotic applications, is that they have at least one pure Nash
equilibrium. Therefore, there is at least one optimum joint action where robots
will not deviate from it unilaterally.

6.2   Robots' Decisions

As any iterative learning algorithm, our algorithm assumes that a specific game
can be iteratively be played and a final decision is reached either when the algorithm converges to an equilibrium or when the maximum number of iterations
is reached. In robotics, this can be seen as the following coordination mechanism. The robots in each iteration choose an action which they intent to play
and makes aware the other robots for its intentions, i.e., by communicating this

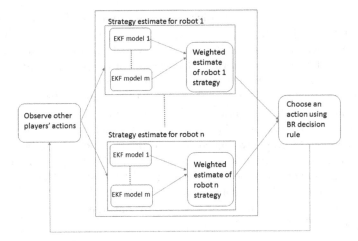

Fig. 3. The MMAF EKFP process [59].

intention to the other robots. Based on this information, they update their estimates about other players strategies and update the action they are intended to choose. The action that the team of robots will execute will be the joint action of the final iteration of the learning algorithm.

6.3 Complexity

The computational complexity of the EKF algorithm is upper bounded by the complexity of inverting a matrix $\mathcal{O}(n^3)$ [7], where n is the rank of the inverted matrix. Therefore the additional computational complexity of EKFFP when it is compared with classic FP is upper bounded by $\mathcal{O}((|\mathcal{I}| - 1)|A^k|^3)$, where A^k ($k \in \mathcal{I}$) is the largest set of actions among all players. Similarly, for MMAF-EKFFP it is $\mathcal{O}(|\mathcal{M}|(|\mathcal{I}| - 1)|A^k|^3)$, where $|\mathcal{M}|$ denotes the number of models which are used. The difference of the two algorithms is of a multiplicative magnitude of $\mathcal{M}$. This computational difference can be vanished if the computations of each model $m \in \mathcal{M}$ are executed in parallel.

6.4 Stopping Criteria

A general and crucial issue with learning algorithms is about stopping criteria, namely, the criteria for which the robots stop the iterative game playing stage (coordination stage) and make a decision. An obvious choice is when a maximum number of iterations is reached. This number should depend on the size of the game, number of robots and their available actions, the problem of interest and constraints which arise from it. For example, in cases where the communication is expensive or robots should make decisions in real time, the maximum number of iterations cannot be arbitrarily large.

If the optimal solutions for the task of interest, and therefore the Nash equilibria, are known, then the coordination state can be terminated before the maximum number of iterations is reached. It can be stopped when the joint action is one of the Nash equilibria or the reward of the selected joint action is not less than a constant ϵ from the equilibrium reward.

Even in cases where no Nash equilibria of the game are known, it is still possible to have a stopping criterion before the maximum number of iterations is reached. Coordination can be established if the learning algorithm has converged to a specific joint action. Convergence to a specific joint action can be defined as the repeated choice for c iterations of his particular joint action. Note here that there is no fixed c which can be used for all games. The size of the game and its nature should be taken into account when c is defined.

Depending on the application and the need to converge to a Nash equilibrium, different combinations of the aforementioned criteria can be used.

6.5   Example of a Sequence of Bayesian Games

In [14], it was shown that dec-POMDPs can be cast as a sequence of Bayesian games. In this section, we present a process of implementing a sequence of Bayesian games to solve a coordination task. Consider the task allocation problem between two robots with rewards shown in Table 3 in Sect. 3. Depending to the type of robot 2, there are two pure Nash equilibria where robots can converge. The first one is (*easy, easy*) when robot 2 is of type A and (*difficult, difficult*) when robot 2 is of type B. In order to accomplish their mission robots should finish both the easy and the difficult task. Independently of the action the robots will choose for this game, they will have accomplish only half of the necessary tasks. Therefore the players will have to play a sequence of games in order to finish both tasks, easy and difficult. The first game is the one with rewards depicted in Table 3. Another game should be defined in order to complete the unselected task, after making a decision based on the first game. An example of such a game is defined in Table 9. There the robots should choose if they will both try to finish the remaining task or only one should try or none of them should try. Note here that the game depicted in Table 9 makes the two robots coordinate and choose to do the remaining task together. Nonetheless, depending on the nature of the problem another reward matrix can be used in order to allow robots having different behaviours.

Table 9. Reward matrices of the Bayesian game for the remaining action.

Type A	do	not do		Type B	do	not do
do	10,10	−5,0		do	10,5	−5,0
not do	−5,0	0,0		not do	0,−10	0,0

7   Simulation Results

7.1   Results in Potential Games (Source: [59])

In this section the performance of the proposed algorithm, MMAF-EKFFP, is compared against the one of EKFFP in a resource allocation task. This is the vehicle-target assignment game which was introduced in [1]. In this potential game, N robots and M targets are placed in an area. The goal of each robot is to engage a target in order to destroy it. The actions of each robot are simply the choice of a target to engage. Each robot can choose only one target to engage, but a target can be engaged by many robots. The probability robot i has to destroy a target m is assumed to be independent of the probability another robot j has to destroy the same target. The probability that a target m will be destroyed is computed as:

$$1 - \prod_{i:a^i=m} (1 - p_{im}),$$

where p_{im} is the probability at which the robot i can destroy target m.

The reward that robots will share is the sum of the rewards each target m will produce if a specific joint action a is selected:

$$r_{global}(a) = \sum_{m \in M} r_m(a), \tag{17}$$

where $r_m(a)$, is defined as the product of target's m value V_m and the probability it can be destroyed by the robots which engage it. More formally, we can express the utility that is produced by target m as follows.

$$r_m(a) = V_m(1 - \prod_{i \in \mathcal{I}:a^i=m} (1 - p_{im})). \tag{18}$$

Multiple cases of the vehicle target assignment game were considered, with varying number of robots. In particular 20 targets and $N = \{20, 30, 40, 50, 60\}$ robots were considered. The simulations were run in a computer with dual Intel Xeon E5-2643 v2 processors (3.50 GHz, 6 cores) and 384 GB memory. The probability that each robot i can destroy a target m was set to be proportional to their euclidean distance. For each case, we run MMAF-EKFFP with six and twelve models respectively. Each model represents a pair of covariance matrices Ξ and Z. In all cases, the values of Ξ and Z were uniformly sampled from the interval $(0, 0.1)$. Comparisons are also made with the classic EKFFP with Ξ and Z defined as in [60]. We reinforce here that there does not exist a universal combination of Ξ and Z which maximises the performance of EKFFP for all games [60]. The parameters which are reported in [60] are suggestive. Therefore, the question which arises is which pair of parameters Ξ and Z maximise the performance of EKFFP for the games of interest. MMAF-EKFFP provides a solution to this problem, since many combinations of Ξ and Z can be used as part of different models. Then the players will select actions based on the weighted sum of these models. The results presented in this paper are averaged over 200 runs for each case. In each run, target values V_m were uniformly chosen from $(0, 10]$. The target and the robot positions were uniformly chosen from $[0, 1]$. This results in different scales of reward function. In order to make comparison feasible, the following normalised version of the global utility was used:

$$r_{total} = \frac{r_{global}}{\sum_m V_m}.$$

As it is depicted in Fig. 4, MMAF-EKFFP with multiple models performs better than the classic EKFFP, which uses only a single model.

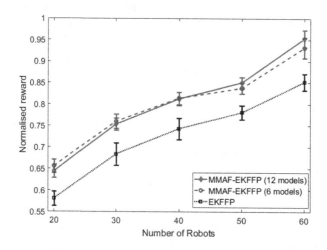

Fig. 4. Average reward over 200 runs of the vehicle target assignment game, [59].

In addition, MMAF-EKFFP with 6 and 12 models perform similarly when cases with up to 40 robots are considered. When more players are considered, having more models improves the results of the algorithm.

It is expected that MMAF-EKFFP has heavier computational cost than EKFFP as the number of models is increased. Nonetheless as it is shown in Table 10, the running time of MMAF-EKFFP is in the same level as EKFFP because it is implemented using parallel computing, taking advantage of the multiple cores which many development platforms already have in robotics. In this experiment, each model is processed by an individual thread, which then runs in an individual physical computation core.

Remark. This game can be also solved by message passing algorithms like max-sum [17]. However, the size of search table and the size of the messages that need to be exchanged between agents render the application of these methods prohibitive complex in real time applications. In particular, if each robot were using maxsum algorithm, then it should update and transmit 20^{50} messages. This is because a robot can engage any of the 20 available targets and the reward of a robot i depends on the joint action a^{-i} of all the other robots.

Table 10. Time in seconds that 20 iterations needed for various number of models EKF fictitious play, from [59].

	20 robots	30 robots	40 robots	50 robots
EKFFP	0.0649 ± 0.0042	0.1133 ± 0.0130	0.1548 ± 0.0109	0.2321 ± 0.0227
MMAF-EKFFP (6 models sequential)	0.3243 ± 0.0263	0.5909 ± 0.2247	1.1428 ± 0.1618	1.6509 ± 0.3116
MMAF-EKFFP (12 models sequential)	0.7773 ± 0.0327	1.3294 ± 0.1102	2.2283 ± 0.2177	3.0378 ± 0.2063
MMAF-EKFFP (6 models parallel)	0.0568 ± 0.0013	0.0906 ± 0.0034	0.1326 ± 0.0059	0.1918 ± 0.0105
MMAF-EKFFP (12 models parallel)	0.0616 ± 0.0030	0.1091 ± 0.0065	0.1619 ± 0.0071	0.2326 ± 0.0192

7.2 Games with Noisy Rewards (Source: [59])

This section contains the simulation results in a scenario where the robots receive noisy observations of the other robots' actions. Noisy observations denote observations which for some reason is incorrect. Consider the case where two UAVs monitor a part of a field in order to decide if fertilisation is needed. The best results are obtained when one UAV flies at the top of the area and the other flies at the sides of the area. This scenario can be modelled as a two player game, which is depicted in Table 11. If both UAVs choose to go at the top of the area of interest, they will collide and they will receive some negative rewards. On the other hand, if they both choose to fly at the side of the area, then they will gain no reward because the quality of the images they gather will be poor. Finally, some positive reward is generated only if the two UAvs make different decisions. Note that the natural choice of the two UAVs is to choose to fly at the side of the area. They change their decision only when they believe with probability greater than 0.8 that the other UAV will choose to go at the side of the area of interest. In addition, each UAV can observe correctly the intention of the other UAV with probability p in every iteration of the coordination process.

Remark. In this paper, we assume that each robot knows the probability distribution of noisy observations, either by having some prior knowledge about its sensors' specification or using some methods to estimate that distribution as the one proposed in [47] to estimate this distribution.

Table 11. UAVs' rewards for the game with noisy observations.

	Top	Sideways
Top	−4,−4	0,1
Sideways	1,0	0,0

Figure 5 shows the results of MMAF-EKFFP and EKFFP for the game with rewards depicted in Table 11. As it is shown here the percentage of times that

MMAF-EKFFP converged to a Nash equilibrium is always greater than 50%. This is significantly better than the results reported in [11], where the results of Generalised Weakened fictitious play (GWFP) [28] and Filtered Fictitious Play (FFP) [11]. The probability of converging to a Nash equilibrium reached zero when the 50% or more of the observations were faulty for FFP. For the case of GWFP the probability of converging to a Nash equilibrium reached zero when the 30% or more of the observations were faulty. Note here that even EKFFP performs better than FFP and GWFP since the probability of converging to a Nash equilibrium reached zero when the 80% or more of the observations were faulty.

The minimum probability of convergence to a Nash equilibrium for the MMAF-EKFFP algorithm is observed when the 50% of the observations were faulty. This is because the observations had exactly the same chance to be correct or faulty. When players know that the probability of a faulty observation is greater than a correct one, they use this information and increase their chances to converge to an equilibrium point.

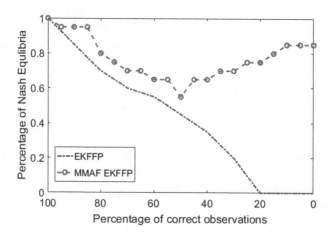

Fig. 5. Probability to converge to Nash equilibrium as a function of the percentage of the correctly observed opponents' actions, [59].

7.3   Results in Bayesian Games (Source: [59])

The majority of the methods that are used to solve Bayesian games, such as Agent Security via Approximate Policies (ASAP) [41], Mixed Integer Programming Nash (MIP Nash) [50], brute force search methods [39] or Multiple Linear Programs [12] tries to find the Bayes Nash equilibrium with the highest reward. In order to solve the Bayesian game in Table 3, we can transform it into a strategic form game using Harsanyi's transformation [20], and search for the Nash equilibrium of this new game. An example of Harsanyi's transformation is depicted in Table 12, where the Bayesian game of Table 3 has been cast as a strategic form game, with probabilities p and $1 - p$ of the second player being of type A or B. In this game, robot 1 is the row player and robot 2 the column player.

Note here that as the second robot can be of any of the two types in the strategic form game, its actions consist of all the possible combinations of its actions in the two games. Therefore, in the strategic form representation of Table 3, the second robot has four possible actions $E_A D_B, E_A E_B, D_A D_B, D_A E_B$, where $E_A D_B$ denotes selecting the easy task if it is of type A and the difficult task if it is of type B etc.

The game with rewards in Table 12 have three Bayes-Nash equilibria. Two pure Bayes-Nash equilibria and one mixed. The joint actions $(difficult, D_A D_B)$ and $(easy, D_A E_B)$ are pure Bayes-Nash equilibria. The mixed Bayes-Nash equilibrium exists when $p > \frac{1}{5}$: robot 1 chooses the difficult task with probability $\frac{5p-1}{5-p}$ and robot 2 chooses $D_A D_B$ with probability $\frac{2}{3}$. Nonetheless, even finding the Bayes-Nash equilibria does not answer to the question which action the robots should choose if they are playing any of the two games. For example if the type of robot 2 is A, then the equilibrium of the actual game which will be played is easy;easy, as it can be seen from Table 3. On the other hand, if the type of the robot 2 is of type B then the equilibrium of the actual game which will be played is difficult, difficult.

Table 12. Strategic form game's rewards, of the Bayesian game of Table 3 as a function of p.

		Robot 2			
		$E_A D_B$	$E_A E_B$	$D_A D_B$	$D_A E_B$
Robot 1	Difficult	$9 + p, 10 - 4p$	$5 + 5p, 4 + 2p$	$9 - 4p, 10$	$5, 4 + 6p$
	Easy	$8, 6 - p$	$7 + p, 5$	$8 + 2p, 6 - 2p$	$7 - p, 5 + 3p$

On the other hand, the proposed algorithm allows robots to learn what the other robots are doing, and evaluate the probability of choosing a particular sequence of actions given that they are of a specific type. Then based on this knowledge, they choose the action that maximises their expected reward conditional to the possible types of the other players.

Now we study the performance of MMAF-EKFFP in two games with incomplete information. The first game had at least one pure strategy Nash equilibrium, and the second has only a mixed strategy Nash equilibrium.

The first game is the one depicted in Tables 3 and 9. MMAF-EKFFP always converged to the pure Nash equilibrium of the game, and therefore, the two robots always chose to work on the same task (easy or difficult) jointly.

The second example which is considered comes from a security problem [41]. In security games, a group of security robots try to secure some areas of interest and an attacker robot tries to invade these areas. In [3,48], the security robots cannot be physically present in all the areas of interest at the same time. Instead, they can choose among various patrol routes. Security robots choose the route and the areas they will patrol based on the importance of the areas or the likelihood at which an attacker robot will be appear etc. The security problem can be cast as a two player game [41]. If there are $\mathcal{M}$ areas of interest, then the action of the security robots will be the d-tuple ($d \leq m$) of the areas which the robots will patrol. The order by which the robots visit the areas is also taking into account. For instance, in the case of three areas $\{1, 2, 3\}$, each petrol order, e.g., $1 \leftarrow 2 \leftarrow 3$ or $1 \leftarrow 3 \leftarrow 2$, is a different action. The attacker robot can choose any of the $\mathcal{M}$ available areas to invade. Assume that the security robots can choose from $\mathcal{K}$ patrolling routes. The reward of the security robots $r_i(k)$ ($k \in \mathcal{K}$) and that of attacking robot $r_j(m)$ ($m \in \mathcal{M}$) are estimated respectively as follows.

$$r_i(k) = \begin{cases} -u_i(a^i) \text{ if } a^j \notin a^i \\ p_{a^i}c_i + (1 - p_{a^i})(-u_i) \text{ if } a^j \in a^i, \end{cases} \tag{19}$$

where $u_i(a^i)$ is the value of area a^i to the security robots, p_{a^i} is the probability that the security robots can catch the attacker in the a^i area, c_i is the reward to the security robots if the attacker is caught:

$$r_j = \begin{cases} u_j \text{ if } a^j \notin a^i \\ -p_{a^j}c_j + (1 - p_{a^j})(u_j) \text{ if } a^j \in a^i, \end{cases} \tag{20}$$

where $u_i(a^j)$ is the value of area a^j to the attacker robot, p_{a^j} is the probability that the security robots can catch the attacker when patrolling area a^j, and c_j is the cost to the attacker robot if it is caught.

Consider the case where two areas are available and the actions available to security robot are $1 \leftarrow 2$ and $2 \leftarrow 1$ respectively. In addition, assume that the attacking robot can be of two types A and B. The above reward function, when similar parameters to [41] are used, can be modelled as a Bayesian game as it is depicted in Table 13.

Table 13. Reward matrices of the attacking and security robot for two different types of attacking robot. The top table is the game played when the attacking robot is of type A.

	Areas 1,2	Areas 2,1
Area 1	−1,0.5	−0.125,−0.125
Area 2	−0.375,0.125	−1,0.5
	Areas 1,2	Areas 2,1
Area 1	−1.2,0.4	−0.025,−0.025
Area 2	−0.275,0.125	−1.2,0.4

When the attacker is type A, the optimal policy for the security robots, which leads to a Nash equilibrium, is to choose a mixed strategy and play action $1 \leftarrow 2$ with probability 0.58 and $2 \leftarrow 1$ with probability 0.42. The mixed strategy for the attacking robot is to choose area 1 with probability 0.375 and area 2 with probability 0.625. If attacker is of type B, the security robots' optimal policy is to choose a mixed strategy by playing action $1 \leftarrow 2$ with probability 0.35 and $2 \leftarrow 1$ with probability 0.65. The mixed strategy for the attacking robot is to choose area 1 with probability 0.39 and area 2 with probability 0.61. The security robots assume that the attacking robot is of type A with probability 0.9 and of type B with probability 0.1. Figure 6 illustrates the probability with which the attacking robot, chose Area 1 when it was of type A. The performance of MMAF-EKFFP was compared with EKFFP and the asynchronous best response algorithm which proposed in [15] in order to solve Bayesian games. As it can be seen from Fig. 6, MMAF-EKFP converged to the Nash equilibrium of the game while the two other algorithms failed to converged to a value close to the Nash equilibrium. Similarly, Fig. 7 depicts the probability with which the security robot chose action $2 \leftarrow 1$. As it can be observed from Fig. 6, MMAF-EKFP converged to the Nash equilibrium, while the other algorithms failed to converged to a value close to the Nash equilibrium. Similar results were obtained for various combinations of the probabilities with which the attacking robot could be of type A or B. In particular, the differences in the results between the case where the attacking robot is of type A with probability 0.9 and the case when it is of type B with probability 0.1, are less than 0.01 from the reported results in Figs. 6 and 7.

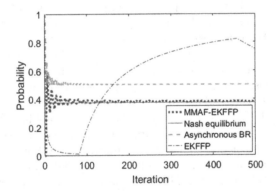

Fig. 6. Probability of the attacking robot to choose area 1 when it is of type A as a function of the number of iterations. The solid line represents the Nash equilibrium, the squared-line the MMAF-EKFFP algorithm, the dashed line the Asynchronous Best response and the dotted line the EKFFP algorithm, [59].

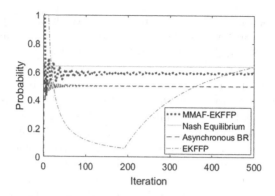

Fig. 7. Probability of the security robot to choose action $2 \leftarrow 1$ when the attacking robot is of type B as a function of the number of iterations. The solid line represents the Nash equilibrium, the squared-line the MMAF-EKFFP algorithm, the dashed line the Asynchronous Best response and the dotted line the EKFFP algorithm, [59].

7.4   Results on Stochastic and State-Based Games

In this section the results obtained for two scenarios of state based games are presented. The first is the game that was described in Tables 6, 7 and 8, with the corresponding transition probabilities of Eq. 3. This state space game was played for 100 replications and in each replication 100 iterations of the state-based game where played. In this game, the players that used EKFMMAF fictitious play, where playing the recurrent equilibrium of the game. In particular, 57% of the times they were selecting the (Not cooperate, Not cooperate) action of the coordination game, and 43% of times they were selecting the (Not cooperate, Not cooperate) of the prisoners' dilemma game.

Consider the game that it is depicted in Fig. 8. In this game two robots located in squares 1 and 3 respectively should reach the square with number 8 where their target is. When a robot is in a particular square this represents a specific state. Even though the available actions of the players are the same in all states, different behaviours can emerge when a robots are in different squares.

The robots can move either one square forward, or one square backwards, or one square at the left or one square at the right. If they both choose to move to the same square, case of possible collision, then only one is can go to the new square with probability $\frac{1}{2}$, while the other one stays at its current cell. In addition, the robots can transition from squares 1 and 3 to squares 4 and 6 respectively with probability p. One iteration of the game finishes when at least one robot reaches the square number 8.

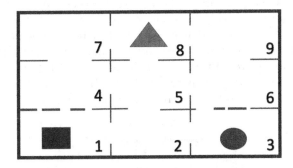

Fig. 8. State-based game of two robots. The robots (brown square and blue cycle) should reach their target on square number eight (orange triangle). (Color figure online)

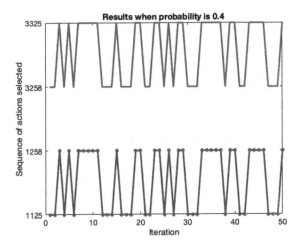

Fig. 9. Sequence of actions when probability p = 0.4. (Color figure online)

Table 14. Percentage of times that each robot reached its target.

p	% of times only robot 1 reached cell #8	% of times only robot 2 reached cell #8	% of times both robots reached cell #8
0.4	0.54	0.46	0
0.5	0.44	0.56	0
0.6	0.48	0.04	0.48
0.7	0.22	0.02	0.76
0.8	0.02	0.04	0.94

Table 14 shows the percentage of times that either only a single robot or both robots managed to reach their target. As expected better coordination achieved when $p \geq 0.6$. In particular, as it is depicted to Figs. 9 and 10, both players where choosing to towards the square number two, since it would give them better chances to reach their target. When $p \geq 0.6$ the robots manage to coordinate and one of was selecting as its first action square 2 while the other was choosing squares 4 and 6 respectively, Figs. 11, 12 and 13.

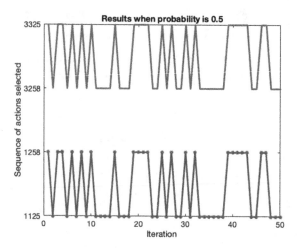

Fig. 10. Sequence of actions when probability p = 0.5. (Color figure online)

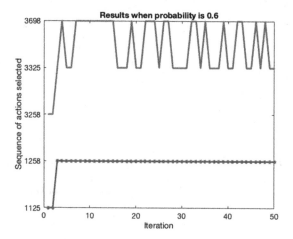

Fig. 11. Sequence of actions when probability p = 0.6. (Color figure online)

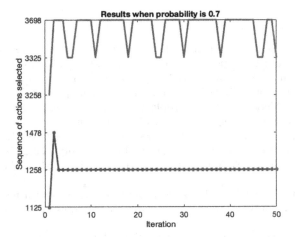

Fig. 12. Sequence of actions when probability p = 0.7. (Color figure online)

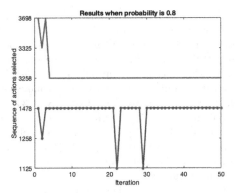

Fig. 13. Sequence of actions when probability p = 0.8. (Color figure online)

8   Conclusions and Future Works

A new game-theoretic learning algorithm based on EKFFP and multi-model adaptive filters has been proposed. This new algorithm can take into account various forms of uncertainty.

The performance of the proposed algorithm was tested in various games, that are related to robotic applications. The experimental results showed that it can provide better solution than the classic EKFFP algorithm and can be run as fast as the latter if implemented using parallel computing.

As future work the proposed algorithm will be applied in robotic platforms with various computing capabilities, in scenarios that can be formulated as games. This will to test the applicability of the proposed methodology in real life scenarios.

References

1. Arslan, G., Marden, J.R., Shamma, J.S.: Autonomous vehicle-target assignment: a game-theoretical formulation. J. Dyn. Syst. Meas. Contr. **129**(5), 584–596 (2007)
2. Ayken, T., Imura, J.i.: Asynchronous distributed optimization of smart grid. In: 2012 Proceedings of SICE Annual Conference (SICE), pp. 2098–2102. IEEE (2012)
3. Beard, R.W., McLain, T.W.: Multiple UAV cooperative search under collision avoidance and limited range communication constraints. In: Proceedings of 42nd IEEE Conference on Decision and Control, vol. 1, pp. 25–30. IEEE (2003)
4. Berger, U.: Fictitious play in 2xn games. J. Econ. Theory **120**(2), 139–154 (2005)
5. Bishop, C.M.: Neural Networks for Pattern Recognition. Oxford University Press, Oxford (1995)
6. Blair, W., Bar-Shalom, T.: Tracking maneuvering targets with multiple sensors: does more data always mean better estimates? IEEE Trans. Aerosp. Electron. Syst. **32**(1), 450–456 (1996)
7. Bonato, V., Marques, E., Constantinides, G.A.: A floating-point extended Kalman filter implementation for autonomous mobile robots. J. Signal Process. Syst. **56**(1), 41–50 (2009)
8. Botelho, S., Alami, R.: M+: a scheme for multi-robot cooperation through negotiated task allocation and achievement. In: 1999 IEEE International Conference on Robotics and Automation, 1999, Proceedings, vol. 2, pp. 1234–1239 (1999)
9. Brown, R.G., Hwang, P.Y.: Introduction to Random Signals and Applied Kalman Filtering: With Matlab Exercises and Solutions. Wiley, New York, 1 (1997)
10. Caputi, M.J.: A necessary condition for effective performance of the multiple model adaptive estimator. IEEE Trans. Aerosp. Electron. Syst. **31**(3), 1132–1139 (1995)
11. Chapman, A.C., Williamson, S.A., Jennings, N.R.: Filtered fictitious play for perturbed observation potential games and decentralised POMDPs. CoRR abs/1202.3705 (2012). http://arxiv.org/abs/1202.3705
12. Conitzer, V., Sandholm, T.: Choosing the best strategy to commit to. In: ACM Conference on Electronic Commerce (2006)
13. Di Mario, E., Navarro, I., Martinoli, A.: Distributed learning of cooperative robotic behaviors using particle swarm optimization. In: Hsieh, M.A., Khatib, O., Kumar, V. (eds.) Experimental Robotics. STAR, vol. 109, pp. 591–604. Springer, Cham (2016). https://doi.org/10.1007/978-3-319-23778-7_39
14. Emery-Montemerlo, R.: Game-theoretic control for robot teams. Ph.D. thesis, The Robotics Institute. Carnegie Mellon University (2005)
15. Emery-Montemerlo, R., Gordon, G., Schneider, J., Thrun, S.: Game theoretic control for robot teams. In: Proceedings of the 2005 IEEE International Conference on Robotics and Automation, ICRA 2005, pp. 1163–1169. IEEE (2005)
16. Evans, J.M., Krishnamurthy, B.: HelpMate®, the trackless robotic courier: a perspective on the development of a commercial autonomous mobile robot. In: de Almeida, A.T., Khatib, O. (eds.) Autonomous Robotic Systems. LNCIS, vol. 236, pp. 182–210. Springer, London (1998). https://doi.org/10.1007/BFb0030806
17. Farinelli, A., Rogers, A., Jennings, N.: Agent-based decentralised coordination for sensor networks using the max-sum algorithm. Auton. Agents Multi-Agent Syst. **28**, 337–380 (2014)
18. Fudenberg, D., Levine, D.: The Theory of Learning in Games. The MIT Press, Cambridge (1998)
19. Govindan, S., Wilson, R.: A global newton method to compute Nash equilibria. J. Econ. Theory **110**(1), 65–86 (2003)

20. Harsanyi, J.C., Selten, R.: A generalized Nash solution for two-person bargaining games with incomplete information. Manage. Sci. **18**(5-part-2), 80–106 (1972)
21. Hennig, P.: Fast probabilistic optimization from noisy gradients. In: ICML, no. 1, pp. 62–70 (2013)
22. Jiang, A.X., Leyton-Brown, K.: Bayesian action-graph games. In: Advances in Neural Information Processing Systems, pp. 991–999 (2010)
23. Kho, J., Rogers, A., Jennings, N.R.: Decentralized control of adaptive sampling in wireless sensor networks. ACM Trans. Sen. Netw. **5**(3), 1–35 (2009)
24. Kho, J., Rogers, A., Jennings, N.R.: Decentralized control of adaptive sampling in wireless sensor networks. ACM Trans. Sen. Netw. (TOSN) **5**(3), 19 (2009)
25. Kitano, H., et al.: RoboCup rescue: search and rescue in large-scale disasters as a domain for autonomous agents research. In:1999 IEEE International Conference on Systems, Man, and Cybernetics, 1999. IEEE SMC 1999 Conference Proceedings, vol. 6, pp. 739–743. IEEE (1999)
26. Koller, D., Milch, B.: Multi-agent influence diagrams for representing and solving games. Games Econ. Behav. **45**(1), 181–221 (2003)
27. Kostelnik, P., Hudec, M., Šamulka, M.: Distributed learning in behaviour based mobile robot control. In: Sinac, P. (Ed) Intelligent Technologies-Theory and Applications IOP press (2002)
28. Leslie, D.S., Collins, E.J.: Generalised weakened fictitious play. Games Econ. Behav. **56**(2), 285–298 (2006)
29. Li, C., Xing, Y., He, F., Cheng, D.: A strategic learning algorithm for state-based games. Automatica **113**, 108615 (2020)
30. Littman, M.L.: Markov games as a framework for multi-agent reinforcement learning. In: Machine Learning Proceedings 1994, pp. 157–163. Elsevier (1994)
31. Madhavan, R., Fregene, K., Parker, L.: Distributed cooperative outdoor multirobot localization and mapping. Auton. Rob. **17**(1), 23–39 (2004)
32. Makarenko, A., Durrant-Whyte, H.: Decentralized data fusion and control in active sensor networks. In: Proceedings of 7th International Conference on Information Fusion, vol. 1, pp. 479–486 (2004)
33. Marden, J.R.: State based potential games. Automatica **48**(12), 3075–3088 (2012)
34. Matignon, L., Laurent, G.J., Le Fort-Piat, N.: Independent reinforcement learners in cooperative Markov games: a survey regarding coordination problems. Knowl. Eng. Rev. **27**(1), 1–31 (2012)
35. Miyasawa, K.: On the convergence of learning process in a 2x2 non-zero-person game (1961)
36. Monderer, D., Shapley, L.: Potential games. Games Econ. Behav. **14**, 124–143 (1996)
37. Nachbar, J.: Evolutionary' selection dynamics in games: convergence and limit properties. Int. J. Game Theory **19**, 59–89 (1990)
38. Nash, J.: Equilibrium points in n-person games. Proc. Nat. Acad. Sci. U.S.A. **36**, 48–49 (1950)
39. Oliehoek, F.A., Spaan, M.T., Dibangoye, J.S., Amato, C.: Heuristic search for identical payoff Bayesian games. In: Proceedings of the 9th International Conference on Autonomous Agents and Multiagent Systems, vol. 1, pp. 1115–1122. International Foundation for Autonomous Agents and Multiagent Systems (2010)
40. Parker, L.: ALLIANCE: an architecture for fault tolerant multirobot cooperation. IEEE Trans. Robot. Autom. **14**(2), 220–240 (1998)
41. Paruchuri, P., Pearce, J.P., Tambe, M., Ordonez, F., Kraus, S.: An efficient heuristic for security against multiple adversaries in Stackelberg games. In: AAAI Spring Symposium: Game Theoretic and Decision Theoretic Agents, pp. 38–46 (2007)

42. Pugh, J., Martinoli, A.: Distributed scalable multi-robot learning using particle swarm optimization. Swarm Intell. **3**(3), 203–222 (2009)

43. Rabinovich, Z., Gerding, E., Polukarov, M., Jennings, N.R.: Generalised fictitious play for a continuum of anonymous players. In: Proceedings of the 21st International Joint Conference on Artificial Intelligence (IJCAI), 01 July 2009, pp. 245–250 (2009)

44. Rabinovich, Z., Naroditskiy, V., Gerding, E.H., Jennings, N.R.: Computing pure Bayesian-Nash equilibria in games with finite actions and continuous types. Artif. Intell. **195**, 106–139 (2013)

45. Raffard, R.L., Tomlin, C.J., Boyd, S.P.: Distributed optimization for cooperative agents: application to formation flight. In: 43rd IEEE Conference on Decision and Control, 2004. CDC. vol. 3, pp. 2453–2459. IEEE (2004)

46. Robinson, J.: An iterative method of solving a game. Ann. Math. **54**, 296–301 (1951)

47. Rosen, D.M., Leonard, J.J.: Nonparametric density estimation for learning noise distributions in mobile robotics. In: 1st Workshop on Robust and Multimodal Inference in Factor Graphs, ICRA (2013)

48. Ruan, S., Meirina, C., Yu, F., Pattipati, K.R., Popp, R.L.: Patrolling in a stochastic environment. In: 10 International Symposium on Command and Control (2005)

49. Sakka, S.: Bayesian Filtering and Smoothing. Cambridge University Press, Cambridge (2013)

50. Sandholm, T., Gilpin, A., Conitzer, V.: Mixed-integer programming methods for finding nash equilibria. In: Proceedings of the National Conference on Artificial Intelligence, vol. 20 (2005)

51. Semsar-Kazerooni, E., Khorasani, K.: Optimal consensus algorithms for cooperative team of agents subject to partial information. Automatica **44**(11), 2766–2777 (2008)

52. Semsar-Kazerooni, E., Khorasani, K.: Multi-agent team cooperation: a game theory approach. Automatica **45**(10), 2205–2213 (2009)

53. Shapley, L.S.: Stochastic games. Proc. Nat. Acad. Sci. **39**(10), 1095–1100 (1953)

54. Sharma, R., Gopal, M.: Fictitious play based Markov game control for robotic arm manipulator. In: Proceedings of 3rd International Conference on Reliability, Infocom Technologies and Optimization, pp. 1–6 (2014)

55. Simmons, R., Apfelbaum, D., Burgard, W., Fox, D., Moors, M., Thrun, S., Younes, H.: Coordination for multi-robot exploration and mapping. In: AAAI/IAAI, pp. 852–858 (2000)

56. Smyrnakis, M., Leslie, D.S.: Dynamic opponent modelling in fictitious play. Comput. J. **53**, 1344–1359 (2010)

57. Smyrnakis, M., Galla, T.: Decentralized optimisation of resource allocation in disaster management. In: Preston, J., et al. (eds.) City Evacuations: An Interdisciplinary Approach, pp. 89–106. Springer, Heidelberg (2015). https://doi.org/10.1007/978-3-662-43877-0_5

58. Smyrnakis, M., Kladis, G.P., Aitken, J.M., Veres, S.M.: Distributed selection of flight formation in UAV missions. J. Appl. Math. Bioinform. **6**(3), 93–124 (2016)

59. Smyrnakis, M., Qu, H., Bauso, D., Veres, S.M.: Multi-model adaptive learning for robots under uncertainty. In: Rocha, A.P., Steels, L., van den Herik, H.J. (eds.) Proceedings of the 12th International Conference on Agents and Artificial Intelligence, ICAART 2020, Valletta, Malta, 22–24 February 2020, vol. 1, pp. 50–61 (2020)

60. Smyrnakis, M., Veres, S.: Coordination of control in robot teams using game-theoretic learning. Proc. IFAC **14**, 1194–1202 (2014)

61. Stranjak, A., Dutta, P.S., Ebden, M., Rogers, A., Vytelingum, P.: A multi-agent simulation system for prediction and scheduling of aero engine overhaul. In: AAMAS 2008: Proceedings of the 7th International Joint Conference on Autonomous Agents and Multiagent Systems, pp. 81–88, May 2008

62. Timofeev, A., Kolushev, F., Bogdanov, A.: Hybrid algorithms of multi-agent control of mobile robots. In: International Joint Conference on Neural Networks, 1999. IJCNN 1999, vol. 6, pp. 4115–4118 (1999)

63. Tsalatsanis, A., Yalcin, A., Valavanis, K.P.: Dynamic task allocation in cooperative robot teams. Robotica **30**, 721–730 (2012)

64. Tsalatsanis, A., Yalcin, A., Valavanis, K.: Optimized task allocation in cooperative robot teams. In: 17th Mediterranean Conference on Control and Automation, 2009. MED 2009, pp. 270–275 (2009)

65. Tsitsiklis, J.N., Athans, M.: On the complexity of decentralized decision making and detection problems. IEEE Trans. Autom. Control **30**(5), 440–446 (1985)

66. Voice, T., Vytelingum, P., Ramchurn, S.D., Rogers, A., Jennings, N.R.: Decentralised control of micro-storage in the smart grid. In: AAAI, pp. 1421–1427 (2011)

67. Wolpert, D., Tumer, K.: A survey of collectives. In: Tumer, K., Wolpert, D. (eds.) Collectives and the Design of Complex Systems, pp. 1–42. Springer, New York. https://doi.org/10.1007/978-1-4419-8909-3_1

68. Zhang, P., Sadler, C.M., Lyon, S.A., Martonosi, M.: Hardware design experiences in ZebraNet. In: Proceedings of SenSys 2004, pp. 227–238. ACM (2004)

69. Zhang, Y., Schervish, M., Acar, E., Choset, H.: Probabilistic methods for robotic landmine search. In: Proceedings of the 2001 IEEE/RSJ International Conference on Intelligent Robots and Systems (IROS 2001), pp. 1525–1532 (2001)

70. Zlot, R., Stentz, A., Dias, M.B., Thayer, S.: Multi-robot exploration controlled by a market economy. In: IEEE International Conference on Robotics and Automation, 2002. Proceedings. ICRA 2002, vol. 3 (2002)

Cooperative Multi-agent Systems for the Multi-target κ-Coverage Problem

Mirgita Frasheri[1]($\boxtimes$) (iD), Lukas Esterle[2] (iD), and Alessandro Vittorio Papadopoulos[1] (iD)

[1] Mälardalen University, Västerås, Sweden
{mirgita.frasheri,alessandro.papadopoulos}@mdh.se
[2] DIGIT, Aarhus University, Aarhus, Denmark
lukas.esterle@eng.au.dk

Abstract. When multiple robots are required to collaborate in order to accomplish a specific task, they need to be coordinated in order to operate efficiently. To allow for scalability and robustness, we propose a novel distributed approach performed by autonomous robots based on their willingness to interact with each other. This willingness, based on their individual state, is used to inform a decision process of whether or not to interact with other robots within the environment. We study this new mechanism to form coalitions in the on-line multi-object κ-coverage problem, and evaluate its performance through two sets of experiments, in which we also compare to other methods from the state-of-art. In the first set we focus on scenarios with static and mobile targets, as well as with a different number of targets. Whereas in the second, we carry out an extensive analysis of the best performing methods focusing only on mobile targets, while also considering targets that appear and disappear during the course of the experiments. Results show that the proposed method is able to provide comparable performance to the best methods under study.

Keywords: κ-coverage problem · Collaborative agents · Coalition formation

1 Introduction

Robots have evolved from performing mundane work to tackling complex tasks with high efficiency. By enabling them to collaborate and interact, they can potentially achieve their tasks faster while requiring less resources. This has reached a level where a group of robots can accomplish tasks that an individual robot would not be able to complete at all. However, collaboration towards a specific goal requires coordination of the all participating robots, and the coordinated formation of coalitions among them. Numerous coalition formation approaches have been proposed which either rely on central components [2,14,37] or focus on a single task to be accomplished [33] in order to achieve meaningful interaction and collaboration. These approaches require dissipation of information about available coalitions as well as negotiations about participation of each potential coalition member [33,37,42]. While coalitions are usually

This work was supported by the DPAC research profile funded by KKS (20150022), the FIESTA project funded by KKS, and the UNICORN project funded by VINNOVA.

formed around single tasks, the use of multiple teams has been shown to be beneficial when pursuing goals that require multiple tasks to be accomplished concurrently [8, 39]. Moreover, when considering autonomously operating robots that aim to achieve multiple tasks, the individuals have to make decisions on when and how to form coalitions, and to what end the coalition is formed.

In this work, we are interested in the ability of autonomously operating robots to interact and collaborate, without a central component involved, in order to provision varying sets of tasks efficiently. We propose an approach where each robot makes individual decisions about whether or not to provision a specific task. For this decision, each robot employs local information about (i) its own status, e.g. its battery level, (ii) its ability (i.e. having the tools to complete the task), and (iii) its interest (i.e. expected performance value the robot contributes to the collective) in performing such task. More specifically, we propose a novel distributed coalition formation and study this approach in the online multi-object κ-coverage problem [9, 10]. This problem is related to the cooperative multi-robot observation of multiple moving targets (CMOMMT) problem proposed by Parker and Emmons [30]. In contrast, the number of target varies throughout the scenario and targets can appear and disappear randomly. Furthermore, the robots do not have any knowledge about the current number of targets at any time nor the number of robots available to interact. For that reason, the set of robots have to tackle the multiple tasks concurrently.

First, the robots need to discover initially unknown moving objects in the environment. They do not possess any *a priori* information about the number or location of these objects. Furthermore, objects may be mobile, requiring robots to change their own location respectively in order to continuously provision them. This introduces an additional degree of complexity as the robots cannot rely on a single solution but have to continuously re-evaluate their performance and find new optimal solutions on an ongoing basis. Second, each object needs to be provisioned with at least κ robots concurrently, i.e. κ robots having the object within their sensing/actuating region at the same time. Here, detecting new targets is considered the first task, however, every newly discovered target generates a new task of covering this known target for the collective. This generates a trade-off between detecting new objects and covering known objects with κ robots when the collective tries to maximise the duration and number of targets covered by κ robots. However, a robot not only needs to decide between provisioning a specific target or exploring the area to discover new targets, but also which of the different known targets it wants to provision. In order to achieve an efficient outcome in this trade-off, the robots are required to form new coalitions for each individual target. According to the taxonomy of Robin and Lacroix [34], the on-line multi-objective κ-coverage problem is hunting mobile search, monitoring multiple targets, with different viewpoints.

In this paper, we extend previous work that presented a novel distributed coalition formation algorithm considering several tasks [12]. At its core, the proposal consisted in introducing a *willingness to interact* to each individual robot as the main driver for the coalition formation. The *willingness* could depend on a robot's local conditions like battery level, and current level of activity. Utilising this *willingness*, robots can make decisions on whether or not to interact and provision a specific object which eventually leads to forming coalitions with other robots. The experimental evaluation of the afore-mentioned work has been extended, by investigating additional scenarios with varying values of the κ-coverage, as well as scenarios in which the targets appear and disappear at random times. Additionally, the willingness and utility functions are refined further, and cover for the distance of agents to the targets. The present paper provides an account on both sets of experiments, over several scenarios of increasing number of targets, considering both static and mobile targets, as well as appearing/disappearing targets. The performance is assessed through different metrics, e.g. the average number of agents covering one target, the average coverage time with at least κ agents. Furthermore, the proposed approach is compared against six other methods presented in the literature. The proposed approach shows performance that is comparable to the best methods considered in the experiments.

The remainder of this paper is structured as follows. Section 2 gives a formal definition of the online multi-object κ-coverage problem, whereas Sect. 3 discusses the related work. Section 4 covers the behaviour of the agents and targets, their interaction as well as our novel coalition formation algorithm. Section 5 gives an overview of the experimental setup, the performed experiments, and the obtained results. Section 6 discusses the generalisation of the proposed approach, while Sect. 7 concludes the paper and outlines future work.

2   Problem Formulation

In the online multi-object κ-coverage problem, we assume a discrete 2D area Z with a given width and height w and h, respectively, and no obstacles. We also consider a set of active robots $A = \{a_1, a_2, \ldots, a_n\}$, and a set of targets or objects of interest $O = \{o_1, o_2, \ldots, o_m\}$ in this problem. Both robots and objects can freely move within Z, with (nonconstant, yet limited) velocities v_i, where $i = 1, \ldots, n$, and v_j, where $j = 1, \ldots, m$; in their motion the robots will always remain in Z. It is assumed that any robot can move faster than the objects, and that the number of robots and targets is constant. Each robot is controlled by an internal, autonomous software agent. We refer to both as a_i. Each robot has a visibility range, with radius r. An object is covered by any robot, only if it is located within its visibility range. At this point, the robot will determine the number of already provisioning robots for this object. Therefore, it will either initiate a new coalition, in the case of no robots following the target, or join the existing coalition, in the case that less than κ agents are following the target. All objects are appointed to a constant interest level l_j. Moreover, levels of interest can be different for different objects, while also shaping the utility $u_{ij}(t)$ of a robot i for following an object j with interest level l_j at a discrete time-step t.

Every agent i can calculate its willingness w_i to interact with others at each time-step (as detailed in Sect. 4.3). This can occur in different situations, e.g. (i) when a robot i first detects an object j entering or leaving its sensing area (ii) when robot i receives a request for help from another robot for following an object j. Thus, the willingness to interact shapes the cooperative behaviour of an agent with respect to other agents, both in terms of asking and giving help. It is assumed that robots are able to change and keep track of their own state and behaviour, as well as the state and behaviour of other robots. Specifically, robot's n state is composed of the following variables: battery level b_i, range d, location $\ell_{x,y}$, and velocity $v_{a,i}$. Without loss of generality, we assume that the level of interest for the targets is equally perceived by all the robots, i.e. the knowledge on the levels of interest for the targets is shared by all agents involved.

The online multi-object κ-assignment problem is solved by having at least κ robots covering any target in the set. Consequently, there are two goals that need to be achieved concurrently: (i) maximising the number of covererd objects, and (ii) covering the targets with at least κ robots. This paper addresses the following questions:

1. What is the average time for which at least κ robots can provision all targets present in Z in an environment when using the proposed coalition formation algorithm?
2. What is the average number of agents that can cover a target with the proposed coalition formation algorithm?
3. How does the motion of the targets affect the obtained performance?
4. How does the defined value for κ affect the performance of the proposed approach?
5. How does allowing for appearing/disappearing targets affect the performance of the proposed approach?
6. How does the proposed method compare with other state-of-the-art techniques for the κ-coverage problem?

We address these questions using two sets of experiments with varying numbers of either mobile or static (immobile) targets, as well as appearing/disappearing targets, according to metrics that analyse the obtainable performance in terms of time to cover targets with at least κ robots, and the average number of robots that cover the targets. Furthermore, we compare our results with six other methods previously proposed in the literature [9].

3   Related Work

The online multi-object κ-coverage problem as introduced by Esterle and Lewis [9] requires moving targets to be detected and afterwards continuously covered by at least κ robots. This is, on one hand a combination of search-and-rescue operations and the κ-coverage problem [18], and on the other hand, an extension to the CMOMMT (Cooperative Multi-robot Observation of Multiple Moving Targets) problem [30].

In search-and-rescue operations, the goal is to coordinate a set of robots to cover a given area and find a set of targets [15]. To achieve this efficiently, Stormont [38] employs a swarming technique to cover a given area rapidly. Bakhshipour et al. [1] employ an heuristic algorithm to optimise and coordinate the movement of individual robots. The combination of supervising robots and subordinate robots for sensing the area enables them to rapidly find all targets and complete the mission successfully. To determine how many searchers are needed for a given operation, Page et al. [29] utilise simulations. They study the trade-off between employed agents and time required to complete a search-and-rescue operation successfully. Yanmaz et al. [41] investigate ad-hoc networks for collaboration in groups of unmanned aerial vehicles and show how these ad-hoc networks allow for more efficient completion of search-and-rescue operations, among others. Ruetten et al. [35] propose using the RSSI of each drone to optimise the area the swarm of robots can cover. This approach is completely distributed and does not require a central component.

Huang and Tseng introduced the idea of κ-coverage to increase the reliability and accuracy in sensor measurements [18]. In addition, the redundancy allows the network nodes to take turns in covering a given area effectively conserving energy resources and increasing the lifetime of the entire network [6,23,28]. However, the deployment of the network is calculated *a priori* to ensure optimal coverage of static areas or specific locations. Elhoseny et al. [7] introduced mobile nodes to cover a set of known targets with κ sensors. Using evolutionary computation on a central controller, they find the optimal location for all nodes to maximise the trade-off between number of nodes and coverage of static targets. Liu et al. [26] take one step further and consider a set of unknown targets. This requires their mobile nodes to detect the target points first before optimisation can take place. Utilising Voronoi diagrams, Li and Kao [25] determine the minimum number of required nodes to achieve κ-coverage. Having the Voronoi diagram at hand, they can also calculate the shortest paths for each node to maximise κ-coverage most efficiently. Instead of using a centralised approach, Hafeeda and Bagheri [16] enable the nodes to approximate optimal κ-coverage using a distributed approach. Fusco and Gupta [13] explore the ability of a simple greedy approach to optimally place and orient directed sensors for κ-coverage of static objects in the environment. Micheloni et al. [27] generate activity density maps to identify highly frequented areas. Utilising the density maps, they employ an expectation-maximisation process to determine optimal orientations of Pan-Tilt-Zoom cameras.

The Cooperative Multi-robot Observation of Multiple Moving Targets (CMOMMT) is an NP-hard problem, first introduced by Paker and Emmons [30]. They used artificial force-fields on the set of known targets to attract robots tasked to track them. While they treated all targets equally, Werger and Matarić [40] assigned weights to each target in order to indicate their importance. Each robot broadcasts its eligibility and coordinates directly with others. To learn where targets are located, Jung and Sukhatme [19] learn density maps during runtime and steer the individual robots accordingly. This clusters robots in those areas, leaving the remaining field of operation open and uncovered. To minimise the time where targets are not covered at all, Kollin and Carpin [22] enable each robot to predict when targets will be lost and notify other robots in the area accordingly. This ensures that available robots can move into position and targets can be observed continuously by at least one robot. However, in CMOMMT the main concern is to maximise the overall coverage of all objects with at least one sensor rather than multiple at once.

In their original work [9], Esterle and Lewis enabled agents to advertise detected objects to other agents in the environment. They further studied the effect of different responses basing decisions on aspects like first-come/first-serve, distance, or simple randomness. They further investigated the benefits of utilising topological interactions by learning neighbourhood relations during runtime. King et al. used an entropy based approach attracting agents towards newly detected targets but repelling them when the coverage condition was satisfied [21]. Considering the trade-off between target detection and following targets, Esterle considered the problem as a team formation problem where each team would tackle different tasks, i.e. detecting new targets and following detected ones. Due to the high dynamics of the problem, agents could switch teams during runtime [8].

The interested reader can find more information on κ-coverage, search-and-rescue operations, and CMOMMT [20, 31, 36].

4   Agent Model

In this section, we describe the operation of a robot, in terms of its motion, the manner in which the agent embodied in the robot updates its willingness to interact, and the manner in which the collective of agents makes decisions and cooperates through the proposed interaction protocols. In the following the terms robot and agent are used interchangeably.

4.1   Robot Kinematics

Every robot $a \in A$ follows a simple unicycle kinematic model

$$
\begin{cases}
\dot{x}_a(t) = v_a(t)\cos(\theta_a(t)) \\
\dot{y}_a(t) = v_a(t)\sin(\theta_a(t)) \\
\dot{\theta}_a(t) = \omega_a(t)
\end{cases}
\tag{1}
$$

where $x_a(t)$ and $y_a(t)$ are the x- and y-coordinate on the map and define the position $p_a = (x_a, y_a)$ of a robot a at time t, θ_a is the orientation of the robot, v_a is the forward velocity of the robot, and ω_a is its angular velocity. We assume that the robot can localise itself within the map, and that it can detect the obstacles within its visibility range.

A robot $a \in A$ follows a set of objects $O_a \subseteq O$, each of which has a different level of interest l. The direction d_a over which the robot moves is thus computed as

$$
d_a(t) = \frac{\sum_{i \in O_a} l_i(p_a(t) - p_i(t))}{\sum_{i \in O_a} l_i}
\tag{2}
$$

making the robot to move towards all the followed objects, weighted by their respective interest. In this way, the robot will prioritise targets with higher level of interest. The target orientation θ_a° and the forward velocity of the robot are therefore computed as:

$$
\theta_a^\circ(t) = \angle d_a(t),
\tag{3}
$$

$$
\tilde{v}_a(t) = \|d_a(t)\|
\tag{4}
$$

where $\angle p \in [0, 2\pi)$ is the angle of the vector $p = (p_x, p_y)$ in its reference frame, and it is obtained as $\angle p = \text{atan2}(p_y, p_x)$. In order to compute the proper value of the angular velocity, we can just use a simple proportional controller with tracking error e_a normalised between $[-\pi, \pi)$:

$$
e_a(t) = \theta_a^\circ(t) - \theta_a(t)
\tag{5}
$$

$$
\tilde{\omega}_a(t) = K_p \, \text{atan2}\left(\sin(e_a(t)), \cos(e_a(t))\right)
\tag{6}
$$

Finally, we include saturations on the forward and angular velocities:

$$v_a(t) = \min(\tilde{v}(t), v_{\max}) \tag{7}$$

$$\omega_a(t) = \min(\max(\tilde{\omega}_a(t), -\omega_{\max}), \omega_{\max}) \tag{8}$$

4.2 Agent Behaviour

Software agents, operate autonomously and their behaviour can be described as a state machine composed of four states: *inspect, evaluate, inspect & follow*, and *evaluate & follow* (Fig. 1). At run-time, all agents start their operation in the state *inspect*, and continue moving in Z according to a given pattern. In case a new target is spotted, or a request is received, an agent switches from *inspect* to *evaluate*. In this state, an agent decides, based on its current state, whether it wants to be involved with the newly detected target or help requests from other agents. The proposed interaction protocol is described in detail in Sect. 4.4. The result of the interaction is a coalition of agents that will follow the spotted target. If the agent is not part of the coalition after the interaction, it will switch back to the *inspect* state, and it will continue scanning Z for other targets. Otherwise, if the agent is part of the coalition, then it will switch to the *inspect & follow* state. In this new state, the agent follows the target, while it simultaneously inspects for new ones. If all targets an agent has been following go outside its visibility range, then the agent switches to *inspect*. In case an agent either has negative willingness, spots a new target, detects that a target is going outside its visibility region, or it gets a request for help, then it switches to the *evaluate & follow* state. In the latter, the agent either generates a help request, or it responds to a help request. In both cases, the agent decides whether to be part of a (new) coalition, or to drop a target altogether. Once the

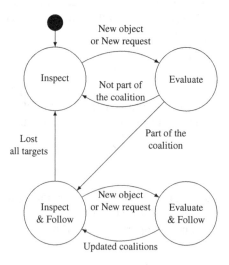

Fig. 1. Agent operation state machine [12].

interaction is complete, an agent switches back to the *inspect & follow* state with an updated set of targets to follow.

Note that an agent can be part of more than one coalition, i.e. can follow several targets at the same time according to their level of interest (as per Eq. 2), but a target is only followed by a single coalition. Also, notice that transitions between states are considered to be instantaneous.

When an agent is following a set of targets, its motion is described by the dynamic model (1), and by the control strategy defined in (3)–(8). The interest level of a target affects the motion of the agent according to (2), i.e. the agent's direction is mostly affected by the level of interest of the targets.

4.3 Willingness to Interact

The willingness to interact w shapes the cooperative behaviour of an agent, i.e. when an agent should ask for help and when it should give help. This parameter reflects the general disposition of any agent to cooperate with the others, without yet considering specific targets. The willingness to interact w takes values in $[-1, 1]$. When $w \geq 0$ the agent is able to help other agents in their provisioning tasks. When $w < 0$, the agent will generate requests for help, and for $w = -1$ it cannot continue with the execution of a task on its own. The value of the willingness is updated by each individual agent i based on several individual factors, at discrete time instants t, according to the dynamics:

$$w_i(t+1) = \min(\max(w_i(t) + B^\top f(t), -1), 1), \tag{9}$$

$f(\cdot) = [f_1(\cdot), \ldots, f_m(\cdot)]^\top$ is an $m \times 1$ vector of the m factors that affect the willingness, while $B = [\beta_1, \ldots, \beta_m]^\top$ is an $m \times 1$ vector that contains the weights of the corresponding factors on the calculation of the willingness.

The calculation of a factor f_i is given by

$$f_i(k) = \phi_i(k) - \phi_{i,\min}, \tag{10}$$

where $\phi(k)$ represents the current measurement of that factor (e.g., the current battery level), while $\phi_{\min}$ is a minimal threshold considered acceptable (e.g., the minimal battery level to perform a task). The terms ϕ and $\phi_{\min}$ take values in $[0, 1]$, where 0 is the minimum value of the measured quantity, and 1 its maximum.

In this work, we consider two factors that affect the willingness to interact. These are the battery level b, and the number of objects in O_a currently provisioned by a. Other factors can be included in the calculation of the willingness, without loss of generality of the proposed approach.

Factors can be divided into two categories: necessary and optional. The battery level is a necessary factor, since a robot with a battery level lower than a certain threshold may not be able to achieve its tasks. Therefore, such agents should rely on the help provided by other agents. On the other hand, the number of targets (n_O) an agent is tracking is considered as optional. This is due to the fact that while an agent can follow several targets, its task will become more difficult, e.g. if $1/n_O$ goes below a certain threshold – the agent is following too many targets – then the agent decreases its willingness to give help and consequently increase its willingness to ask for help. The effect of different factors can be modulated by their corresponding weights. The weight for a necessary factor β_{nec} is defined as:

$$\beta_{nec}(t) = \begin{cases} 1/m, & \phi_{nec}(t) - \phi_{nec,min} > 0, \\ -(1 + w(t)), & \text{otherwise,} \end{cases} \qquad (11)$$

where m is the number of all the factors, whereas the weight for an optional factor β_{opt} is defined as:

$$\beta_{opt}(t) = \begin{cases} 0, \text{ if } \exists\phi_{nec}, \phi_{nec}(t) - \phi_{nec,min} < 0, \\ \dfrac{sgn(\phi_{opt}(t) - \phi_{opt,min})}{m}, \text{ otherwise.} \end{cases} \qquad (12)$$

This ensures that necessary factors have the highest impact on the willingness to interact. As an example, in the case the battery level is below a threshold, then the agent should ask for help, irrespective of other factors ($w = -1$). Thus, the weights of other factors should be set to zero. While we provided an example for factors approaching a minimum, factors approaching a maximum can also be applicable. Nevertheless, the corresponding calculations for the factors and weights have to be adapted accordingly. More examples on factors that can affect the willingness can be found in [11].

4.4 Interaction Protocol

The interaction protocol defines how agents create coalitions for any given target and elect the corresponding leaders for these coalitions. The proposed protocol mostly complies with the Self-organising Coordination Regions (SCR) design pattern [4], however differently from SCR an agent can belong to different coalitions, hence it can have more than one leader. An agent can trigger a help request either when it spots a new target, or it wants to extend an existing coalition to reach $\kappa-$coverage, or it perceives that targets in its visibility range are moving away from itself, or if it is necessary to ask for help (e.g., battery level is under the accepted minimum). Furthermore, agents make decisions on whether to interact with one another when they receive help requests from others. The interaction protocol is illustrated in Fig. 2.

When an agent spots a new target, an *information request* is broadcast to other agents, which contains the agent's willingness and respective utility for provisioning the target. Thereafter, the agent waits for a specified time Δt to receive a response from other robots. We assume that agents can identify commonly observed objects and assign common labels. In case a coalition already exists for the given target, the corresponding leader will reply whether more agents are needed to reach the κ-coverage. If no help is needed, then the sending the information request drop the targets and continues its operation. If help is needed, then the agent will receive an assignment from the leader of the coalition, based on the previously sent willingness and utility. In case the agent does not receive a response within time Δt to its initial information request, it assumes there is no other coalition provisioning the target. Subsequently, the process for creating a coalition and electing a leader responsible for following the target is triggered. Initially, the agent calculates its own willingness to help in the future coalition, and the utility for following the target. The mechanism follows the logic of a fast bully algorithm [24],

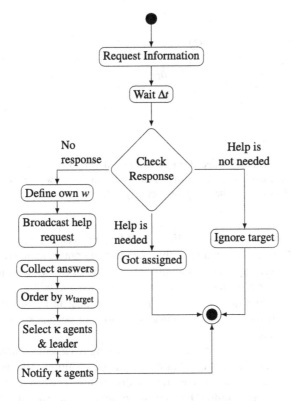

Fig. 2. Activity diagram of the agent's behaviour when a new target is spotted [12].

well-known in distributed systems. A request for help to follow the object is broadcast to all other agents. Other agents respond with their willingness to help, i.e. the willingness to enter the coalition, and their utility for following the specific target. After the responses are collected, agents with a negative willingness $w < 0$ are discarded. The positive willingness of an agent i to interact is combined with its utility u_{ij} to form the willingness to interact to provision a specific object j at time t:

$$w_{ij}(t) = w_i(t) + u_{ij}(t). \tag{13}$$

Utilities are defined by each agent for the individual target and can generally vary from agent to agent as well as between the different targets. Examples for this could be the size, speed, or direction of movement of the object. In our experiments, we consider different interest levels that are agent-independent, i.e. the agents share the same interest for the same targets. The received values $w_{ij}(t)$ are ordered in decreasing value, and the κ agents with highest $w_{ij}(t)$ are selected for the coalition. The agent with the highest $w_{ij}(t)$ is elected the leader. The outcome is propagated to the other agents via broadcast. The initiating agent does not necessarily need to be part of the coalition.

Furthermore, agents keep track of whether the targets in their visibility range are moving outside the visibility range. We introduce another internal threshold with radius

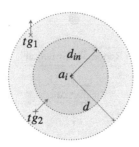

Fig. 3. Agent a_i with visibility range d, indicated with the red circle, and internal range d_{in}, indicated with the blue circle. The targets tg_1 and tg_2 are indicated with crosses, and they are moving towards and away from the agent, respectively [12].

d_{in} around the robots, where $d_{in} < d$ (Fig. 3). When a target, e.g. tg_2 in Fig. 3, moves out of the internal range, yet remains within the visibility range, then a request for help is triggered. If a target, e.g. tg_1, is moving towards the agent while being within the internal and visibility range, no request is issued. In case the willingness of an agent becomes negative, help requests are generated, and the agent considers dropping its targets one by one. If the willingness remains negative or becomes -1, eventually all targets will be dropped.

A help request means that either an agent is looking for a replacement for itself, or it is looking for an additional agent that can enter the coalition. This is illustrated in Fig. 4. If an agent needs to leave a coalition, we distinguish between leading agents and ordinary members of the coalition. Leader agents should take care of replacing themselves, as such the leader election needs to be repeated. The process can include other agents not yet in the coalition, if κ-coverage is not achieved at that point in time. On the other hand, common agents need only notify the respective leaders when they are dropping a target. Leaders are also responsible for triggering continuously the extension of a coalition in order to reach or maintain κ-coverage, following a monotonically increasing period.

5   Simulation Setup

The behaviour of the agents was evaluated with computer simulations[1], that model the agents' kinematics, behaviour, and interaction. The communication between agents is realised through the robot operating system (ROS) [17,32]. Two sets of experiments were conducted, namely Set I and Set II. The purpose of the experiments in Set I[2] is to compare the willingness to interact approach against a selection of methods in the state-of-art [9], across several scenarios differing in the number of targets and their mobility – static or dynamic. Whereas, the purpose of the experiments in Set II is to

---

[1] The code for running the simulations is publicly available at https://github.com/gitting-around/kcoverage_ICAART21.git.

[2] The present paper is an extension of previous work [12], which contains the account on the experiments and results for Set I.

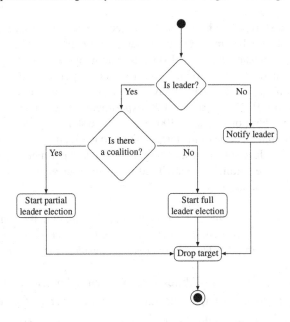

Fig. 4. Activity diagram of the agent's behaviour when it needs to replace itself in a coalition [12].

focus the analysis on the best performing methods identified in Set I, for mobile targets, considering also scenarios in which targets may appear or disappear from the area Z.

5.1   Set I Experiments and Results

In these experiments the method utilising the willingness to interact, was compared to six other methods that were previously proposed in the literature for solving the multi-object κ-coverage problem [9]. Each method is a combination of one communication model and one response model. Two communication models are considered, broadcast BC and random RA. In BC an agent broadcasts a help request to everyone, whereas in RA it sends a help request to κ agents chosen randomly. Regarding response models, the following three are considered: (i) newest-nearest NN, (ii) available AV, and (iii) received calls RE. In NN an agent will answer to the newest request, and in case of simultaneous requests, it will respond to the nearest one. In AV the agent answers to requests according to the newest-nearest strategy only if it is not following other target(s). In RE, an agent will answer to requests for objects with the least coverage, only if it is not following other targets. The six methods chosen for comparison, based on these models, are: BC-NN, BC-AV, BC-RE, RA-NN, RA-AV, and RA-RE. Such selection is due to previous results [9], where the broadcast and random communication models were evaluated better with respect to the rest, while the response models were reported to have a significant impact on the κ-coverage.

In all simulations, we consider a total number of $n_A = 10$ robots starting from the same initial position $(0,0)$, with a random direction, and $v_{i,\max} = 2$ units per time-step. If an agent hits any boundary in Z, it will bounce back at a $90°$ angle, i.e. Z is assumed to be a limited area surrounded by walls. The objects to be covered are generated uniformly in area Z of size 100 m $\times$ 100 m. In our experiments, we consider 7 different scenarios with an increasing number of objects. The number of objects distributed in the environment are 1, 4, 7, 13, 16 and 19 for the corresponding scenarios $S0$ to $S6$. For each simulation the interest level of any target was randomly sampled from a set of levels $\mathcal{L} = \{0.3, 0.6, 0.9\}$. We performed 20 experiments for each scenario, with each experiment having a duration of $T_{\text{sim}} = 300$ discrete time steps and a specified seed. The latter impacts the initial location of the targets, the initial direction for agents and mobile targets, as well as the level of interest of targets for each experiment corresponding to a scenario. Given these settings, we analysed the behaviour of our agents to achieve κ-coverage where $\kappa \geq 3$, and $\kappa \geq 5$.

Results for Static Targets. In these experiments, targets remain in their initial locations ($v_j = 0$). Once targets are covered, they remain covered for the rest of the simulation, as such, the time for reaching the desired coverage is considered one of the performance indicators for evaluation.

For every scenario, we run N different experiments. For every experiment $e = 1, \ldots, N$, we compute for every target j the time to reach 1-coverage $t_{j,e}^{(1)}$, and the time to reach κ-coverage $t_{j,e}^{(\kappa)}$. Based on this information we can calculate: (i) the average time to get one target to be covered by at least κ agents $t_{\text{avg}}^{(\kappa)}$, and (ii) the average minimum time to get all the targets covered by at least κ agents $t_{\text{min}}^{(\kappa)}$. These two metrics give an indication of a minimum coverage, and a complete coverage. They are formally defined as:

$$t_{\text{avg}}^{(\kappa)} = \frac{1}{N} \sum_e \frac{1}{|O|} \sum_j t_{j,e}^{(\kappa)} \tag{14}$$

$$t_{\text{min}}^{(\kappa)} = \frac{1}{N} \sum_e \max_j t_{j,e}^{(\kappa)} \tag{15}$$

In particular, in these experiments we study (i) the average time to get one target to be covered by at least by 1 agent, $t_{\text{avg}}^{(1)}$, (ii) the average time to get one target to be covered by at least by κ agent, $t_{\text{avg}}^{(\kappa)}$, (iii) the average minimum time to get all the targets covered by at least 1 agent, $t_{\text{min}}^{(1)}$, and (iv) the average minimum time to get all the targets covered by at least κ agents, $t_{\text{min}}^{(\kappa)}$. In all the metrics, the lower, the better.

Results for $\kappa \geq 3$ as well as $\kappa \geq 5$ are shown in Fig. 5, where $t_{\text{min}}^{(\kappa)}$ is given on the x-axis, and $t_{\text{avg}}^{(\kappa)}$ is given on the y-axis. For both metrics, the lowest the value, the better. In the graph the corresponding Pareto frontier is included in order to highlight the best performing methods. We also compare this directly to the cases for $\kappa \geq 1$ (only a single agent covers the target), however, the agents still aim to cover all targets with $\kappa \in \{3, 5\}$ and therefore might cluster at specific objects even when reporting results for $\kappa \geq 1$.

It can be observed that on average there are no differences between the utilised methods for scenario $S0$ for $\kappa \geq 1$, as shown in Fig. 5. This is due to the fact that the only static target in the environment will be discovered at the exact same time by any method for an experiment initiated with the same seed. There could be a shift with a couple of

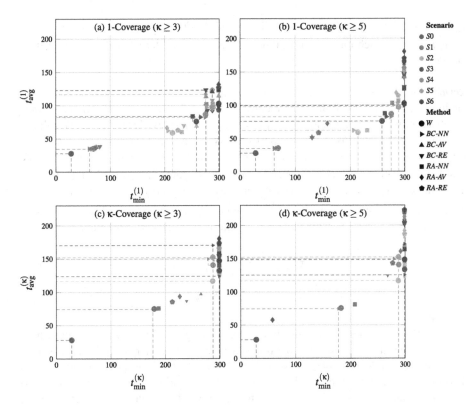

Fig. 5. Average time vs minimum time to cover all stationary targets (i.e., not moving) with 1 (top) or κ agents (bottom), for κ ≥ 3 and κ ≥ 5 [12].

time-steps in the discovery times, in case there is an occasional failure or delay in the ROS service calls or broadcast used by agentst when handling targets that appear in the visibility range. Nevertheless, for κ ≥ 5, Fig. 5d, the minimum times are not necessarily the same, e.g. the result for method *RA-AV* as compared to the six other methods. With the increase of number of targets in each scenario, the average and minimum times to coverage also increase. For each scenario S1–S6, a difference on average between the different methods is observed. Mostly, the proposed method, indicated with the 'W' in the legend, is either the best on average or at least on the Pareto frontier, for scenarios S3 in Fig. 5c; S2 and S5 in Fig. 5b; S2, S5, and S6 in Fig. 5d; and for scenarios S2 and S3 in Fig. 5a; S2 in Fig. 5c; S4 and S6 in Fig. 5b; and S4 in Fig. 5d, respectively. Similar performance is displayed by the *BC-NN* method, which is the best performing method among the ones considered in this study.

When only one target is involved, the average minimum time to coverage is lowest. In all cases, the agents will move in Z and eventually find and cover the targets. However, when increasing the number of targets (S1–S6), agents can gather on the first targets found, leaving remaining targets undiscovered for the rest of the simulation. As such, all metrics are affected, and the $t_{j,e}^{(\kappa)}$ is saturated to the duration of the simulation

$T_{\text{sim}} - 1^3$ for the targets that were not discovered. In Fig. 5, the points are accumulated at the $t_{\text{min}}^{(\kappa)} - 1$, which means that in those scenarios not all targets were discovered by the agents.

Results for Dynamic Targets. In these experiments, targets move within map Z by randomly changing direction, with velocity $v_{t,\text{max}} = 1.5\ m$ per time-step. In both cases, agents move with a higher velocity $v_{a,\text{max}} = 2\ m$ per time-step. Nevertheless, we still use the same sets of scenarios. As for the performance, for a single experiment $e = 1, \ldots, N$, we consider the time for which a target j is covered with at least κ agents over the simulation duration, $\tau_{j,e}^{(\kappa)}$, and the average amount of agents that cover the target j over the simulation $\alpha_{j,e}$. Based on these two quantities we compute the following metrics: (i) the average time for which at least κ agents cover the targets, $\tau_{\text{avg}}^{(\kappa)}$, and (ii) the average amount of agents that cover the targets α_{avg}. These quantities are computed as

$$\tau_{\text{avg}}^{(\kappa)} = \frac{1}{N} \Sigma_e \frac{1}{|O|} \Sigma_j \tau_{j,e}^{(\kappa)} \tag{16}$$

$$\alpha_{\text{avg}} = \frac{1}{N} \Sigma_e \frac{1}{|O|} \Sigma_j \alpha_{j,e} \tag{17}$$

While in the experiments featuring static targets, a target will be covered for the whole duration of the simulation once a coalition is formed, in the dynamic case, such assumption cannot be made, because agents can lose targets as all objects are moving in Z. Furthermore, these metrics are calculated twice for *active* and *passive coverage*, i.e. by (i) considering the targets which are actively being followed by agents, and (ii) considering targets that are within the visibility range of agents, but are not being actively followed. In other words, agents are actively following targets when they adjust their own motion based on the motion of the targets.

Results are shown in Fig. 6, where the average time of coverage is given along the *x*-axis, and the average number of agents is given on the *y*-axis. The method with the willingness indicated with W in the legends of Fig. 6 is overall on the Pareto frontier for $\kappa \geq 3$, with an exception for scenario $S3$. With respect to $\kappa \geq 5$, the method with the willingness is on the Pareto frontier for scenarios $S0$–$S4$, and the best on average for $S5$–$S6$. The same is observed in the results for passive provisioning. Furthermore, our approach tends toward maximising the number of agents covering a target, thus it lies on the left side of the Pareto frontier. Similarly to the results in the static case, the performance of the *BC-NN* strategy is comparable to the method with the willingness.

We can observe that for both $\kappa \geq 3$ and $\kappa \geq 5$ the average coverage time is highest when the number of targets is lower, in $S0$ and $S1$, falls for $S2$–6 when the number of targets to be covered increases. We speculate that an increase in the number of targets, whilst the size of the area is unchanged, might increase the average coverage time as agents can join multiple coalitions, i.e. are able to follow more tasts concurrently. However, this remains subject to further research. The impact of the chosen values for κ can be observed as well in Fig. 6, by inspecting the average coverage times, which are lower

---

[3] In the final time-step the multi-agent system shuts down, hence this time-step is not considered when dealing with the results.

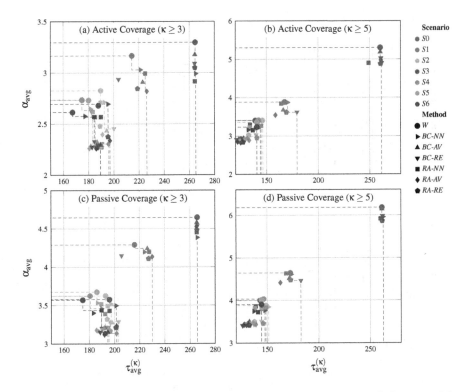

Fig. 6. Average number of agents covering targets vs average coverage time of all targets of the entire duration of the simulation for κ ≥ 3 and for κ ≥ 5. On the top we show active coverage where we only consider the agents actively following a target while the bottom includes passive coverage—agents having multiple targets in their visibility range while following another target [12].

for κ ≥ 5 than κ ≥ 3. Taking into account what is being covered passively increases the average number of agents that cover a target.

Note that, the averages are taken over all time-steps of the simulation including the time to discover the objects in the first place. Naturally, the lack of coverage prior discovery penalises the shown results.

In our current approach, the agents are not aiming to exceed the desired coverage. Nevertheless, race-conditions in the coalition formation process can result in coalitions that extend the κ-coverage. Furthermore, this can also take place when an agent detects that a target is moving away, and finds a replacement agent which also joins the coalition. Note that, the target is not dropped by the former agent until it actually goes out of its visibility range.

5.2 Set II Experiments and Results

Extension of Set I Experiments. Results from the experiments in Set I indicate that the best performing methods across the investigated scenarios are the willingness approach,

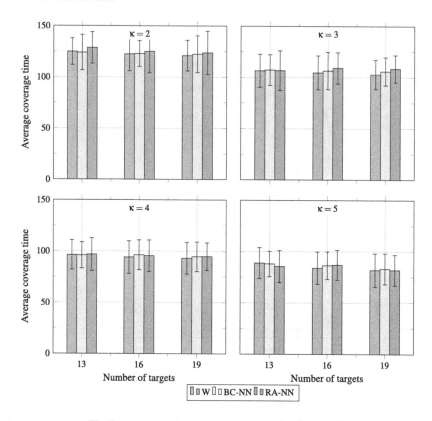

Fig. 7. Average active coverage time for $\kappa \in \{2,3,4,5\}$.

$BC - NN$, followed by $RA - NN$. In order to gain a better insight on the performance of these methods, additional experiments with different values of κ were run, specifically for $\kappa \in \{2,3,4,5\}$. In these experiments, only mobile targets are considered with the metrics adopted in Set I, and scenarios with number of targets in $\{13, 16, 19\}$, i.e. scenarios S4-S6. Furthermore, instead of running 20 experiments with different seeds, 10 different seeds were used, where for each seed 5 runs were performed, for a total of 50 experiments. The reason behind this choice is that experiments initiated with the same seed do not necessarily produce the same exact results since it cannot be guaranteed that the same coalitions will be formed every-time. Based on which message arrives in time when an agent is gathering responses, a specific coalition will be created. Therefore, affecting the rest of the simulation in terms of which targets are followed or discovered next.

The results of these experiments are given in Figs. 7, 8 for active coverage, and Figs. 9, 10 for passive coverage. Note that the metrics have been weighed based on the interest level of the targets. It can be observed that as κ increases, the average coverage time decreases (Fig. 7), as is expected. The average agents per target metric decreases in the same manner (Fig. 8). Additionally, for $\kappa = 2$ the coverage is achieved and surpassed, while in the other cases it is not reached by any method. For $\kappa = 3$ the results are

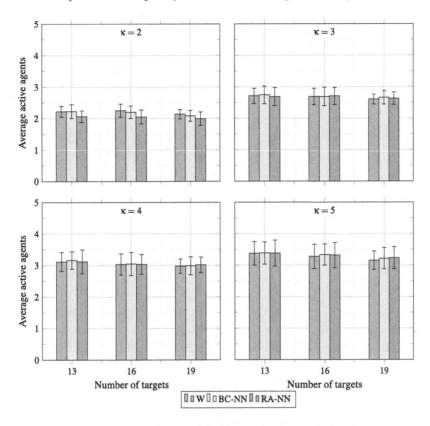

Fig. 8. Average active number of agents per target for κ ∈ {2, 3, 4, 5}.

quite close to the desired coverage, however for κ = 4, 5 the achieved coverage is rather below the desired values. Results improve overall when considering passive coverage (Figs. 9, 10), and the average agents per target metric lies in (3, 4] across the different experiments. Conclusively, the performance of the methods is comparable, with slight differences in average across the different scenarios.

Experiments with Appearing/Disappearing Targets. A more relaxed version of the κ-coverage problem, in which the targets are not only mobile but are also allowed to appear/disappear during the simulation, is used to further evaluate the three methods considered in the previous paragraph. For these experiments, it is assumed that area Z is confined, however it is possible for new targets to come in. The decisions concerning the removal and insertion of targets are made at every time-step. Furthermore, these decisions are sequential, i.e. first it is decided on whether to remove an existing target, thereafter it is decided on whether to insert a new one. The probabilities for removal and insertion are set to the same value $p_R = p_I = 0.2$. Targets appear and disappear on the spot. The rationale behind such implementation is that, a target disappears when there is no interest associated to it, and appears when the interest jumps from 0.0 to

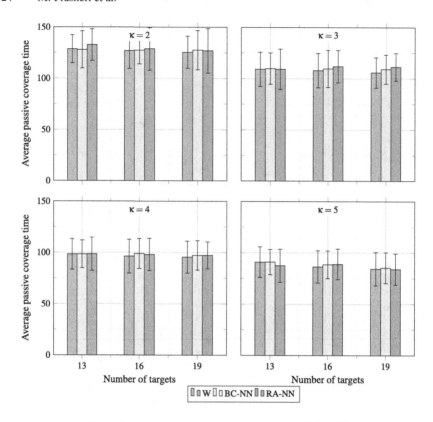

Fig. 9. Average passive coverage time for $\kappa \in \{2,3,4,5\}$.

$I_j \in I = \{0.3, 0.6, 0.9\}$. Initially, the number of targets present in the simulation is equal to 19, corresponding to the *S6* scenario in the previous experiments. Simulations were run for values of κ in $\{2,3,4,5,6,7,8\}$.

The willingness to interact function has been simplified to account only for the state of the robot at a given time-step, thus Eq. 20 is modified as follows:

$$w_i(t+1) = \max(\min(\mathbf{B}^\top \mathbf{f}(t), -1), 1). \tag{18}$$

Furthermore, only one factor shapes the willingness in these experiments, that is the level of activity calculated as:

$$l_A = \frac{O_a}{O_{ALL}}, \tag{19}$$

where O_a is the number of objects provisioned by robot a, whereas O_{ALL} is the number of all objects of interest in Z. Note that, for experiments with appearing/disappearing targets, it is assumed that agents know how many targets need to be provisioned at a given time. This assumption is not made in the other experiments. Depending on how much knowledge agents have access to, the utility functions need to be modified accordingly.

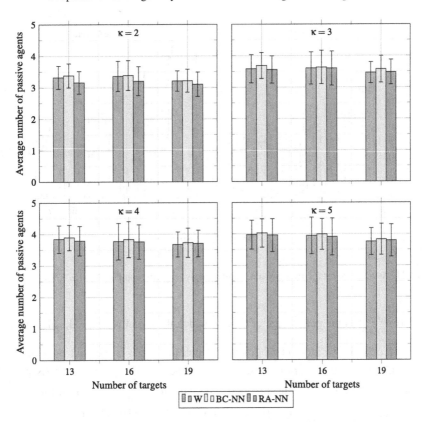

Fig. 10. Average passive number of agents per target for $\kappa \in \{2,3,4,5\}$.

For these experiments, the utility for following a given target is modified to also account for the distance to such target, where the distance is weighed based on the interest level.

$$u_{o_i} = \min\left(\frac{1}{(1 - I_{o_i}) \cdot d_{a \to o_i}}, 1\right), \tag{20}$$

where u_{o_i} represents the utility for following target o_i, I_{o_i} is the interest level of o_i, and $d_{a \to o_i}$ is the distance between robot a and target o_i. The intuition behind the equation is that, given the same distance, the utility will be higher for a higher interest level, and lower otherwise.

There are two metrics of interest in these experiments: (i) the average coverage time percentage of all targets $\tau_{\text{avg}\%}^{(\kappa)}$ (Eq. 21), and (ii) the average amount of agents covering the targets β_{avg} (Eq. 22). The first metric (i) is calculated as

$$\tau_{\text{avg}\%}^{(\kappa)} = \frac{1}{N} \sum_e \frac{1}{|O|} \sum_j \tau_{j,e(\%)}^{(\kappa)}, \tag{21}$$

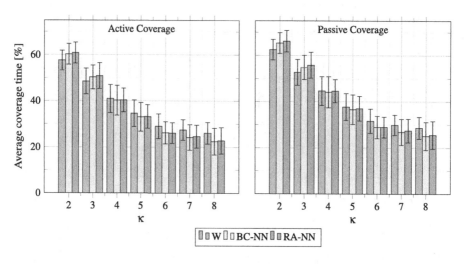

Fig. 11. Average coverage time for active and passive coverage and $\kappa \in \{2,3,4,5,6,7,8\}$.

where $\tau^{(\kappa)}_{j,e(\%)}$ is the percentage of time in which the target is covered, calculated as $\frac{c^{(\kappa)}_j}{tp_j}$, where $c^{(\kappa)}_j$ is the amount of time for which the target is covered by κ or more agents, and tp_j is the amount of time for which the target is present in Z (Note that $tp_j <= T_{sim}$). We also compute this metric by weighing $\tau^{(\kappa)}_{j,e(\%)}$ based on the interest level of target o_j, i.e. $\tau^{(\kappa)}_{j,e(\%)} \cdot I_{oj}$. The second metric (ii) is calculated as

$$\beta_{avg} = \frac{1}{N}\sum_e \frac{1}{|O|}\sum_j \beta_{j,e},\qquad (22)$$

where $\beta_{j,e}$ is the average amount of agents that cover target o_j during the part of the simulation in which it is present in Z.

It is possible to observe that the three methods produce comparable results across the different values of κ, considering both active and passive coverage (Fig. 11). Slight differences in average are noted, and as κ increases the method with the willingness has a slight improvement compared to the other two. These trends are consistent when weighing $\tau^{(\kappa)}_{j,e(\%)}$ by the interest level of target o_j (Fig. 12). Comparing active and passive coverage, it is possible to see that the latter achieves a slight improvement, circa 7% for $\kappa = 2$ (Fig. 11).

Regarding the average agents per target, the three methods remain comparable across the different values of κ, considering both active and passive coverage (Fig. 13). There are slight differences in average, more notable in the passive case. Furthermore, it is possible to observe that when considering passive coverage as well, the average number of agents per target remains quite close to 3 for all the values of κ under study. This result gives an indication of the physical limit with respect to how many agents can cover a target, given a particular setting, in terms of area size, number of agents,

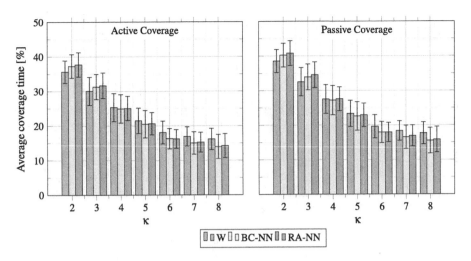

Fig. 12. Average coverage time for active and passive coverage and κ ∈ {2,3,4,5,6,7,8}, weighed by interest level.

and targets, there is Whereas, in the active case the metric increases with the increase of the value of κ.

6   Generalization of the Approach

In this paper, a collaborative approach based on the willingness to interact has been adopted in order to solve the κ-coverage problem for a multi-robot system. The described framework, composed of the agent behaviour, willingness to interact, combined with the interaction protocols can be applied in other problems as well. Regarding the agent behaviour, the state machine presented in Sect. 4.2 can be generalised by considering the following abstract states: *idle*, *interact*, *idle & execute*, and *interact & execute* adapted from [11]. Such states can be specialised depending on the desired behaviours robots should display when tackling different problems, e.g. moving by randomly changing direction and inspecting the space for new targets can be used to instantiate the *idle* state into the *inspect* state as done in this paper for solving the κ-coverage problem. Whereas the *execute* state can be instantiated into either the *inspect & follow* or *evaluate & follow*, by adding the target following behaviour to the agents.

The willingness to interact formalism can be easily modified to account for additional relevant factors in a given application domain. Additionally, it is possible to differentiate between different types of factors, such as necessary and optional, as well as giving a specific weight to each factor. In this paper we have considered factors such as the battery level and the level of activity of an agents, which correspond to the necessary and optional factors respectively. Weights are determined in a simple way, i.e. if no necessary factor is under the minimum threshold, then factors are weighted the same, otherwise the necessary factors will override the optional ones, thus determining the final value of the willingness.

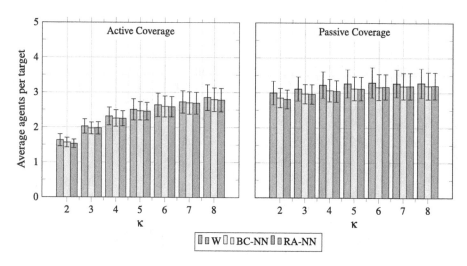

Fig. 13. Average agents per target for active and passive coverage and $\kappa \in \{2, 3, 4, 5, 6, 7, 8\}$.

Finally, the interaction protocol is independent of the application and problem to be solved, apart for the κ parameter which can be adjusted depending on the desired size of coalitions for provisioning targets, and the triggers that agents use to initiate the interaction. In the current application domain agents are tasked with discovering and tracking targets in their environment. Therefore, the triggers for executing the interaction protocol are application dependent such as (i) spotting a new target in the visibility range, (ii) detecting that a target is moving away and might soon be outside of the visibility range, and (iii) extending an existing coalition in order to reach κ-coverage. The fourth trigger captures the moment when an agent decides that it needs to ask for help, which is based on the willingness to interact. This trigger is not application dependent.

7   Conclusion and Future Work

This paper presented a novel, distributed, agent-centric coalition formation approach, based on the willingness to interact for adaptive cooperative behaviour. We showed that we can use this novel approach to solve the κ-coverage problem for a group of targets. The performance of this approach is evaluated in two sets of experiments, and is compared with six methods previously proposed in the literature. The purpose of the first set of experiments is to investigate scenarios with static and mobile targets, while also considering a different number of such targets. For static targets, the analysed metrics are the average time to get one target covered with κ agents, and the average minimum time to κ-cover all objects are considered. Whereas, for mobile targets, we considered the average coverage time and average number of agents per target. Results show that our approach either performs comparably good in the case of static targets with respect to the *BC-NN* method (the best performing among the ones considered in the paper), followed by *RA-NN*, and that it performs better than the other methods in terms of achieving a higher level of coverage when it comes to moving targets. The purpose of the second set of experiments was to further compare the proposed approach with the best performing methods, across several values of κ for mobile targets. Additionally, the performance of the methods was evaluated in scenarios where targets would appear/disappear with a given probability. Results from these experiments show that the three methods are comparable to one another.

There are two main lines of inquiry for future work. First, it is of interest to investigate different rates of appearance and disappearance for targets, in order to understand which method makes for a better coping mechanism in a dynamic environment. Furthermore, issues related to how the studied models scale up in terms of, e.g. bandwidth capacity and latency, can also be considered in the analysis. Second, security aspects can be introduced, by considering the trustworthiness of agents. Such information can be included in the calculation of the willingness to interact, in order to facilitate the cooperation between agents that are more trustworthy, e.g. open systems where new agents may be introduced or removed, similarly to recent approaches [3,5].

References

1. Bakhshipour, M., Jabbari Ghadi, M., Namdari, F.: Swarm robotics search & rescue: a novel artificial intelligence-inspired optimization approach. Appl. Soft Comput. **57**, 708–726 (2017)
2. Burgard, W., Moors, M., Schneider, F.: Collaborative exploration of unknown environments with teams of mobile robots. In: Beetz, M., Hertzberg, J., Ghallab, M., Pollack, M.E. (eds.) Advances in Plan-Based Control of Robotic Agents. LNCS (LNAI), vol. 2466, pp. 52–70. Springer, Heidelberg (2002). https://doi.org/10.1007/3-540-37724-7_4
3. Calvaresi, D., Dubovitskaya, A., Calbimonte, J.P., Taveter, K., Schumacher, M.: Multi-agent systems and blockchain: results from a systematic literature review. In: Demazeau, Y., An, B., Bajo, J., Fernández-Caballero, A. (eds.) PAAMS 2018. LNCS (LNAI), vol. 10978, pp. 110–126. Springer, Cham (2018). https://doi.org/10.1007/978-3-319-94580-4_9
4. Casadei, R., Pianini, D., Viroli, M., Natali, A.: Self-organising coordination regions: a pattern for edge computing. In: Riis Nielson, H., Tuosto, E. (eds.) COORDINATION 2019. LNCS, vol. 11533, pp. 182–199. Springer, Cham (2019). https://doi.org/10.1007/978-3-030-22397-7_11
5. Castelló Ferrer, E.: The blockchain: a new framework for robotic swarm systems. In: Arai, K., Bhatia, R., Kapoor, S. (eds.) FTC 2018. AISC, vol. 881, pp. 1037–1058. Springer, Cham (2019). https://doi.org/10.1007/978-3-030-02683-7_77
6. Eickstedt, D.P., Benjamin, M.R.: Cooperative target tracking in a distributed autonomous sensor network. In: OCEANS 2006, pp. 1–6 (2006)
7. Elhoseny, M., Tharwat, A., Yuan, X., Hassanien, A.E.: Optimizing K-coverage of mobile WSNs. Expert Syst. Appl. **92**, 142–153 (2018)
8. Esterle, L.: Goal-aware team affiliation in collectives of autonomous robots. In: International Conference on Self-Adaptive and Self-Organizing Systems (SASO), pp. 90–99 (2018)
9. Esterle, L., Lewis, P.R.: Online multi-object k-coverage with mobile smart cameras. In: International Conference on Distributed Smart Cameras, pp. 1–6. ACM (2017)
10. Esterle, L., Lewis, P.R.: Distributed autonomy and trade-offs in online multiobject k-coverage. Comput. Intell. **36**(2), 720–742 (2019)
11. Frasheri, M., Cürüklü, B., Ekström, M., Papadopoulos, A.V.: Adaptive autonomy in a search and rescue scenario. In: International Conference on Self-Adaptive and Self-Organizing Systems, pp. 150–155 (2018)

12. Frasheri, M., Esterle, L., Papadopoulos, A.V.: Modeling the willingness to interact in cooperative multi-robot systems. In: 12th International Conference on Agents and Artificial Intelligence (ICAART), vol. 1, pp. 62–72 (2020)
13. Fusco, G., Gupta, H.: Selection and orientation of directional sensors for coverage maximization. In: Proceedings of the International Conference on Sensor, Mesh and Ad Hoc Communications and Networks, pp. 1–9 (2009)
14. García, S., Menghi, C., Pelliccione, P., Berger, T., Wohlrab, R.: An architecture for decentralized, collaborative, and autonomous robots. In: International Conference on Software Architecture, pp. 75–7509 (2018)
15. Guarnieri, M., Debenest, R., Inoh, T., Fukushima, E., Hirose, S.: Development of Helios VII: an arm-equipped tracked vehicle for search and rescue operations. In: IEEE/RSJ International Conference on Intelligent Robots and Systems (IROS), pp. 39–45 (2004)
16. Hefeeda, M., Bagheri, M.: Randomized k-coverage algorithms for dense sensor networks. In: International Conference on Computer Communications, pp. 2376–2380 (2007)
17. Hellmund, A., Wirges, S., Ş. Taş, O., Bandera, C., Salscheider, N.O.: Robot operating system: a modular software framework for automated driving. In: International Conference on Intelligent Transportation Systems, pp. 1564–1570 (2016)
18. Huang, C.F., Tseng, Y.C.: The coverage problem in a wireless sensor network. Mob. Netw. Appl. **10**(4), 519–528 (2005). https://doi.org/10.1007/s11036-005-1564-y
19. Jung, B., Sukhatme, G.S.: Cooperative multi-robot target tracking. In: Gini, M., Voyles, R. (eds.) Distributed Autonomous Robotic Systems, vol. 7, pp. 81–90. Springer, Tokyo (2006). https://doi.org/10.1007/4-431-35881-1_9
20. Khan, A., Rinner, B., Cavallaro, A.: Cooperative robots to observe moving targets: review. IEEE Trans. Cybern. **48**(1), 187–198 (2018)
21. King, D.W., Esterle, L., Peterson, G.L.: Entropy-based team self-organization with signal suppression. In: Artificial Life Conference Proceedings, vol. 31, pp. 145–152 (2019)
22. Kolling, A., Carpin, S.: Cooperative observation of multiple moving targets: an algorithm and its formalization. Int. J. Robot. Res. **26**(9), 935–953 (2007)
23. Kumar, S., Lai, T.H., Balogh, J.: On k-coverage in a mostly sleeping sensor network. In: International Conference on Mobile Computing and Networking, pp. 144–158 (2004)
24. Lee, S.-H., Choi, H.: The fast bully algorithm: for electing a coordinator process in distributed systems. In: Chong, I. (ed.) ICOIN 2002. LNCS, vol. 2344, pp. 609–622. Springer, Heidelberg (2002). https://doi.org/10.1007/3-540-45801-8_58
25. Li, J.S., Kao, H.C.: Distributed k-coverage self-location estimation scheme based on Voronoi diagram. IET Commun. **4**(2), 167–177 (2010)
26. Liu, B., Dousse, O., Nain, P., Towsley, D.: Dynamic coverage of mobile sensor networks. Trans. Parall. Distrib. Syst. **24**(2), 301–311 (2013)
27. Micheloni, C., Rinner, B., Foresti, G.L.: Video analysis in pan-tilt-zoom camera networks. Sign. Process. Mag. **27**(5), 78–90 (2010)
28. Navarro-Serment, L.E., Dolan, J.M., Khosla, P.K.: Optimal sensor placement for cooperative distributed vision. International Conference on Robotics and Automation, vol. 1, pp. 939–944 (2004)
29. Page, J., Armstrong, R., Mukhlish, F.: Simulating search and rescue operations using swarm technology to determine how many searchers are needed to locate missing persons/objects in the shortest time. In: Naweed, A., Bowditch, L., Sprick, C. (eds.) ASC 2019. CCIS, vol. 1067, pp. 106–112. Springer, Singapore (2019). https://doi.org/10.1007/978-981-32-9582-7_8
30. Parker, L.E., Emmons, B.A.: Cooperative multi-robot observation of multiple moving targets. In: International Conference on Robotics and Automation, vol. 3, pp. 2082–2089 (1997)

31. Piciarelli, C., Esterle, L., Khan, A., Rinner, B., Foresti, G.L.: Dynamic reconfiguration in camera networks: a short survey. IEEE Trans. Circ. Syst. Video Technol. **26**(5), 965–977 (2016)

32. Quigley, M., et al.: ROS: an open-source robot operating system. In: ICRA Workshop on Open Source Software, vol. 3, p. 5 (2009)

33. Qureshi, F., Terzopoulos, D.: Distributed coalition formation in visual sensor networks: a virtual vision approach. In: Aspnes, J., Scheideler, C., Arora, A., Madden, S. (eds.) DCOSS 2007. LNCS, vol. 4549, pp. 1–20. Springer, Heidelberg (2007). https://doi.org/10.1007/978-3-540-73090-3_1

34. Robin, C., Lacroix, S.: Multi-robot target detection and tracking: taxonomy and survey. Auton. Robots **40**(4), 729–760 (2015). https://doi.org/10.1007/s10514-015-9491-7

35. Ruetten, L., Regis, P.A., Feil-Seifer, D., Sengupta, S.: Area-optimized UAV swarm network for search and rescue operations. In: Computing and Communication Workshop and Conference (CCWC), pp. 0613–0618 (2020)

36. SanMiguel, J.C., Micheloni, C., Shoop, K., Foresti, G.L., Cavallaro, A.: Self-reconfigurable smart camera networks. Computer **47**(5), 67–73 (2014)

37. Shehory, O., Kraus, S.: Methods for task allocation via agent coalition formation. Artif. Intell. **101**(1), 165–200 (1998)

38. Stormont, D.P.: Autonomous rescue robot swarms for first responders. In: IEEE International Conference Computational Intelligence for Homeland Security and Personal Safety, pp. 151–157 (2005)

39. Theraulaz, G., Bonabeau, E., Deneubourg, J.L.: Response threshold reinforcements and division of labour in insect societies. Roy. Soc. B Biol. Sci. **265**(1393), 327–332 (1998)

40. Werger, B.B., Matarić, M.J.: From insect to internet: Situated control for networked robot teams. Ann. Math. Artif. Intell. **31**(1), 173–197 (2001). https://doi.org/10.1023/A:1016650101473

41. Yanmaz, E., Yahyanejad, S., Rinner, B., Hellwagner, H., Bettstetter, C.: Drone networks: communications, coordination, and sensing. Ad Hoc Netw. **68**, 1–15 (2018)

42. Ye, D., Zhang, M., Sutanto, D.: Self-adaptation-based dynamic coalition formation in a distributed agent network: a mechanism and a brief survey. IEEE Trans. on Parallel Distrib. Syst. **24**(5), 1042–1051 (2013)

A Dynamic Scheduling Multiagent System for Truck Dispatching in Open-Pit Mines

Gabriel Icarte Ahumada[1,2(✉)] (ID), Jean Diaz Pinto[3] (ID),
and Otthein Herzog[4,5,6] (ID)

[1] International Graduate School for Dynamics in Logistics (IGS),
University of Bremen, Bremen, Germany
gicartea@uni-bremen.de
[2] Faculty of Engineering and Architecture, Arturo Prat University - UNAP,
Iquique, Chile
gicarte@unap.cl
[3] Science Faculty, Arturo Prat University - UNAP, Iquique, Chile
jeadiaz@unap.cl
[4] TZI - Center for Computing Technologies, University of Bremen,
Bremen, Germany
herzog@tzi.de
[5] Jacobs University, Bremen, Germany
[6] Tongji University Shanghai, Shanghai, People's Republic of China

Abstract. Material handling is an important process in the mining industry because of its high operational cost. In this process, shovels extract and load materials that must be transported by trucks to different destinations at the mine. When a truck ends an unloading operation, it requires a new loading destination. If a centralized system provides destinations by following dispatching criteria, then one of the main disadvantages of this kind of systems is not being able to provide a precise dispatching solution without knowledge about potentially changed external conditions and the dependency on a central node. In this paper, we describe a distributed approach based on Multiagent Systems (MAS) to alleviate these disadvantages. In this approach, the real-world equipment items such as shovels and trucks are represented by intelligent agents. The agents interact with each other to generate schedules for the machines that they represent. For this interaction, a Contract Net Protocol with a confirmation stage was implemented. In addition, when a machine failure occurs, the agents are able to update their schedules. In order to evaluate the MAS, an agent-based simulation with data from a Chilean open-pit mine was used. The results show that the MAS is able to generate the schedules in a practical computation timeframe. The schedules generated by the MAS decrease the truck cost by 17% on average. Moreover, when a machine failure occurs, the agents are able to repair their schedules in a short period of time.

Keyword: Truck dispatching · Open-pit mine · Multiagent systems · Scheduling · Rescheduling

© Springer Nature Switzerland AG 2021
A. P. Rocha et al. (Eds.): ICAART 2020, LNAI 12613, pp. 132–148, 2021.
https://doi.org/10.1007/978-3-030-71158-0_6

1 Introduction

Material handling is an important process in open-pit mines since its cost can represent up to 50% of the entire operational cost in these kinds of mines [1]. In this process shovels and trucks work together to extract and to transport all the material required in the operational plan at minimum cost. If the material extracted is ore, it must be transported and unloaded into a crusher or onto a stockpile. If the extracted material is waste, it must be transported to a waste dump. Figure 1 depicts the operations that a truck must perform to transport materials from a shovel to a crusher, stockpile, or waste dump. This cycle is performed and repeated by each truck until the shift ends.

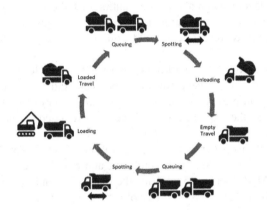

Fig. 1. The truck cycle. Adapted from [2, p. 2]

The material handling process is performed in a dynamic environment that affects the performance and availability of the involved equipment. For example, changes in weather conditions or to the state of the routes as well as equipment failures are some of the reasons for delays in material handling [3].

During the material handling process, each time a truck ends an unloading operation it requires a new loading destination, i.e., it requires a new assignment to a shovel where the truck must go for a new loading. This is called truck dispatching. Determining the new destination for the truck is not easy because of the stochasticity of the material handling process and the dynamics of the environment where the equipment items perform their operations.

Different centralized systems have been implemented to support truck dispatching in open-pit mines [4]. Most of these systems use a multistage approach [1], which computes a guideline in the first stage. A later stage uses this guideline to dispatch the trucks in real-time each time that a truck ends an unloading operation.

One example of the application of the multistage approach is a system with two stages. The first stage determines, before the shift starts, the number of travels to transport the required materials by the production plan from shovels to unloading points. Then, when the trucks are working and when a truck requires a new destination, the later stage determines the destination based on a dispatching criterion (e.g., the number of trips performed) and the current information on the process.

The strengths of these centralized systems are their maturity and their well-known implementation. However, the weaknesses that can be observed are using estimated information [5–8], and not being able to provide a precise solution [9]. In addition, using dispatching criteria in this way is myopic, and it is hard to predict the performance of the entire system since decisions are made locally in real-time [10]. Due to these weaknesses, the material handling process is not performed efficiently, since queues of trucks can form in front of shovels and crushers, and there can also be shovel idle times. Therefore, the question remains as how to improve the efficiency of the material handling process.

Icarte et al. [2] developed an alternative solution that allows the equipment items to operate more efficiently. The solution is based on a Multiagent system in which intelligent agents that represent real-world equipment interact with each other to generate schedules.

In this paper, we extend the work presented in [2] by performing and evaluating extended experiments for the generation of schedules, and by the evaluation of the MAS when a major unforeseen event occurs at the mine. In order to demonstrate the validity of the MAS, the experiments were performed based on actual data from a Chilean open-pit mine.

The remainder of this paper is structured as follows: Sect. 2 presents related work, Sect. 3 presents the formulation of the problem, and Sect. 4 presents the distributed solution based on MAS. Section 5 presents the evaluation and discussion of the proposed MAS. Finally, conclusions and outlook are presented in Sect. 6.

2   Related Work

In the past years, many articles deal with the truck dispatching problem in open-pit mines. These articles show different methods that try to achieve two goals: improve productivity and reduce operating costs [1]. These methods are based on Operations Research, simulation modelling or heuristic procedures and follow a centralized approach. For instance, Bakhtavar and Mahmoudi [11] developed a two-phase scenario-based robust optimization (SBRO) model by considering the maximization of production, control of ore grade sent to the crusher, minimization of waiting times for trucks and shovels, and trucks with different capacities. Koryagin and Voronov [12] presented a heuristic algorithm to dispatch trucks after unloading. The algorithm uses priority parameters for choosing the shovel to which the truck will be allocated, and the corresponding route for material transportation is considered. In addition, the algorithm applies a minimizing truck waiting time criterion. Chaowasakoo et al. [13] illustrated the differences between the dispatching strategies by conducting a stochastic simulation study based on the data gathered from an actual big-size mine.

Most of the articles on the truck dispatching problem in open-pit mines propose a method that determines the next destination of a truck after the completion of an unloading activity. To do this, the methods use a previously calculated guideline, the current status of the mine, and some dispatching criteria. Although these methods are easy to implement, they are not able to provide a precise description of the activities of shovels and trucks. Therefore, they cannot guarantee a good synchronization between the activities of the equipment items [9]. In scheduling theory, this kind of method is called "Completely reactive scheduling" [10, 14].

In "Completely reactive scheduling" no schedule is generated. The decision on what is the next task to be performed is made locally in real-time [10] considering the available information at the moment and some dispatching criteria. This way of dynamic scheduling is quick, usually intuitive, and easy to implement. However, a schedule of the tasks to perform has the potential to significantly improve the performance of a system [10].

Few articles have proposed to generate schedules for the truck dispatching problem in open-pit mines. Chang et al. [3] and Patterson et al. [7] proposed algorithms that generate an initial schedule which is improved by using a metaheuristic method. Their results show that these algorithms generate schedules for different size instances with good results and performance in practical frame times. Icarte et al. [2] developed a distributed approach based on multiagent systems to generate schedules for the equipment item involved in the material handling process. Their results show that a MAS approach provides schedules in practical frame times for the mining industry. However, none of these articles mention how the schedules could be rescheduled when a major unforeseen event occurs in a mine.

There are several articles that use multiagent systems for scheduling and rescheduling problems. Most of them are applied in manufacturing [15–18] and for vehicles [19–24]. All these authors mention the good performance of MAS to generate schedules and, some of them, a good reaction when an event occurs [16, 19–21, 23, 25]. These articles demonstrate the applicability of MAS to scheduling and rescheduling problems.

3 Problem Representation

Truck dispatching in open-pit mines as a scheduling problem is represented by the following notations, constraints, and objective functions:

3.1 Notations

- $S = \{s_1, \ldots, s_n\}$. It is the set of shovels.
- $T = \{t_1, \ldots, t_m\}$. It is the set of trucks.
- $J = \{j_1, \ldots, j_p\}$. It is the set of the material extracted by a shovel.
- C_t^s. It is the loading time that the shovel s takes for loading the truck t.
- C_j^t. It is the unloading time that the truck t takes for unloading at destination j.
- C_loaded_t. It is the cost matrix $(C_{s,j})$ of truck t that represent the cost of traveling from shovel s to destination j.
- C_empty_t. It is the cost matrix $(C_{j,s})$ of truck t that represent the cost of traveling from destination j to shovel s.

- *TargetPlan* $= \{(s,j,x)|s \in S, j \in J, x \in \mathbb{N}\}$. It is the material that must be extracted by shovel s and transported to destination j.
- *TruckOperation* $= \{$'emptyTrip','*loading*','*loadedTrip*','*unloading*'$\}$. The operation that a truck can perform.
- *TruckSchedule* $= \{(t, operation, startTime, \quad endTime, from, to)|t \in T, operation \in TruckOperation, startTime \in \mathbb{N}, \text{endTime} \in \mathbb{N}, from \in (S \cup J), to \in (S \cup J)\}$. It is the schedule of the trucks.
- *ShovelSchedule* $= \{(s, startTime, endTime, quantityLoaded)|s \in S, startTime \in \mathbb{N}, \text{endTime} \in \mathbb{N}\}$. It is the schedule of the shovels.

The following constraints set the sequence and times of the operations scheduled and avoiding overlapping them.

$$startTime + C\_empty_t(j,s)$$
$$= endTime \forall x_{(t,emptyTrip,starTime,endTime,s,j)} \tag{1}$$
$$\in TruckSchedule$$

$$startTime + C\_loaded_t(s,j)$$
$$= endTime \forall x_{(t,loadedTrip,starTime,endTime,j,s)} \tag{2}$$
$$\in TruckSchedule$$

$$startTime + C_t^s = endTime \forall x_{(t,loading,starTime,endTime,s,s)} \tag{3}$$
$$\in TruckSchedule$$

$$startTime + C_j^t = endTime \forall x_{(t,unloading,starTime,endTime,j,j)} \tag{4}$$
$$\in TruckSchedule$$

$$x_{(t,emptyTrip,startTime,endTime,s,j)}$$
$$\leq y_{(t,loading,startTime',endTime',s,s)} iff\ endTime \tag{5}$$
$$\leq startTime' \forall x, y \in TruckSchedule$$

$$x_{(t,loading,startTime,endTime,s,s)}$$
$$\leq y_{(t,loadedTrip,startTime',endTime',s,j)} iff\ endTime \tag{6}$$
$$\leq startTime' \forall x, y \in TruckSchedule$$

$$x_{(t,loadedTrip,startTime,endTime,s,j)}$$
$$\leq y_{(t,unloading,startTime',endTime',j,j)} iff\ endTime \tag{7}$$
$$\leq startTime' \forall x, y \in TruckSchedule$$

$$x_{(t,unloading,startTime,endTime,j,j)}$$
$$\leq y_{(t,emptyTrip,startTime',endTime',j,s)} iff\ endTime \tag{8}$$
$$\leq startTime' \forall x, y \in TruckSchedule$$

$$startTime + C_t^s = endTime \forall x_{(s,starTime,endTime)} \in ShovelSchedule \tag{9}$$

$$x_{(s,startTime,endTime)} \leq y_{(s,startTime',endTime')} iff\ endTime \tag{10}$$
$$\leq startTime' \forall x, y \in ShovelSchedule$$

3.2   Objective Functions

The truck dispatching problem pursues two objectives: to achieve the production targets and the minimization of the truck travel costs. These objectives can be formulated as follows:

$$max \sum_{x \in ShovelSchedule} (quantityLoaded) \tag{11}$$

$$min \sum_{x \in TruckSchedule} (endTime - starTime) \tag{12}$$

4   Dynamic Scheduling Multiagent System for Truck Dispatching in Open-Pit Mines

The objective of the developed MAS is to achieve the goals of the production plan at minimum cost. In order to do this, the agents must interact with each other to generate schedules for each equipment item involved in the material handling process. Moreover, the agents must update the generated schedules when a major unforeseen event occurs at the mine. Table 1 shows the implemented agents, their objectives, and properties.

Our developed multiagent system for truck dispatching in open-pit mines has the following advantages over current centralized systems:

- Efficient Dispatching Solution: The schedules generated by the MAS are more efficient than a "Completely reactive scheduling", which is applied by the current systems.
- Use of Specific Data from Equipment Items: This allows the MAS to generate more precise schedules.

Table 1. Agent description. Adapted from [2, p. 4].

Agent	Real-world representation	Objective	Properties
truckAgent	Trucks	Create a schedule of the activities of the truck at minimum cost	Capacity, loaded velocity, empty velocity, spotting time and unloading time, layout of the mine
shovelAgent	Shovels, front loaders	Create a schedule of the activities of the equipment that it represents considering its target in the production plan	Capacity, dig velocity, load velocity and the destination of extracted material
unloadingPointAgent	Crusher, stockpiles, waste dumps	Create a schedule of the activities of the equipment that it represents	Number of trucks unloading simultaneously

- Robustness: As there is not a central node, if any node is out of order, the system continues working without it.
- Flexibility: An agent can change its behavior to adapt to the new conditions in its environment and, in this way, to achieve its own objectives or the objectives of the entire system.
- Reactiveness: The agents are able to update the schedules when a major unforeseen event occurs at the mine.

The following subsections describe the interactions among the agents and their decision-making processes.

4.1 Interactions for Scheduling

In order to generate the schedules, the agents negotiate among them by using the adapted Contract Net Protocol presented in [2]. In this protocol, a *shovelAgent* plays the role of the initiator and *truckAgents* play the role of participants. The *shovelAgents* in the system start this negotiation process in parallel, therefore the protocol must manage concurrent negotiations.

To manage concurrent negotiations, the original CNP is adapted by including a confirmation stage. The state transitions in the negotiation process between a *shovelAgent* and *truckAgents* are depicted in Fig. 2. The process starts when a *shovelAgent* sends a *call-for-proposal* message (CFP) to *truckAgents*. After sending the CFP, the process passes to the first state "Evaluating CFP". In this state, *the truckAgents* evaluate the received CFP and decide on sending a *proposal* or a *refuse* message as the answer. Meanwhile the *shovelAgent* is waiting for the messages from the *truckAgents*.

When a *shovelAgent* receives a message from a *truckAgent*, the negotiation process passes to the state "Receiving proposals". In this state, the *shovelAgent* receives and stores the proposals sent by the *truckAgents* and keeps a count of the received messages from the *truckAgents*. The negotiation keeps in this state until a deadline expires or when the *shovelAgent* has received all the messages (*propose* or *refuse*) from the *truckAgents*. In the "Receiving proposals" state two situations can happen: having received proposals or not. If it has not received any proposals, the negotiation process finishes without a contract. If it has received proposals, the negotiation process passes to the state "Selecting best proposal".

In the state "Selecting best proposal", the *shovelAgent* selects the best proposal and sends a message with the performative *requestConfirmation* to the truckAgent that sent the best proposal, and the negotiation process passes to the state "Waiting for answer".

In the state "Waiting for answer", three situations can happen: receiving a message with the performative *acceptConfirmation*, receiving a message with the performative *refuseConfirmation*, or a deadline expires. In the first case, the negotiation process passes to the state "Sending results". In the "Sending results" state the *shovelAgent* sends a *reject-proposal* message to those *truckAgents* that were not awarded, and the negotiation process ends with a contract. In the second and third cases, the negotiation process passes to the "Removing proposal" state. In this state, the *shovelAgent* removes the proposal from its storage. If there are more proposals, the negotiation process

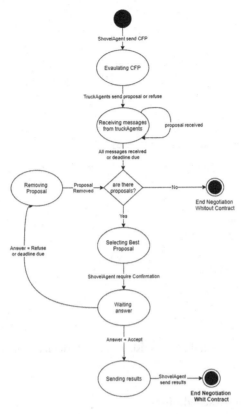

Fig. 2. State machine diagram of the negotiation process by applying the adapted Contract Net Protocol.

Table 2. Example of schedule created for a truck.

Assignment	Destination	Start time of the Trip	Arrival time	Start time of the loading/unloading	End time of the assignment
0	Shovel.04	05:57:01	06:10:23	06:10:36	06:15:12
1	WasteDump.03	06:15:12	06:32:33	06:38:23	06:40:23
2	Shove l.04	06:45:25	06:58:47	07:00:10	07:05:35
3	WasteDump.02	07:05:35	07:22:24	07:26:38	07:27:12
4	Shovel.02	07:37:44	07:41:25	07:43:18	07:48:32

passes to the state "Selecting best proposal" and repeats the cycle. If there are no more proposals, the negotiation process ends without a contract. Figure 3 depicts the interaction between the agents using the adapted Contract Net Protocol and Table 2 shows a schedule example for a truck generated by the agents by applying this protocol.

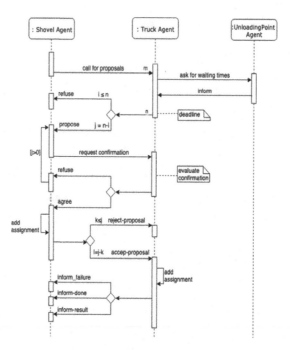

Fig. 3. The interaction between the agents using the CNP with the confirmation stage. Adapted from [2, p. 4].

4.2 Interactions for Rescheduling

In the scheduling literature, two main rescheduling strategies are mentioned: schedule repair, and complete rescheduling [10]. scheduling repair refers to some local adjustment of the current schedule. complete rescheduling regenerates a new schedule from scratch.

In the context of the MAS for the truck dispatching in open-pit mines, the agents can use both strategies, depending on the type event that triggers the rescheduling. In both strategies, the agents apply the adapted CNP described previously. For the schedule repair strategy, some agents may apply changes to their schedules. For instance, in the case of a truck failure, the *truckAgent* that represents the broken truck informs *shovelAgents* and *unloadingAgents* that the truck will not be able to perform the assignments. The *shovelAgent* must cancel the affected assignment and its production will decrease. Here, the *shovelAgent* starts new a negotiation process cycle to try to reach its production goals again. In the case of complete rescheduling, all agents must generate a new schedule from the point in time where the failure occurred. All agents cancel their assignments and the agents interact with each other by applying the adapted CNP to generate new schedules.

4.3   Decision Making

In the MAS for truck dispatch in open-pit mines, *ShovelAgents* and *TruckAgents* make decisions at different moments in the negotiation process. The following subsections describe the decision-making process for these types of agents.

ShovelAgent. *ShovelAgents* only must make one decision during a negotiation process: what is the best proposal received. to make this decision, the *shovelagents* use the utility function proposed in [2], which promotes those proposals that decrease the shovel's waiting time and minimize the cost to perform the truck operations. formally:

$$offer = number \in \{0\} \cup \mathbb{N}. \text{ It represents the time offered by a} shovelAgent \quad (13)$$

to start a new loading.

$$P = set \, of \, received \, proposals \, p_1 \ldots p_n \quad (14)$$

The decision is a multicriteria problem as

$$Decision = arg_{min}(p_i \in P)\{U(p_1), \ldots, U(p_n)) \quad (15)$$

$$U = U(arrivalTime)\prime + U(cost)\prime \quad (16)$$

$$\delta = (arrivalTime - offer) \in \mathbb{Z} \quad (17)$$

$$U(arrivalTime) = \begin{cases} \delta, \; if \, \delta < 0 \; (the \, truck \, arrives \, earlier) \\ 0, \; if \, \delta = 0 \; (the \, truck \, arrives \, just \, on \, time) \\ 2 * \delta, \; if \, \delta > 0 \; (the \, truck \, arrives \, later) \end{cases} \quad (18)$$

Where *U(arrivalTime)'* is the normalized value of *U(arrivalTime)* and *U(cost)'* is the normalized value of *U(cost)*. The normalization applied is

$$x' = \frac{x - \min(x)}{\max(x) - \min(x)} \quad (19)$$

TruckAgent. A *truckagent* must make two decisions. the first one is deciding whether or not to send a proposal to a *shovelagent* that sent a *call-for-proposal* message. the second one is to decide on whether or not to confirm a previously sent proposal. Figure 4 depicts both decision-making processes.

To decide whether or not to send a proposal, the *truckAgent* uses the *call-for-proposal* message's information and its current schedule. The *shovelAgents* send *a call-for-proposal* offering the next available time to load a truck. After receiving a CFP, the *truckAgent* checks its schedule and determines if there is a free time slot for the offered time. If not, it sends a *reject* message. If yes, it calculates the total time to perform all the operations and determines if it fits into its schedule. If it does not fit into the schedule, it sends a *reject* message. If it fits into the schedule, it sends a proposal. This decision-making process is shown in Fig. 4a.

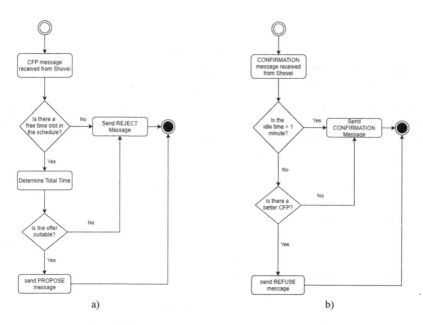

Fig. 4. Decision-making processes for a *TruckAgent*.

To decide whether or not to confirm a proposal sent previously, the *truckAgent* must consider two aspects: the shovel idle time (informed by the *requestConfirmation* message sent by the *shovelAgent*), and the negotiations which the *truckAgent* is taking part in. If the shovel idle time is higher or equal than one minute, the truckAgent sends an *acceptConfirmation* message. If the shovel idle time is less than one minute, the *truckAgent* considers the negotiations which it is taking part in. If there is a negotiation with more potential benefit for the truck (i.e., with a lower cost to perform the operations), the *truckAgent* sends a *refuseConfirmation* message. Otherwise, it sends an *acceptationConfirmation* message. This decision process is depicted in Fig. 4b.

5 Experiments and Discussion

In order to validate the MAS, two types of experiments were performed. On the one hand, some experiments evaluated the performance and quality of the schedules generated by the MAS. On the other hand, additional experiments evaluated the ability of the MAS to reschedule when a machine failure occurs at the mine. The following subsections describe the experiments and their results.

5.1 Experimental Setup

Our experiments were based on actual data from an open-pit copper mine in Chile. The material handling process at the mine is performed using a heterogeneous fleet of trucks and shovels in twelve-hour shifts. The truck dispatching is supported by DISPATCH

(TM), which is a well-known dispatch system in the mining industry. This system follows a centralized approach and Completely Reactive Scheduling. The actual data, such as velocities and capacities, is used to set the properties of the agents. Table 3 shows the property sets of the agents.

The experiments were performed by simulations run in PlaSMA [29], which is an agent-based event-driven simulation platform created for the simulation and evaluation of multiagent systems. It focuses on simulating logistics processes and is based on the FIPA-compliant Java Agent DEvelopment Framework (JADE) [30]. All simulations have been run on a laptop computer with an Intel Xeon 3 GHz CPU, 32 GB of RAM, and Windows 10.

5.2   Experiment on Schedule Generation

The aim of this experiment was to determine the required time by the MAS to generate the schedules. In order to do this, we simulated several scenarios of different sizes. The scenarios had the same characteristics, i.e. the same layout of the mine and equipment items with the same properties (velocity, capacity, etc.). The differences between the scenarios were the size of the fleet and the length of the shift (column H). Table 4 shows the scenarios and the time it took the MAS to generate the schedules.

Table 3. Property values for the simulations.

Equipment	Property	Unit	Min value	Max value
Trucks	Velocity loaded	[km/hr]	20	25
	Velocity empty	[km/hr]	40	55
	Capacity	[tons]	300	370
	Spotting time	[sec]	20	80
	Current load	[tons]	0	370
Shovel	Capacity	[tons]	35	80
	Load time	[sec]	8	30
	Dig time	[sec]	8	20
	Destination	Location at mine (crusher, stockpile, or waste dump)		
Crusher	Equipment discharging	[number of trucks]	1	1
Stockpile	Equipment discharging	[number of trucks]	1	20
Waste Dump	Equipment discharging	[number of trucks]	1	20

Table 4. Required time to generate the schedules by the MAS.

Scenario	H	Shovels	Trucks	Minutes
1	1	1	10	0.04
2	3	3	25	0.22
3	6	5	40	0.90
4	9	7	60	3.35
5	12	10	90	13.28

The results show that the required time for the MAS to generate the schedules increases with a bigger problem. However, the required time for the last scenario, which is a common scenario of a big-size open-pit mine, is a practical timeframe to generate schedules in the context of the mining industry.

5.3 Experiment on the Quality of the Generated Schedules

In this experiment, the aim was to analyze the quality of the generated schedules by the MAS, by comparing the production and cost of simulated shifts against real shifts. We simulated five shifts based on the actual data. Table 5 shows the amount of transported material and the truck cost to transport those materials.

Table 5. Comparison of transported material and truck cost between MAS and actual data.

Shift (hours)	Shovels	Trucks	Actual material transported (Tons)	Actual travel time (Hours)	Simulated material transported (Tons)	Simulated travel time (Hours)	Delta material transported	Delta travel time
12	11	99	367.623	863,00	368.215	702,24	+0,16%	−18,63%
12	11	96	360.505	820,25	361.254	688,42	+0,21%	−16,07%
12	12	99	392.773	824,47	394.259	691,93	+0,38%	−16,08%
12	12	101	405.459	804,88	406.254	655,26	+0,20%	−18,59%
12	12	95	379.234	767,82	381.245	648,69	+0,53%	−15,52%

The results show that if the trucks had been dispatched according to the schedules, the material handling process had been more efficient. This is because the schedules generated by the MAS allow the trucks to transport the same amount of material as the actual data (even a little bit more), decreasing the truck travel costs by 17% on average in comparison to the actual data.

The main reason for these savings is that the agents decrease their travel times by applying a shortest path algorithm, whereas the truck operators in the real world decide by themselves which path to follow. Another reason is the use of specific data to allow for calculations better adapted to the activity times of each equipment item, and in this way, the agents can create more appropriate and efficient schedules.

Table 6. Performance of rescheduling strategies.

	Production (tons)	Cost (hours)	Required time (sec)
Initial schedule	512,049	844,048	796,800
Simple schedule update	467,949	781,354	0.002
Schedule repair	494,633	818,339	15,215
Complete rescheduling	496,927	821,121	785,500

5.4 Experiment on Rescheduling

The objective of this experiment was to evaluate the reaction of the MAS when a machine failure occurs in the mine. In this context, we compared a simple schedule update (cancelation of the affected assignments), a schedule repair, and a complete reschedule when truck failures occur. We simulated truck failures because it is a common situation in open-pit mines.

In the simulated scenario, the fleet is compounded by 90 trucks and 10 shovels and operates in a twelve-hours shift. Two trucks have a failure at the beginning of the shift and are not available anymore. Table 6 shows the performance of the new schedules (in terms of production level and the cost) and the required time to get them by applying a simple schedule updating, schedule repair, and complete rescheduling.

These results show that the simple schedule update achieves the lowest production level in a very short time. This was predictable because the agents update only their own schedules canceling the affected assignments. It was calculated in order to contrast it with the increase in the production level by applying schedule repair and Complete rescheduling.

Schedule repair increases the production level by 5,7% and requires more time to regenerate the schedules than the simple schedule update. This happens because the affected *shovelAgents*, start the negotiation processes with the cancelation of some loading assignments to achieve their production goals.

Complete rescheduling achieves the highest production level, but the required time to generate all schedules is much higher in comparison to schedule repair. This happens because all *shovelAgents* cancel all their assignments and initiate the negotiation processes to regenerate the schedules from scratch. As it was described before, in schedule repair only a subset of *shovelAgents* (the affected ones) start the negotiation processes. In addition, in complete rescheduling, since the *truckAgents* do not have schedules, they take more time to evaluate and decide on whether to send a proposal. In schedule repair, as the *truckAgents* have schedules, they are more restricted to send proposals, and therefore it takes them less time to evaluate and decide on whether to send a proposal. Basically, a negotiation process takes more time in complete rescheduling than in schedule repair.

At first sight, it looks like schedule repair is the most suitable strategy to apply by the MAS when truck failures occur since in a short period of time the schedules are repaired. However, total regeneration is also a suitable alternative to be applied by the MAS in spite the longer time it requires. This is because the adapted CNP is implemented by anytime algorithms, i.e., complete rescheduling returns a valid schedule even if it is interrupted before it ends.

6   Conclusions

A major process in open-pit mines is material handling. In this process, dispatching a truck when it completes an unloading operation becomes a complex decision because of the stochasticity of the process and the dynamics of the environment where the equipment items operate. In general, a centralized system supports this process. However, most of them follow a reactive scheduling strategy to dispatch the trucks. This strategy does not guarantee a correct synchronization between the operations of the equipment items. In order to address this situation, we developed a multiagent system (MAS) with agents that represent equipment items from the real world. The agents interact with each other using an extended Contract Net Protocol with a confirmation stage to generate initial schedules for their represented equipment items. Schedules are a more precise way to organize and synchronize the equipment item activities than those proposed by a reactive scheduling strategy. In addition, the agents are able to repair their schedules when trucks have failures.

In order to evaluate the MAS, we made experiments based on simulations to determine the efficiency of the schedules generated by the MAS, and the reaction of the agents to repair the schedules when truck failures occur. Regarding the efficiency of the schedules, the simulations show that the trucks achieved the production level of the actual data by following the schedules with decreasing truck cost by 17% on average. In addition, the MAS generated the schedules in a practical frame time for the mining industry.

Regarding the reactiveness of the MAS when trucks have failures, the experiments demonstrate that both, scheduling repair and complete repair strategies, are suitable even if the second one takes more time for scheduling than the first one.

Our results demonstrate that an agent-based system for truck dispatching in open-pit mines is a suitable alternative to existing systems. Several characteristics of the agent technology such as flexibility, robustness, and autonomy allow the agents to generate a dispatch solution that is more precise and robust than the current approaches.

In our further research, we will compare our approach also against a metaheuristic algorithm for both scheduling and rescheduling. In addition, we will consider other events such as shovel and truck delays.

References

1. Alarie, S., Gamache, M.: Overview of solution strategies used in truck dispatching systems for open pit mines. Int. J. Surf. Min. Reclam. Environ. **16**(1), 59–76 (2002)
2. Icarte, G., Rivero, E., Herzog, O.: An agent-based system for truck dispatching in open-pit mines. In: ICAART (2020)

3. Adams, K.K., Bansah, K.K.: Review of operational delays in shovel-truck system of surface mining operations. In: 4th UMaT Biennial International Mining and Mineral Conference, pp. 60–65 (2016)
4. Icarte, G., Herzog, O.: A multi-agent system for truck dispatching in an open-pit mine. In: Second International Conference Mines of the Future (2019)
5. Chang, Y., Ren, H., Wang, S.: Modelling and optimizing an open-pit truck scheduling problem. Discret. Dyn. Nat. Soc. **2015** (2015)
6. Da Costa, F.P., Souza, M.J.F., Pinto, L.R.: Um modelo de programação matemática para alocação estática de caminhões visando ao atendimento de metas de produção e qualidade. Rem Rev. Esc. Minas **58**(1), 77–81 (2005)
7. Krzyzanowska, J.: The impact of mixed fleet hauling on mining operations at Venetia mine. J. South. Afr. Inst. Min. Metall. **107**(4), 215–224 (2007)
8. Newman, A.M., Rubio, E., Caro, R., Weintraub, A., Eurek, K.: A review of operations research in mine planning. Interfaces (Providence) **40**(3), 222–245 (2010)
9. Patterson, S.R., Kozan, E., Hyland, P.: Energy efficient scheduling of open-pit coal mine trucks. Eur. J. Oper. Res. **262**(2), 759–770 (2017)
10. Ouelhadj, D., Petrovic, S.: A survey of dynamic scheduling in manufacturing systems. J. Sched. **12**(4), 417–431 (2009)
11. Bakhtavar, E., Mahmoudi, H.: Development of a scenario-based robust model for the optimal truck-shovel allocation in open-pit mining. Comput. Oper. Res. **115**, 104539 (2020)
12. Koryagin, M., Voronov, A.: Improving the organization of the shovel-truck systems in open-pit coal mines. Transp. Probl. **12**(2), 113–122 (2017)
13. Chaowasakoo, P., Seppälä, H., Koivo, H., Zhou, Q.: Digitalization of mine operations: scenarios to benefit in real-time truck dispatching. Int. J. Min. Sci. Technol. **27**(2), 229–236 (2017)
14. Vieira, G.E., Herrmann, J.W., Lin, E.: Rescheduling manufacturing systems: a framework of strategies, policies, and methods. J. Sched. **6**(1), 39–62 (2003)
15. Lopes Silva, M.A., de Souza, S.R., Freitas Souza, M.J., Bazzan, A.L.C.: A reinforcement learning-based multi-agent framework applied for solving routing and scheduling problems. Expert Syst. Appl. **131**, 148–171 (2019)
16. Gehlhoff, F., Fay, A.: On agent-based decentralized and integrated scheduling for small-scale manufacturing. At-Automatisierungstechnik **68**(1), 15–31 (2020)
17. Wang, J., Zhang, Y., Liu, Y., Wu, N., Member, S.: Multiagent and bargaining-game-based real-time scheduling for internet of things-enabled flexible job shop. IEEE Internet Things J. **6**, 2518–2531 (2018)
18. Martin, S., Ouelhadj, D., Beullens, P., Ozcan, E., Juan, A.A., Burke, E.K.: A multi-agent based cooperative approach to scheduling and routing. Eur. J. Oper. Res. **254**(1), 169–178 (2016)
19. Chargui, K., El fallahi, A., Reghioui, M., Zouadi, T.: A reactive multi-agent approach for online (re)scheduling of resources in port container terminals. IFAC-PapersOnLine **52**(13), 124–129 (2019)
20. Whitbrook, A., Meng, Q., Chung, P.W.H.: Reliable, distributed scheduling and rescheduling for time-critical, multiagent systems. IEEE Trans. Autom. Sci. Eng. **15**(2), 732–747 (2018)
21. Seitaridis, A., Rigas, E.S., Bassiliades, N., Ramchurn, S.D.: An agent-based negotiation scheme for the distribution of electric vehicles across a set of charging stations. Simul. Model. Pract. Theory **100**, 102040 (2020)
22. Madhyastha, M., Reddy, S.C., Rao, S.: Online scheduling of a fleet of autonomous vehicles using agent-based procurement auctions. In: Proceeding - 2017 IEEE International Conference on Service Operation Logistics and Informatics, SOLI 2017, vol. 2017, pp. 114–120 (2017)

23. Skobelev, P., Budaev, D., Brankovsky, A., Voschuk, G.: Multi-agent tasks scheduling for coordinated actions of unmanned aerial vehicles acting in group. Int. J. Des. Nat. Ecodyn. **13** (1), 39–45 (2018)

24. Granichin, O., Skobelev, P., Lada, A., Mayorov, I., Tsarev, A.: Cargo transportation models analysis using multi-agent adaptive real-time truck scheduling system. In: ICAART 2013 - Proceeding 5th International Conference Agents Artificial Intelligence, vol. 2, pp. 244–249 (2013)

25. Lin, F., Dewan, M.A.A., Nguyen, M.: Optimizing rescheduling intervals through using multi-armed bandit algorithms. In: 2018 IEEE International Conference on Internet of Things (iThings) and IEEE Green Computing and Communications (GreenCom) and IEEE Cyber, Physical and Social Computing (CPSCom) and IEEE Smart Data (SmartData), pp. 746–753 (2018)

26. Smith, R.G.: The Contract Net Protocol: high-level communication and control in a distributed problem solver. IEEE Trans. Comput. **29**(12), 1104–1113 (1980)

27. Schillo, M., Kray, C., Fischer, K.: The eager bidder problem: a fundamental problem of DAI and selected solutions. In: Proceeding 1st International Joint Conference on Autonomous Agents Multiagent System, pp. 599–606, January 2002

28. Aknine, S., Pinson, S., Shakun, M.F.: An extended multi-agent negotiation protocol. Auton. Agent. Multi. Agent. Syst. **8**(1), 5–45 (2004)

29. Warden, T., Porzel, R., Gehrke, J.D., Herzog, O., Langer, H., Malaka, R.: Towards ontology-based multiagent simulations : plasma approach (2010)

30. Bellifemine, F., Caire, G., Greenwood, D.: Developing multi-agent systems with JADE (2007)

Time Matters: Exploring the Effects of Urgency and Reaction Speed in Automated Traders

Henry Hanifan, Ben Watson, John Cartlidge$^{(\boxtimes)}$, and Dave Cliff

Department of Computer Science, University of Bristol, Bristol, UK
{hh15092,bw15485}@my.bristol.ac.uk
{john.cartlidge,csdtc}@bristol.ac.uk

Abstract. We consider issues of time in automated trading strategies in simulated financial markets containing a single exchange with public limit order book and continuous double auction matching. In particular, we explore two effects: (i) *reaction speed* - the time taken for trading strategies to calculate a response to market events; and (ii) *trading urgency* - the sensitivity of trading strategies to approaching deadlines. Much of the literature on trading agents focuses on optimising pricing strategies only and ignores the effects of time, while real-world markets continue to experience a *race to zero* latency, as automated trading systems compete to quickly access information and act in the market ahead of others. We demonstrate that modelling reaction speed can significantly alter previously published results, with simple strategies such as SHVR outperforming more complex adaptive algorithms such as AA. We also show that adding a *pace* parameter to ZIP traders (ZIP-Pace, or ZIPP) can create a sense of urgency that significantly improves profitability.

Keywords: Agent based modelling · Auctions · Automated trading · Financial markets · Simulation · Trading agents

1 Introduction

The academic literature on financial trading agents is predominately focused on strategies to determine the price at which an agent should submit the next order (often, the price most likely to maximise profit), given current market conditions. These *pricing strategies* are usually developed and tested in a controlled experimental environment that has changed little in form since the experimental design was first introduced in 1955 by the seminal work of Vernon L. Smith [29]. Smith—now regarded as the "father of experimental economics"—borrowed techniques from psychology laboratory experiments to perform a series of trading experiments, using student volunteers at Purdue University. Smith created virtual markets by designating half the participants as buyers and half the participants as sellers. Buyers and sellers were given a range of limit prices (a private value associated with each assignment to trade) and participants interacted and

© Springer Nature Switzerland AG 2021
A. P. Rocha et al. (Eds.): ICAART 2020, LNAI 12613, pp. 149–170, 2021.
https://doi.org/10.1007/978-3-030-71158-0_7

negotiated freely via a simple open outcry mechanism until trade prices converged towards the market equilibrium.

In subsequent years, the majority of work on trading agents has followed Smith's deliberately simple experimental design; and with good reason, as doing so enables strict performance comparisons with earlier work. Each time a new agent design is introduced (e.g., ZIC [19]; ZIP [9]; GD [18]; AA [36]), Smith's framework is used to demonstrate the relative profitability of the new agent and to measure the equilibration behaviours of markets containing the new agent, and markets containing mixtures of agent types. Over the decades, extensions to Smith's framework have been made, e.g., the use of limit order books [12]; real-time markets with humans and agents [4,12–14]; and more realistic market dynamics such as continuous replenishment of assignments [4,14], and continuously varying equilibria [11,30]. However, these extensions remain focused on studying pricing strategies, and rarely address issues of strategy timing: how long a strategy takes to compute (i.e., the *reaction time*), and how strategies adapt prices when there are constraints on time available (i.e., the trading *urgency*).

Overlooking issues of time in trading experiments is anachronistic. In 21st century financial markets, speed is king. Competition between automated trading systems (ATS), looking to capitalise on fleeting opportunities ahead of rivals, has resulted in a proliferation of high frequency trading (HFT) algorithms capable of executing many thousands of trades each second [15]. Market dynamics reflect this general acceleration in trading speed: individual stocks frequently exhibit *ultra extreme events*, with ten percent price swings in less than one tenth of a second [23]; *flash crashes* cause markets to lose a trillion dollars in value in five minutes [1]; and when an ATS *malfunctions*, it can lose hundreds of millions of dollars in under an hour and drive the owners into administration [1].

Here, we address the gap between research and reality by exploring reaction speed and trading urgency on a suite of reference algorithms (AA, GDX, GVWY, SHVR, ZIC, and ZIP) using the *Bristol Stock Exchange* simulation platform (for open source download, see [2]; for platform description, see [10]). In Sect. 2, we review related work and introduce key economic concepts and technical details of the financial trading agents and simulation platform used in this study. Section 3 explores *reaction time* of traders through a speed proportional selection mechanism. In Sect. 4, we explore *trading urgency*, and introduce a method for modelling trading urgency in ZIP traders, inspired by Gjerstad's "pace" parameter [17]. Finally, in Sect. 5, we discuss findings and conclude that since reaction speed and trading urgency can improve trading profits, and since time is such an important factor in real-world trading, the trading agents' research community will benefit from focusing more attention on these timing issues in future.

This paper extends work by Hanifan and Cartlidge on *reaction time* of traders, originally published in the 2020 Proceedings of the International Conference on Agents and Artificial Intelligence (ICAART) [21]. Much of the background material presented in Sect. 2 is reproduced from [21], while Sect. 3 presents a condensed version of the key results in [21]. Section 4 presents entirely new experiments and results, exploring the consequences of adding "urgency" or "pace" to the ZIP strategy, and draws from Watson's MSc thesis [38].

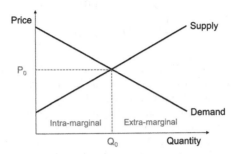

Fig. 1. Supply and demand. The intersection of supply and demand determines the markets' competitive equilibrium price P_0 and quantity Q_0. *Intra-marginal* units to the left of Q_0 (i.e., quantity demanded with limit prices higher than P_0 and quantity supplied with limit prices lower than P_0) expect to transact; *extra-marginal* demand and supply will be unable to transact when the market is trading at equilibrium price.

2 Background

2.1 Trading Agent Experiments

In 1962, Vernon Smith published his landmark study, which reported on a series of trading experiments conducted with small groups of untrained human participants (i.e., students) to investigate competitive market behaviours [29]. He was able to demonstrate that these simple simulations of financial markets produced surprisingly efficient equilibration behaviours, with trade prices quickly tending to the theoretical equilibrium value predicted by the underlying market supply and demand. Intriguingly, three decades later, Gode and Sunder were able to reproduce similar results, but this time using 'zero intelligence' (ZI) algorithmic traders that generate random quote prices [19]. Despite their simplicity, markets of ZIC traders (the letter 'C' indicating traders are *constrained* to not make a loss) were shown to exhibit equilibration behaviours similar to that of humans, suggesting that intelligence is not necessary for competitive markets to behave efficiently: the market mechanism (the rules of the continuous double auction) performs much of the work.

However, Gode and Sunder's result was later shown to only hold when market demand and supply are symmetric (i.e., when the magnitude of the gradient—the *price elasticity*—of supply and demand schedules are similar, such as the example shown in Fig. 1). For asymmetric markets, such as when the supply curve is horizontal, Cliff showed that 'zero' intelligence is not enough to provide human-like levels of market efficiency [9]. To account for this, Cliff introduced a new

Bids		Asks	
Volume	**Price**	**Price**	**Volume**
1	0.97	0.99	2
2	0.96	1.01	1
1	0.94	1.03	3
1	0.90	1.04	1

Fig. 2. A Limit Order Book (LOB), presenting the current market state. Bids (orders to buy) are presented on the left hand side, ordered by price *descending*. Asks (orders to sell) are presented on the right hand side, ordered by price *ascending*. Volume indicates the quantity available at each price. The top line presents the Best Bid ($BB = 0.97$) and Best Ask ($BA = 0.99$) prices in the market, and the difference between these prices is called the *spread* $= BA - BB = 0.02$. The *midprice* of the book is $(BB + BA)/2 = 0.98$; the *microprice* is volume weighted midprice, calculated as: $(2/3)0.97 + (1/3)0.99 = 0.977$. Orders can be submitted at any price, subject to a minimum resolution, or tick size (*tick* $= 0.01$). Aggressive orders that *cross the spread* (i.e., an ask with price $p_a \leq 0.97$, or a bid with price $p_b \geq 0.99$) will immediately execute at the price presented in the LOB (i.e., the ask will transact at price $BB = 0.97$; the bid will transact at price $BA = 0.99$). Passive orders that do not cross the spread will rest in the LOB, with position determined by price (Reproduced from [21]).

minimally-intelligent trading algorithm, which he named *Zero Intelligence Plus* (ZIP). ZIP maintains an internal profit margin, μ, which is increased or decreased by traversing a decision tree that considers the most recent quote price, the direction of the quote (buy or sell) and whether it resulted in a trade. Margin, μ, is then adjusted with magnitude proportional to a learning rate parameter, similar to that used in Widrow-Hoff or in back-propagation learning. Cliff successfully demonstrated that markets containing only ZIP traders will exhibit human-like behaviours in all of Smith's original experimental market configurations, both symmetric and asymmetric [9].

Other intelligent trading agents have been developed to maximise profits in experimental markets that follow Smith's framework. Most notably, these include: GD, named after its inventors, Gjerstad and Dickhaut [18]; and *Adaptive-Aggressive* (AA), developed by Vytelingum [36]. GD selects a quote price by maximising a 'belief' function of the likely profit for each possible quote, formed using historical quotes and transaction prices in the market. Over time, the original GD algorithm has been successively refined: first by Das et al. [12] and Tesauro and Das [34] (named *Modified GD*, or MGD) to enable trading using an order book (see example in Fig. 2), and to reduce belief function volatility; and then by Tesauro and Bredin [33], who used dynamic programming to optimise cumulative long-term discounted profitability rather than immediate profit (*GD eXtended*, or GDX). In contrast, AA incorporates a combination of short-term and long-term learning to update an internal profit margin, μ. In the short-term, μ is updated using rules similar to ZIP. Over the long-term, AA calculates a moving average of historical transaction prices to estimate the market equilibrium

Table 1. Summary of trading agent strategies.

Trader	Method used by buyers to determine new bid price to quote, Q
AA	$Q = L(1 - \mu)$, where $0 \leq \mu < 1$ is an internal profit margin. Estimate P_0 to determine if L is intra-marginal ($L \geq P_0$) or extra-marginal ($L < P_0$). If extra-marginal, increase aggressiveness (decrease μ); else increase μ [36]
GDX	Q selected by dynamic programming to maximise cumulative long-term discounted profitability of a belief function that calculates likely outcome of each price, q, based on the success of previous quotes and trade prices [33]
GVWY	$Q = L$. Always post quote at price equal to limit price, i.e., "tell the truth"
SHVR	$Q = min(BB + T, L)$. Quote one tick inside current best bid
ZIC	$Q = q \in U[T, L]$. Quote selected randomly from a Uniform distribution with minimum value one tick ($T = 0.01$) and maximum value limit price, L [19]
ZIP	$Q = L(1 - \mu)$, where $0 \leq \mu < 1$ is an internal profit margin When a new trade occurs with price p, if $Q > p$ decrease μ (i.e., raise quote), else increase μ. If new best bid has price $BB > Q$, decrease μ (i.e., raise quote) [9]

Q is new quote price; L is limit price; T is tick size; BB is best bid price on the LOB. Traders cannot make a loss, i.e., $Q \leq L$. Routines for sellers are symmetric to buyers

value, P_0, and current price volatility calculated as root mean square deviation of transaction prices around the estimate P_0. If the AA trader estimates that it is extra-marginal (and will therefore find it difficult to trade profitably: see Fig. 1) it trades more aggressively (by reducing μ), if it is intra-marginal (and will therefore find it easier to profit) it trades more passively (by increasing μ). For a summary of trading strategies, see Table 1.

2.2 Trading Strategy "Dominance"

For the last two decades, a research theme has emerged: to develop the best trading agent that can successfully beat human participants and other trading agents in Smith-style experiments (see [30] for a detailed historical account). In 2001, Das et al. first demonstrated that trading agents, specifically ZIP and MGD, outperform humans when directly competing in human-agent markets [12]. This announcement quickly generated global media coverage and significant industry interest. Shortly afterwards, Tesauro and Bredin [33] suggested that GDX *"may offer the best performance of any published CDA bidding strategy"*. Subsequently, after its introduction in 2006 [36], AA was shown to dominate ZIP and GDX [37] and also humans [13]: *"we therefore claim that AA may offer the best performance of any published strategy"*. And so, for several years, AA held the undisputed algo-trading crown.

The King Is Dead? More recently, the dominance of AA has been questioned in several works. Using the discrete-event simulation mode of OpEx, Vach [35] used simple Smith-style markets to compare efficiencies of traders in markets containing AA, GDX, and ZIP, as the proportion of each trader type in the market was varied. For large regions of this 3-trader mixture space, GDX was shown to be the dominant strategy, with AA only dominating in markets where there are significant proportions of other AA agents. This finding was supported by Cliff [11], through exhaustive testing of markets containing mixtures of MAA (a slightly *modified* version of AA which utilises *microprice* of the orderbook; see Fig. 2), ZIC, ZIP, and SHVR (a simple non-adaptive strategy that quotes prices one tick inside the current best price on the order book; see Table 1).

Further, Cliff demonstrated that introducing more *realistic* market dynamics—continuous replenishment of assignments rather than periodic replenishments at regular intervals; and also a dynamic equilibrium, P_0, which was set to follow real world historical trade price data—MAA did *not* dominate, with SHVR and ZIP generating significantly more profits [11]. A related study by Snashall and Cliff [30] also showed that GDX dominates in these more realistically complex markets containing ASAD (*Assignment-Adaptive*, developed by Stotter et al. [31]), GDX, MAA, and ZIP traders; and moreover, GDX also outperforms AA in simpler Smith-style markets.

In summary, these works suggest that AA's previously perceived dominance is sensitive to the mixture of competing strategies in the market, and the complexity of the underlying market dynamics.

2.3   Speed and Urgency

Throughout the previous works, the primary motivation has been focused on pricing strategies for trading efficiency (i.e., profit maximisation and market equilibration behaviours). However, if we are to better understand the behaviour of these algorithms in more realistic environments, it is important to consider *latency*, a key real-world factor that is missing in most of these studies. In real-world financial markets, *communication latency* (the differential delays in which traders can access trading information and initiate trades with an exchange, e.g., [25]), and *trading latency* (or *reaction time*: the time it takes for a human or algorithmic trader to react to new information) are major determinants of trading behaviours and market dynamics [15,30]. In real markets, the proliferation and profitability of high frequency trading (HFT) evidences the efficacy of harnessing reduced latency, enabling traders to capitalise on fleeting opportunities ahead of competitors. McGroarty et al. introduced an agent model of financial markets with agents that operate on different timescales to simulate common strategies and behaviours, such as market makers, fundamental traders, high frequency momentum and mean-reversion traders, and noise traders [24].

Reaction Time. Several studies have conducted human-agent and agent-agent trading experiments using real-time asynchronous trading platforms. For their seminal demonstration of agents outperforming human traders, Das et al. [12] used a hybrid platform consisting of two of IBM's proprietary systems: GEM, a distributed experimental economics platform; and Magenta, an agent environment. Although real-time asynchronous, trading agents were constrained to operate on a sleep-wake cycle of $\bar{s}$ seconds, with *fast* agents having mean sleep time $\bar{s} = 1$, and *slow* agents having mean sleep time $\bar{s} = 5$. A random jitter was introduced for each sleep s such that: $s \in [0.75\bar{s}, 1.25\bar{s}]$. Fast agents were set to wake on all new orders and trades, slow traders were set to wake only on trades. Therefore, although this real-time system enabled asynchronous actions, algorithmic traders were artificially slowed to have reaction times comparable with human traders.

Following Das et al. [12], other real-time human-agent experiments have invoked a similar sleep-wake cycle. Using the *Open Exchange* (OpEx) platform (download available: [27]), De Luca et al. [14] demonstrated AA, GDX, and ZIP outperform humans when agents have sleep-wake cycle $\bar{s} = 1$; agent-agent experiments, demonstrating AA dominance, were performed using a discrete event model (such that reaction times were ignored). OpEx has also been used for further human-agent experiments, for example, to demonstrate that: aggressive (*spread-jumping*) agents that are faster (i.e., those with lower $\bar{s}$ values) can perform less well against humans [14]; faster trading agents can reduce the efficiencies of human traders in the market [8]; and agents with reaction speeds much quicker than humans can lead to endogenous fragmentation within a single market, such that fast (slow) traders are more likely to execute with fast (slow) traders ([4]; a result that has analogies with the *robot phase transition* demonstrated in real-world markets [23]).

Agent-only real-time asynchronous experiments have also been conducted using the *Exchange Portal* (ExPo) platform (download available: [16]). Stotter et al. [31,32] used ExPo to introduce a new Assignment-Adaptive (ASAD) trading agent. They demonstrated that in ASAD:ZIP markets (with sleep-wake cycle, $\bar{s} = 4$), signals produced by the trading behaviour of ASAD are beneficially utilised by ZIP traders, to the detriment of ASAD themselves.

These works are representative of the literature relevant to reaction time and in automated trading algorithms. In general, we see that reaction times are either skewed by enforced sleep, directly encoded, or drawn from a probability distribution. As far as the authors are aware, there are no previously-published attempts to systematically understand the effects of reaction time using accurate computation times of individual trading strategies.

Urgency. In March 1990, the Santa Fe Institute held a computerised discrete-time double auction tournament. Todd Kaplan, an economist at the University of Minnesota, won the competition with a simple rule-of-thumb strategy: *wait in the background and let others do the negotiating, but when bid and ask get sufficiently close, or when time is running out, jump in and 'steal the deal'* [28]. This strategy is now widely referred to as "Kaplan's sniper". To steal the deal, Kaplan's snipers submit a bid (ask) with price equal to the last best ask (bid); thereby crossing the spread. Since Kaplan's snipers tend to wait in the background, this parasitic strategy does not help price formation. Therefore, when too many traders follow the same strategy, market efficiency falls. However, in many markets, hiding in wait for an opportunity to present itself (i.e., *sniping*) can be profitable. Such behaviour is typically observed in online auction venues with fixed deadlines (such as eBay), where snipers wait until the auction is about to close before urgently posting bids. In contrast, a similar sniping effect is not observed in venues (such as Amazon) where auctions have no fixed deadline [26].

Apart from Kaplan's sniper, the only other trading agent with an explicit sense of trading urgency is Gjerstad's extension of GD (named Heuristic Belief Learning, or HBL), which includes a "pace" parameter to alter the submission rate and quote price as a function of time remaining before deadline [17]. In human-agent trials, Gjerstad demonstrated that the performance of faster paced HBL traders is comparable to that of humans; suggesting trading urgency can be beneficial [17]. Since urgency can be roughly approximated as aggressiveness (urgent traders anxious to trade will submit a more aggressive quote price), one could consider AA agents as having a sense of urgency, as aggressiveness is dynamically tuned based on prevailing market conditions [36]. However, AA aggressiveness was not described as a mechanism for modelling temporal urgency, and does not explicitly consider trading deadlines.

In summary, we see that despite its importance in real world trading, the literature on urgency and reaction speed in financial trading agents is relatively sparse. In this paper, we attempt to address these gaps.

3 Reaction Time

This section presents a condensed version of an exploration on *reaction time* of traders, originally published in the 2020 Proceedings of the International Conference on Agents and Artificial Intelligence (ICAART) [21]. For further exploration (including *fixed ordering* and *tournament selection* models), we refer the reader to [21] and also Hanifan's MSc thesis [20].

3.1 Modelling Reaction Time

For all experiments performed in this paper, we use the *Bristol Stock Exchange* (BSE), a teaching and research platform designed for running controlled financial trading experiments (for details, see [10]). BSE is a minimal, discrete-time simulation of a centralised financial market, containing a single exchange with public limit order book (LOB). Trading experiments can be quickly configured by defining supply and demand schedules, the times that assignments are given to traders, and the strategies that each trader will follow. The BSE repository has reference implementations of a selection of trading strategies from the literature, including six that we consider in this paper: AA, GDX, GVWY, SHVR, ZIC, and ZIP. Python source-code for BSE is available open-source on the GitHub repository [2].[1]

---

[1] In this paper, we use BSE version dated 22/07/18, with commit hash: c0b6a1080b6 f0804a373dbe430e34d062dc23ffb.

Random Order Selection. Each time step, BSE ensures that all traders have exactly one opportunity to act. This is achieved by selecting traders at random, and without replacement. When not selected, a trader cannot act. Therefore, when a profitable opportunity is presented in the market, a trader is likely to miss that opportunity unless it is lucky enough to be selected soon. Over a long simulation with many time steps, profitable opportunities will tend to be shared equally between traders, making random selection a fair process for comparing performance of strategies. However, in the real world, when a profitable opportunity is presented, traders that can recognise and act on that opportunity most quickly, are the most likely to profit. Therefore, the random order selection process is *unrealistic*, as it models all trading algorithms to have the same reaction speed.

Random order selection suffers from the following unrealistic outcomes:

1. All traders have the same number of opportunities to act, irrespective of relative speed; and
2. Each trader has an equal chance to get *lucky* by being selected next.

To address these issues, we introduce a more *realistic* proportional selection model to simulate reaction time in the BSE framework.

Speed Proportional Selection. We assign each trader t with a *reaction time* R^t to represent the time taken for trader t to react to new market information (i.e., t's computation time). We adapt the BSE simulation so that, each time step, traders are selected to act in proportion to their relative speeds. For example, fast trader F with reaction time $R^F = 1$ acts twice as often as slow trader S with reaction time $R^S = 2$. To achieve this, we select traders from a biased pool containing multiple references to each trader, such that the number of references to trader t is inversely proportional to t's relative reaction time R^t. For example, if $R^F = 1$ and $R^S = 2$, we generate a biased pool, $P = \{F, F, S\}$, containing two references to fast trader F and one reference to slow trader S. Each time step, traders are randomly selected, without replacement, until the pool is empty. We use notation $R_S^F = 1/2$ to indicate F's reaction time is half S's reaction time (i.e., F is *twice as fast* as S); similarly $R_F^S = 2$ indicates S's reaction time is twice as long as F's (i.e., S has *half the speed* of F). Therefore, for a market containing two strategies F and S, with $R_S^F = 1/n$, the biased pool P will contain traders F and S in a ratio of $n : 1$, respectively.

Speed proportional selection provides several benefits of added realism:

1. faster agents have more opportunities to act than slower agents;
2. faster agents can act multiple times before a slower trading agent acts; and
3. since ordering is random, slower traders can get *lucky* by being selected next, but the likelihood of this diminishes as the difference in relative speeds increase.

Notice that, when all traders in market M have the same relative speed (i.e., when $\forall i, j \in M, R_j^i = 1$), the speed proportional selection model reduces to the BSE default random order selection model.

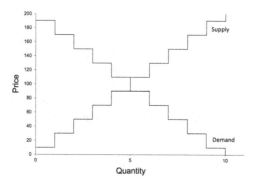

Fig. 3. Symmetric supply and demand schedules for reaction speed experiments. The market has $n = 10$ buyers (demand) and $n = 10$ sellers (supply) with limit prices evenly distributed between 10 and 190, giving a theoretical equilibrium price $P_0 = 100 \pm 10$ and quantity transacted $Q_0 = n/2 = 5$.

3.2 Experimental Configuration

We performed a series of experiments, with markets containing an equal number of n buyers and n sellers, and with assignment limit prices distributed evenly between minimum value of 10 and maximum value of 190, as shown graphically in Fig. 3. Market sessions lasted 330 time steps, with assignments replenished periodically every 30 time steps. This simple, static, symmetric market is deliberately chosen to enable comparisons with the literature. We use the speed proportional selection model (described in Sect. 3.1) to explore the effects of varying the reaction time of trading agents. Each simulation configuration was repeated 100 times, with results graphs plotting mean ±95% confidence intervals. Where p values are presented, statistical significance is calculated using Student's t-test.

3.3 Sensitivity Analysis

Figure 4 presents results of speed sensitivity analysis of AA performance in heterogeneous balanced-group tests against each of four other trading strategies: (a) GVWY, (b) SHVR, (c) ZIC, (d) ZIP. The reaction time of AA relative to the competing trader strategy is varied from $R_*^{AA} = 1$ (i.e., equal speed) to $R_*^{AA} = 40$ (i.e., AA is forty times *slower* than the competing strategy). Graphs show the effect of increasing R_*^{AA} (x-axis: as we move right, AA is increasingly slowed). In each case, we see that when $R_*^{AA} = 1$ (i.e., equal reaction times, equivalent to the default random order selection model used in the literature), AA (light blue line) outperforms the competing trader (purple dashed line). This is the BSE default setting, and the result confirms previous findings, which suggest AA dominates in symmetric markets with balanced numbers of traders [13].

However, as relative AA reaction time R_*^{AA} is increased (i.e., as AA becomes relatively *slower*), we see that AA performance gradually falls, until a point is

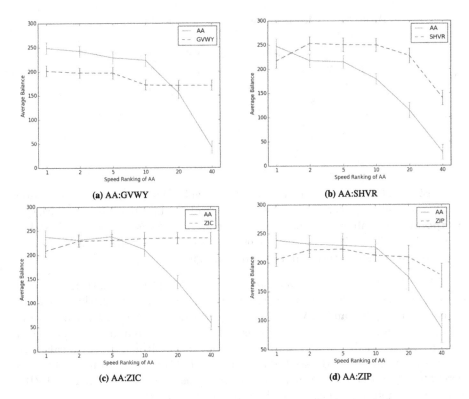

Fig. 4. Sensitivity analysis of AA using speed proportional selection in heterogeneous balanced tests. Reaction time of AA relative to the competing trader type is varied from $R_*^{AA} = 1$ to $R_*^{AA} = 40$ (x-axis). Each test, AA (light blue) outperforms the competitor (purple dash) when compute times are equal $(R_*^{AA} = 1)$. As R_*^{AA} increases, AA performance falls, until an inversion point is reached where AA no longer outperforms the competitor. For SHVR, inversion occurs between $1 < R_{SHVR}^{AA} < 2$ (Figures reproduced from [21]). (Color figure online)

reached where *AA* performs *worse* than the strategy it is competing against. This inversion point varies depending on which pair of strategies are being tested: (a) for GVWY, inversion is between $10 < R_{GVWY}^{AA} < 20$; (b) for SHVR, between $1 < R_{SHVR}^{AA} < 2$; (c) for ZIC, between $5 < R_{ZIC}^{AA} < 10$; and (d) for ZIP, between $10 < R_{ZIP}^{AA} < 20$.

Most noticeable is the low inversion value for SHVR (between 1 and 2), suggesting that AA's dominance over SHVR is particularly sensitive to small variations in relative trader speeds.

3.4   Profiling Reaction Times

Having demonstrated that trading performance is sensitive to relative speed, we attempt to accurately profile the reaction times of each trading agent strategy. In BSE, the computation time of an agent is composed of two methods:

Table 2. Profiled reaction times (reproduced from [21]).

Trader	Time (µs)	Stateful	Reactive	R^*_{SHVR}
GVWY	4.2	N	N	0.61
SHVR	6.9	N	Y	1.00
ZIC	7.1	N	N	1.03
ZIP	8.4	Y	Y	1.22
AA	9.5	Y	Y	1.38

getOrder called when a trader is selected to act. This requires the calculation of a new quote price, Q, if a new order is to be submitted into the market;

respond called after each market event (e.g., a new trade, or a new best bid or ask on the LOB). Traders can use the event data to update any internal parameters they have (such as a profit margin).

GVWY, SHVR, and ZIC are *stateless* traders: strategies have no internal parameters and therefore no action is taken when the respond method is called. In comparison, ZIP and AA are *stateful*: strategies use the respond method to update internal variables and to calculate a new profit margin, μ. When getOrder is called, ZIP and AA use their current profit margin, μ, to calculate a new quote price; SHVR uses the current best bid (or best ask) in the LOB to generate a new quote price; while the *nonreactive* strategies, GVWY and ZIC, generate a quote price without making reference to market data.

We profiled the reaction times of each trading agent across a variety of market conditions, including varied population size, mix of trading strategies in the market, assignment replenishment schedules, supply and demand schedules, etc. (see [20] for details). In Table 2, we present mean time calculated across more than 52 million method calls. Unsurprisingly, we see that the traders with the longest computation times, ZIP and AA, are those with an internal state that requires continuous updating. The relative reaction times between the fastest and slowest traders is roughly a factor of two: $R^{AA}_{GWVY} = 2.26$. The relative reaction times between AA and ZIP is $R^{AA}_{ZIP} = 1.13$. This result is consistent with the average relative time $R^{AA}_{ZIP} = 1.19$ presented by [30], and we take this as confirmatory evidence that our profiling is accurate. The final column of Table 2, headed R^*_{SHVR}, presents the reaction time of each trader relative to SHVR. Generating a quote price relative to the current LOB, SHVR is the only stateless (and therefore *fast*) trader that *reacts* to market information; although it does so in a simplistic non-adaptive fashion (unlike the slower AA and ZIP).

3.5   Results Using Profiled Reaction Times

We used profiled computation times (see Table 2) for proportional selection in heterogeneous balanced-group tests for pairwise comparisons between all trader types. The majority of results showed no significant difference, suggesting the

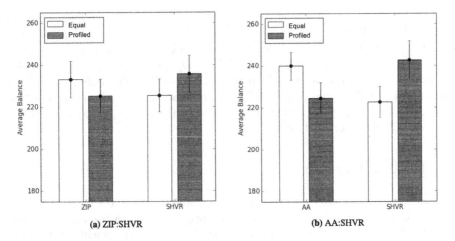

Fig. 5. When traders have equal speed (white bars), SHVR is outperformed by ZIP (not significant) and AA (significant). When traders have profiled speeds (grey bars), SHVR outperforms ZIP (not significant) and AA (significant).

relative differences in reaction speeds between the trader agents are not large enough to have an impact. However, results for ZIP:SHVR and AA:SHVR were particularly interesting (see Fig. 5). For ZIP:SHVR (Fig. 5a), under BSE's default random order selection process (white bars), ZIP outperforms SHVR. However, when selecting traders proportional to their true relative speeds (grey bars) SHVR outperforms ZIP (although the difference is not significant; $p > 0.05$). A similar, but more pronounced trend emerges between AA:SHVR (Fig. 5b). Here, AA significantly ($p < 0.05$) outperforms SHVR under the default randomised selection (white), and significantly ($p < 0.05$) underperforms SHVR under speed proportional selection (grey).

This is a novel result. By accurately accounting for the relative reaction times of the two algorithms, we have demonstrated that, in balanced tests, SHVR—the simple non-adaptive order book strategy—is able to generate more profit than AA in a Smith-style static symmetric marketplace; exactly the kind of market that AA was specifically designed to succeed in [36], and in which several studies have previously demonstrated AA as being the dominant known strategy [13,37].

We believe that this finding is significant, not only because it contributes to the recent body of evidence suggesting that AA is non-dominant (refer to Sect. 2.2), but also because it demonstrates that the performance of adaptive trading algorithms (AA and ZIP) are sensitive to reaction time; and once reaction time considered, SHVR may be relatively superior. In more complex markets designed to emulate real-world financial dynamics, SHVR has previously been shown to outperform AA and to perform similarly to ZIP [11]. Here, we extend this result to show that SHVR can also outperform in simple markets, once we account for speed.

In this study, we have not considered the GDX trading strategy and we reserve this for future work. However, we note that Snashall and Cliff [30] have recently published profiled reaction times of GDX and report it to be an order of magnitude slower than AA (i.e., $R_{AA}^{GDX} \approx 10$), due to its relatively complex internal optimisation process. It is therefore likely that GDX would also perform less well than SHVR (and AA and ZIP), once we accurately account for reaction times, as each competing strategy would have roughly ten opportunities to act, for every GDX trader's action.

4 Trading Urgency

Here, we turn our attention to *trading urgency* and return to the default random order selection method of BSE. The speed proportional selection model introduced in Sect. 3 is not used here. For further details on experiments and results presented in this section, we refer the reader to Watson's MSc thesis [38].

4.1 Pace

To introduce trading urgency, we follow Gjerstad's "pace" approach for modelling wait times between posting orders in the HBL model [17, p. 14]. Assume $\kappa - 1$ asks/bids have occurred at times $\{t_1, t_2, \ldots t_{\kappa-1}\}$. Each trader i calculates a time t_{κ_i} to wait until posting next bid/ask, described by the following probability distribution:

$$p_r[t_{\kappa_i} < t_{\kappa_{i-1}} + \tau] = 1 - e^{-\tau/\lambda_i} \tag{1}$$

Parameter λ_i depends on trader i's current maximum expected surplus S_i^*; current time that has elapsed in the trading period t_{k-1}; and on total time in the trading period T. Specifically:

$$\lambda_i(S_i, t_{\kappa-1}, T) = \frac{\beta_i(T - \alpha_i t_{\kappa-1})}{S_i^* T} \tag{2}$$

where $\alpha_i \in (0, 1)$ determines trader i's acceleration in pace as the trading period progresses; $\beta_i \in (0, \infty)$ is a linear scale factor for the timing decision (where $\beta_i = 250$ is "fast", and $\beta_i = 400$ is "slow"); and S_i^* is the maximum expected surplus for agent i. Therefore, λ_i signifies the mean wait time between i's orders, and decreases in S_i^*, as traders with greater expected surplus are more anxious (i.e., have more *urgency*) to trade.

4.2 ZIP with Pace (ZIPP)

We modify ZIP to have urgency by incorporating Gjerstad's *pace* formulation. However, since ZIP does not calculate a maximum expected surplus, we instead calculate S_i^* as trader i's current surplus (i.e., profit). We name this algorithm ZIP-Pace, or ZIPP, and use parameter values $\alpha = 0.95$ and $\beta = 400$, which Gjerstad demonstrated to yield highest profits [17].

Each time ZIPP trader i submits a new order, a maximum wait time t_{κ_i} is generated using Eqs. (1) and (2). Trader i must submit a new order *before* time t_{κ_i} is reached. Either: (i) market updates trigger a new order submission from trader i before t_{κ_i} (using the standard ZIP logic), in which case a new maximum wait time t_{κ_i} is generated; or (ii) if no order is submitted before t_{κ_i}, then at time t_{κ_i} trader i is forced to submit a new "urgent" order. This stops ZIPP traders from waiting for long periods between posting orders when there is little or no market activity, and enables ZIPP traders to react with urgency as the market close (or some other client-imposed) deadline approaches.

When ZIPP trader i posts an *urgent* order (i.e., when time t_{κ_i} is reached), a new (more *aggressive*) quote price q_i^t is calculated by shaving δ_i off the previous quote price q_i^{t-1}. For sellers, the quote price is decreased, i.e., $q_i^t = q_i^{t-1} - \delta_i$; for buyers, the quote price is increased, i.e., $q_i^t = q_i^{t-1} + \delta_i$. For trader i, the amount to shave δ_i is defined as:

$$\delta_i = \frac{|L_i - q_i^{t-1}|}{T - t} \tag{3}$$

where L_i is current limit price, q_i^{t-1} is the previous quote price, T is auction close (or *deadline*), and t is current time. Therefore, δ_i increases as t approaches T (i.e., as auction close draws near), and decreases as q_i^{t-1} approaches L_i (i.e., as quote price nears limit price). Since minimum tick size in BSE is 1, if $\delta_i < 1$, we set $\delta_i = 1$; and to ensure traders do not make a loss, q_i^t is restricted to a maximum bid value (or minimum ask value) equal to L_i.

4.3   ZIPP Bidding Behaviour

To demonstrate the behaviour of ZIPP, we compare homogeneous markets: (i) containing only ZIP traders (Fig. 6a); and (ii) containing only ZIPP traders (Fig. 6b). Each market contains 20 traders (10 buyers and 10 sellers), with assignments distributed using symmetric demand and supply schedules (see Fig. 7a) with minimum/maximum limit order values $(L_{min}, L_{max}) = (75, 125)$. A trading day lasts 180 s, and each trader receives a new assignment to trade every 30 s (we call this the *assignment period*, represented by blue vertical lines). Therefore, traders receive 5 assignments to trade each day, and if an assignment has not been completed before a new assignment is received (i.e., before the assignment period ends), the original assignment is cancelled and opportunities for making profit from the assignment are lost. Figure 6 presents the trading behaviours of the 5 intra-marginal buyers (i.e., those *expected* to trade) in each market (note that behaviours for sellers, not shown, are symmetric). The y-axis plots trader i's quote price q_i as a percentage of limit price L_i, such that $y = 100(q_i/L_i)$, with a dot representing an unexecuted order (resting in the order book), and a cross representing order execution. In each assignment period, there can be at most one order execution per trader.

In Fig. 6a, ZIP traders begin by posting quotes with relatively small margin (around 90% of limit price, or above), which quickly results in all traders executing their orders (crosses). In each subsequent assignment period, ZIP traders

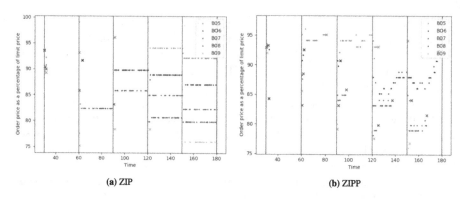

Fig. 6. Bid quote prices, q_i, as a percentage of limit price, L_i; i.e., $y = 100q_i/L_i$.

tend to increase their margin (and therefore post a lower quote price), with little or no variation in quote price during the period (indicated by horizontal banding of dots). As a result, during the final period, no ZIP trader executes a trade, even though each has a significant profit margin that can be relaxed (B09 continues to maintain a margin of nearly 25% throughout the final period). In contrast, ZIPP traders (Fig. 6b) continue to explore different quote prices during each assignment period (indicated by horizontal zig-zagging of dots), with every trader executing a trade (cross) in the final period. Notice how B06 increasingly reduces margin during the final period (from 13% to 5%) as the deadline approaches, eventually executing a trade shortly before close (cross obscured by legend). Overall, homogeneous markets of ZIPP traders execute more transactions than homogeneous markets of ZIP traders, resulting in a more efficient market and greater profit for ZIPP traders. This is the behaviour we desire.

4.4   ZIPP Performance Testing

Method. For testing the performance of ZIPP (and comparing performance against other trading agents), we use five different supply and demand schedules (see Fig. 7), each displaying different market properties: (a) symmetric supply and demand; (b) price elastic demand, with all buyers having the same limit price; (c) price elastic supply; (d) an excess demand, with more buyers than sellers; and (e) excess supply, with more sellers than buyers. Each market contains exactly 10 buyers and 10 sellers. In homogeneous markets we have 20 traders of one type. In heterogeneous balanced-test markets, containing multiple trader types, we have 5 buyers of each type, and 5 sellers of each type. Each test is run over one day, lasting 180 s, with assignments distributed every 30 s (i.e., each day contains five assignment periods). For each condition, we perform 25 repeated trials.

Homogeneous Markets. Figure 8 shows mean profits ($\pm$ standard deviation) generated in homogeneous markets containing only one trader type. In Fig. 8a, we

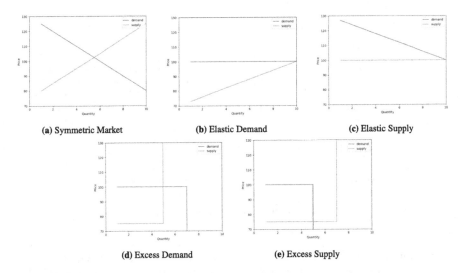

Fig. 7. Supply and demand schedules used for trading urgency experiments.

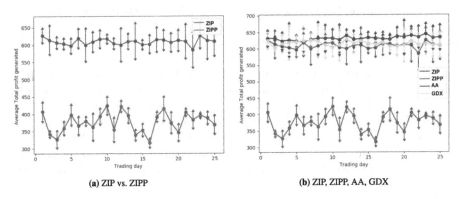

Fig. 8. Average total profit generated each trading day (homogeneous markets).

see that ZIPP traders consistently achieve significantly higher profits than ZIP traders. Figure 8b presents the same results, but with results for homogeneous AA and GDX markets overlaid. Visually, profits of AA, GDX, and ZIPP fall in a similar region, with all gaining profits significantly higher than the profits attained by ZIP. AA profits are slightly, but significantly higher than GDX and ZIPP (Mann-Whitney U test; $p < 0.05$), while profits of GDX and ZIPP have no significant difference (Mann-Whitney U test; $p > 0.05$), suggesting both have similar performance.

Heterogeneous Markets. Figure 9 shows mean profits ($\pm$ standard deviation) generated in heterogeneous markets containing multiple trader types. Figure 9a shows ZIPP generates significantly more profit than ZIP (Mann-Whitney U test;

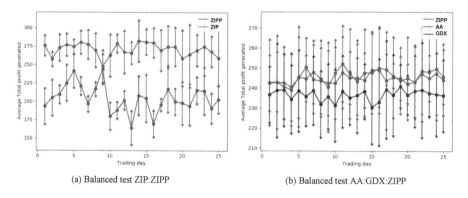

(a) Balanced test ZIP:ZIPP   (b) Balanced test AA:GDX:ZIPP

Fig. 9. Average total profit generated each trading day (heterogeneous markets).

$p < 0.05$) in markets containing both agents. Markets containing AA/ZIPP and GDX/ZIPP demonstrated that AA significantly outperforms ZIPP and ZIPP significantly outperforms GDX (results not shown). Figure 9b shows results from a market containing three agent types: AA, GDX, and ZIPP. Here, ZIPP and AA significantly outperform GDX (Mann-Whitney U test; $p < 0.05$); while there is no significant difference between AA and ZIPP (Mann-Whitney U test; $p > 0.05$).

Results demonstrate that adding *pace* to ZIP—thereby creating a ZIPP trader with a sense of urgency—increases performance; with ZIPP significantly outperforming ZIP in both homogeneous and heterogeneous markets, across a variety of market conditions. By comparing ZIPP with other leading strategies (AA and GDX), results show that AA tends to be the most profitable, but does not always outperform ZIPP; while ZIPP outperforms GDX in heterogeneous environments. Therefore, adding urgency to ZIP results in a more profitable strategy.

5   Conclusions

We have presented an exploration of reaction speed and urgency in financial trading agents. Results demonstrate that SHVR (a simple but quick strategy) generates significantly more profit than AA (a more complex and therefore slower strategy) when reaction speed is accurately modelled. We also demonstrated that ZIPP (a ZIP trader that adjusts pace as a deadline approaches) generates significantly more profit than ZIP. These results confirm that time matters, and if we are to better understand real-world markets it is necessary for reaction speeds and urgency to be considered more thoroughly.

Our results add to the mounting body of evidence that suggests SHVR could be a surprisingly successful trading strategy, despite being so simple. SHVR is the only agent considered in this paper that determines quote price solely on the basis of current order book information. Unlike AA, GDX, and ZIP, SHVR has no internal state and so does not consider *where* the market is trading (i.e., at what price the market is trading). This demonstrates that considering only the current order book dynamics can result in a profitable trading strategy, without considering long term price trends, or estimations of some fundamental equilibrium value. We therefore intend to more fully explore the use of order book metrics in trading strategies (e.g., Volume Imbalance [3]; Order Book Imbalance [22]) as future work. We note that the MAA (*modified* AA) strategy introduced by Cliff [11] considers the order book *microprice*, which is a useful first step towards this goal.

In real financial markets, order book information is known to be strategically useful, as it exposes the trading intentions of market participants. In order to hide one's intention to trade, some trading venues, described as *dark pools*, do not reveal market quotes and all order information remains hidden (see, e.g., [6,7], for a summary of dark pools and methods for implementing cryptographically secure dark pool mechanisms using multi-party computation (MPC)). This ensures no information "leakage", and can therefore result in a better execution price. However, orders can take much longer to execute in a dark pool as trading counterparties are more difficult to discover. Therefore, dark pools offer a trade off between immediacy and risk. Trading urgency, as we introduced in ZIPP, can help an automated strategy determine which trading venue ("lit", for immediacy; or "dark", for best execution) is most appropriate to use at any given time. We intend to explore this research avenue more fully in future.

Several works have demonstrated that altering the design of trading agent experiments can raise doubt over previously established results, and how well these results translate to the real world. This has led several authors to call for more experimental *realism* (e.g., [4,5,11,14,30]). Here, we have addressed that challenge by introducing minimal models of time into the standard experimental framework. Our demonstration of significantly different outcomes when reaction times are realistically modelled adds to this growing body of evidence.

References

1. Baxter, G., Cartlidge, J.: Flying by the seat of their pants: what can high frequency trading learn from aviation? In: Proceedings of the 3rd International Conference on Application and Theory of Automation in Command and Control Systems, ATACCS, pp. 56–65. (2013). https://dl.acm.org/doi/10.1145/2494493.2494501
2. BSE: The Bristol Stock Exchange. GitHub public source-code repository (2012). https://github.com/davecliff/BristolStockExchange
3. Cartea, Á., Donnelly, R., Jaimungal, S.: Enhancing trading strategies with order book signals. Appl. Math. Financ. **25**(1), 1–35 (2018). https://doi.org/10.1080/1350486X.2018.1434009
4. Cartlidge, J., Cliff, D.: Exploring the 'robot phase transition' in experimental human-algorithmic markets. In: The Future of Computer Trading in Financial Markets, Driver Review DR25. Foresight, Government Office for Science, London (2012). https://bit.ly/2llHjbh+

5. Cartlidge, J., Cliff, D.: Modelling complex financial markets using real-time human–agent trading experiments. In: Chen, S.-H., Kao, Y.-F., Venkatachalam, R., Du, Y.-R. (eds.) CEF 2015. SPC, pp. 35–69. Springer, Cham (2018). https://doi.org/10.1007/978-3-319-99624-0_3

6. Cartlidge, J., Smart, N.P., Alaoui, Y.T.: MPC joins the dark side. In: Proceedings of the 14th ACM Asia Conference on Computer and Communications Security, pp. 148–159. AsiaCCS (2019). https://doi.org/10.1145/3321705.3329809

7. Cartlidge, J., Smart, N.P., Alaoui, Y.T.: Multi-party computation mechanism for anonymous equity block trading: a secure implementation of Turquoise Plato Uncross. Cryptology ePrint Archive, Report 2020/662 (2020), https://ia.cr/2020/662

8. Cartlidge, J., Szostek, C., De Luca, M., Cliff, D.: Too fast too furious: faster financial-market trading agents can give less efficient markets. In: Proceedings of the 4th International Conference on Agents and Artificial Intelligence, volume 2, pp. 126–135. ICAART (2012). https://doi.org/10.5220/0003720301260135

9. Cliff, D.: Minimal-intelligence agents for bargaining behaviours in market-based environments. Technical report HPL-97-91, Hewlett-Packard Labs (1997). https://www.hpl.hp.com/techreports/97/HPL-97-91.html

10. Cliff, D.: An open-source limit-order-book exchange for teaching and research. In: IEEE Symposium Series on Computational Intelligence, SSCI, pp. 1853–1860 (2018). https://doi.org/10.1109/SSCI.2018.8628760

11. Cliff, D.: Exhaustive testing of trader-agents in realistically dynamic continuous double auction markets: AA does not dominate. In: Proceedings of the 11th International Conference on Agents and Artificial Intelligence, ICAART, volume 2, pp. 224–236 (2019). https://doi.org/10.5220/0007382802240236

12. Das, R., Hanson, J.E., Kephart, J.O., Tesauro, G.: Agent-human interactions in the continuous double auction. In: Proceedings of the 17th International Joint Conference on Artificial Intelligence, IJCAI, volume 2, pp. 1169–1176 (2001). https://dl.acm.org/doi/10.1145/501158.501183

13. De Luca, M., Cliff, D.: Human-agent auction interactions: adaptive aggressive agents dominate. In: Proceedings of the 22nd International Joint Conference on Artificial Intelligence, IJCAI, volume 1, pp. 178–185 (2011). https://doi.org/10.5591/978-1-57735-516-8/IJCAI11-041

14. De Luca, M., Szostek, C., Cartlidge, J., Cliff, D.: Studies of interactions between human traders and algorithmic trading systems. In: The Future of Computer Trading In Financial Markets, Driver Review DR13. Foresight, Government Office for Science, London (2011). https://bit.ly/2llv52c+

15. Duffin, M., Cartlidge, J.: Agent-based model exploration of latency arbitrage in fragmented financial markets. In: IEEE Symposium Series on Computational Intelligence, SSCI, pp. 2312–2320 (2018). https://doi.org/10.1109/SSCI.2018.8628638

16. ExPo: The Exchange Portal. SourceForge public source-code repository (2011). https://sourceforge.net/projects/exchangeportal/

17. Gjerstad, S.: The strategic impact of pace in double auction bargaining. In: Econometric Society 2004 North American Winter Meetings 190. Econometric Society (2004). https://ideas.repec.org/p/ecm/nawm04/190.html

18. Gjerstad, S., Dickhaut, J.: Price formation in double auctions. Games Econ. Behav. **22**(1), 1–29 (1998). https://doi.org/10.1006/game.1997.0576

19. Gode, D.K., Sunder, S.: Allocative efficiency of markets with zero-intelligence traders: market as a partial substitute for individual rationality. J. Polit. Econ. 101(1), 119–137 (1993). https://doi.org/10.1086/261868

20. Hanifan, H.: Investigating the impact speed has on the performance of algorithmic traders within the BSE simulation. Master's thesis, Department of Computer Science, University of Bristol, UK (2019)

21. Hanifan, H., Cartlidge, J.: Fools rush. In: Competitive Effects of Reaction Time in Automated Trading. In: Proceedings of the 12th International Conference on Agents and Artificial Intelligence, ICAART, volume 1, pp. 82–93 (2020). https://doi.org/10.5220/0008973700820093

22. Imaev, D.D., Imaev, D.H.: Automated trading systems based on order book imbalance. In: XX IEEE International Conference on Soft Computing and Measurements (SCM), pp. 815–819 (2017). https://doi.org/10.1109/SCM.2017.7970733

23. Johnson, N., et al.: Abrupt rise of new machine ecology beyond human response time. Sci. Rep. **3**(2627), 1–7 (2013). https://doi.org/10.1038/srep02627

24. McGroarty, F., Booth, A., Gerding, E., Chinthalapati, V.L.R.: High frequency trading strategies, market fragility and price spikes: an agent based model perspective. Ann. Oper. Res. **282**(1), 217–244 (2019). https://doi.org/10.1007/s10479-018-3019-4

25. Miles, B., Cliff, D.: A cloud-native globally distributed financial exchange simulator for studying real-world trading-latency issues at planetary scale. In: Proceedings of the 31st European Modelling and Simulation Symposium, EMSS, pp. 294–303 (2019). https://arxiv.org/abs/1909.12926

26. Ockenfels, A., Roth, A.E.: Ending rules in internet auctions. In: Vulkan, N., Roth, A.E., Neeman, Z. (eds.) The Handbook of Market Design, chap. 13. Oxford University Press (2013). https://doi.org/10.1093/acprof:oso/9780199570515.003.0014

27. OpEx: The Open Exchange. SourceForge public source-code repository (2011). https://sourceforge.net/projects/open-exchange/

28. Rust, J., Miller, J.H., Palmer, R.: Characterizing effective trading strategies: insights from the computerized double auction tournament. Econ. Dyn. Control **18**(1), 61–96 (1994). https://doi.org/10.1016/0165-1889(94)90069-8

29. Smith, V.L.: An experimental study of competitive market behavior. J. Polit. Econ. **70**(2), 111–137 (1962). https://doi.org/10.1086/258609

30. Snashall, D., Cliff, D.: Adaptive-aggressive traders don't dominate. In: van den Herik, J., Rocha, A.P., Steels, L. (eds.) ICAART 2019. LNCS (LNAI), vol. 11978, pp. 246–269. Springer, Cham (2019). https://doi.org/10.1007/978-3-030-37494-5_13

31. Stotter, S., Cartlidge, J., Cliff, D.: Exploring assignment-adaptive (ASAD) trading agents in financial market experiments. In: Proceedings of the 5th International Conference on Agents and Artificial Intelligence, ICAART, volume 1, pp. 77–88 (2013). https://doi.org/10.5220/0004248000770088

32. Stotter, S., Cartlidge, J., Cliff, D.: Behavioural investigations of financial trading agents using exchange portal (ExPo). In: Nguyen, N.T., Kowalczyk, R., Fred, A., Joaquim, F. (eds.) Transactions on Computational Collective Intelligence XVII. LNCS, vol. 8790, pp. 22–45. Springer, Heidelberg (2014). https://doi.org/10.1007/978-3-662-44994-3_2

33. Tesauro, G., Bredin, J.L.: Strategic sequential bidding in auctions using dynamic programming. In: Proceedings of the 1st International Joint Conference on Autonomous Agents and Multiagent Systems: Part 2, AAMAS, pp. 591–598 (2002). http://doi.acm.org/10.1145/544862.544885

34. Tesauro, G., Das, R.: High-performance bidding agents for the continuous double auction. In: Proceedings of the 3rd ACM Conference on Electronic Commerce, pp. 206–209 (2001). https://doi.org/10.1145/501158.501183

35. Vach, D.: Comparison of double auction bidding strategies for automated trading agents. Master's thesis, Faculty of Social Sciences, Charles University in Prague, CZ (2015). https://is.cuni.cz/webapps/zzp/detail/152184
36. Vytelingum, P.: The structure and behaviour of the continuous double auction. Ph.D. thesis, School of Electronics and Computer Science, University of Southampton, UK (2006). https://eprints.soton.ac.uk/263234/
37. Vytelingum, P., Cliff, D., Jennings, N.R.: Strategic bidding in CDAs. Artif. Intell. **172**(14), 1700–1729 (2008). https://doi.org/10.1016/j.artint.2008.06.001
38. Watson, B.A.: Algorithmic trading on multiple trading platforms. Master's thesis, Department of Computer Science, University of Bristol, UK (2019)

Artificial Intelligence

Cost-Sensitive Semi-supervised Classification for Fraud Applications

Sulaf Elshaar and Samira Sadaoui[✉]

Department of Computer Science, University of Regina, 3737 Wascana Parkway,
Regina, SK S4S 0A2, Canada
{elshaars,Samira.Sadaoui}@uregina.ca

Abstract. This research explores Cost-Sensitive Learning (CSL) in the
fraud detection domain to decrease the fraud class's incorrect predictions and increase its accuracy. Notably, we concentrate on shill bidding
fraud that is challenging to detect because the behavior of shill and legitimate bidders are similar. We investigate CSL within the Semi-Supervised
Classification (SSC) framework to address the scarcity of labeled fraud
data. Our paper is the first attempt to integrate CSL with SSC for fraud
detection. We adopt a meta-CSL approach to manage the costs of misclassification errors, while SSC algorithms are trained with imbalanced
data. Using an actual shill bidding dataset, we assess the performance
of several hybrid models of CSL and SSC and then compare their misclassification error and accuracy rates statistically. The most efficient
CSL+SSC model was able to detect 99% of fraudsters and with the lowest total cost.

Keywords: Cost-sensitive learning · MetaCost · Cost matrix ·
Semi-supervised classification · Misclassification errors · Imbalanced
data · Fraud detection

1 Introduction

1.1 Problem and Motivations

Even though the auction industry is a lucrative marketplace, e-auction sites are,
however, attractive to dishonest moneymakers due to the anonymity of bidders,
flexibility of bidding, and cheap auction services [1]. In 2015, the Internet Crime
Complaint Center reported 21,510 auction fraud complaints and a monetary
loss of $19 million [12]. The illicit activities can occur before the auctions take
place (ex. misrepresentation of items), during the bidding period (ex. shill bidding and bid shielding), and after the auctions are completed (ex. no delivery
of items and fee stacking). Among the auction scams, Shill Bidding (SB) is considered the most difficult fraud to detect due to its similarity to the normal
bidding behaviour. Consequently, the SB fraud goes undetected by the victims.
Via alternate accounts, shill bidders compete on behalf of a seller (the auction

A. P. Rocha et al. (Eds.): ICAART 2020, LNAI 12613, pp. 173–187, 2021.
https://doi.org/10.1007/978-3-030-71158-0_8

owner) by elevating the item price without being detected. SB is still plaguing the auction sector, as shown by several lawsuits that have been filed against dishonest sellers because SB fraud led to substantial financial losses for honest consumers [1]. SB detection is a challenging problem to address due to the following aspects: 1) thousands of auctions are held every day in auction companies, like eBay and TradeMe, 2) auctions may involve a large number of bids and bidders, 3) auctions may have long biding duration, like seven or ten days, and 4) SB identification must be made in real-time to avoid financial losses for buyers. Therefore, we adopt Machine Learning (ML) to tackle these real-life fraud scenarios. Nevertheless, we are confronted with three significant classification problems:

- **Unavailability of Labeled SB Data:** Annotating multi-dimensional SB data is a challenging operation. Generally speaking, labeling training data is carried out by the experts of the application domain, sometimes with the help of ML techniques [1]. Still, this operation is very time-consuming.
- **Absence of Misclassification Costs:** Classical ML algorithms do not take into account the costs of misclassification errors and treat errors of all the classes equally. This behaviour is not appropriate in fraud detection applications where the incorrectly predicted fraud data should possess a penalty. The latter should be the highest one as the fraud data is the target for investigation.
- **Presence of Class Imbalance:** Fraud datasets are imbalanced. The skewed class distribution degrades the accuracy of ML algorithms [1]. Additionally, the fraud class, which is the most significant output, is misrepresented since the learning methods are influenced by the majority (normal) class.

In the previous paper [9], we addressed the labeled data scarcity problem using Semi-Supervised Classification (SSC) algorithms because they require only a few labeled data to be trained. Hence, we were able to check the ground truth of the few annotated SB data. Moreover, we empirically demonstrated that having a few annotated data during the training stage returned a satisfactory performance. We also determined the optimal amount of labeled SB data that leads to the highest accuracy. Besides, SSC can outperform supervised classification, as shown in [8]. However, SSC algorithms do not consider the costs of the misclassification errors of the two classes (Normal and Fraud). In fraud detection, this lack means that there is no difference between misclassifying a legitimate activity (normal bidding behaviour) and misclassifying a fraudulent activity (shill bidding). Nevertheless, we know that the risk of predicting a shill bidder as a normal bidder is more serious than the opposite case. Therefore, it becomes essential to take into account the misclassification costs for our fraud classification problem.

1.2   Contributions

In this present study, we explore Cost-Sensitive Learning (CSL) to manage both the misclassification costs and imbalanced data on the one hand, and reduce the incorrect predictions of the two classes on the other hand. In this case, we can assign a higher penalty for the fraud data that went undetected (false negatives). Indeed, we are more concerned about detecting fraudulent activities, so that we can take action against auctions infected by SB by canceling the auction before processing the payment of the item and suspending the accounts of shill bidders. We incorporate CSL into the Semi-Supervised Classification (SCC) framework. However, an SSC algorithm utilizes one or more baseline supervised classifiers that require data to be balanced. CSL addresses the skewed class imbalance at the algorithm level, i.e., without modifying the training datasets. Over- and under-sampling methods can also tackle imbalance data [1,9]. When adjusting the class distribution, over-sampling adds synthetic data to the minority class, but these data do not represent actual observations. Under-sampling method deletes some data from the majority class, which may discard essential data for the learning task. Hence, adopting CSL can be beneficial in handling the imbalanced learning problem since it employs only real bidding behaviour. We use a real SB dataset for which a small subset has been already labeled and evaluated in [9].

In our work, we take advantage of a meta-CSL approach, called MetaCost, to train semi-supervised classifiers with few labeled data that are imbalanced. We select this approach for several reasons: 1) it can be used by any type of classification algorithm, 2) it is easy to combine with a SSC algorithm, and 3) it uses ensemble learning to achieve much stronger performance, especially for unstable classifiers. With MetaCost, SSC algorithms will be able to consider the costs of misclassification errors of both classes while learning from the SB dataset. For this purpose, we define a cost matrix specifically for our SB detection problem.

We develop multiple hybrid classification models of CSL and SCC based on the cost matrix. More precisely, by varying the cost penalties of the fraud class, the most important class as it is the target for investigation, we assess and compare the accuracy and misclassification error rates of several CSL+SSC models using statistical testing. In this present study, we employ two different SSC collective packages: Chopper and Yatsi. Since in [9], CollectiveIBK returned an average performance, so in this present paper, we consider a new approach called Yatsi. We keep Chopper as it produced a very good performance. Moreover, we also show that the CSL+SSC model outperforms the non cost-sensitive SSC model developed in [9] with the same SB dataset. This research is the first attempt to integrate CSL to the SSC environment in the fraud detection domain. Besides, to the best of our knowledge, we found only one recent paper that merged CSL with SSC but outside the fraud detection field, as discussed in the related work section.

We organize our paper as follows. In Sect. 2, we examine recent studies on CSL in the fraud detection domain and one study combining CSL and SSC. In Sect. 3, we describe the SB training dataset developed from commercial auctions and bidder history. In Sect. 4, we specify the cost matrix and describe the Meta-Cost method for our fraud detection application. In Sect. 5, we discuss multiple

SSC algorithms based on two different approaches, Yatsi and Chopper, as well as the hyper-parameter tuning of both CSL and SSC methods. In Sect. 6, we conduct an experimental evaluation and comparison of several CSL+SSC models trained on a few labeled data that are imbalanced. In Sect. 7, we present essential findings of our work as well as some future research directions.

2   Related Work

This section reviews representative studies on cost-sensitive learning, specifically in the fraud detection domain. This review will allow us to examine the costs assigned to the incorrect prediction of the fraud class. Nevertheless, prior works have almost exclusively focused on detecting fraud in credit card transactions. We believe this limitation is due to the availability of training datasets, on the one hand, and complaints of victims who reported the fraud on the other hand. Moreover, the ability to label transactions as normal or fraud provided valuable support to the research. Several studies examined SSC for fraud detection, but we found only one recent paper that combined CSL and SSC to the best of our knowledge.

The study [3] investigated the ensemble of CSL and Bayesian network to detect credit card fraud. The annotated training dataset was provided by "UOL PagSeguro", a Brazilian online payment company. For the CSL task, the authors adopted two methods to deal with imbalanced data: instance re-weighing and class probability threshold. To assess the fraud model's performance, they considered two metrics only: F1-score and the cost named "economic efficiency". However, due to data privacy, they did not mention the actual values of costs. Instead, they provided an equation to compute the costs from the transactions, which is used in the current system of PagSeguro company. The class probability threshold led to the best accuracy. Moreover, the authors stated that a model with a high accuracy does not necessarily have a low cost.

Another research [17] also detected credit card fraud based on CSL. First, the authors collected labeled data from an anonymous bank from 2012 to 2013. Additionally, they considered the deviation from the normal behavior of customers as a sign of fraud. Next, they defined an equation to calculate the costs from the transactions, but they did not provide the cost amounts in the experiments. For the classification task, they employed Random Forest (RF) and then the hybrid version of CSL and RF. The findings demonstrates that utilizing CSL reduced the misclassification errors of the fraud class by 23%.

The paper [10] incorporated CSL to Neural Networks to detect credit card fraud. The dataset was supplied by the company "BBVA Data & Analytics," which consists of anonymous card transactions for 2014 and 2015. Besides, the company also provided the fraud claims, which made it easier to label customers as normal or fraud. The authors removed a large number of transactions because the dataset was highly imbalanced, with a ratio of fraudulent to normal data equals to 1:5000. They considered the cost as the amount of money associated with the fraud activities detected by the model. Based on the monetary cost, the experiment showed that the fraud model achieved similar accuracy that was previously attained by other costly models. However, the values of the cost were not given in this study, and it was not clear how the CSL matrix was employed in the supervised framework.

The study [11] examined how different values of the cost of False Negatives (i.e., fraud wrongly classified as normal) can affect the performance of CSL models. The authors trained the Bayes Minimum Risk algorithm along with several base CSL classifiers using different values of FN costs. They trained the CSL classifiers with a credit card dataset published in 2009 by the UCSD repository. First, they adopted the average number of transactions as the value of the FN cost, and then used numerous random values that are lower or larger than the average value. The results showed that CSL models produced different results when using different costs of FNs. The lower the FN cost, the better the model performance.

In [18], the authors utilized a cost-sensitive Decision Tree method to minimize the misclassification errors when detecting fraud in credit card data. The labeled dataset was provided by an anonymous bank. The authors varied the costs of FNs based on the available limit of the credit card transactions. The experiments demonstrated that the hybrid model CSL+Decision Tree outperformed traditional classifiers, such as Artificial Neural Networks, Decision Trees and SVM, in terms of accuracy, true positive rate, and misclassification errors.

Very recently, [23] developed an ensemble GMDH Neural Network method based on CSL and SSC to identify customers with good or bad credit. This scoring can assist financial companies to make decisions regarding customer loan approval. The authors assessed the proposed method with an old public labeled credit scoring dataset (from 2009 to 2011). Intending to fill the gap in the literature, they used CSL to handle imbalanced data and SSC because, in many cases, the labels were not provided. The accuracy results showed that the developed model was superior to standard SSC models, such as CoBag, Semi-bagging, and Tri-training. The experiments also proved that fewer labeled samples led to a better scoring performance.

3   Fraud Dataset Overview

We developed a reliable SB dataset using a large collection of commercial auctions of eBay and their bidder history too [7] (see Table 1). We rigorously preprocessed the two crawled datasets, auctions and bidders. Then, we implemented a collection of nine SB strategies exposed in Table 1. For more details about the fraud patterns and their measurement algorithms, consult the article [7]. Subsequently, for each bidder in each auction, we evaluated the metric of each SB pattern. This measurement task resulted in an SB dataset consisting of 9291 samples (after removing outliers). An SB sample denotes the behaviour of a bidder in an individual auction, which is Normal or Fraud. It is a vector of eleven elements: Bidder ID, Auction ID, and the nine SB patterns. With this granularity, we can act against each auction infected by fraud to avoid a monetary loss for the winning bidder.

In a subsequent work [9], we appropriately labeled a small portion of the SB dataset to conduct the semi-supervised classification task. For this purpose, we first combined two data clustering techniques, X-means and Hierarchical clustering, to produce clusters of bidders of high quality. Then, we proposed a new approach to detect fraudulent activities or anomalies in each cluster based on the biddersŚB scores in that cluster and the Three Sigma Rule. Lastly, we experimented to determine the minimal sufficient amount of labeled data statistically to achieve the highest accuracy [9]. In Table 1, we can observe that the SB labeled subset is imbalanced with a ratio of Normal to Fraud samples equals to 5:1.

4   Cost-Sensitive Learning Framework

4.1   Cost Matrix for SB Fraud

Real-life detection applications can be endowed with different types of costs that can be utilized to improve further their prediction outcome. The costs are mostly financial, as the cost of hiring experts, or using specific devices, or conducting additional tests. However, the cost can also be non-financial but paramount, such as the cost of identifying the disease carrier as not carrying it, or the cost of classifying a fraudster as a genuine bidder. In our specific problem, we cannot estimate the monetary cost because we do not know objectively the loss that occurs when the classification result is erroneous. However, we know for sure that the risk of classifying a shill bidder as a normal bidder is higher than the

Table 1. Fraud dataset and its labeled subset.

Number of auctions	1399	
Number of bidders	1100	
Bidding duration	1, 3, 5, 7 and 10 days	
Number of samples	9291	
Fraud predictors	- Bidder tendency	
	- Bidding ratio	
	- Last bidding	
	- Auction bids	
	- Starting price	
	- Early bidding	
	- Winning ratio	
	- Buyer rating based on items	
	- Bid retraction	
Labeled subset	Normal	Fraud
(total: 945)	791	154
Unlabeled subset	8346	

risk of classifying a normal bidder as a shill bidder. So, it becomes essential to consider the penalties for the wrong predictions in our SB detection application.

In a two-class classification problem, a prediction can be one of four outcomes: True Positive (TP) and True Negative (TN) are the correct predictions whereas False Positive (FP) and False Negative (FN) are the incorrect predictions. In our application, FPs represent honest bidders misclassified as shill bidders, and FNs shill bidders mislabeled as honest bidders. CSL-based models utilize a cost matrix to assign relevant costs for the misclassification errors. Generally speaking, if the costs are known apriori or can be provided by the experts of the application domain, we can assign different costs for the incorrect predictions and different benefits for the correct predictions. In this case, the cost matrix can be provided directly to the cost-sensitive classifiers. Nevertheless, in our classification problem, the costs are unknown. We are more interested in detecting fraudulent bidding behaviour so that we can take action against infected auctions. Therefore, we put more penalty on the fraud samples that went undetected (i.e., FNs).

As presented in Table 2, we set the cost matrix to 2×2 because we have two target classes. Since we are not studying the profits of the correct predictions, we assign to their penalties the default value i.e., $Cost_{TP} = Cost_{TN} = 0$. Regarding the mislabelled instances, we set the penalty of FPs to "1"; however no rules can be found in the literature for choosing the values for the FN penalty. After examining the literature, the most common costs employed in past empirical studies ranged from 1 to 10. As an example, the paper [15] used the values of 1, 2, 3, 4, 6 and 10, [5] selected 2, 5 and 10, and [14] chose 2, 3, 4, 5, 6, 7, and 8. We note that no reasons have been mentioned for choosing certain values over others.

We vary the FN costs from 2 to 5 and keep FP cost equal to 1 with the sole purpose of preventing more penalties on the SSC models when they predict instances incorrectly. First, we choose the values of 2, 3, 4 and 5 because they are the most common in previous research. Second, we do not consider values that are higher than the class imbalance ratio of 5:1 of our labeled SB subset (see Table 1). A higher value means too many penalties on the classifiers, which may lead to many errors when classifying normal bidders as fraudsters. Table 2 presents our cost matrix for the CSL+SSC models.

Table 2. Cost matrix for SB classification.

		Predicted class	
		Normal	Fraud
Actual class	Normal	0	1
	Fraud	2, 3, 4, 5	0

The goal of the CSL is to develop a classifier with the lowest total cost, which is calculated as follows [15]:

$$TotalCost = Count_{FNs} * Cost_{FN} + Count_{FPs} * Cost_{FP} \qquad (1)$$

where $Count_{FNs}$ denotes the count of FNs and $Count_{FPs}$ the count of FPs.

On another note, CSL models are capable of dealing efficiently with imbalanced data at the algorithm level. Consequently, the SSC algorithms will learn from the real bidding behavior of users since we are not altering the SB subset, unlike with data sampling techniques.

4.2   MetaCost Learning

Traditionally, to make a two-class classifier cost-sensitive, a CSL algorithm modifies the proportion of training samples when the misclassification errors have different penalties. This technique, called data stratification, consists of modifying the proportion of the minority class because it has the highest risk. The goal here is to minimize the prediction errors of this class [6]. Changing the proportion of the minority class can be done by either duplicating the instances or re-weighting the instances to the relative cost of errors of FNs and FPs [13]. The disadvantage of the first option is that it changes the training dataset, but our goal is to consider only the real behaviour of bidders. On the other hand, if data stratification is done by re-weighing the instances, we are forced to utilize only those algorithms that possess this capability. Thus, we prefer not to be restricted to a specific type of learning algorithm that has the ability of re-weighting data samples.

Due to the disadvantages mentioned above, we adopt a meta-CSL approach, called "MetaCost", which can make any classifier cost-sensitive but without data stratification [5]. MetaCost is appropriate for our fraud classification problem owning to the following factors:

- It can be utilized by any type of classification algorithm, supervised and semi-supervised, and algorithms that can re-weight or not the instances.
- It is the best candidate to manage the penalties of multi-class classifiers [13]. MetaCost works by wrapping the cost-minimizing concept around the classifier but without knowing its internal procedures [5].
- It uses the concept of bagging together with the costs. Bagging produces very accurate probability estimates for unstable classifiers, which are achieved by creating many bootstrapping randomly. Bootstrapping together with the cross-validation optimization method allows a classifier to be trained with a wide variety of samples.
- It employs ensemble learning in which the final prediction decision is made by several classifiers using the weighted majority voting. A fraud model based on multiple classifiers' decisions is much stronger than the best model obtained by one classifier.

We first specify the misclassification costs of both classes in MetaCost as shown in the cost matrix. We then develop four CSL+SSC models by integrating MetaCost into each classification algorithm. Each SSC algorithm employs base classifiers that are trained with the labeled SB subset (imbalanced).

5   Experiment Framework

5.1   SSC Algorithms

Regarding the SSC framework, we select two different collective packages, called "Chopper" [21] and "Yatsi" (Yet Another Two-Stage Idea) [4]. Chopper is an ensemble learner that works only for the two-class classification task. It employs a first classifier to label the testing data after being trained with the labeled subset. This classifier determines the distributions for all the testing data and then ranks the data based on the difference between two confidences (classes). The new training dataset is then supplied to a second classifier, which again determines the distributions for the remaining testing data. The Yatsi approach conducts the classification in two phases: 1) it trains the first classifier with the small portion of labeled data, 2) it employs the classifier to transform the unlabeled data into weighted data (called pre-labeled data), and lastly 3) after merging the original labeled data and pre-labeled data, it uses KNN to produce the classes of the pre-labeled data using the following approach: KNN sums the weights of the nearest neighbours of the pre-labeled data, and then label those data with the class that has the largest summation of weights.

We customize Chopper and Yatsi with the classification algorithms that are commonly adopted in the field of fraud detection, including Naive Bayes (NB), Random Forest (RF), J48 (implementation of Decision Trees C4.5) and IBK (implementation of KNN). More precisely, we develop Chopper with NB as the first classifier and RF as the second classifier. With Yatsi, we train Yatsi-J48, Yatsi-KNN, and Yatsi-NB.

5.2   Parameter Tuning

We optimize the hyper-parameters of the SSC models using a predefined class named "CVParameter" of Weka toolkit. This class determines the optimal values of the parameters using Cross-Validation (CV). However, we need to supply which parameters to be tuned, and their range of values. We train the SSC algorithms using 10-fold CV and perform ten runs to obtain more stable SB classifiers.

For the second classifier of Chopper, we first set the range of the two RF hyper-parameters: the Number of Iterations (NI) from 50 to 300 and the Maximum Tree Depth (MTD) from 1 to 50. CVParameter returns the optimal classifier with the lowest FNR using the best parameter values: 100 for NI and 12 for MTD. We train Yatsi-KNN classifier by setting the number of Nearest Neighbours (NNs) to 5 because this value led to the lowest FNR. We choose the

KDTree search algorithm to accelerate the NN search. We also assign the value of 1.0 (default value) to the weighting factor for unlabeled data. Lastly, we tune the two hyper-parameters of J48: the pruning tree confidence factor with the optimal value of 0.75, and the minimum number of data per leaf with the best value of 2.

For the ensemble learning task used by MetaCost, we assign the number of bagging iterations to 10 and the batch size to 100. These default values are the most preferred when the prediction is performed [21].

5.3 Performance Metrics

Since we are more concerned about detecting shill bidders, we, therefore, focus on the fraud data. Moreover, the CSL+SSC models that we develop are trained directly with the imbalanced SB subset. Hence, we choose the most relevant performance metrics for imbalanced data and correctly predicted fraudsters.

- Recall returns the ratio of shill bidders correctly and wrongly classified.

$$Recall = \frac{TP}{TP + FN} \tag{2}$$

- False Negative Rate (FNR) measures the ratio of shill bidders wrongly classified as normal bidders.

$$FNR = \frac{FN}{FN + TP} \tag{3}$$

- False Positive Rate (FPR) calculates the ratio of normal bidders wrongly classified as fraudulent.

$$FPR = \frac{FP}{FP + TN} \tag{4}$$

- Kappa Statistic (Kappa) computes the agreement between actual and predicted classes while correcting the agreement that happens by chance.

$$KappaStat = \frac{P_{observed} - P_{chance}}{1 - P_{chance}} \tag{5}$$

- Area Under the ROC Curve (AUC) informs us of how much a classifier can differentiate between the normal and fraud class. The closer the AUC value is to 1, the better is the classification model.

6 Evaluation and Comparison

6.1 Performance Results

We first report in Table 3, 4, 5 and 6 the performance results of the four SB classifiers by varying the misclassification cost of the fraud class. The results are then discussed and compared in the next sections.

Table 3. CSL+SSC performance when Penalty is 2, "*" indicates the model is significantly worse while "**" significantly better.

	CSL+Yatsi-KNN	CSL+Yatsi-NB	CSL+Yatsi-J48	CSL+Chopper
Kappa	0.66	0.14*	0.71	0.76**
FNR	0.03	0.1*	0.04	0.01
FPR	0.36	0.77*	0.27	0.28
Recall	0.97	0.9	0.96	0.99
AUC	0.92	0.76*	0.86*	0.97
Cost	137	308	177	**100**

Table 4. CSL+SSC Performance when Penalty is 3, "*" indicates the model is significantly worse.

	CSL+Yatsi-KNN	CSL+Yatsi-NB	CSL+Yatsi-J48	CSL+Chopper
Kappa	0.65	0.19*	0.7	0.75
FNR	0.05	0.12*	0.05	0.03
FPR	0.31	0.69*	0.25	0.27
Recall	0.95	0.88	0.95	0.97
AUC	0.93	0.79*	0.86*	0.96
Cost	182	398	**147**	151

Table 5. CSL+SSC Performance when Penalty is 4, "*" indicates the model is significantly worse while "**" significantly better.

	CSL+Yatsi-KNN	CSL+Yatsi-NB	CSL+Yatsi-J48	CSL+Chopper
Kappa	0.62	0.27*	0.67	0.72**
FNR	0.07	0.15*	0.07	0.04**
FPR	0.29	0.56*	0.23	0.25**
Recall	0.93	0.85*	0.93	0.96**
AUC	0.93	0.79*	0.88*	0.96
Cost	231	449	**174**	191

Table 6. CSL+SSC Performance when Penalty is 5; "*" indicates the model is significantly worse while "**" significantly better.

	CSL+Yatsi-KNN	CSL+Yatsi-NB	CSL+Yatsi-J48	CSL+Chopper
Kappa	0.62	0.28*	0.66	0.7
FNR	0.09	0.19*	0.08	0.05**
FPR	0.24	0.48*	0.22	0.23**
Recall	0.91	0.81*	0.92	0.95**
AUC	0.93	0.79*	0.88*	0.95
Cost	280	511	**216**	238

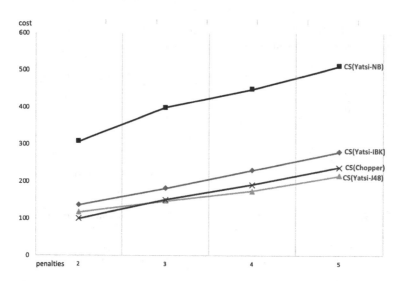

Fig. 1. Learning curves of CSL+SSC models with different penalties.

6.2 Misclassification Errors

In terms of minimizing the misclassification error of the fraud class, the classification model with the lowest cost is the best. As presented in Table 3, when the cost penalty is 2, CSL+Chopper provided the lowest cost of 100 followed by CSL+Yatsi-KNN with 137. Regarding the other penalties of 3, 4 and 5, CSL+Yatsi-J48 returned the lowest cost of 147, 174 and 216 respectively, which is followed by CSL+Chopper with a gap of 4, 17 and 22 respectively. On the other hand, CSL+Yatsi-NB has the highest cost across all the penalties. Moreover, as illustrated in Fig. 1, the learning curves of the CSL+SSC models demonstrate that the misclassification errors increase dramatically when the penalties are increasing. Therefore, the best performing model is CSL+Chopper with the cost penalty of 2.

6.3 Statistical Comparison

We also compare all the accuracy of the four classifiers based on the statistical testing T-test. The symbol "*" indicates significant worse performance while "**" significant better performance.

- When the cost penalty is 2, the accuracy of CSL+Chopper is significantly better with KappaStat because 76% of data are really correctly classified, and not by chance. There is no significant difference with the other metrics. CSL+Yatsi-NB is significantly worse across all the metrics.
- When the cost penalty is 3, we observe no significant difference between CSL+Yatsi-KNN, CSL+Yatsi-J48 and CSL+Chopper. However, CSL+Yatsi-J48 returned the worse AUC of 0.86. CSL+Yatsi-NB is again the worst across all the metrics.

- When the cost penalty is 4, the performance of CSL+Chopper is again significantly better with KappaStat because it outperforms CSL+Yatsi-KNN by 10%, produced 3% less false negatives, and detected 99% of fraud. CSL+Yatsi-NB is the worst across all the metrics.
- When the cost penalty is 5, CSL+Chopper is significantly better in terms of FNR, FPR and Recall. However, there is no statistical difference between CSL+Chopper and CSL+Yatsi-KNN in terms of KappaStat and AUC. The worst AUC values were generated by CSL+Yatsi-J48 and CSL+Yatsi-NB.

In conclusion, the most performing hybrid model is CSL+Chopper, which provided the lowest total cost of 100 when penalizing the classifier with the cost of 2. We observe that 76% of the predictions are really correctly classified and not by chance, only 1% of shill bidders are undetected, and 28% of normal bidders are misclassified. Moreover, by comparing CSL+Yatsi-IBK with CSL+Chopper, we find out that both models are very accurate in classifying bidders into normal and fraudsters with a Recall of 0.97 and 0.99 respectively.

Furthermore, the classifier CSL+Chopper outperforms the regular Chopper model developed in [9] by minimizing the misclassification error of the fraud class by 14% and increasing the accuracy by 17%. Indeed, Chopper (using re-balanced data) returned a FNR of 0.15 and CSL+Chopper (using original imbalanced data) a FNR of 0.01. Chopper provided a Recall of 0.82 and CSL+Chopper a Recall of 0.99. Since these gaps are significant in the fraud detection field, we can conclude that CSL+SSC classifier is the best fit for our fraud detection problem.

7 Conclusion and Future Work

In our study, we successfully incorporated a meta cost-sensitive learning method into the semi-supervised classification environment to achieve three essential benefits: 1) learn with few labeled data because it is time-consuming to annotate multi-dimensional fraud data, 2) manage the costs of misclassification errors so that the fraud class, which is the target of the investigation, has the highest penalty, and 3) tackle the imbalanced learning problem at the algorithm level, so that only the real behaviour of bidders/users is considered during training. Using a real fraud dataset, we conducted an in-depth evaluation and comparison of the performance of several hybrid models of cost-sensitive and semi-supervised classifiers. CSL+Chopper (based on Naive Bayes and Random Forest) is the most performing model concerning the error minimization and accuracy maximization. This fraud model was able to detect 99% of shill bidders with the lowest total cost of 100. Also, CSL+Chopper outperforms the regular Chopper.

For future work, we plan to investigate the interactive active learning method. The latter first chooses the most relevant data and then asks the developer or expert to suggest a label for the chosen data. Our goal is to examine how semi-supervised classifiers would be affected by the selected labeled data. We are also interested in conducting a comparison of our semi-supervised classifiers with the chunk-based incremental classification method defined in [2]. The latter has also been used to tackle the scarcity of labeled data in the fraud detection domain.

References

1. Anowar, F., Sadaoui, S.: Detection of auction fraud in commercial sites. J. Theor. Appl. Electron. Commer. Res. JTAER **15**(1), 81–98 (2020)
2. Anowar, F., Sadaoui, S.: Chunk-based incremental classification of fraud data. In: Proceedings of the 33rd International FLAIRS Conference, pp. 176–179. AAAI Press (2020)
3. de Sá, A.G.C., Pereira, A.C.M., Pappa, G.L.: A customized classification algorithm for credit card fraud detection. J. Eng. Appl. Artif. Intell. **72**, 21–29 (2018)
4. Driessens, K., Reutemann, P., Pfahringer, B., Leschi, C.: Using weighted nearest neighbor to benefit from unlabeled data. In: Ng, W.-K., Kitsuregawa, M., Li, J., Chang, K. (eds.) PAKDD 2006. LNCS (LNAI), vol. 3918, pp. 60–69. Springer, Heidelberg (2006). https://doi.org/10.1007/11731139_10
5. Domingos, P.: Metacost: a general method for making classifiers cost-sensitive. In: Proceedings of the 5th ACM SIGKDD International Conference on Knowledge Discovery And Data Mining, pp. 155–164 (1999)
6. Elkan. C.: The foundations of cost-sensitive learning. In: Proceedings of the International Joint Conference on Artificial Intelligence, Lawrence Erlbaum Associates Ltd., pp. 973–978 (2001)
7. Elshaar, S., Sadaoui, S.: Building high-quality auction fraud dataset. J. Comput. Inf. Sci. **12**(4) (2019). https://doi.org/10.5539/cis.v12n4p1
8. Elshaar, S., Sadaoui, S.: Semi-supervised Classification of Fraud Data in Commercial Auctions, Applied Artificial Intelligence. Taylor & Francis (2020). https://doi.org/10.1080/08839514.2019.1691341
9. Elshaar, S., Sadaoui, S.: Detecting bidding fraud using a few labeled data. In: Proceedings of the 12th International Conference on Agents and Artificial Intelligence - Volume 2: ICAART, Malta, pp. 17–25 (2020). ISBN 978-989-758-395-7. https://doi.org/10.5220/0008894100170025
10. Gómez, J.A., Arévalo, J., Paredes, R., Nin, J.: End-to-end neural network architecture for fraud scoring in card payments. Patt. Recogn. Lett. **105**, 175–181 (2018)
11. Hassan, D.: The impact of false negative cost on the performance of cost sensitive learning based on bayes minimum risk: a case study in detecting fraudulent transactions. Int. J. Intell. Syst. Appl. **9**(2), 18 (2017)
12. Internet Crime Complaint Center-IC3. 2015 internet crime annual report. https://www.ic3.gov/search.aspx?q=job%20offer&p=1. Accessed Oct 2019
13. Witten, I.H., Frank, E., Hall, M.A., Pal, C.J.: Data Mining, Fourth Edition: Practical Machine Learning Tools and Techniques. Morgan Kaufmann Publishers Inc., United States (2016)
14. Kulluk, S., Özbakır, L., Tapkan, P.Z., Baykasoğlu, A.: Cost-sensitive meta-learning classifiers: MEPAR-miner and DIFACONN-miner. Knowl.-Based Syst. **98**, 148–161 (2016)
15. McCarthy, K., Zabar, B., Weiss, G.: Does cost-sensitive learning beat sampling for classifying rare classes? In: Proceeding of the 1st International Workshop on Utility-based Data Mining, pp. 69–77. ACM (2005)
16. Narayan, R., Rout, J.K., Jena, S.K.: Review SPAM detection using semi-supervised technique. In: Sa, P.K., Sahoo, M.N., Murugappan, M., Wu, Y., Majhi, B. (eds.) Progress in Intelligent Computing Techniques: Theory, Practice, and Applications. AISC, vol. 519, pp. 281–286. Springer, Singapore (2018). https://doi.org/10.1007/978-981-10-3376-6_31

17. Nami, S., Shajari, M.: Cost-sensitive payment card fraud detection based on dynamic random forest and k-nearest neighbors. Expert Syst. Appl. **110**, 381–392 (2018)
18. Sahin, Y., Bulkan, S., Duman, E.: A cost-sensitive decision tree approach for fraud detection. Expert Syst. Appl. **40**(15), 5916–5923 (2013)
19. Sedhai, S., Sun, A.: Semi-supervised SPAM detection in twitter stream. IEEE Trans. Comput. Soc. Syst. **5**(1), 169–175 (2018)
20. Salazar, A., Safont, G., Vergara, L.: Semi-supervised learning for imbalanced classification of credit card transaction. In: Proceedings of the International Joint Conference on Neural Networks (IJCNN), pp. 1–7. IEEE (2018)
21. Bernhard, P., Driessens, K., Reutemann, P.: Collective and Semi-supervised Classification. Technical Report, University of Waikato, pp. 1–21 (2014)
22. Viegas, J., Cepeda, N., Vieira, S.: Electricity fraud detection using committee semi-supervised learning. In: Proceeding of the International Joint Conference on Neural Networks (IJCNN), pp. 1–6. IEEE (2018)
23. Xiao, J., Zhou, X., Zhong, Y., Xie, L., Gu, X., Liu, D.: Cost-sensitive semi-supervised selective ensemble model for customer credit scoring. Knowl. Based Syst. **189**, 105118 (2020)
24. Yilmaz, C., Durahim, A.: SPR2EP: a semi-supervised spam review detection framework. In: Proceedings of the IEEE/ACM International Conference on Advances in Social Networks Analysis and Mining (ASONAM), pp. 306–313. IEEE (2018)

Blending NLP and Machine Learning for the Development of Winograd Schemas

Nicos Isaak[1]([✉])[iD] and Loizos Michael[1,2]

[1] Open University of Cyprus, Nicosia, Cyprus
nicos.isaak@st.ouc.ac.cy, loizos@ouc.ac.cy
[2] CYENS Center of Excellence, Nicosia, Cyprus

Abstract. The Winograd Schema Challenge (WSC), a novel litmus test for machine intelligence, has been proposed to advance the field of AI. Over the last decade, AI researchers have become increasingly interested in this challenge. While a common and trivial task for humans, studies have shown that the WSC is still difficult for current AI systems. Tackling the challenge would likely require access to a sufficiently rich set of Winograd schema examples, which are currently limited in their number and too cumbersome to create completely manually. Towards addressing these limitations, we propose a machine-driven approach for the development of large numbers of schemas. Our empirical evaluation suggests that our developed system, which blends the advantages of Machine Learning and Natural Language Processing, is able to automatically develop Winograd schemas autonomously, or considerably help humans in the development task.

Keywords: Winograd Schema Challenge · Schema development · machine learning · Deep learning

1 Introduction

The Winograd Schema Challenge (WSC) [15], the task of resolving definite pronouns in carefully-constructed sentences, has been proposed to advance the field of AI [16]. It is believed that systems able to tackle the WSC will be able to support a wide range of commonsense and reasoning tasks that will help us understand human behaviour itself [16]. It seems that tackling the WSC will play a significant role in a wide range of current AI applications, as a step towards the development of machines that will automate or enhance basic human abilities—a traditional goal of AI that was laid back in the late 1950s [19].

Scholars seem to agree that the WSC is quite trivial for humans, but at the same time it is quite difficult for machines [21,28], due to the acknowledged lack of their commonsense reasoning abilities. In this line of research, in a recent work we have demonstrated the possibility of using the WSC as a novel form of CAPTCHAs [10]. This kind of challenge might spur research interest in

© Springer Nature Switzerland AG 2021
A. P. Rocha et al. (Eds.): ICAART 2020, LNAI 12613, pp. 188–214, 2021.
https://doi.org/10.1007/978-3-030-71158-0_9

anaphora resolution which remains an essential task for the Natural Language Understanding (NLU) community [6]. Although the use of the WSC as a means to bring more researchers in the AI field is very important [10,22], it would seem necessary that for this to happen one would require access to a good source of newly developed Winograd schemas, which itself has its challenges [21].

Aiming to develop a new system that is able promote the original goals of the WSC through the development of high quality schemas, this work presents Winventor (see Fig. 1). Winventor is a machine-driven approach that automates the schema development process and considerably helps humans in the development task. It combines NLP tools and deep learning into a flexible system able to produce efficiently a number of new Winograd schemas, which could be used to enhance the creativity and motivation of human experts for the development of schemas that were formerly designed by Winventor.

To lay a foundation for a machine-aided schema development process, we start by explaining the key challenge of the task, and continue by describing our system. Winventor's architecture is based on three major approaches: based on NLP, based on deep learning, and a blended approach. In each case, we undertake several experiments regarding the a priori appropriateness of our system as a schema development mechanism. Our empirical evaluation suggests that the blended approach, which combines deep learning and NLP, can provide us with more schemas than the other two approaches. Finally, we review the implications of our results along with potential directions for future research.

The current paper extends an earlier version [12] presented at the 12th International Conference on Agents and Artificial Intelligence (ICAART). Compared to the conference paper, which was based on NLP-only techniques, we enhanced the schema development process through Deep Learning. In this regard, we developed some original ideas to blend Deep Learning with NLP, and the resulting system was able to provide larger numbers of schemas, while being 92% faster than our initial approach.

2   Problem Definition

The WSC consists of pairs of halves and the objective is to resolve a definite pronoun in each half. Each half comprises a sentence, a question and two possible pronoun targets or answers. The pronoun targets belong to the same gender and both are either plural or singular. Ostensibly, in each half there is a special word that when replaced by another word the answer also changes.

The WSC was named after Terry Winograd because of a well known example that was taken from his doctoral thesis [4], justified in terms of machine translation ("The city councilmen refused to give the women a permit for a demonstration because they [feared/advocated] violence"). The following schema (a pair of halves) illustrates the modified example, which meets the challenge rules:

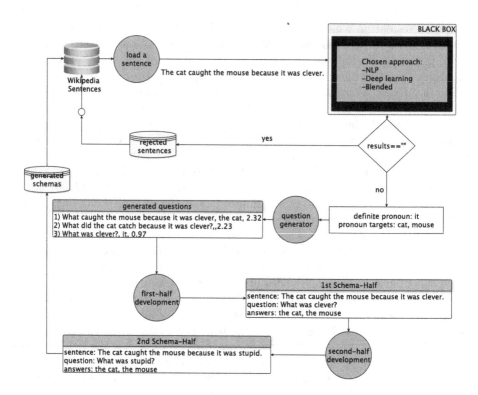

Fig. 1. Winventor's high-level architecture: a system that automates the schema development process (adapted from [12]).

- First-half: Sentence: The city councilmen refused the demonstrators a permit because they feared violence. Question: Who feared violence? Answers: The city councilmen, The demonstrators. Correct Answer: The city councilmen.
- Second-half: Sentence: The city councilmen refused the demonstrators a permit because they advocated violence. Question: Who advocated violence. Answers: The city councilmen, The demonstrators. Correct Answer: The demonstrators.

It is believed that the WSC can provide a meaningful measure of machine intelligence, exactly because of the presumed necessity of reasoning with commonsense knowledge to identify how the special word or phrase affects the resolution of the definite pronoun [15,16]. According to Levesque [15], in every schema you need to have background knowledge that is not revealed in the words of the sentence to be able to clarify what is going on. By extension, it is believed that a system that contains the commonsense knowledge to correctly resolve Winograd schemas should be capable of supporting a wide range of AI applications (e.g., machine translation).

As stated in the literature, constructing a WSC corpus is a laborious job, requiring creativity, motivation, and inspiration [21]. In addition to this, as far as we know, only two WSC datasets are widely available: the Rahman and Ng's dataset [25], consisting of 943 schemas (1886 halves), and the Levesque et al.'s dataset [15], consisting of 150 schemas (300 halves). It seems that a machine-driven approach for the development of schemas, which is a fertile area of research, would presumably help the community work on those WSC problems that require schemas, supporting and promoting at the same time further research on the WSC.

3   High-Level Architecture

In this section, we start with a high-level overview of Winventor by presenting how the engine works (see Fig. 1). If Winventor cannot develop a schema, it only develops a schema half that consists of a sentence, a definite pronoun, a question that indirectly points to the definite pronoun, and the two pronoun targets. Schemas that do not obey all constraints are known as "Winograd Schemas in the broad sense" [15]. In this regard, we developed Winventor to work in two different modes: strict or relaxed. With the strict mode enabled, Winventor develops schemas that strictly follow the WSC rules, whereas with the relaxed mode it may also develop schemas where the pronoun targets do not have to share the same gender.

3.1   A Simplified Example

At first Winventor loads an English sentence to evaluate if it can develop a schema. Winventor utilizes the sentence to output the definite pronoun and the two pronoun targets with one of the three specified approaches: using only NLP, using only deep learning, and a blended approach (see BlackBox in Fig. 1). If this is not possible, the current sentence is rejected. Otherwise: i) it proceeds with the question development, using a tool from the literature; ii) it constructs the first schema half by placing together the sentence, the question, and the two pronoun targets; iii) it finds the special word in the first sentence, generates the question, and develops the second schema half. More details on this procedure are given next.

Wikipedia Sentences: To be able to automatically develop schemas it is important to have access to a source of sentences. The Winventor framework can use any source, local or online, which can provide a bulk amount of English sentences. In its current version, Winventor is built on an extensible framework that allows access to a broad collection of nearly 88 million sentences from the English Wikipedia [9].

Developing the Schema-Half Questions: One of the most difficult parts of the challenge is to come up with appropriate questions [15]. According to Levesque, while doing so we must avoid two major pitfalls: i) The first pitfall concerns questions whose answers are in a certain sense too obvious; ii) The second and more troubling pitfall concerns questions whose answers are not obvious enough. It might be a stretch to do that since the question generation task is a very challenging and tedious process that dates back to 1976 [30].

To tackle this, Winventor uses the Heilman and Smith question generator[1] [7], a system able to generate questions based on a given piece of text. This question generator is freely available, easily customizable, and, at the same time, able to generate questions with a ranking strategy. Specifically, *Winventor* uses the question generator with the *"–keep-pro and –just-wh"* flags enabled. *Keep-pro* keeps questions with unresolved pronouns and *Just-wh* excludes boolean questions from the output. At the end, it selects the pronoun targets that relate to the pronoun that is given as the answer of the best question. For instance, in the next example *"The cat caught the mouse because it was clever"*, Winventor, via Heilman and Smith's question generator, returns the following questions: i) "What caught the mouse because it was clever, the cat, 2.32"; ii) "What did the cat catch because it was clever?, ,2.23"; iii) "What was clever?, it, 0.97". In the end, it selects the third question, as it is the only one that has as answer a definite pronoun: it.

Completing the Schema-Half: The next step for Winventor is the development of schema halves, meaning, pairs of sentences, questions, and pronoun targets. For each sentence and depending on the returned results (based on the approach used), Winventor might construct several schema halves. The number of the schema halves relates to the question generator results and the possible pronoun-target pairs. Specifically, for each valid pronoun-target pair, Winventor develops a number of schema halves, reordered by their significance (see *first schema-half* in Fig. 1).

Completing the Schema: Winventor develops schemas by keeping in mind that they are constructed so that there is a special word, in each sentence, which when replaced by another word, the answer also changes [21]. Hence, for every schema half it considers the following: i) it parses the question to identify the special word, which is a verb/adjective that participates in the questions' triple relation (e.g., the word clever from the question "Who was clever"); ii) it returns the antonym of the special word, found in the previous step (e.g., from "clever" to "careless"), and iii) it modifies the returned word, in the question and the sentence, to match the tense of the second schema half (see *second-half* in Fig. 1). Regarding the triples, these are semantic scenes of the type *subject, verb, object* that are created through the sentence/question's subjects and objects [9]. For instance, the triples [cat, caught, mouse] and [who, was, clever], which were used for the development of the schema in Fig. 1, were created from the parser's *nsubj and dobj* relations *(abbreviations of "nominal-subject" and "direct-object")*.

---

[1] http://www.cs.cmu.edu/~ark/mheilman/questions/.

In the next sections, we will show how Winventor analyzes Wikipedia sentences to select the definite pronoun and the pronoun targets, based on three different approaches. In the first part, we will discuss how the engine handles its semantics to develop schemas with various NLP tools, and, in the second part, we will show how deep learning comes into play. In the third part, we will show how the blending of the two approaches can be used to enhance the schema development process.

3.2 Developing Schemas Through NLP

Winventor makes use of various NLP tools to determine the meaning of each sentence [3]. This approach helps select the definite pronoun along with the pronoun targets based on the semantic analysis of a given piece of text. For instance, via various NLP tools, Winventor will be able to acquire sentences with good structure to select pronoun targets that agree in gender, number, and participate in relations with other words. In the sequel, we will introduce the major NLP components of Winventor by presenting how it generates schemas from scratch (see Fig. 2).

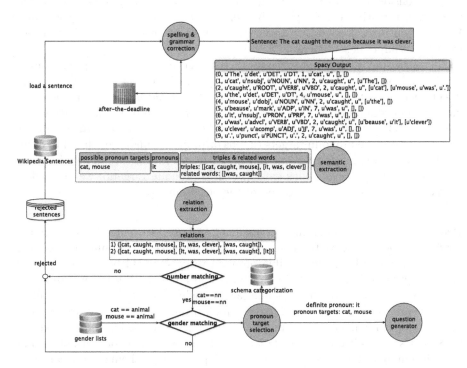

Fig. 2. A schema development process by Winventor using various NLP tools (adapted from [12]). The NLP section ends just before the question generator comes into play (see question-generator in Fig. 1).

Orthography and Spelling Correction: It is well-known that sentences found from online sources, like Wikipedia, might suffer from abbreviations, spelling errors, and misspellings of words. For instance, it was found that the percentage of misspellings of words on Wikipedia, relative to content, consistently increases year after year [29]. To avoid these kinds of problems, Winventor makes use of two tools from the literature. The first is the Google language-detection[2] library, which helps Winventor acquire only English sentences. The second is the After-the-Deadline[3] language-checker, which automatically corrects spelling and grammar errors. Tools like After-the-Deadline offer efficient and effective ways of enhancing grammar accuracy and learning [23].

Sentence Word Relations: With the term word-relations we refer to semantic relations that can be concluded from a given text. While this task, which is necessary for the development of schemas, is very common and trivial for humans, it is quite challenging and difficult for machines. According to the literature, semantic relations of any given piece of text, are considered good if they can output essential relationships between the events and their participants [28], albeit, there is still no clear path to this goal [27]. To built good relations we have to consider various facts, like grammatical role, number, gender, and syntactic structure that can be given by dependency parsers [1,9]. In this regard, Winventor utilizes the spaCy[4] dependency parser to develop semantic relations from the Wikipedia sentences.

Through spaCy, Winventor parses each sentence to develop triples, related-words, and pronoun relations. *Related Words* are based on verbs that have a direct relation between them. For instance, the *caught-was* relation shows an indirect connection of the *nsubj* cat and the *dobj* mouse to the *adjective* clever (see *2nd and 7th line of the spaCy output* in Fig. 2). *Pronoun Relations* are relations where the pronoun targets (nouns or proper-nouns) are related to other words, via pronouns (see *relations* in Fig. 2). If at least one pronoun exists, and two nouns or two proper nouns exist (possible pronoun targets), we proceed to the next step, otherwise we proceed to the next sentence.

Pronoun-Target Selection: A challenging task for Winventor is to obtain the possible pronoun targets from each examined sentence. According to what the challenge dictates [15], the possible pronoun targets should be either a pair of nouns or proper-nouns that agree in gender and number. Winventor's approach to discerning a list of possible pronoun targets includes the following: i) it utilizes spaCy's entity recognition system to search for proper nouns, ii) it searches some pre-downloaded gender-lists to find nouns that have the same gender, and, iii) via spaCy's dependency parser, it selects only nouns and/or proper-nouns that agree in number. The final result is to develop as many schemas as it can from

---

[2] https://pypi.org/project/langdetect/.
[3] http://www.afterthedeadline.com.
[4] https://spacy.io.

each examined sentence. For each developed schema, Winventor keeps track of three variables/flags, showing the relations that govern the pronoun targets:

- NumberAgreement: This variable equals 1 if the two nouns/proper-nouns agree in number, otherwise 0.
- GenderAgreement: Likewise, this equals 1 if the two pronoun targets have the same gender.
- PronounGenderAgreement: This variable equals 1 if the two pronoun targets' gender agree with the target pronoun, otherwise 0. To complete this task we consider the following: The third-person singular personal pronouns, *he/him/his*, refer to the masculine gender, whereas *she/her(s)* refer to the feminine gender. On the other hand, the singular pronouns *they/them/their(s)* refer to the neutral gender, and the pronouns *it/its* refer to the neuter gender (in the case of companion animals, the pronouns *he/she* may also be used).

Pronoun-Target Appropriateness: In order to identify the appropriateness of each pronoun target pair, Winventor does the following: i) as previously mentioned, it keeps a track of number, gender, and the pronoun-gender agreement, ii) it stores the number of the triple relations that the pronoun targets participate in, and iii) it utilizes the Mitkov aggregation score [20], which is able to create a ranking list of nouns, according to some preferences. Mitkov's work showed that when we have limited background knowledge, like in our case, we can consider five salience indicators to select the best pronoun targets: 1.) *Definiteness* refers to definite nouns, meaning that this kind of nouns should get a higher preference, in comparison to other nouns. Definite noun phrases' score equals 0, whereas indefinite ones are penalized by −1. 2.) *Indicating verbs* relate with nouns that are followed by verbs that are members of a specific Verb set (e.g., discuss, consider, investigate). These nouns' score equals 1, otherwise 0. 3.) *Lexical Reiteration* refers to repeated synonymous noun phrases where they get a higher preference. A noun's score equals 2 if it is repeated twice or more, 1 if it is repeated once, and 0 if not. 4.) *Non-prepositional* nouns are given a higher preference than prepositional nouns. A non-prepositional noun's score equals 0, whereas a prepositional noun's score equals −1. 5.) *Collocation and Immediate-Reference* refers to nouns with identical collocation patterns, where they get a higher preference (Collocation nouns' score equals 2, otherwise 0).

Completing the Schema: As shown in Sect. 3.1, after the selection of the best pronoun target, Winventor parses the sentence through the Heilman and Smith question generator and selects the one that has as answer the definite pronoun (see Sect. 3.1). Finally, it develops the two schema halves, constructs the schema and adds it to the Schema Database. Based on this approach, each developed schema is automatically classified into predefined categories and added to a schema-categorization DB (see Fig. 2). The categorization is done according to each sentence subject (e.g., Schwarzenegger - terminator - protection, birds - food) and the types of the pronoun target pairs (e.g., gpe, gerund, loc, country, facility, norp, org, etc.). Additionally, *Winventor* keeps track of the rejected sentences with the following flags: 1.) Nouns and proper-nouns have not been found; 2.) Target Pronoun relations have not been found; 3) Questions have not been formed; 4.) not an English sentence; 5.) This was artificially created for previous WSC (see rejected-sentences DB in Fig. 2).

3.3   Developing Schemas via Deep Learning

Deep learning refers to a class of different techniques that allow computational models to learn representations of data through multiple levels of abstraction [14]. As stated in the literature, deep learning is extremely good at finding complex data structures and is, therefore, suitable for different fields [14]. In this regard, we aim to train three deep learning models to help Winventor in the schema development process. Specifically, we train: 1.) the sentence model for the selection of sentences, 2.) the pronoun model for the selection of the definite pronoun, and 3.) the pronoun-targets model for the selection of the best pronoun-target pair, from each examined sentence.

For the development of a schema-half/schema, our algorithm starts with the sentence model to select an appropriate sentence, continues with the pronoun model to select the best definite pronoun from the previously selected sentence, and, finally, ends with the pronoun-targets model to select the best possible pair of answers. In the sequel, we will introduce the deep learning models with the datasets used for their training and testing (see Fig. 3).

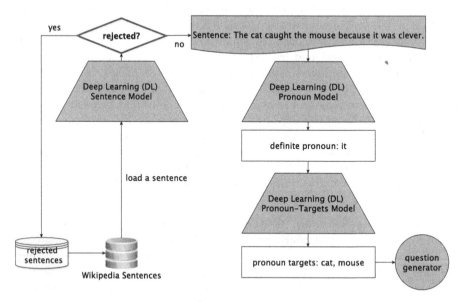

Fig. 3. A schema development process by Winventor using deep learning. The deep learning section ends just before the question generator comes into play (see question-generator in Fig. 1).

Dataset Preparation: The central aspect of deep learning is that the layers of a deep neural network are automatically learned from data using a general-purpose learning process [14]. In this sense, deep learning algorithms are not capable of understanding the text models but only map the statistical structure of written language, which is supposedly sufficient to solve simple textual tasks [2]. On the other hand, we know that in problems where data are limited, deep learning often is not an ideal solution [18]. In this regard, we employed a data synthesis/augmentation procedure to increase the size of our training data. In an attempt to use a different training set than that of Rahman and Ng's, we begun with Levesque et al.'s dataset [15], which consists of 150 schemas, and ended up with 30,000 schemas.

Sentence Model: This model utilizes a classifier that is responsible for selecting appropriate sentences for the development of schemas (see *DL-Sentence-Model* in Fig. 3). Given any English sentence, our sentence model returns a value in the range of 0–1, where values >0.5 indicate high-grade (suitable) sentences for the development of schemas. Valid or high-grade sentences are eligible for further processing for the development of schemas, whereas non-valid are not.

To train our classifier, we used training data with positive and negative examples. Positive examples refer to sentences that were used in the development of the Levesque et al.'s dataset [15], whereas negative examples refer to sentences that cannot be used in the development of schemas. To increase the number of positive-examples we proceeded as follows: 1.) we parsed each sentence and removed the punctuation characters, 2.) for every noun, adjective, verb, and adverb, we developed a list with their synonyms, and, 3.) based on a random combination of their synonyms, we developed a list of new sentences, 4.) via spaCy, we replaced the words of each examined sentence with their part of speech (part-of-speech tagging). Through the part-of-speech tagging, our model does not need to use knowledge transfer between various domains which is a characteristic feature for many deep learning approaches [17]. Regarding the negative examples, for every positive sentence, we developed a negative one: i) by randomly removing some words, and ii) by randomly reordering its tagging (see Table 1).

Table 1. A sentence transformation example for the development of the training and testing dataset of our sentence model.

	Part of speech tagging
Sentence	The city councilmen refused the demonstrators a permit because they feared violence
Part of speech	DET NOUN NOUN VERB DET NOUN DET NOUN ADP PRON VERB NOUN
Synonym-positive example	DET ADJ NOUN NOUN VERB DET NOUN DET PROPN NOUN ADP PRON VERB NOUN
Synonym-negative example	DET NOUN VERB PART DET DET ADP PRON VERB

Pronoun Model: A key problem within the schema development process is the selection of the definite pronoun, as this directly relates with the selection of the pronoun targets. To that end, we developed the pronoun-model, which is responsible for selecting the definite pronoun in sentences that were returned by the sentence model. Given any tagged-English sentence with multiple pronouns, this model returns the best possible pronoun, which could be used as our definite pronoun. Specifically, for each sentence with a (marked) pronoun, this model returns a confidence score in the range of 0–1; the higher the score, the higher the confidence for the specific pronoun.

To increase our training set we have followed a similar procedure to the previous model. Regarding the construction of the positive examples, we have used the valid sentences from our sentence model but with the position of the definite pronoun marked. For instance, for the schema-half sentence *The city councilmen refused the demonstrators a permit because they feared violence* our algorithm would return "DET NOUN NOUN VERB DET NOUN DET NOUN ADP <PRON> VERB NOUN". For the construction of the negative examples, we have followed a similar procedure, where, for each positive sentence, we build a new negative one with its tagging shuffled. For instance, in our previous example, this would result in "DET NOUN DET NOUN <PRON> NOUN VERB ADP NOUN VERB DET NOUN".

Pronoun-Targets Model: This model is responsible for the selection of the best pronoun target pair (answers), in sentences that were selected by the pronoun model. Recall that the WSC is about resolving the definite pronoun to one of *two* possible pronoun targets, in each schema. Hence, in each examined sentence, this model aims to output the best answer pair to be used in the construction of the schema. Given any tagged English sentence, with two words marked, this model returns a confidence score in the range of 0–1 that indirectly shows the best pair for the development of the schema.

For training purposes and specifically for the building of our positive examples, in all of the synonym sentences the correct pronoun target pair was marked. This resulted in pairs of multiple words, as in some schemas the correct answers consisted of compound nouns. For instance, in the example used in our previous models our algorithm would return "DET <NOUN NOUN> VERB DET <NOUN> DET NOUN ADP PRON VERB NOUN", with the position of the two pronoun targets marked. For the construction of the negative examples, we have followed a similar procedure, where, for each positive sentence, we build a new negative one with its tagging shuffled.

Schema Development: We continue to discuss how Winventor develops schemas via the deep learning approach. At the start, each Wikipedia sentence is validated by the sentence-model, where for every *valid* sentence (>0.5) it proceeds to the next step to search for the definite pronoun (see Algorithm 1). Winventor replaces every sentence word by its part-of-speech, marks the pronoun (<PRON>) and parses it though the pronoun-model to retrieve its score; this process is repeated for every pronoun in the sentence and at the end it selects the pronoun with the biggest score. The next step is to find the best pronoun-target pair of the sentence that indirectly relates to the definite pronoun. To that end, Winventor randomly creates all the combinations of two, three, and four words. Then, for every combination, it marks the combination's words in the sentence (part-of-speech) and parses it through the pronoun-targets model to retrieve its score. At the end, it selects as the best pair the pair with the highest score. After the selection of the sentence, the definite pronoun, and the pronoun target pair, Winventor develops the two schemas halves, following the same procedure as stated in the previous sections (see Sect. 3.2). The only difference within this approach, is that each developed schema cannot be automatically classified into predefined categories to be added to the schema-categorization DB.

Algorithm 1. Schema development via deep learning.

1: sentences = loadDatasetHalf1Sentences (RahmanNg)
2: **for** *sentence in sentences* **do**
3:     validSentence = checkSentMODEL (sentence)
4:     **if** validSentence $<= 0.5$ then continue
5:     bestPronoun = findTheBestPronoun (sentence, pronounMODEL)
6:     bestAnswerPair = findBestAnswerPair (sentence, answerMODEL)
7:     question = buildQuestion (sent)
8:     half1 = finalizeSchema (sent, bestPronoun, bestAnswerPair, question)
9:     half2 = buildHalf2 (sent, bestPronoun, bestAnswerPair, question)
10: **end for**

3.4   The Blended Approach

In this section, we describe how we blended the NLP and deep learning approaches with the ultimate goal of developing a more efficient and more effective solution. In particular, we modified the pronoun-target selection process based on factors described in the previous sections (see Algorithm 2), by replacing the deep learning solution for that task with the gender, number, pronoun-gender, and triple factors, in order to select the best answer pair (see Fig. 4).

Thus, the blended approach proceeds as follows: 1.) via the sentence model it parses Wikipedia sentences to select an appropriate sentence for the development of a schema; 2.) through the pronoun model it returns the definite pronoun of the examined sentence; 3.) from the sentence it selects only nouns or proper-nouns and builds all the possible combinations (see *relations* in Algorithm 2); 4.) at the same time, it searches for possible compound-nouns and replaces each noun accordingly; 5.) next, for every pair of answers, it estimates a score value where it adds 1 if they are both members of the same number-class. It does the same, in case the two candidates share the same gender, participate in triples (*as subj and dobj*), and have a pronoun-gender agreement with the definite pronoun; 6.) it adds the score to a list of scores (see *answersScore* in Algorithm 2); 7.) In the last step, it returns the best answer pair, which is the pair with the highest score.

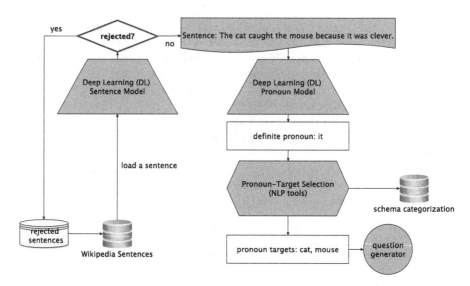

Fig. 4. A schema development process by Winventor using deep learning and NLP tools (for a further explanation on the NLP tools, see Algorithm 2). The process ends just before the question generator comes into play (see question-generator in Fig. 1).

Completing the Schema: The blended approach generates the questions and develops the two schema halves following the same procedure as stated in the previous sections (see Sect. 3.2). Furthermore, similarly to the NLP approach and contrary to the deep learning approach, each developed schema is automatically classified into predefined categories and added to the schema-categorization DB (see Fig. 4).

4   Experiments and Results

In this section, we describe the results from several studies that we undertook to evaluate Winventor's performance on the development of schemas, based on the aforementioned approaches. Each of the following subsections reports on one of the approaches.

4.1   NLP Approach

Here we describe the results from three studies that we undertook to evaluate Winventor's performance, on replicating existing Winograd Schemas from a well-known WSC dataset, on developing new Winograd Schemas from scratch, and on helping humans develop new Winograd Schemas.

Algorithm 2. Blended pronoun-target pair selection.

```
 1: function FINDBESTANSWERPAIR(sentence)
 2:     relations = returnPairs (["NOUN", "PROPN"], doubleRelations)
 3:     compounds = findCompoundNouns ()
 4:     pairs=match (compounds, relations )
 5:     for pair in pairs do
 6:         num = checkNumberAgreement (pair)
 7:         gnd = checkGenderAgreement (pair)
 8:         pga = checkPronounGenderAgreement (pair)
 9:         trp = checkTriples(pair)
10:         score = m1+m2+num+gnd+pga+trp
11:         answersScore.append(score)
12:     end for
13:     return bestAnswerPair = pairs[answersScore.index(max(answersScore))]
14: end function
```

Schema Replication: In this experiment, we have tested Winventor on replicating schemas from Rahman and Ng's dataset [25], which is a challenging dataset of 943 schemas, where each schema half consists of a sentence, a definite pronoun (instead of question), and two possible pronoun targets. The average sentence length of the database was 14 words. For the purpose of this experiment the *strict* mode was disabled, as this is a dataset that was developed under the "broad" flag. By giving Winventor the sentence of the first half of each schema, we wanted to evaluate if it can produce similar results as in the dataset. For each sentence, Winventor was requested to develop all the possible schemas, storing at the same time all of the developed relations and factors (e.g., Mitkov-score, gender, number, and pronoun-gender-agreement variables).

Schemas: The results revealed that 416 sentences resulted in 990 halves where 848 were schemas. More than two hundred schemas (254 schema halves of which 214 are schemas) were found to match with the Rahman and Ng's dataset, meaning that they have the same definite pronoun and the same pronoun targets. At the same time our system rejected 527 sentences, for the following reasons: 1.) Nouns and proper-nouns have not been found (10 sentences) 2.) Target Pronoun relations have not been found (502 sentences) 3.) Questions have not been formed (13 sentences) 4.) Not an English sentence (2 sentences were wrongly identified). Regarding the big number of rejected sentences, it shows that further gains could be achieved via more accurate semantic analysis of each sentence. For instance, over fifty percent of the sentences were rejected because of pure parsing: *Target Pronoun relations have not been found.*

Pronoun Targets: Regarding the pronoun targets, 122 schema halves were identified as proper-noun problems, and 132 as noun problems. Among the proper-noun schema halves, it was found that 33% had more than two proper-nouns, in each sentence. Similarly, 70% of the noun problems were found to have more than two nouns, in each sentence. The positive difference in favor of the

Table 2. A snapshot of *Winventor's* developed questions on Rahman and Ng dataset.

	Sentence	Pronoun	Question
1	Tony helped Jeff because he wanted to help	He	Who wanted to help?
2	The security team locked the scientists inside the building because they had to keep confidential information inside	They	Who had to keep confidential information inside?
3	Sam helped Davey fortify their bunker because he thought the Mexicans were invading?	He	Who thought the Mexicans were invading?
4	Tiger Woods dropped Randy as his caddy because he was not satisfied with his work?	He	Who was not satisfied with his work?

noun problems might suggest that resolving proper-nouns is more challenging than resolving nouns [1].

Definite Pronoun: We further analyzed our results regarding the cases where Winventor was able to correctly resolve the definite pronoun but not the correct pronoun targets. Broadly speaking, we have found that: i) on average, each sentence that was identified as a proper-noun problem contains four proper-nouns, and ii) each sentence that was identified as a noun problem contains five nouns. It seems that the increased number of possible pronoun targets might have led Winventor to wrong conclusions. Further analysis has shown that the average sentence length for the examined sentences was increased. Specifically, on the one hand, schemas that were characterized as proper-noun problems contain, on average, thirteen words, and, on the other hand, schemas characterized as noun problems, contain nineteen words. At the same time, in the halves where Winventor correctly identified both, the definite pronoun and the pronoun targets, the average length is twelve words for the proper-noun problems, and fourteen words for the noun problems.

Question Development: Although the original dataset did not include questions, *Winventor* was able to produce schemas with valid questions (see Table 2). This shows that the parsing of sentences through the question generator, and, at the same time, the selection of the best appropriate question, returned useful results.

Non-matching Schemas: Our results showed that Winventor was able to develop 990 halves from 416 sentences, meaning that for each sentence multiple schemas were developed. On the other hand, our analysis showed that only 254 halves (214 schemas) were found to match the original dataset, meaning that 74% of the schema halves were among those that were rejected as non-matching schema halves. Recall that there are sentences that contain multiple number of nouns, proper-nouns and pronouns, which means that there is a big chance to have sentences that could lead to more than one schema. For instance, in the original schema dataset we have the following halves: i) *Sentence: Arnold Schwarzenegger cannot terminate John Conner, because he is protecting him. Definite-Pronoun: he, Answers: Arnold Schwarzenegger, John Conner*, and, ii) *Sentence: Arnold Schwarzenegger cannot terminate John Conner, because he is the leader of the resistance. Definite-Pronoun: he, Answers: Arnold Schwarzenegger, John Conner*. Although Winventor did not manage to build the requested schema, it returned the following results: i) *Sentence: Arnold Schwarzenegger cannot terminate John Conner, because he is protecting him. Definite-Pronoun: he, Question: Who is protecting him? Answers: Arnold Schwarzenegger, John Conner*, and ii) *Sentence: Arnold Schwarzenegger cannot terminate John Conner, because he is protecting him. Definite-Pronoun: him, Question: Who is he protecting? Answers: Arnold Schwarzenegger, John Conner*. As we can see, the question of the second schema half, which was returned by Winventor, refers to a different pronoun than the original schema half. Given that the original dataset was developed under the "broad" flag, these two halves can be taken together to consist a new valid schema, albeit different from the original one.

Selecting the Best Schemas: Given that for any sentence multiple schemas might be created, many open questions remain regarding the fastest way to select the best ones (for instance, to select the 254 halves from our database of 990 halves). To that end, we further analyzed the relation between the developed halves and different *factors* (e.g., Mitkov-score, triple, gender and pronoun-gender agreement). The results showed a direct relation between our factors and the selection of the best schema halves. For instance, if we select all the schema halves that agree on gender, number, participate in triples, and have a pronoun-gender agreement, we have an 89% success rate. Furthermore, our results showed the importance of the triple factor (nsubj-dobj); it was shown that if we remove the triple factor the success rate drops to 85%. Additionally, our analysis showed that if we select the schemas according to their Mitkov-score, we have an 82% success rate, meaning that Mitkov's theory works well when we have limited background knowledge.

Schema Development: Within this experiment, we investigated Winventor's appropriateness on developing new Winograd Schemas from scratch. To that end, we analyzed schemas developed from Wikipedia sentences, with a survey that we designed and undertook. The schemas were developed with the *strict* flag enabled, meaning that they had to consist of a sentence, a question, and two possible pronoun-targets that agreed in gender, number, and had a pronoun-gender agreement. At the time of the experiment *Winventor* had already searched 20000 sentences from the Wikipedia dataset and developed 500 schemas.

Design: For our experiments we selected the Microworkers (MW) platform[5], which can be considered as one of the best available crowdsourced platforms [8,24]. Specifically, we designed a questionnaire using LimeSurvey[6] and posted the link on the MW platform. We divided our questionnaire into two sections, where the first section consisted of twenty randomly selected Winograd halves, whereas the second consisted of ten Winograd *schemas*; every single example was automatically developed by Winventor. Examples that were included in the first section were excluded from the second one. The questionnaire started with the first section and continued with the second one, where each half/schema was displayed on a single screen, followed by the question; in each example three choices were displayed side-by-side: i) Valid Schema - Easy to Solve, ii) Valid Schema - Hard to Solve, iii) Non-Valid Schema. Furthermore, all participants were informed that once the survey started, they could not change a submitted answer. Additionally, before taking the survey, each participant had to do the following: i) read a consent form and agree to participate, ii) select their age and their English language literacy level, and iii) pass a training phase to get familiarized with the task. In the training task, which consisted of few examples similar to that of our questionnaire, immediate feedback (correct or incorrect) was given after each trial.

Participants: Our experiment was performed during May 2019, where a total of one hundred MW workers were recruited, aged between 18 and 65. Our participants were residents of English speaking countries, and were screened by means of a qualification task from the Microworkers platform. The total cost of our campaign was $250.

Results: In the first section the participants characterized the schema halves as *valid* with a mean of 69% ($\sigma = 0.15$). In the second section they characterized the schemas as *valid* with a mean of 73% ($\sigma = 0.17$). It seems that the positive difference in favor of the schemas might have happened not because of the quality of the schemas, which are harder to develop, but because of the following reasons: i) the participants were able to see the two halves at the same time, which seems to help them understand the meaning of the schema, and ii) sentences that were found appropriate for the development of schemas might have simpler structure. Generally speaking, we believe that our results must be taken with a grain of salt. Specifically, we are not claiming that this system can be used to develop schema/halves without the need of reviewing. For instance, in order to validate the next schema-half we need to change a word in the question (*is* to *causes*): *sentence: If the back side of the stick is used, it is a penalty and the other team will get the ball back. question: What is a penalty? answers: the stick, the ball.*

Winventor as an Assistant: Within this experiment we evaluated if Winventor can assist humans in the schema development process. To delineate it from

---

[5] www.microworkers.com.

[6] http://limesurvey.org.

the previous experiment, we asked ten colleagues who have prior experience in developing schema halves to design new schemas from scratch, in a specified period of time. For the sake of simplicity, participants were asked to develop only schema halves. In order to identify Winventor's a priori appropriateness as a *teammate*, we divided the experiment in two sections. The experiment started with the first section, where participants were asked to develop as many schema-halves as they can without Winventor's help, in ten minutes; these were called non-guided schema-halves. They continued with the second section where the experiment was then replicated under conditions in which we gave them access to fifteen randomly selected schema halves, developed by Winventor; the results were called guided schema halves.

Results: On average, we found that Winventor helped participants develop twenty schema halves, whereas without Winventor's help, they only developed seven schema-halves. Ostensibly, a schema sentence analysis that we undertook, showed that Winventor helped them develop schema halves that are based on different sentence patterns/types (see Table 3). These tests revealed that the guided developed schemas have a variety of sentence types (29% based compound sentences, 44% on complex sentences, 26% on compound-complex sentences, 1% on simple sentences). On the other hand, regarding the non-guided schema-halves, results showed that 33% of them are based on compound sentences, 63% on complex sentences and 4% on compound-complex sentences.

Furthermore, we analyzed our results based on the sentence structure of each schema-half. Regarding the complex and compound-complex sentences, this is a list of six different types of relationships along with the connectors they use: 1.) Cause/Effect 2.) Comparison/Contrast 3.) Place/Manner 4.) Possibility/Condition 5.) Relation 6.) Time. Results highlighted that the guided schema-halves are based on a variety of relationships, which is much richer than the non-guided schema-halves (see Fig. 5). All in all, non-guided schemas were mostly designed using the cause/effect relationship (70.5%) with the connectors "because, since, so that". The rest of them were designed by using connectors of "Time" relationship (e.g., after, as, before, since, when, whenever, while, until). Regarding the guided schemas, our results showed that they were designed based on a much richer set of connectors: 6% "Cause/Effect", 11.5% "Comparison/Contrast", 6% "Place/Manner", 7.5% "Possibility/Condition", 39% "Relation", and 30% "Time" relationship (see Fig. 5). We also incorporated a similar analysis for the schema-halves that are based on compound sentences. As anticipated, our analysis showed that the guided schema-halves, compared to non-guided schema-halves, were developed based on a variety of relationships. Specifically, 19% of them are arranged as "SV, and SV" (S: subject, V:verb), 37% as "SV, but SV", 18% as "SV; but, SV", 14% as "SV, or SV" and 12% as "SV, so SV". On the other hand, 58% of non-guided schema-halves are arranged as "SV, but SV", 37% as "SV, and SV" and 5% as "SV, for SV" (see Fig. 6).

Our observations show that Winventor seems to motivate and inspire participants develop richer and more diverse schema halves, in the shortest time

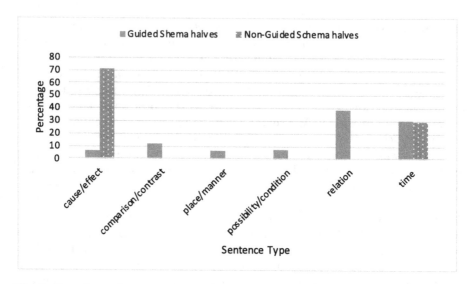

Fig. 5. Complex and compound-complex sentence types that were developed based on guided-schema halves (designed with Winventor's help) and non-guided schema halves.

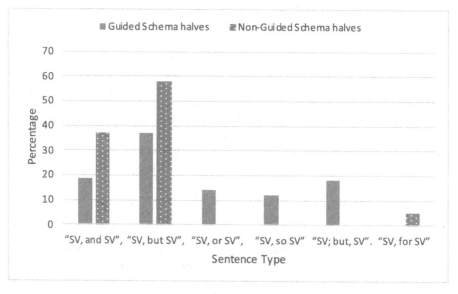

Fig. 6. Compound sentence types that were developed based on guided-schema halves (designed with Winventor's help) and non-guided schema halves.

possible. The results are inline with a recent work that we undertook [11], where it was shown that schemas developed by crowdworkers have a similar hardness to those developed by experts.

4.2   Deep Learning Approach

In this section, we present the results of the deep learning approach. We begin by presenting the results regarding our models' training and then continue by applying the methodology on the development of schemas. For the purpose of these experiments, we trained and evaluated our system on Levesque et al.'s dataset [15]. We divided our samples into a training and a testing set following the ratio of 70%–30% and evaluated our three models. Initials results showed an accuracy of 89% on the sentence selection process, 94% on the pronoun selection process, and 91% on the pronoun-target selection process.

Schema Replication: Within this experiment, we have tested if our proposed approach is able to replicate schemas from Rahman and Ng's dataset. That is, Winventor loads all sentences from the first half of each schema, and tests if it can produce the same or similar results as the second half of each schema. Here, in contrast to the NLP approach, Winventor develops one schema/schema-half for each examined sentence (see Algorithm 1).

Sentence-Model: The results revealed that the sentence-model rejected only 170 sentences, achieving 82% of accuracy, which is very near to our initial training and testing results. Compared to our previous results (527 rejected sentences) it seems that the deep learning approach works better, meaning that it is able to correctly validate which sentences are appropriate for the development of schemas.

Definite Pronoun: In 96% of the cases (745 sentences) Winventor returned the correct pronoun. The results are in line with our training and testing results, meaning that our model is able to correctly identify the definite pronoun in sentences with multiple pronouns.

Pronoun Targets: Contrary to our expectations, Winventor returned the correct answers in only 9% of the cases (74 sentences). On the other hand, this is in line with the challenge difficulties and design purposes. Recall that the whole idea behind the WSC is to develop systems that can resolve the definite pronoun to one of its two conferences, in each schema-half. In this regard, it seems that it might be a stretch to find the correct pronoun targets in sentences with multiple candidates.

Schemas: Results showed that 745 sentences resulted in 162 schemas. This is in line with our Pronoun-Target results as the question generator automatically rejects questions that have as answers possible pronoun targets (e.g., the notification "A noun is in the question" was returned in 1698 cases). Regarding our previous results, which showed that 416 sentences resulted in 254 valid schemas, it seems that our NLP-approach can provide us with more schemas than our deep learning models. On the other hand, considering the fact that: i) the deep learning method achieved better results on the selection of both sentences and

Table 3. A subset of the schemas that were developed by humans with and without Winventor's help. The first five examples are a subset of the schemas that were given in order to inspire humans in the development of new Winograd schemas.

	Sentence	Question	Answers
	Automatically developed schemas		
1	Your governors are unjustifiably killing people and they only write the crime of the killed person to inform you	Who only write the crime of the killed person to inform you?	The governors, The people
2	This river may have been shaped by God, or glaciers, or the remnants of the inland sea, or gravity or a combination of all, but the Army Corps of Engineers controls it now	What does the Army Corps of Engineers control now?	The river, the island sea
3	Some do not eat grains, believing it is unnatural to do so, and some fruitarians feel that it is improper for humans to eat seeds as they contain future plants, or nuts and seeds, or any foods besides juicy fruits	What contain future plants?	The grains, The nuts
4	The Greeks hiding inside the Trojan Horse were relieved that the Trojans had stopped Cassandra from destroying it, but they were surprised by how well she had known of their plan to defeat Troy	Who were surprised by how well she had known of their plan to defeat Troy?	Greeks, Trojans
5	The reintroduction of a permanent diaconate has permitted the Church to allow married men to become deacons but they may not go on to become priests	Who may not go on to become priests?	The men, The deacons
	Schemas that were developed from humans with Winventor's help		
1	Because of a misunderstanding Hitler had with Stalin, he attacked his country, misjudging the level of preparation needed to withstand harsh weather conditions, and subsequently that misunderstanding had cost him the war	Who the misunderstanding cost the war?	Hitler; Stalin
2	Even though Meredith was the one who had committed the fraud, Andrea Wanted to fix everything, so she confessed and went to jail	Who went to jail?	Meredith; Andrea
3	Some fruitarians feel that it is improper for humans to eat seeds as they contain future plants	What contain future plants?	Grains, humans
4	This river may have been shaped by God, or glaciers, or the remnants of the inland sea, but the Army Corps of Engineers controls it now	What does the Army Corps of Engineers control now?	the river; the island sea
5	It is allowed by the Church married men to become deacons but they may not go on to become priests	Who may not go on to become priests?	Men; deacons
6	Since everybody could always rely on Tommy, they expected him to have a plan, and so did John, but unfortunately he got shot during this specific operation by their worst enemy	Who got shot?	John; Tommy
	Schemas that were developed from humans without Winventor's help		
1	Jack gave John the book, although he didn't need it	Who didn't need the book?	Jack; John
2	My cat hates my dog because it is jealous	Who is jealous?	My cat; My dog
3	Alice tried to reach her mother's head but she was too short	Who was too short?	Alice; her mother
4	Mary tried to calm her mother, but she was really stressed	Who was stressed?	Mary; her mother
5	Kids talk to their parents but sometimes they are too busy to listen	Who are busy?	The kids; the parents
6	Ice cream is really nice with sirup, especially when it's caramel flavoured	What is caramel flavoured?	The ice cream; the sirup

Table 4. Number of developed schemas/schema-halves based on various approaches (NLP, deep learning, and blended approach) that match Rahman and Ng's dataset (943 schemas). Regarding the initially-rejected sentences of the deep learning and blended approaches, there is an additional number of 28 sentences where our pronoun-model did not manage to correctly identify the definite pronoun.

	Rejected sentences	Used sentences	Matching answers	Matching schemas	Matching halves
NLP	527	416	254	212	254
DL	170	745	75	27	38
BL	170	745	389	234	332

definite pronouns, and ii) the question generator directly relates with the selection of the best pronoun targets, it seems that better pronoun targets could lead to the development of more schemas. That is, it appears that the pronoun-targets model is the one that thwarts the full potential of our deep learning approach.

4.3 Blended Approach

Below, we present the results by applying the methodology described in the blended approach section (see Sect. 3.4). Specifically, we performed an analysis regarding Winventor's ability in replicating and developing schemas from scratch. Additionally, we performed a speed analysis comparison between the blended and the NLP approach, which indirectly relates to the availability of schemas.

Schema Replication: Within this experiment, we report results based on Winventor's blended-mechanism on replicating schemas from Rahman and Ng's dataset. Like before, the results are expressed in terms of accuracy.

Results showed that in 50% of the cases (389) Winventor selected the correct answer pair, which is 40% more than the deep learning approach (see Table 4). Regarding the schema development process, our analysis showed that Winventor was able to develop 332 schema halves that match the Rahman and Ng's dataset; 70% of them (234) were found to be schemas. In the case of schema halves, this means 27% more than the NLP, and 158% more than the deep learning approach. Furthermore, in the case of schemas, this means 10% more than the NLP, and 159% more than the deep learning approach.

We observed that if we remove any of the NLP factors the performance is further reduced, showing the importance of every single factor in the schema development process. The results ultimately show that our blended approach replicates more schemas than both the other methods, which is very important considering the challenge difficulties. On the other hand, our findings would seem to show that the development/sentence ratio of the NLP approach is better than the blended approach. According to our findings, 61% of the sentences of the NLP approach were successfully used in the development of schema halves, whereas in the blended approach only 43% of the sentences resulted in schema halves. This suggests that the NLP approach works better with the question generator mechanism. This may have occurred because the question generator needs to successfully output the semantic relations of a given piece of text in order to develop the questions; It seems that sentences that were rejected by the NLP approach are very difficult to be used with the question generator [7]. The results might suggest that a better question generator could lead to the development of more schemas.

We also performed a speed analysis. Since the availability of more schemas directly relates to the ability to run a WSC-based CAPTCHA service [10], it is important for Winventor to be able to develop schemas at a sufficiently fast pace. Our results showed that the blended approach is able to return results in 1.5 h instead of 5 h for the NLP approach, meaning that Winventor can develop, on average, 3 schemas per minute.

Schema Development: Within this experiment, we report results of Winventor's blended-approach, on developing schemas from scratch. In this regard, we fed Winventor with the same Wikipedia dataset, like in Sect. 4.1, and compared the two approaches. Specifically, we randomly selected 2000 Wikipedia sentences that were previously used for the NLP approach.

In contrast to previous findings—recall that the NLP approach returned 23 schema halves of which 16 were schemas—the blended approach returned 39 schema halves of which 25 were schemas. At the same time, 1587 sentences were rejected from our sentence model (79%), whereas 1978 sentences were rejected by the NLP approach (99%). On average, the blended approach provided 52% more schema-halves and 44% more schemas than the NLP approach. In general, regarding the number of the developed schemas, the performance was a little disappointing. The prime cause of this discrepancy seems to be due to the structure of the sentences found on the Web. This realization is in line with the previous section, where Winventor was able to replicate more schemas, as the sentences that were used were designed by humans. Furthermore, not surprisingly though, there were some discrepancies due to our sentence model limitations. Recall that in previous examples all of the sentences were validated as they were manually designed by humans. On the other hand, as some Wikipedia sentences did not include pronouns, our deep learning sentence-model mistakenly identified them as valid sentences. This might lead to the conclusion that our data augmentation process was not sufficient, meaning that more valid sentences are required in order to do better training.

One of the most surprising results to emerge from our analysis is the number of the developed schemas compared to the time needed. According to our results, the blended approach parsed 20000 sentences in 1 h, whereas the NLP approach required 12 h; the results show that the blended approach is 91.67% faster than the NLP approach. In general, although performance was not perfect, we still believe that results highlighted the importance of mixing machine learning and semantic analysis to achieve better results. In this regard, and based on both the Wikipedia dataset at hand (88 million sentences) and our current results (39 schema halves from 20000 sentences), it seems that Winventor could provide us, approximately, with 1.7 million schema halves or 1 million schemas when applied on the entire Wikipedia dataset. However, we are aware that these numbers are not guaranteed, as this depends on the structure of the sentences found on the Web. Overall, the results ultimately show that via the interaction between the two approaches we were able to enhance the schema development process. This also shows the possibilities of combining the two approaches in future challenges, which is already in full swing with recent research in the field of AI [18].

5   Related Work

The first and only Winograd Schema Challenge that took place in 2016 required the organizers to manually develop a collection of 89 Winograd schemas. For evaluation purposes they designed a questionnaire where participants were requested to resolve the schemas [5]. As stated in the literature, the development of Winograd schemas was found to be troublesome, difficult and too burdensome to do on a yearly or biennial basis [21]. The challenge, which was designed based on the questionnaire results, consisted of two rounds, where, the first one included 60 Winograd halves (as pronoun disambiguation problems, or PDPs) and the second 60 Winograd schemas.

In a recent work, which in part served as a motivation for this one, we have demonstrated the possibility of using the WSC as a novel form of CAPTCHA [10]. While designing good CAPTCHAs is a tedious task, through an experiment that we designed and undertook we showed that a Winograd CAPTCHA is generally faster to solve than, and equally entertaining with, the most typical existing CAPTCHA tasks. The ultimate goal of that work was to attract security researchers to participate in future challenges for tackling the WSC. As this CAPTCHA service requires multiple Winograd schemas to be displayed on a daily basis, it is in direct relation with what Winventor seeks to do: to offer a continuously-replenished pool of Winograd schemas.

Davis [4] demonstrated the possibility of using the Winograd schemas as a machine translation challenge. According to the author, Winograd schemas with special gender characteristics of their answers could be used to advance the machine translation field. Consider, for instance, the following schema-half, a slightly modified example from Davis et al.'s dataset, to see how it can be used in a translation from English to French: "The city councilmen refused to give the women a permit for a demonstration because they [feared/advocated] violence". In the first sentence (with "feared" as the special word), the definite pronoun "they" would refer to councilmen and would be translated to "ils" in French, whereas in the second sentence (with "advocated" as the special word), "they" would refer to women and would be translated to "elles" in French. In this regard, Winventor could be used to provide us with schemas that could enhance a translation-schema database.

Our experimental set up bears a resemblance to the one proposed in another work [11], where it was shown that workers who collaborate on crowdsourcing platforms could develop Winograd schemas of high quality, similar to that of experts. Compared to this work, where we are able to construct high numbers of draft machine-generated schemas, workers are able to produce a limited number of schemas but of higher quality. It seems that the collaboration of the crowd with systems like Winventor could potentially help overcome the limitations of the automated development of Winograd schemas.

Recent work has shown a significant improvement on the WSC by fine-tuning large pre-trained language models, such as BERT (Bidirectional Encoder Representations from Transformers) [13]. That work introduces a method for generating large-scale WSC-like examples—although not exactly WSC schemas, like in our work—by masking repeated occurrences of nouns (130 million examples, downscaled to 2.4 million). Their large developed dataset (MASKEDWIKI) indirectly shows that an automated way for the development of schemas will be helpful to the research community.

The importance of an automated way to develop Winograd schemas is not unrelated to WINOGRANDE, a large-scale dataset of 44 thousand examples collected via crowdsourcing [26]. To prevent the development of the same schemas, workers are primed by a randomly chosen topic from a WikiHow article. The idea of a randomly chosen topic shows the importance of Winventor's categorization dataset.

6   Conclusion and Future Work

We have presented Winventor, a machine-driven approach for the development of Winograd schemas. Given that the development of schemas is hard and troublesome even for humans, Winventor comes into play as a schema replenishment mechanism, and as an assistant for the schema design process. Our experiments offer evidence that this can be achieved with two different approaches, the pure NLP approach, which provides a limited number of schemas, albeit with multiple variations, and a blended approach, which provides a bigger number of schemas, albeit one for every single sentence. In either case, the variability generally stems from which method is used. The evidence from this study suggests that systems like Winventor could act as teammates to further enhance the schema development process by humans. Winventor does not purport to replicate the thought process of humans in the development of schemas, as there is still no clear path yet on how this could be achieved. Future studies will have to identify other mechanisms to help humans and machines produce efficiently more schemas. Perhaps a better question generator, able to develop questions for more schema halves, would further help the schema development process. Furthermore, schemas could be offered to the crowd for further validation, leading to an interaction that would amplify human and machine intelligence by combining their complementary strengths.

Acknowledgments. This work was supported by funding from the EU's Horizon 2020 Research and Innovation Programme under grant agreements no. 739578 and no. 823783, and from the Government of the Republic of Cyprus through the Directorate General for European Programmes, Coordination, and Development. The authors would like to thank Ernest Davis for sharing his thoughts and suggestions on this line of research.

References

1. Budukh, T.U.: An Intelligent Co-reference Resolver for Winograd Schema Sentences Containing Resolved Semantic Entities. Master's thesis, Arizona State University (2013)
2. Chollet, F.: The future of deep learning. Future **8**, 2 (2017)
3. Chowdhury, G.G.: Natural language processing. Ann. Rev. Inf. Sci. Technol. **37**(1), 51–89 (2003)
4. Davis, E.: Winograd schemas and machine translation (2016)
5. Davis, E., Morgenstern, L., Ortiz, C.: Human tests of materials for the winograd schema challenge 2016 (2016)
6. Deepa, K.A., Deisy, C.: Statistical pair pruning towards target class in learning-based anaphora resolution for tamil. Int. J. Adv. Intell. Paradigms **9**(5–6), 437–463 (2017)
7. Heilman, M., Smith, N.A.: Question Generation via Overgenerating Transformations and Ranking. Carnegie-Mellon Univ Pittsburgh Pa Language Technologies Inst, Technical report (2009)
8. Hirth, M., Hoßfeld, T., Tran-Gia, P.: Anatomy of a crowdsourcing platform – using the example of microworkers.com. In: Proceedings of the 5th International Conference on Innovative Mobile and Internet Services in Ubiquitous Computing, pp. 322–329. IEEE (2011)
9. Isaak, N., Michael, L.: Tackling the Winograd schema challenge through machine logical inferences. In: Pearce, D., Pinto, H.S. (eds.) STAIRS. Frontiers in Artificial Intelligence and Applications, vol. 284, pp. 75–86. IOS Press (2016). http://dblp.uni-trier.de/db/conf/stairs/stairs2016.html$?$IsaakM16
10. Isaak, N., Michael, L.: Using the Winograd schema challenge as a CAPTCHA. In: Lee, D., Steen, A., Walsh, T. (eds.) GCAI-2018. 4th Global Conference on Artificial Intelligence. EPiC Series in Computing, vol. 55, pp. 93–106. EasyChair (2018). https://doi.org/10.29007/rnk8. https://easychair.org/publications/paper/pV9V
11. Isaak, N., Michael, L.: WinoFlexi: a crowdsourcing platform for the development of winograd schemas. In: Liu, J., Bailey, J. (eds.) AI 2019. LNCS (LNAI), vol. 11919, pp. 289–302. Springer, Cham (2019). https://doi.org/10.1007/978-3-030-35288-2_24
12. Isaak., N., Michael., L.: Winventor: a machine-driven approach for the development of winograd schemas. In: Proceedings of the 12th International Conference on Agents and Artificial Intelligence - Volume 2: ICAART, pp. 26–35. INSTICC, SciTePress (2020). https://doi.org/10.5220/0008902600260035
13. Kocijan, V., Cretu, A.M., Camburu, O.M., Yordanov, Y., Lukasiewicz, T.: A urprisingly robust trick for winograd schema challenge. arXiv preprint arXiv:1905.06290 (2019)
14. LeCun, Y., Bengio, Y., Hinton, G.: Deep learning. Nature **521**(7553), 436–444 (2015)

15. Levesque, H., Davis, E., Morgenstern, L.: The winograd schema challenge. In: Thirteenth International Conference on the Principles of Knowledge Representation and Reasoning (2012)
16. Levesque, H.J.: On our best behaviour. Artif. Intell. **212**, 27–35 (2014)
17. Liu, Q., et al.: Probabilistic reasoning via deep learning: neural association models. arXiv preprint arXiv:1603.07704 (2016)
18. Marcus, G.: Deep learning: a critical appraisal (2018)
19. Michael, L.: Machines with websense. In: Proceeding of 11th International Symposium on Logical Formalizations of Commonsense Reasoning (Commonsense 13) (2013)
20. Mitkov, R.: Robust pronoun resolution with limited knowledge. In: Proceedings of the 17th International conf. on Computational linguistics-Volume 2, pp. 869–875. Association for Computational Linguistics (1998)
21. Morgenstern, L., Davis, E., Ortiz, C.L.: Planning, executing, and evaluating the winograd schema challenge. AI Mag. **37**(1), 50–54 (2016)
22. Morgenstern, L., Ortiz, C.: The winograd schema challenge: evaluating progress in commonsense reasoning. In: Twenty-Seventh IAAI Conference (2015)
23. Mudge, R.: The design of a proofreading software service. In: Proceedings of the NAACL HLT 2010 Workshop on Computational Linguistics and Writing: Writing Processes and Authoring Aids, pp. 24–32. Association for Computational Linguistics (2010)
24. Peer, E., Samat, S., Brandimarte, L., Acquisti, A.: Beyond the Turk: An Empirical Comparison of Alternative Platforms for Crowdsourcing Online Research. In: Diehl, K., Carolyn Yoon, D. (eds.) NA - Advances in Consumer Research, vol. 43, pp. 18–22. MN, Association for Consumer Research (2015)
25. Rahman, A., Ng, V.: Resolving complex cases of definite pronouns: the winograd schema challenge. In: Proceedings of the 2012 Joint Conference on Empirical Methods in Natural Language Processing and Computational Natural Language Learning, pp. 777–789. EMNLP-CoNLL 2012, Association for Computational Linguistics, Stroudsburg, PA, USA (2012). http://dl.acm.org/citation.cfm?id=2390948. 2391032
26. Sakaguchi, K., Bras, R.L., Bhagavatula, C., Choi, Y.: WINOGRANDE: an adversarial winograd schema challenge at scale. arXiv preprint arXiv:1907.10641 (2019)
27. Schubert, L.K.: Semantic representation. In: Twenty-Ninth AAAI Conference on Artificial Intelligence (2015)
28. Sharma, A., Vo, N.H., Aditya, S., Baral, C.: Towards addressing the winograd schema challenge - building and using a semantic parser and a knowledge hunting module. In: Proceedings of the Twenty-Fourth International Joint Conference on Artificial Intelligence, IJCAI, pp. 25–31 (2015)
29. Stacey, J.: Text mining wikipedia for misspelled words (2011)
30. Wolfe, J.H.: Automatic question generation from text-an aid to independent study. In: Proceedings of the ACM SIGCSE-SIGCUE Technical Symposium on Computer Science and Education, pp. 104–112 (1976)

Cognitive Map Query Language
for Temporal Domains

Adrian Robert, David Genest[(✉)], and Stéphane Loiseau

LERIA, Université d'Angers, Angers, France
{adrian.robert,david.genest,stephane.loiseau}@univ-angers.fr

Abstract. This article introduces the temporal cognitive maps model and its associated query language.

A cognitive map is a graph used to model strategies or influence systems. Each node represents a concept and each edge represents an influence.

One limit of cognitive maps is that temporal features cannot be taken account in the model.

This article proposes an extended model of cognitive map, called temporal cognitive maps, that includes temporal features in a cognitive map.

This article also proposes a temporal cognitive map query language that accesses all the components of a temporal cognitive map: concept, influence and temporal features.

Keywords: Time representation · Cognitive map · Query language · OWL

1   Introduction

This article is an improved and extended version of [27]. These extensions have been made: *(i)* bibliography in cognitive maps, temporal models and query languages are extended, *(ii)* seven primitives, instead of two, are presented in detail, *(iii)* the TCMQL language, along with its syntax and semantics is presented.

The *cognitive map* [1] model is a semantic model coming from cognitive psychology. This model represents strategies expressed in an influence system. A cognitive map is an oriented graph whose nodes are labeled by *concepts* and edges, called *influences*, are labeled by an *influence value*. Influence values belong to a predefined value set. A sequence of influences from a node to another makes a *path*. The model can infer a *propagated influence value* from a node to another. A *taxonomic cognitive map* [18] is a cognitive map defined on a *taxonomy*. The taxonomy organizes the concepts with'kind of' type relations: the nodes of the taxonomic cognitive map are labeled by concepts of the taxonomy.

The Kifanlo project aimed to study the evolution of the fishing strategies in the Atlantic coast from 1970 to 2016. About fifty cognitive maps have been designed with fishermen to model their fishing strategies. Half of those maps represents fishing strategies in the seventies, the other half represent current

© Springer Nature Switzerland AG 2021
A. P. Rocha et al. (Eds.): ICAART 2020, LNAI 12613, pp. 215–235, 2021.
https://doi.org/10.1007/978-3-030-71158-0_10

fishing strategies, each map contains 25 to 50 nodes. A cognitive map edition software, VSPCC, has been used and improved[1]. In the Kifanlo project, there is a significant number of concepts that have a temporal semantics. These concepts usually repeat periodically over time like seasons, fishing seasons and so on... This periodicity of the concepts should be taken into account in cognitive maps; that was not the case in VSPCC. So, this paper introduces temporal cognitive maps, which is a new model that extends taxonomic cognitive maps with a temporal ontology for representation and reasoning. No previous works including temporal aspects in concepts of cognitive maps has been proposed in bibliography.

As seen in [27], because of the periodicity of the concept's semantics, the *temporal ontology* aims to represent *periodic intervals* [22]. It uses *temporal assertions* that are triples made of two periodic intervals related by a *comparison predicate*. A *temporal cognitive map* is defined on a temporal ontology; it contains a set of temporal assertions that link the nodes of the cognitive map to the temporal ontology. The nodes can thus be temporally characterized, meaning that a certain influence holds with respect to the temporal assertions of its nodes. To reason with a temporal cognitive map, this article presents the 'Temporal Cognitive Map Query Language' *TCMQL*, which is an extension of the query language for cognitive maps CMQL [25]. TCMQL is made with seven primitives which two of them are temporal *primitives* presented in [27]: *TimeInfo* and *Compare*. *TimeInfo* lets the user access the periodic interval associated with a node. *Compare* infers new information using temporal assertions of nodes and the temporal ontology. This extension provides a way to use the temporal information of the model for a further analysis of cognitive maps. TCMQL, as well as VSPCC extended to temporal cognitive maps, have been delivered to the researchers in geography that work in the Kifanlo project for further analysis[2].

The article is composed of five parts. The first is the bibliographic part. The second recalls the taxonomic cognitive map model. The third introduces the temporal cognitive map model. The fourth presents primitives. The fifth describes the TCMQL language.

2 Bibliography

The bibliography related with cognitive map query language for temporal domains can be connected to three kinds of works. First and principally, the works that focus on cognitive maps. Second, the numerous works that are related on temporal models. Third, the research works about query languages.

Cognitive maps and Bayesian networks [23] are two models that stem on causal graphical networks. While Bayesian networks focus on the computation of influences based on conditional probabilities, cognitive maps focus mainly on the visualization. So cognitive maps are easier to understand for several types

---

[1] VSPCC [19] has been implemented after the thesis of Aymeric LeDorze [17], for the project Kifanlo.

[2] This work is being led in the project *Analyse Cognitive de Savoirs (ACS)* granted by the french region Pays de la Loire from 2017 to 2020.

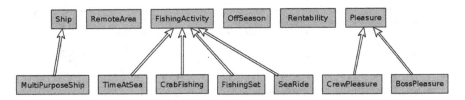

Fig. 1. A taxonomy T_1 [27].

of user. The semantic of the influence, called propagated influence in cognitive map model can vary depending on the subject and users. It also can be seen as a drawback of cognitive maps versus Bayesian networks that stem always on the same theoretical basis. In cognitive map models, depending on the problem, various sets of influence values can be used: $\{-, +\}$ and $[-1, 1]$ are the most used; there are also $\{none, some, much, alot\}$ [15] or $\{-4, -3, -2, -1, 0, 1, 2, 3, 4\}$ [17]. Cognitive maps are used in many fields such as social sciences [1], biology [21] and geography [4].

An important domain for artificial intelligence research is a study of temporal concepts. Many aspects of time exist, and many solutions to model them and make some inferences with them have been proposed. No cognitive map model takes into account temporal concepts, but few articles integrates temporal aspects on the influences: they explain the delay needed to make an influence from a concept to another one, for instance [3,29] provides a way to describe an approximation of the time needed for making an influence. For our applications, the core of the temporal aspects needed to be modelled are periodic. A periodic interval [7,8,22] is a type of non-convex interval [16], which is an interval composed of several unconnected convex subintervals. Periodic intervals have the particularity to be composed of subintervals that have the same length and are equally spaced. For instance 'winter' is a periodic interval.

The relational model [6] is the standard model to manage databases. Relational databases are queried with the popular query language SQL that is a standard; SQL [14] is known by many people, including non-engineer's ones. So, the syntax of SQL provides the bases of many query languages for databases or knowledge bases. It is the case of SPARQL [11] that is the language used to query RDF knowledge bases; it is also the case for query languages for property graphs, like GraphQL, PGQL, Cypher [9]. There is no query language to query cognitive maps, except CMQL [26] that is the base of TCMQL, the query language presented in this paper. CMQL is a query language whose syntax is close to the one of SQL and whose semantics is similar to the one of the domain relational calculus [20,26]. CMQL's particularity resides in the use of many primitives that allow to access the various features of a taxonomic cognitive map set.

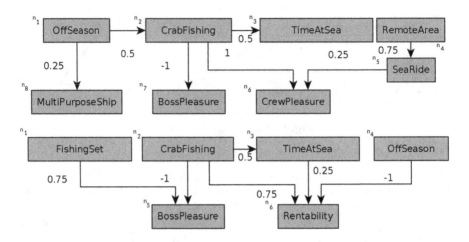

Fig. 2. Two taxonomic cognitive maps, $CC1$ (top) and $CC2$ (bottom) [27].

3 Taxonomic Cognitive Map

A taxonomic cognitive map is a graph whose nodes and edges are respectively labeled by a concept of a taxonomy and by an influence value; the taxonomy aims to organize the concepts. The taxonomy is even more useful when using a set of cognitive maps, to make sure that different cognitive maps use the same concepts [5].

3.1 Taxonomic Cognitive Map Model

The taxonomy organizes the concepts by specifying a specialization relation between them

Definition 1 (Taxonomy). *Let C be a concept set. A taxonomy $\mathcal{T} = (C, \leq)$ is a set of rooted trees of concepts that represents a partial order relation $\leq$ whose meaning is 'kind of'.*

Example 1. $\mathcal{T}_1$ is the taxonomy of the Fig. 1. Some concepts are ordered by a relation of specialization. For instance, the relation $MultiPurposeShip \leq Ship$, meaning that $MultiPurposeShip$ is a kind of $Ship$, is represented by an arrow in the figure.

The most specialized concepts of the taxonomy are said elementary.

Definition 2 (Elementary Concepts). *Let $\mathcal{T} = (C, \leq)$ be a taxonomy. The elementary concepts of $\mathcal{T}$ are: $elem_{\mathcal{T}} = \{c \in C / \ \forall c' \in C, c' \leq c \implies c' = c\}$.*

Example 2. In $\mathcal{T}_1$, the elementary concepts are $elem_{\mathcal{T}_1} = \{MultiPurposeShip, RemoteArea...\}$; only the concepts $Ship$, $FishingActivity$ and $Pleasure$ are not elementary.

A taxonomic cognitive map is a graph whose nodes and edges are respectively labeled by an elementary concept of a taxonomy and an influence value. The influence value represents the strength of the influence and belongs to a defined value set which can be qualitative or quantitative, discrete or continuous.

Definition 3 (Taxonomic Cognitive Map). *A taxonomic cognitive map defined on a taxonomy* $T = (C, \leq)$ *and a value set* I *is an oriented labeled graph* $CM = (N,E,labelN, labelE)$ *such that:*

- N : *the nodes of the graph.*
- $E \subseteq N \times N$: *the edges are called influences.*
- $labelN : N \rightarrow elem_T$ *is a label function on the nodes.*
- $labelE : E \rightarrow I$ *is a label function on the edges.*

Example 3. $CC1$ and $CC2$ are the two taxonomic cognitive maps of the Fig. 2. They are defined on the taxonomy T_1 of the Fig. 1 and the value set $I = [-1, 1]$. Note that, in the figure, each node has a unique identifier per map $n_1, n_2...$ that is displayed only for clarity in this paper. An influence labeled by 1 (resp. -0.25) means that the source node influences strongly (resp. weakly) and positively (resp. negatively) the destination node. In our application, each fisherman designs a cognitive map: $CC1$ has been designed by *fisherman1*, and $CC2$ by *fisherman2*. In $CC2$, the node n_2 (*CrabFishing*) influences strongly and negatively (-1) the node n_5 (*BossPleasure*); which means that the boss does not like fishing crab.

3.2   Taxonomic Cognitive Map Inference

A path is a sequence of influence which represents a way a node of the map influences another. A path is said minimal if it does not contain any cycle. Notice that between two nodes, there can be more than one minimal path.

Definition 4 (Path, *source*, *dest*, *Paths$_{CM}$*). *Let* $CM = (N,E,labelN,labelE)$ *be a taxonomic cognitive map defined on* $T = (C, \leq)$ *and* I. *Let* $a, b \in N$ *be two nodes of CM.*

- *A* path P *from* a *to* b *is a sequence of length length$_P \geq 1$ of influences* $(u_i, u_{i+1}) \in E$ *(with* $i \in [0; length_P - 1]$*) such that* $a = u_0$ *is the source of* P *and* $b = u_{length_P}$ *is the destination of* P. *This path is denoted by* $a \rightarrow u_1 \rightarrow \cdots \rightarrow b$.
- *source$_P$* $= labelN(a)$ *is the source concept of* P *and* *dest$_P$* $= labelN(b)$ *is the destination concept of* P.
- *A path* P *is said* minimal *if* $\forall i, j \in [0; length_P], i \neq j \Rightarrow u_i \neq u_j$.
- *The set of all minimal paths on CM is denoted by Paths$_{CM}$. Let* S *be a set of taxonomic cognitive maps, the set of paths on* S, *denoted by Paths$_S$, is defined as Paths$_S = \bigcup_{s \in S} Paths_s$.*

Example 4. This example is based on $CC2$ (Fig. 2). $p_1 = n_2(CrabFishing) \rightarrow n_3$ ($TimeAtSea$) $\rightarrow n_6$ ($Rentability$) is a minimal path from the source node n_2 to the destination node n_6, $length_{p_1} = 2$. $p_2 = n_2$ ($CrabFishing$) $\rightarrow n_6$ ($Rentability$) is a minimal path, $length_{p_2} = 1$, $source_{p_2} = CrabFishing$.

One of the main features of cognitive maps is their ability to infer the propagated influence from any node to any other one, which denotes a value of influence. To do that, every influence path from the node to the other is involved. The propagated influence from a node to another can be calculated differently depending on the map's semantics and on the value set on which it is defined. In all cases, the computation of the propagated influence first assigns a path value for each path with a function, then secondly aggregates those values with an other function.

Definition 5 (Propagated Influence, PV). *Let CM=(N,E,labelN,labelE) be a taxonomic cognitive map defined on $\mathcal{T} = (C, \leq)$ and I.*

- *The* path value *is a function $PV_{path} \colon Paths_{CM} \rightarrow I$ which infers the propagated influence of a path.*
- *The* propagated influence value *is a function $PV \colon N \times N \rightarrow I$ which infers the propagated influence from a node to another one, aggregating the path values of each path between the two nodes.*

In this paper, we will use the value set $I = [-1, 1]$. A product function will be used as path value and a mean function for the propagated influence value as it is often done in cognitive maps [10].

Example 5. This example is based on $CC2$ (Fig. 2). The paths p_1 and p_2 come from the example 4. Let's infer the propagated influence value between n_2 and n_6, respectively labeled by *CrabFishing* and *Rentability*. The set of all minimal paths between those two nodes is $\{p_1, p_2\}$. To infer the propagated influence value between n_2 and n_6 we need $PV_{path}(p_1)$ and $PV_{path}(p_2)$. From the chosen product function, we have $PV_{path}(p_1) = 0.5 * 0.25 = 0.125$ and $PV_{path}(p_2) = 0.75$. Then, aggregating the path values, $PV(n_2, n_6) = \frac{(0.125 + 0.75)}{2} = 0.44$. So the propagated influence value from n_2 to n_6 is 0.44.

The taxonomic cognitive map model can also infer a taxonomic influence value which is used to infer the influence value between any pair of concepts of the taxonomy. Note that the propagated influence value is a particular case of the taxonomic influence value where the concepts are elementary. The taxonomic influence value is not presented in this article, but is described in [5].

4   Time Representation

This section introduces the periodic intervals, then proposes a temporal ontology defined on those periodic intervals and temporal assertions that compare pairs of them. So, the temporal cognitive map can be introduced, it is a taxonomic cognitive map defined on a temporal ontology.

4.1 Periodic Intervals

The periodic intervals of Osmani and Balbiani [2, 22] that also considers qualitative relations between them are chosen. This approach is relevant to the Kifanlo project and, in general, seems suited for cognitive maps as it offers more flexibility and handles the lack of precise information.

Definition 6 (Periodic Interval). *A periodic interval is a non-convex interval whose subintervals are equally spaced and have equal length.*

Example 6. January is a periodic interval since all its subintervals last one month and occur every year. *Summer* is also a periodic interval, with subintervals lasting three months and occurring every year.

This paper proposes to specify those periodic intervals with qualitative relations between two intervals using a comparison predicate. Those predicates are the 16 relations of Osmani [22] plus 5 relations. The relations of Osmani are very similar to the 13 relations of the Allen's intervals, except that the precedence and its inverse are replaced by 5 relations which consider the periodicity. This paper also considers two relations (*inside/disjoint*) that combine some of Osmani's relations and three relations ($<,>,=$) that compare duration of intervals, which can not be done with Osmani's intervals.

Definition 7 (Comparison Predicate). *A comparison predicate is a binary relation whose domain and range are periodic intervals. $\mathcal{P}$ is the set of the 21 comparison predicates:* $\{m,mi,s,si,d,di,f,fi,o,oi,eq,ppi,mmi,moi,omi,ooi,in,dis,<,=,>\}$

Fig. 3. Two cyclic representations of relations between periodic intervals [27].

The table below shows the 16 relations of Osmani & Balbiani, the column *meaning* explains the relations through an ordering of the boundaries ($A1,A2,B1,B2$) of the periodic intervals A and B. This ordering comes from the CYCORD theory [28]. Two added relations are: '*in*' (Inside) which is the disjunction of '*s*', '*d*', '*f*', '*eq*' and '*dis*' (Disjoint) which is the disjunction of '*m*', '*mi*', '*mmi*', '*ppi*'.

To these relations are also added three relations to compare the duration of periodic intervals: '<', '>' and '='.

Periodic intervals and comparison predicates defined above are used to represent temporal knowledge through temporal assertions. A temporal assertion is an assertion which represents a relation between two periodic intervals. It is a triple (*interval, predicate, interval*).

Definition 8 (Temporal Assertion). $\mathcal{P}$ *is the set of the 21 comparison predicates. A* temporal assertion *is an assertion which constitute a triple* (e_1, p, e_2) *such that* $p \in \mathcal{P}$ *and* e_1 *and* e_2 *are periodic intervals.*

Example 7. Relations between periodic intervals are often represented on a circle (Fig. 3) which is to be read clockwise. The first circle represents the temporal assertion (*Spring, meets, Summer*) and it matches the ordering ('*SpringBegins*', '*SpringEnds*' = '*SummerStarts*', '*SummerEnds*') of the second row of the table. Its inverse relation is *mi* (*is met by*), so we have (*Summer, is met by, Spring*). The second circle illustrates the temporal assertion (*CrabSeason, meets & is met, Summer*). *CrabSeason* is related to *Summer* by the relation '*meets & is met*' which means that the crab season starts when summer ends and ends when summer starts. Some comparison predicates are used to compare duration, for instance in the temporal assertion (*Day, <, Month*) the comparison predicate '<' is used to compare the duration of *Day* and *Month*.

name	meaning	inverse
eq (*equals*)	$A1 = B1$, $A2 = B2$	(*eq*)
m (*meets*)	$A1$, $A2 = B1$, $B2$	**mi**
s (*starts*)	$A1 = B1$, $A2$, $B2$	**si**
d (*during*)	$A1$, $A2$, $B2$, $B1$	**di**
f (*finishes*)	$A1$, $A2 = B2$, $B1$	**fi**
o (*overlaps*)	$A1$, $B1$, $A2$, $B2$	**oi**
ppi (*precedes & is preceded*)	$A1$, $A2$, $B1$, $B2$	(*ppi*)
mmi (*meets & is met*)	$A1 = B2$, $A2 = B1$	(*mmi*)
moi (*meets & is overlapped*)	$A1$, $B2$, $A2 = B1$	**omi**
ooi (*overlaps & is overlapped*)	$A1$, $B2$, $B1$, $A2$	(*ooi*)
in (*inside*)	$s \vee d \vee f \vee eq$	
dis (*disjoint*)	$m \vee mi \vee mmi \vee ppi$	
< (*is shorter*)	$\overline{A1A2} < \overline{B1B2}$	**>**
= (*has same length*)	$\overline{A1A2} = \overline{B1B2}$	(**=**)

Fig. 4. Meaning of comparison predicates [27].

4.2 Time Ontology

Many temporal ontologies exist, amongst those, OWL-Time ontology [13] is a W3C reference and one of the most used. It turns out that time ontologies do not take into account periodic intervals and certainly not the qualitative relations to compare them. That is why this paper introduces a new temporal ontology that considers periodic intervals and could be added to existing heavier temporal ontologies like OWL-Time. Our light-weight temporal ontology is composed of the class *PeriodicInterval*, the 21 comparison predicates as object properties, a set of instances of *PeriodicInterval* and a set of temporal assertions on these individuals.

Definition 9 (Temporal Ontology). *A temporal ontology $\mathcal{O} = (\mathcal{P}, \mathcal{E}, \mathcal{A})$ is an ontology such that:*

- *$\mathcal{P}$ is the set of the comparison predicates.*
- *$\mathcal{E}$ is a set of periodic intervals.*
- *$\mathcal{A}$ is a set of temporal assertions of the ontology.*

Example 8. The Fig. 5 represents the temporal ontology $\mathcal{O}_1$. The periodic intervals of this ontology are $\mathcal{E}=\{Spring,\ CrabSeason,\ Year\ \dots\}$ and the temporal assertions are $\mathcal{A} = \{(Season, <, Year),\ (CrabSeason,\ meets\ \&\ is\ met,\ Summer)\ \dots\}$.

4.3 Temporal Cognitive Map

A temporal cognitive map is a taxonomic cognitive map defined on a temporal ontology. Each node of the map is labeled by a periodic interval and a set of temporal assertions links those periodic intervals to the ontology. This way, nodes may be temporally characterized.

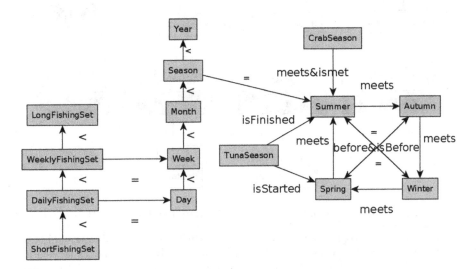

Fig. 5. A partial representation of the temporal ontology $\mathcal{O}_1$ [27].

Definition 10 (Temporal Cognitive Map). *Let $\mathcal{O} = (\mathcal{P}, \mathcal{E}, \mathcal{A})$ be a temporal ontology, let $T = (C, \leq)$ be a taxonomy and I a value set. A temporal cognitive map TCM defined on $\mathcal{O}$ is a sextuplet $(N, E, labelN, labelE, labelT, \mathcal{A}_{TCM})$ such that:*

- *$(N, E, labelN, labelE)$ is a taxonomic cognitive map defined on $T(C, \leq)$ and I.*
- *labelT is a label function on the nodes of the map which attaches a unique periodic interval e_n to a node n.*
- *$\mathcal{A}_{TCM}$ is a set of temporal assertions (e_1, p, e_2) where $labelT^{-1}(e_1) \in N$ and $e_2 \in \mathcal{E}$.*

Example 9. This example[3] describes the two temporal cognitive maps of the Fig. 6: *TCM*1 and *TCM*2. A temporal assertion (in yellow) of a temporal cognitive map is visually represented below the node (in blue) that it characterizes. The periodic interval attached to the node is visually omitted, that is why temporal assertions are written as couples and not triples. For instance in *TCM*1, the node labeled by *OffSeason* is characterized by the temporal assertion (*TCM1_OffSeason, si, Summer*) where *TCM1_OffSeason* is the omitted periodic interval attached to this node and '*si*' is the comparison predicate '*isStartedBy*'. Notice that several temporal assertions can be attached to the same node,

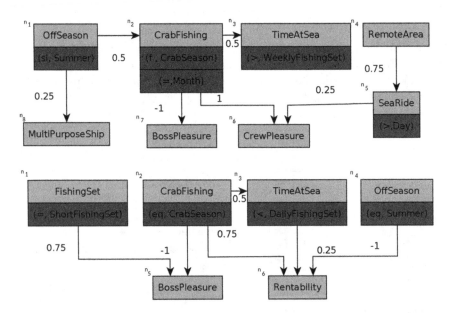

Fig. 6. Two temporal cognitive maps, *TCM*1 (top) and *TCM*2 (bottom) [27].

---

[3] A set of temporal cognitive maps based on the same taxonomy, value set and temporal ontology will be considered. Since many maps may contain nodes labeled by the same concept, the following notation is used: The periodic interval associated with a node labeled by a concept '*c*' of a map '*m*' is noted '*m_c*'.

as it is the case for the node labeled by *CrabFishing* in *TCM1*. This node is characterized by a periodic interval that lasts one month ($=$, *Month*) at the end of the *CrabSeason* (f, *CrabSeason*). *fisherman1* fishes crab for one month at the end of the crab season.

5 Primitives

In this section, we first define what a primitive is and how it can be used. Then we recall the basic primitives of the model, concerning the presence of concepts in a map (*IsInMap*), taxonomy (*KindOf*), paths (*Path*, *PathValue*) and influences (*InfluenceValue*). Finally, we present in detail primitives concerning the temporal aspects: *TimeInfo* and *Compare*, which allow to access the concepts' temporal assertions and compare them.

5.1 Primitive and Primitive Formula

A primitive is defined as a relation indexed by its attributes, definitions and notations are based on those of the domain relational calculus: an element of a relation, i.e. a tuple, is seen as a mapping from the attributed of the relation to values of the domains.

Definition 11 (Primitive). *Let $A = \{A_1, \ldots A_n\}$ be a set of attributes and $D = \{D_1, \ldots D_n\}$ be a set of domains. A primitive is a relation $R(A_1 : D_1, \ldots, A_n : D_n)$ of arity n, its value is a subset of the cartesian product of its domains indexed by its attributes : $val(R) \subseteq \{t : A \to D_1 \cup \ldots \cup D_n / \forall i \in [1,n] t(A_i) \in D_i\}$.*

In order to provide examples in this section, we also introduce primitive formulas. A primitive formula can be seen as a very simple query and will be used in the condition clause of TCMQL queries. A primitive formula is a syntactic construction based on a primitive, whose arguments are the attributes of the primitive, they can be variables or constants.

Definition 12 (Primitive Formula). *A primitive formula f on a n-ary primitive P is an expression $P(X_1, \ldots X_n)$ where each X_i, called term, is either a variable, i.e. a syntactic expression prefaced with "?" or a constant.*
Let $f = P(X_1, \ldots, X_n)$ be a primitive formula, let m be the number of variables in $X_1 \ldots X_n$. The value of f is the set of tuples of arity m : $\{t / \exists t_1 \in val(P), \forall i \in [1,n] \ t_1(A_i) = X_i$ if X_i is a constant; $t_1(A_i) = t(X_i)$ if X_i is a variable\}.

5.2 The Path Primitive

The *Path* primitive links a path with its source concept and destination concept, it provides an access to paths and concepts.

Definition 13 (Path). *Let S be a set of temporal cognitive maps defined on the same temporal ontology $\mathcal{O} = (\mathcal{P}, \mathcal{E}, \mathcal{A})$, taxonomy $T = (C, \leq)$ and I. Path(m : $S, c_1 : C, c_2 : Cp : Paths_S$) is a primitive whose value is $\{(m, c_1, c_2, p)/\ m \in S, p \in Paths_m, source_p = c_1\ and\ dest_p = c_2\}$.*

Example 10. – The following examples uses the maps $TCM1$ and $TCM2$ (Fig. 6).

– *Path(TCM2,CrabFishing,Rentability, ?p)* is a primitive formula. Its value is a unary relation whose set of tuples (?p) is:

$?p$
$CrabFishing \rightarrow TimeAtSea \rightarrow Rentability$
$CrabFishing \rightarrow Rentability$

– *Path(TCM2,CrabFishing, ?c2, ?p)* is a primitive formula. It uses $TCM2$. Its value is a relation whose set of tuples (?c2,?p) is:

$?c2$	$?p$
$TimeAtSea$	$CrabFishing \rightarrow TimeAtSea$
$Rentability$	$CrabFishing \rightarrow TimeAtSea \rightarrow Rentability$
$Rentability$	$CrabFishing \rightarrow Rentability$
$BossPleasure$	$CrabFishing \rightarrow BossPleasure$

5.3 The PathValue Primitive

The primitive *PathValue* links a path with its value.

Definition 14 (PathValue). *Let S be a set of temporal cognitive maps defined on the same temporal ontology $\mathcal{O} = (\mathcal{P}, \mathcal{E}, \mathcal{A})$, taxonomy $T = (C, \leq)$ and I. PathValue(m : $S, p : Paths_S, i : I$) is a relation whose value is $\{(m, p, i)/m \in S, p \in Paths_m\ and\ i = PV_{path}(p)\}$.*

Example 11. PathValue*(TCM2,CrabFishing $\rightarrow$ TimeAtSea $\rightarrow$ Rentability, ?i)* is a primitive formula. Its value is a unary relation whose set of tuples (?i) is:

$?i$
0.125

5.4 The InfluenceValue Primitive

The primitive *InfluenceValue* links two concepts of the taxonomy with the propagated influence value from the first to the second.

Definition 15 (InfluenceValue). *Let S be a set of temporal cognitive maps defined on the same temporal ontology $\mathcal{O} = (\mathcal{P}, \mathcal{E}, \mathcal{A})$, taxonomy $T = (C, \leq)$ and I. InfluenceValue($m : S, c_1 : C, c_2 : C, i : I$) is a relation whose value is $\{(m, c_1, c_2, i)/m = (N, E, labelN, labelE, labelT, \mathcal{A}_m) \in S, c_1, c_2 \in C, \exists n_1, n_2 \in N, labelN(n_1) = c_1, labelN(n_2) = c_2 \text{ and } i = PV(n_1, n_2)\}$.*

Example 12. InfluenceValue(TCM2, CrabFishing, Rentability, ?i) is a primitive formula. Its value is a unary relation whose set of tuples is:

?i
0.44

5.5 The IsInMap Primitive

The primitive *IsInMap* links a map and a concept of this map.

Definition 16 (IsInMap). *Let S be a set of temporal cognitive maps defined on the same temporal ontology $\mathcal{O}$, taxonomy $T = (C, \leq)$ and I. IsInMap($m : S, c : C$) is a relation whose value is $\{(m, c)/m = (N, E, labelN, labelE, labelT, \mathcal{A}_m) \in S, \exists n \in N \text{ such that } labelN(n) = c\}$.*

Example 13. IsInMap(?m, Rentability) is a primitive formula querying for maps that contains the concept *Rentability*. Its value is a unary relation whose set of tuples is:

?m
TCM2

5.6 The KindOf Primitive

KindOf is a binary primitive with two concepts of the taxonomy where the first is a kind of the second.

Definition 17 (KindOf). *Let $T = (C, \leq)$ be a taxonomy. KindOf($c_1 : C, c_2 : C$) is a relation whose value is $\{(c1, c2)/c_1 \leq c_2\}$.*

Example 14. KindOf(?c, Pleasure) is a primitive formula querying for specializations of *Pleasure*. Its value is a unary relation whose set of tuples is:

?c
Pleasure
CrewPleasure
BossPleasure

5.7   The TimeInfo Primitive

The extraction primitive *TimeInfo* links a cognitive map, a concept of this map, and the periodic interval associated with the node labeled by this concept in this map.

Definition 18 (TimeInfo). *Let S be a set of temporal cognitive maps defined on the same temporal ontology $\mathcal{O} = (\mathcal{P}, \mathcal{E}, \mathcal{A})$, taxonomy $T = (C, \leq)$ and I. Let $\mathcal{E}_S$ be the set of all periodic intervals associated with the nodes of the maps in S. The primitive TimeInfo$(m : S, c : C, i : \mathcal{E}_S)$ is a relation whose value is $\{(m, c, i)/m = (N, E, labelN, labelE, labelT, \mathcal{A}_m) \in S, \exists n \in N, labelT(n) = i$ and $labelN(n) = c\}$*

Example 15. *TimeInfo(?map, TimeAtSea, ?interval)* is a primitive formula. Its value is a binary relation whose value is the set of tuples *(?map, ?interval)* in which *?interval* is associated with the node labeled by the concept *TimeAtSea* in *?map*:

?map	?interval
$TCM1$	$TCM1\_TimeAtSea$
$TCM2$	$TCM2\_TimeAtSea$

The primitive *TimeInfo* is used here to link concepts and maps to associated periodic intervals, *TimeAtSea* is then used in $TCM1$ and $TCM2$.

Used alone the usefulness of this primitive is limited, it is often used in conjunction with the primitive *Compare* defined below.

5.8   The Compare Primitive

When the designer of a temporal cognitive map adds his domain knowledge, he adds the least amount of temporal assertions and expects the implicit ones to be taken into account: an inference is thus necessary. 151 inference rules are used for these inferences, they are OWL2 [12] rules. The comprehensive list of rules is not given in the paper as it is too long but available online [24]. The rules about the 16 Balbiani's relations can be found also in the references [2], a few other rules about the new predicates are added.

Example 16. Here are some inference rules:

- *SubObjectPropertyOf(during inside)* which means $(e_1,\ during,\ e_2) \rightarrow (e_1,\ inside, e_2)$
- *SubObjectPropertyOf(starts $<$)* which means $(e_1,\ starts,\ e_2) \rightarrow (e_1,\ <, e_2)$
- *SubObjectPropertyOf(ObjectPropertyChain(meets startedBy) meets)* which means $(e_1,\ meets,\ e_2) \wedge (e_2,\ startedby,\ e_3) \rightarrow (e_1,\ meets, e_3)$

Using the ontology of the Fig. 5 and the cognitive maps Fig. 6, new assertions are inferred:

- *(CrabSeason, disjoint, Summer)* which means that the crab season is outside the summer. This assertion comes from the assertion *(CrabSeason, mmi, Summer)* of $\mathcal{O}_1$ and the rule $(e_1, \text{mmi}, e_2) \rightarrow (e_1, \text{disjoint}, e_2)$.
- *(TunaSeason, >, Season)* which means that the season of tuna is longer than a calendar season. This assertion comes from the assertions *(TunaSeason, fi, Summer)*, *(Season, =, Summer)* of $\mathcal{O}_1$ and the rules $(e_1, \text{fi}, e_2) \rightarrow (e_1, <, e_2)$ and $(e_1, >, e_2) \wedge (e_2, =, e_3) \rightarrow (e_1, >, e_3)$.
- *(TCM1_CrabFishing, meets, Summer)* which means that Summer starts when the crab season ends. This assertion comes from the assertions *(TCM1_CrabFishing, f, CrabSeason)* of TCM1, *(CrabSeason, mmi, Summer)* of $\mathcal{O}_1$ and the rule $(e_1, \text{f}, e_2) \wedge (e_2, \text{mmi}, e_3) \rightarrow (e_1, \text{meets}, e_3)$.

Inferences can be carried out on a set that contains the temporal assertions of the ontology and the temporal assertions of each temporal cognitive map. The saturated set is the set of temporal assertions that can be deduced from all these temporal assertions and the inference rules.

Definition 19 (Saturated Set). *Let $\mathcal{R}$ a set of rules and $S = \{(CM_1, labelT_1, \mathcal{A}_1), \ldots, (CM_k, labelT_k, \mathcal{A}_k))\}$ be a set of k temporal cognitive maps defined on $\mathcal{O} = (\mathcal{P}, \mathcal{E}, \mathcal{A})$, $\mathcal{I}_S$ is the saturated set of temporal assertions resulting from the inference of the rules of $\mathcal{R}$ on the set $\mathcal{A} \cup \bigcup_{i=1}^{k} \mathcal{A}_i$.*

The primitive *Compare* uses the saturated set of temporal assertions, it is a relation between two periodic intervals and a comparison predicate which is a valid comparison between these intervals.

Definition 20 (Compare). *Let S be a set of temporal cognitive maps defined on the same ontology $\mathcal{O} = (\mathcal{P}, \mathcal{E}, \mathcal{A})$ where $\mathcal{P}$ is the set of comparison predicates. Let $\mathcal{E}_S$ be the set all periodic intervals associated with the nodes of the maps in S. Let $\mathcal{I}_S$ the saturated set of all temporal assertions.*

The primitive Compare(e1: $\mathcal{E}_S \cup \mathcal{E}$, p: $\mathcal{P}$, e2: $\mathcal{E}_S \cup \mathcal{E}$) is a relation whose value is $\{(e_1, p, e_2)/(e_1, p, e_2) \in \mathcal{I}_S\}$.

Example 17. The following examples use the ontology $\mathcal{O}_1$ (Fig. 5) and the temporal cognitive maps $TCM1$ and $TCM2$ (Fig. 6).

- *Compare(TunaSeason, ?pred, ?interval)* is a primitive formula which aims to compare the periodic interval *TunaSeason* (which is from *Spring* to *Summer* according to $\mathcal{O}_1$) to any other periodic interval. There are many result tuples like *(>, Summer)* since the *Summer* finishes the *TunaSeason*:

?pred	?interval
isStarted	Spring
isFinished	Summer
>	Summer
>	Week
isFinished	TCM2_OffSeason
...	...

– *Compare(TCM1_ TimeAtSea, ?pred, Month)* is a primitive formula. There is no answer since we can not evaluate the comparison of two durations both greater than a week *(TCM1_ TimeAtSea, >, Week)* and *(Month, >, Week)* with no more information:

?pred

– *Compare(Winter, ?pred, CrabSeason)* is a primitive formula. This primitive formula asks the relations between the *Winter* and the *CrabSeason*. Since the *CrabSeason* starts at the end of the summer and ends at its beginning, the *Winter* is during the *CrabSeason* and thus shorter. We obtain the three following tuples:

?pred
during
Inside
<

Although the complexity of the inferences is high (at least EXPTIME), it has not been a problem in our system for two reasons. Firstly, a cognitive map is hand designed and it is a visual model so it is usually quite a small graph, for instance in the Kifanlo project a thirty nodes map is a big one. Secondly, the saturated set is precomputed and queries give an answer in an acceptable time in our application. Nevertheless, to go one step further, a study should be done to evaluate the theoretical complexity and how to face it depending on maps structure.

6   Temporal Cognitive Map Query Language

TCMQL is the extension of CMQL that integrates the temporal primitives *Time-Info* and *Compare*. TCMQL is designed to query a set of temporal cognitive maps defined on the same temporal ontology.

TCMQL's syntax is close to SQL's syntax : SELECT selects variables ?x...,
FROM indicates the maps to query and WHERE describes the conditions. Four examples are given here along with their results and comments, they are based on T_1 (Fig. 1), O_1 (Fig. 5) and $TCM1, TCM2$ (Fig. 6).

Our aim is to provide a simple and intuitive language: a user does not need to precisely understand the underlying semantics. In this section we first describe examples of TCMQL queries and their result, then we provide syntax and semantics.

6.1 Queries

Example 18. The primitives `IsInMap` and `KindOf` are used in this example. In plain English this query means: 'In which maps are used the concepts types of Pleasure?'.

```
SELECT ?map,?concept FROM TCM1,TCM2 WHERE{
KindOf(?concept, Pleasure)
AND IsInMap(?map,?concept)
}
```

The first condition allows to obtain the concepts that are types of Pleasure in the taxonomy. The second condition gets the couples (map, concept) such that the concept belongs to the map. The result of this query is the list of the following tuples (?map,?concept):

?map	?concept
$TCM1$	$BossPleasure$
$TCM1$	$CrewPleasure$
$TCM2$	$BossPleasure$

The result shows what are the types of the concept pleasure and in which maps they appear.

Example 19. In plain English this query means: 'When does fisherman1(TCM1) fish crabs in comparison to fisherman2(TCM2)?'.

```
SELECT ?pred FROM TCM1,TCM2 WHERE{
TimeInfo(TCM1, CrabFishing, ?e1) AND
TimeInfo(TCM2, CrabFishing, ?e2) AND
Compare(?e1,?pred,?e2) }
```

The first two conditions allow to get the temporal entities of the concept CrabFishing in TCM1 and TCM2. The third condition allows to get all comparison predicates between those two temporal entities that are characterized by "finishes CrabSeason" and "= Month" for the one in TCM1 and by "equals CrabSeason" for the other. The result is made of the tuples (?pred):

?pred
$finishes$
$<$

The result shows that the fisherman1 fishes at the end of the fisherman2's fishing period, for a shorter period.

Example 20. In plain English this query means: 'Which duration of FishingSets influences BossPleasure?'.

```
SELECT ?p, ?e2, ?map FROM TCM1,TCM2 WHERE{
Path(?map,FishingSet,BossPleasure,?path)
AND TimeInfo(?map,FishingSet,?e1)
AND Compare(?e1, ?p, ?e2))}
```

The first condition allows to get the maps in which FishingSet influences BossPleasure (TCM2). The two following conditions allow to get the temporal information about FishingSet in the right map.

$?p$	$?e2$	$?map$
$=$	$ShortFishingSet$	$TCM2$
$<$	Day	$TCM2$
$\ldots$	$\ldots$	$\ldots$

The result shows that according to the fisherman2 (TCM2), the BossPleasure is influenced by a short period of fishingset.

Example 21. This query asks the concepts in summer which influence a concept kind of `Pleasure`.

```
SELECT ?map,?c1,?i,?c2 FROM TCM1,TCM2
WHERE{KindOf(?c2,Pleasure) AND
Value(?map,?c1,?c2,?i) AND ?i != 0 AND
TimeInfo(?map,?c1,?e1) AND
Compare(?e1,in,Summer)}
```

The first condition allows to get all concepts ?c2 kind of Pleasure. The second and third ones allow to get the concepts ?c1 that influences ?c2 with their influence value. The two last conditions filter only the concepts ?c1 in summer.

$?map$	$?c1$	$?i$	$?c2$
$TCM1$	$OffSeason$	-0.5	$BossPleasure$
$TCM1$	$OffSeason$	0.5	$CrewPleasure$

The results show that, according to the fisherman1, the OffSeason which is in Summer influences negatively the pleasure of the boss and positively the pleasure of the crew.

6.2 Syntax and Semantics

Generally speaking, a query is mainly composed of variables to be returned, a data source and formulas. These formulas are recursive and can be combined with each other according to different rules. The atomic formulas are either primitive formulas or expression formulas. The primitive formulas, presented in the previous section, are composed of a primitive name and terms being either variables or constants. Expression formulas are composed of two terms and of an operator. We present here a (simplified) syntax of the TCMQL language in the Backus-Naur form (BNF).

Query ::= SelectClause FromClause WhereClause
SelectClause ::= 'SELECT' ResultsClause (',' ResultClause)*
ResultClause ::= 'DISTINCT'? Variable
FromClause ::= 'FROM' ('ALL'| *MapName* (',' *MapName*)*)
WhereClause ::= 'WHERE' "FormulaClause"
FormulaClause ::= '(' FormulaClause ')'   (1)
    | FormulaClause 'AND' FormulaClause   (2)
    | FormulaClause 'OR' FormulaClause   (3)
    | AtomicClause
AtomicClause ::= ExpressionClause | PrimitiveClause
ExpressionClause ::= T Operator T   (4)
Operator ::= '<' | '<=' | '=' | '!=' | '>=' | '>'
T ::= Variable | *Constant*
Variable ::= '?' *VariableName*
PrimitiveClause ::= *PrimitiveName* '(' T (',' T) + ')'   (5)

The semantics of TCMQL is based on the semantics of the domain relational calculus. We describe here an partial and simplified version of the semantics. The main idea behind this definition of semantics is that each numbered formula above denotes a relation whose attributes are the variables of the formula. We need to introduce some notations first:

- Let F be a formula and let $v(F)$ be the set of variables of F, each variable v_i has an associated domain $d(v_i)$.
- Let V be a set of variables, $d(V)$ is the set of associated domains.
- Let $V = \{V_1, \ldots, V_n\}$ be a set of variables, $\Pi(V : d(V))$ denotes the cartesian product of domains $d(V_1) \times \ldots \times d(V_n)$ indexed by the elements of V.

Let F be a formula, the meaning of F, denoted $mng(F)$, is a relation of arity $|v(F)|$ such that:

(1) $mng((F)) = mng(F)$
(2) $mng(F_1 \text{ AND } F_2) = mng(F_1) \times \Pi(v(F_2) - v(F_1) : d(v(F_2) - v(F_1))) \cap mng(F_2) \times \Pi(v(F_1) - v(F_2) : d(v(F_1) - v(F_1)))$
(3) $mng(F_1 \text{ OR } F_2) = mng(F_1) \times \Pi(v(F_2) - v(F_1) : d(v(F_2) - v(F_1))) \cup mng(F_2) \times \Pi(v(F_1) - v(F_2) : d(v(F_1) - v(F_1)))$
(4) $mng(T_1 \text{ op } T_2) =$
   - $\{t \in \Pi(T_1 : d(T_1))/t(T_1) \text{ op } T_2\}$ if T_1 is a variable and T_2 is a constant.
   - $\{t \in \Pi(T_2 : d(T_2))/T_1 \text{ op } t(T_2)\}$ if T_1 is a constant and T_2 is a variable.
   - $\{t \in \Pi(\{T_1, T_2\} : d(\{T_1, T_2\}))/t(T_1) \text{ op } t(T_2)\}$ if both T_1 and T_2 are variables.
(5) $mng(\text{PrimitiveName}(T_1, \ldots, T_n)) =$ value of the primitive formula (cf. definition 12)

7   Conclusion

This paper introduces a new model of cognitive map, called temporal cognitive map, that allows to extend cognitive maps with temporal features, using an ontology which includes periodic intervals. This paper also proposes a language, called TCMQL, which allows to query sets of temporal cognitive maps.

The temporal features of temporal cognitive maps are issued of real needs. The ACS project uses temporal cognitive maps to better modelling fishermen's strategies that were expressed in the Kifanlo project with simple cognitive maps. The VSPCC software has been developed to edit and use temporal cognitive maps. VSPCC can also execute TCMQL queries. The implementation uses the temporal ontology owl-time to which is added a class PeriodicInterval as a subclass of the main class TemporalEntity and comparison predicates as properties. VSPCC is available online [19].

Two perspectives of the research can be given. First, we are currently working with geographers of the LETG laboratory (University of Nantes, CNRS UMR(6554). TCMQL is used to analyze the fishing strategy in Atlantic from 1970 to nowadays. These results will be published in a geographical journal. The promotion of TCMQL in international laboratories of geography is one of our aims. Second, in our computer science laboratory, evolution of TCMQL should be considered in the next years. The merge of temporal aspects in TCMQL with geographical aspects is in progress. A reflection on how to compare automatically maps to provide learning abilities to our system has to be taken.

References

1. Axelrod, R.M.: Structure of Decision: The Cognitive Maps of Political Elites. Princeton University Press, Princeton (1976)
2. Balbiani, P., Osmani, A.: A model for reasoning about topologic relations between cyclic intervals. In: Principles of Knowledge Representation and Reasoning, pp. 378–385 (2000)
3. Carvalho, J.P., Tome, J.A.B.: Rule based fuzzy cognitive maps-expressing time in qualitative system dynamics. In: 10th IEEE International Conference on Fuzzy Systems, vol. 1, pp. 280–283. IEEE (2001)
4. Çelik, F.D., Ozesmi, U., Akdogan, A.: Participatory ecosystem management planning at Tuzla lake (Turkey) using fuzzy cognitive mapping. arXiv preprint q-bio/0510015 (2005)
5. Chauvin, L., Genest, D., Loiseau, S.: Ontological cognitive map. Int. J. Artif. Intell. Tools 18(05), 697–716 (2009)
6. Codd, E.F.: The Relational Model for Database Management: Version 2. Addison-Wesley Longman Publishing Co. Inc., Boston (1990)
7. Ermolayev, V., Batsakis, S., Keberle, N., Tatarintseva, O., Antoniou, G.: Ontologies of time: review and trends. Int. J. Comput. Sci. Appl. 11(3), 57–115 (2014)
8. Ermolayev, V., Keberle, N., Matzke, W.-E., Sohnius, R.: Fuzzy time intervals for simulating actions. In: Kaschek, R., Kop, C., Steinberger, C., Fliedl, G. (eds.) UNISCON 2008. LNBIP, vol. 5, pp. 429–444. Springer, Heidelberg (2008). https://doi.org/10.1007/978-3-540-78942-0_42

9. Francis, N., et al.: Cypher: an evolving query language for property graphs. In: Proceedings of the 2018 International Conference on Management of Data, SIGMOD 2018, pp. 1433–1445. Association for Computing Machinery (2018)
10. Genest, D., Loiseau, S.: Modélisation, classification et propagation dans des réseaux d'influence. Technique et Science Informatiques **26**, 471–496 (2007)
11. Harris, S., Seaborne, A., Prud'Hommeaux, E.: SPARQL 1.1 Query Language. W3C recommendation (2013)
12. Hitzler, P., Krötzsch, M., Parsia, B., Patel-Schneider, P.F., Rudolph, S.: OWL 2 web ontology language primer. W3C recommendation (2009)
13. Hobbs, J.R., Pan, F.: Time ontology in OWL. W3C Candidate Recommendation (2020). https://www.w3.org/TR/owl-time/
14. International Organization for Standardization: ISO IEC 9075:2016: Information Technology - Database languages SQL. ISO, Geneva, Switzerland (2016)
15. Kosko, B.: Fuzzy cognitive maps. Int. J. Man Mach. Stud. **24**, 65–75 (1986)
16. Ladkin, P.B.: Time representation: a taxonomy of internal relations. In: AAAI, pp. 360–366 (1986)
17. Le Dorze, A.: Validation, synthèse et paramétrage des cartes cognitives. Ph.D. thesis, LERIA, Université d'Angers, France, November 2013
18. Le Dorze, A., Chauvin, L., Garcia, L., Genest, D., Loiseau, S.: Views and synthesis of cognitive maps. In: Ramsay, A., Agre, G. (eds.) AIMSA 2012. LNCS (LNAI), vol. 7557, pp. 119–124. Springer, Heidelberg (2012). https://doi.org/10.1007/978-3-642-33185-5_13
19. LeDorze, A., Robert, A.: https://sourcesup.renater.fr/projects/vspcc (2016)
20. Louis, G., Pirotte, A.: A denotational definition of the semantics of DRC, a domain relational calculus. In: VLDB, pp. 348–356 (1982)
21. Martin, B.L., Mintzes, J.J., Clavijo, I.E.: Restructuring knowledge in biology: cognitive processes and metacognitive reflections. Int. J. Sci. Educ. **22**(3), 303–323 (2000)
22. Osmani, A.: Introduction to reasoning about cyclic intervals. In: Imam, I., Kodratoff, Y., El-Dessouki, A., Ali, M. (eds.) IEA/AIE 1999. LNCS (LNAI), vol. 1611, pp. 698–706. Springer, Heidelberg (1999). https://doi.org/10.1007/978-3-540-48765-4_74
23. Pearl, J.: Probabilistic Reasoning in Intelligent Systems: Networks of Plausible Inference. Elsevier, Amsterdam (2014)
24. Robert, A.: (2019). http://www.info.univ-angers.fr/pub/adrian/rules/rules.html
25. Robert, A., Genest, D., Loiseau, S.: A query language for cognitive maps. In: Agre, G., van Genabith, J., Declerck, T. (eds.) AIMSA 2018. LNCS (LNAI), vol. 11089, pp. 218–227. Springer, Cham (2018). https://doi.org/10.1007/978-3-319-99344-7_20
26. Robert, A., Genest, D., Loiseau, S.: The taxonomic cognitive map query language: a general approach to analyse cognitive maps. In: 30th ICTAI, pp. 999–1006. IEEE (2019)
27. Robert, A., Genest, D., Loiseau, S.: Temporal cognitive maps. In: Proceedings of the 12th International Conference on Agents and Artificial Intelligence (ICAART 2020), vol. 2, pp. 58–68. INSTICC, SciTePress (2020)
28. Röhrig, R.: A theory for qualitative spatial reasoning based on order relations. In: Proceedings of the Twelfth AAAI National Conference on Artificial Intelligence, AAAI 1994, pp. 1418–1423. AAAI Press (1994)
29. Zhong, H., Miao, C., Shen, Z., Feng, Y.: Temporal fuzzy cognitive maps. In: 2008 IEEE International Conference on Fuzzy Systems (IEEE World Congress on Computational Intelligence), pp. 1831–1840. IEEE (2008)

Choose Your Words Wisely: Leveraging Embedded Dialog Trajectories to Enhance Performance in Open-Domain Conversations

Nancy Fulda[(✉)] [ID], Tyler Etchart, and Will Myers

Brigham Young University, Provo, UT 84602, USA
{nfulda,tyler.etchart,william_myers}@byu.edu
http://DRAGN.ai

Abstract. Human conversations are notoriously nondeterministic, and identical conversation histories can nevertheless accept dozens, if not hundreds, of distinct valid responses. In this paper, we present and expand upon *Conversational Scaffolding*, a response scoring method that capitalizes on this fundamental linguistic property. We envision a conversation as a set of trajectories through embedding space. Our method leverages the analogical structure encoded within language model representations to prioritize possible conversational responses with respect to these trajectories. Specifically, we locate candidate responses based on their linear offsets relative to the scaffold sentence pair with the greatest cosine similarity to the current conversation history. In an open-domain dialog setting, we are able to show that our method outperforms both an Approximate Nearest-Neighbor approach and a naive nearest neighbor baseline. We demonstrate our method's performance on a retrieval-based dialog task using a retrieval dataset containing 19,665 randomly-selected sentences. We further introduce a comparative analysis of algorithm performance as a function of contextual alignment strategy, with accompanying discussion.

Keywords: Response prioritization · Utterance retrieval · Word embeddings · Conversational AI

1 Overview

The one-to-many hypothesis of dialog as explored by Zhao et al. [30] asserts that the correct next response to for a given dialog history is not dependent on the dialog history alone, but is instead a function of many variables related to user state, world state, and dialog state, and that it is nontrivial to extract them all. This leaves connectionist approaches to dialog modeling with an interesting predicament. How can one apply a classic training paradigm to dialog modeling when there is no single right answer to the question of "what should I say next?"

© Springer Nature Switzerland AG 2021
A. P. Rocha et al. (Eds.): ICAART 2020, LNAI 12613, pp. 236–253, 2021.
https://doi.org/10.1007/978-3-030-71158-0_11

A commonly-applied solution includes the use of variational autoencoders [2, 21, 26, 28, 30], which model the unknown conversational elements as a stochastic process. While often effective, this method is data-hungry, and high-quality conversational data is scarce. Consequently, it is often necessary to train the language models on larger datasets of lesser quality, such as lightly pre-processed exchanges from online chat forums, rather than on small but high quality datasets.

In [27] we presented an alternate approach: a *Conversational Scaffolding* method that leveraged the conversational patterns in a small, high-quality scaffold corpus in order to rank candidate responses in a retrieval-based conversation system. This paper expands and improves upon that work by presenting a more detailed analysis of the scaffolding approach as well as a comparative study of algorithm performance as a function of contextual alignment method. We frame the conversational scaffolding method in terms of dialog trajectories, with linear offsets between the embedded representations of context sentences used in order to find the most appropriate match.

A key advantage of this approach is its ability to leverage the power of connectionist systems while still adhering to the conversational norms and patterns exemplified by a small, highly curated dataset. Specifically, the language model used to embed context sentences is a classic connectionist system trained on large scale, broad-topic text corpora, and is able to leverage the inherent linguistic knowledge common to such models during the embedding process. Once each sentence has been localized within an 512-dimensional linguistic space, however, the process of analyzing the dialog history and scoring candidate responses is handled via a low-resource algorithm.

1.1 The Challenge of Large Conversational Datasets

While the internet era has provided unprecedented access to large-scale text corpora across a variety of styles and topics, high-quality conversational data is more difficult to come by. Unmoderated online interactions, while plentiful and easy to harvest, often fail to exhibit the topical continuity, common courtesy, and social restraint that one might like to replicate in an automated chat system. This is caused not only by the unfortunate prevalence of trolling [6, 9, 24], but also by the varying personalities, ideologies, and social competencies of the conversation participants themselves. Dialogs extracted from movie scripts [32] or technical support forums [18] are often more coherent, but fail to exhibit the conversational patterns of common, everyday speech. (It would seem odd indeed if an automated personal assistant trained using such data were to provide unsolicited technical advice, or profess its newly-discovered love toward its conversation partner).

A further complication arises from the crowd-sourced nature of all such online conversational data. The life histories, demographics, political opinions, and general likes and dislikes of the conglomerate chatters are so disparate that any language model trained using them is almost guaranteed to seem schizophrenic, producing mutually incompatible statements with distressing frequency.

We seek to alleviate these challenges by introducing a conversational response-scoring method that does not require such massive amounts of data, and can instead be used in conjunction with a relatively small scaffold corpus. Our method also does not require any network updates or fine-tuning of the Incorporated language models, and is often able to respond appropriately to conversation histories that are not well represented in the scaffold corpus because it relies, not on the specific embedding locations of individual sentences, but rather on their locations relative to one another. It is the general *patterns* of language, the dialog trajectories that describe the transition from question to answer and back again, that we seek to emulate.

1.2   The Analogical Structure of Embedding Spaces

In addition to generating and categorizing text, it has become increasingly popular to extract the hidden layer activations of large language models for the purpose of semantic evaluations. Favorite models for this purpose include Sentence-level embedding spaces such as skip-thought vectors [15], quick-thought vectors [17], InferSent [10], and Google's Universal Sentence Encoder [8], as well as contextualized word embedding models such as BERT [12] and ELMo [23].

A driving force behind this tendency is the phenomenal and fascinating ability of word-level embedding spaces to encode human-interpretable knowledge in the relative locations of embedded texts. For example, the word2vec [19], GLoVE [22], and FastText [4] models can be used to solve linguistic analogies of the form *a:b::c:d*. This is generally accomplished using vector offsets such as [*Madrid - Spain + France ≈ Paris*] or [*walking - walked + swimming ≈ swam*] [14,20]. The sums and differences between the embedded representations of the first three words are calculated, and then a nearest-neighbor search across the model's vocabulary (excluding the three source words) produces the solution to the analogical query.

Our research extends this notion of analogical relationships into the realm of multi-word embeddings. We postulate (and show via our results) that sentence-level embedding spaces can contain similar analogical relationships, and that these relationships can be utilized to select plausible responses in open-domain dialogs. Thus, rather than evaluating candidate responses based on their strict distance to exemplars in the scaffold corpus, we instead rely on the relative distance between pairs of sentences in order to locate an idealized response vector which corresponds to point *d* in the classic *a:b::c:d* analogical form. Candidate responses are scored based on their cosine distance from this target point.

2   Embeddings, Scaffolds, and Dialog Trajectories

We begin our response-ranking process by encoding a reference corpus, called our *scaffold*, using one of many available pre-trained embedding models. Incoming utterances are matched against the scaffold corpus, and the top *n* contextual matches are used to calculate an analogically coherent response, or *target point*

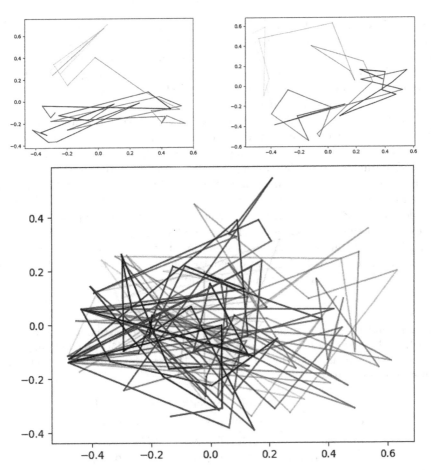

Fig. 1. PCA Reduction: Dialog trajectories from three conversations in the Chit-Chat Dataset, encoded using Google's universal sentence encoder lite [8]. Blue lines indicate chat partner 1, red lines are chat partner 2. Alpha values correspond to the index of each utterance over time, with faint lines representing earlier messages and dark lines representing later ones. The objective of our scaffolding algorithm is to find subpaths within the scaffold corpus which match the general location and trajectory of the current dialog history, then user the next point on the highest-ranking subpaths to select the best response candidate. (Color figure online)

within the embedding space. The candidate response with the lowest cosine distance from the target point is selected as our agent's dialog output.

Figure 1 shows sample dialog trajectories from three conversations. In each, it is possible to observe the meandering of the conversation topic and utterance type over time. Critically, one can observe a certain tendency toward repetition, both within each plot and between the plots as a whole, and this behavior is equally visible when dimensionality reductions other than PCA are used. In short, while language is combinatorial in nature and thus able to represent a nearly infinite span of ideas, the *patterns* of language are far more tractable. Certain types of statements encourage certain types of responses, regardless of the specific conversation topic. These patterns can be detected and imitated via the use of analogical relations within a pre-trained embedding space. Thus, a relatively small corpus of exemplars can be used to guide the response ranking system of a conversational agent.

After due consideration, we selected Google's Universal Sentence Encoder Lite [8] as the embedding model of choice for this application. This decision was based primarily on its unusually high performance as a heuristic for semantic distance. Experiments in our laboratory revealed that USE Lite was able to achieve a Pearson's r score of 0.751 on the 2017 Semantic Textual Similarity benchmark, the highest score of any model we tried, as shown in Table 1. It is possible that Google's large model would have performed even better, but exploratory applications found the large model too slow to implement on a sentence-by-sentence basis. In a real-time conversational scenario, there is no possibility of batch-processing utterances, and so we opted to consider only those models which might reasonably be employed in a real-world setting.

Table 1. Model performance on the SemEval 2017 Semantic Textual Similarity Benchmark [7] and the Stanford Natural Language Inference Corpus [5] evaluated using Pearson's *r* and Spearman's *rho* (higher is better). The greatest value in each column is shown in bold-face text.

	STS r	STS rho	SNLI r	SNLI rho
GPT-2	−0.052	0.092	−0.007	0.019
InferSent	0.718	0.702	0.273	0.279
Google use lite	**0.751**	**0.737**	**0.366**	**0.367**
Transformer-XL	0.341	0.341	0.112	0.112
Skip-thought	0.214	0.296	0.046	0.108
BERT BoW	0.495	0.490	0.166	0.174
FastText BoW	0.547	0.543	0.248	0.257
Glove BoW	0.404	0.440	0.241	0.247

2.1   Conversational Scaffolding

Conversational Scaffolding [27] is a response-ranking algorithm that relies on the structural properties of an analogically coherent embedding space in order to select high-quality candidates from a repository of possible responses. In this paper, the embedding space used is that provided by Google's universal sentence encoder lite [8].

Figure 2 gives an overview of our conversational scaffolding algorithm. Given a dialog context of variable length, our algorithm first locates a set of high-quality

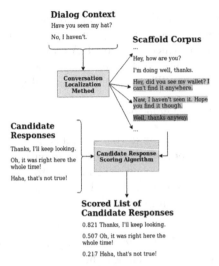

Fig. 2. Workflow diagram: The dialog context is converted to an array of sentence embeddings using Google's Universal Sentence Encoder, then passed to an embedded concatenation localization function to determine the best contextual match(es). The matched utterances (orange) along with their direct successors (red) are then passed to the Response Scoring Algorithm, which assigns a numerical value to each candidate response. Image originally published in [27]. (Color figure online)

contextual matches within the scaffold corpus. These contextual matches, along with the dialog sentence directly following each context match, are then passed to one of several scoring algorithms.

2.2   Contextual Alignment

We use a *contextual alignment* process to match incoming sentences against similar sentence patterns within a scaffold corpus. This can be done naively by using an Approximate Nearest Neighbor algorithm based on a simple Euclidean distance metric. In this paradigm, for a dialog context of length n, the optimal contextual match can be identified as follows:

$$min_z \sum_{i=1}^{n} ||v_i - s_{z+i}|| \qquad (1)$$

where $\{v_1, ..., v_n\}$ are the vector embeddings of the n most recent sentences in the current dialog and $\{s_{z+1}, ..., s_{z+n}\}$ represent the vectors located within a sliding window of length n beginning at element z of the pre-embedded scaffold corpus. The notation $||x||$ represents the Euclidean norm of vector x.

This Euclidean distance approach is easy to calculate, but it ignores the powerful analogical structure inherent within the embedding space [27]. In order to capture such subtleties, we compare this approach against two alternate method of contextual alignment: *Embedded Concatenation* and *Difference Vectors*.

Embedded Concatenation. *Embedded Concatenation* leverages the structure of the embedding space by concatenating the input sentences prior to encoding them via Universal Sentence Encoder Lite [8]. A naive Euclidean distance metric is then used to match the embedded concatenation against each element in the pre-embedded scaffold corpus. The optimal contextual match is:

$$min_z \; ||embed(h_1 + ... + h_n) - s_z|| \tag{2}$$

where $\{h_1, ..., h_z\}$ are the plain text (i.e. *un*embedded) utterances in the dialog history, the $+$ symbol represents string concatenation (with an extra space inserted between sentences), s_z is an arbitrary vector located within the pre-embedded scaffold corpus, and $embed(x)$ denotes the process of embedding a plain text utterance x to obtain its corresponding vector representation.

Difference Vectors. The *Difference Vectors* approach embeds each sentence in the dialog history separately, then searches for a contextual match with the smallest average distance across all sentences:

$$min_{\sum_i} \; (\; ||embed(h_{i+1}) - embed(h_i)|| \; - \; ||s_{i+1} - s_i|| \;)^2 \tag{3}$$

Note that the described localization methods assume that only a single, optimal, contextual match is desired. This was done for simplicity. In reality, it is often beneficial to take the k best matches, and in fact many of the scoring algorithms in Sect. 3.2 require $k > 1$. The scattershot diagram in Sect. 2.3 assumes a value of $k = 3$ for clarity. In our empirical experiments, a value of $k = 5$ was used.

2.3 Candidate Response Scoring

In [27] we presented three candidate response scoring algorithms for conversational scaffolding, each of which assumes a set of candidate responses g_i and a recent dialog sentence c. We briefly review these algorithms here.

1. *Naive Analogy*. This algorithm is based on the simplifying assumption that the closest context match within the scaffold dataset must of necessity be paired with an optimal response. (In reality, a scaffold sentence with a slightly larger distance from the user utterance might actually be paired with a superior response; this is addressed in the scattershot and flow vector methods, below). Using a value of $k = 1$, the naive analogy locates the sentence in the scaffold corpus whose embedded representation is closest to the most recent dialog utterance, then follows the conversational trajectory between that sentence and its (embedded) successor in order to find a target point.

2. *Flow Vectors*. The flow vectors approach is based on the idea that conversations tend to "flow" from certain regions of embedding space into others, and that all matching utterance pairs will reflect the same general flow direction. Accordingly, rather than simply taking the most promising dialog, we average

the dialog trajectories from multiple contextual matches and then look for a candidate utterance that lies along the resulting flow direction.

3. *Scattershot.* The scattershot scoring algorithm takes the one-to-many property of language into account by assuming that there are many valid responses for each dialog context, and searches for a candidate response that matches *any* of several high-scoring context matches. In this method, the vector differences between each context match and its respective successor are calculated separately, then added to the vector embedding of the most recent utterance in the dialog history. The result is a set of k target points, each of which represents a possible response. The candidate nearest to *any one* of these targets receives the highest score.

Of these three algorithms, we found in prior work that the *scattershot* algorithm performed most impressively with respect to the baselines as well as to the other conversational scaffolding algorithms. We expand upon that result in this paper by comparing the algorithms across a variety of context lengths and contextual matching strategies, and show that *scattershot* continues to be the strongest method.

3 The Scattershot Algorithm

The *scattershot* algorithm (Fig. 3, Algorithm 1) is based on three key principles: (a) the idea that dialog modeling is a nondeterministic task, and there are many correct responses to a given dialog history, (b) under most dialog control paradigms, the selection of possible response candidates is finite, and (c) in many conversational settings, it is not necessary to find the *optimal* response for a given context; you merely have to be good enough to satisfy the user.

Accordingly, the scattershot method examines a number of trajectories identified in the scaffold conversation as being a good contextual match for the current dialog history, and then extends each trajectory to find the target point, or 'ideal response', that would be implied by this trajectory. The repository of candidate responses is then examined to find the candidate which has the minimum distance of any sentence to any target point, and this response is given the highest ranking. Intuitively, this process can be described as seeking a candidate response that is related to the dialog history in the same way that the scaffold corpus successor is related to the sentences that precede it. It is an extension at the sentence level of the classic A:B::C:D analogy structure commonly used in conjunction with word embeddings [14,20].

3.1 Scattershot Performance as a Function of Contextual Matching

No algorithm exists in isolation. The effectiveness of the scattershot algorithm (and other conversational scaffolding methods) is impacted by the methods used to select the contextual matches to be used as its starting points. We evaluate this impact on a response prioritization task across four datasets, which were cleaned and pre-processed as described in [27].

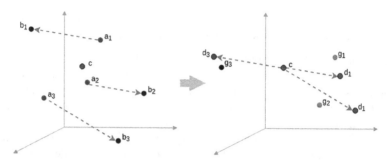

Fig. 3. Diagrammatic depiction of the *scattershot* algorithm for conversational scaffolding. c (green) represents the embedded input sentence, a_i (blue) represent the nearest embedded sentences from the scaffold corpus, b_i (red) represent the associated embedded successors to a_i in the scaffold, $d_i = c + (b_i - a_i)$ (yellow) represent the 'ideal' responses, and g_i (grey and black) represent embedded candidate responses with g_3 (black) representing the response selected by the scattershot scoring algorithm. Image originally from [13]. (Color figure online)

Algorithm 1. Scattershot.

Inputs:
h = Embedded conversation history.
r = Embedded candidate responses produced by the enerators.
$C_{n \times \|h\| - 1}$ = Embedded Chit-Chat dataset

Output:
$S = \{s_1 \ldots s_i \mid s \in [0, 1]\}$ where s_i is the score for r_i

```
1:  c ← [h_1 − h_0, ..., h_n − h_{n−1}]
2:  for i in 1..5 do                                    ▷ Find the n closest points in C to c.
3:      a_i ← min_i(dist(u, C))                         ▷ Where dist is any valid distance metric.
4:      b_i ← Find the utterance in C that directly follows a_i
5:      d_i ← b_i − a_i + c                             ▷ Where d_i is the "ideal" response vector to b_i.
6:  end for
7:  for r_i in r do
8:      g_i ← min(dist(r_i, d))
9:  end for
10: return 1.0 − g/‖g‖
```

The response prioritization tasks was set up as follows. 13,244 windowed conversations were selected from four text corpora, with equal representation from each corpus:

1. Chit-Chat[1] [27]
2. Daily Dialog[2] [16]
3. A 33 million word subset of Reddit[3] [25]
4. Ubuntu Dialogue Corpus[4] [18]

---

[1] https://github.com/BYU-PCCL/chitchat-dataset.
[2] https://aclanthology.coli.uni-saarland.de/papers/I17-1099/i17-1099.
[3] http://files.pushshift.io/reddit/.
[4] https://www.kaggle.com/rtatman/ubuntu-dialogue-corpus.

The Chit-Chat dataset, collected locally via a university competition, contains 483,112 dialog turns between university students using an informal online chat framework. The Daily Dialog dataset simulates common, real-life interactions such as shopping or ordering food at a restaurant. Reddit[5] covers an array of general topics, with copious instances of web links, internet acronyms, and active debate. Finally, the Ubuntu Dialogue Corpus contains 966,400 dialog turns taken from the Ubuntu Chat Logs, with a heavy emphasis on troubleshooting and technical support.

We then set aside 3,311 conversations (about 5% of the smallest corpus) from each dataset to create the evaluation corpus, with the unused portions of each dataset remaining as scaffolding. The scaffold corpus was embedded using Google's Universal Sentence Encoder lite [8], an embedding algorithm that strikes a strong balance between semantic coherence and speed of computation.

We then windowed the evaluation corpus so that rather than 3,311 long conversations, we instead had 13,244 windowed conversations with 5 dialog turns each. Each dialog from this windowed evaluation set was paired with six candidate responses: (a) the correct follow-on sentence for the given dialog context, and (b) five distractors randomly chosen from the same text corpus as the correct answer. The scaffolding algorithms in Sect. 2.3, along with several baselines described in Sect. 3.1, were tasked with identifying the true response.

Baselines. We selected three baselines to compare along with our conversational scaffolding algorithms, the objective being to determine whether performance improves when conversational trajectories are taken into consideration.

Naive Nearest
This algorithm naively selects the successor of the best context match as the 'ideal response' or target point. In other words, rather than calculating the ideal response as $d_1 = c + b_i - a_i$, the naive-nearest algorithm calculates $d_1 = b_i$. This approach ignores the analogical nature of language by assuming that the successor to the best context match represents an optimal response, even if the contexts do not match exactly.

Approximate Nearest Neighbor (ANN)
This algorithm implements an Approximate Nearest Neighbor scoring strategy. Its ideal target point is calculated in the same way as the flow vectors algorithm, but with $d_1 = 1/n \sum b_i$. The impact of conversational trajectories are ignored, and the algorithm instead orients itself based on the successor utterances extracted from the scaffold corpus.

Random
This baseline randomly selects one of the candidate responses without reference to the dialog history. As there are six candidate responses for each evaluation

---

dialog, only one of which is correct, we can expect the random algorithm to perform with an accuracy of approximately $\frac{1}{6} \approx 16.7\%$.

Neural Network
We also implemented a multilayer regression network using Tensorflow [1]. As input it accepts two utterances from the dialog history, each embedded as a 512 dimensional vector using the Universal Sentence Encoder Lite. It then predicts the ideal target point as a 512 dimensional output vector. The hidden layer sizes were 2048 and 2014 units respectively, with exponential linear unit activation functions, MSE loss, and 25% dropout.

Table 2. Retrieval accuracy on a dialog control task with 13,244 distinct conversations. A context size of $n = 2$ was used for the dialog history. The highest-scoring algorithm in each column is shown in bold-face text. The neural network baseline was unable to select a response for embedded concatenation because it requires two distinct vectors as input, and embedded concatenation provides only one reference vector.

	euclidean dist.	diff. vectors	embed. concat.	average
scattershot	59.30%	**63.99%**	**68.07%**	**63.79%**
flow vectors	60.41%	61.53%	62.47%	61.47%
naive-analogy	56.16%	61.88%	62.29%	60.11%
naive-nearest	56.15%	36.45%	58.97%	50.52%
ANN classifier	**65.54%**	37.71%	64.96%	56.07%
network	50.41%	50.41%	n/a	33.61%
random	17.13%	16.60%	16.06%	16.60%

Results. Experimental results are shown in Table 2. We note with interest that the contextual matching method chosen has a high impact on all scoring algorithms except for flow vectors and the neural network baseline. With a peak accuracy of 68.07% when paired with embedded concatenation, the scattershot algorithm shows a clear advantage over all other methods, outperforming the nearest baseline by 2.53%. We believe that this is because scattershot takes the one-to-many nature of language into account, allowing the system to select a candidate that closely matches one of many possible valid responses.

It is also useful to compare our naive-analogy algorithm with the naive-nearest baseline. These two algorithms are identical except for their analogical content. Our results show that leveraging the inherent analogical properties of the embedding space results in an overall accuracy improvement of 3.32% when using embedded concatenation and by 25.43% when using difference vectors. Additionally, we observe that the naive-analogy algorithm outperforms the naive-nearest algorithm in 2/3 scenarios, supporting the theory that response accuracy can be improved by leveraging the inherent analogical structure of the embedding space.

Surprisingly, the same pattern was not observed when comparing the flow vectors and ANN classifier algorithms. Like naive-analogy and naive-nearest, these two algorithms differ primarily in their use of analogical structure. The fact that ANN tends to outperform flow vectors suggests that in this case, the averaging of multiple dialog trajectories (a.k.a. "flow vectors") results in a target point that lies far from the manifold of valid responses, whereas the averaging of multiple actual sentence embeddings (as per ANN) remains closer to the valid manifold. Further research is needed to understand this phenomenon and quantify the complex structures found in semantic embedding spaces, and in this direction we applaud the work of [31] and [11].

3.2   Generalization Across Datasets

We found ourselves curious as to what extent each dialog corpus was able to generalize to the other corpora in the evaluation set. We therefore implemented the following experiment: Using the scattershot algorithm and embedded concatenation localization method, we created a confusion matrix showing how well the algorithm performed when using only one of our four corpora as its scaffold.

Table 3. Confusion matrix showing how well each dataset, when used as a scaffold corpus, is able to select appropriate responses for dialogs drawn from the other corpora. Each column contains a scaffold corpus, each row an evaluation corpus. The scattershot algorithm was used in conjunction with the embedded concatenation localization method, with a context size $n = 2$ and with 3,311 evaluation dialogs drawn from each corpus. The highest accuracy level in each column is shown in bold-face text.

	Chit-Chat	Daily Dialog	Reddit	Ubuntu
Chit-Chat	.5826	**.6563**	.6068	.3455
Daily Dialog	.5421	.6540	.5847	.3582
Reddit	**.5886**	.6261	**.7508**	.3860
Ubuntu	.4971	.4666	.5639	**.7523**

Results are shown in Table 3. The unusually high performance seen when both the scaffold and evaluation corpus were taken from the Ubuntu dataset can be explained by the high level of overlap within the Ubuntu dialog corpus. An investigation of the data downloaded from Kaggle reveals that between the three files ("dialogueText_301.csv", "dialogueText_196.csv", and "dialogueText.csv") there was an overlap of 53.35% in the original data (14,318,055 non-unique turns out of a total of 26,839,031 turns). As a result, the evaluation corpus drawn from the Ubuntu dataset contained exact copies of dialogs in the Ubuntu scaffold corpus. The other corpora had little or no overlap.

3.3 Retrieval from Large Data Repositories

The end objective of our research is to facilitate the creation of versatile conversational systems that are able to select dialog responses the conform to a friendly, upbeat and courteous conversational style. Candidate utterances for such systems may be generated by an ensemble of response generators, retrieved from a databank of possible utterances, or created algorithmically via a context-free grammar or template system, but in all cases there must be a means of deciding which candidate utterance is "best", i.e., which one should be delivered to the user. In generative systems, too, it is critical that we develop more and better methods for conversational scoring. Metrics such as n-gram matching, METEOR [3], BERTScore [29] and perplexity are helpful, but not yet sufficient for the aspirations of the research community.

To explore the effectiveness with which our system ranks responses and the types of conversations it is able to produce, we allowed a human to type the opening line of dialog with an agent executing the scattershot algorithm. The objective was to see whether a dialog agent choosing from among ca. 10,000 candidate responses could leverage the analogical structure of language in order to create a plausible conversation. A randomly-selected sentence from a repository this size would, of course, be meaningless and generally widely off-topic. We wanted to see if our system could do better.

Figures 4 and 5 show typical conversations generated using the method described above. Interestingly, although the 19,665 randomly-selected candidate utterances were drawn from all four conversational datasets, almost all of the ones chosen by the scattershot algorithm came from the Chit-Chat dataset. This suggests that the Chit-Chat dataset was an unusually good stylistic match for the informal conversation patterns used by the human chatter.

We permitted one augmentation to our algorithms for this experiment: Candidate responses that were too similar to the most recent statement in the dialog history were excluded from consideration[6]. This constitutes an extension at the sentence level of the traditional exclusion of source words when solving analogical queries via word embeddings [14,20]. Without it, the scaffolding algorithm tends to select sentences that parrot or reflect the content of the dialog history rather than progressing to new topics.

4 Analysis and Future Work

A key insight to be taken from our results is the observation that the average of several valid responses cannot be assumed to *also* represent a valid response. This amounts to taking the centroid of a (possibly oddly-shaped) manifold, resulting in a vector that might easily represent a nonsense sentence. For example, it is important to realize that the 'ideal' responses d_i depicted in Fig. 3 do not necessarily represent an optimal reply; they may in fact be the vector embedding

---

[6] Similarity was defined as Euclidean distance $< \tau$, where τ is a hand-selected threshold value.

```
> Hey. What's up?
Hey, whats up?
> Not much. How is your day going so far?
Hi, it's good!
> Good to hear. What are you working on?
I'm figuring out my budget .
> Oh that sounds fun. What are you going to do after you finish?
Well I plan to get into the accounting program
> Oh cool! Do you like accounting?
I've thought about going into cardiology, that seems interesting, but also I'm
considering anesthesiology.
> Oh wow. Those are both very different from accounting. Are they hard?
semester for you and me. Is your next semester seeming to look like its going to
be a little easier?
> I think this semester will be fun but a little challenging.
That it does! Even though you may not be getting everything out of your classes
now but oh well...;)
> Do you think you will have any time to go to see a movie this semester?
That it does! Even though you may not be getting everything out of your classes
now but oh well...;)
> So, where are you from originally?
Haha well I'm from Arkansas
> Oh cool. I have never been there. Do you like it?
Ya actually I did enjoy the shreveport one when I lived there last year (2012
Mardi gras) but you're right, it's almost nothing Compared to most of the NO ones.
Still very enjoyable. My of my friends lives right on the route so it was nice
having somewhere to go for it lol
> haha fun. Do you like it here then?
Cool
> If you could vacation anywhere, where would it be?
well,its like 1 am here,i should get to bed, it was nice talking to you, have a
great day.
> Oh wow. Goodnight. Talk to you later.
Thanks. You too!
```

Fig. 4. Conversation generated using the scattershot scaffolding algorithm, the embedded concatenation localization method, and distance threshhold $\tau = 0.6$. Human-generated text is preceded by the $>$ symbol. In this example, even the τ threshhold is not sufficient to keep the agent from getting caught in a sentence repetition, however, it successfully switches to a new topic on the next utterance. Conversation originally published in [27].

of a nonsense sentence. Rather, these 'ideal' responses, or target points, function as a heuristic to gauge whether a specific candidate response is conversationally appropriate.

A future direction for this research should include the use of a sufficiently-trained decoder to render the target point directly into text, thus enabling researchers to probe the structure and behavior of the embedding space in more detail.

```
> Hello.
Hey!
> How are you doing today?
How are you?
> I am good. How has your day been so far?
I've been pretty good, I was sick earlier, but better now.
> Oh man, that stinks. What were you sick with? I am glad you are feeling better
though!
I had like ten servings of it.
> Uh oh. That sounds like a lot. Was it good food?
I had such tasty food too.
> Yum. What is your favorite food?
yum sounds so good right now haha! I love every fruit! I like rice and pickles too
haha. but like you I like just about everything
> I love fruit too. So, have you seen any good movies lately?
Black panther is so good!!!
> Yeah I really liked it too. I think that or, Thor Ragnarok might be my favorite
Marvel movie.
No , I haven't . This is my first time to watch it .
> Oh yeah?
*It flips him off.*
> What are some of your favorite books?
It's a little bit of romance and comedy.
> Cool. Well, I have to go. It has been nice talking to you!
Okay ! Bye !
```

Fig. 5. Conversation generated using the scattershot scaffolding algorithm and Euclidean distance localization method, and distance threshold $\tau = 0.5$. Human-generated text is preceded by the > symbol. In this example, the agent is able to maintain several fairly coherent dialog turns, then pivots appropriately to the topic of movies in response to user cues. It also successfully detects and responds to an indication that the conversation is over. Conversation originally published in [27].

Another useful direction for future research would be the use of a dynamic context length depending on the content of the dialog history. For example, generic sentences such as "yes", "of course not", or "i'm not sure" provide little conversational context, and are generally meaningless in isolation, whereas other sentences may require little or no context at all in order to enable an optimal response. The taks of dynamically determining when further context is needed, and how much of it to include, is a fertile area for future research.

Going forward, we imagine a possible future agent which generates responses via a neural architecture, but which has been trained to adhere as closely as possible to a scaffold corpus in its utterance patterns. Future work in this area should explore neural dialog models that utilize a scaffold corpus during loss calculations. A comprehensive study of distance metrics should also be undertaken, as it is not necessarily certain that the *de facto* standards of Euclidean and cosine distance are the best possible heuristics for semantic similarity; L1 distance or correlation coefficients might be more effective.

As new language models and embedding algorithms are constantly being developed, another important area for future work involves the testing and analysis of new semantic embedding spaces, with an eye towards identifying the ones that are most appropriate for conversational scaffolding, analogical reasoning, and other processes that depend on the semantic properties and innate geometry of the embedding space itself.

5   Conclusion

As automated personal assistants become more prevalent, developers will need to strike a balance between control and spontaneity. We want our conversational systems to behave in unexpected, even surprising ways, even pushing humans out of their comfort zone at times. But we also want them to be kind and courteous, and refrain from insulting their users, making broadly offensive statements, or giving inaccurate information. Striking this balance requires *finesse*, and we believe that conversational scaffolding strikes a good balance between leveraging the power of connectionist systems and maintaining the continuity of a heavily curated system.

The methods outlined in this paper describe an enticing middle ground, allowing a scaffold corpus to define an overall personality or conversational style for the agent without directly restricting its responses. In this paper, we have presented a scaffolding algorithm that uses pre-trained sentence embeddings to (a) leverage the inherent analogical properties of the embedding space and (b) account for the one-to-many property of language while (c) encouraging responses that closely align with the scaffold corpus. Our scattershot algorithm is able to predict the correct follow-on sentence for a given dialog history with nearly 70% accuracy, outperforming both ANN and naive nearest-neighbor baselines. It is also able to produce engaging and (sometimes) believable conversations with topical coherence a relaxed, conversational feel. We believe that conversational scaffolding and the scattershot algorithm offer a unique and valuable new paradigm for response ranking in open-domain dialog settings, and we look forward to future work in this area.

Acknowledgements. We wish to thank David Wingate and his students in the BYU Perception, Control and Cognition laboratory for their role in creating and hosting the Chit-Chat dataset, and Daniel Ricks for his contributions to Fig. 3.

References

1. Abadi, M., et al.: TensorFlow: large-scale machine learning on heterogeneous systems, software available from tensorflow.org (2015). https://www.tensorflow.org/
2. Bak, J., Oh, A.: Variational hierarchical user-based conversation model. In: Proceedings of the 2019 Conference on Empirical Methods in Natural Language Processing and the 9th International Joint Conference on Natural Language Processing (EMNLP-IJCNLP), pp. 1941–1950. Association for Computational Linguistics, Hong Kong, China, November 2019. https://doi.org/10.18653/v1/D19-1202, https://www.aclweb.org/anthology/D19-1202

3. Banerjee, S., Lavie, A.: Meteor: an automatic metric for MT evaluation with improved correlation with human judgments. In: Proceedings of the ACL Workshop on Intrinsic and Extrinsic Evaluation Measures for Machine Translation and/or Summarization, pp. 65–72 (2005)

4. Bojanowski, P., Grave, E., Joulin, A., Mikolov, T.: Enriching word vectors with subword information. arXiv preprint arXiv:1607.04606 (2016)

5. Bowman, S.R., Vilnis, L., Vinyals, O., Dai, A.M., Jozefowicz, R., Bengio, S.: Generating sentences from a continuous space. CoRR abs/1511.06349 (2015). http://arxiv.org/abs/1511.06349

6. Buckels, E.E., Trapnell, P.D., Paulhus, D.L.: Trolls just want to have fun. Pers. Individ. Differ. **67**, 97–102 (2014)

7. Cer, D., Diab, M., Agirre, E., Lopez-Gazpio, I., Specia, L.: Semeval-2017 task 1: semantic textual similarity - multilingual and crosslingual focused evaluation. In: Proceedings of SemEval, vol. 2017 (2017)

8. Cer, D., et al.: Universal sentence encoder. CoRR abs/1803.11175 (2018). http://arxiv.org/abs/1803.11175

9. Cho, D., Acquisti, A.: The more social cues, the less trolling? an empirical study of online commenting behavior (2013)

10. Conneau, A., Kiela, D., Schwenk, H., Barrault, L., Bordes, A.: Supervised learning of universal sentence representations from natural language inference data. arXiv preprint arXiv:1705.02364 (2017)

11. Conneau, A., Kruszewski, G., Lample, G., Barrault, L., Baroni, M.: What you can cram into a single vector: Probing sentence embeddings for linguistic properties. arXiv preprint arXiv:1805.01070 (2018)

12. Devlin, J., Chang, M.W., Lee, K., Toutanova, K.: Bert: Pre-training of deep bidirectional transformers for language understanding. arXiv preprint arXiv:1810.04805 (2018)

13. Fulda, N., et al.: Byu-eve: mixed initiative dialog via structured knowledge graph traversal and conversational scaffolding. In: Proceedings of the 2018 Amazon Alexa Prize, November 2018

14. Gladkova, A., Drozd, A., Matsuoka, S.: Analogy-based detection of morphological and semantic relations with word embeddings: what works and what doesn't. In: Proceedings of the NAACL Student Research Workshop, pp. 8–15 (2016)

15. Kiros, R., et al.: Skip-thought vectors. CoRR abs/1506.06726 (2015)

16. Li, Y., Su, H., Shen, X., Li, W., Cao, Z., Niu, S.: DailyDialog: A Manually Labelled Multi-turn Dialogue Dataset. arXiv e-prints arXiv:1710.03957 (2017)

17. Logeswaran, L., Lee, H.: An efficient framework for learning sentence representations. In: International Conference on Learning Representations (2018). https://openreview.net/forum?id=rJvJXZb0W

18. Lowe, R., Pow, N., Serban, I., Pineau, J.: The Ubuntu Dialogue Corpus: A Large Dataset for Research in Unstructured Multi-Turn Dialogue Systems. arXiv e-prints arXiv:1506.08909 (2015)

19. Mikolov, T., Chen, K., Corrado, G., Dean, J.: Efficient estimation of word representations in vector space. CoRR abs/1301.3781 (2013)

20. Mikolov, T., tau Yih, W., Zweig, G.: Linguistic regularities in continuous space word representations. Association for Computational Linguistics, May 2013

21. Park, Y., Cho, J., Kim, G.: A hierarchical latent structure for variational conversation modeling. In: Proceedings of the 2018 Conference of the North American Chapter of the Association for Computational Linguistics: Human Language Technologies (Long Papers), vol. 1, pp. 1792–1801. Association for Computational Linguistics, New Orleans, Louisiana, June 2018. https://doi.org/10.18653/v1/N18-1162, https://www.aclweb.org/anthology/N18-1162

22. Pennington, J., Socher, R., Manning, C.D.: Glove: global vectors for word representation. In: Empirical Methods in Natural Language Processing (EMNLP), pp. 1532–1543 (2014). http://www.aclweb.org/anthology/D14-1162

23. Peters, M.E., et al.: Deep contextualized word representations. In: Proceedings of NAACL (2018)

24. Rainie, H., Anderson, J.Q.: The future of free speech, trolls, anonymity and fake news online (2017)

25. Reddit: Reddit datasets. https://www.reddit.com/r/datasets/

26. Shen, X., Su, H., Niu, S., Demberg, V.: Improving variational encoder-decoders in dialogue generation. In: Thirty-Second AAAI Conference on Artificial Intelligence (2018)

27. Will, M., Tyler, E., Nancy, F.: Conversational scaffolding: an analogy-based approach to response prioritization in open-domain dialogs. In: Proceedings of the 12th International Conference on Agents and Artificial Intelligence (ICAART) (2020)

28. Xupeng Tong, Y.L., Yen, C.M.: Variational neural conversational model. In: ICML (2014). https://www.cs.cmu.edu/epxing/Class/10708-17/project-reports/project12.pdf

29. Zhang, T., Kishore, V., Wu, F., Weinberger, K.Q., Artzi, Y.: Bertscore: evaluating text generation with bert. arXiv preprint arXiv:1904.09675 (2019)

30. Zhao, T., Zhao, R., Eskenazi, M.: Learning discourse-level diversity for neural dialog models using conditional variational autoencoders. In: Proceedings of the 55th Annual Meeting of the Association for Computational Linguistics (Long Papers), vol. 1, pp. 654–664. Association for Computational Linguistics, Vancouver, Canada, July 2017. https://doi.org/10.18653/v1/P17-1061, https://www.aclweb.org/anthology/P17-1061

31. Zhu, X., Li, T., De Melo, G.: Exploring semantic properties of sentence embeddings. In: Proceedings of the 56th Annual Meeting of the Association for Computational Linguistics (Short Papers), vol. 2, pp. 632–637 (2018)

32. Zhu, Y., et al.: Aligning books and movies: towards story-like visual explanations by watching movies and reading books. In: Proceedings of the IEEE International Conference on Computer Vision, pp. 19–27 (2015)

Heuristic Learning in Domain-Independent Planning: Theoretical Analysis and Experimental Evaluation

Otakar Trunda$^{(\boxtimes)}$ (ID) and Roman Barták (ID)

Faculty of Mathematics and Physics, Charles University, Prague, Czech Republic
Otakar.Trunda@mff.cuni.cz, Bartak@ktiml.mff.cuni.cz

Abstract. Automated planning deals with the problem of finding a sequence of actions leading from a given state to a desired state. The state-of-the-art automated planning techniques exploit informed forward search guided by a heuristic which is used to estimate a distance from a state to a goal state.

In this paper, we present a technique to automatically construct an efficient heuristic for a given domain. The proposed approach is based on training a deep neural network using a set of solved planning problems as training data. We use a novel way of extracting features for states developed specifically for planning applications. Our experiments show that the technique is competitive with state-of-the-art domain-independent heuristic. We also introduce a theoretical framework to formally analyze behaviour of learned heuristics. We state and prove several theorems that establish bounds on the worst-case performance of learned heuristics.

Keywords: Heuristic learning · Automated planning · Machine learning · State space search · Knowledge extraction · Zero-learning · STRIPS · Neural networks · Feature extraction

1 Introduction

Automated planning deals with finding a sequence of actions that leads from a given initial state to a desired goal state. Nowadays, the most successful approaches to automated planning are based on informed forward search algorithms which exploit *heuristics*. Heuristic is an efficiently computable function that assigns to each state an estimate of the distance to the nearest goal state. More accurate estimates lead to better performance of the search algorithm.

Heuristic learning (HL) is a relatively new field which studies how machine learning (ML) can be utilized to construct such heuristics automatically. The objective is to train a regression-based ML model to be able to estimate goal-distances of states and then to use the trained model as a heuristic function during search.

In this paper, we present a ML technique that automatizes the process of developing domain-specific heuristics for planning. We work with the standard STRIPS planing and we use supervised learning, with a multi-layered feed-forward neural network as

© Springer Nature Switzerland AG 2021
A. P. Rocha et al. (Eds.): ICAART 2020, LNAI 12613, pp. 254–279, 2021.
https://doi.org/10.1007/978-3-030-71158-0_12

the ML model. Expert knowledge about the domain is extracted automatically from a set of training samples. Heuristic learned in this way is applicable to any problem from the domain, i.e., it is able to generalize over problems of different sizes and with different goal conditions.

This paper extends our previous work on the topic [29] where we've introduced our features extraction technique. In this paper, our contribution is twofold. We compare properties of standard and learned heuristics and we describe how the loss function, features extractor and distribution of the training data affects the resulting heuristic. These findings should provide a useful guideline for future research in the field.

Second, we propose a theoretical framework that allows to formally analyze behaviour of learned heuristics. Currently, authors rely mostly on empirical results when arguing for applicability of HL. We present here three theorems that provide theoretical bounds on the worst-case performance of learned heuristics together with their proofs.

Paper is structured as follows. Section 2 defines the classical planning problem, specifies the variant of HL that we work with and provides some related works. In Sect. 3, we compare standard heuristics with the ones produced by HL systems and we describe impact of choice of the loss function and features extractor on behavior of the learned heuristic. We also propose a data-driven heuristic-adjustments as an alternative to heuristic weighting. Section 4 presents our HL framework and Sect. 5 describes the features extractor that we use. In Sect. 6, we establish a theoretical model for learned heuristics and prove some of their properties. The paper is then concluded by an experimental evaluation and final discussion.

2 Background and Related Works

2.1 Classical Planning

Planning deals with finding a sequence of decisions (actions) which - when executed in the given environment - leads to achieving the given goal. Performing decisions affects state of the environment. We work with classical planning [22] which means that the environment is fully observable, deterministic and static, executing actions is instantaneous, i.e. duration is not taken into account and the solver is *domain-independent*, in a sense that it accepts its inputs in a standardized format and is applicable to a wide range of different environments.

A classical planning task T is a tuple $T = (S, A, \gamma, s_0, goal, c)$, where S is a set of *states*, A is a set of *actions*, $\gamma : S \times A \mapsto S$ is a partially defined *successor function*, $s_0 \in S$ is the *initial state*, $goal : S \mapsto \{0, 1\}$ is a goal condition and $c : A \mapsto \mathbb{R}$ is a *cost function*.

We use the predicate representation of the problem, that is, we are given a set of constants C, and a set of predicate symbols Ψ. Each predicate symbol has assigned its arity $ar : \Psi \mapsto \mathbb{N}^0$. A set Q of all *instantiated predicates* is defined as
$$Q = \{(p, c_1, c_2, \ldots, c_{ar(p)}) \mid p \in \Psi, c_i \in C\}.$$

A *state* is defined as an assignment of values $\{true, false\}$ to all predicates of Q, i.e. $s : Q \mapsto \{true, false\}$. Goal condition is a partial assignment of the same kind. State s *meets* the goal condition if $\forall q \in Q : goal(q) = s(q)$ or $goal(q)$ is not defined.

Each action a is tuple $a = (prec_a, eff_a)$ where $prec_a$ and eff_a are partial assignments. Action a is applicable to s if s meets $prec_a$, otherwise $\gamma(s, a)$ is not defined. If a is applicable to s, then $\gamma(s, a) = s'$ where $s'(q) = eff_a(q)$ if $eff_a(q)$ is defined and $s'(q) = s(q)$ otherwise.

A plan is a sequence of actions $\pi = \langle a_1, a_2, \ldots, a_n \rangle$ such that applying each action $a_i \in \pi$ sequentially starting from s_0 leads to a state that meets *goal*. Cost of the plan π is $\sum_{a_i \in \pi} c(a_i)$.

In practice, the planning problem is specified in two components: a *planning domain file* and a *planning problem file*. The domain file specifies predicate symbols and templates for actions. The problem file then specifies a particular goal condition and an initial state and hence it also gives the set of constants.

In the rest of the text we use the following notation. P denotes a planning problem, s_0^P denotes the initial state of P, S^P the set of all states of P, $Dom(P)$ a set of all planning problems from the same domain as P and $S^{Dom(P)}$ a set of states of all problems from the same domain as P. For a state $s^P \in S^P$, $h^*(s^P)$ denotes minimal cost of a plan from s^P to some goal state of P or ∞ if no such plan exists. We call it the goal-distance of s^P.

2.2 Heuristic Learning

Heuristic learning (HL) is an application of supervised Machine learning (ML) to estimate goal-distance of states of some planning problem. It works with a set of training samples in a form of $(s_i^P, h^*(s_i^P))$ and the objective is to train an ML model that approximates the mapping $s \mapsto h^*(s)$. The trained model is then used as a heuristic function during search.

As standard ML models work with fixed-size real valued vectors as their inputs, another component is required that transforms states into this form. We call this component a *features extractor* and denote it by F. We call $F(s)$ the *features* of s.

HL can be used for several different purposes based on the generalization capabilities that are required of the model.

Type I HL: By *Type I* we denote the variant of HL that aims at constructing a heuristic tailored for a single problem. In this case the model will only generalize over different states of the same problem, i.e. the set of predicates, predicate symbols and constants as well as the goal condition will always be the same.

Given a problem P and a set of training data, $(s_i^P, h^*(s_i^P))$ the goal is to construct a heuristic $h : S^P \mapsto \mathbb{R}$ and then use it to solve the problem P as fast as possible. Typically, the time required to construct the heuristic is considered part of the solving process hence we want to minimize the sum of *training time* and *search time*.

The usage scenario is similar to the one of *Pattern database heuristics* (PDBs) (see [24] pages 106–107) where given the problem, we first construct PDBs based on the problem's state space and then use them to solve the problem.

Type II HL: In the *Type II* scenario we aim at constructing a heuristic applicable to a whole domain, i.e. we generalize over problems from the same domain. In this case, the model needs to be able to handle inputs with variable set of constants and variable goal conditions. The set of predicate symbols as well as action-templates will remain the same in all inputs.

We are given several problems $\mathcal{P} = \{P_1, P_2, \ldots P_k\}$ from the same domain *Dom* and a set of training data $\{(s_i^{P_j}, h^*(s_i^{P_j})) \mid P_j \in \mathcal{P}\}$, the task is to construct a heuristic h applicable to any problem from *Dom*.

Typically, the time required for training the model is **not** considered a part of the solving process. It is considered a pre-processing, or a domain analysis phase that could take several hours or even days. After the model is trained, new problems from the same domain can be solved quickly.

Unlike with the *Type I*, here the ML model needs to be able to handle problems of different size and with different goal conditions hence the features extractor must be much more sophisticated.

Type III HL: *Type III* deals with a hypothetical task of automatically constructing a domain-independent heuristic, i.e. to construct a model capable of generalizing across domains. The setting is similar as in the previous case except that the training data come from different domains.

This would require an even more flexible features extractor and an ML model with huge expressive power like a *Neural Turing machine* or some Turing-complete model used in *Genetic programming*. To our best knowledge, no serious attempt has been made in this area.

2.3   Related Works

Many attempts have been made to utilize ML in planning or search [19]. ML has been used to learn reactive policies [12,13,21], control knowledge [31], for plan recognition [3] and for other planning-related tasks [20]. ML tools are also often used to combine several heuristics [8,25] and in particular to help portfolio-based planners to efficiently combine multiple search algorithms [5]. A lot of papers exist that utilize ML in neoclassical planning paradigm (partial observability, non-deterministic actions, extended goals etc.), like *robotics* [26]. These are not directly related to our work.

Heuristic learning was investigated by [1] where the authors use a bootstrapping procedure with a NN to successively learn stronger heuristics using a set of small planning problems for training. The paper proposed an efficient way of generating training data based on switching between learning and search phases. The technique become popular and was successfully used by other authors [6,27]. We use a modified version of this technique as well. A domain-independent generalization of this approach was published later [9].

Most papers deal with the *Type I HL* scenario and almost all of them use a set of simple heuristics as features [2,4,30] or a SAS^+ representation of the state [7,27]. A serious attempt to use other kind of features was made in [31]. A *Type II* HL systems were studied in [9,28].

Authors mostly use simple ML models like linear regression or a shallow NN. ML models are often just used as a tool and ML-related issues like generalization capabilities, number and distribution of training samples, choice of loss function, etc. are not analyzed at all. Few exceptions exist: in [27] the authors proposed a modification to the loss function used during the training to bias the model towards under-estimation which increased quality of solutions found during the subsequent search. In [7] the authors study hyper-parameters of the NN and compare it with other ML models as well. They conclude that simpler models are not well suited for HL.

3   Heuristics in an ML Age

Before we present our framework, we review the role of heuristics in forward search, define several notions that we will be using and compare the "standard" heuristics with the ones produced by HL systems. Our analysis is general and can be applied to any heuristic constructed from training data by statistical ML.

We also present a data-driven heuristic-adjustment technique as an alternative to heuristic weighting.

3.1   Heuristics and Search Algorithms

The heuristic imposes an order on the set of open nodes which determines what nodes will be expanded first by the A* algorithm. Properties of the heuristic have significant impact on performance of the search algorithm. The most important performance guarantees are presented in Theorems 1 and 2.

Definition 1 (Cost of A* Solution). *Let P be a planning problem and h a heuristic. For a state $s \in S^P$, we denote by $A_h(s)$ the cost of plan that A* algorithm finds from s to some goal state of P using h as heuristic. If no such plan exists, we set $A_h(s) = \infty$.*

Definition 2 (Admissible Heuristic). *Given a planning problem P, heuristic h is called admissible $\forall s^P \in S^P : h(s^P) \leq h^*(s^P)$.*

Theorem 1 (Optimality of A^*). *Let P be a planning problem and h an admissible heuristic then $A_h(s_0^P) = h^*(s_0^P)$.*

Definition 3 (ε-admissible Heuristic). *Given a planning problem P and $\varepsilon \geq 1$, heuristic h is called ε-admissible on P if $\forall s^P \in S^P : h(s^P) \leq \varepsilon \cdot h^*(s^P)$. The heuristic is called ε-admissible if it is ε-admissible on all problems to which it can be applied.*

Theorem 2 (Bounded Suboptimality of A^*). *Let P be a planning problem and h an ε-admissible heuristic then $A_h(s_0^P) \leq \varepsilon \cdot h^*(s_0^P)$.*

Time complexity of A^* on a planning problem depends on accuracy of the heuristic used. Theorem 3 in [23] (page 186) states that if $\forall s \in S^P : h(s) = h^*(s)$ then A^* with h finds optimal solution to P in polynomial time. Given the fact that *NP-hard* planning problems do exist and assuming that $P \neq NP$, it is not possible for a polynomial-time computable h to be equal to h^* on all states. We rely here on an intuitive notion of complexity. For more exact definitions of complexity of planning domains see [15].

3.2   Standard vs. Learned Heuristics

The process of calculating the heuristic estimate can be divided to two steps. Given the set of states S, we first split them into categories and then assign an estimate to each category. There is a set of categories Δ, a *dividing* component $d : S \mapsto \Delta$ and an *estimating* component $e : \Delta \mapsto \mathbb{R}$.

Every existing heuristic h can be disassembled into these two components d, e such that $\forall s \in S : h(s) = e(d(s))$ and $|\Delta| << |S|$.

Definition 4 (**Heuristic Equivalence**). *Let h be a heuristic and P a problem. A heuristic equivalence $\sim_h$ is an equivalence relation on S^P defined as*
$$s_1 \sim_h s_2 \Leftrightarrow h(s_1) = h(s_2).$$

Given a heuristic h, we can define Δ as a set of equivalence classes of $\sim_h$.

This view on heuristics is very useful as heuristics constructed by HL systems work in the similar way. They assign features to states using the features extractor $F : S \mapsto \mathbb{R}^d$ and then use an ML model $M : \mathbb{R}^d \mapsto \mathbb{R}$ to produce the estimate.

It is possible to analyze the two components of a heuristic separately. Ideally, the d-component should divide the states to categories with the same h^*, i.e., ideally it should hold that $d(s_1) = d(s_2) \Leftrightarrow h^*(s_1) = h^*(s_2)$. Using the same computational complexity argument as before, however, it can be shown that for an $NP - hard$ planning domain such function d cannot be computed in polynomial time unless $P = NP$. This indicates that the dividing component is actually the hard and interesting part of any heuristic estimation.

From the HL perspective, the d-component is fully determined by the choice of features extractor. The training data or even the choice of model itself (neural network, linear regression, etc.) have no impact on it.

As for the e-component, the desired behaviour depends on the usage scenario. If the d-component is fixed, we need to assign an estimate to each set $\Delta_k = \{s_i \in S \mid d(s_i) = k\}$. To guarantee admissibility, we need $e(\Delta_k) \leq \min_{s_i \in \Delta_k}(h^*(s_i))$.

It's never useful to produce an estimate $e(\Delta_k) < \min_{s_i \in \Delta_k}(h^*(s_i))$ or $e(\Delta_k) > \max_{s_i \in \Delta_k}(h^*(s_i))$ so the most informed admissible heuristic (with the given d-component) would produce $e(\Delta_k) = \min_{s_i \in \Delta_k}(h^*(s_i))$. If optimality is not required, a different value from the interval might be preferred.

Comparing again with HL approach, the e-component is determined mostly by the choice of the loss function. Using MSE, the model would prefer $e(\Delta_k) = \beta$ such that $\sum_{s_i \in \Delta_k}(h^*(s_i) - \beta)^2$ is minimal. Other loss functions might lead to producing an average of $\{h^*(s_i) \mid s_i \in \Delta_k\}$, median or some other value. In [29] we have showed that $LogMSE$ is a much better choice for HL applications than MSE. The $LogMSE$ minimizes $\sum_{s_i \in \Delta_k}\left[\log\left(\frac{(h^*(s_i)+1)}{\beta+1}\right)\right]^2$ where β is the produced estimate.

The loss function is not evaluated over the whole S but only over the given set of training sample hence the choice of training data and other techniques like regularization also affect the e-component. Furthermore, ML models are able to interpolate the features space, i.e. when calculating $e(\Delta_k)$, they take into account also data points in other categories than just Δ_k.

3.3 Heuristic Modifications

Every heuristic h provides a tradeoff between informedness (speed of the search) and admissibility (quality of the solution). Based on the usage scenario, it is often desirable to adjust the informedness vs. admissibility ratio in favor of one or the other component. A popular way of doing so is heuristic weighting.

Weighting increases the heuristic estimate for all states evenly. It uses the same d-component and adjusts the e-component by a multiplicative constant. There is, however, no guarantee that the new value will be closer to h^* or that the weighted heuristic will perform any better during search than the original. There is also no guideline on how to choose the weight nor any theoretical reasoning why weighting is the proper way to improve the heuristic. There are many other transformation we could apply to the heuristic, like $h(s) + c$, $[h(s)]^2$, $h(s) \cdot \log(h(s))$, etc.

Having access to training data, we can come up with a much more efficient way of adjusting the informedness vs. admissibility ratio. Given a heuristic h and a set of training samples $T = \{(s_i, h^*(s_i))\}_i$, we keep the heuristic's d-component to perform the grouping while replacing its e-component by some other estimate constructed from the data. We propose three ways of doing so. We define $\Delta_s = \{s_i \in T \mid h(s_i) = h(s)\}$,

$$h^{min}(s) = \min\{h^*(s_i) \mid s_i \in \Delta_s\}$$

$$h^{avg}(s) = average\{h^*(s_i) \mid s_i \in \Delta_s\}$$

$$h^{shift}(s) = \begin{cases} \min\{h^*(s_i) \mid s_i \in \Delta_s\}, & if\ h(s) < \min\{h^*(s_i) \mid \Delta_s\} \\ \max\{h^*(s_i) \mid s_i \in \Delta_s\}, & if\ h(s) > \max\{h^*(s_i) \mid \Delta_s\} \\ h(s) & otherwise \end{cases}$$

h^{min} is the most informed "admissible" heuristic possible when using the grouping provided by h. h^{avg} has the lowest average absolute error, given the grouping and h^{shift} corrects some obvious errors of h. h^{shift} will always have the same or lower average absolute error than h without compromising its admissibility nor informedness.

We use "admissible" with quotes as we can only guarantee that on states from T. If the set of training samples is too small or poorly chosen then the heuristics will not exhibit the advertised behavior when deployed.

Unlike weighting, these data-driven modifications allow targeting a specific types of states and provide theoretical guarantees of the behaviour. They give the user a direct control over the distribution of $P[h^*(s) = x \mid h(s) = y]$. E.g., it is possible to modify the heuristic in such a way that $\forall s : h^{modified}(s) - h^*(s) < 2$ or that the number of states on which the heuristic overestimates is less than 5% of all states, etc.

We've conducted several experiments with these modifications. The results are provided in Sect. 7.

4 Heuristic Learning Framework

We will use heuristic learning in automated planning using the following framework. First, during the *training phase*, the deep NN will learn the heuristic from given training sample. Then, during the *deployment phase*, the obtained NN will be used to calculate heuristic values that will be exploited by A* search to find plans. The focus of this paper is on the training phase, in particular, on novel approach to generating features for training.

We work with the *Type II HL* (see Subsect. 2.2) and our approach is domain independent in a sense that the domain from which the training problems come might be arbitrary. Once the model is trained on data from some specific domain, it will only be applicable to problems from that domain but the process can be repeated on any domain of interest. Our approach can therefore be described as an automatic creation of domain-specific heuristic for any domain.

4.1 Obtaining the Training Data

Ideally, the training data should be given as inputs. That might be possible in some specific situations when historical data are available, but in general the training data need to be generated. This involves three tasks: obtaining states s_i, extracting features $F(s_i)$ and computing $h^*(s_i)$ for those states.

Computing $h^*(s_i)$ is very time-consuming hence majority of existing works only use states for which it is easy to compute $h^*(s_i)$, such as states close to the goal or states on goal-paths [7]. Typically samples are collected using backward search from the goal.

From the ML perspective, however, this is very problematic since training data must come from the same probability distribution as the data encountered during the deployment. Evaluating the model on completely different type of inputs would lead to poor performance and unpredictable behaviour, especially when using a *high variance* model [14] such as deep neural network.

In the HL scenario, we would like to train the model on the same type of states that it will encounter during the search phase. This would require to predict what kind of states will A* expand. Making such predictions is tricky as the set of expanded nodes depends on the heuristic used which depends on how well the model is trained and that depends back on the choice of training data. We adopt a popular technique by [1], which solves this issue by an iterative procedure that combines training and search steps.

The first set of training samples is empty. Then, in each iteration, the model is trained on current set of samples and a time-limited search is performed on all training problems using the trained model as a heuristic. States that the algorithm expanded are collected and used as training samples in the next iteration. The time limit is increased in each successive iteration, and the process continues until sufficient amount of samples is generated or all training problems can be solved within the time limit. In the first iteration where the set of training samples is empty, the model is not actually trained but a blind heuristic is used instead.

Pseudocode for the training phase is presented as Algorithm 1.

5 Extracting Features

An important step in any ML application is selecting features that will be used in learning. Given a set of planning problems $\{P_1, P_2, \ldots P_j\} \subset Dom$, the feature extractor F

realizes a mapping $F : S^{Dom} \mapsto \mathbb{R}^k$, i.e., assigns a real valued vector to any state of any problem from the domain of interest.

Length of the feature vector needs to be *fixed* and independent of the specific planning problem. Features should also be *informative* in a sense that states with different goal-distances should have different features, and *comparable* among problems from the whole domain so that knowledge is transferable to previously unseen problems.

When assigning features to state $s \in S^P$, properties of P that affect $h^*(s)$ have to be taken into account, namely the set of available actions and the goal condition. The model is trained on problems from a single domain and for such problems the set of actions is always the same so it is not necessary to encode it into features of states. Goal conditions, however, must be encoded so that the learned knowledge is transferable to problems with different goal states.

Algorithm 1. Training phase.

    Input: Set of planning problems $\{P_j\} \subset Dom$ used for training
    features extractor F
    Output: Trained model M that realizes mapping $F[S^{Dom}] \mapsto \mathbb{R}$

1 $L := 1$;
2 *trainingStates* := $\emptyset$;
3 **repeat**
4   compute $h^*(s_i)$ for each state $s_i \in trainingStates$;
5   assign features $f_i = F(s_i)$ to all states $s_i \in trainingStates$;
6      $M :=$ train neural net on data $\{(f_i, h^*(s_i))\}$;
7   **foreach** *problem* $P \in \{P_j\}$ **do**
8   run IDA* on P with time limit L minutes using M as heuristic;
9          $T :=$ states of P that were expanded during the search;
10   *trainingStates* := *trainingStates* $\cup\, T$;
11   **end**
12      $L := L + 1$;
13 **until** *termination criterion is met*;
14 **return** M;

5.1 Simple Features

Majority of papers on HL use either a fixed set of simple heuristics or a SAS^+ representation of the state as features. Given a sequence of heuristics $\mathcal{H} = (h_1, h_2, \ldots h_k)$, we can define $F^{\mathcal{H}}(s) = (h_1(s), h_2(s), \ldots, h_k(s))$. Most papers use a set of *pattern database heuristics* (PDBs). This approach is popular as the feature vector has fixed length, is quite informative and its computation is fast.

The SAS^+ representation encodes states using multi-valued state variables instead of predicates [15]. There is a fixed number of variables $v_1, \ldots v_k$ each with a fixed domain $\{0, 1, \ldots, \mathcal{D}(v_i)\}$ and assignment of values to those variables uniquely represents a state. There is a translator [16] that can automatically create a concise state variables representation of a state space of any problem. Using vector of state variables' values as features can again be advantageous as it has fixed length (for states of the same problem), and is very informative. In fact, it is maximally informative as it assigns unique features to each state.

These approaches are useful in the *Type I* HL scenario but not so in *Type II* that we deal with. PDB is based on a pattern: a set of objects from the planning problem. It is possible to us it if all the problems are given in advance. In the *Type II* scenario, however, the model needs to be applicable to *new*, unseen problems from the domain. If we use a fixed set of PDBs, new problems might not contain the same objects, and even if they do, meaning of those objects might be different so the features would not be comparable. The SAS^+ encoding is not usable at all as length of the vector varies for different problems.

Also we want to avoid dependency on existing human-designed heuristics as such dependence might prevent the model from achieving super-human performance. Development in the fields of sound, image, and language processing during the last ten years showed that ML systems with little to none expert knowledge encoded might achieve better results than sophisticated human-designed tools.

5.2   Graph-Based Features

We use a direct encoding of the state to an integer-valued vector. We transform the PDDL representation of both the current state and the goal condition to a labeled graph and use this graph to generate features. We select a set of small connected graphs and then use the number of occurrences of these graphs in the original graph as features. The idea is loosely inspired by the *Bag-Of-Words* model [10] that assigns fixed-length feature vectors to variable-length texts by counting number of occurrences of selected words or phrases.

Object Graph. We work with the PDDL representation of the problem, so we are given a set of constants C, a set of predicate symbols Ψ, a set Q of all *instantiated predicates* and a goal condition $G \subset Q$. We don't support negative goal conditions as they can be compiled-away so the goal condition is just a set of predicates. We are also given a state s which is represented as a set of predicates that are true in the state, i.e. $s \subset Q$.

An *object graph* for a state s of a planning problem P (denoted $G(s^P)$) is a vertex labeled graph $G(s^P) = (V, E, w)$ defined as follows.

The set of vertices is composed by four disjoint sets:

1. there is a vertex v_c for every constant $c \in C$
2. there is a vertex v_ψ for every predicate symbol $\psi \in \Psi$
3. there is a vertex v_q for every instantiated predicate $q \in Q$ that is true in s
4. there is a vertex v_q^g for every predicate $q \in G$

The set E contains an edge $e_{q\psi}$ from v_q or v_q^g to v_ψ if instantiated predicate q uses the predicate symbol ψ, and an edge e_{cq} from v_c to v_q or v_q^g if instantiated predicate q contains constant c.

Every vertex of the graph is labeled by an integer using a labelling function $w : V \mapsto \mathbb{N}^0$ that looks as follows.

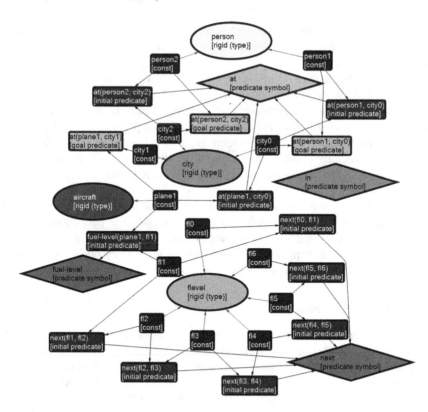

Fig. 1. Example of an object graph for the initial state of problem *pfile1* of the *zenotravel* domain.

- every v_c is assigned number 0
- every v_q is assigned number 1
- every v_q^g is assigned number 2
- every v_ψ is assigned a unique number from $[3, 4, \ldots, |\Psi| + 3]$ where $|\Psi|$ is the number of predicate symbols

If types are present, they are treated as unary predicate symbols. E.g. if a constant *plane1* has type *Plane*, we add a predicate symbol *Plane* to Ψ and we set instantiated predicate *Plane*(*plane1*) to be true in all states.

In Fig. 1 there is an example of object graph for the initial state of the problem *pfile1* of the *zenotravel* domain. Colors represent labels. Constants are colored red (label 0), initial predicates are green (label 1) and goal predicates gold (label 2). There are 8 predicate symbols that are represented by 8 nodes with mutually different colors. These have labels 3–10. Unary predicates are drawn as circles, binary ones as diamonds.

Size of the graph $G(s^P)$ is linear in the size of s and in the number of goal conditions. Number of vertices is $|C| + |G| + |s| + |\Psi|$. Every predicate (initial or goal) is connected to the corresponding predicate symbol and a constants where a is the arity of the predicate symbol. Hence, number of edges is at most $(a_m + 1) \cdot (|s| + |G|)$ where a_m is the maximum arity of some predicate symbol from Ψ.

The graph need not to be connected as seen in the example, but it often is. Number of constants, initial and goal predicates is problem-specific. Number of predicate symbols, on the other hand, is domain-specific and will be the same for all problems within the domain. The object graph is an equivalent representation of the current state and goal condition. The original PDDL representation of the state and the goal can be reconstructed back from the graph.

Extracting Features. We use object graph to extract features by counting the number of occurrences of specific subgraphs taking into account labels of nodes.

Let B_α^k be a sequence of all connected non-isomorphic vertex-labeled graphs containing at most α vertices where the labels are from $\{0, 2 \ldots k - 1\}$. See Fig. 2 for an example of graphs B_2^2 - colors represent labels.

Definition 5 (Occurrence of a Graph in Another Graph). *Occurrence of a graph G_1 in graph G_2 is a set of vertices T of G_2 such that induced subgraph of G_2 on T is isomorphic to G_1.*

Given a state s and $\alpha \in \mathbb{N}$, the feature vector of s (denoted $F_\alpha(s)$) is an integer-valued vector of size $|B_\alpha^k|$ whose i-th component is the number of occurrences of the i-th graph from B_α^k in $G(s)$. Parameter k is the number of labels present in $G(s)$ which is uniquely determined by the domain from which s comes.

Consider the graph G in the left-hand side of Fig. 2 with two different labels represented by colors. We use $\alpha = 2$, i.e. we count occurrences of connected subgraph of size up to 2. On the right-hand side of Fig. 2 there are graphs from B_2^2 that we will use to assign features to G. The resulting vector is $F_2(G) = (5, 3, 5, 2, 1)$ which corresponds to number of occurrences of the individual graphs in G.

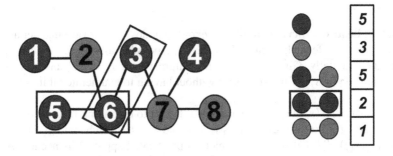

Fig. 2. Left-hand side: a simple graph used to demonstrate computation of features. Right-hand side: a set of graphs B_2^2 together with number of their occurrences in the example graph. Occurrences of one of the graphs are marked.

The length of $F_\alpha(.)$ can be controlled by adjusting the parameter α. With low α, the vector will be short and will contain less information about the state but its computation will be faster, and vice versa. Given a graph with n vertices, it is not known whether or not $F_\alpha(G)$ uniquely determines the graph for some $\alpha < n$. It is an open problem in graph theory known as the *Reconstruction conjecture*.

Length of the vector is at most $\sum_{i=1}^{\alpha} 2^{\frac{i(i-1)}{2}} C_i'(k)$, where k is the number of labels, α is the maximum size of subgraphs considered, $2^{\frac{i(i-1)}{2}}$ is the number of graphs on i vertices and $C_i'(k) = \frac{(k+i-1)!}{i!(k-1)!}$ is the number of combinations with repetition of size i from k elements. In practice, $|F_\alpha(.)|$ is much lower since we only use subgraphs that occurred at least once in the training data and most graphs do not occur due to the way how the object graph is defined. E.g. every predicate symbol has its own label l_i and every object graph contains exactly one vertex with such label so subgraphs that contain more than one vertex labeled l_i can never occur.

The object graph is defined in such a way that the number of labels k is the same for all problems from the same domain. This is very important as it means that length of the features vector doesn't vary across problems. From the planning perspective, features capture relations between objects in the given state. E.g. in blocksworld, occurrence of a certain subgraph of size 4 can capture the fact, that there are 2 blocks A on top of B and B is not correctly placed (so both of them have to be moved), etc.

Computing Features from Scratch. Given the object graph $G(s)$, feature vector $F_\alpha(s)$ can be computed by a recursive procedure that iterates through all connected subgraphs with size up to α in the graph and its time complexity is proportional to the number of such subgraphs. It is difficult to estimate the number in general as it strongly depends on the structure of the graph. E.g. a cycle with n vertices contains just n connected induced subgraphs of size $\alpha < n$, while a clique on n vertices contains $\binom{n}{\alpha}$ such subgraphs. The number depends on the edge-connectivity of the graph as well as on degrees of vertices. Experiments show that the time complexity grows exponentially in both n (size of the graph) and α. Due to the high computational complexity, the method is not competitive on larger problems.

Computing Features Incrementally. A^* expands nodes in a forward manner and two successive states differ only locally. It is therefore possible and useful to compute the features incrementally. Given a state s, its feature vector $F(s)$ and an action a, we can compute $F(\gamma(a,s))$ of the successor without having to enumerate all its subgraphs again.

Unfortunately, $F(s)$ and a alone are not sufficient to determine features of the successor. For any fixed α there exist states $s_1 \neq s_2$ and action a_1 such that $F_\alpha(s_1) = F_\alpha(s_2)$ but $F_\alpha(\gamma(a_1,s_1)) \neq F_\alpha(\gamma(a_1,s_2))$ so a more sophisticated approach is needed. Applying action to a state s can be viewed as performing some local changes in $G(s)$. These changes can be decomposed into a sequence of atomic graph operations of 3 types: *AddVertex*, *RemoveVertex* and *AddEdge*. For example, in Zenotravel, there is an action $a = load(person1, city1, plane1)$. Given $G(s)$, we can construct $G(\gamma(a,s))$ by first removing vertex that represents predicate $at(person1, city1)$, then adding vertex for predicate $in(person1, plane1)$ and then successively adding edges between the new vertex and vertices for in, $person1$ and $plane1$.

Given graph G, its vertex v and a set of graphs B_α, we define *contribution* of a vertex v to $F(G)$ denoted by $C(v)$ as a set of all occurrences of graphs from B_α in G which intersect with v.

We use a data structure that for given state s contains the following

1. Object graph $G(s)$
2. Set of all occurrences of subgraphs from B_α^k in $G(s)$
3. Features vector $F_\alpha(s)$
4. The i-th element of $F_\alpha(s)$ hold reference to all occurrences of the i-th subgraph
5. Each vertex v holds reference to its *contribution* $C(v)$
6. Every pair of vertices (v_i, v_j) holds reference to $C(v_i) \cap C(v_j)$

We call this data structure an *extended object graph* (EOG). We will now show how each of the three atomic operations can be performed incrementally over the EOG.

Input to each step is an EOG and argument of the operation (i.e. a vertex or an edge). Output is EOG with the operation applied.

Remove Vertex
For each $c \in C(v)$, remove c from every $C(v_i)$ that contains it, decrease values in $F(s)$ accordingly. Remove v from $G(s)$.

Add Vertex
Add v to $G(s)$, add one new occurrence of a subgraph containing a single vertex with the given label to $C(v)$, increment the the corresponding element of $F(s)$.

Add Edge
1. replace every occurrence $c \in C(v_1) \cap C(v_2)$ by occurrence of a graph with the same vertex set and one more edge added at the corresponding location.
2. for every occurrence $c \in C(v_1) \setminus C(v_2)$ such that $|c| \leq \alpha - 1$ create a new occurrence on vertices $c \cup \{v_2\}$. If c contained some vertex adjacent to v_2, edges between these vertices and v_2 will be taken into account when determining which graph from B_α occurred on $c \cup \{v_2\}$.
3. repeat the previous step symmetrically for v_2
4. add the edge to $G(s)$

Using the *extended object graph* data structure, we can perform *AddVertex*, *RemoveVertex* as well as the step 1 of *AddEdge* in time $O(1)$, steps 2 and 3 can be performed in time $O(|C(v_1)|)$ and $O(|C(v_2)|)$ respectively.

EOG for the initial state is constructed from scratch, every other EOG is constructed from the EOG of its predecessor via applying a sequence of atomic graph operations that corresponds to the action used. This allows us to compute $F_\alpha(s)$ in polynomial time for every state given EOG of its predecessor.

6 Stochastic Heuristics

The learned heuristics often work well in practice but in general they are not admissible nor ε-admissible. They don't provide any theoretical guarantees on the performance as the standard heuristics do via Theorems 1 and 2. These theorems are not applicable to learned heuristics as they require the error to be bounded on *all* states. ML techniques don't provide these types of guarantees. After the ML model is trained, it typically achieves low error on *average* but there could be a very small percentage of inputs on which the error is high.

We would like leverage the fact that on *average* the error of a learned heuristic is low in order to generalize Theorem 2 in a probabilistic manner, i.e., saying that the quality of the solution will be good with some high probability.

Requirements in Theorem 2 are tight in a sense that even if a single state would violate the requirements, there would exist a problem for which the stated bound does not hold. Formally, $\forall \varepsilon, h \; \exists P, s' \in S^P : h(s') > \varepsilon \cdot h^*(s') \Rightarrow A_h(s_0^P) > \varepsilon \cdot h^*(s_0^P)$. This is problematic for our probabilistic generalization as we have no control over distribution of problems, i.e. we can't average over problems. We must assume that the problem will be given by an adversary and provide a worst-case probabilistic bound that will hold for every problem.

We will now define a formal notion of *Stochastic heuristic* and formulate some of its properties. We will later show how heuristics obtained by HL can be modeled as stochastic heuristics.

Definition 6 (Stochastic Heuristic). *Given a problem P, a stochastic heuristic H is a set of independent non-negative random variables $H(s_i)$ for each $s_i \in S^P$.*

When we use H in search, we first sample each $H(s_i)$ to obtain a fixed estimate for each state, i.e. a standard heuristic. Then we use the standard heuristic for search so during the search, there is no randomness involved. Running another search on the same problem could of course produce different results as we could obtain a different standard heuristic via the initial sampling. When analyzing properties of a stochastic heuristic, we always work the situation *before* the initial sampling hence both $H(s)$ and $A_H(s)$ are random variables (RV).

6.1 Properties of Stochastic Heuristics

We formulate and prove three theorems that provide bounds on solution quality when using stochastic heuristic with A*. In general, we show how distributions of $H(s_i)$ affect distribution of $A_H(s_0)$. We work with a restricted planning problem, that is a problem that contains exactly one goal state and exactly one optimal path from s_0 to the goal, cost of each action is 1 and the initial state is not a goal state. These restrictions simplify the proof but the theorems also hold in the non unit-costs scenario.

Theorem 3. *Let P be a planning problem and H be a stochastic heuristic. If $\forall s \in S^P :$ $E[H(s)] = h^*(s)$, then $\forall c > 1 : P[A_H(s_0) \geq c \cdot (h^*(s_0))^2] < \frac{1}{c}$.*

Proof. Let's first state several inequalities that we will use in the proof.

Lemma 1 (Markov's Inequality). *Let X be a random variable, such that $X > 0$, then $\forall a > 0 : P[X \geq a] \leq \frac{E[X]}{a}$.*

Lemma 2 (Boole's Inequality). *Let A_i be events, then $P[\bigcup A_i] \leq \sum P[A_i]$.*

Lets denote by $Opt(s_0)$ the optimal path from s_0 to the nearest goal (a sequence of states) except the initial and the goal state. Since we work with unit-cost actions, $|Opt(s_0)| = h^*(s_0) - 1$ and $\forall s_i \in Opt(s_0) : h^*(s_i) = h^*(s_0) - i$.
By a contraposition of Theorem 2, we have

$$\forall \varepsilon \geq 1 : A_H(s_0) > \varepsilon \cdot h^*(s_0) \Rightarrow \tag{1}$$

$$\exists s_i \in Opt(s_0) : H(s_i) > \varepsilon \cdot h^*(s_i) \tag{2}$$

hence

$$P[A_H(s_0) > \varepsilon \cdot h^*(s_0)] \leq \tag{3}$$

$$P[\exists s_i \in Opt(s_0) : H(s_i) > \varepsilon \cdot h^*(s_i)] \leq \tag{4}$$

$$\sum_{s_i \in Opt(s_0)} P[H(s_i) > \varepsilon \cdot h^*(s_i)] \tag{5}$$

(3) $\leq$ (4) comes from (1) $\Rightarrow$ (2), while (4) $\leq$ (5) can be achieved by applying Boole's inequality.

Now, Markov's inequality states that

$$\forall s_i : P[H(s_i) \geq \varepsilon \cdot h^*(s_i)] \leq \frac{E[H(s_i)]}{\varepsilon \cdot h^*(s_i)} = \frac{h^*(s_i)}{\varepsilon \cdot h^*(s_i)} = \frac{1}{\varepsilon} \tag{6}$$

By substituting (6) to (5) we get:

$$\sum_{s_i \in Opt(s_0)} P[H(s_i) > \varepsilon \cdot h^*(s_i)] \leq$$

$$\sum_{s_i \in Opt(s_0)} \frac{1}{\varepsilon} = |Opt(s_0)| \cdot \frac{1}{\varepsilon} \leq \frac{h^*(s_0)}{\varepsilon}$$

We've created a chain of inequalities. When we put together the first and the last element of the chain, we get

$$\forall \varepsilon > 1 : P[A_H(s_0) > \varepsilon \cdot h^*(s_0)] < \frac{h^*(s_0)}{\varepsilon}$$

Now for given $c > 1$, we set $\varepsilon = c \cdot h^*(s_0)$ which gives us the required bound. $\square$

Bound in Theorem 3 is quite loose as it uses $[h^*(s_0)]^2$. If we take variance of $H(s)$ into account, we can come up with a tighter bound.

Theorem 4. *Let P be a search problem and H be a stochastic heuristic such that $\forall s \in S^P : E[H(s)] = h^*(s), var[H(s)] = \sigma^2 < \infty$. Then*

$$\forall c > 1 : P[A_H(s_0) > c \cdot (h^*(s_0))] < \frac{\sigma}{c-1} \cdot \frac{\pi}{2}$$

Proof. We will use the following inequalities in the proof.

Lemma 3 (Cantelli's Inequality). *Let X be a random variable, such that $E[X] = \mu < \infty$ and $var[X] = \sigma^2 < \infty$, then $\forall a > 0 : P[X - \mu \geq a] \leq \frac{\sigma^2}{\sigma^2 + a^2}$.*

Lemma 4 (Integral Approximation of a Sum). *Let f be a non-decreasing function on $[a - 1, b + 1]$, then:*

$$\int_{s=a-1}^{b} f(s) \, ds \leq \sum_{i=a}^{b} f(i) \leq \int_{s=a}^{b+1} f(s) \, ds$$

We proceed in the same way as in the previous proof up to Eq. (5). We have

$$\forall \varepsilon > 1 : P[A_H(s_0) > \varepsilon \cdot h^*(s_0)] < \sum_{s_i \in Opt(s_0)} P[H(s_i) > \varepsilon \cdot h^*(s_i)]$$

Lets denote $k = h^*(s_0)$. When we use Cantelli's inequality, we have:

$$P[H(s_i) \geq \varepsilon \cdot h^*(s_i)] = P[H(s_i) \geq \varepsilon \cdot (k - i)] \leq \frac{\sigma^2}{\sigma^2 + (\varepsilon - 1)^2(k - i)^2}$$

When we substitute that to the sum, we get

$$\sum_{s_i \in Opt(s_0)} P[H(s_i) > \varepsilon \cdot h^*(s_i)] < \sum_{i=1}^{k-1} \frac{\sigma^2}{\sigma^2 + (\varepsilon - 1)^2(k - i)^2} \leq$$

Using Lemma 4, we get

$$\leq \int_1^k \frac{\sigma^2}{\sigma^2 + (\varepsilon - 1)^2(k - i)^2} \, di =$$

$$\frac{\sigma}{\varepsilon - 1} \arctan \frac{(k - 1)(\varepsilon - 1)}{\sigma} \leq \frac{\sigma}{\varepsilon - 1} \cdot \frac{\pi}{2}$$

Now given $c > 1$, we just set $\varepsilon = c$.

□

Theorem 4 is a direct generalization of Theorem 2 as it imposes the same bound on $A_h(s)$. If we calculate $\lim_{var[H(s)] \to 0}$ of the bound, we get a weaker version of Theorem 1. The probability bound, however, is quite loose hence the theorem is only applicable for large c. Specifically for $c > \frac{\sigma \cdot \pi}{2} + 1$. Since σ is the standard deviation of $H(s)$, is could be quite large in practice: between 5 and 10 or even larger depending on the problem.

Theorems 3 and 4 make no assumptions about distribution of $H(s_i)$, i.e. they work for any distribution. They don't even require that $H(s_i)$ are identically distributed. A much better bound can be obtained when we take the distribution of $H(s_i)$ into account.

Theorem 5. *Let P be a search problem and H be a distribution heuristic such that $\forall s \in S^P : H(s) \sim N(h^*(s), \sigma^2), \sigma^2 < \infty$. Then*

$$\forall c > 1 : P[A_H(s_0) \geq c \cdot (h^*(s_0))] < \frac{\sigma^2}{\exp\left(\frac{(c-1)^2}{2\sigma^4}\right) \sqrt{2\pi}(c - 1)}$$

Proof. We again make use of several well known notions and inequalities.

Definition 7 (Gauss Error Function). *The Gauss error function erf is defined as* $erf(x) = \frac{2}{\sqrt{\pi}} \int_x^\infty \exp\left(-t^2\right) dt$. *By erfc we denote the complementary error function:* $erfc(x) = 1 - erf(x)$.

Erf can be used to calculate cumulative distribution function for normally distributed random variables.

Lemma 5 (CDF of Normally Distributed Random Variable). *Let* $X \sim N(\mu, \sigma^2)$, *then* $\forall q : P[X > q] = 1 - \frac{1}{2} erfc\left(\frac{\mu-q}{\sqrt{2\sigma^2}}\right)$.

There is no closed-form formula for $erf(x)$, so various approximations are used:

Lemma 6 (Bounds on Gauss Error Function).
For all $x > 0$:

$$\frac{2\exp\left(-x^2\right)}{\sqrt{\pi}\left(\sqrt{x^2+2}+x\right)} < erfc(x) < \frac{\exp\left(-x^2\right)}{\sqrt{\pi}x}$$

We again proceed in the same way as in the proof of Theorem 3 up to Eq. (5) which gives us

$$\forall \varepsilon > 1 : P[A_H(s_0) > \varepsilon \cdot h^*(s_0)] < \sum_{s_i \in Opt(s_0)} P[H(s_i) > \varepsilon \cdot h^*(s_i)] =$$

Using $k = h^*(s_0)$, $|Opt(s_0)| = k - 1$ and $\forall s_i \in Opt(s_0) : h^*(s_i) = k - i$, we get

$$= \sum_{i=1}^{k-1} P[H(s_i) > \varepsilon \cdot (k-i)] \leq$$

By applying Lemma 4 we get

$$\leq \int_1^k P[H(s_i) > \varepsilon \cdot (k-i)] di \leq$$

we can just calculate this directly using Lemmata 5 and 6 to obtain

$$\leq \frac{\sigma^2}{\exp\left(\frac{(\varepsilon-1)^2}{2\sigma^4}\right)\sqrt{2\pi}(\varepsilon-1)} - \frac{\exp\left(-\frac{(\varepsilon-1)^2}{2\sigma^4}\right)}{\sqrt{\pi}\left(\frac{\varepsilon-1}{\sqrt{2\sigma^2}}+\sqrt{\frac{(\varepsilon-1)^2}{2\sigma^4}+2}\right)}$$

Now we can drop the second term which is negative hence by doing so we only increase the value. That gives us the required bound. □

Theorem 5 is based on a strong assumption of normality but it also provides a very strong bound: the probability of producing a solution whose cost is c-times greater than the optimal cost is exponentially small with respect to c.

6.2 Applicability of the Model

After the NN is trained, it is possible to analyze it, discover its weaknesses and come up with an adversary example: a planning problem on which the learned heuristic performs poorly. We can overcome this by defining the stochastic heuristic in the way we did. First the adversary produces the problem and only after that the stochastic heuristic is sampled. Since the adversary has no control over the sampling, the probabilistic bounds will hold.

In practice, sampling the stochastic heuristic corresponds to training the network. The training algorithm is randomized so we don't know the result beforehand but once the NN is trained, it operates in a deterministic manner. When stating the probabilistic bounds, we don't average over problems but rather over all possible outcomes of the randomized training algorithm. When we are given an adversary example, we can just re-train the network using the same training data and chances are that the new network will no longer have any difficulties with that example.

The theorems are based on several preconditions: independence of $H(s_i)$ and $H(s_j)$ for $s_i \neq s_j$, unbiasedness, i.e. $\mathsf{E}[H(s)] = h^*(s)$ and non-negativity: $\forall s : \mathsf{P}[H(s) < 0] = 0$.

We can easily guarantee non-negativity of estimates by restricting outputs of the NN only to positive values, i.e. replacing any negative output by zero. Assumptions of independence and unbiasedness of $H(s_i)$ can be justified by analyzing the bias-variance tradeoff for NNs [14]. NNs are universal approximators [18] and in general they have high variance and low bias hence for a large enough network, $H(s)$ should be unbiased and $\forall s_i, s_j : H(s_i)$ and $H(s_j)$ should be close to independent.

The independence and unbiasedness, however, is only achievable if the network is "well trained", i.e. if it is large enough to represent the target function, it doesn't over-fit, features are well chosen, there is enough data samples and they are properly distributed in the input space, there is enough time to train the network, etc. It is not possible to formally specify and verify all these requirements so we have to rely on empirical results which show that NNs can often behave like this in practice.

The normality assumption in Theorem 5 is even stronger and can't be guaranteed in practice either. Again, we have to rely on empirical results. Output of the network is computed by combining outputs of many independent neurons hence if we are going to assume it has some distribution, the normal distribution should be the most likely candidate.

We don't require that all $H(s_i)$ are identically distributed. In theorems 4 and 5 we're assuming that $\text{var}[H(s_i)]$ is the same for all states but even if it wasn't, the theorem would still hold with an identical proof. In fact, we can just use $\sigma^2 = \max_{s_i \in S} \text{var}[H(s_i)]$. If the actual variance is lower for some states, it will only improve the bound.

Theorems stated here are not tied to our particular HL framework. They can be applied to any HL system and also to other kinds of heuristics that were constructed by stochastic optimization algorithms like Monte-Carlo Tree Search, heuristic-selection approaches, genetic algorithms, hyper-heuristics and others, as long as they fulfill the requirements of independence, unbiasedness and non-negativity.

7   Experiments

We conducted experiments on two standard benchmark domains: *zenotravel* and *blocks* because it is easy to obtain training data for these domains. For the purpose of the experiments, we implemented ad-hoc solvers for the two domains and used them to generate training data. Our solvers are based on a genetic algorithm combined with a greedy search, they are capable of solving most problems within a few seconds and provide optimal or close-to-optimal solutions. We test the method on 20 problems available for *zenotravel*[1] and the first 27 problems from *blocks*[2].

7.1   Heuristic Analysis and Adjustments

We've performed the analysis described in Sect. 3.3 on two heuristic: *GoalCount* and *FastForward*.

GoalCount (h_{GC}) is a very simple heuristic: it just counts the number of goal predicates that are not yet accomplished in current state. The heuristic is admissible if no action can accomplish multiple goal predicates simultaneously.

FastForward heuristic (h_{FF}) [17] is a much more sophisticated heuristic based on so called *delete relaxation*. The *Fast Forward* planning system won the International Planning Competition (IPC) in 2000 and performed well also in the following IPCs. Since then h_{FF} has become a popular benchmark to test new heuristics against.

Our main goal is to perform the heuristic learning as described in Sect. 4. To achieve that, we've collected the training data using the technique presented in Sect. 4.1 which gives us a set states $\{s_i^P\}$. For each of those states, we compute h^* using our ad-hoc solvers and the two heuristic values h_{GC} and h_{FF}. This gives us a set of tuples $\{(s_i, h_{GC}(s_i), h_{FF}(s_i), h^*(s_i))\}_i$. In total, we obtained 31,434,617 unique data samples for *Blocks* and 25,977,816 for *Zenotravel*. Raw data can be accessed via *https://github.com/otaTrunda/PADD/tree/master/HeuristicAnalysisData*.

We can use the data to perform various data-analysis tasks. Figure 3 shows correlation between heuristic estimates and real goal-distances for each heuristic and each domain.

The blue area represents the data as a scatter plot. The X axis is goal distance, Y axis is the heuristic estimate. The red line represents a perfect match. The closer to the red line the more informed the heuristic is. Data points above the red line indicate overestimation.

Based on the data, we've constructed the three adjusted heuristics h^{min}, h^{avg} and h^{shift} as defined in Sect. 3.3 and tested them on a set of problems. For every combination of $h \in \{h_{GC}, h_{FF}\}$ and $domain \in \{blocks, zenotravel\}$ we run an A^* search with heuristics h, h^{min}, h^{avg} and h^{shift} on all available problems in *domain*. Time was capped at 30 min per problem and there was a memory limit of 5 million nodes per problem (sum of sizes of the open list and the closed list).

When solving a problem P, we use only data from *other* problems - all from the domain except P - to construct the adjusted heuristics. This should resemble our use case scenario where we are interested in transferring the knowledge across problems.

---

[1] api.planning.domains/json/classical/problems/17.

[2] api.planning.domains/json/classical/problems/112.

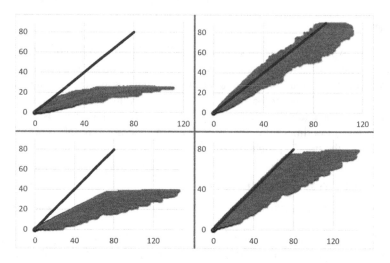

Fig. 3. Correlation between heuristic estimates and real goal-distances. Top part: zenotravel, bottom part: blocks. Left hand side: h_{GC}, right hand side: h_{FF}. (Color figure online)

Figure 4 shows results for *blocks* and Fig. 5 for *zenotravel*. We measure *TotalNodes* - sum of number of expanded nodes and the number of nodes present in the open list at the end of the search, *SolutionCost* which in this case is the number of actions in the plan, number of problems solved and search time. Blank spaces in *SolutionCost* means that the problem was not solved within time or memory limit. We've only included problems that were solved by at least one of the heuristics.

Problem	NodesTotal				SolutionCost				SearchTime (s)			
	GC	GC+avg	GC+min	GC+shift	GC	GC+avg	GC+min	GC+shift	GC	GC+avg	GC+min	GC+shift
probBLOCKS-4-0.sas	54	48	27	27	6	10	6	6	0	0	0	0
probBLOCKS-5-0.sas	241	46	46	46	12	12	12	12	0	0	0	0
probBLOCKS-6-0.sas	304	79	48	48	12	12	12	12	0	0	0	0
probBLOCKS-7-0.sas	6040	233	602	602	20	22	20	20	0	0	0	0
probBLOCKS-8-0.sas	73194	2114	1680	1680	18	22	18	18	1	0	0	0
probBLOCKS-9-0.sas	4E+06	1E+06	264398	264398	30	34	30	30	83	22	4	4
probBLOCKS-10-0.sas	5E+06	4E+06	3E+06	3E+06		36	34	34	98	71	56	56
probBLOCKS-11-0.sas	5E+06	5E+06	2E+06	2E+06			32	32	101	97	30	29
probBLOCKS-12-0.sas	5E+06	5E+06	4E+06	4E+06			34	34	105	96	67	65

Problem	FF	FF+avg	FF+min	FF+shift	FF	FF+avg	FF+min	FF+shift	FF	FF+avg	FF+min	FF+shift
probBLOCKS-4-0.sas	20	18	18	20	6	6	6	6	0	0	0	0
probBLOCKS-5-0.sas	45	29	40	45	12	12	12	12	0	0	0	0
probBLOCKS-6-0.sas	38	36	33	38	12	12	12	12	0	0	0	0
probBLOCKS-7-0.sas	215	89	226	215	20	22	20	20	0	0	0	0
probBLOCKS-8-0.sas	927	572	650	927	18	22	18	18	0	0	0	0
probBLOCKS-9-0.sas	35585	104938	38200	35585	30	30	30	30	21	58	20	19
probBLOCKS-10-0.sas	1E+06	820863	685206	1E+06	34	38	34	34	885	602	472	817
probBLOCKS-11-0.sas	128839	160648	209636	128839	32	34	32	32	123	88	183	114
probBLOCKS-12-0.sas	137680	53302	221442	137680	34	36	34	34	175	65	259	167
probBLOCKS-14-0.sas	615017	902475	398023	615017	38		38	38	1283	1800	768	1214

Fig. 4. Performance of h_{FF}, h_{GC} and their modified versions in *blocks*.

GoalCount is an admissible but very week heuristic hence the adjusted heuristics outperform it in all criteria except plan length on all problems in *blocks*. The heuristic is admissible, so the *min* adjustment and the *shift* adjustment will yield the same result.

In *blocks* the h_{GC} heuristic systematically and unnecessarily underestimates most states. The heuristic counts the number of blocks that are misplaced. Moving a block, however, requires two actions hence $\forall s : h_{GC}(s) = k \Rightarrow h^*(s) \geq 2k - 1$. (We subtract 1 as one of the k blocks could already by lifted in the state.) When using the estimate $2k - 1$ instead of k, the heuristic is more informed and still admissible. This is exactly what h_{GC}^{min} and h_{GC}^{shift} are doing.

Underestimation such as this should never occur in any state-of-the-art domain-specific heuristic as it harms the performance and is avoidable. Author of the heuristic should be able to identify and remove such anomaly.

With domain-independent heuristics, however, this can happen. The systematical underestimation could only occur on some specific domain and shifting the value could make the heuristic inadmissible on other domains. It is not possible for the author of heuristic to manually check its behaviour on all existing domains and adjust it to each such domain. With the ML approach we can do exactly that as those adjustments are created automatically.

In *zenotravel* domain the h_{GC} heuristic counts the number of passengers that are not yet at their destinations. When $h_{GC}(s) = k$, it could be that there are k passengers in the plane that is already at their destination so just performing the *disembark* action k-times will lead to goal. Due to this, the heuristic estimate is actually tight and can't be improved without loosing admissibility. In this case $h_{GC}^{min} = h_{GC}^{shift} = h_{GC}$.

h_{GC}^{avg} on the other hand is more informed that the others, solves more problems and requires less time and memory. It is not admissible hence it doesn't guarantee optimality of solutions.

FF heuristic is much more sophisticated and it is hence unlikely that these simple adjustments will significantly improve it. h_{FF}^{Shift} seems to be working exactly like h_{FF} which suggests that there are no obvious errors in h_{FF} that could be repaired by shifting. None of the *Avg* and *Min* adjustments outperform h_{FF} in all criteria. h_{FF}^{Min} is admissible unlike h_{FF} hence can improve the solution quality and provide optimality guarantee. h_{FF}^{Avg} can sometimes be faster, especially in the *blocks* domain. These modification can be used to adjust the informedness vs. admissibility tradeoff of the heuristic.

7.2   Heuristic Learning

For each problem P in our set, we train the model using the other problems from the domain (except P) as the training data, and then use the trained model as a heuristic with an A* algorithm to solve P. We compare the quality of the resulting heuristic with the *Fast-Forward* heuristic h_{FF} [17].

The NN we used have 5 hidden layers with sizes of $(256, 512, 128, 64, 32)$ neurons respectively, and two *DropOut* layers. We used *ReLU* activation function, *Xavier* weight initialization and *Adam* as the training algorithm [11]. The last layer contained a single neuron with a linear activation to compute the output. Architecture of the network was chosen according to best practices for this kind of scenario.

Problem	NodesTotal				SolutionCost				SearchTime (s)			
	GC	GC+avg	GC+min	GC+shift	GC	GC+avg	GC+min	GC+shift	GC	GC+avg	GC+min	GC+shift
pfile1.sas	5	5	5	5	1	1	1	1	0	0	0	0
pfile2.sas	88	107	88	88	6	6	6	6	0	0	0	0
pfile3.sas	1377	843	1377	1377	6	6	6	6	0	0	0	0
pfile4.sas	4042	4426	4042	4042	8	8	8	8	0	0	0	0
pfile5.sas	15802	4275	15802	15802	11	13	11	11	0	0	0	0
pfile6.sas	97502	22345	97502	97502	11	13	11	11	1	0	2	1
pfile7.sas	172953	46596	172953	172953	15	16	15	15	2	1	3	2
pfile8.sas	596687	35040	596687	596687	11	12	11	11	9	0	10	9
pfile9.sas	5E+06	1E+06	5E+06	5E+06		21			114	20	114	115
pfile10.sas	5E+06	4E+06	5E+06	5E+06		23			105	59	97	104
pfile11.sas	5E+06	268131	5E+06	5E+06		14			117	4	109	119

Problem	FF	FF+avg	FF+min	FF+shift	FF	FF+avg	FF+min	FF+shift	FF	FF+avg	FF+min	FF+shift
pfile1.sas	5	5	5	5	1	1	1	1	0	0	0	0
pfile2.sas	41	41	43	41	6	6	6	6	0	0	0	0
pfile3.sas	97	97	293	97	6	6	6	6	0	0	0	0
pfile4.sas	123	123	412	123	8	8	8	8	0	0	0	0
pfile5.sas	122	122	1378	122	11	11	11	11	0	0	0	0
pfile6.sas	185	231	4010	185	12	12	11	12	0	0	1	0
pfile7.sas	2870	2826	25968	2870	15	15	15	15	1	1	8	1
pfile8.sas	594	594	8356	594	12	12	11	12	0	0	6	0
pfile9.sas	2146	5185	3E+06	2146	21	21		21	1	3	1800	1
pfile10.sas	9430	39215	2E+06	9430	23	23		23	8	36	1800	8
pfile11.sas	4157	9863	780032	4197	14	14	14	14	6	15	968	6
pfile12.sas	29221	63698	1E+06	29221	21	21		21	43	96	1800	44
pfile13.sas	130732	172523	899246	130732	26	26		26	226	335	1800	225
pfile14.sas	39666	247819	193657	39666	30			30	304	1800	1800	305

Fig. 5. Performance of h_{FF}, h_{GC} and their modified versions in *zenotravel*.

We experimented with values of parameter α (size of subgraphs) from 2 to 4. For values larger that 4, computing features of states is too costly and the heuristic is not competitive. We also tried to include value of the h_{FF} among the features of states. I.e., we first trained the network having only the graph-based features as its inputs and then another network that used both graph-based features and h_{FF} value of the state as its inputs. We conducted experiments for all combinations of these parameters: $\alpha \in \{2,3,4\}$ and $FFasFeature \in \{true, false\}$. This gives us 6 different neural net-based heuristics.

We compared performance of heuristics using the *IPC-Score*. Given a search problem P, a minimization criterion R (e.g. length of the plan) and algorithms $A_1, A_2, \ldots, A_k$, the IPC-Score of A_i on problem P is computed as follows: $IPC_R(A_i, P) = 0$ if A_i didn't solve P, or $\frac{R^*}{R_i}$ otherwise, where R_i is value of the criterion for the i-th algorithm and $R^* = \min_i\{R_i\}$.

For every problem P, $IPC_R(A_i, P) \in [0, 1]$ and higher means better. The IPC-Score takes into account both number of problems solved and quality of solutions found. We can then sum up the IPC-Score over several problems to get accumulated results. We monitor the following criteria: total number of problems solved, IPC-Score of time, IPC-Score of plan length and IPC-Score of number of expansions.

Figure 6 shows results for the two domains.

As expected, higher values of α lead to a more accurate heuristic: the number of expanded nodes as well as plan length are better. The difference is apparent especially

heuristic	α	FF used	IPC Score - Time		IPC Score - Plan length		IPC Score - Expansions		Solved problems	
			blocks	zenotravel	blocks	zenotravel	blocks	zenotravel	blocks (27 total)	zenotravel (20 total)
NN heuristic	2	FALSE	5.31	2.01	9.98	5.92	1.79	0.74	10	6
		TRUE	14.99	4.16	24.75	9.30	10.89	3.96	25	9
	3	FALSE	8.43	2.37	11.98	10.52	4.82	3.26	12	11
		TRUE	21.57	5.31	25.94	11.08	17.77	5.53	26	11
	4	FALSE	18.67	4.46	25.94	12.08	20.68	4.77	26	12
		TRUE	19.57	8.49	25.94	15.08	22.61	10.10	26	16
FF heuristic			5.03	13.00	5.06	10.72	0.32	9.37	8	13

Fig. 6. Results of experiments.

for values 2 and 3. Using value $\alpha = 4$ still helps but computing features in this case is slower and so A* expands less nodes per second and overall results are not that much better than for $\alpha = 3$.

Adding h_{FF} as feature has a mixed effect. It is very helpful on *blocks* domain for $\alpha \in \{2,3\}$, but not much helpful for $\alpha = 4$. See Fig. 7. This indicates that subgraphs of size 2 and 3 cannot capture useful knowledge about a blocks problem hence the network relies on h_{FF} as the source of information. Subgraphs of size 4 are be able to provide the required knowledge already and adding h_{FF} doesn't help anymore. In general, adding h_{FF} improves accuracy of the NN so the resulting heuristic is more informed which improves both number of expansions and plan length. Due to the slow-down, though, adding h_{FF} doesn't often improve number of problems solved.

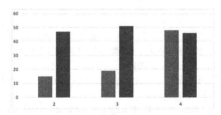

Fig. 7. Number of problems solved in *blocks* domain. Taken from [29]. On the X-axis there is value of α, blue columns correspond to networks trained without using h_{FF} as feature, orange columns show networks trained with h_{FF} included.

Among the neural-based heuristics, the setting with $\alpha = 4$ and h_{FF} added performs best. If we compare it with the h_{FF}, we see that our method vastly outperforms the baseline on *blocks* where it solved 26 out of 27 problems while h_{FF} can only solve 8 problems. Even on problems solved by both methods, the NN heuristic finds shorter plans and expands less nodes. On the *zenotravel* domain, our method outperforms h_{FF} in all criteria except *Time*. h_{FF} can find suboptimal plans very quickly in this domain hence it is difficult to achieve better score even though our method solved more problems.

8   Conclusions and Future Work

We presented a technique to automatically construct a strong heuristic for a given planning domain. Our technique is domain-independent and can extract knowledge about any domain from a given set of solved training problems without any assistance from a human expert. The knowledge in represented by a trained neural network and is transferable to previously unseen problems of any size.

We are using a novel technique for extracting features for states. The method allows to compute features incrementally which is very useful in the planning application. The presented technique significantly outperforms a popular domain-independent heuristic h_{FF} in both number of problems solved and solution quality.

We have proposed a data-driven heuristic-adjustment techniques that have several advantages over the popular heuristic-weighting approach. We believe that data-driven tools have a great undiscovered potential in the field of heuristic design.

We have also established a theoretical model that allows us to formally analyze properties of learned heuristics. Using that model, we formulated and proved bounds on the worst-case performance of learned heuristics.

As a feature work, we will perform experimental evaluation of our technique over a larger set of planning domains and we will try to extend our model to domains with action costs.

Acknowledgments. Research is supported by the Czech Science Foundation project P103-18-07252S.

References

1. Arfaee, S.J., Zilles, S., Holte, R.C.: Bootstrap learning of heuristic functions. In: Felner, A., Sturtevant, N.R. (eds.) Proceedings of the Third Annual Symposium on Combinatorial Search, SOCS 2010. AAAI Press (2010)
2. Arfaee, S.J., Zilles, S., Holte, R.C.: Learning heuristic functions for largestate spaces. Artif. Intell. **175**(16), 2075–2098 (2011)
3. Bisson, F., Larochelle, H., Kabanza, F.: Using a recursive neural network to learn an agent's decision model for plan recognition. In: Twenty-Fourth International Joint Conference on Artificial Intelligence (2015)
4. Brunetto, R., Trunda, O.: Deep heuristic-learning in the Rubik's cube domain: an experimental evaluation. In: Hlaváčová, J. (ed.) Proceedings of the 17th Conference ITAT 2017, pp. 57–64. CreateSpace Independent Publishing Platform (2017)
5. Cenamor, I., De La Rosa, T., Fernández, F.: Learning predictive models to configure planning portfolios. In: Proceedings of the 4th Workshop on Planning and Learning (ICAPS-PAL 2013) (2013)
6. Chen, H.C., Wei, J.D.: Using neural networks for evaluation in heuristic search algorithm. In: AAAI (2011)
7. Ferber, P., Helmert, M., Hoffmann, J.: Neural network heuristics for classical planning: a study of hyperparameter space. In: ECAI (2020)
8. Fink, M.: Online learning of search heuristics. In: Artificial Intelligence and Statistics, pp. 115–122 (2007)
9. Geissmann, C.: Learning heuristic functions in classical planning. Master's thesis, University of Basel, Switzerland (2015)
10. Goldberg, Y.: Neural network methods for natural language processing. Synth. Lect. Hum. Lang. Technol. **10**(1), 1–309 (2017)
11. Goodfellow, I., Bengio, Y., Courville, A.: Deep Learning. MIT Press, Cambridge (2016)

12. Groshev, E., Goldstein, M., et al.: Learning generalized reactive policies using deep neural networks. In: Symposium on Integrating Representation, Reasoning, Learning, and Execution for Goal Directed Autonomy (2017)
13. Groshev, E., Tamar, A., Goldstein, M., Srivastava, S., Abbeel, P.: Learning generalized reactive policies using deep neural networks. In: 2018 AAAI Spring Symposium Series (2018)
14. Hastie, T., Tibshirani, R., Friedman, J.: The Elements of Statistical Learning. Springer Series in Statistics. Springer New York Inc., New York (2001). https://doi.org/10.1007/978-0-387-21606-5
15. Helmert, M.: Understanding Planning Tasks: Domain Complexity and Heuristic Decomposition. LNCS (LNAI), vol. 4929. Springer, Heidelberg (2008). https://doi.org/10.1007/978-3-540-77723-6
16. Helmert, M.: Concise finite-domain representations for PDDL planning tasks. Artif. Intell. **173**(5), 503–535 (2009). https://doi.org/10.1016/j.artint.2008.10.013. http://www.sciencedirect.com/science/article/pii/S0004370208001926. Advances in Automated Plan Generation
17. Hoffmann, J., Nebel, B.: The FF planning system: fast plan generation through heuristic search. J. Artif. Intell. Res. **14**, 253–302 (2001)
18. Hornik, K.: Approximation capabilities of multilayer feedforward networks. Neural Netw. **4**(2), 251–257 (1991). https://doi.org/10.1016/0893-6080(91)90009-T. http://www.sciencedirect.com/science/article/pii/089360809190009T
19. Jiménez, S., De la Rosa, T., Fernández, S., Fernández, F., Borrajo, D.: A review of machine learning for automated planning. Knowl. Eng. Rev. **27**(4), 433–467 (2012)
20. Konidaris, G., Kaelbling, L.P., Lozano-Perez, T.: From skills to symbols: learning symbolic representations for abstract high-level planning. J. Artif. Intell. Res. **61**, 215–289 (2018)
21. Martín, M., Geffner, H.: Learning generalized policies from planning examples using concept languages. Appl. Intell. **20**(1), 9–19 (2004)
22. Nau, D., Ghallab, M., Traverso, P.: Automated Planning: Theory & Practice. Morgan Kaufmann Publishers Inc., San Francisco (2004)
23. Pearl, J.: Heuristics: Intelligent Search Strategies for Computer Problem Solving. The Addison-Wesley Series in Artificial Intelligence. Addison-Wesley (1984). https://books.google.cz/books?id=0XtQAAAAMAAJ
24. Russell, S.J., Norvig, P.: Artificial Intelligence: A Modern Approach, 3rd edn. Prentice Hall, Upper Saddle River (2010)
25. Samadi, M., Felner, A., Schaeffer, J.: Learning from multiple heuristics. In: Fox, D., Gomes, C.P. (eds.) AAAI, pp. 357–362. AAAI Press (2008)
26. Takahashi, T., Sun, H., Tian, D., Wang, Y.: Learning heuristic functions for mobile robot path planning using deep neural networks. In: Proceedings of the International Conference on Automated Planning and Scheduling. vol. 29, pp. 764–772 (2019)
27. Thayer, J., Dionne, A., Ruml, W.: Learning inadmissible heuristics during search. In: Proceedings of International Conference on Automated Planning and Scheduling (2011)
28. Toyer, S., Trevizan, F., Thiébaux, S., Xie, L.: Action schema networks: generalised policies with deep learning. In: Thirty-Second AAAI Conference on Artificial Intelligence (2018)
29. Trunda, O., Barták, R.: Deep learning of heuristics for domain-independent planning. In: Rocha, A.P., Steels, L., van den Herik, H.J. (eds.) Proceedings of the 12th International Conference on Agents and Artificial Intelligence, ICAART 2020, vol. 2, pp. 79–88. SCITEPRESS (2020)
30. Virseda, J., Borrajo, D., Alcázar, V.: Learning heuristic functions for cost-based planning. Planning and Learning, p. 6 (2013)
31. Yoon, S., Fern, A., Givan, R.: Learning control knowledge for forward search planning. J. Mach. Learn. Res. **9**(Apr), 683–718 (2008)

Knowledge Injection to Neural Networks with Progressive Learning Strategy

Ha Thanh Nguyen$^{(\boxtimes)}$, Trung Kien Vu, Teeradaj Racharak, Le Minh Nguyen, and Satoshi Tojo

Japan Advanced Institute of Science and Technology, Ishikawa, Japan
{nguyenhathanh,kienvu,racharak,nguyenml,tojo}@jaist.ac.jp

Abstract. Nowadays, deep learning has become the most modern and practical approach to solve a wide range of problems. With the ability to automatically extract the hierarchy of semantic level from the data, neural networks often outperform other techniques in complex issues. However, to perform well, the models need a vast amount of data, which is not always available. To overcome that problem, we propose an approach of injecting knowledge into the neural network instead of letting it struggles by itself. Our proposed policy for the training process is guiding the model to learn the label from a similarity distribution. Finally, we conduct experiments in the chord modeling problem to show the effectiveness of our method.

Keywords: Knowledge injection · Simlarity distribution · Chord2Vec · Neural networks · Progressive training

1 Introduction

Our knowledge about the world is a model itself. We percept nature and sociality by our senses, process the information by our brain, and remember the conclusion as experience. When a new situation comes, we compare it with our experience and conduct an appropriate judgment for the case. The artificial neural network is much more straightforward but has the same mechanism. Given input/output pairs in the training data, the model tries to predict the answer, correct the prediction from feedbacks, and remember the hidden rules in the data.

Different architectures of neural networks share the same mechanism. Specifically, given input/output pairs, the model during the training process needs to learn to minimize the designed loss function to achieve better and better predictions. Theoretically, after being trained, the parameters of the model make it able to output the correct label similar to what it has learned from the data. However, in practice, there are often situations that the data is not enough for the model to formulate an excellent interpretation to make the right prediction for unseen samples.

© Springer Nature Switzerland AG 2021
A. P. Rocha et al. (Eds.): ICAART 2020, LNAI 12613, pp. 280–290, 2021.
https://doi.org/10.1007/978-3-030-71158-0_13

Many authors came up with different methods to overcome this challenge. Most of them are about adding more information to the input. Pretrained embeddings (*cf.* [12,14,16]) are the methods that enhance the information about relationship between the tokens via learned vectors. Transfer learning methods use pre-trained models like BERT [4] and fine-tune them later according to downstream tasks.

Those approaches are suitable for the problems in a domain containing a large amount of material like problems in Natural language processing or Computer vision. Nevertheless, in a field in which the training data is limited even for training pre-trained models, the transfer learning technique is useless. In such situations, to improve the learning performance of the model, there must be a way to inject the domain knowledge into its learning progress. Song et al. [18] uses an ontology to train parameters of the model selectively. In the work of [2], instead of using a single target vector, the authors let the model guided by multiple vectors.

The deep learning models often update their parameters directly from the label of training data. This optimization has a potential drawback. The feedback for the model is only whether right or wrong and the model need to look up a different value set of parameter randomly. This *try-and-error* progress takes a lot of resource for training and possibly lead to overfitting when the model only tries to remember the training data. Based on such observation, we propose a progressive training method that injects the domain knowledge to the neural network by similarity metric. For that purpose, we implement a training method that gradually turns the similarity target, which is obtained from the domain knowledge, into the original distribution, which is annotated in the training data.

In this lecture note, besides the contributions presented at ICAART 2020 [22], we study and convey the theoretical basis of using similarity as an element of knowledge. We also introduce an approach to extract the knowledge when the corpus is given automatically. Our experiment shows that our method is effective and general.

2   Backgrounds

2.1   Similarity in Cognitive Science

The similarity is a field of research in cognitive science. There are lots of research approaches to the concept of similarity. They are strongly related to knowledge representation; each of them focuses on a set of assumptions.

Shepard et al. [17] bases on the assumption that points within the space can represent the concepts and the distances between the points represent the similarity between concepts. This approach is a vital basis for machine learning techniques like clustering or latent semantic analysis.

The distance approach is straightforward to understand, but it has the limitation as the distance is symmetric. In the featural approach, Tversky et al. [20] define a function $s(a, b)$ as a metric of similarity from a to b. We need to notice that this function is asymmetry and comparable. $s(a, b) > s(b, a)$ is valid following this theory. In detail, the authors propose this approach based on two assumptions: Matching and Monotonicity. Let A and B be the set of features of a and b. The matching assumption is that similarity of a to b is a function accepting three arguments: $A \cap B$, $A - B$, and $B - A$. Figure 1 illustrates how these subsets affect the similarity function. Monotonicity assumption states that $s(a, b) \geq s(a, c)$ whenever: $A \cap C \subset A \cap B$, $A - B \subset A - C$, and $B - A \subset C - A$.

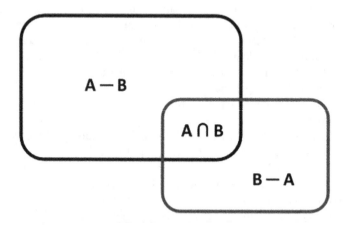

Fig. 1. Illustration of arguments of similarity function.

Another theory of similarity, Gentner et al. [5] develops structural mapping. In this theory, there are two kinds of differences which are the non-alignable difference and the alignable difference. The alignable difference comes from the commonality, for example, both dogs and chickens have legs, but dogs have four legs while chickens have two legs. Non-alignable differences are the features that do not belong to both entities. Another approach, Hahn et al. [7] evaluate the similarity based on the minimum number of transformation steps to make one representation into another.

2.2   Neural Network Models

The most classical deep learning model is multiple layer perceptron (MLP) or feedforward neural network. An MLP consists of at least three layers known as the input layer, hidden layer(s), and output layer. This simple model can approximate a wide range of functions and classify nonlinear separable data. Each node in this neural network is assigned with a weight value. Learning is about adjusting these weights to fit the data. When the model makes a wrong prediction, a signal in the form of the loss function is calculated. Based on that, the model updates the weights to improve the predictions.

The limitation of MLP is that it cannot capture the relation of entities in an input sequence because each input is feed through the network separately.

The relation information is essential to obtain a good prediction. As a result, the vanilla version of the neural network as MLP does not perform well on sequential data.

A different well-known neural network class is recurrent neural networks. The precursor of this class is the Hopfield Networks [11]. This architecture makes use of the information from the previous step in the prediction of the current phase. Consequently, this neural network is able to handle consecutive inputs. LSTM [9] and GRU [3] are the better versions of RNN.

Although the recurrent neural network can handle the sequential input, it faces a challenge, namely "vanishing gradients". This architecture maintains the relationship between entities in a long sequence. As a result, the feedback signals have to pass through a dense bundle of layers, which leads to the loss value becomes zero at the first layers. Overcome such challenge, LSTM is the neural network that can skip some unnecessary input in the sequence and focus only on the critical parts. This architecture contains an input gate, an output gate, and a forget gate, as shown in Fig. 2. This model can choose which input to remember and ignore others. GRU is another architecture, which has a similar principle of design but contains less number of parameter than LSTM.

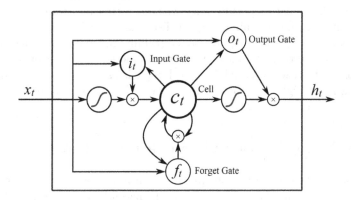

Fig. 2. LSTM architecture can capture longer input sequence [22].

LSTM models are widely used and bring good performance in many tasks like sequence tagging [10], speech recognition [6], or language modeling [19].

The lastest well-known architecture of deep learning is the transformer models [21]. They were invented with the idea of attention mechanism. This mechanism helps the model to choose the most relevant part in the sequence to pay attention to. The advantage of this approach is that the distance between the word does not limit the relationship probability.

2.3 Related Works

This work is not the first research to try to enhance learning efficiency by exploiting knowledge at training progress. We can mention some of the well-known approaches, such as multi-task learning, transfer learning, curriculum learning, and knowledge compilation.

The aim of multi-task learning is leveraging the relationship between classes at the training time. For example, Vural et al. [23] proposed a classification model to extract interclass relationships. Wu et al. [24] built a classifier that can learn the relationship features using deep learning architecture in the video classification task.

The idea behind transfer learning is to make use of learned parameters from one domain to another domain. Compared to the target domain, the source domain often contains more resources and is more feasible for deep learning models to exploit knowledge. This approach is natural as the way humans learn. For example, if a person has experience in learning a foreign language, such experience can help to learn other foreign languages faster. Pre-trained models like BERT [4] or GPT-2 [15] are good examples of transfer learning.

Curriculum learning approaches try to use a metric for measuring the difficulty of each sample. The model then can choose to learn the sorted example based on that metric. Gradually increasing the complexity of the learning problem makes the model learn and build the hierarchy of concepts instead of trying to remember precisely the samples. [2] makes use of curriculum learning to make their model achieve better performance without increasing training time.

Along with transfer learning, we can distill the knowledge from a model to another model. For instance, [8] proposes a training procedure in which there are two models. This procedure allows the student model to learn from the output distribution of the teacher model. This technique is useful for model compression for creating lightweight but robust models. Besides, knowledge distillation can help to avoid overfitting (*cf.* [1]).

3   Knowledge Injection via Simlarity Metric

In a multi-class classification problem, there are K classes of the instances, and the model needs to predict which class each instance belongs to. At first, the features of each sentence are fed into the model as a vectorized representation. The model then needs to predict the output by producing a K-dimension vector $\hat{\mathbf{y}} := [\hat{y}_1, \ldots, \hat{y}_K]$. This vector represents the probability distribution of the confidence over K classes. If the prediction is far from the gold distribution, the neural network needs to update its weights θ to reduces the loss calculated by KL divergence between the predicted distribution $\hat{\mathbf{y}}$ and the gold distribution $\mathbf{y}$ (*cf.* Eq. 1 [22]).

$$D_{\mathrm{KL}}(\mathbf{y}, \hat{\mathbf{y}}) := \sum_{i=1}^{K} y_i \log \frac{y_i}{\hat{y}_i} \tag{1}$$

In general, one-hot representation is the format for the target distribution $\mathbf{y} := [y_1, \ldots, y_K]$ *i.e.*, the true distribution. However, this distribution is not always straightforward for the model to learn. The feedback signal is simply whether right and wrong, which does not reflect the fact that among wrong predictions, some of them are better than the others. As mentioned in Sect. 1, the feedback signal for each class should be unequal. The loss value between two similar classes should be smaller than the very different ones. At that point, the knowledge of similarity between classes is essential for improving training performance. We propose the training process containing two steps as following:

1. Calculate the similarity between classes and form a distribution based on that information.
2. Apply a progressive learning start from the similarity distribution and gradually turn to the true distribution.

The similarity score between two classes is calculated following the Eq. 2 [22]. In which, $s(a, b)$ is the similarity score between two classes a and b, $w(p)$ is the weighted common properties of the classes.

$$s(a, b) := \sum_{p \in \mathcal{P}_a \cap \mathcal{P}_b} w(p) \tag{2}$$

Continuing the previous work on chord data [22], in this paper, we propose a knowledge extraction method named Chord2Vec. Chord2Vec is built on statistics of the occurrence of chords with contexts. Initially, each chord is represented by a random vector. After the training process, the updated vector can reflect the relationship and distance between chords. Given the context, which are previous chords in a sequence, the model needs to predict the next one. Let $\boldsymbol{v}_a$ and $\boldsymbol{v}_b$ are the chord vectors of chord a and chord b, the similarity function $s(a, b)$ is calculated by the Eq. 3.

$$s(a, b) = 1 + cos(\boldsymbol{v}_a, \boldsymbol{v}_b) \tag{3}$$

In the formula, we add 1 into the cosine similarity to make sure the outputs of the function is greater or equal to 0.

After calculating the pairwise similarity score, we construct the similarity vector representation, in which each unit calculated following the Eq. 4 [22].

$$s_{ak} := \frac{s(i, k)}{\sum_{j=1}^{K} s(i, j)} \tag{4}$$

Finally, the mass distribution is calculated from the similarity vectors following the Eq. 5 [22]. To make use of the knowledge of similarity in the training period, we apply a progressive learning process.

$$t_{ak} := \text{softmax}(s_{ak}) := \frac{\exp(s_{ak}/T)}{\sum_{j=1}^{K} \exp(s_{aj}/T)} \tag{5}$$

We use a variable T to control the learning temperature. At the beginning of the process, we use a high value of T and gradually decrease it following Eq. 6 [22]. As a result, the model is forced to learn from the similarity distribution and slowly turns to the actual distribution.

$$T_t := \frac{T_{t-1}}{1 + \lambda t} \tag{6}$$

4   Experiments

This section has two main purposes. First, we verify the effectiveness of knowledge injection in a training process when similarity knowledge is given by the user. Second, we aim at showing that similarity knowledge can be automatically learnt from a dataset. For that, we introduce an approach called Chord2Vec. Note that this idea of automatic knowledge extraction is new and has not well investigated in [22].

4.1   Experimental Settings

To verify the effectiveness of our method, we choose the chord modeling problem. We use the ABC dataset [13] which are from 17 Beethoven string quartets. For the experimental setup purpose, we split all pieces into phrases. And because we do not model the duration of each chord, repetitions of phrases are removed. Table 1 represents some important properties of the final dataset.

Table 1. Properties of the final dataset.

Property	Value
Number of phrases	968
Average length of phrases	21
Number of keys	21
Number of chord types	13

We used 5-fold cross-validation and two metrics as perplexity and accuracy to assess the model. We use 200 phrases as the evaluation data in each fold, and the rest to train the model. We use the data augmentation technique for the data in the training set. Each phrase is transposed into 12 keys. At last, we got 8000 samples in the training set.

The deep learning model in our experiments is LSTM. The embedding size, hidden size is set to 128. We optimized the model with Adam Optimizer. Learning rate is 10^{-3}. The early stopping patience is 10 and maximum number of epochs is 200.

As described in Sect. 3, we conduct experiments to confirm whether it is feasible to extract knowledge directly from the corpus to improve model efficiency in specific tasks. This has two meanings. Firstly, we can cross-evaluate the effectiveness of knowledge injection in our method. Secondly, it gives a hint about how to guide the model using knowledge injection in domains where people do not have much experience.

The idea is borrowed from Word2Vec [12]. The musician places the chords in a music sheet intentionally. If the placement is random, the creation is not called music, it is just a sequence of noise. By such observation, we have a hypothesis that there must be a kind of grammar in the music, and the machine learning model can learn such knowledge.

We sort the chord by descending frequency and the chord appearing less than 5 times in the corpus is eliminated. We train the Chord2Vec with the starting learning rate is 0.025 and is linearly reduced to zero. We stop the training process as soon as the loss stop decreasing.

4.2   Experimental Results

As reported in our previous paper [22], training model with our proposed knowledge injection overperformed using the one-hot vector as the target. The chord properties which we use to calculate the similarity score includes: *token name, key name, key number, triad form, figured bass*, and *note pair*. Besides, the weights for properties make the performance of the model better than using uniform weights. The optimal weight setting for this approach is $(16, 32, 16, 4, 4, 32)$. Interestingly, our novel approach using Chord2Vec achieved state-of-the-art results with hyperparameter value $T_0 = 0.025$ and $\lambda = 0.01$. Although this value does not create a big gap with the performance of knowledge injection with chord properties, this result still can confirm that injecting knowledge with chord property is reasonable and the knowledge can be learned automatically from the corpus.

Table 2. Performance of different approaches.

Approach	Perplexity
One-hot vector	3.48
Uniform weight set	2.49
Optimal weight set	2.39
Chord2Vec	**2.37**

Figure 3 shows similarity matrices calculated by chord properties with weight sets $(1, 1, 1, 1, 1, 1)$ and $(16, 32, 16, 4, 4, 32)$ as well as calculated by cosine similarity of Chord2Vec vectors according to Eq. 3. Axis X and Y of the matrices are the ids of the chords. In all three matrices, high similarity points often gather in the diagonal (Table 2).

The figure of the similar pattern calculated by cosine has more diverse similarity points. However, there are rows and columns with all null values because of some chords which do not exist in the corpus used to train Chord2Vec embedding. It is one of the limitations of this approach compared to human knowledge.

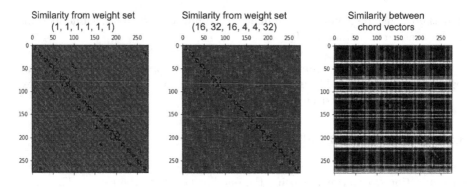

Fig. 3. Similarity matrices are calculated base on weighted properties and chord vectors.

5   Conclusion

This work leverages the proposal in our previous paper [22]. Human knowledge is a model about the world, and such information can guide the neural network to learn better. In this paper, we have introduced the theory basis for knowledge encoding as a similarity metric and propose an approach to make use of knowledge during the training time of the model.

To experiment with our idea, we defined a similarity encoding based on the common weighted properties of chords to deal with the problem of chord prediction. There is an interesting finding in our experiment that turning similarity target to one-hot target using appropriate temperature and decay can significantly improve the performance of the model.

In this paper, we also make an additional experiment to extract the knowledge from the corpus, then compare its performance with expert knowledge. The result confirms the effectiveness of our method and gives us a hint to use this method as a transfer learning approach in a suitable domain. The model can learn to construct the similarity encoding if there is a large enough corpus. The proposed method in this paper can be applied to a wide range of works using neural networks.

References

1. Asami, T., Masumura, R., Yamaguchi, Y., Masataki, H., Aono, Y.: Domain adaptation of dnn acoustic models using knowledge distillation. In: 2017 IEEE International Conference on Acoustics, Speech and Signal Processing (ICASSP), pp. 5185–5189, March 2017. https://doi.org/10.1109/ICASSP.2017.7953145
2. Bengio, S., Vinyals, O., Jaitly, N., Shazeer, N.: Scheduled sampling for sequence prediction with recurrent neural networks. In: Proceedings of the 28th International Conference on Neural Information Processing Systems, NIPS 2015, vol. 1. pp. 1171–1179. MIT Press, Cambridge (2015). http://dl.acm.org/citation.cfm?id=2969239.2969370

3. Cho, K., et al.: Learning phrase representations using RNN encoder-decoder for statistical machine translation. arXiv preprint arXiv:1406.1078 (2014)
4. Devlin, J., Chang, M.W., Lee, K., Toutanova, K.: BERT: pre-training of deep bidirectional transformers for language understanding. arXiv preprint arXiv:1810.04805 (2018)
5. Gentner, D., Markman, A.B.: Structure mapping in analogy and similarity. Am. Psychol. **52**(1), 45 (1997)
6. Graves, A., Mohamed, A.r., Hinton, G.: Speech recognition with deep recurrent neural networks. In: 2013 IEEE International Conference on Acoustics, Speech and Signal Processing, pp. 6645–6649. IEEE (2013)
7. Hahn, U., Chater, N., Richardson, L.B.: Similarity as transformation. Cognition **87**(1), 1–32 (2003)
8. Hinton, G., Vinyals, O., Dean, J.: Distilling the knowledge in a neural network. arXiv preprint arXiv:1503.02531 (2015)
9. Hochreiter, S., Schmidhuber, J.: Long short-term memory. Neural Comput. **9**(8), 1735–1780 (1997)
10. Huang, Z., Xu, W., Yu, K.: Bidirectional LSTM-CRF models for sequence tagging. arXiv preprint arXiv:1508.01991 (2015)
11. John, J.H.: Neural network and physical systems with emergent collective computational abilities. Proc. Nat. Acad. Sci. U.S.A. **79**, 2554–2558 (1982)
12. Mikolov, T., Chen, K., Corrado, G., Dean, J.: Efficient estimation of word representations in vector space. arXiv preprint arXiv:1301.3781 (2013)
13. Neuwirth, M., Harasim, D., Moss, F.C., Rohrmeier, M.: The Annotated Beethoven Corpus (ABC): a dataset of harmonic analyses of all Beethoven string quartets. Front. Digit. Hum. **5**, 16 (2018). https://doi.org/10.3389/fdigh.2018.00016. https://www.frontiersin.org/article/11.3389/fdigh.2018.00016
14. Pennington, J., Socher, R., Manning, C.: GloVe: global vectors for word representation. In: Proceedings of the 2014 Conference on Empirical Methods in Natural Language Processing (EMNLP), Doha, Qatar, pp. 1532–1543. Association for Computational Linguistics, October 2014. https://doi.org/10.3115/v1/D14-1162
15. Radford, A., Wu, J., Child, R., Luan, D., Amodei, D., Sutskever, I.: Language models are unsupervised multitask learners. OpenAI Blog **1**(8), 9 (2019)
16. Radford, A., Wu, J., Child, R., Luan, D., Amodei, D., Sutskever, I.: Language models are unsupervised multitask learners. OpenAI Blog **1**(8), 9 (2019)
17. Shepard, R.N.: The analysis of proximities: multidimensional scaling with an unknown distance function. i. Psychometrika **27**(2), 125–140 (1962)
18. Song, L., Cheong, C.W., Yin, K., Cheung, W.K., Fung, B.C.M., Poon, J.: Medical concept embedding with multiple ontological representations. In: Proceedings of the Twenty-Eighth International Joint Conference on Artificial Intelligence, IJCAI 2019, pp. 4613–4619. International Joint Conferences on Artificial Intelligence Organization (7 2019)
19. Sundermeyer, M., Schlüter, R., Ney, H.: LSTM neural networks for language modeling. In: Thirteenth Annual Conference of the International Speech Communication Association (2012)
20. Tversky, A.: Features of similarity. Psychol. Rev. **84**(4), 327 (1977)
21. Vaswani, A., et al.: Attention is all you need. In: Advances in Neural Information Processing Systems, pp. 5998–6008 (2017)
22. Vu, T.K., Racharak, T., Tojo, S., Nguyen, H.T., Nguyen, L.M.: Progressive training in recurrent neural networks for chord progression modeling. In: Proceedings of the 12th International Conference on Agents and Artificial Intelligence (2020)

23. Vural, V., Fung, G., Rosales, R., Dy, J.G.: Multi-class classifiers and their under-lying shared structure. In: IJCAI (2009)
24. Wu, Z., Jiang, Y.G., Wang, J., Pu, J., Xue, X.: Exploring inter-feature and inter-class relationships with deep neural networks for video classification. In: Proceedings of the 22Nd ACM International Conference on Multimedia, MM 2014, pp. 167–176. ACM, New York (2014). https://doi.org/10.1145/2647868.2654931

A Scalable and Automated Machine Learning Framework to Support Risk Management

Luís Ferreira[1,2(✉)] ⓘ, André Pilastri[2] ⓘ, Carlos Martins[3] ⓘ, Pedro Santos[3] ⓘ, and Paulo Cortez[2] ⓘ

[1] EPMQ - IT Engineering Maturity and Quality Lab, CCG ZGDV Institute, Guimarães, Portugal
{luis.ferreira,andre.pilastri}@ccg.pt
[2] ALGORITMI Centre, Department of Information Systems, University of Minho, Guimarães, Portugal
pcortez@dsi.uminho.pt
[3] WeDo Technologies, Braga, Portugal
{carlos.mmartins,pedro.santos}@mobileum.com

Abstract. Due to the growth of data and widespread usage of Machine Learning (ML) by non-experts, automation and scalability are becoming key issues for ML. This paper presents an automated and scalable framework for ML that requires minimum human input. We designed the framework for the domain of telecommunications risk management. This domain often requires non-ML-experts to continuously update supervised learning models that are trained on huge amounts of data. Thus, the framework uses Automated Machine Learning (AutoML), to select and tune the ML models, and distributed ML, to deal with Big Data. The modules included in the framework are task detection (to detect classification or regression), data preprocessing, feature selection, model training, and deployment. In this paper, we focus the experiments on the model training module. We first analyze the capabilities of eight AutoML tools: Auto-Gluon, Auto-Keras, Auto-Sklearn, Auto-Weka, H2O AutoML, Rminer, TPOT, and TransmogrifAI. Then, to select the tool for model training, we performed a benchmark with the only two tools that address a distributed ML (H2O AutoML and TransmogrifAI). The experiments used three real-world datasets from the telecommunications domain (churn, event forecasting, and fraud detection), as provided by an analytics company. The experiments allowed us to measure the computational effort and predictive capability of the AutoML tools. Both tools obtained high-quality results and did not present substantial predictive differences. Nevertheless, H2O AutoML was selected by the analytics company for the model training module, since it was considered a more mature technology that presented a more interesting set of features (e.g., integration with more platforms). After choosing H2O AutoML for the ML training, we selected the technologies for the remaining components of the architecture (e.g., data preprocessing and web interface).

Keywords: Automated machine learning · Distributed machine learning · Supervised learning · Risk management

© Springer Nature Switzerland AG 2021
A. P. Rocha et al. (Eds.): ICAART 2020, LNAI 12613, pp. 291–307, 2021.
https://doi.org/10.1007/978-3-030-71158-0_14

1   Introduction

Nowadays, Machine Learning applications can make use of a great amount of data, complex algorithms, and machines with great processing power to produce effective predictions and forecasts [11]. Currently, two of the most important features of real-world ML applications are distributed learning and AutoML. Distributed learning is particularly useful for ML applications in the context of Big Data or when there are hardware constraints. Distributed learning consists of using multiple machines or processors to process parts of the ML algorithm or parts of the data. The fact that it is possible to add new processing units enables ML applications to surpass time and memory restrictions [29]. AutoML intends to allow people that are not experts in ML to efficiently choose and apply ML algorithms. AutoML is particularly relevant since there is a growing number of non-specialists working with ML [31]. It is also important for real-world applications that require constant updates to ML models.

In this paper, we propose a technological architecture that addresses these two ML challenges. The architecture was adapted to the area of telecommunications risk management, which is a domain that mostly uses supervised learning algorithms (e.g., for churn prediction). Moreover, the ML models are constantly updated by people that are not experts in ML and may involve Big Data. Thus, the proposed architecture delineates a set of steps to automate the typical workflow of a ML application that uses supervised learning. The architecture includes modules for task detection, data preprocessing, feature selection, model training, and deployment.

The focus of this work is the model training module of the architecture, which was designed to use a distributed AutoML tool. In order to select the ML tool for this module, we initially evaluated the characteristics of eight open-source AutoML tools (Auto-Gluon, Auto-Keras, Auto-Sklearn, Auto-Weka, H2O AutoML, Rminer, TPOT, and TransmogrifAI). We then performed a benchmark to compare the two tools that allowed a distributed execution (H2O AutoML and TransmogrifAI). The experiments used three real-world datasets from the domain of telecommunications. These datasets were related to churn (regression), event forecasting (time series), and fraud detection (binary classification).

This paper consists of an extended version of our previous work [14]. The main novelty of this extended version is the technological architecture that is presented in Sect. 6. This section describes the particular technologies that were used to implement the components of the proposed AutoML distributed framework apart from model training. Also, this section describes the REST API that was developed to mediate the communication between the end-users and the proposed framework.

The paper is organized as follows. Section 2 presents the related work. In Sect. 3, we detail the proposed ML architecture. Next, Sect. 4 describes the analyzed AutoML technologies and the datasets used during the experimental tests. Then, Sect. 5 discusses the experimental results. Section 6 details the technological architecture. Finally, Sect. 7 presents the main conclusions and future work directions.

2 Related Work

In a Big Data context, it is critical to create and use scalable ML algorithms to face the common constraints of memory and time [29]. To face that concern, classical distributed ML distributes the work among different processors, each performing part of the algorithm. Another current ML problem concerns the choice of ML algorithms and hyperparameters for a given task. For ML experts, this selection of algorithms and hyperparameters may use domain knowledge or heuristics, but it is not an easy task for non-ML-experts. AutoML was developed to combat this relevant issue [22]. The definition of AutoML can be described as the search for the best algorithm and hyperparameters for a given dataset with minimum human input.

In recent years, a large number of AutoML tools was developed, such as Auto-Gluon [3], Auto-Keras [23], Auto-Sklearn [15], Auto-Weka [24], H2O AutoML [21], Rminer [10], TPOT [27], and TransmogrifAI [30]. Within our knowledge, few studies directly compare AutoML tools. Most studies compare one specific AutoML framework with state-of-the-art ML algorithms [15], do not present experimental tests [12,35], or are related to ML automation challenges [18–20].

Recently, some studies focused on experimental comparisons of AutoML tools. In 2019, [17,32] compare a set of AutoML tools using different datasets and ML tasks. In 2020, a benchmark was conducted using publicly available datasets from OpenML [33], comparing different types of AutoML tools, which were grouped by their capabilities [36]. None of the mentioned comparison studies considered the distributed ML capability for the AutoML tools. Furthermore, none of the studies used datasets from the domain of telecommunications risk management, such as churn prediction or fraud detection.

3 Proposed Architecture

This paper is part of "Intelligent Risk Management for the Digital Age" (IRMDA), a R&D project developed by a leading Portuguese company in the area of software and analytics. The purpose of the project is to develop a ML system to assist the company telecommunications clients. Both scalability and automation are central requirements to the ML system since the company has many clients with diverse amounts of data (large or small) and that are typically non-ML-experts.

The ML technological architecture that is proposed by this work identifies and automates all typical tasks of a common supervised ML application, with minimum human input (only the dataset and the target column). Also, since the architecture was developed to work within a cluster with several processing nodes, the users can handle any size of datasets just by managing the number of cluster nodes. The architecture is illustrated in Fig. 1.

3.1 Phases

The proposed architecture assumes two main phases (Fig. 1): a training phase and a testing phase.

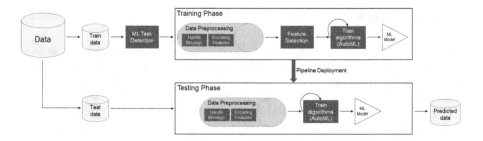

Fig. 1. The proposed automated and scalable ML architecture (adapted from [14]).

Training Phase: The training phase includes the creation of a pipeline instance and the definition of its stages. The only human input needed by the user is the selection of the training dataset and the identification of the target column. Depending on the dataset columns, each module defines a set of stages for the pipeline. Each stage either transforms data or also creates a model based on the training data that will be used on the test phase to transform the data. When all stages are defined, the pipeline is fitted to the training data, creating a pipeline model. Finally, the pipeline model is exported to a file.

Testing Phase: The execution of the testing pipeline assumes the same transformations that were applied to the training data. To execute the testing pipeline the user only needs to specify the test data and a pipeline model (and a forecasting horizon in the case of time series forecasting task). The last stage of the testing pipeline is the application of the best model obtained during training, generating the predictions. Performance metrics are also computed and presented to the user.

3.2   Components

The proposed architecture includes five main components: task detection, data preprocessing, feature selection, model training (with the usage of AutoML), and pipeline deployment.

Machine Learning Task Detection: Set to detect the ML task of the pipeline (e.g., classification, regression, time series). This detection is made by analyzing the number of levels of the target column and the existence (or not) of a time column.

Data Preprocessing: Handles missing data, the encoding of categorical features, and the standardization of numerical features. The applied transformations depend on the data type of the columns, number of levels, and number of missing values.

Feature Selection: Deletes features from the dataset that may decrease the predictive performance of the ML models, using filtering methods. Filtering methods are based on individual correlations between each feature and the target, removing several features that present the lowest correlations [4].

Model Training: Automatically trains and tunes a set of ML models using a set of constraints (e.g., time limit, memory usage). The component also identifies the best model to be used on the test phase.

Pipeline Deployment: Manages the saving and loading of the pipelines to and from files. This module saves the pipeline that will be used on a test set, ensuring that the new data will pass through the same transformations as the training data. Also, the component stores the best model obtained during the training to make predictions, discarding all other ML models.

4   Materials and Methods

4.1   Experimental Evaluation

For the experimental evaluation, we first examined the characteristics of the open-source AutoML tools. Then, we used the tools that could be implemented in our architecture to perform a benchmark study. In order to be considered for the experimental evaluation, the tools have to implement distributed ML.

4.2   AutoML Tools

We first analyzed eight recent open-source AutoML tools, to verify their compliance with the project requirements.

Auto-Gluon: AutoGluon is an open-source AutoML toolkit with a focus on Deep Learning. It is written in Python and runs on Linux operating system. AutoGluon is divided into four main modules: tabular data, image classification, object detection, and text classification [3]. In this article, only the tabular prediction functionalities are being considered.

Auto-Keras: Auto-Keras is a Python library based on Keras [6] that implements AutoML methods with Deep Learning algorithms. The focus of Auto-Keras is the automatic search for Deep Learning architectures and hyperparameters, usually named Neural Architecture Search [13].

Auto-Sklearn: Auto-Sklearn is an AutoML Python library based on Scikit-Learn [28] that implements methods for automatic algorithm selection and hyperparameter tuning. Auto-Sklearn aims to free the user from the choice of an algorithm and the tuning of its hyperparameters using Bayesian optimization, meta-learning, and Ensemble Learning [16].

Auto-Weka: Auto-Weka is a module of WEKA, a ML tool that provides data preprocessing functions and ML algorithms that allow users to quickly compare ML models and create predictions using new data [34]. Auto-Weka aims to solve the Combined Algorithm Selection and Hyperparameter Optimization (CASH) problem, first established in [31].

H2O AutoML: H2O AutoML is one of the open-source modules of H2O, a ML analytics platform that uses in-memory data and implements a distributed and scalable architecture [7]. H2O AutoML uses H2O's infrastructure to provide functions to automate algorithm selection and hyperparameter optimization [21].

Rminer: Rminer is a package for the R tool, intending to facilitate the use of Machine Learning algorithms. The focus of Rminer are the CRISP-DM phases of Modeling and Evaluation [8,9]. In the most recent version, Rminer uses more than 20 classification and regression algorithms. Also, since version 1.4.4, Rminer implements AutoML functions.

TPOT: Tree-Based Pipeline Optimization Tool (TPOT) is an open-source AutoML written in Python. TPOT automates the phases of feature selection, feature engineering, algorithm selection, and hyperparameter tuning. It uses algorithms such as Decision Trees, Random Forest, and XGBoost, most of them from the Scikit-Learn library [25, 27].

TransmogrifAI: TransmogrifAI is a tool that uses Apache Spark framework to automate ML applications. It is written in Scala and focused on the automation of several phases of the ML workflow, such as algorithm selection, feature selection, and feature engineering [30].

AutoML Tool Comparison: Table 1 presents the characteristics of the analyzed AutoML related to interface language, associated platforms, current version and if it contains a Graphical User Interface and distributed ML mode.

For the experimental study, we selected H2O AutoML and TransmogrifAI, as these were the only tools from Table 1 that meet the distributed ML requirement. Table 2 presents the ML algorithms implemented by both tools. The last two rows are related to the stacking ensembles implemented by H2O AutoML: all, which combines all trained algorithms; and best, which only combines the best algorithm per family.

4.3 Data

For the benchmark study, we used three real-world datasets from the domain of telecommunications, provided by the IRMDA project analytics company. The datasets are related to customer churn prediction (regression), event forecasting (univariate time series), and telecommunications fraud detection (binary classification).

Table 1. Main characteristics of the analyzed AutoML tools (extended from [14]).

	Interface language	Associated platforms	Current version	Graphical user interface	Distributed mode
Auto-Gluon	Python	-	0.0.14	-	-
Auto-Keras	Python	-	1.0.9	-	-
Auto-Sklearn	Python	-	0.10.0	-	-
Auto-Weka	Python R	WEKA	2.6.1	✓	-
H2O AutoML	Python R Scala	AWS Azure Google Cloud Apache Spark	3.30.1.3	✓	✓
Rminer	R	-	1.4.6	-	-
TPOT	Python	-	0.11.5	-	-
TransmogrifAI	Scala	Apache Spark	0.7.0	-	✓

Table 2. Algorithms implemented by H2O AutoML and TransmogrifAI (adapted from [14]).

Algorithm	H2O AutoML	TransmogrifAI
Decision Trees	-	✓
Deep Learning	✓	-
Extremely Randomized Forest	✓	-
Gradient-Boosted Trees (GBT)	-	✓
Gradient Boosting Machine (GBM)	✓	-
Generalized Linear Model (GLM)	✓	-
Linear Regression	-	✓
Linear Support Vector Machine	-	✓
Logistic Regression	-	✓
Naive Bayes	-	✓
Random Forest (RF)	✓	✓
XGBoost	✓ (only fully supported in Linux)	-
Stacking All (SA)	✓	-
Stacking Best (SB)	✓	-

Churn Prediction: The churn dataset contains 189 rows and 21 attributes. The attributes of each row characterize a client and the probability for canceling the company's analytics service (churn), as defined by the company. Table 3 describes each attribute of the churn dataset.

Table 3. Description of the attributes of the churn dataset (adapted from [14]).

Attribute	Description
tenure	Time passed since the beginning of the contract
streaming_quality	Contractualized display resolution
ott_video	If OTT video is contractualized or not
contract	Duration of the contract
payment_method	Contractualized method of payment
product_name	Identification of the product
platform	Type of connectivity present in the contract
financial_status	If the payment is late or regularized
service_latency	Latency of the service
dropped_frames	Number of dropped frames
volume	Information about volume
duration	Information about duration
account_number	Account identification number
service_latency category	Category of the service latency attribute
dropped_frames category	Category of the dropped frames attribute
volume category	Category of the volume attribute
duration category	Category of the duration attribute
tenure category	Category of the tenure attribute
account_segment	Age segment of the client
equipment	Equipment used by the client
churn_probability	Probability of canceling the service ($\in [0, 1]$)

Table 4. Description of the attributes of the event forecasting dataset (adapted from [14]).

Attribute	Description
Time	Timestamp (format: yyyy-mm-dd hh:mm)
Datapoints	Number of events

Event Forecasting: The event forecasting dataset contains 1,418 rows that correspond to records about telecommunication events of a certain type (e.g., phone calls). The events occurred from February to April of 2019, aggregated on an hourly basis, ranged from 3,747 to 56,320. The only attributes are the timestamp and the number of events in that interval, as described in Table 4.

Fraud Detection: Each row of the fraud detection dataset contains the identification of A (sender) and B (receiver), and the classification of the phone call ("fraud" or "normal"). The dataset contains more than 1 million examples, which correspond to one day of phone calls from one of the company clients. The dataset attributes are described in Table 5.

Table 5. Description of the attributes of the fraud dataset (adapted from [14]).

Attribute	Description
A	Identification of the call sender
B	Identification of the call receiver
Result	Classification of the call ("fraud" or "normal")

5   Results

5.1   Experimental Setup

The benchmark consisted of several computational experiments that used three real-world datasets to compare the selected AutoML tools (H2O AutoML and Transmogri-fAI). The benchmark was executed on a machine with an i7-8700 Intel processor with 6 cores. Every AutoML experiment considered a holdout split that used 3/4 of the data as training set and 1/4 as test set. The split between train and test sets was random for two of the datasets (churn and fraud). For the event forecasting dataset, the division between train and test was ordered in time (since the data is ordered in time). Every AutoML execution implemented a 10-fold cross-validation during the training of the algorithms.

Each AutoML tool optimizes a performance metric to select the best algorithms and tune the hyperparameters. We selected the Mean Absolute Error (MAE) for the regression tasks and Area Under Curve (AUC) for the classification data. Also, we computed additional metrics for the test data in order to further compare the tools.

Additionally, we disabled time limits to allow the execution of all selected ML algorithms. From the algorithms presented in Table 2, we only disabled Deep Learning from the experiments, from H2O AutoML. First, because it required a greater computational effort, especially for the fraud detection dataset. Second, to achieve a more fair comparison with TransmogrifAI, since this tool does not include Deep Learning algorithms.

For the churn dataset, the performance of the AutoML tools was measured with two scenarios. The first scenario (1) considered all the attributes of the dataset as input features for the ML algorithms. The second scenario (2) only uses a subset of the attributed as input features, derived from a previous feature selection phase. For Transmogri-fAI the intention was to test the automatic feature selection characteristic. For H2O AutoML, the features of scenario 2 were the most relevant features identified by the best performing algorithm of scenario 1.

For event forecasting, we transformed the dataset, creating time lags as inputs for a regression task. The dataset could not be used as a univariate time series, since neither H2O AutoML nor TransmogrifAI implement native time series algorithms (e.g., ARIMA, Holt-Winters). We created three scenarios with different combinations of time lags: 1 – with time lags $t - 1$, $t - 24$, and $t - 25$, where t is the current time (corresponding to the previous hour, day, and hour before that day); 2 – with all the time lags from the last 24 h (from $t - 1$ to $t - 24$); and 3 – with the time lags $t - 12$, $t - 24$, $t - 36$, and $t - 48$.

For the fraud detection dataset, we designed three training scenarios. Since the fraud detection dataset only has around 0.01% of illegitimate calls, we used the Synthetic Minority Oversampling Technique (SMOTE) technique [5] to balance the two classes in two of the scenarios. Scenario 1 used a simple undersampling that considered all "fraud" records and a random selection (with replacement) of "normal" cases. Scenarios 2 and 3 used SMOTE to generate extra fraud examples (100% and 200%, respectively). For each training scenario, we also considered three test scenarios of unseen data with different class balancing (with "normal"/"fraud" ratio): A – 50%/50%, thus balanced; B – 75%/25%; and C – 80%/20%.

5.2   Discussion

A summary of the overall results is presented in Table 6. For each AutoML tool, the execution times and test error metric values were aggregated by considering the average of the dataset scenario executions.

Table 6. Summary of the experimental results, best values in **bold** (adapted from [14]).

Dataset	Number of scenarios	AutoML tool	Avg. execution time (mm:ss)	Used metric	Avg. test metric
Churn prediction	2	H2O AutoML	**00:27**	MAE	**0.119**
		TransmogrifAI	03:40	MAE	0.160
Event forecasting	3	H2O AutoML	**02:25**	MAE	**2467**
		TransmogrifAI	04:41	MAE	2765
Fraud detection	9	H2O AutoML	07:11	AUC	**0.973**
		TransmogrifAI	**01:46**	AUC	0.963

The experimental results show that both AutoML tools require a small execution time to select the best ML model, with the highest average execution time being slightly higher than 7 min. The low training time can be justified with the usage of distributed ML, datasets with a small number of rows or columns, and the removal of Deep Learning algorithms. However, if the benchmark included datasets with more examples or attributes, an addition of machines or cores to the cluster would maintain the execution time low.

The metrics obtained during the predictions show that H2O AutoML obtained the best average results for all three datasets. In particular, H2O AutoML was better on three of the five regression scenarios and in seven of the nine classification scenarios. TransmogrifAI obtained the best predictive results in two regression scenarios and two classification scenarios. Although the AutoML tools present minor predictive differences, the results of all scenarios can be considered of high quality.

After analyzing the results, the risk management software and analytics company decided to select H2O AutoML for the model training module of the architecture. This choice was supported by two main reasons. First, H2O AutoML obtained better predictive results for most of the scenarios. Second, the analytics company considered H2O AutoML a "more mature" technology. This classification was due to the fact that H2O AutoML is available in more programming languages than TransmogrifAI (as shown in Table 1), it can be integrated with more platforms and it provides an easy to use Graphical User Interface.

6 Technological Architecture

After the comparative ML experiments, the analytics company selected the H2O AutoML tool for the model training component. The remaining technological modules were then designed in cooperation with the company. Since one of the prerequisites of the architecture is that it is distributed, we tried to identify technologies with distributed capabilities. Given that H2O can be integrated with Apache Spark (using the Sparkling Water module) and that Spark provides functions for data processing, we relied on Spark's Application Programming Interface (API) functions to implement the remaining components of the architecture. The updated architecture, with references to the technologies used, is illustrated in Fig. 2.

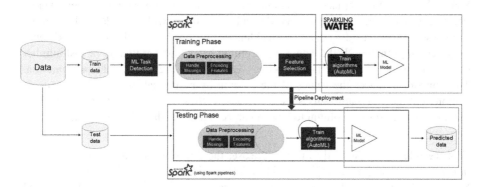

Fig. 2. The technological automated and scalable ML architecture (adapted from [14]).

6.1 Components

This subsection describes the current implementation of each module of the architecture. The updated technological architecture changed some of the modules initally described in Sect. 3. These changes were related to feedback received from the analytics company or due to technological restrictions.

Machine Learning Task Detection: Currently set to detect if the ML pipeline should be considered a binary classification, multi-class classification, pure regression, or a univariate time series task since these are the typical telecommunications risk management ML tasks used by the company.

The detection of the ML task can be overridden by the user. This is due to the fact that it could be useful to consider an ML task different than the one suggested by the module. For example, the end-user might want to consider a regression task, although the target column of the dataset only has a few number of levels, which could be automatically considered a multi-class classification. If the user specifies an ML task before running the pipeline, this component is skipped.

The type of supervised tasks handled will be expanded according to feedback provided by the software company clients and the AutoML tools capabilities. Interesting future possibilities of tasks to be addressed are multivariate time series, ordinal classification, or multi-target regression.

Data Preprocessing: Currently, the preprocessing transformations (e.g., dealing with missing data, the encoding of categorical features, standardization of numerical features) are done using Apache Spark's functions for extracting, transforming and selecting features [1].

To deal with missing data in numerical columns we use the `Imputer` function from Spark. This function replaces the unknown values of a column with its mean value. For categorical columns, we replace the unknown fields with a predefined tag (e.g., "Unknown"). The encoding of categorical features is done by default using Spark's one-hot Encoding function. If the categorical column has a high cardinality (a vast number of levels), instead of the one-hot encoding we apply the `String Indexer` function. This function replaces the values of the column by numerical indices. The standardization of numerical features uses the `Standard Scaler` function from Spark. This function normalizes the column to have mean zero and standard deviation one.

Feature Selection: Currently, this module uses the Chi-Squared feature selection function from Apache Spark. This method decides what features to keep based on Chi-Squared statistical test. Depending on the dataset and the ML task, we filter a fixed number of features or a percentage of features with the most correlation.

Additionally, we added the possibility for the user (usually a domain expert) to influence this step. Thus, the user can specify beforehand the features that will be used as inputs by the model training module. Such features cannot be removed by the feature selection step, although other features can be added to the ones that the user selected. If no features were chosen by the user, this component works without restrictions. Also

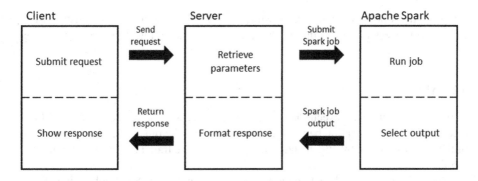

Fig. 3. Adopted scheme for handing of requests and responses.

by request of the company, we created an auxiliary pipeline that performs a simple feature filtering, outputting a list of the most relevant features for a particular supervised learning dataset but without fitting an ML model (e.g., usage of the simple correlation statistic).

Model Training: Currently, this module uses one of two AutoML approaches we implemented, depending on the ML task that is being considered. For classification (binary or multi-class) and regression tasks, we use H2O AutoML to automatically find and tune the best model. Since none of the AutoML tools we analyzed support native univariate time series forecasting algorithms, we implemented our own AutoML for the time series task.

In order to create the AutoML for time series, we used the algorithms implemented by the GitHub repository scalaTS[1] as a base. The repository includes a set of time series algorithms, such as autoregressive integrated moving average (ARIMA), autoregressive moving average (ARMA), autoregression (AR), and moving average (MA). Also, the package includes hyperparameter optimization capabilities, with the algorithms Auto ARIMA, Auto ARMA, Auto AR, and Auto MA, which pick the best parameters for each algorithm. The repository is built on top of Apache Spark using the distributed DataFrames objects, allowing distributed training and forecasting.

In order to select the best algorithm for a time series task, we run each Auto algorithm with the training data and select the one that performs best on the validation data by using a rolling window validation [26].

Pipeline Deployment: Currently, the pipeline management module uses an Apache Spark API related to ML pipelines [2]. To create a Spark ML pipeline it is necessary to detail a list of stages and then fit the pipeline to the training data. After fitting the pipeline to the training data, the Spark API allows the export of the pipeline to the disk. This process is applied during the training phase of the architecture.

To apply a pipeline to test data it is necessary to load the model from a file. Then,

---

[1] https://github.com/liao-iu/scalaTS/.

using the transform function, it is possible to apply the pipeline to previously unseen data. This process is applied during the test phase of the architecture, generating a set of predictions.

6.2 API

In order to facilitate the execution of the architecture, we also created a REST API to mediate the communication between the end-users and the pipelines. The development of the API resulted in two main endpoints: one to run the train pipeline and the other to run the test pipeline.

Since the execution of each request consists of one Apache Spark job (using H2O's capabilities through the Sparkling Water module), the API works as an intermediary between the end-user and the execution of the code inside Spark. This way, the API server receives the client's requests and uses the parameters of the body of the request to initiate a Spark job inside the server (using the spark-submit command). After the execution of the application that was submitted to Spark, the server receives the output of the job (e.g., metrics of training, predictions). The server formats the response to the appropriate format (e.g., XML, JSON) and sends the response to the client interface.

Figure 3 depicts this process. We highlight that the current version of the overall architecture, which received positive feedback from the Portuguese software company of the IRMDA project, is expected to be incrementally improved in future research. In particular, we intend to evolve and test the non AutoML components by using more real-world datasets and feedback from the analytics company clients.

7 Conclusions

This paper proposes a ML framework to automate the typical workflow of supervised ML applications without the need for human input. The framework includes the modules of task detection, data preprocessing, feature selection, model training, and pipeline deployment. The framework was developed within project IRMDA, a R&D project developed by a leading Portuguese software and analytics company that provides services for the domain of telecommunications risk management. The company clients work with datasets of variable sizes (large or small) and are mostly non-ML-experts. Thus, the proposed framework uses distributed ML to add computational scalability to the process and AutoML to automate the search for the best algorithm and hyperparameters.

In order to assess the most appropriate AutoML tools for this model training module, we initially conducted a benchmark experiment. First, we analyzed the features of eight open-source AutoML tools (Auto-Gluon, Auto-Keras, Auto-Sklearn, Auto-Weka, H2O AutoML, Rminer, TPOT, and TransmogrifAI). Then, we selected the tools that allowed a distributed execution for the experiments (H2O AutoML and TransmogrifAI). The benchmark study used three real-world datasets provided by the software company from the domain of telecommunications risk management. The proposed framework was positively evaluated by the analytics company, which selected H2O AutoML as the best tool for the model training module.

After the selection of H2O AutoML for the model training module, we developed the technological architecture. We selected technologies with distributed capabilities for the remaining modules of the initially proposed framework. Most of the remaining modules were implemented using Apache Spark's API functions. Then, we describe the current implementation of each module of the architecture. Finally, we describe the REST API that was created to facilitate the communication between the end-users (the company clients) and the implemented pipelines.

In future work, we intend to use more telecommunications datasets to provide additional benchmarks for the model training module. Moreover, new AutoML tools can be considered, as long as they provide distributed capabilities. Besides, we intend to add more ML tasks to the framework, such as ordinal classification, multi-target regression, or multivariate time series. For the remaining modules, we expect to conduct similar studies to evaluate the most appropriate technologies to use (e.g., for handling missing data, for choosing the best features). Finally, even though the framework was developed specifically for the telecommunications risk management domain, we intend to study the applicability of the framework to other areas.

Acknowledgements. This work was executed under the project IRMDA - Intelligent Risk Management for the Digital Age, Individual Project, NUP: POCI-01-0247-FEDER-038526, co-funded by the Incentive System for Research and Technological Development, from the Thematic Operational Program Competitiveness of the national framework program - Portugal2020.

References

1. Apache Spark: extracting, transforming and selecting features - Spark 2.4.5 documentation (2020) https://spark.apache.org/docs/latest/ml-features
2. Apache Spark: ML pipelines - Spark 2.4.5 documentation (2020). https://spark.apache.org/docs/latest/ml-pipeline.html
3. Auto-Gluon: AutoGluon: AutoML toolkit for deep learning — AutoGluon documentation 0.0.1 documentation (2020). https://autogluon.mxnet.io/
4. Blum, A.L., Langley, P.: Selection of relevant features and examples in machine learning. Artif. Intell. **97**(1–2), 245–271 (1997). https://doi.org/10.1016/s0004-3702(97)00063-5
5. Chawla, N.V., Bowyer, K.W., Hall, L.O., Kegelmeyer, W.P.: SMOTE: synthetic minority over-sampling technique. J. Artif. Intell. Res. **16**, 321–357 (2002). https://doi.org/10.1613/jair.953
6. Chollet, F., et al.: Keras (2015). https://keras.io
7. Cook, D.: Practical Machine Learning with H2O: Powerful, Scalable Techniques for Deep Learning and AI. O'Reilly Media, Inc., Sebastopol (2016)
8. Cortez, P.: Data mining with neural networks and support vector machines using the R/rminer tool. In: Perner, P. (ed.) ICDM 2010. LNCS (LNAI), vol. 6171, pp. 572–583. Springer, Heidelberg (2010). https://doi.org/10.1007/978-3-642-14400-4_44
9. Cortez, P.: A tutorial on using the rminer r package for data mining tasks, Technical report, Universidade do Minho, Escola de Engenharia (EEng) (2015)
10. Cortez, P.: Package 'rminer' (2020). https://cran.r-project.org/web/packages/rminer/rminer.pdf
11. Darwiche, A.: Human-level intelligence or animal-like abilities? Commun. ACM **61**(10), 56–67 (2018). https://doi.org/10.1145/3271625

12. Elshawi, R., Maher, M., Sakr, S.: Automated machine learning: state-of-the-art and open challenges. arXiv preprint arXiv:1906.02287 (2019)

13. Elsken, T., Metzen, J.H., Hutter, F.: Neural architecture search: a survey. arXiv preprint arXiv:1808.05377 (2018)

14. Ferreira, L., Pilastri, A., Martins, C., Santos, P., Cortez, P.: An automated and distributed machine learning framework for telecommunications risk management. In: Proceedings of the 12th International Conference on Agents and Artificial Intelligence - Volume 2: ICAART, pp. 99–107. INSTICC, SciTePress (2020). https://doi.org/10.5220/0008952800990107

15. Feurer, M., et al.: Efficient and robust automated machine learning. In: Cortes, C., Lawrence, N.D., Lee, D.D., Sugiyama, M., Garnett, R. (eds.) Advances in Neural Information Processing Systems 28: Annual Conference on Neural Information Processing Systems 2015, 7–12 December 2015, Montreal, Quebec, Canada, pp. 2962–2970 (2015). http://papers.nips.cc/paper/5872-efficient-and-robust-automated-machine-learning

16. Feurer, M., Springenberg, J.T., Hutter, F.: Initializing Bayesian hyperparameter optimization via meta-learning. In: Bonet, B., Koenig, S. (eds.) Proceedings of the Twenty-Ninth AAAI Conference on Artificial Intelligence, 25–30 January 2015, Austin, Texas, USA, pp. 1128–1135. AAAI Press (2015). http://www.aaai.org/ocs/index.php/AAAI/AAAI15/paper/view/10029

17. Gijsbers, P., LeDell, E., Thomas, J., Poirier, S., Bischl, B., Vanschoren, J.: An open source automML benchmark. arXiv preprint arXiv:1907.00909 (2019)

18. Guyon, I., et al.: Design of the 2015 chalearn automML challenge. In: 2015 International Joint Conference on Neural Networks, IJCNN 2015, Killarney, Ireland, 12–17 July 2015, pp. 1–8. IEEE (2015). https://doi.org/10.1109/IJCNN.2015.7280767

19. Guyon, I., et al.: A brief review of the chalearn automl challenge: any-time any-dataset learning without human intervention. In: Hutter, F., Kotthoff, L., Vanschoren, J. (eds.) Proceedings of the 2016 Workshop on Automatic Machine Learning, AutoML 2016, co-located with 33rd International Conference on Machine Learning (ICML 2016), New York City, NY, USA, 24 June 2016. JMLR Workshop and Conference Proceedings, vol. 64, pp. 21–30. JMLR.org (2016)

20. Guyon, I., et al.: Analysis of the AutoML challenge series 2015–2018. In: Hutter, F., Kotthoff, L., Vanschoren, J. (eds.) Automated Machine Learning. TSSCML, pp. 177–219. Springer, Cham (2019). https://doi.org/10.1007/978-3-030-05318-5_10

21. H2O.ai: H2O AutoML, June 2017. http://docs.h2o.ai/h2o/latest-stable/h2o-docs/automl.html, h2O version 3.30.0.1

22. He, X., Zhao, K., Chu, X.: AutoML: a survey of the state-of-the-art. arXiv preprint arXiv:1908.00709 (2019)

23. Jin, H., Song, Q., Hu, X.: Auto-keras: an efficient neural architecture search system. In: Teredesai, A., Kumar, V., Li, Y., Rosales, R., Terzi, E., Karypis, G. (eds.) Proceedings of the 25th ACM SIGKDD International Conference on Knowledge Discovery & Data Mining, KDD 2019, Anchorage, AK, USA, 4–8 August 2019, pp. 1946–1956. ACM (2019). https://doi.org/10.1145/3292500.3330648

24. Kotthoff, L., Thornton, C., Hoos, H.H., Hutter, F., Leyton-Brown, K.: Auto-weka 2.0: automatic model selection and hyperparameter optimization in WEKA. J. Mach. Learn. Res. **18**, 25:1–25:5 (2017). http://jmlr.org/papers/v18/16-261.html

25. Le, T.T., Fu, W., Moore, J.H.: Scaling tree-based automated machine learning to biomedical big data with a feature set selector. Bioinformatics **36**(1), 250–256 (2020)

26. Oliveira, N., Cortez, P., Areal, N.: The impact of microblogging data for stock market prediction: Using twitter to predict returns, volatility, trading volume and survey sentiment indices. Expert Syst. Appl. **73**, 125–144 (2017). https://doi.org/10.1016/j.eswa.2016.12.036

27. Olson, R.S., Urbanowicz, R.J., Andrews, P.C., Lavender, N.A., Kidd, L.C., Moore,J.H.: Automating biomedical data science through tree-based pipeline optimization. In: Squillero, G., Burelli, P. (eds.) EvoApplications 2016. LNCS, vol. 9597, pp. 123–137. Springer, Cham (2016). https://doi.org/10.1007/978-3-319-31204-0_9

28. Pedregosa, F., et al.: Scikit-learn: machine learning in python. J. Mach. Learn. Res. **12**, 2825–2830 (2011). http://dl.acm.org/citation.cfm?id=2078195

29. Peteiro-Barral, D., Guijarro-Berdiñas, B.: A survey of methods for distributed machine learning. Prog. Artif. Intell. **2**(1), 1–11 (2013). https://doi.org/10.1007/s13748-012-0035-5

30. Salesforce: Transmogrifai (2019). https://docs.transmogrif.ai/en/stable/

31. Thornton, C., Hutter, F., Hoos, H.H., Leyton-Brown, K.: Auto-weka: combined selection and hyperparameter optimization of classification algorithms. In: Proceedings of the 19th ACM SIGKDD International Conference on Knowledge Discovery and Data Mining, pp. 847–855 (2013). https://doi.org/10.1145/2487575.2487629

32. Truong, A., Walters, A., Goodsitt, J., Hines, K., Bruss, B., Farivar, R.: Towards automated machine learning: Evaluation and comparison of autoML approaches and tools. arXiv preprint arXiv:1908.05557 (2019)

33. Vanschoren, J., van Rijn, J.N., Bischl, B., Torgo, L.: OpenML: networked science in machine learning. SIGKDD Explor. **15**(2), 49–60 (2013). https://doi.org/10.1145/2641190.2641198

34. Witten, I.H., Frank, E., Hall, M.A., Pal, C.J.: Data Mining: Practical Machine Learning Tools and Techniques. Morgan Kaufmann, Amsterdam (2016)

35. Yao, Q., et al.: Taking human out of learning applications: a survey on automated machine learning. arXiv preprint arXiv:1810.13306 (2018)

36. Zöller, M.A., Huber, M.F.: Benchmark and survey of automated machine learning frameworks. Technical report. https://www.researchgate.net/publication/332750780

Designing New Data Replication Strategies Automatically

Syed Mohtashim Abbas Bokhari[✉] and Oliver Theel

Department of Computer Science, University of Oldenburg, Oldenburg, Germany
{syed.mohtashim.abbas.bokhari,oliver.theel}@uni-oldenburg.de

Abstract. A distributed system is a paradigm indispensable to the current world due to countless requests with every passing second. In distributed systems, reliability is of extreme importance. In this regard, data replication plays a vital role in making systems more reliable by increasing the availability of the access operations at a lower cost. However, availability and cost both cannot be achieved at the same time. Certainly, there are compromises between these objectives, thereby making different application-scenarios that may not be easily satisfied by contemporary strategies. This requires designing new strategies and the question still stands which strategy is the best for a given scenario or application class assuming a certain workload, its distribution across a network, availability of the individual replicas, and cost of the access operations. For this, the research exploits the heterogeneity between the strategies to generate new data replication strategies automatically through genetic programming. It uses and extends this genetic programming-based automatic mechanism to subsequently demonstrate its usefulness by reducing the cost significantly while not comprising too much on the availabilities of the access operations. It generates replication strategies there are innovative and such combinations have not been explored yet.

Keywords: Distributed systems · Fault tolerance · Data replication · Quorum protocols · Operation availability · Operation cost · Voting structures · Optimization · Machine learning · Evolutionary strategies · Genetic programming

1 Introduction

To provide highly available data access operations is a widely discussed prevalent problem in computer science. Relying on a single replica significantly confines the availability of the data. Therefore, the increase in the number of replicas to store the data objects is inevitable, which, when smartly applied, increases the availability of the data object and makes it more fault-tolerant. Because now, it can be accessed by approaching other replicas, too. But then the challenge comes up of managing those replicas and maintain consistency so that replicas always yield correct values [7]. The goal of the operations is also to behave in a replicated system the same as they would do in a non-replicated system. This is known as one-copy serializability (1SR) [1]. As for this, these replicas are managed by protocols known as data replication strategies (DRSs).

© Springer Nature Switzerland AG 2021
A. P. Rocha et al. (Eds.): ICAART 2020, LNAI 12613, pp. 308–331, 2021.
https://doi.org/10.1007/978-3-030-71158-0_15

These strategies impose a threshold of a minimal number of replicas known as read quorum (rq) and write quorum (wq) to be accessed to perform the preferred access operations. These access operations are either a read or a write operation. The decisions to choose suitable DRSs are trade-offs between choosing various quality metrics such as load, capacity, availability [2], scalability, and cost [3]. The availabilities of read and write operations are optimally point symmetrical to each other [4]. For instance, an increased availability for a write operation would compromise the availability of a read operation to a certain extent and vice versa. It is more like the same case with the cost of the read and write operations, too. The questions arise that what are those compromises, to what extent particular values can be compromised, and at the expense of what? These compromises could be highly application-specific and comprised of many scenarios, which will be discussed further in Sect. 2. This research intends to provide application-optimized DRSs to fulfill such specified scenarios. In this regard, this research is an extension of our research [5, 7] particularly to demonstrate new instances by tweaking the algorithm slightly. It generates replication strategies there are innovative and such combinations have not been explored yet, which could significantly reduce the cost. This automatic mechanism evolves strategies as computer programs over many generations of evolution and also provides desirable trade-offs between the availability and cost of the access operations while restricting total nodes to the desirable limit. This can be visualized by a 3D representation, i.e., given in Fig. 17, where trade-offs are overt and relevant strategies can be easily picked at run-time. In this regard, details on a multi-objective optimization approach to data replication in distributed systems can be found here [6].

The paper is written as follows. Section 2 specifies and discusses the problem statement. Section 3 discusses the state-of-the-art DRSs and other contemporary approaches to address the problem and their limitations. Section 4 defines the fault model, describes the adopted methodology to approach the problem, and argues about the reason for picking this approach over others. Section 5 states the implementation aspects of the research. Section 6 presents the results and their comparisons, followed by a conclusion.

2   Problem Statement

The problem is illustrated by a triangle given in Fig. 1 where the consistency part is static because 1SR is maintained all the time. This leaves us room to fully operate around the availability and cost of the access operations (provided a threshold of the total number of replicas and the probability of individual replicas). It can be seen that there are many scenarios between the availability and cost of the access operations in a distributed paradigm. There exist many contemporary strategies to manage those distributed replicas, but the question still stands which strategy is best for a given scenario or application class. Considering the fact that not every strategy fulfills each scenario, leaves many scenarios unaddressed, for which no optimal strategy exists. Hence, there is no best solution (in terms of a global optima), but solutions that serve a particular purpose (i.e., local optima). Our research focuses on the automatic identification and design of such an optimized data replication strategy.

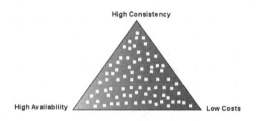

Fig. 1. Data replication scenarios [7].

3   Related Work

DRSs in general are categorized into two major classes: unstructured and structured DRSs. Unstructured DRSs, for instance, the Majority Consensus Strategy [9] use combinatorics and minimum quorum cardinalities to specify a quorum system. The Majority Consensus Strategy requires $\lceil n/2 \rceil$ replicas for the read and $\lceil (n+1)/2 \rceil$ for the write quorum to execute any operation in a system comprising n replicas. This threshold-based quorum system allows all the replicas an equal opportunity to be in a read or write quorum. However, it succumbs to high operational cost and scalability issues because of linearly increasing quorum cardinalities. This is not the case in structured replication strategies where structural properties and patterns are used to specify the quorum system. For instance, the Grid Protocol [13] imposes a logical rectangular i * j grid structure where i indicates column and j rows for a system comprised of i * j = n replicas. A read quorum consists of replicas from each column while a write quorum constitutes all the replicas from a column along with one replica from each column to satisfy the quorum system intersection property. There exist many other contemporary strategies such as Read-One-Write-All [8], the Tree Quorum Protocol (TQP) [10], the Weighted Voting Strategy [11], the Hierarchical Quorum Consensus [12], the Triangular Lattice Protocol (TLP) [14], etc., but the state-of-the-art has not much focused on a hybrid approach to explore new strategies.

There have been only a few limited efforts made towards hybrid strategies because of its cumbersome nature. So, there are some attempts, i.e., [5, 17–19] on hybrid approaches, which manually design DRSs but lack automation. Moreover, there exist only a few papers, i.e., [15, 16], etc., on hybrid approaches that primarily attempt to combine Tree Quorum Protocols with Grid Protocols, but they do not impose any unified structure on the nodes, which greatly limits the operability of the approach. Because of the diverse nature of topologies, there is less room for a hybrid approach to work effectively as it cannot incorporate the varied strategies freely [5]. As a consequence, many scenarios could be left unaddressed. Whereas, to address this issue, if a hybrid approach is applied to such a diverse nature of topologies, the problem easily goes out of hand. For this, this paper is an extension of our current [7] overall line of research. As it is ongoing research, it uses, extends, and optimizes the same foundational mechanism and follows the same research methodology to derive new results.

4   Methodology

Figure 2 shows the adopted methodology in a simplified manner. It starts with replication strategies being injected into a database repository and a scenario. Both, the nature of the repository and the scenario will be explained in detail in this section. The analysis and simulations (shown later in this paper) are performed on the repository until the desired solution is met, which then is inserted back to the repository for future use. Here, the question also arises of selecting the appropriate machine learning and simulation techniques for the identification and design of optimized data replication strategies. Let us dissect all these components one by one in the following.

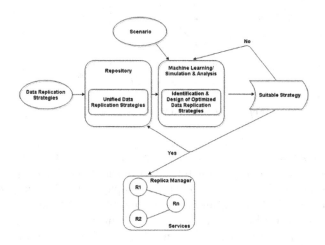

Fig. 2. Methodology [7].

4.1   Fault Model

Prior to discussing the components, we state the fault model and other assumptions first. The access operations are either read or write and are performed only when the proper quorum is acquired. The replicas are supposed to manifest a fail-silent behavior. All failures are assumed to be independent of each other. The network is supposed to be fully connected without communication failures. Only nodes (machines) with replicas can fail and the probability that a node has failed at any particular point in time is $(1 - p)$. p gives the probability that a node is available at an arbitrary point in time. The strategies are supposed to be version-based to avoid additional time synchronization issues, i.e., a replica does not only consist of some "payload" data but also a version number. A replica with the highest version number has the up-to-date payload.

4.2   Voting Structures

To address the mentioned topological and diversity issues between DRSs, a unified representation of these strategies by a concept like General Structured Voting [20] is required for the simulation and machine learning approaches to be applied over it. Expert-based manual designs of optimized DRSs using the concept of voting structures have been presented in [18, 19]. Figure 3 represents a quorum system by a directed acyclic graph (DAG) named a voting structure.

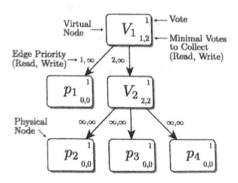

Fig. 3. Example of a voting structure [21].

A voting structure is traversed recursively by an algorithm to derive the quorums for respective access operations at run time independent of the varied topologies of the strategies. The nodes of a voting structure are either physical nodes representing actual replicas or virtual nodes that constitute the groupings of physical and virtual nodes. The virtual nodes are labeled V_i where $i = 1, 2, \ldots$ while the physical nodes are labeled p_j where $1 \leq j \leq n$ and n represents the total number of replicas of a system. Irrespective of being a physical or virtual node, every node is endowed with votes comprised of a natural number (top right corner), which could also be comprehended as the weightage of that node. Furthermore, each node is equipped with a pair of minimal quorums (called "minimal votes" in the figure) to collect from its child nodes to build the read and write quorums. The minimal quorums for each node to gather per operation has to be less than or equal to the sum of the votes of its children. Some replication strategies, i.e., the Tree Quorum Protocol imposes a partial order on the quorums by which to use quorums for operation execution. The specification of such an ordering allows certain quorums to be used prior to others. In such cases, the directed edges of voting structures can be marked with operation-specific priorities imposing such orderings. An edge priority of 1 annotates the highest while the symbol ∞ represents the lowest priority. This voting structure is traversed by the recursive algorithm to derive respective quorums. It starts from the root node and queries as many of its child nodes as specified in the minimal quorums to orchestrate the quorums of physical replicas for the respective access operations. On each level, if the voting structure has a total number of votes V, then the quorums for intersection abide by the following rules in general:

$$rq + wq > V \ (to \ avoid \ read - write \ conflict) \tag{1}$$

$$wq > V/2 \ (to \ avoid \ write - write \ conflict) \tag{2}$$

Here, rq (wq) is a number representing the minimal read (write) quorum. For instance, the voting structure shown in Fig. 3 produces the following read (RQ) and write quorum sets (WQ):

$$RQ = \{\{p1\}, \{p2, p3\}, \{p2, p4\}, \{p3, p4\}\}$$
$$WQ = \{\{p1, p2, p3\}, \{p1, p2, p4\}, \{p1, p3, p4\}\}$$

4.3 Scenario Parameters

A scenario for DRSs consists of constraints that determine the fitness of a strategy holistically to judge the goodness of a solution. These constraints may vary among different applications depending upon their nature, requirements, and resources. It comprises the following parameters [7].

Consistency of Operations. There exists a variety of data consistency models for DRSs ranging from strict data consistency to relatively weaker notions. As already stated, the consistency model opted for our approach is static and strictly meets the 1SR property. The 1SR property is maintained in a DRS when 1) every read quorum intersects every write quorum, 2) all write quorums intersect with each other, 3) replicas can be locked exclusively for write operations and locked shared for read operations.

Number of Replicas. There is a threshold imposed on the total number of replicas n that for any strategy, n cannot exceed the specified threshold value ϵ. This is because it certainly costs to create new nodes to host replicas.

$$n, \epsilon \in \mathbb{N}^+$$
$$\wedge n \leq \epsilon \tag{3}$$

Availability of Access Operations. The probability that the data access operations are available for a DRS depends on the characteristics of the strategy, the probability of individual replicas p, and the number of replicas n. It is defined by A_r(p, n) and A_w(p, n) respectively, where A_r(p, n), A_w(p, n) $\in$ [0,1]. For some DRSs, there exist closed formulas to calculate the availability as well as the costs. However, generally, the equations given below are used to analyze the data access operations' availability of a DRS. All the RQs and WQs are derived from a DRS to calculate A_r(p, n) and A_w(p, n) for given p and n values. Equations 4 and 5 calculate the read and write operation availabilities respectively. For this, they rely on a so-called set of all possible read (write) quorums RQS (WQS). In the scope of the example given in Fig. 3, RQS equals (RQ $\cup$ {{p1, p2, p3, p4}}) and WQS equals (WQ $\cup$ {{p1, p2, p3, p4}}). The equations take the sum of the probability of all elements of RQS or WQS being available for a given probability p of individual replicas.

$$A_r\left(p, n\right) = \sum_{\forall q \in RQS} p^{|q|} \left(1 - p\right)^{n - |q|} \tag{4}$$

$$A_w(p, n) = \sum_{\forall q \in WQS} p^{|q|} (1 - p)^{n - |q|} \tag{5}$$

These availabilities are probabilities and constraints restrict them to be within the specified thresholds α, β.

$$A_r, A_w, \alpha, \beta \in [0, 1]$$
$$\wedge A_r \geq \alpha \tag{6}$$
$$\wedge A_w \geq \beta$$

Cost of Access Operations. The average minimal costs for the data access operations are represented by $C_r(p, n)$ and $C_w(p, n)$ respectively. The read $C_r(p, n)$ and write $C_w(p, n)$ costs reckon the average minimal number of replicas out of the total number of replicas n, which are mandatory to perform an operation for a given probability of individual replicas p. This cost is calculated by taking the sum of the minimum number of replicas minRQ (minWQ) obligatory to form a read (write) quorum for each replica set in RQS (WQS) with the probability of the replica set appearing. Furthermore, the resulted sum has to be divided by $A_r(p, n)$ or $A_w(p, n)$ depending upon the particular access operation.

$$C_r(p, n) = \frac{\sum_{\forall q \in RQS} p^{|q|} (1 - p)^{n - |q|} * minRQ(q)}{A_r(p, n)} \tag{7}$$

$$C_w(p, n) = \frac{\sum_{\forall q \in WQS} p^{|q|} (1 - p)^{n - |q|} * minWQ(q)}{A_w(p, n)} \tag{8}$$

These costs are real positive numbers and constraints restrict them to be within the specified thresholds γ, δ.

$$C_r, C_w, \gamma, \delta \in \mathbb{R}^+$$
$$\wedge C_r \leq \gamma \tag{9}$$
$$\wedge C_w \leq \delta$$

Fitness Weightage. We use a so-called fitness weightage (fw) that suggests a scenario to be biased towards either cost or availability (or even being neutral), to be able to convert a multi-objective into a single objective problem. This makes the optimization problem somewhat easier to solve.

$$fw \in [0, 1] \tag{10}$$

Probability of Individual Replicas. There is a subtle difference between the availability of access operations and the availability of individual replicas p. p refers to the probability by which the replicas are available, which means the probability that a replica has failed at any particular point in time is $(1 - p)$ while the user performs the operations with access operations' probability. In a scenario, we restrict p to be in the interval between $p_{min} \leq p \leq p_{max}$.

$$p_{min}, p, p_{max} \in [0, 1]$$
$$\wedge \ p_{min} \leq p \leq p_{max} \tag{11}$$

4.4 Database Repository

Figure 4 shows the data replication strategies Grid Protocol (left) and Triangular Lattice Protocol (right) being represented in a unified representation of a voting structure each. These voting strategies are stored in a scalable database repository in the form of JSON documents and can be queried upon any desirable criteria.

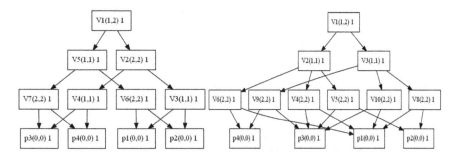

Fig. 4. Voting structures as DAGs representing DRSs [7].

4.5 Genetic Programming

The research proposes genetic programming (GP) [22,23] as a subset of machine learning to automatically identify or design application-optimized DRSs. The major difference between GP and other genetic variants of machine learning is the representation. GP is used to evolve computer programs. It consists of an encoding scheme, random crossover, mutation, a fitness function, and multiple generations of evolution to solve the specified task on its termination condition. The encoding scheme consists of a genotype (coding space) carrying an underlying set of traits and a phenotype (solution space), which is the behavioral expression of this genotype in a specific environment. Hence, the question arises which encoding scheme should be used since poor representations may lead to poor results. The crossover [24] operator mixes up the genetic material of parents in anticipation of forming a better offspring. It splits up the genome of two existing solutions at an arbitrary point and swaps them to create the offspring solutions inheriting properties from both of the parent solutions. The mutation operator changes the solution randomly but slightly, i.e., by flipping one or more bits from the previous offspring to generate a new altered child solution. In the pursuit of a solution, the questions of crossover and mutation types as well as points are also thought-provoking to address. Moreover, the population size also matters because a very small size implies a few possibilities of executing the crossovers. Therefore, only a fraction of the search space can be explored. Alternatively, a very large size may slow down the genetic approach. Although, it is highly problem-specific but very large populations do not solve the problem faster than moderate-sized populations. Figure 5 illustrates the problem in the context of genetic programming where we start from a scenario and an accordingly initial population. The initial population is analyzed based on its fitness to the scenario in order to choose better strategies to perform crossover and sometimes also mutation in anticipation of a constant evolutionary trajectory until a solution is found.

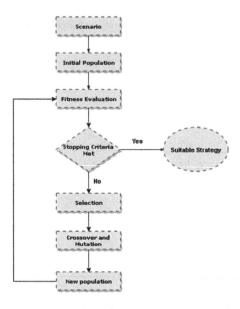

Fig. 5. Genetic programming [7].

5   Implementation

Having discussed the methodology, terminologies, and semantics, next we examine the implementation aspect comprising the parameters, functions, and the algorithm itself in detail. Once the scenario is specified to find a suitable DRS to fulfill it, the system parameters are set for the algorithm to run.

5.1   Mu, μ, and Lambda, λ

Having provided the repository to select the respective DRSs, the μ and λ values are also set as system parameters for the algorithm to start. μ is the restriction on the number of parents that are used to form the next generation and λ is the restraint on the number of offspring strategies generated using μ number of parent DRSs.

5.2   Crossover

There are various ways in which the DRSs can be combined and the resulting hybrid strategy will certainly exhibit different properties than the parents. The virtual nodes of two parent strategies are swapped to form new offspring strategies. Additionally, there are crossover points in every DRS represented by a Boolean variable which allows the crossover to be performed only on those points and in such a way that it maintains the DRSs' 1SR property throughout the process. While performing crossovers, the algorithm also restricts the number of replicas not to grow beyond a certain threshold ϵ specified in the scenario.

5.3   Mutation

The algorithm also performs mutation on the DRSs with the probability specified in the system parameters. This mutation modifies the votes of the strategies allowing some replicas to be more important in the weightage than other replicas. Once the votes are changed, the quorum also needs to be updated accordingly under the conditions (1) and (2) to uphold the 1SR property. In addition, the algorithm identifies the mutation points by a Boolean variable to avoid the DRS to be inconsistent and thereby, again, maintaining 1SR all the time.

5.4   Algorithm

Having specified a scenario and given it to the program, scenarioFitness is calculated. μ and λ are defined along with mutation probability. The list μList contains parent DRSs, the list λList comprises offspring DRSs, whereas the list initPopList consists of an initial population of DRSs. The Boolean variable isFit determines whether a strategy has achieved the expected level of fitness. The genetic program loops through all the passed on DRSs, calculates the fitness of every individual strategy, and selects the μ best strategies to the μList, in case, there is no satisfactory solution found in the initial population. This λList is then sent to the while loop to select the DRSs randomly from it (or from the initial population) and perform the crossovers and mutations to create λ offspring strategies. The use of the initial population here is for not letting the existing solutions vanish away in the next generations as the algorithm proceeds. The λList constitutes newly created strategies that are evaluated again to check if they satisfy the standard criteria. If the criteria are met, then the relevant newly generated optimized strategy is stored in the repository, the while loop terminates and so does the program. If not, it selects the μ best DRSs to the μList from (μList + λList) for the next generation. This process continues until a suitable strategy is found.

6   Experiments and Results

Figure 6 gives a relatively simple example of a hybrid DRS generated by the algorithm, which consists of 11 replicas. It can be seen that although the DRS is not very complex and maintains a tree-like structure rather than an acyclic one, yet it is so powerful and

---

Algorithm 1.

---

1 *Specify* a scenario;
2 *Specify* μ and λ;
3 *Specify* mutationProb;
4 *Specify* initPopListProb;
5 *Define* rand;
6 *Initialize* initPopList;
7 *Initialize* μList;
8 *Initialize* λList;
9 *Double* scenarioFitness = 0.0;
10 *Boolean* isFit = false;
11 *Generate* initial population of DRSs to the repository;
12 *Retrieve, parse & store* the generated DRSs to initPopList;
13 *geneticProgrammingFunc* () {
14   scenarioFitness = *calculateFitness*(scenario);
15   *Loop* through initPopList
16   *Calculate* fitness;
17   *if* (fitness $\geq$ scenarioFitness) {
18   isFit = true;
19   *return*;
20   }
21   END
22   *Choose* μ best DRSs to the μList;
23   Do{
24   *Empty* λList;
25   *Loop* to λ
26   *Select* randomly DRS1 from μList;
27   *Select* randomly DRS2 from (μList || initPopList);
28   Perform crossover1 of DRS1, DRS2;
29   *Generate* offspring DRSs;
30   *if* ($rand(0,1) \leq$ mutationProb) {
31   *Perform* mutation on the offspring;
32   }
33   *Calculate* fitness;
34   *if* (fitness $\geq$ scenarioFitness){
35   isFit = true;
36   *Store* offspring DRS into the repository;
37   }
38   *Add* offspring DRSs to the λList;
39   END
40   Select μ best DRSs to the μList from (μList + λList) for next generation;
41   }
42   *While* (! isFit);
43 }

---

optimized in terms of its availability and cost that it is competing with the Majority Consensus Strategy (MCS), which is believed to be the best in terms of its availability of write access operations. When compared, the hybrid DRS in terms of its availability is so close to MCS. It is almost the same for higher values of p, however, it is far better when it comes to the cost comparison.

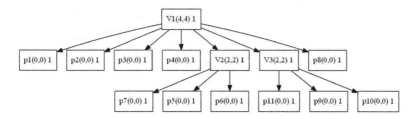

Fig. 6. Hybrid strategy 1 [7].

The availability and cost graphs on the discretized values of p are shown in Fig. 7 and Fig. 8, respectively, where Strategy 1 indicates the MCS while the Strategy 2 represents a hybrid DRSs. Both strategies consist of 11 replicas each. It can be seen that in terms of operational availability the hybrid strategy is converging on to the same values as MCS for higher values of p. This is a quite good availability but more importantly, it outclasses the MCS in terms of its cost in all the cases. Hence, it covers a scenario that could have been left unaddressed otherwise.

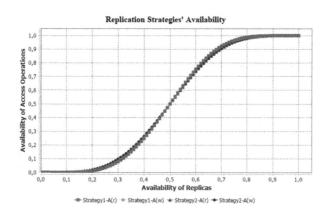

Fig. 7. Hybrid DRS 1, availability of the access operations [7]. (Color figure online)

In the best case, out of 11, it only takes four replicas each to perform a read and a write operation while the total cost for MCS is 12 for all the cases. This is a good example of a relatively less complicated DRS where we have not compromised the availability and yet reduced the cost significantly by using the hybrid approach via genetic programming.

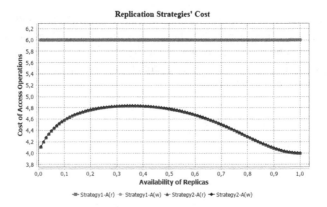

Fig. 8. Hybrid DRS 1, cost of the access operations [7].

Figure 9 shows a relatively complex but more economical example of an up-to-now unknown hybrid replication strategy designed via GP, exploiting the voting structures. It is comprised of both the Grid Protocol and the Triangular Lattice Protocol (TLP) where it unprecedentedly combines Grid Protocol comprising four replicas with TLP of six replicas, resulting in a total of ten replicas. It demonstrates an instance of a horizontal crossover, which has lowered the cost by a great value while maintaining a very good availability of the access operations.

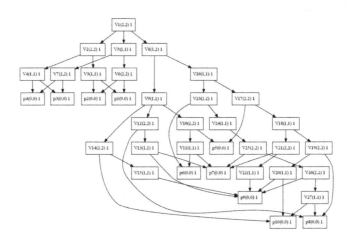

Fig. 9. Hybrid strategy 2.

Figure 10 presents and compares the availability of MCS with our hybrid approach of the same number of replicas. Red and pink lines represent the availabilities of the read and write operations, respectively, for the MCS. Whereas blue and green lines show availabilities of read and write operations, respectively, for the hybrid strategy.

The latter (hybrid) is competing fairly with the former (MCS), considering the fact that MCS is known to be the best for its availability, particularly for the critical write availability. In comparison, it can be noticed that availabilities are almost the same for the later values of p.

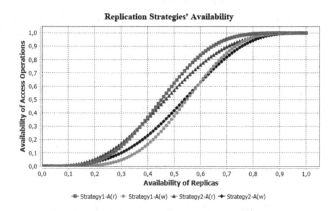

Fig. 10. Hybrid DRS 2, availability of the access operations. (Color figure online)

Figure 11 enables us a closer view where it can be observed that for hybrid strategy, the respective availabilities of the access operations converge onto almost the same values for later values of p, which is a very good operation availability considering the strong hardware nowadays.

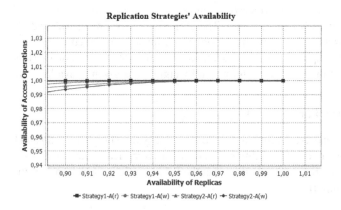

Fig. 11. Hybrid DRS 2, zoom-in availability graph.

As for the cost, as shown in Fig. 12, hybrid DRS is much cheaper as compared to the MCS. It costs almost half of the MCS, where in best cases, it only takes three replicas to perform an access operation, whereas the cost of the access operations for

MCS remains a constant of 11 replicas in total. Here, again, it is evident that we have significantly reduced the cost while not sacrificing on availability too much, covering another prospective scenario where a further reduced cost could be required.

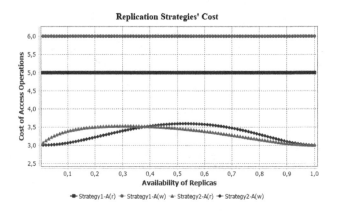

Fig. 12. Hybrid DRS 2, cost of the access operations.

We have demonstrated powerful examples of newly generated unknown voting structures via genetic programming, now we move on to specifying scenarios, explained earlier.

6.1 Scenario 1

Let us specify a sample scenario and apply our approach to find out whether a suitable replication strategy can be found. The scenario consists of the desired read and write availabilities and their respective costs, which must be achieved within the threshold of maximum 16 replicas and some availability p of individual replicas. However, cost is not important in this case, therefore, full weightage is given to availability.

6.2 Scenario Parameters 1

The desired read availability and write availability thresholds are 0.80 and 0.72, respectively, using a node availability of 0.6 inside a 16 replicas limit. Cost is specified being less than seven for each operation, but the fitness weightage determines the availability to be fully important.

$$p = 0.6, \quad \epsilon = 16, \quad \alpha = 0.80, \quad \beta = 0.72,$$
$$\gamma = 7.0, \quad \delta = 7.0, \quad fw = 1.0$$

6.3   System Parameters 1

Having defined the scenario, now the system parameters are set to run the algorithm accordingly. Here, the number of parent and offspring strategies are set to six and 15, respectively. The initial population is only used once, namely in the crossover process in the very first generation. The crossovers are performed all the time while the mutation is performed with a probability of 0.2.

$$\mu = 6, \lambda = 15,$$
$$\text{mutationProb} = 0.2$$

6.4   Results 1

This section shows the graphical visualization of the results generated by the algorithm on the provided parameters. It analyzes the fitness of every individual, every generation, and designs new strategies in the course of fulfilling the specified criteria when it is not found in the repository.

Fitness Analysis. Figure 13 depicts the fitness of every individual DRS and the way it evolves. The x-axis represents the number of DRSs and the y-axis denotes the fitness value of every individual strategy. The red line indicates the fitness of the DRSs while the pink and blue lines represent the availabilities of read and write operations, respectively. It can be noticed that it starts with only a few strategies of low fitness, which implies that the repository does not have a satisfactory solution to the problem. Then, the fitness improves and begins to evolve gradually through crossover and mutation operators of genetic programming until the loop stops over the desired termination condition.

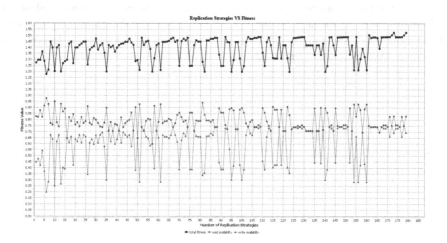

Fig. 13. Scenario 1, fitness of the DRSs [7]. (Color figure online)

Population Analysis. Figure 14 illustrates how the fitness of DRSs grows by every generation. The graph shows the fitness of the best DRSs among every generation. The x-axis represents the number of generations while the y-axis indicates the fitness value of the best replication strategy of a respective generation. It took 10 generations for the system to find a suitable DRS that satisfies the given scenario. It starts from a fitness of 1.365 and gradually but consistently continues to climb up until the desired fitness of 1.525 is achieved.

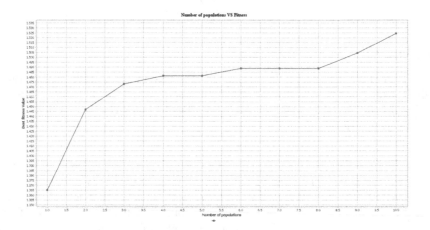

Fig. 14. Scenario 1, populations' evolution [7].

Hybrid Data Replication Strategy. Figure 15 shows the identified suitable strategy optimized for the mentioned scenario of Sect. 6.2. This strategy is comprised of 16 replicas that meet our threshold criterion ϵ. Moreover, the variable votes, quorums, and the structure itself reflect its hybrid nature that works together to serve the purpose and provide an up-to-now unknown replication strategy.

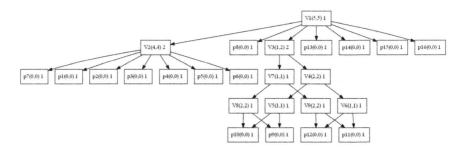

Fig. 15. Optimized hybrid DRS for scenario 1 [7].

Availability Analysis. Figure 16 shows the availability graph for the access operations of the identified DRS on discretized values of p. The newly designed DRS fulfills the specified scenario of thresholds. The x-axis represents the node availability while the y-axis indicates the availability of the access operations. The point symmetry of the graph overtly displays an extremely high availability for the access operations.

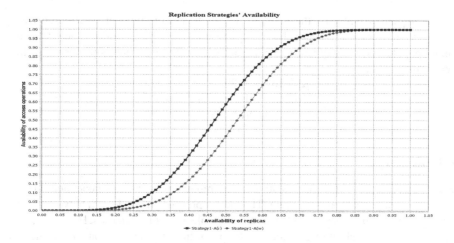

Fig. 16. Availability graph of read and write operations [7].

This availability is, again, very close to MCS (particularly for higher p values), which is considered the best in terms of the critical write operations' availability, and at the same time, our hybrid approach is reasonably economical in terms of cost. In best cases, it takes only five replicas each for the access operations out of 16 unlike MCS with a cost of 17 replicas in total for read and write, which is very expensive. A detailed comparison of this strategy is performed here [6].

6.5 Scenario 2

Having found a suitable optimized strategy for the specified scenario, now we specify a different, but relatively challenging scenario, as compared to the former one to show the effectiveness of our approach. Here, cost is also being taken into consideration, previously (Scenario 1) full weightage was given to availability, and cost was ignored in the evolutionary process.

6.6 Scenario Parameters 2

In this scenario, the probability of individual replicas is set to 0.7 and the total number of replicas is confined to 12, to achieve a read and a write availability of at least 0.85, whereas the expected cost for each operation is set to be no more than three replicas.

For this, 70% is being given to the availability of the access operations and rest to the cost.

$$p = 0.7, \quad \epsilon = 12, \quad \alpha = 0.85, \quad \beta = 0.85,$$
$$\gamma = 3.0, \quad \delta = 3.0, \quad \text{fw} = 0.7$$

6.7 System Parameters 2

As for system parameters, the number of parents and the number of children DRSs are set to 13 and 30, respectively, to explore the search space more. The use of the initial population in every generation is set to 30%. The mutation is performed with a probability of 0.2.

$$\mu = 13, \quad \lambda = 30,$$
$$\text{probInitialParentList} = 0.3,$$
$$\text{mutationProb} = 0.2$$

6.8 Results 2

Figure 17 presents a 3D representation of the replication strategies generated through the process of genetic programming. The view represents the trade-offs between different objectives of the DRSs, making several possible trade-off scenarios. Here, the x-axis represents the availability while the y-axis cost of the access operations. Each strategy in this representation is given a unique color and clicking on it gives the relevant information about the DRS. The view can be divided into four equal quadrants. Quadrant 1 (top right) presents strategies with higher availabilities at higher costs. Quadrant 2 (top left) represents the strategies with lower availabilities at higher costs. Quadrant 3 (bottom left) presents strategies with lower availabilities at lower costs. Quadrant 4 (bottom right) presents strategies with higher availabilities and lower costs. The strategies are

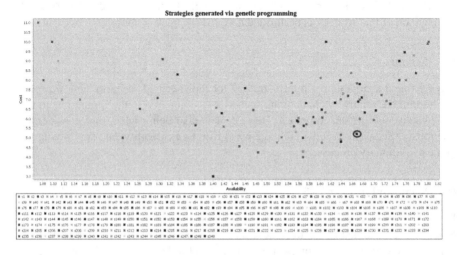

Fig. 17. Trade-off replications strategies.

getting closer to the total availability of 1.82 while the cheapest of the strategy takes three replicas in total for both the access operations to be executed. For the specified case, considering the desirable trade-offs, a DRS circled in red satisfying the criteria is chosen.

The graphs shown in Fig. 18, represent the fitness, read availabilities, and write availabilities of every individual strategy involved in the whole GP process. It is overt that it starts from a lower fitness and slowly with every passing generation it evolves. The parent strategies for the next generation are becoming better and better in terms of getting closer to the desired criteria until it hits the success.

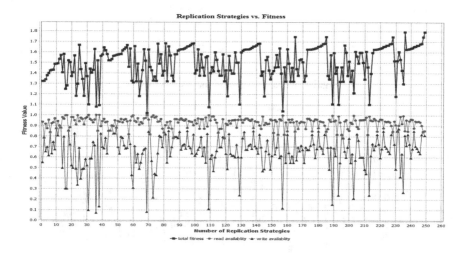

Fig. 18. Scenario 2, fitness of the DRSs.

Figure 19 shows selected strategies of best fitness among each generation. It shows an explicitly evolving trend among every generation starting from a lower fitness of 1.57 to the desired level 1.79. In this case, it takes six generations to find the respective solution.

Figure 20 displays the total number of replicas (y-axis, pink line) and the average minimal costs of read and write operations (y-axis, red line) for every DRS involved in the genetic process. The x-axis represents the strategy numbers to uniquely identify them. The graph starts with the strategies where there is not much difference between the total cost and the total number of replicas, which gradually fades away for the later strategies proving that the system is optimizing the DRSs in terms of their cost. Because now it takes less replicas to execute the access operations out of total replicas. The algorithm stops over a desired optimized strategy comprised of 11 replicas (better than the specified threshold of 12) with a total cost (sum of read and write costs) of almost five on given p.

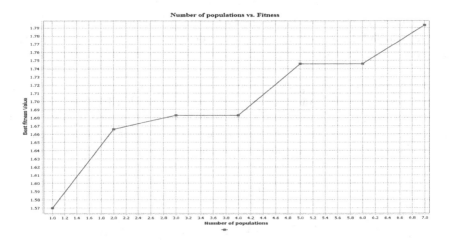

Fig. 19. Scenario 2, evolutionary trajectory.

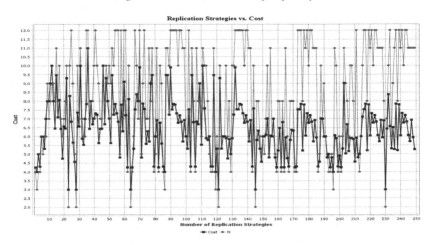

Fig. 20. Scenario 2, cost of the DRSs.

This specified scenario boils down to a fitness of 1.79 to be achieved. The algorithm finds a solution DRS achieving a total availability closer to 1.7 and total cost not more than six replicas (at best four replicas). The system takes six generations to evolve the strategies from a lower fitness 1.57 to the desired fitness of 1.793. Figure 21 shows the generated hybrid replication strategy, comprising MCS, TLP, and TQP (top to bottom, respectively). The system mixes up those strategies automatically in an intelligent way through vertical crossovers in order to satisfy the termination condition.

This instance demonstrates a very economical combination of these different strategies, which merely takes two replicas each to perform an operation in the best case, which is even cheaper than the famous TLP for both the access operations. This automatic mechanism to glue strategies together, in a certain fashion, on certain locations,

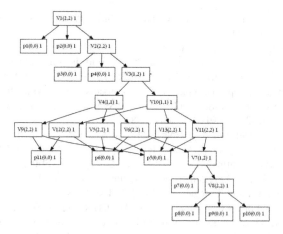

Fig. 21. Optimized hybrid DRS for scenario 2.

to make them optimized, opens up new possibilities of designing new replication strategies, until now unknown. In this manner, the proposed machine learning framework provides a strong opportunity to explore and design new unknown DRSs for any specified scenario and optimize them over several generations of evolution to meet the specified scenario-specific criteria.

7 Conclusion

The research demonstrates the use of machine learning, particularly, genetic programming for the data replication and fault tolerance. It uses this genetic programming-based automated mechanism for designing new hybrid optimized DRSs for specified application-specific scenarios for which no optimal strategy may exist. It designs new DRSs efficiently (without brute-forcing all the possible combinations) and evolve their population as computer programs to make them optimized. The novel approach does not only consider the availability aspect, but also the cost aspect and successfully models a scenario into a replication strategy. This paper demonstrates its usefulness by specifying different scenarios and accordingly designing innovative DRSs to date unknown, satisfying the criteria. This unification of the concepts of fault tolerance with the genetic programming has the potential to open whole new doors of exploring unknown replication strategies. As for future work, this research shall act as a building block to introduce new multi-type crossover as well as mutation operators to gain some more fine-grained control over the algorithm in anticipation of designing appropriate solutions, accordingly. More complex scenarios may also be taken into consideration, thereby indicating the sheer effectiveness of our approach as well as comparing with the state-of-the-art.

References

1. Bernstein, P., Hadzilacos, V., Bernstein, P.: Concurrency Control and Recovery in Database Systems. Addison Wesley, Boston (1987)

2. Naor, M., Wool, A.: The load, capacity, and availability of quorum systems. SIAM J. Comput. **27**(2), 423–447 (1998)
3. Ricardo, J., Marta, P., Bettina, K., Gustavo, A.: How to select a replication protocol according to scalability, availability, and communication overhead. In: Proceedings of the 20th IEEE Symposium on Reliable Distributed Systems (SRDS), New Orleans, LA, USA (2001)
4. Theel, O., Pagina, H.: Optimal replica control protocols exhibit symmetric operation availabilities. In: Proceedings of the 28th International Symposium on Fault-Tolerant Computing (FTCS-28), pp. 252–261. IEEE, Munich (1998)
5. Bokhari, S.M.A., Theel, O.: A flexible hybrid approach to data replication in distributed systems. In: Arai, K., Kapoor, S., Bhatia, R. (eds.) SAI 2020. AISC, vol. 1228, pp. 196–207. Springer, Cham (2020). https://doi.org/10.1007/978-3-030-52249-0_13
6. Bokhari, S.M.A., Theel, O.: A genetic programming-based multi-objective optimization approach to data replication strategies for distributed systems. In: Proceedings of the IEEE Congress on Evolutionary Computation (CEC, WCCI), Glasgow, Scotland (2020)
7. Bokhari, S.M.A., Theel, O.: Design of scenario-based application-optimized data replication strategies through genetic programming. In: Proceedings of the 12th International Conference on Agents and Artificial Intelligence (ICAART), pp. 120–129. SCITEPRESS, Valletta (2020)
8. Bernstein, P., Goodman, N.: An algorithm for concurrency control and recovery in replicated distributed databases. ACM Trans. Database Syst. (TODS) **9**(4), 596–615 (1984)
9. Thomas, R.H.: A majority consensus approach to concurrency control for multiple copy databases. ACM Trans. Database Sys. (TODS) **4**(2), 180–207 (1979)
10. Agrawal, D., Abbadi, A.: The tree quorum protocol: an efficient approach for managing replicated data. In: Proceedings of the 16th International Conference on Very Large Data Bases (VLDB), pp. 243–254 (1990)
11. Gifford, D.: Weighted voting for replicated data. In: Proceedings of the Seventh ACM Symposium on Operating Systems Principles (SOSP), pp. 150–162. ACM (1979)
12. Kumar, A.: Hierarchical quorum consensus: a new algorithm for managing replicated data. IEEE Trans. Comput. **40**(9), 996–1004 (1991)
13. Cheung, S.Y., Ammar, M.H., Ahamad, M.: The grid protocol: a high performance scheme for maintaining replicated data. IEEE Trans. Knowl. Data Eng. **4**(6), 582–592 (1992)
14. Wu, C., Belford, G.G.: The triangular lattice protocol: a highly fault tolerant and highly efficient protocol for replicated data. In: Proceedings of the 11th Symposium on Reliable Distributed Systems (SRDS), pp. 66–73. IEEE Computer Society Press, Houston (1992)
15. Arai, M., et al.: Analysis of read and write availability for generalized hybrid data replication protocol. In: Proceedings of the 10th IEEE Pacific Rim International Symposium on Dependable Computing (PRDC), pp. 143–150. IEEE, Papeete (2004)
16. Choi, S.C., Youn, H.Y.: Dynamic hybrid replication effectively combining tree and grid topology. J. Supercomput. **59**(3), 1289–1311 (2012)
17. Theel, O.: Meeting the application's needs: a design study of a highly customized replication scheme. In: Proceedings of the Pacific Rim International Symposium on Fault Tolerant Computing, Australia, pp. 111–117 (1993)
18. Theel, O.: Rapid replication scheme design using general structured voting. In: Proceedings of the 17th Annual Computer Science Conference, New Zealand, pp. 669–677 (1994)
19. Pagnia, H., Theel, O.: Priority-based quorum protocols for replicated objects. In: Proceedings of the 2nd International Conference on Parallel and Distributed Computing and Networks (PDCN), Brisbane, Australia, pp. 530–535 (1998)
20. Theel, O.: General structured voting: a flexible framework for modelling cooperations. In: Proceedings of the 13th International Conference on Distributed Computing Systems, pp. 227–236. IEEE, Pittsburgh (1993)

21. Theel, O.: General Structured Voting: A Flexible Framework for Modelling Cooperations. Springer Vieweg, pp. 1–350 (2012)
22. Koza, J.: Genetic Programming: On the Programming of Computers by Means of Natural Selection. MIT Press, Cambridge (1992)
23. Banzhaf, W., Frank, D.F., Keller, R.E., Nordin, P.: Genetic Programming: An Introduction: On the Automatic Evolution of Computer Programs and its Applications, pp. 387–398. Morgan Kaufmann Publishers Inc., San Francisco (1998)
24. Syswerda, G.: Simulated crossover in genetic algorithms. In: Foundations of Genetic Algorithms (FOGA), pp. 239–255. Elsevier (1993)

Trading Bias for Expressivity in Artificial Learning

George D. Montañez[(✉)], Daniel Bashir, and Julius Lauw

AMISTAD Lab, Department of Computer Science, Harvey Mudd College,
Claremont, CA 91711, USA
{gmontanez,dbashir,julauw}@hmc.edu

Abstract. Bias, arising from inductive assumptions, is necessary for successful artificial learning, allowing algorithms to generalize beyond training data and outperform random guessing. We explore how bias relates to algorithm flexibility (expressivity). Expressive algorithms alter their outputs as training data changes, allowing them to adapt to changing situations. Using a measure of algorithm flexibility rooted in the information-theoretic concept of entropy, we examine the trade-off between bias and expressivity, showing that while highly biased algorithms may outperform uniform random sampling, they cannot also be highly expressive. Conversely, maximally expressive algorithms necessarily have performance no better than uniform random guessing. We establish that necessary trade-offs exist in trying to design flexible yet strongly performing learning systems.

Keywords: Machine learning · Search · Algorithmic bias · Inductive bias · Entropic expressivity

1 Introduction

Assumptions are essential for learning [7,9,10]. Unless a learning algorithm is biased towards certain outcomes, it cannot outperform random guessing [10]. However, biased algorithms are less flexible; increasing performance comes at a price. Being predisposed towards some outcomes means being predisposed away from others. The degree to which an algorithm can respond to data and output a variety of different responses is its *expressivity*. We investigate the inherent tension between bias and expressivity in learning algorithms, presenting a number of theorems which show that the two are at odds. Flexible and expressive algorithms can change their outcomes in response to changes in data, but highly flexible algorithms cannot widely deviate in performance from uniform random sampling. Conversely, highly biased algorithms can be successful on only a narrow set of problems, limiting their expressivity. Biased algorithms are specialized and our work explores the costs of this specialization in terms of reduced flexibility.

We build on existing research in theoretical machine learning viewing machine learning, AI, and optimization as black-box search processes [8], allowing us to prove

This work was supported in part by a generous grant from the Walter Bradley Center for Natural and Artificial Intelligence.

A. P. Rocha et al. (Eds.): ICAART 2020, LNAI 12613, pp. 332–353, 2021.
https://doi.org/10.1007/978-3-030-71158-0_16

theorems simultaneously applying to many different types of learning, including classification, regression, unsupervised clustering, and density estimation. Within the algorithmic search framework, we define a form of expressivity, *entropic expressivity*, which measures the information-theoretic entropy of an algorithm's induced probability distribution over its search space. An algorithm with high entropic expressivity will spread its probability mass more uniformly on the search space, allowing it to sample widely and without strong preference within that space, displaying flexibility. Conversely, an algorithm with low entropic expressivjty concentrates its mass on few regions of the search space, displaying bias towards those outcomes. No algorithm can be both highly expressive and highly biased.

2   Bias in Machine Learning

The word "bias" used in this paper may call a number of associations to the reader's mind. In this section, we seek to disambiguate between different definitions of bias as they arise in machine learning, clarify how we use the term bias, and discuss how our notion interacts with other definitions.

Definition 1. *(Prejudicial Bias (Tim Jones, IBM)) Prejudicial Bias is a prejudice in favor of or against a person, group, or thing that is considered to be unfair. Such bias can result in disparate outcomes when machine learning algorithms, such as facial recognition systems, behave differently when applied to different groups of people.*

Definition 2. *(Inductive Bias (Tom Mitchell)) In the case of a machine leaning algorithm, Inductive Bias is any basis for choosing one generalization over another, other than strict consistency with the observed training instances.*

Informally, the definition of bias that we will employ in this paper quantifies the predisposition an algorithm has towards certain outcomes over others. This controls how an algorithm interprets data and influences how "well-suited" an algorithm is to a particular task, resulting in performance deviations from uniform random sampling. For example, the naïve Bayes classifier is predisposed towards hypotheses that interpret the training data as a set of conditionally independent inputs, where each feature depends only on its output label.

Our mathematical definition of bias is inspired by Definition 2, and is similar to the notion of bias used in statistical parameter estimation, being the difference between an expected random outcome and a baseline value. Bias, as used in this paper, is quite different from the notion of bias in Definition 1. The machine learning community has paid a great deal of attention to confronting the problematic and unethical consequences of prejudicial bias in our field. We believe any applications that use insights from our work and similar work on bias should reflect the responsible consideration of the potential for prejudicial bias and seek to eliminate, or at least minimize, its impact.

As an illustrative example, prejudicial bias can arise when either the researchers designing a machine learning system or the data used to train that system themselves exhibit problematic bias. For example, in the facial recognition case, a vision model being used to recognize people might be trained on images of those that are mostly of

European descent. As a result, the vision model might have trouble recognizing people of non-European racial backgrounds and skin tones.

We would also like to briefly comment on how our notion of bias interacts with prejudicial bias. As we have discussed, a facial recognition system may not work as well for some groups of people as it does for others either because it chose a hypothesis based on training data that reflects such a bias, because it was predisposed towards prejudicially biased hypotheses in the first place (inductive bias), or some combination of both. Under our definition of bias, the algorithm that is inductively biased towards prejudicially biased hypotheses would indeed be considered more biased than a "baseline" algorithm that is not more likely to select one hypothesis over another. At the same time, and perhaps less intuitively, we would also consider an algorithm strongly predisposed *not* to select a racially biased hypothesis more biased than the baseline, precisely because this reflects the algorithm's predisposition towards certain outcomes (and away from others).

We strongly oppose the use of prejudicial biases in learning systems, and support continued efforts to expose and eliminate them. Knowledge that all nontrivial systems must be biased is some way can help us identify and critically evaluate the biases inherent in our own systems, removing prejudicial biases wherever we find them.

3   Related Work

Our notion of algorithmic expressivity stands among many other measures of expressivity found in the statistical learning literature. Among the most well-established are the Vapnik-Chernovekis (VC) dimension [15], a loose upper bound based on the number of points that can be perfectly classified by a learning algorithm for any possible labeling of the points; the Fat-shattering VC dimension, an extension to the VC dimension developed by Kearns and Schapire that solves the issue of dependence on dimensionality when the algorithm operates within a restricted space [4]; and Rademacher complexity, a measure of algorithmic expressivity developed by Barlett and Mendelson that eliminates the need for assuming restrictions on the distribution space of an algorithm [1]. More recent work has attempted to capture the expressivity of deep neural networks in particular, by using structural properties of neural networks to consider their representative power [11]. While this more recent work is of interest, we seek a much more general notion of algorithmic expressivity under which other such notions might be captured.

This paper delves into the relationships between algorithmic (inductive) bias, a concept explored by Mitchell due to its importance for generalization [7], and algorithmic expressivity. Towards this end, we build on the search and bias frameworks developed in [10], where Montañez et al. prove the necessity of bias for better-than-random performance of learning algorithms and that no algorithm may be simultaneously biased towards many distinct target sets. In addition to giving explicit bounds on the trade-offs between bias and algorithmic expressivity, we establish a general measure of algorithmic flexibility that applies to clustering and optimization [9] in addition to the problems considered in Vapnik's learning framework [16], such as classification, regression, and density estimation. Our framework's generality is conducive to applying theoretical derivations of algorithmic expressivity to many different types of learning algorithms.

3.1   Relation to Lauw et al.'s "The Bias-Expressivity Trade-off"

This manuscript is most closely related to Lauw et al.'s "The Bias-Expressivity Trade-off" [6], being an extended presentation of that work. Our discussion of the various uses of the term "bias" in machine learning acts as a helpful supplement to the space-constrained introduction made there. We also provide an improved presentation and motivation for the concepts of algorithmic bias and entropic expressivity found in that paper. The theorems from that work, along with their proofs and key figures, are reproduced here.

4   Algorithmic Search Framework

4.1   The Search Problem

The framework used in this paper views machine learning problems as instances of algorithmic search problems [8]. In the algorithmic search framework, a search problem is defined as a 3-tuple, (Ω, T, F). An algorithm samples elements from a finite **search space** Ω in order to find a particular nonempty subset T of Ω, called the **target set**. The elements of Ω and T are encoded in a **target function**, a $|\Omega|$-length binary vector where an entry has value 1 if it belongs to the target set T and 0 otherwise. The **external information resource** F provides initialization information for the search and evaluates points in Ω to guide the search process. In a traditional machine learning scenario, the search space Ω corresponds to a hypothesis space an algorithm may have available (such as the space of linear functions). The external information resource F would be a dataset with an accompanying loss function. The target set T would correspond to those hypotheses which achieve sufficiently low empirical risk on a dataset given some desired threshold. The loss function included in F guides the algorithm in searching through Ω for a hypothesis in T.

4.2   The Search Algorithm

Black-box search algorithms can be viewed as processes that induce probability distributions over a search space and subsequently sample according to those distributions, in order to locate target elements within the space. Black-box algorithms use their search history to produce a sequence of distributions. The search history contains information gained during the course of the search by sampling elements of Ω and evaluating them according to the external information resource F, along with any information given as initialization information. As the search proceeds, a sequence of probability distributions gets generated, one distribution per iteration, and a point is sampled from each distribution at every iteration. The sampled point and its evaluation under F are added back to the search history, and the algorithm updates its sampling distribution over Ω. A search algorithm is *successful* if at any point of the search it samples an element $\omega \in T$ contained in the target set. Success is determined retrospectively, since the algorithm has no knowledge of the target T during its search apart from that information given by F. Figure 1 gives a graphical representation of the search process.

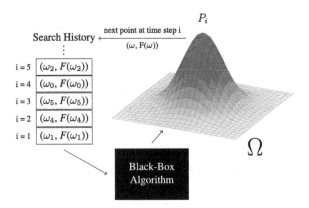

Fig. 1. Graphical representation of the search process. As a black-box algorithm searches a space by sampling from Ω, it induces a probability distribution P_i at each time step, based on its current search history. A sampled point $\omega \in \Omega$ is evaluated according to the external information resource F, and the tuple $(\omega, F(\omega))$ is added to the search history. The process repeats until a termination criterion is met. Figure reproduced from [6].

4.3   Measuring Performance

A more fine-grained measure of search performance is given by the expected per-query probability of success [8], which normalizes the expected total cumulative probability of success by the number of queries taken. Different algorithms may choose to terminate their searches using different criteria, taking a different number of sampling steps. Using the expected total probability of success without normalization would unfairly reward algorithms making a larger number of queries. As an additional benefit, the expected per-query probability of success gracefully handles algorithms which may repeatedly resample the same points, such as genetic algorithms [3, 12].

Following Montañez [8], **the expected per-query probability of success** is defined as

$$q(T, F) = \mathbb{E}_{\tilde{P}, H}\left[\frac{1}{|\tilde{P}|}\sum_{i=1}^{|\tilde{P}|} P_i(\omega \in T)\,\bigg|\,F\right] \tag{1}$$

where $\tilde{P} = [P_1, P_2, \ldots, P_N]$ is a sequence of induced probability distributions on search space Ω (with P_i denoting the distribution at the ith iteration), H is the search history, T is the target set, and F is the external information resource. Thus, the expected per-query probability of success measures the expected amount of probability mass placed on the target set, averaged over the entire search. As Lauw et al. explain [6], *"The outer expectation accounts for stochastic differences in multiple runs of the algorithm, whereas the inner quantity is equivalent to the expected probability of success for a uniformly sampled time step of a given run."*

5 Inductive Orientation and Algorithmic Bias

We begin by introducing a geometric concept of algorithm behavior, the *inductive orientation*, which will allow us to define algorithmic bias in a way that is simultaneously quantitative and geometric. We then review the definition of algorithmic bias introduced in Lauw et al. [6], and define it in terms of inductive orientation.

5.1 Inductive Orientation

The definition of expected per-query probability of success given in Eq. 1 naturally suggests a way of characterizing the behavior of an algorithm based on its expected average probability distribution on the search space. For a fixed target set t, define a corresponding $|\Omega|$-length binary target vector $\mathbf{t}$, which has a 1 at its ith index if the ith element of Ω is in the target set t, and has a zero otherwise. For a random information resource $F \sim \mathcal{D}$, we can see that

$$q(t, F) = \mathbb{E}_{\tilde{P}, H}\left[\frac{1}{|\tilde{P}|}\sum_{i=1}^{|\tilde{P}|} P_i(\omega \in t)\middle| F\right]$$

$$= \mathbb{E}_{\tilde{P}, H}\left[\frac{1}{|\tilde{P}|}\sum_{i=1}^{|\tilde{P}|} \mathbf{t}^\top \mathbf{P}_i\middle| F\right]$$

$$= \mathbf{t}^\top \mathbb{E}_{\tilde{P}, H}\left[\frac{1}{|\tilde{P}|}\sum_{i=1}^{|\tilde{P}|} \mathbf{P}_i\middle| F\right]$$

$$= \mathbf{t}^\top \overline{\mathbf{P}}_F$$

where we have defined $\overline{\mathbf{P}}_F := \mathbb{E}_{\tilde{P}, H}[\frac{1}{|\tilde{P}|}\sum_{i=1}^{|\tilde{P}|} \mathbf{P}_i \mid F]$ as the expected average conditional distribution on the search space given F. We notice two things. First, the expected per-query probability of success is equivalent to an inner product between two vectors, one representing the target and the other representing where the algorithm tends to place probability mass in expectation. As Montanez et al. note [10], the degree to which the expected distribution aligns geometrically to the target vector is the degree to which a search algorithm will be successful. Second, as Sam et al. have shown, this implies that the expected per-query probability of success is a decomposable probability-of-success metric [13].

The **inductive orientation** of an algorithm is then defined as

$$\overline{\mathbf{P}}_\mathcal{D} = \mathbb{E}_{F \sim \mathcal{D}}[\overline{\mathbf{P}}_F] \tag{2}$$

given a marginal distribution $\mathcal{D}$ on the information resource F. From this definition, we see that

$$\mathbb{E}_\mathcal{D}[q(t, F)] = \mathbb{E}_\mathcal{D}[\mathbf{t}^\top \overline{\mathbf{P}}_F] \tag{3}$$

$$= \mathbf{t}^\top \mathbb{E}_\mathcal{D}[\overline{\mathbf{P}}_F] \tag{4}$$

$$= \mathbf{t}^\top \overline{\mathbf{P}}_\mathcal{D}. \tag{5}$$

Thus, the expected per-query probability of success relative to a randomized F can be computed simply and geometrically, by taking an inner product of the inductive orientation with the target vector.

We can further extend the concept of inductive orientation with regards to any decomposable probability-of-success metric ϕ, since we can take any weighted average of the probability distributions in a search, not just the uniform average. We define the ϕ-**inductive orientation** for decomposable metric $\phi(t, F) = \mathbf{t}^\top \mathbf{P}_{\phi,F}$ as

$$\mathbf{P}_{\phi,\mathcal{D}} = \mathbb{E}_{F \sim \mathcal{D}}[\mathbf{P}_{\phi,F}], \tag{6}$$

of which $\overline{\mathbf{P}}_\mathcal{D}$ is simply a special case for uniform weighting [13].

5.2 Algorithmic Bias

We now review the definition of bias introduced in [10] and show how it can be defined as a linear function of the inductive orientation. We then restate some existing results for bias, which show the need for bias in learning systems.

Definition 3. *(Algorithmic Bias) Given a fixed target function* $\mathbf{t}$ *(corresponding to target set* t*), let* $p = \|\mathbf{t}\|^2/|\Omega|$ *denote the expected per-query probability of success under uniform random sampling, let* $\mathbf{P}_\mathcal{U} = \mathbf{1} \cdot |\Omega|^{-1}$ *be the inductive orientation vector for a uniform random sampler, and let* $F \sim \mathcal{D}$, *where* $\mathcal{D}$ *is a distribution over a collection of information resources* $\mathcal{F}$. *Then,*

$$\begin{aligned}
\mathrm{Bias}(\mathcal{D}, \mathbf{t}) &= \mathbb{E}_\mathcal{D}[q(t, F) - p] \\
&= \mathbf{t}^\top(\overline{\mathbf{P}}_\mathcal{D} - \mathbf{P}_\mathcal{U}) \\
&= \mathbf{t}^\top \mathbb{E}_\mathcal{D}[\overline{\mathbf{P}}_F] - \mathbf{t}^\top(\mathbf{1} \cdot |\Omega|^{-1}) \\
&= \mathbf{t}^\top \int_\mathcal{F} \overline{\mathbf{P}}_f \mathcal{D}(f)\, df - \frac{\|\mathbf{t}\|^2}{|\Omega|}.
\end{aligned}$$

The above definition is in complete agreement with that given by Lauw et al. [6], but makes clearer the relation of bias to inductive orientation, the bias being a linear function of the orientation vector. The first equality in the definition highlights the semantic meaning of bias, being a deviation in performance from uniform random sampling. The second equality highlights the cause of this deviation, namely the algorithm's inductive orientation encoding assumptions concerning where target elements are likely to reside, distributing its probability mass unevenly within the search space. The larger the deviation from uniform mass placement, the greater the opportunity for improved (or degraded) performance.

As a special case, we can define bias with respect to a finite set of information resources, as follows.

Definition 4. *(Bias for a finite set of information resources) Let $\mathcal{U}[\mathcal{B}]$ denote a uniform distribution over a finite set of information resources $\mathcal{B}$. Then,*

$$\mathrm{Bias}(\mathcal{B}, \mathbf{t}) = \mathrm{Bias}(\mathcal{U}[\mathcal{B}], \mathbf{t})$$

$$= \mathbf{t}^{\top} \left(\frac{1}{|\mathcal{B}|} \sum_{f \in \mathcal{B}} \overline{\mathbf{P}}_f \right) - \frac{\|\mathbf{t}\|^2}{|\Omega|}.$$

6 Existing Bias Results

We restate a number of theorems given in Montañez et al. [10] which are useful for understanding the results in the present paper.

Theorem 1 (Improbability of Favorable Information Resources). *Let $\mathcal{D}$ be a distribution over a set of information resources $\mathcal{F}$, let F be a random variable such that $F \sim \mathcal{D}$, let $t \subseteq \Omega$ be an arbitrary fixed k-sized target set with corresponding target function $\mathbf{t}$, and let $q(t, F)$ be the expected per-query probability of success for algorithm $\mathcal{A}$ on search problem (Ω, t, F). Then, for any $q_{\min} \in [0, 1]$,*

$$\Pr(q(t, F) \geq q_{\min}) \leq \frac{p + \mathrm{Bias}(\mathcal{D}, \mathbf{t})}{q_{\min}}$$

where $p = \frac{k}{|\Omega|}$.

This theorem tells us that sampling highly favorable information resources remains unlikely for any distribution without high algorithmic bias for the given target. Given that we typically search for very small targets in very large spaces (implying a tiny p), the bound is restrictive for values of $q_{\min}$ approaching 1, unless the bias is strong. The upper bound is controlled linearly by the bias of the sampling distribution with respect to the fixed target and algorithm. Furthermore, bias is a conserved quantity: to be highly biased towards one target means to be equally biased against other targets. Thus, choosing an inductive orientation and bias represents a zero-sum game, as the next result shows.

Theorem 2 (Conservation of Bias). *Let $\mathcal{D}$ be a distribution over a set of information resources and let $\tau_k = \{\mathbf{t} | \mathbf{t} \in \{0, 1\}^{|\Omega|}, \|\mathbf{t}\| = \sqrt{k}\}$ be the set of all $|\Omega|$-length k-hot vectors[1]. Then for any fixed algorithm $\mathcal{A}$,*

$$\sum_{\mathbf{t} \in \tau_k} \mathrm{Bias}(\mathcal{D}, \mathbf{t}) = 0.$$

This result can be viewed as a special case of No Free Lunch [14, 17] behavior, since bias is a relative performance measure between two algorithm strategies, and the set of all k-sized targets is closed under permutation [14], a necessary and sufficient condition for the original No Free Lunch theorems.

---

[1] k-hot vectors are binary vectors containing exactly k ones.

Theorem 3 (Famine of Favorable Information Resources). *Let $\mathcal{B}$ be a finite set of information resources and let $t \subseteq \Omega$ be an arbitrary fixed k-size target set with corresponding target function* $\mathbf{t}$. *Define*

$$\mathcal{B}_{q_{\min}} = \{f \mid f \in \mathcal{B}, q(t, f) \geq q_{\min}\},$$

where $q(t, f)$ is the expected per-query probability of success for algorithm $\mathcal{A}$ on search problem (Ω, t, f) and $q_{\min} \in [0, 1]$ represents the minimum acceptable per-query probability of success. Then,

$$\frac{|\mathcal{B}_{q_{\min}}|}{|\mathcal{B}|} \leq \frac{p + \mathrm{Bias}(\mathcal{B}, \mathbf{t})}{q_{\min}}$$

where $p = \frac{k}{|\Omega|}$.

By the above theorem, the proportion of $q_{\min}$-favorable information resources is bounded by the problem difficulty and the average bias of the set as a whole. For any fixed value of bias, fixed target, and fixed algorithm, the proportion of highly favorable information resources remains strictly bound.

Lastly, we see that without bias, the single-query probability of success for any algorithm is equivalent to uniform random sampling: it is the same as flipping coins. Algorithms must have nonuniform inductive orientations to perform well, and any choice of inductive orientation is a choice against some targets sets, thus encoding trade-offs among the various possible targets.

Theorem 4 (Futility of Bias-free Search). *For any fixed algorithm $\mathcal{A}$, fixed target $t \subseteq \Omega$ with corresponding target function $\mathbf{t}$, and distribution over information resources $\mathcal{D}$, if $\mathrm{Bias}(\mathcal{D}, \mathbf{t}) = 0$, then*

$$\Pr(\omega \in t; \mathcal{A}) = p$$

where $\Pr(\omega \in t; \mathcal{A})$ represents the single-query probability of successfully sampling an element of t using $\mathcal{A}$, marginalized over information resources $F \sim \mathcal{D}$, and p is the single-query probability of success under uniform random sampling.

At this point, we remind the reader that although the above theorems are stated with reference to search and sampling, they apply far more widely to most forms of artificial learning, such as AI methods and other types of machine learning [9], being formalized within the algorithmic search framework for that purpose [8].

7   Main Results

In this section, we present results building on the definitions of algorithmic bias and inductive orientation given in Sect. 5. We reproduce the main results of Lauw et al. [6] and add new discussion concerning the relevance of each result. These results include upper bounds on the bias of a learning algorithm in relation to its minimum value over the set of possible targets, a concentration bound on the difference between estimated and actual bias, and bounds relating algorithmic bias to entropic expressivity. These bounds capture an inherent trade-off between the expressivity and bias for artificial learning systems.

7.1 Bias Bounds

Theorem 5 (Bias Upper Bound). *Let* $\tau_k = \{t | t \in \{0,1\}^{|\Omega|}, ||t|| = \sqrt{k}\}$ *be the set of all* $|\Omega|$-*length k-hot vectors and let* $\mathcal{B}$ *be a finite set of information resources. Then,*

$$\sup_{t \in \tau_k} \text{Bias}(\mathcal{B}, t) \leq \left(\frac{p-1}{p}\right) \inf_{t \in \tau_k} \text{Bias}(\mathcal{B}, t)$$

where $p = \frac{k}{|\Omega|}$.

This result presents limitations on the amount of bias that can be induced within a learning algorithm from all possible target sets of a fixed size. From Theorem 5, we see that the maximum amount of bias that can be induced in a learning algorithm is related to the minimum amount that can be induced. The two are related by, at most, a constant factor $\frac{p-1}{p}$, where p is the proportion of elements in the $|\Omega|$-sized search space that are in the target set.

Figure 2 demonstrates the relationship between the value of p and the upper bound on bias in Theorem 5. We see that as p increases, the upper bound on bias tightens considerably. This is due to the fact that the target set k increases in size relative to the size of Ω, which substantially increases the probability that the algorithm will do well on a greater number of target sets because of target element density in the search space. This indicates that the algorithm is not predisposed towards any particular target set, giving evidence against the presence of strong bias (Theorem 2).

Theorem 6 (Difference between Estimated and Actual Bias). *Let* t *be a fixed target function, let* $\mathcal{D}$ *be a distribution over a set of information resources* $\mathcal{B}$, *and let* $X = \{X_1, \ldots, X_n\}$ *be a finite sample independently drawn from* $\mathcal{D}$. *Then,*

$$\mathbb{P}(|\text{Bias}(X, t) - \text{Bias}(\mathcal{D}, t)| \geq \epsilon) \leq 2e^{-2n\epsilon^2}.$$

While the bias with respect to an underlying distribution over information resources may not be accessible, it may be possible to estimate it by drawing, independently at random, a sample from that distribution. Theorem 6 quantifies how well the empirical bias estimates the true bias with high probability.

7.2 Entropic Expressivity

Just as the bias of an algorithm can be defined as a function of inductive orientation, so can the expressivity. We now formalize such a definition.

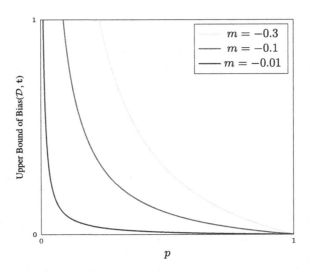

Fig. 2. As plotted for different values of $m = \frac{p-1}{p}$, the upper bound of the supremum of bias changes with different values of p, where the supremum is over all possible target sets of some fixed size k. Figure reproduced from [6].

Definition 5 (Entropic Expressivity). *The entropic expressivity of a search algorithm is the information-theoretic entropy of its inductive orientation, namely,*

$$H(\overline{\mathbf{P}}_{\mathcal{D}}) = H(\mathcal{U}) - D_{\mathrm{KL}}(\overline{\mathbf{P}}_{\mathcal{D}} \,\|\, \mathcal{U})$$

where $D_{\mathrm{KL}}(\overline{\mathbf{P}}_{\mathcal{D}} \,\|\, \mathcal{U})$ is the Kullback-Leibler divergence between distribution $\overline{\mathbf{P}}_{\mathcal{D}}$ and the uniform distribution $\mathcal{U}$, both being distributions over search space Ω.

Informally, the expressivity of an algorithm is how well it responds to changes in data: different datasets produce different probability distributions over the search space. More formally, expressivity is the degree to which an algorithm's inductive orientation vector blurs towards uniformity, meaning that in expectation it places probability mass on many different regions of the search space, in reaction to changing information resources. Again, expressive algorithms will shift mass around different regions of the space as the dataset changes. This stands in contrast to a highly biased algorithm, which places substantial mass in a limited number of regions of the search space. Consequently, the inductive orientation of the more flexible algorithm will be closer to uniform than that of the highly biased algorithm. Using the information-theoretic entropy for discrete probability mass functions, our notion of entropic expressivity characterizes this aspect of algorithmic flexibility.

7.3 Expressivity and Bias Trade-off

We now present results relating entropic expressivity to algorithmic bias, bounding expressivity in terms of bias and bias in terms of expressivity, demonstrating a trade-off between the two quantities.

Theorem 7 (Expressivity Bounded by Bias). *Let* $\epsilon := \text{Bias}(\mathcal{D}, \mathbf{t})$. *Given a fixed k-hot target vector* $\mathbf{t}$ *and a distribution over information resources* $\mathcal{D}$, *the entropic expressivity,* $H(\overline{\mathbf{P}}_{\mathcal{D}})$, *of a search algorithm can be bounded in terms of bias,* ϵ, *by*

$$H(\overline{\mathbf{P}}_{\mathcal{D}}) \in \left[H(p+\epsilon), \left((p+\epsilon) \log_2 \left(\frac{k}{p+\epsilon} \right) \right.\right.$$
$$\left.\left. + (1-(p+\epsilon)) \log_2 \left(\frac{|\Omega| - k}{1 - (p+\epsilon)} \right) \right) \right].$$

Theorem 7 gives the minimum and maximum amount of entropic expressivity for a given amount of bias and fixed target set size. We see that bias limits the entropic expressivity of a learning algorithm, by reducing the uniformity of its inductive orientation. To get a better sense of this result, we show how the range of entropic expressivity varies in response to plugging in different values of algorithmic bias. In Table 1, we consider some exemplar cases, where a learning algorithm has minimum bias, zero bias, as well as maximum bias, and present the entropic expressivity range computed based on Theorem 7.

Table 1. As computed for cases where there is minimum bias, zero bias, and maximum bias, the bound for the range of entropic expressivity changes with different levels of bias relative to target function $\mathbf{t}$. Table reproduced from [6].

Bias$(\mathcal{D}, \mathbf{t})$	$\mathbf{t}^{\top} \overline{\mathbf{P}}_{\mathcal{D}}$	Expressivity range
$-p$ (Minimum bias)	0	$[0, \log_2(|\Omega| - k)]$
0 (No bias)	p	$[H(p), \log_2 |\Omega|]$
$1 - p$ (Maximum bias)	1	$[0, \log_2 k]$

As an algorithm's bias increases, its entropic expressivity becomes more tightly bounded. In the majority of cases, the size k of the target set is substantially smaller than the size $|\Omega|$ of the search space. Therefore, in the case of minimum bias, entropic expressivity has only a loosely bounded range of $[0, \log_2(|\Omega| - k)]$. Similarly, when there is no bias, the expressivity can take on values up to $\log_2 |\Omega|$. In the case of maximum bias, however, the algorithm becomes extremely predisposed towards a particular outcome. Given that $k \ll |\Omega|$, $\log_2 k \ll \log_2(|\Omega - k|)$, indicating a considerable tightening of the bound. With these observations in hand, we now present our main result, which demonstrates a quantifiable trade-off between the algorithmic bias and entropic expressivity of artificial learning systems.

Theorem 8 (Bias-Expressivity Trade-off). *Given a distribution over information resources $\mathcal{D}$ and a fixed target $t \subseteq \Omega$, entropic expressivity is bounded above in terms of bias,*

$$H(\overline{\mathbf{P}}_{\mathcal{D}}) \le \log_2 |\Omega| - 2\mathrm{Bias}(\mathcal{D}, t)^2.$$

Additionally, bias is bounded above in terms of entropic expressivity,

$$\mathrm{Bias}(\mathcal{D}, t) \le \sqrt{\frac{1}{2}(\log_2 |\Omega| - H(\overline{\mathbf{P}}_{\mathcal{D}}))}$$

$$= \sqrt{\frac{1}{2}D_{KL}(\overline{\mathbf{P}}_{\mathcal{D}} \| \mathcal{U})}.$$

This theorem extends the results of Theorem 7 to demonstrate a mathematical relationship between algorithmic bias and entropic expressivity. As in Theorem 7, entropic expressivity is bound from above in terms of algorithmic bias. As the level of algorithmic bias on a specified target set increases, the level of entropic expressivity in the underlying inductive orientation decreases. We see that there is an opposing relationship between entropic expressivity and bias, such that higher values of algorithmic bias result in smaller values of entropic expressivity, and vice versa. We upper-bound algorithmic bias in terms of entropic expressivity, which again demonstrates this trade-off. The higher the entropic expressivity of a learning algorithm, the lower the bias. This result establishes that if a learning algorithm is strongly oriented towards any specific outcome, the algorithm becomes less flexible and less expressive over all elements, and the more flexible an algorithm, the less it can specialize towards specific outcomes.

Finally, we present a bound for algorithmic bias in terms of the expected entropy of induced strategy distributions. Similar to the trade-off relationship between algorithmic bias and entropic expressivity, the following corollary further establishes a trade-off between algorithmic bias and the expected entropy of induced strategy distributions.

Corollary 1 (Bias Bound Under Expected Expressivity)

$$\mathrm{Bias}(\mathcal{D}, t) \le \sqrt{\frac{1}{2}(\log_2 |\Omega| - \mathbb{E}_{\mathcal{D}}[H(\overline{\mathbf{P}}_F)])}$$

$$= \sqrt{\mathbb{E}_{\mathcal{D}}\left[\frac{1}{2}D_{KL}(\overline{\mathbf{P}}_F \| \mathcal{U})\right]}.$$

8   Conclusion

We extend the algorithmic search framework to consider a new notion of bias, being the difference in performance from uniform random sampling caused by the inductive assumptions encoded within an algorithm. We also define the entropic expressivity of a learning algorithm and characterize its relation to bias. Given an underlying distribution on information resources, entropic expressivity quantifies the expected degree of uniformity for strategy distributions, namely, the uniformity of the resulting inductive orientation. In addition to upper-bounding the bias on an arbitrary target set and the probability of a large difference between the estimated and true biases, we upper- and lower-bound the entropic expressivity with respect to the bias on a given target. These bounds concretely demonstrate the trade-off between bias and expressivity.

The bias-variance trade-off [2,5] is well-known in machine learning. Our results present a similar trade-off, providing bounds for bias and expressivity in terms of one another. Our notion of bias corresponds to the expected deviation from uniform random sampling that results from an algorithm's inductive assumptions, while expressivity, similar to variance, captures how an algorithm's output distribution over its search space changes in expectation with regards to the underlying distribution on information resources (e.g., training data).

As shown by Mitchell [7] and later Montañez et al. [10], bias is necessary for learning algorithms to perform better than random chance. However, this comes at the cost of reducing the algorithm's ability to respond to varied training data. A maximally biased algorithm will have very little flexibility, while a maximally flexible algorithm, making no assumptions about its input, cannot perform better than uniform random sampling (Theorem 4). Fundamentally, bias and expressivity are both functions of an algorithm's inductive orientation: the more strongly pronounced its inductive orientation, the better an algorithm can generalize, but the less flexible it will be. Understanding the nature of this trade-off can help us design the type of behavior we want, according to the situation at hand.

Appendix

For completeness, in this appendix we reproduce all proofs from Lauw et al. [6] in their entirety, without modification.

Lemma 1 (Existence of Subset with at Most Uniform Mass). *Given an n-sized subset S of the sample space of an arbitrary probability distribution with total probability mass M_S, there exists a k-sized proper subset $R \subset S$ with total probability mass M_R such that*

$$M_R \leq \frac{k}{n} M_S.$$

Proof. We proceed by induction on the size k.

Base Case: When $k = 1$, there exists an element with total probability mass at most $\frac{M_S}{n}$, since for any element in S that has probability mass greater than the uniform mass $\frac{M_S}{n}$, there exists an element with mass strictly less than $\frac{M_S}{n}$ by the law of total probability. This establishes our base case.

Inductive Hypothesis: Suppose that a k-sized subset $R_k \subset S$ exists with total probability mass M_{R_k} such that $M_{R_k} \leq \frac{k}{n} M_S$.

Induction Step: We show that there exists a subset $R_{k+1} \subset S$ of size $k + 1$ with total probability mass $M_{R_{k+1}}$ such that $M_{R_{k+1}} \leq \frac{k+1}{n} M_S$.

First, let $M_{R_k} = \frac{k}{n}M_S - s$, where $s \geq 0$ represents the slack between M_{R_k} and $\frac{k}{n}M_S$. Then, the total probability mass on $R_k{}^c := S \setminus R_k$ is

$$M_{R_k^c} = M_S - M_{R_k} = M_S - \frac{k}{n}M_S + s.$$

Given that $M_{R_k^c}$ is the total probability mass on set $R_k{}^c$, either each of the $n - k$ elements in $R_k{}^c$ has a uniform mass of $M_{R_k^c}/(n-k)$, or they do not. If the probability mass is uniformly distributed, let e be an element with mass exactly $M_{R_k^c}/(n-k)$. Otherwise, for any element e' with mass greater than $M_{R_k^c}/(n-k)$, by the law of total probability there exists an element $e \in R_k{}^c$ with mass less than $M_{R_k^c}/(n-k)$. Thus, in either case there exists an element $e \in R_k{}^c$ with mass at most $M_{R_k^c}/(n-k)$.

Then, the set $R_{k+1} = R_k \cup \{e\}$ has total probability mass

$$
\begin{aligned}
M_{R_{k+1}} &\leq M_{R_k} + \frac{M_{R_k^c}}{n-k} \\
&= \frac{k}{n}M_S - s + \frac{M_S - \frac{k}{n}M_S + s}{n-k} \\
&= \frac{kM_S(n-k) + n(M_S - \frac{k}{n}M_S + s)}{n(n-k)} - s \\
&= \frac{knM_S - k^2M_S + nM_S - kM_S + ns}{n(n-k)} - s \\
&= \frac{(n-k)(kM_S + M_S) + ns}{n(n-k)} - s \\
&= \frac{k+1}{n}M_S + \frac{s}{n-k} - s \\
&= \frac{k+1}{n}M_S + \frac{s(1+k-n)}{n-k} \\
&\leq \frac{k+1}{n}M_S
\end{aligned}
$$

where the final inequality comes from the fact that $k < n$. Thus, if a k-sized subset $R_k \in S$ exists such that $M_{R_k} \leq \frac{k}{n}M_S$, a $k+1$-sized subset $R_{k+1} \in S$ exists such that $M_{R_{k+1}} \leq \frac{k+1}{n}M_S$.

Since the base case holds true for $k = 1$ and the inductive hypothesis implies that this rule holds for $k + 1$, we can always find a k-sized subset $R_k \in S$ such that

$$M_{R_k} \leq \frac{k}{n}M_S.$$

Lemma 2 (Maximum Probability Mass over a Target Set). *Let $\tau_k = \{t | t \in \{0,1\}^{|\Omega|}, \|t\| = \sqrt{k}\}$ be the set of all $|\Omega|$-length k-hot vectors. Given an arbitrary probability distribution* $\mathbf{P}$,

$$\sup_{t \in \tau_k} t^\top \mathbf{P} \leq 1 - \left(\frac{1-p}{p}\right) \inf_{t \in \tau_k} t^\top \mathbf{P}$$

where $p = \frac{k}{|\Omega|}$.

Proof. We proceed by contradiction. Suppose that

$$\sup_{t \in \tau_k} t^\top P > 1 - \left(\frac{1-p}{p}\right) \inf_{t \in \tau_k} t^\top P.$$

Then, there exists some target function $t \in \tau_k$ such that

$$t^\top P > 1 - \left(\frac{1-p}{p}\right) \inf_{t \in \tau_k} t^\top P.$$

Let **s** be the complementary target function to **t** such that **s** is an $|\Omega|$-length, $(|\Omega| - k)$-hot vector that takes value 1 where **t** takes value 0 and takes value 0 elsewhere. Then, by the law of total probability,

$$s^\top P < \left(\frac{1-p}{p}\right) \inf_{t \in \tau_k} t^\top P.$$

By Lemma 1, there exists a k-sized subset of the complementary target set with total probability mass q such that

$$
\begin{aligned}
q &\le \frac{k}{|\Omega| - k}(s^\top P) \\
&< \frac{k}{|\Omega| - k}\left(\left(\frac{1-p}{p}\right) \inf_{t \in \tau_k} t^\top P\right) \\
&= \frac{k}{|\Omega| - k}\left(\left(\frac{|\Omega| - k}{k}\right) \inf_{t \in \tau_k} t^\top P\right) \\
&= \inf_{t \in \tau_k} t^\top P.
\end{aligned}
$$

Thus, we can always find a target set with total probability mass strictly less than $\inf_{t \in \tau_k} t^\top P$, which is a contradiction.

Therefore, we have proven that

$$\sup_{t \in \tau_k} t^\top P \le 1 - \left(\frac{1-p}{p}\right) \inf_{t \in \tau_k} t^\top P.$$

Theorem 5 (Bias Upper Bound). *Let $\tau_k = \{t | t \in \{0,1\}^{|\Omega|}, ||t|| = \sqrt{k}\}$ be the set of all $|\Omega|$-length k-hot vectors and let $\mathcal{B}$ be a finite set of information resources. Then,*

$$\sup_{t \in \tau_k} \text{Bias}(\mathcal{B}, t) \le \left(\frac{p-1}{p}\right) \inf_{t \in \tau_k} \text{Bias}(\mathcal{B}, t)$$

where $p = \frac{k}{|\Omega|}$.

Proof. First, define

$$m := \inf_{t \in \tau_k} \mathbb{E}_{\mathcal{U}[\mathcal{B}]}[t^\top \overline{P}_F] = \inf_{t \in \tau_k} \text{Bias}(\mathcal{B}, t) + p$$

and

$$M := \sup_{\mathbf{t} \in \tau_k} \mathbb{E}_{\mathcal{U}[\mathcal{B}]}[\mathbf{t}^\top \overline{\mathbf{P}}_F] = \sup_{\mathbf{t} \in \tau_k} \text{Bias}(\mathcal{B}, \mathbf{t}) + p.$$

By Lemma 2,

$$M \le 1 - \left(\frac{1-p}{p}\right)m.$$

Substituting the values of m and M,

$$\sup_{\mathbf{t} \in \tau_k} \text{Bias}(\mathcal{B}, \mathbf{t}) \le 1 - p - \left(\frac{1-p}{p}\right)$$
$$\left(\inf_{\mathbf{t} \in \tau_k} \text{Bias}(\mathcal{B}, \mathbf{t}) + p\right)$$
$$= \left(\frac{p-1}{p}\right) \inf_{\mathbf{t} \in \tau_k} \text{Bias}(\mathcal{B}, \mathbf{t}).$$

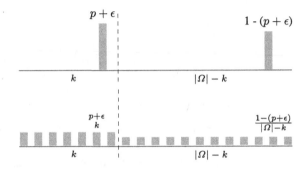

Fig. 3. Assuming positive bias, this figure shows two discrete probability distributions over Ω. The top is of an algorithm with high KL divergence while the bottom is of an algorithm with low KL divergence. Figure reproduced from Lauw et al. [6].

Theorem 6 (Difference between Estimated and Actual Bias). *Let* $\mathbf{t}$ *be a fixed target function, let* $\mathcal{D}$ *be a distribution over a set of information resources* $\mathcal{B}$, *and let* $X = \{X_1, \ldots, X_n\}$ *be a finite sample independently drawn from* $\mathcal{D}$. *Then,*

$$\mathbb{P}(|\text{Bias}(X, \mathbf{t}) - \text{Bias}(\mathcal{D}, \mathbf{t})| \ge \epsilon) \le 2e^{-2n\epsilon^2}.$$

Proof. Define

$$\overline{B}_X := \frac{1}{n}\sum_{i=1}^{n} \mathbf{t}^\top \overline{\mathbf{P}}_{X_i}$$
$$= \text{Bias}(X, \mathbf{t}) + p.$$

Given that X is an iid sample from $\mathcal{D}$, we have

$$
\begin{aligned}
\mathbb{E}[\overline{B}_X] &= \mathbb{E}\left[\frac{1}{n}\sum_{i=1}^{n}\mathbf{t}^\top \mathbf{P}_{X_i}\right] \\
&= \frac{1}{n}\sum_{i=1}^{n}\mathbb{E}\left[\mathbf{t}^\top \mathbf{P}_{X_i}\right] \\
&= \text{Bias}(\mathcal{D},\mathbf{t}) + p.
\end{aligned}
$$

By Hoeffding's inequality and the fact that

$$
0 \le \overline{B}_X \le 1
$$

we obtain

$$
\mathbb{P}(|\text{Bias}(X,\mathbf{t}) - \text{Bias}(\mathcal{D},\mathbf{t})| \ge \epsilon) = \mathbb{P}(|\overline{B}_X - \mathbb{E}[\overline{B}_X]| \ge \epsilon)
$$
$$
\le 2e^{-2n\epsilon^2}.
$$

Theorem 7 (Expressivity Bounded by Bias). *Let $\epsilon := \text{Bias}(\mathcal{D},\mathbf{t})$. Given a fixed k-hot target vector $\mathbf{t}$ and a distribution over information resources $\mathcal{D}$, the entropic expressivity, $H(\overline{\mathbf{P}}_\mathcal{D})$, of a search algorithm can be bounded in terms of bias, ϵ, by*

$$
H(\overline{\mathbf{P}}_\mathcal{D}) \in \left[H(p+\epsilon), \left((p+\epsilon)\log_2\left(\frac{k}{p+\epsilon}\right)\right.\right.
$$
$$
\left.\left. + (1-(p+\epsilon))\log_2\left(\frac{|\Omega|-k}{1-(p+\epsilon)}\right)\right)\right].
$$

Proof. Following Definition 5, the expressivity of a search algorithm varies solely with respect to $D_{\text{KL}}(\overline{\mathbf{P}}_\mathcal{D} \parallel \mathcal{U})$ since we always consider the same search space and thus $H(\mathcal{U})$ is a constant value. We obtain a lower bound of the expressivity by maximizing the value of $D_{\text{KL}}(\overline{\mathbf{P}}_\mathcal{D} \parallel \mathcal{U})$ and an upper bound by minimizing this term.

First, we show that $H(p+\epsilon)$ is a lower bound of expressivity by constructing a distribution that deviates the most from a uniform distribution over Ω. By the definition of $\text{Bias}(\mathcal{D},\mathbf{t})$, we place $(p+\epsilon)$ probability mass on the target set t and $1-(p+\epsilon)$ probability mass on the remaining $(n-k)$ elements of Ω. We distribute the probability mass such that all of the $(p+\epsilon)$ probability mass of the target set is concentrated on a single element and all of the $1-(p+\epsilon)$ probability mass of the complement of the target set is concentrated on a single element. In this constructed distribution where $D_{\text{KL}}(\overline{\mathbf{P}}_\mathcal{D} \parallel \mathcal{U})$ is maximized, the value of expressivity is

$$
\begin{aligned}
H(\overline{\mathbf{P}}_\mathcal{D}) &= -\sum_{\omega \in \Omega}\overline{P}_\mathcal{D}(\omega)\log_2 \overline{P}_\mathcal{D}(\omega) \\
&= -(p+\epsilon)\log_2(p+\epsilon) \\
&\quad - (1-(p+\epsilon))\log_2(1-(p+\epsilon)) \\
&= H(p+\epsilon)
\end{aligned}
$$

where the $H(p + \epsilon)$ is the entropy of a Bernoulli distribution with parameter $(p + \epsilon)$. The entropy of this constructed distribution gives a lower bound on expressivity,

$$H(\overline{\mathbf{P}}_D) \geq H(p + \epsilon).$$

Now, we show that

$$(p + \epsilon) \log_2 \left(\frac{k}{p + \epsilon} \right) + (1 - (p + \epsilon)) \log_2 \left(\frac{|\Omega| - k}{1 - (p + \epsilon)} \right)$$

is an upper bound of expressivity by constructing a distribution that deviates the least from a uniform distribution over Ω. In this case, we uniformly distribute $\frac{1}{|\Omega|}$ probability mass over the entire search space, Ω. Then, to account for the ϵ level of bias, we add $\frac{\epsilon}{k}$ probability mass to elements of the target set and we remove $\frac{\epsilon}{n-k}$ probability mass to elements of the complement of the target set. In this constructed distribution where $D_{\mathrm{KL}}(\overline{\mathbf{P}}_D \parallel \mathcal{U})$ is minimized, the value of expressivity is

$$
\begin{aligned}
H(\overline{\mathbf{P}}_D) &= - \sum_{\omega \in \Omega} \overline{P}_D(\omega) \log_2 \overline{P}_D(\omega) \\
&= - \sum_{\omega \in t} \left(\frac{1}{|\Omega|} + \frac{\epsilon}{k} \right) \log_2 \left(\frac{1}{|\Omega|} + \frac{\epsilon}{k} \right) \\
&\quad - \sum_{\omega \in t^c} \left(\frac{1}{|\Omega|} - \frac{\epsilon}{|\Omega| - k} \right) \log_2 \left(\frac{1}{|\Omega|} - \frac{\epsilon}{|\Omega| - k} \right) \\
&= - \sum_{\omega \in t} \left(\frac{p + \epsilon}{k} \right) \log_2 \left(\frac{p + \epsilon}{k} \right) \\
&\quad - \sum_{\omega \in t^c} \left(\frac{1 - (p + \epsilon)}{|\Omega| - k} \right) \log_2 \left(\frac{1 - (p + \epsilon)}{|\Omega| - k} \right) \\
&= - k \left(\frac{p + \epsilon}{k} \right) \log_2 \left(\frac{p + \epsilon}{k} \right) \\
&\quad - (|\Omega| - k) \left(\frac{1 - (p + \epsilon)}{|\Omega| - k} \right) \log_2 \left(\frac{1 - (p + \epsilon)}{|\Omega| - k} \right) \\
&= (p + \epsilon) \log_2 \left(\frac{k}{p + \epsilon} \right) \\
&\quad + (1 - (p + \epsilon)) \log_2 \left(\frac{|\Omega| - k}{1 - (p + \epsilon)} \right).
\end{aligned}
$$

The entropy on this constructed distribution gives an upper bound on expressivity,

$$
\begin{aligned}
H(\overline{\mathbf{P}}_D) &\leq (p + \epsilon) \log_2 \left(\frac{k}{p + \epsilon} \right) \\
&\quad + (1 - (p + \epsilon)) \log_2 \left(\frac{|\Omega| - k}{1 - (p + \epsilon)} \right).
\end{aligned}
$$

These two bounds give us a range of possible values of expressivity given a fixed level of bias, namely

$$H(\overline{\mathbf{P}}_\mathcal{D}) \in \left[H(p+\epsilon), \left((p+\epsilon) \log_2 \left(\frac{k}{p+\epsilon} \right) \right. \right.$$
$$\left. \left. + (1 - (p+\epsilon)) \log_2 \left(\frac{|\Omega| - k}{1 - (p+\epsilon)} \right) \right) \right].$$

Theorem 8 (Bias-expressivity Trade-off). *Given a distribution over information resources $\mathcal{D}$ and a fixed target $t \subseteq \Omega$, entropic expressivity is bounded above in terms of bias,*

$$H(\overline{\mathbf{P}}_\mathcal{D}) \leq \log_2 |\Omega| - 2\mathrm{Bias}(\mathcal{D}, \mathbf{t})^2.$$

Additionally, bias is bounded above in terms of entropic expressivity,

$$\mathrm{Bias}(\mathcal{D}, \mathbf{t}) \leq \sqrt{\frac{1}{2}(\log_2 |\Omega| - H(\overline{\mathbf{P}}_\mathcal{D}))}$$
$$= \sqrt{\frac{1}{2} D_{KL}(\overline{\mathbf{P}}_\mathcal{D} \,\|\, \mathcal{U})}.$$

Proof. Let $\omega \in t$ denote the measurable event that ω is an element of target set $t \subseteq \Omega$, and let Σ be the sigma algebra of measurable events. First, note that

$$\mathrm{Bias}(\mathcal{D}, t)^2 = |\mathrm{Bias}(\mathcal{D}, t)|^2$$
$$= |\mathbf{t}^\top \mathbb{E}_\mathcal{D}[\overline{\mathbf{P}}_F] - p|^2$$
$$= |\mathbf{t}^\top \overline{\mathbf{P}}_\mathcal{D} - p|^2$$
$$= |\overline{P}_\mathcal{D}(\omega \in t) - p|^2$$
$$\leq \frac{1}{2} D_{KL}(\overline{\mathbf{P}}_\mathcal{D} \,\|\, \mathcal{U})$$
$$= \frac{1}{2}(H(\mathcal{U}) - H(\overline{\mathbf{P}}_\mathcal{D}))$$
$$= \frac{1}{2}(\log_2 |\Omega| - H(\mathbb{E}_\mathcal{D}[\overline{\mathbf{P}}_F]))$$

where the inequality is an application of Pinsker's Inequality. The quantity D_{KL} $(\overline{\mathbf{P}}_\mathcal{D} \,\|\, \mathcal{U})$ is the Kullback-Leibler divergence between distributions $\overline{\mathbf{P}}_\mathcal{D}$ and $\mathcal{U}$, which are distributions on search space Ω.

Thus,

$$H(\mathbb{E}_\mathcal{D}[\overline{\mathbf{P}}_F]) \leq \log_2 |\Omega| - 2\mathrm{Bias}(\mathcal{D}, \mathbf{t})^2$$

and

$$\mathrm{Bias}(\mathcal{D}, t) \leq \sqrt{\frac{1}{2}(\log_2 |\Omega| - H(\overline{\mathbf{P}}_\mathcal{D}))}$$
$$= \sqrt{\frac{1}{2} D_{KL}(\overline{\mathbf{P}}_\mathcal{D} \,\|\, \mathcal{U})}$$
$$= \sqrt{\frac{1}{2}(\log_2 |\Omega| - H(\mathbb{E}_\mathcal{D}[\overline{\mathbf{P}}_F]))}.$$

Corollary 2 (Bias Bound under Expected Expressivity)

$$\text{Bias}(\mathcal{D}, \mathbf{t}) \leq \sqrt{\frac{1}{2}(\log_2 |\Omega| - \mathbb{E}_{\mathcal{D}}[H(\overline{\mathbf{P}}_F)])}$$

$$= \sqrt{\mathbb{E}_{\mathcal{D}}\left[\frac{1}{2}D_{KL}(\overline{\mathbf{P}}_F \| \mathcal{U})\right]}.$$

Proof. By the concavity of the entropy function and Jensen's Inequality, we obtain

$$\mathbb{E}_{\mathcal{D}}[H(\overline{\mathbf{P}}_F)] \leq H(\mathbb{E}_{\mathcal{D}}[\overline{\mathbf{P}}_F]) \leq \log_2 |\Omega| - 2\text{Bias}(\mathcal{D}, \mathbf{t})^2.$$

Thus, an upper bound of bias is

$$\text{Bias}(\mathcal{D}, \mathbf{t}) \leq \sqrt{\frac{1}{2}D_{\text{KL}}(\overline{\mathbf{P}}_{\mathcal{D}} \| \mathcal{U})}$$

$$= \sqrt{\frac{1}{2}(\log_2 |\Omega| - H(\mathbb{E}_{\mathcal{D}}[\overline{\mathbf{P}}_F]))}$$

$$\leq \sqrt{\frac{1}{2}(\log_2 |\Omega| - \mathbb{E}_{\mathcal{D}}[H([\overline{\mathbf{P}}_F])])}$$

$$= \sqrt{\mathbb{E}_{\mathcal{D}}\left[\frac{1}{2}D_{\text{KL}}(\overline{\mathbf{P}}_F \| \mathcal{U})\right]},$$

where the final equality follows from the linearity of expectation and the definition of KL-divergence.

References

1. Bartlett, P.L., Mendelson, S.: Rademacher and Gaussian complexities: risk bounds and structural results. J. Mach. Learn. Res. **3**, 463–482 (2003). http://dl.acm.org/citation.cfm?id=944919.944944
2. Geman, S., Bienenstock, E., Doursat, R.: Neural networks and the bias/variance dilemma. Neural Comput. **4**(1), 1–58 (1992)
3. Goldberg, D.: Genetic Algorithms in Search Optimization and Machine Learning. Addison-Wesley Longman Publishing Company, Reading (1999)
4. Kearns, M.J., Schapire, R.E.: Efficient distribution-free learning of probabilistic concepts. In: Proceedings [1990] 31st Annual Symposium on Foundations of Computer Science, vol. 1, pp. 382–391 (1990). https://doi.org/10.1109/FSCS.1990.89557
5. Kohavi, R., Wolpert, D.H., et al.: Bias plus variance decomposition for zero-one loss functions. In: ICML 1996, pp. 275–283 (1996)
6. Lauw, J., Macias, D., Trikha, A., Vendemiatti, J., Montañez, G.D.: The bias-expressivity trade-off. In: Rocha, A.P., Steels, L., van den Herik, H.J. (eds.) Proceedings of the 12th International Conference on Agents and Artificial Intelligence, ICAART 2020, Valletta, Malta, 22–24 February 2020, vol. 2, pp. 141–150. SCITEPRESS (2020). https://doi.org/10.5220/0008959201410150
7. Mitchell, T.D.: The need for biases in learning generalizations. In: CBM-TR-117, Rutgers University (1980)

8. Montañez, G.D.: The famine of forte: few search problems greatly favor your algorithm. In: 2017 IEEE International Conference on Systems, Man, and Cybernetics (SMC), pp. 477–482. IEEE (2017)

9. Montañez, G.D.: Why machine learning works. Dissertation, Carnegie Mellon University (2017)

10. Montañez, G.D., Hayase, J., Lauw, J., Macias, D., Trikha, A., Vendemiatti, J.: The futility of bias-free learning and search. In: Liu, J., Bailey, J. (eds.) AI 2019. LNCS (LNAI), vol. 11919, pp. 277–288. Springer, Cham (2019). https://doi.org/10.1007/978-3-030-35288-2_23

11. Raghu, M., Poole, B., Kleinberg, J., Ganguli, S., Sohl-Dickstein, J.: On the expressive power of deep neural networks. In: Precup, D., Teh, Y.W. (eds.) Proceedings of the 34th International Conference on Machine Learning. Proceedings of Machine Learning Research, vol. 70, pp. 2847–2854. PMLR, International Convention Centre, Sydney (2017). http://proceedings.mlr.press/v70/raghu17a.html

12. Reeves, C., Rowe, J.E.: Genetic Algorithms: Principles and Perspectives. A Guide to GA Theory, vol. 20. Springer, London (2002)

13. Sam, T., Williams, J., Abel, T., Huey, S., Montañez, G.D.: Decomposable probability-of-success metrics in algorithmic search. In: Rocha, A.P., Steels, L., van den Herik, H.J. (eds.) Proceedings of the 12th International Conference on Agents and Artificial Intelligence, ICAART 2020, Valletta, Malta, 22–24 February 2020, vol. 2, pp. 785–792. SCITEPRESS (2020). https://doi.org/10.5220/0009098807850792

14. Schumacher, C., Vose, M.D., Whitley, L.D.: The no free lunch and problem description length. In: Proceedings of the Genetic and Evolutionary Computation Conference (GECCO-2001), pp. 565–570 (2001)

15. Vapnik, V.N., Chervonenkis, A.Y.: On the uniform convergence of relative frequencies of events to their probabilities. Theory Probab. Appl. **16**(2), 264–280 (1971)

16. Vapnik, V.N.: An overview of statistical learning theory. IEEE Trans. Neural Netw. **10**(5), 988–999 (1999)

17. Wolpert, D.H., Macready, W.G.: No free lunch theorems for optimization. IEEE Trans. Evol. Comput. **1**(1), 67–82 (1997)

A Multi-modal Audience Engagement Measurement System

Miguel Sanz-Narrillos$^{(\boxtimes)}$ (iD), Stefano Masneri$^{(\boxtimes)}$ (iD), and Mikel Zorrilla$^{(\boxtimes)}$ (iD)

Vicomtech Foundation, Basque Research and Technology Alliance,
San Sebastian, Spain
{msanz,smasneri,mzorrilla}@vicomtech.org

Abstract. During live events the organizers often would want to deploy audience engagement systems to analyze people behaviour, perform user profiling or modify the show according to the participant feedback. Such systems usually need computer vision algorithms whose performance are severely affected by constraints such as illumination and cameras position. In this paper we present a fully automatic audience engagement system, optimized for live music events with rapidly changing illumination conditions. The system uses a multi-modal approach which combines wireless-based person detection together with computer vision algorithms for pose and face analysis. We show that such hybrid approach, while running in real-time, performs better than standard approaches that only employ computer vision techniques. The system has been tested both in a laboratory environment as well as in a concert hall and it will be deployed in distributed live events.

Keywords: Multi-modal analysis · Wireless detection · Computer vision · Audience engagement

1 Introduction

The rapid evolution of broadband and streaming technologies in the last few years has had a profound impact on the entertainment industry, which has seen a strong increase in revenues coming from internet deployed services. Such implementations have given the opportunity to reach even more customers [11], and increase exponentially the data collected from the customers, using these services to boost the user engagement. The data collected is used not only to increase the revenue through direct advertising [16], but also to understand users' behaviour, feedback and preferences to improve the general experience.

The development of new technologies is obviously a key component for industry growth, but especially in the entertainment sector this is a crucial factor as it has allowed to reach wider audiences and to make shows more appealing, interactive and enjoyable. It wasn't until very recently, for example, that live events could also be experience by an online audience in an active way.

In online events such as e-sports the organizers collect a huge amount of data from the audience, such as the number of people connected at every second, location data, or the average amount of time watching the streams.

© Springer Nature Switzerland AG 2021
A. P. Rocha et al. (Eds.): ICAART 2020, LNAI 12613, pp. 354–377, 2021.
https://doi.org/10.1007/978-3-030-71158-0_17

This kind of data is currently not collected in traditional live events [32]. People in charge of organizing live events (concerts, festivals, sport events) are becoming more and more interested in obtaining users' data, due to its intrinsic value and the insights that can be extracted from it, but in this case in the real world, as the data obtained can be even more important.

In this paper, we describe a passive, non-invasive system for measuring audience engagement in live events. The data collected by the system allows us to identify when and where the users are the most involved in the show, as well as what are they most interested in. As the metrics normally used to measure engagement (as movement detection, person recognition, gaze detection and emotion detection) require to accurately detect and track the different body parts of the people attending the event, the system developed include methods for performing these tasks in the challenging illumination conditions typical of live events, where off-the-shelf implementations fail.

Standard techniques for person and body keypoint detection usually feed the camera stream to a convolutional neural network (CNN) [37]. CNNs are very powerful but they also require a lot of training data to provide meaningful results. Collecting and labeling data is usually expensive and time-consuming but it is often necessary, as the detection accuracy of CNNs typically plummets when they are used to analyse data coming from different distributions.

A relevant example where standard CNN based techniques do not return good results is in live events. CNN architectures trained on existing datasets are able to accurately detect faces position or the pose and movements of the people, but in settings with constantly changing illumination conditions, such as concerts, such systems perform very poorly. A system relying only on video data would require extensive fine-tuning, performing training on additional data with abrupt changes in illumination. A further issue with such approaches is that most of the times different regions of the image to analyze contain both bright and dark spots, making it very hard for the CNN to properly generalize and detect all the people in the scene.

A more sensible way to deal with those issues is to preprocess the images captured by the cameras in order to eliminate or at least reduce the factors affecting the performances of the CNN. The preprocessing step varies depending on the input and thus it requires information from other sources, for example localization data estimated from the wireless signals emitted by the users' smartphones.

The main contribution of this paper is the description of a hybrid system which uses both computer vision and wireless signal analysis techniques for detection and tracking of people in live events and, from that, derives audience engagement measures. The use of a hybrid approach, apart from providing more user information, allows higher detection and tracking accuracy than using the two methods separately. Furthermore, the system is robust to sudden illumination changes and noisy environments without requiring additional training, making it useful for a wide range of applications.

This works improves the system described in [42] and describes in detail the development and deployment process of a complete solution for obtaining the engagement in live shows.

The code of the system and the data used during the experiments are available on Github[1]. The rest of the paper is organized as follows, Sect. 2 will cover the related work with the two techniques used for the hybridization, engagement and multi-modal systems, in Sect. 3 a comparison of the capabilities and possible obtainable metrics between different systems that perform engagement detection is done, in Sect. 4 a explanation of each method and the hybridization characteristics is explained, including the improvements and extra functionalities added, and in Sect. 5 a comparison between the results of the hybrid method, the computer vision method and the computer vision with the improvements implemented.

2   Related Work

2.1   Vision-Based Human Analysis

The detection of people in still images and video has long been one of the most studied problems in computer vision. Prior to the advent of deep learning based techniques, the standard approach was to create a human model using image keypoints and descriptors, for example Haar cascades methods [26], Support Vector Machines [5,29] or Histogram of oriented gradients [9]. In recent years, thanks to the availability of datasets such as ImageNet [12] or Microsoft COCO (Common Objects in COntext) [27] and the increase of computational CPU and GPU power, convolutional neural networks became the standard tool used for objects detection and tracking. The architectures most commonly used for this task are R-CNN and its evolutions [13,14,40], You Only Look Once (YOLO) [38,39] or Single Shot multibox Detector (SSD) [28]. More advanced architectures can provide a pixel-level segmentation of the person detected [19], while others detect the position of the joints in order to estimate the person pose [6,8,46,47]. Such algorithms rely on datasets specifically created for the task such as MPII Human Pose [2] and Leeds Sports Pose [21].

2.2   Wireless-Based Human Analysis

The standard approach for detecting and tracking people using wireless signals is to rely on the Wi-Fi and Bluetooth signals provided by a smartphone or other wireless capable devices carried by the user. One of the possible approaches relies on Received Signal Strength Indicator (RSSI) fingerprinting [49], where the communication signal strength is used to determine the distance of the device from the receptor. In order to obtain a reliable position trilateration must be used, combining the data from several receptors [33]. Other approaches rely on wireless time of flight [25], which uses the time between the emission and reception to determine the distance between the devices and from that infer the persons position. Another technique is the wireless angle of arrival [17,35], where an antenna array measures the angle of arrival of the signal instead of the ToF. In this case the angle from the device to the receptor is calculated by having an antenna array as receptor and with the difference on the reception time between each of the antennas the angle of the signal can be calculated, and with trilateration the position

---

[1] Indoor person localization hybrid system in live events https://bit.ly/3cYmvz2.

can be approximated. A technique that does not need the person to carry a device is the ones used in WI-SEE and WI-VI [24], where the shape of objects in the room is computed by analyzing the reflection of the Wi-Fi waves, and uses those to detect the position of the persons.

2.3 Audience Engagement Systems

As mentioned in Sect. 1 most of the engagement systems are designed for online events because in those cases the infrastructure necessary is already available. Systems for online learning [23, 31], social media [43] or news [4] already implement tools for measuring user engagement. In the case of live events the infrastructure and the system have to be built separately, although some interactions can be created with electronic devices such as lights or screens. Most current engagement systems depends on the usage of an external device to provide the information about the engagement. One example of engagement system is the glisser app [15], in which the event manager can implement questionnaires, slide sharing or a Twitter wall. In this case only the information that the person writes in the app is considered as engagement. Another approach to have a more truthful information has been the usage of electroencephalograms to measure the signals produced in the brain as in the engageMeter [18]. Such systems are not very suitable to be used in events such as concerts where multiple people are moving and user engagement has to be measured in an indirect way.

2.4 Multi-modal Systems

The usage of different techniques and methods together has been used for many years in the development of new systems to improve the final results. In the detection field this type of systems has been used in recent years for autonomous vehicles [3], combining a CNN and Lidar, person detection systems [45], which uses laser and camera data, and some datasets has been created for this type of systems such as a fall detection [30], which combines information from video and wearable sensors.

3   Engagement Measurement Systems

As the system is meant to be installed in the entertainment industry in order to measure the engagement of the people to a determined show, we are going to compare theoretically all the methods that could have useful metrics related to the engagement as number of people in the room, movements of the people or emotions. The analysis is portrayed in order to chose the methods to take part in the hybridization and it will be taken into account the accuracy, performance, hardware used and possibility to be used at distance and with crowds.

CNN. There are several networks that perform this type of detection but the technique that gives better results is the ones using pose detection, in which it detects several joints as in some cases some face points in order to locate a person, this techniques is a good candidate to be one of the bases of the hybrid system that is explained and from which results are analysed in this paper. This technique has good result when the conditions of the environment are previously known and are included in the training data, in other case the result is not as good as expected. The computing power out of the box of this type of techniques is quite high, having several GPUs to be able to perform the detection on 720p footage at real time. If we take into account the improvements included in the technique described in this paper the main problem is the conditions, that if one is not present in the preprocessing data it will not be good, so the preprocessing would need to be dependable on the conditions, reason that our system has the hybrid method. The main metrics obtained directly when this system is working in good conditions are the position of the different joints, which from that several variables such as movement or person localization can be obtained.

WiFi/Bluetooth Localization. In this case the localization of the person has huge dependency on carrying a device, as this is the thing located, and the performance is only average, having only an approximate position. Another drawback of this system is the number of devices that are detected, reason to use the filter, but the main drawback is the time between probes, that depending on the device to be tracked can change from twenty seconds to several minutes, as well as the necessity of having one of those signals activated in the devices. This method allow us to obtain the approximate localization of a device, that is normally attached to a person, so with this the number of people in a determined zone can be approximated, although the accuracy will decrease as the area of the zone decrease. The main metric obtained is the number of people inside a zone, so it could be used in cope with the CNN in order to refine the results and lower the number of false detections and people no detected.

RFID. This technique is more a barrier detector than a locator, which means that it detects when a person or an object goes through some point but it can not detect the number of people at some distance. It also requires special hardware to be in both the detected and detector devices. This technique is more suitable to maintain an stock list rather than a person locator. The main metric obtained from this method is the number of people that has crossed an invisible barrier, data that is less accurate than any of the previous methods and this even needs more specialised hardware, being in both the tracker and the detected person, than in the case of the CNN is not necessary and in the wireless is so common that is virtually not necessary.

Accelerometers. This technique can be used to measure the movement and it can perform well detecting movement and direction of movement, but the main problem with this technique is the calibration as to have reliable lectures of position we need to have an initial point. It requires to have specialized hardware in the person to be detected. The main metrics obtained from this method are in reverse as in the CNN, while in this we obtain the movement directly and the position can be computed from that data, in the CNN we obtain the position and with the historic data the movement can be computed, the main difference from those technique is the necessity of specialised hardware in the detected person to perform the detection, than also needs to be calibrated to obtain a reliable detection.

Emotion Detection by Camera. This technique make use of the detection of facial landmarks, as eye borders or lips borders, as the detection of other facial points, such as eyes or ears, this will mean that at least 100 points in the face are obtained, all this points are introduced in a neural network that has been trained with faces related to several emotions from several people, in order to reduce the bias of only having few people data, the results of this neural network are two variables, the valence and arousal, depending on the values of this two variables an emotion between the six primal ones (Happiness, sadness, fear, disgust, anger and surprise) can be obtained, the relation of the arousal and valence with the primal emotions is done by using different models as Bayesian networks, Gaussian models or Markov models and with that the emotion can be obtained. Nowadays this method can not be used with a high number of people as it needs both huge computing power and a good view of the faces to perform well. Another problem is the reliability of the data as the primal emotions are very different in each person, as well as needing to have very exaggerated expressions to be able to read the emotion. Although the metrics of this method is very unique and very related to the engagement, but the problems to the implementation surpass the increase in accuracy, the improvements of this technology has to be taken into account but nowadays the implementation in this system is not worth it.

Emotion Detection by Body Signals. This method is very related to the previous one as it is also based on obtaining the emotion of the people out of one of the primal ones from the valence and arousal, which is done the same way, the difference between this methods is the way that the variables are obtained, while in the previous one was done reading the facial points with a camera, in this case some of the body signals are measured, which normally several are taken into account to have a higher accuracy. Some of the signals that could be taken into account are the temperature, hearth rate or breath rate, in this case the reliability is greater, and technically could analyse several people at the same time, but the main drawback is the hardware that is needed, that in most of the cases needs to be in direct contact with the body. As before the metrics of this method is very unique and very related to the engagement, but the problems to the implementation surpass the increase in accuracy.

Our Hybrid Approach. As the analysis has shown the methods to be implemented in the hybrid approach are the CNN, as this is the most used technique to locate people and the metrics obtained are numerous, and the wireless detection, as the reliability is high with the localization metric. In order to obtain other metrics some additions could be done, as obtaining the gaze direction of a person, but the main additions to be done to each of the techniques is to try to reduce the drawbacks explained in this section with the hybridization, as the lightning condition of the CNN or the number of devices in the wireless method, which will be explained in the Sect. 4.1 and 4.2, while the way both methods communicate to make a real hybrid method is placed in the Sect. 4.3.

4   Methods

4.1   CNN-Based Detection and Tracking

CNN architectures are the de facto standard for tasks like people detection and tracking. Usually, one or more cameras are used as input source for the CNN, while the output consists of a vector of bounding boxes describing the people position or, depending on the architecture, the position of specific joints. The reference technique used in this work is the one described in [34], a technique for person detection that detects the person position as well as that of different body parts such as face, shoulders or hips. This technique provides average accuracy in densely packed scenes (with more than 30 people in the same scene). The base implementation used in this project is based on [48] and in order to improve its detection accuracy we implemented new functionalities related to preprocessing of the input, tracking additional keypoints and improving the performance.

The addition of a preprocessing step is the contribution that improved the detection accuracy the most. Using this module, we were able to accurately detect people and their body parts without fine-tuning the architecture using a dedicated training set. The preprocessing is done in three steps. First, the input frame is sliced into several rectangular area. Each area is then processed separately (and in parallel) to the others. Then, the contrast of each area is improved by applying the CLAHE (Contrast Limited Adaptive Histogram Equalization) algorithm, to make the borders of the objects more noticeable. Finally, gamma correction and normalization is applied to each image slice. This helps in cases where some slices are illuminated while others are not, as it is often the case during concerts or other live events. The results of preprocessing can be appreciated in Fig. 1, where while in the first part the illumination is on the low-right part of the frame the preprocessing intensifies the borders and regulate the light in the overall picture.

(a) Original Frame   (b) After CLAHE and Gamma correction

Fig. 1. Preprocessing of input frames.

Apart from the position of the person and its keypoint, our system detects gaze and movement. The gaze detection tool infers approximately the gaze direction (front, right or left) from the position of the eyes and nose detected by the CNN. It is calculated analysing the angle formed by the segments connecting the two eyes and the nose with the midpoint between the eyes. Movement data, on the other hand, is computed by performing tracking of the different keypoints so that we could evaluate average and maximum speed of a person over time.

Changes in performance has been implemented to reduce the processing of all the parts that are nor necessary as reducing the number of joints to detect, in cases that is impossible to see them as the knees in crowded concerts. This project also allows to eliminate zones from the image that are impossible to contain people as ceilings.

The part that improves the performance more is the implementation of tracking which puts a tracker in the detected people, this allow the system to only perform the detection in one out of several frames instead of on everyone.

The dataset used for training this CNN is COCO, which contains more than 200K labeled images although not all of them are fully annotated. The images are usually taken with good to excellent illumination conditions and no preprocessing (except for the standard data augmentation procedures) was applied during training.

The implementation in [48] shows a steep decline in the accuracy of detections when the illumination conditions of the scene are not represented in the training set. An example of such performance decay can be seen in Fig. 2, where the detection is perfect in the upper figure, while in the bottom image a very small percentage of the people gets detected. This is caused by not having the network trained with all the possible illumination conditions, making it almost unusable without the aforementioned preprocessing step.

(a) Good illumination and positioning

(b) Illumination changing and strange positioning

Fig. 2. Pose and person detection under different illumination conditions [42].

Comparing the two images in Fig. 2 we can easily appreciate that the main difference between them is the illumination conditions as the image on top has higher brightness and contrast than the one on the bottom. In audience monitoring applications (such as during live events) it is highly likely that the illumination conditions change over time, and often different parts of the scene have different brightness and contrast. In this case any person detection algorithm is doomed to fail unless the input frames are preprocessed so that they provide the same illumination conditions across the whole image as well as over time. Section 4.3 describes in detail how our implementation chooses the parameters used to preprocess the input frames before feeding them to the neural network.

4.2 Wireless Data

Nowadays almost every person carries at least one device capable of receiving wireless signals such as Wi-Fi or Bluetooth. These types of signals have already been used to perform device localization tasks [1, 10, 24] because they offer several advantages compared to computer vision based applications, as they require much less computation capability and they are not affected by problems like occlusions.

A device can be localized even though it is not connected to a network, the only requirement is that it is in the range of the router. This occurs because the devices periodically scan the environment to check for available networks, while at the same time the access points (APs) send broadcast messages to make their network discoverable. When a device detects that it is in the range of an available network, it exchanges with the AP the MAC addresses and the connection properties. By analysing such properties and the intensities of the signal received by the AP, we can estimate the distance between them.

Knowing the distance between the device and the detector is not enough to locate the device in a room, but with trilateration (using three or more detectors) the position of the object can be calculated. The process for the localization can be seen in Fig. 3a, where the persons position is approximated by four trackers (in our case the APs). Our implementation is based on Find3 [44], with some modifications allowing us to perform device filtering and to deal with devices performing MAC randomization.

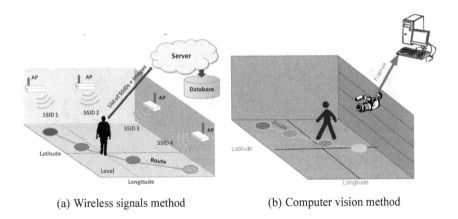

(a) Wireless signals method   (b) Computer vision method

Fig. 3. Device positioning and communication diagram [42].

We modified the original implementation of Find3, adding two new functionalities to make its adoption more suitable for usage in live events settings. The first add-on is device filtering and it was developed to improve the performances of the system, while the second is zone differentiation, which allows us to know in which part of the room each person is located.

As we mentioned before, the number of wireless capable devices has dramatically increased in the last few years, so when an AP looks for available devices, it could detect not only mobile phones or smartwatches, but also other device types such as printers, TVs, smart balances etc. This is a problem as we are only interested in a device if it's being carried by a person, otherwise the estimation of the number of people would be skewed. For this reason we filter the list of available devices twice. First, by removing all the device that are not detected by all the APs, as we assume that such devices lie outside our region of interest (as we show in Fig. 4).

Then, we filter a second time according to the device manufacturer. This information is encoded in the MAC address of the device, since the Organization Unique Identifier (OUI) is a 24-bit identifier encoded in the first three octets of a MAC address. By using the company ID list provided on the IEEE website [20], we filter the results by excluding all the devices not associated with companies producing smartphones or smartwatches.

This filtering based on MAC address could pose an issue though, as in recent version of the Android and iOS operating systems the devices implement MAC randomization. For security reasons, before a connection to the network is established, the devices share with the AP a random MAC address, and communicate the real one only once the habdshake is completed and the connection to the network is established. In Apple devices running iOS 8 or above the MAC address is completely random and changes periodically, thus making MAC filtering uneffective. For devices running Android 10 (currently the most recent OS version), device filtering still works since the randomized MAC addresses are chosen from a known range bought by Google and available in the IEEE list.

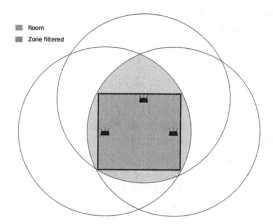

Fig. 4. Filter zone of interest.

We implemented the two filters both in the server and on the detectors. We first developed a Python version of the filters and then, to improve the performances, we also ported the code to Go. Table 1, summarizes the results obtained where, unsurprisingly, the fastest implementation of the filters is the one written in Go and running on the server. The results of the table are the average between 20 detections with an average of 35 MACs in the input and 10 when the filtering is done.

Table 1. Time (s) spent in the MAC comparison.

Server with python	Server with Go	Scanner with python	Scanner with Go
0.16454	0.03668	28.36	2.5

Another addition introduced over the original implementation is the possibility to classify the position of the devices into different areas (customizable by the end user). The classification can be performed in three different ways:

- Manual: this method is based on having the RSSI measured in the room by one device before the detection then with that having a map of the RSSI in the room, and compare the measurements of each device with that map to position each of the devices. This method has low computational requirements, but changes in the environment, such as moving obstacles or reflections, can severely affect its accuracy.
- Weighted: this method tries to improve the precision by using a group of measurements instead of only the most recent. We tried several weighting strategies and we found out that logarithmic weight averaging offered the best accuracy. This method improves the results but also the computing power needed.
- Automatic: the main focus of this method is to make the zone differentiation non dependable on the conditions of the room. This is achieved by using reference devices in selected locations of the room to obtain the measurements of known positions and compare them with the ones of unknown devices. Reference devices can be distinguished by their MAC address as long as they remain connected to the network. This method outperforms both the manual and weighted approach in terms of accuracy and it can even be combined with the weighted method for a further boost in accuracy.

4.3   Hybridization

Once the results from vision and wireless based detection systems are available, the hybridization step is responsible for processing and combining them in order to obtain a higher accuracy. The main idea is that the data provided by the wireless person detection system can represent a rough estimation of the number of people in the scene and, comparing it with the previous result from the vision system, it can steer the preprocessing of the frames to improve the subsequent vision-based detection and tracking results of the system.

Consider for example the image in Fig. 2. In this case the wireless detection system could estimate that there are more than 30 people in the range of the router, while the vision-based system only detects 3 people (due to poor illumination condition, varying image contrast in different region of the image, etc.). The work-flow of the hybridization is summed up in Fig. 5.

Apart from the detection and the tracking data from both systems, the hybridization system takes as input a function which maps the 3D regions in which the wireless detection splits the room and the 2D regions in the camera frames where the preprocessing will be applied.

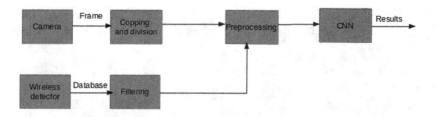

Fig. 5. Workflow for the hybrid system.

Preprocessing. The aim of the preprocessing is twofold, as it should both speed-up the detection times and modify the input images with the aim of maximizing the detection accuracy.

The preprocessing performed is composed by several steps. First, the image is cropped to remove the parts of the frame where no person could appear (see Fig. 6 for an example). The cropping process is performed manually, as it depends on the camera positioning, and it is a one-time operation which is then applied to every frame of the video. This improves the performance since there is a lower quantity of pixels to evaluate and the neural network is able to process more frames in a single pass. Then, the input frame is divided into different slices. Figure 7 shows an example where the input frame, after cropping, is split into six parts. Each slice will be then preprocessed separately by applying different brightness and contrast changes. In this way the system is able to cope with the fact that different parts of the frame may have different color

Fig. 6. Elimination of non-person parts of the frame [42].

Fig. 7. Preprocessing slicing of the frame [42].

and brightness statistics. There is a 5% overlap between each slice (represented by the orange lines in Fig. 7) to counter the fact that people moving in the scene from one slice to the adjacent one may be lost when crossing from one slice to the other. The way the frame is split into different slices depends on the camera position as well as on the geometry of the regions identified by the wireless detection system.

The processing of each slice is done by applying contrast stretching using the CLAHE transformation [36], followed later by Gamma correction [41] to reduce or increase the number of bits of luminance and so dynamically increase or decrease the processing power needed. The parameters used for performing CLAHE and gamma correction are dynamically chosen by comparing the detection results of the wireless and vision-based system.

Tracking Strategies. In order to speed-up the processing times of the vision system, the detection step is performed once every 10 frames, while in the remaining frames people are only tracked using MedianFlow [22].

To avoid tracking false detections indefinitely, the tracking is periodically reset, while correct assignments keep being tracked by performing a simple nearest-neighbor assignment from previous frames. Figure 8 shows a visualization of the tracking of a person's face: the green rectangle shows the current position of the face, while a curve shows the path followed by the face center. The most recent positions (the latest 20 frames) are drawn in blue, while older positions are shown in green and, for positions older than 50 frames, in red.

The wireless detection system does not implement a tracking mechanism, but data from previous measurement is used to increase the robustness of the detection mechanisms. Previous measurements are exponentially weighted, with a higher weight associated to more recent measures.

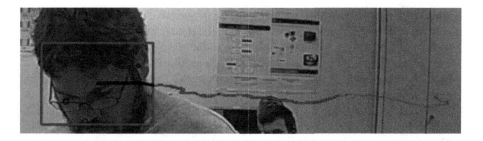

Fig. 8. Tracking path drawing in the frame [42]. (Color figure online)

Zone Relation. The wireless method divides the room in several zones, while the computer vision method divides the frame in several slices. In the tests we performed, we used three zones for the wireless system and six for the computer vision one. Before the processing starts, a function maps the zones from the camera to a zone in the 3D space. The mapping is not perfect but, as the precision of the wireless technique is in the range of centimeters, the relation does not need to be exact.

The number of zones in the wireless method depend on the accuracy needed and the conditions of the room, such as size and shape. It is possible to have a different number of zones and trackers: in our tests we used 2 trackers for classifying into 3 zones.

Depending on how the image is split, it may happen that if the person is very close to the camera, or the person does not wear his device, the computer vision system detects one person in one zone while the wireless method detects it in another. Some of that issues can be avoided with a good camera positioning, which is at a medium distance from the people and at a height of 2.5 m approximately. If the camera cannot be moved, the detection difference between the methods can be changed. This difference compares the total detections between the methods and in the case that is greater than a threshold the preprocessing conditions (gamma and contrast), are changed.

4.4   Engagement

The information collected from the combination of computer vision and wireless signals techniques can be used to measure the engagement of the people attending the live event. We are aware that the information available is only a proxy of the user engagement and that our measurements are not perfect. For this reason we are more interested in average user behaviour patterns and we decided to analyze the results also from a qualitative point of view. Below is a list of the parameters used to estimate the user engagement:

– Number of people in the room: This is the simplest metric we collect. It is computed by averaging the estimation from the vision and wireless based system, and gives a rough indication of how successful a specific event has been. It is useful when compared with data from previous events or for events happening in other rooms or venues.

- Number of people in each zone: As explained in Sect. 4.3, we can also estimate the number of people in specific areas. Analyzing the change of population per area over time (for example, the ratio of people close to the stage vs. people in the bar area) can provide information about what parts of the show were the most engaging.
- Movement patterns: since people can be tracked, we can analyze their movement patterns and study the dynamic of people movements in the venue over time.
- Movement of a person thought the entire session: This is related to the previous metric, but in this case we focus on a single person instead of checking group dynamics. This metric can provide detailed information about the engagement of the user, especially when comparing it with the information about the event (lists of songs played, performers etc.)
- Movement of the different limbs: This metric is a proxy indicator for how much a person has been dancing. In many cases when people are dancing we noticed a small movement across the venue but a high movements of the joints detected by the system.
- Direction where a person is looking to: Gaze information, especially its variation over time, is also very relevant for determining the user engagement. By analyzing when the people change their gaze direction towards the stage we could detect the most interesting moment of the event.

5   Results

We conducted fifteen tests in a controlled environment, changing the following variables:

Number of people on camera: controls the number of people that can be seen in the image retrieved from the camera. This variable can take the values from four to eleven in the test. It has been included to see if the system loses precision when increasing the number of people in the room.

Separation between the people: controls the distance between the people in the room. It is treated as a binary variable as people could be either close (distance is less than 30 cm) or separated (distance is greater than 70 cm). This variable has been included to see the impact of occlusions in the vision-based system and to measure the reliability of the tracking system.

Wi-Fi connection: controls if the mobile device of the people are connected to the same network as the scanning devices, allowing the system to know the real MAC address of the device and to retrieve more data from it.

Illumination: controls the state of the lights on the room, either turned on or changing over time. This variable has been included to see if both the preprocessing with segmentation and the hybrid approach can reduce the effect of the change of illumination in the computer vision techniques.

Number of people moving: controls the quantity of people moving from one zone to another. This variable is expressed in percentage of the total people in the image.

Table 2 shows the different conditions under which the fifteen tests were ran.

In order to simplify the testing and the further proving of results, we ran the test in offline mode, that is we first recorded the electromagnetic environment and the room

Table 2. Test variables [42].

Test	People	Separation	Wi-Fi	Lights	People moving
1	11	30 cm	✗	Turn on	3
2	11	30 cm	✗	Turn on	5
3	11	30 cm	✗	Changing	5
4	11	70 cm	✗	Changing	3
5	6	70 cm	✗	Turn on	2
6	11	30 cm	✓	Changing	5
7	11	30 cm	✓	Turn on	3
8	11	70 cm	✓	Changing	3
9	6	30 cm	✓	Changing	2
10	11	30 cm	✓	Turn on	5
11	11	70 cm	✓	Changing	7
12	11	70 cm	✓	Turn on	4
13	6	70 cm	✓	Changing	1
14	6	70 cm	✓	Turn on	1
15	11	30 cm	✓	Turn on	11

with the camera, and then later we processed the data. The video was taken in two modalities, a low-quality one (360p resolution, 10 fps and 400 kbps bitrate) and a high-quality one (1080p, 10 fps and 5 Mbps) to compare security camera quality to consumer grade cameras. Each test lasted five minutes, both for video and recording of the electromagnetic environment. As expected, using low quality videos the detection rate decreases, having more false detections and less people detected. Strangely, we noticed that double detections, person being detected two times in the same frame were more probable with the high quality video. This double detections happens when the system does not detect that two detected joints are from the same person and attributes them to different people, by supposing that the rest of the person is not detected because is being covered.

In the tests we compare, when possible, the out of the box computer vision algorithm without any of the improvements that has been exposed in this text, the computer vision algorithm with all the improvements that has been covered and the hybrid method with also the improvements exposed. In the case of analysing the tracking we only use the computer vision with the improvements, as this is the only one that implements the tracking mechanism.

The tests measured the following:

– True positive detections: measures the number of persons correctly detected at each frame. This variable is related to the maximum number of people that the system is able to track.

– Number of false detections: measures false detection at each frame. This variable will take into account both the false negatives (missing detections) and the false positives (detecting a person when it is not there, or detecting the same person twice).
– Tracking: This variable takes into account the movement of the people across different zones in the room and their location. This variable will measure if the system can track the movement of a person through the time.
– Processing time: This variable analyses the average time that is necessary for the processing of a frame in the video.

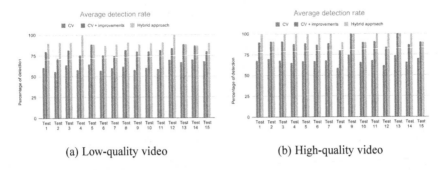

(a) Low-quality video   (b) High-quality video

Fig. 9. Average person detection rate.

In Fig. 9 we show the average (per frame) percentage of people detected on the videos in each of the tests, while in Fig. 10 we report the average number of false detections, both for the low and high bit-rate videos.

Figure 9a shows that, for the low-quality video, the hybrid approach in most cases performs better than the vision-only system (and in two cases correctly detects all the people in the scene), while in three cases it shows the same performance. Figure 10a shows a strong improvement in terms of false detections across almost every test, and no false detections at all in one case. In both cases it can be seen that the performance with computer vision is worse when the improvements and add-ons mentioned in this paper are not included, although the conditions of the test were not as changing as in the entertainment shows both detection rates, for low and high quality videos, has increased.

Similar conclusions can be drawn when analyzing the results on the high-quality video. Figure 9b shows that the hybrid system improves over the vision-only method and in 11 cases, reaching 100% detection rate. Figure 10b shows a similar trend: with the exceptions of tests #4 and #15 (where one of the participants is detected twice by the system), the false detections are lower when using the hybrid approach. In this case the difference of the computer vision before and after the improvements are noticeable, reducing the double detection in more than half in the majority of the cases and improving the detection rate by 10%.

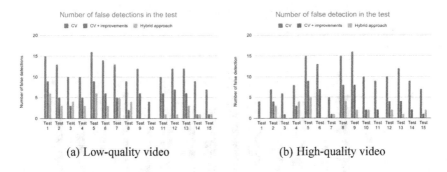

(a) Low-quality video   (b) High-quality video

Fig. 10. Average false detections.

We measure the quality of the tracking using the *tracking length* metric [7]. In Fig. 11 we show the tracking length when using the hybrid approach (red) and the vision-only based system. The tracking length is fairly consistent across the different tests, and the results clearly show that the hybrid approach improves over the vision-only system, with an approximate gain of 25%. As the tracking is an addition included in the computer vision there is no data for the computer vision without improvements or add-ons.

Figure 12 and Fig. 13b show some examples of the difference in detection and tracking quality between the vision-only system and the hybrid one according to different metrics:

- Tracking performance - Fig. 12a shows that the movement of the person is recorded for much longer time when using the hybrid approach.
- Number of detections - Fig. 12b shows how the hybrid approach is able to detect more people and how the vision-only approach may fail, by detecting a group of people as a single person.
- False and double detections - Fig. 13a shows that the double detection of the person does not take place on the hybrid method.
- Body parts detections - Fig. 13b shows that, even if both methods fail to detect the person, the hybrid method is able to detect at least some body parts

We measured the difference in processing time between the hybrid system and the computer vision with and without improvements techniques. The results, displayed in the Table 3, show that the hybrid approach is marginally slower than the vision-only based method when it has the improvements added, but without them it is many times better, this is due to the tracking functionality, which reduces the number of complete frames that has to be analysed completely. Performance were measured on an Intel i5 PC with 16 GB of RAM and a Nvidia 1080 GPU, taking the average over 20 runs.

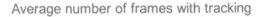

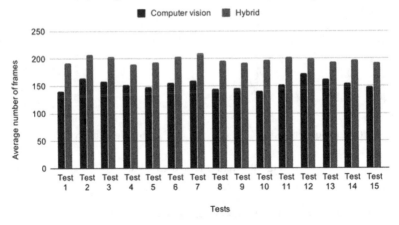

Fig. 11. Average tracking length across all tests. (Color figure online)

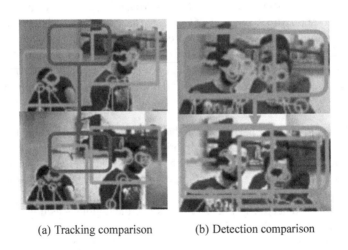

(a) Tracking comparison   (b) Detection comparison

Fig. 12. Comparison between computer vision technique (Left) and hybrid approach (Right) [42].

Table 3. Average processing times over 20 runs.

Quality	CV-only (fps)	CV-improved (fps)	Hybrid (fps)
High	0.46	2.73	2.51
Low	0.67	3.79	3.70

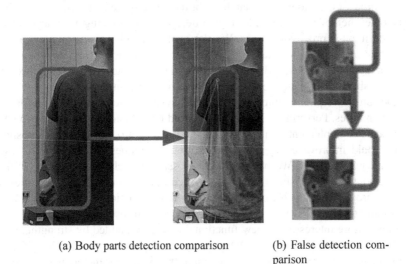

(a) Body parts detection comparison

(b) False detection comparison

Fig. 13. Comparison between CV (Left) and hybrid approach (Right) [42].

Finally, we also measured the ability of the system to determine the location of the people in the different zones of the room. We measured the average number of people in each zone across every test video, and compared it to the localization results when using only the vision system with and without the improvements, only the Wi-Fi method, or the hybrid approach. As detailed in Table 4, the hybrid approach is the one that matches the ground truth data more closely.

Table 4. Average number of people detected per zone, using CV-only, Wi-Fi only, hybrid methods and ground truth [42].

Zone	CV	CV improved	Wi-Fi	Hybrid	GT
1	3.2	3.4	3.6	**3.7**	3.9
2	0.7	1.0	1.4	**1.1**	1.2
3	2.8	2.9	3.3	**3.2**	3.2

6 Conclusions and Future Work

In this work we presented an out of the box solution for person detection, tracking and counting based on computer vision and WiFi signal analysis techniques. The system presented improves over a previous prototype [42] by modifying the preprocessing of the data in the computer vision based task. We have compared the hybrid solution, using both CV and WiFi signal techniques, with the improved CV-only and the WiFi-only implementations.

The comparison demonstrates that the hybrid method presented here performs better than the other methods, as it provides higher detection and tracking accuracy with only a small detriment in processing times. We also applied the improved preprocessing step to the hybrid solution. In this case we noticed a negligible improvement when testing the system in lab conditions, and slightly improved tracking accuracy in complex setups such as live shows with many people and poor lighting conditions.

In the future we plan to improve the hybrid system in terms of both performance and functionalities. Performance-wise, gains could be obtained by switching to newer, better models or implementing improved methods for localization via wireless signals. Tracking could improve using face-identification techniques which allow to resume tracking after occlusions. We believe that is possible to achieve real-time (25 fps or better) without compromising the detection accuracy. Regarding functionalities, one obvious improvement is to increase the amount of information extracted, for example running emotion analysis (which correlates directly with user engagement) or action recognition. More interestingly, new functionalities can be added by strengthening the interaction between the vision and wireless systems: for example, the hybrid implementation could use the data from the camera to tweak the parameters used to perform wireless localization, or to reshape the zones of interest based on people movements.

References

1. Altini, M., Brunelli, D., Farella, E., Benini, L.: Bluetooth indoor localization with multiple neural networks. In: ISWPC 2010 - IEEE 5th International Symposium on Wireless Pervasive Computing, 1 June 2010, pp. 295–300 (2010). https://doi.org/10.1109/ISWPC.2010.5483748
2. Andriluka, M., Pishchulin, L., Gehler, P., Schiele, B.: 2D human pose estimation: new benchmark and state of the art analysis. In: Proceedings of the IEEE Computer Society Conference on Computer Vision and Pattern Recognition (2014). https://doi.org/10.1109/CVPR.2014.471
3. Asvadi, A., Garrote, L., Premebida, C., Peixoto, P., Nunes, U.J.: Multimodal vehicle detection: fusing 3D-LIDAR and color camera data. Pattern Recogn. Lett. **115**, 20–29 (2018). https://doi.org/10.1016/j.patrec.2017.09.038
4. Bodd, B.: Means, not an end (of the world) the customization of news personalization by European news media. SSRN Electron. J. (2018). https://doi.org/10.2139/ssrn.3141810
5. Bourdev, L., Malik, J.: Poselets: body part detectors trained using 3D human pose annotations. In: 2009 IEEE 12th International Conference on Computer Vision (2010). https://doi.org/10.1109/iccv.2009.5459303
6. Cao, Z., Hidalgo, G., Simon, T., Wei, S.E., Sheikh, Y.: OpenPose: realtime multi-person 2D pose estimation using Part Affinity Fields. In: arXiv preprint arXiv:1812.08008 (2018)
7. Čehovin, L., Leonardis, A., Kristan, M.: Visual object tracking performance measures revisited. IEEE Trans. Image Process. **25**(3), 1261–1274 (2016)
8. Chang, J.Y., Moon, G., Lee, K.M.: V2V-PoseNet: voxel-to-voxel prediction network for accurate 3D hand and human pose estimation from a single depth map. In: Proceedings of the IEEE Computer Society Conference on Computer Vision and Pattern Recognition (2018). https://doi.org/10.1109/CVPR.2018.00533
9. Dalal, N., Triggs, B.: Histograms of oriented gradients for human detection. In: Proceedings - 2005 IEEE Computer Society Conference on Computer Vision and Pattern Recognition, CVPR 2005 (2005). https://doi.org/10.1109/CVPR.2005.177

10. Dari, Y.E., Suyoto, S.S., Pranowo, P.P.: CAPTURE: a mobile based indoor positioning system using wireless indoor positioning system. Int. J. Interact. Mob. Technol. (JIM) **12**(1), 61 (2018). https://doi.org/10.3991/ijim.v12i1.7632
11. Deloitte: 2018 Media and Entertainment Industry Trends — Deloitte US (2018)
12. Deng, J., Dong, W., Socher, R., Li, L.J., Li, K., Fei-Fei, L.: Imagenet: a large-scale hierarchical image database. In: 2009 IEEE Conference on Computer Vision and Pattern Recognition, pp. 248–255. IEEE (2009)
13. Girshick, R.: Fast R-CNN. In: Proceedings of the IEEE International Conference on Computer Vision, pp. 1440–1448 (2015)
14. Girshick, R., Donahue, J., Darrell, T., Malik, J.: Rich feature hierarchies for accurate object detection and semantic segmentation. In: Proceedings of the IEEE Computer Society Conference on Computer Vision and Pattern Recognition (2014). https://doi.org/10.1109/CVPR. 2014.81
15. Glisser (2019). https://www.glisser.com/features/. Accessed 24 Sept 2019
16. Granados, N.: Digital Video and Social Media Will Drive Entertainment Industry Growth in 2019 (2018)
17. Gupta, P., Kar, S.P.: MUSIC and improved MUSIC algorithm to estimate direction of arrival. In: 2015 International Conference on Communication and Signal Processing, ICCSP 2015 (2015). https://doi.org/10.1109/ICCSP.2015.7322593
18. Hassib, M., Schneegass, S., Eiglsperger, P., Henze, N., Schmidt, A., Alt, F.: EngageMeter: a system for implicit audience engagement sensing using electroencephalography. In: Conference on Human Factors in Computing Systems - Proceedings (2017). https://doi.org/10. 1145/3025453.3025669
19. He, K., Gkioxari, G., Dollár, P., Girshick, R.: Mask R-CNN. In: Proceedings of the IEEE International Conference on Computer Vision, pp. 2961–2969 (2017)
20. IEEE OUI MAC registries (2019). https://regauth.standards.ieee.org/standards-ra-web/pub/ view.html#registries. Accessed 24 Sept 2019
21. Johnson, S., Everingham, M.: Clustered pose and nonlinear appearance models for human pose estimation. In: Proceedings of the British Machine Vision Conference (2010) https:// doi.org/10.5244/C.24.12
22. Kalal, Z., Mikolajczyk, K., Matas, J.: Forward-backward error: automatic detection of tracking failures. In: 2010 20th International Conference on Pattern Recognition, pp. 2756–2759. IEEE (2010)
23. Khalil, M., Ebner, M.: Clustering patterns of engagement in Massive Open Online Courses (MOOCs): the use of learning analytics to reveal student categories. J. Comput. High. Educ. **29**(1), 114–132 (2016). https://doi.org/10.1007/s12528-016-9126-9
24. Nanani, G.K., Prasad Kantipudi, M.V.V.: A study of WI-FI based system for moving object detection through the wall. Int. J. Comput. Appl. **79**(7), 15–18 (2013). https://doi.org/10. 5120/13753-1589
25. Lanzisera, S., Zats, D., Pister, K.S.: Radio frequency time-of-flight distance measurement for low-cost wireless sensor localization. IEEE Sens. J. (2011). https://doi.org/10.1109/JSEN. 2010.2072496
26. Lienhart, R., Maydt, J.: An extended set of Haar-like features for rapid object detection. In: Proceedings, International Conference on Image Processing (2003). https://doi.org/10.1109/ icip.2002.1038171
27. Lin, T.-Y., et al.: Microsoft COCO: common objects in context. In: Fleet, D., Pajdla, T., Schiele, B., Tuytelaars, T. (eds.) ECCV 2014, Part V. LNCS, vol. 8693, pp. 740–755. Springer, Cham (2014). https://doi.org/10.1007/978-3-319-10602-1_48
28. Liu, W., et al.: SSD: single shot MultiBox detector. In: Leibe, B., Matas, J., Sebe, N., Welling, M. (eds.) ECCV 2016. LNCS, vol. 9905, pp. 21–37. Springer, Cham (2016). https://doi.org/ 10.1007/978-3-319-46448-0_2

29. Malisiewicz, T., Gupta, A., Efros, A.A.: Ensemble of exemplar-SVMs for object detection and beyond. In: Proceedings of the IEEE International Conference on Computer Vision (2011). https://doi.org/10.1109/ICCV.2011.6126229

30. Martínez-Villaseñor, L., Ponce, H., Brieva, J., Moya-Albor, E., Núñez-Martínez, J., Peñafort-Asturiano, C.: UP-fall detection dataset: a multimodal approach. Sensors (2019). https://doi.org/10.3390/s19091988

31. Meyer, K.A.: Student engagement in online learning: what works and why. ASHE High. Educ. Rep. (2014). https://doi.org/10.1002/aehe.20018

32. Mitchell, J.: Hollywood's Latest Blockbuster: Big Data and The Innovator's Curse (2014)

33. Oguejiofor, O.S., Okorogu, V.N., Adewale, A., Osuesu, B.O.: Outdoor localization system using RSSI measurement of wireless sensor network. Int. J. Innov. Technol. Explor. Eng. **2**, 1–6 (2013)

34. Papandreou, G., Zhu, T., Chen, L.-C., Gidaris, S., Tompson, J., Murphy, K.: PersonLab: person pose estimation and instance segmentation with a bottom-up, part-based, geometric embedding model. In: Ferrari, V., Hebert, M., Sminchisescu, C., Weiss, Y. (eds.) ECCV 2018, Part XIV. LNCS, vol. 11218, pp. 282–299. Springer, Cham (2018). https://doi.org/10.1007/978-3-030-01264-9_17

35. Peng, R., Sichitiu, M.L.: Angle of arrival localization for wireless sensor networks. In: 2006 3rd Annual IEEE Communications Society on Sensor and Adhoc Communications and Networks, Secon 2006 (2007). https://doi.org/10.1109/SAHCN.2006.288442

36. Pizer, S.M., Johnston, R.E., Ericksen, J.P., Yankaskas, B.C., Muller, K.E.: Contrast-limited adaptive histogram equalization: speed and effectiveness. In: Proceedings of the First Conference on Visualization in Biomedical Computing (1990)

37. Razavian, A.S., Azizpour, H., Sullivan, J., Carlsson, S.: CNN features off-the-shelf: an astounding baseline for recognition. In: IEEE Computer Society Conference on Computer Vision and Pattern Recognition Workshops (2014). https://doi.org/10.1109/CVPRW.2014.131

38. Redmon, J., Divvala, S., Girshick, R., Farhadi, A.: You only look once: unified, real-time object detection. In: Proceedings of the IEEE Computer Society Conference on Computer Vision and Pattern Recognition (2016). https://doi.org/10.1109/CVPR.2016.91

39. Redmon, J., Farhadi, A.: Yolov3: An incremental improvement. CoRR abs/1804.02767 (2018). http://arxiv.org/abs/1804.02767

40. Ren, S., He, K., Girshick, R., Sun, J.: Faster R-CNN: towards real-time object detection with region proposal networks. In: Advances in Neural Information Processing Systems, pp. 91–99 (2015)

41. Richter, R., Kellenberger, T., Kaufmann, H.: Comparison of topographic correction methods. Remote Sens. (2009). https://doi.org/10.3390/rs1030184

42. Sanz Narrillos, M., Masneri., S., Zorrilla, M.: Combining video and wireless signals for enhanced audience analysis. In: Proceedings of the 12th International Conference on Agents and Artificial Intelligence - Volume 2: ICAART, pp. 151–161. INSTICC, SciTePress (2020). https://doi.org/10.5220/0008963101510161

43. Schivinski, B., Christodoulides, G., Dabrowski, D.: Measuring consumers' engagement with brand-related social-media content: development and validation of a scale that identifies levels of social-media engagement with brands. J. Advert. Res. (2016). https://doi.org/10.2501/JAR-2016-004

44. Schollz, Z.: High-precision indoor positioning framework, version 3 (2019). https://github.com/schollz/find3. Accessed 10 Apr 2019

45. Spinello, L., Triebel, R., Siegwart, R.: Multimodal people detection and tracking in crowded scenes. In: Proceedings of the National Conference on Artificial Intelligence (2008)

46. Su, Z., Ye, M., Zhang, G., Dai, L., Sheng, J.: Cascade feature aggregation for human pose estimation. In: CVPR (2019)

47. Sun, K., Xiao, B., Liu, D., Wang, J.: Deep High-Resolution Representation Learning for Human Pose Estimation (2019). http://arxiv.org/abs/1902.09212
48. Wightman, R.: posenet-pytorch (2018). https://github.com/rwightman/posenet-pytorch
49. Yiu, S., Dashti, M., Claussen, H., Perez-Cruz, F.: Wireless RSSI fingerprinting localization (2017). https://doi.org/10.1016/j.sigpro.2016.07.005

Learning Latent Variable Models
with Discriminant Regularization

Jing Peng[1(✉)] and Alex J. Aved[2]

[1] Department of Computer Science, Montclair State University, Montclair, NJ 07043, USA
pengj@montclair.edu
[2] Information Directorate, AFRL, Rome, NY 13441, USA
alexander.aved@us.af.mil

Abstract. In many machine learning applications, data are often described by a large number of features or attributes. However, too many features can result in overfitting. This is often the case when the number of examples is smaller than the number of features. The problem can be mitigated by learning latent variable models where the data can be described by a fewer number of latent dimensions. There are many techniques for learning latent variable models in the literature. Most of these techniques can be grouped into two classes: techniques that are informative, represented by principal component analysis (PCA), and techniques that are discriminant, represented by linear discriminant analysis (LDA). Each class of the techniques has its advantages. In this work, we introduce a technique for learning latent variable models with discriminant regularization that combines the characteristics of both classes. Empirical evaluation using a variety of data sets is presented to verify the performance of the proposed technique.

Keywords: Classification · Dimensionality reduction · Latent variable models

1 Introduction

In many machine learning applications, a large number of features or attributes is often used to describe examples. However, too many features can cause overfitting, resulting in poor generalization performance. This is the case when there are more features than examples. Poor generalization performance can be attributed to the curse of dimensionality [6], which implies that to avoid overfitting, the number of examples must increase exponentially with the number of features. For example, it is shown that there are $O(2^q)$ unknowns that must be estimated to learn a binary distribution in a space with q correlated features [8].

The above problem can be mitigated by learning latent variable models where the data can be described by a fewer number of latent dimensions. In fact, learning latent variable models has been one of the key building blocks in machine learning, which in turn will benefit many practical applications [4, 20, 24, 27, 40].

One of the goals of learning latent variable models is to compute the intrinsic dimensionality of the input space represented by high dimensional input examples. There are both linear and non-linear techniques for learning latent variable models in the literature. In this work, we are concerned with linear techniques for their simplicity. Many linear techniques can be extended to non-linear cases.

A. P. Rocha et al. (Eds.): ICAART 2020, LNAI 12613, pp. 378–398, 2021.
https://doi.org/10.1007/978-3-030-71158-0_18

Many techniques for learning latent variable models have been developed over the years [3,5,15,21,22,28,29,43]. There are two major categories of techniques for learning latent variable models. The first category of techniques is represented by principal component analysis (PCA), where the objective is to minimize information loss. The second category of techniques is represented by linear discriminant analysis (LDA), where the objective is to maximize class separation. Each has its advantages. For example, latent positions computed by PCA do not rely on class label information, while latent positions computed by LDA do. And as such, one expects LDA to be able to perform better than PCA in classification applications. However, when there are insufficient training examples per class in face recognition problems, empirical evidence shows that PCA can perform better [26].

In this paper, we propose a technique for learning latent variable models that combine some of the characteristics of both PCA and LDA. The proposed technique draws upon ideas from probabilistic latent variable models [25,33,38], where the negative log prior can be viewed as regularization (or penalty) in a non-Bayesian context. The technique minimizes a minimum information loss objective with discriminant regularization. As a result, the technique represents a trade-off between PCA and LDA, resulting in better generalization performance in many applications. Empirical evaluation using a number of data sets is presented to verify the proposed technique for learning latent variable models.

Note that an earlier version of the current work appeared in [30]. While the technical idea presented here is along the lines of the one described in [30], the technical discussion is carried out in a general probabilistic context, rather than Gaussian processes. Thus the technical presentation is more refined in the present paper. Furthermore, we have included more examples in the empirical evaluation section in the present paper. These diverse examples, ranging from biometric (such as iris and fingerprint) and image classification problems to hyperspectral image analysis, have provided strong empirical evidence to support the technique proposed in the present paper.

The rest of the paper is organized as follows. Section 2 discusses related work. Section 3 introduces a probabilistic framework for learning latent variable models to motivate the introduction of out proposal. Section 4 introduces a linear technique for learning latent variable models with discriminant regularization. The technique can be interpreted as regularized PCA, where discriminant analysis is the regularizer. It can also be viewed as regularized discriminant analysis, where the regularizer is PCA. Section 5 provides the empirical evaluation of the proposed technique against several competing techniques. Finally, Sect. 6 summarizes our contributions and points out future research directions.

2   Related Work

There are many techniques in the literature that aim to exploit the inherent low dimensional nature of the data [12,17,34,41]. Linear techniques for learning latent variable models can be broadly categorized into two classes, represented by PCA and LDA, respectively. These techniques can learn the intrinsic geometry of the input space, along with its global Euclidean structure.

Note that PCA is closely related to auto-encoders in neural networks. In its very basic form (one hidden layer with linear outputs), the q hidden units span the same latent space as the first q components found by PCA [7,18]. The components of PCA are orthogonal, while the weight vectors of the basic auto-encoder may not. A deep auto-encoder can learn a non-linear subspace, which can be desirable in many applications. The challenge is that it can be very difficult to optimize deep auto-encoders using backpropagation. Techniques have been proposed to address this challenge in the literature [18]. In addition, studies have been done comparing deep auto-encoders with kernel PCA, which can also produce a non-linear subspace.

Locality preserving projection (LPP) is a linear technique for learning the locality structure of input space [19]. The technique constructs an adjacency matrix from input examples that describes the local neighborhood information of the input space. The optimal projection can then be computed that preserves the neighborhood information in the latent space. It has been noted that the basis functions, resulting from LPP, may not be orthogonal [9]. Thus, the data reconstruction can be a challenge in many applications.

Orthogonal locality preserving projection (OLPP) is a linear technique for learning latent variable models [9]. It is proposed to address some of the problems associated with LPP [19]. As in LPP, OLPP first constructs an adjacency matrix that contains locality information. OLPP then computes a latent subspace, where its basis functions are orthogonal. These orthogonal basis functions preserve the metric structure of latent space. OLPP has been shown to perform better than LPP in several applications [9].

Gaussian Process (GP) latent variable models are probabilistic techniques for learning latent variable models from high dimensional input examples [16,23,25,38]. GP latent variable models have been shown to be successful in a number of problems such as image reconstruction and facial expression recognition [1,10,14,35].

GP latent variable models are generative techniques [25,33,38]. Similar to PCA, these techniques are unsupervised [25]. GP latent variable models are useful in many applications, such as data visualization and regression analysis. However, GP latent variable models may not be suitable for classification applications. One possible solution is to introduce priors over latent variables to bias their positions in latent space [38]. One potential problem associated with GP latent variable models require an inference process for a test example in order to estimate its position in latent space. This separate inference process can complicate GP latent variable model computation, due to increased computational complexity.

Techniques for combining PCA and LDA for dimensionality reduction have been introduced in the literature [42,44]. The objective function is formulated as a linear combination of the objectives of PCA and LDA in these techniques. In this work, we aim to learn latent variable models with discriminant regularization. This formulation is closely related to the maximum a posteriori estimation in a Gaussian framework, where the negative log prior can be viewed as regularization (or penalty) [33,38].

3   Latent Variable Models

In this work, we use $\mathbf{x}$ to represent the input, and use y to represent the output or target. We let

$$D = \{(\mathbf{x}_i, y) | i = 1, \cdots, n\}^t \tag{1}$$

be a set of n centered examples, where $\mathbf{x}_i \in \Re^q$. The vector inputs are aggregated in the $n \times q$ matrix X

$$X = [\mathbf{x}_1, \mathbf{x}_2, \cdots, \mathbf{x}_n]^t, \tag{2}$$

where t represents transpose. We denote the corresponding latent variables as $\mathbf{h} \in \Re^d$. The vector latent variables are aggregated in the $n \times d$ matrix H

$$H = [\mathbf{h}_1, \mathbf{h}_2, \cdots, \mathbf{h}_n]^t.$$

We note that $d \ll q$.

The input $\mathbf{x}$ and its latent variable $\mathbf{h}$ can be described in the following way

$$\mathbf{x} = F\mathbf{h} + \varepsilon, \tag{3}$$

where F is a $q \times d$ matrix of weights or parameters of the model, and ε represents the error term. We assume that this error term follows a Gaussian distribution with zero mean and uniform variance

$$p(\varepsilon) = N(0, \beta^{-1}\mathbf{I}),$$

where β is a constant. We further assume that the error term is independent and identically distributed (i.i.d.). The model (3) along with the Gaussian error term gives us the following likelihood, conditional probability density of the input examples

$$p(\mathbf{x}|\mathbf{h}, F, \beta) = N(F\mathbf{h}, \beta^{-1}\mathbf{I}).$$

The above shows that X (2) follows a matrix variate normal distribution

$$\begin{aligned} p(X|H, F, \beta) &= \prod_{i=1}^{n} p(\mathbf{x}_i|\mathbf{h}_i, F, \beta) \\ &= \frac{\beta^{\frac{qn}{2}}}{(2\pi)^{\frac{qn}{2}}} \exp(-\frac{1}{2}tr(\beta(X^t - FH^t)(X^t - FH^t)^t)). \end{aligned} \tag{4}$$

Here the underlying assumption is that input examples $\mathbf{x}_i$ are independent and identically distributed. If we integrate out the latent variables H, we obtain the probabilistic PCA solution for F [36].

An alternative approach is to integrate out F and optimize with respect to H to obtain a solution for the latent variables. This dual approach has been studied in [25, 38]. In this approach, $\mathbf{f}_i$, the ith row of F, is assumed to follow a Gaussian distribution with zero mean and uniform variance

$$p(\mathbf{f}_i) = N(0, \alpha^{-1}\mathbf{I})$$

where α is a constant. It follows that $p(F)$ is also Gaussian and given by

$$p(F) = \prod_{i=1}^{q} p(\mathbf{f}_i) = \frac{1}{C_q} \exp(-\frac{1}{2}tr(\alpha F^t F))$$

$$= \frac{\alpha^{\frac{dq}{2}}}{(2\pi)^{\frac{dq}{2}}} \exp(-\frac{1}{2}tr(\alpha F^t F)). \tag{5}$$

where C_q is a normalization factor. Combining (4) and (5) and integrating out F, we obtain the marginalized likelihood of X

$$p(X|H,\beta) = \int p(X|H,F,\beta)p(F)dF$$

$$\propto \frac{1}{|K|^{q/2}} \exp(-\frac{1}{2}tr(\Sigma^{-1}XX^t)), \tag{6}$$

where

$$\Sigma = (\alpha^{-1}HH^t + \beta^{-1}\mathbf{I}),$$

and $|\Sigma|$ denotes the determinant of matrix Σ.

The above (6) shows that the likelihood of the input examples X is Gaussian, given the latent variables H. The log likelihood of X is

$$L = -\frac{qn}{2} \ln(2\pi) - \frac{q}{2}|\Sigma| - \frac{1}{2}tr(\Sigma^{-1}XX^t).$$

It is shown that optimization of the log likelihood respect to latent variables H results in a solution that is equivalent to the PCA solution [25, 36].

We note that it is possible to further constrain the latent variables H by introducing priors over H. For example, if we introduce an uninformed prior on H, we obtain the following log prior

$$\ln p(H) = -\frac{1}{2}\sum_{i=1}^{n} \mathbf{h}_i^t \mathbf{h}_i.$$

This simple prior constrains the latent variables to be closer to the origin [38]. For classification problems, class labels can be incorporated into priors [14, 35]. For example, priors can be based on linear discriminant analysis [15]. If Σ_w and Σ_b represent the sample between- and within-class matrices in the latent space, respectively, the LDA based criterion $J(H) = tr(\Sigma_w^{-1}\Sigma_b)$ can be implemented. We use tr to represent the matrix trace operator. This leads us to the following prior [38]

$$p(H) = C\exp(-J^{-1}).$$

One of the problems with the latent variable models discussed above is that to estimate the latent position for an unseen test example, a separate inference process is required. And as such, additional uncertainties can be introduced in the estimate with increased computational complexity.

4 Latent Variable Models with Discriminant Regularizers

In the previous section, we discussed a general technique for learning latent variable models. In this section, we introduce an algorithm for learning latent variable models for classification problems without a separate process and increased computational complexity.

As discussed in the previous section, the optimization of the likelihood (6) with respect to latent variables H gives rise to the probabilistic PCA solution to the latent variables H. Additional constraints can be placed on the latent variables H by introducing priors. The introduction of priors over latent variables $p(H)$ results in the log posterior (terms that the posterior depends on)

$$L = \frac{q}{2} \ln |\Sigma| + \frac{1}{2} tr(\Sigma^{-1} X X^t) - \ln p(H). \qquad (7)$$

In a non-Bayesian setting, the negative log prior $-\ln p(H)$ can often be regarded as a penalty term [33,38]. This is also related to ridge regression [28] and weight decay [39]. If the prior $p(H)$ is discriminant, optimization of (7) produces a solution to the latent variables Z that is both informative, as in PCA, and discriminant, as in LDA. While the idea is appealing for many applications, an inference must be made for each test example, which potentially introduces uncertainty and additional computational complexity [25,38].

We address this problem by describing a simple algorithm for learning latent variable models with discriminant regularization. The algorithm achieves the desired representation balance shown in (7), without separate inference for test examples.

We begin with PCA. Recall that PCA computes linear projection P by optimizing

$$J_{PCA}(P) = tr(P^t X X^t P), \qquad (8)$$

where $X X^t$ represents the sample covariance matrix, assuming that the examples are centered (2). The resulting linear projection P has the following property that

$$\sum_i^n \|\mathbf{x}_i - P P^t \mathbf{x}_i\|^2$$

is minimum. That is, the latent representations of the examples X estimated from PCA are optimal in terms of information loss.

We note that PCA is entirely unsupervised. For classification problems, we want to leverage class label information to compute latent variable models. To do so, we explore the idea behind the joint distribution of the latent variables (7), where the prior distribution over the latent variables imposes conditions on their positions in the resulting latent space. As discussed in the previous section, the negative log prior can be simply interpreted as a penalty term, or regularization. Therefore, we can introduce a discriminant regularization or penalty term in (8)

$$J_{PCA_r}(P) = tr(P^t X X^t P) + \lambda r(P), \qquad (9)$$

where $r(\cdot)$ denotes a regularization term, and λ is a regularization parameter. In this work, we examine two discriminant regularization schemes: Locality Preserving regularizer and Linear Discriminant regularizer.

4.1 Locality Preserving Regularizer

The locality preserving projection (LPP) is a technique introduced in [19]. The technique first constructs a graph of the input examples (2). LPP then computes a linear projection from the graph that preserves the locality information.

Suppose that A is a $n \times n$ matrix, where the entry A_{ij} (ith row and jth column) is computed according to

$$A_{ij} = \begin{cases} \exp(-\eta\|\mathbf{x}_i - \mathbf{x}_j\|^2) & i \neq j \text{ and } l(\mathbf{x}_i) = l(\mathbf{x}_j) \\ 0 & \text{otherwise.} \end{cases} \tag{10}$$

In the above, $\mathbf{x}_i$ denotes the ith training example, $l(\mathbf{x})$ is the label of $\mathbf{x}$, and η is a parameter. That is, A represents the adjacency matrix of the input examples. Let $\mathbf{p} \in \Re^q$ such that $h_i = \mathbf{p}^t \mathbf{x}_i$. Also, let

$$J_{LPP} = \sum_{i,j} (h_i - h_j)^2 A_{ij}. \tag{11}$$

As can be seen, when examples $\mathbf{x}_i$ and $\mathbf{x}_j$ that are in the same class are projected far apart by $\mathbf{p}$, they contribute to J_{LPP}. On the other hand, J_{LPP} completely ignores examples that are in different classes. The locality preserving technique computes a linear projection $\mathbf{p}$ by minimizing (11).

We rewrite the above objective (11) by simple algebraic manipulation

$$\begin{aligned} J_{LPP} &= \frac{1}{2} \sum_{i,j} (h_i - h_j)^2 A_{ij} \\ &= \frac{1}{2} \sum_{i,j} (\mathbf{p}^t \mathbf{x}_i - \mathbf{p}^t \mathbf{x}_j)^2 A_{ij} \\ &= \mathbf{p}^t X^t L X \mathbf{p}, \end{aligned} \tag{12}$$

where $L = \Lambda - A$ is the graph Laplacian, and Λ is a diagonal matrix with diagonal entries $\lambda_{ii} = \sum_j A_{ij}$. Often Λ_{ii} can be regarded as the volume of h_i. Thus, LPP aims to solve the following constraint optimization problem

$$\min_{\mathbf{p}} \mathbf{p}^t X^t L X \mathbf{p} \tag{13}$$
$$\text{s.t. } \mathbf{p}^t X^t \Lambda X \mathbf{p} = 1$$

Therefore, the optimal $\mathbf{p}$ can be obtained by solving the following generalized eigenvalue problem

$$X^t L X \mathbf{p} = \lambda X^t \Lambda X \mathbf{p}, \tag{14}$$

where λ denotes the eigenvalue corresponding to $\mathbf{p}$. In many applications, LPP has been demonstrated to be effective [9, 19].

The above discussion naturally suggests that locality preserving can be exploited as a regularizer to the PCA objective (8). Therefore, the proposed PCA with locality preserving regularization becomes

$$J(\mathbf{p}) = tr(\mathbf{p}^t X X^t \mathbf{p}) + \lambda tr(\mathbf{p}^t (X^t L X)^{-1} (X^t \Lambda X) \mathbf{p}). \tag{15}$$

It follows that the optimal projection $\mathbf{p}$ can be computed by maximizing

$$J_{PCA-LPP} = tr(XX^t + \lambda((X^tLX)^{-1}(X^t\Lambda X))). \tag{16}$$

The resulting linear projection algorithm is denoted as *P-Lpp*. It is interesting to note that we can interpret (16) as regularized PCA, where locality preserving is the regularizer. We can also interpret (16) as regularized locality preserving projection, where PCA is the regularizer.

4.2   Linear Discriminant Regularizer

In this section, we consider an alternate regularizer-linear discriminant analysis (LDA) [15]. Recall that LDA finds a linear projection $\mathbf{p}$ by optimizing

$$J(\mathbf{p}) = tr((\mathbf{p}^t\Sigma_w\mathbf{p})^{-1}(\mathbf{p}^t\Sigma_b\mathbf{p})), \tag{17}$$

where

$$\Sigma_w = \sum_{c=1}^{C} \sum_{i=1,\mathbf{x}_i \in c}^{n_c} (\mathbf{x}_i - \mathbf{m}_c)(\mathbf{x}_i - \mathbf{m}_c)^t \tag{18}$$

and

$$\Sigma_b = \sum_{c=1}^{C} (\mathbf{m}_c - \mathbf{m})(\mathbf{m}_c - \mathbf{m})^t \tag{19}$$

are the within and between class matrices, $\mathbf{m}$ is the overall mean of the input examples, and $\mathbf{m}_c$ denotes the mean of class c. It turns out that maximizing (17) is equivalent to maximizing

$$J_{LDA} = tr(\Sigma_w^{-1}\Sigma_b).$$

This allows us to propose PCA (8) with linear discriminant regularization

$$J_{IP-LDA} = tr(XX^t + \lambda\Sigma_w^{-1}\Sigma_b). \tag{20}$$

We call the resulting linear projection algorithm *P-Lda*. Note that similar to P-Lpp (16), we can interpret (20) as regularized PCA, where the regularizer is LDA. We can also view (20) as regularized LDA. In this case, PCA is the regularizer.

5   Empirical Evaluation

In this section, we provide empirical evaluation using a number of problems that validates performance of the proposed technique. We also include several competing techniques for comparison.

5.1 Competing Methods

The following competing methods are evaluated in our empirical evaluation.

1. P-Lpp–Regularized PCA, where locality preserving is the regularizer (Eq. 16).
2. P-Lda–Regularized PCA, where LDA is the regularizer (Eq. 20).
3. PCA–Laten variable model that maximizes (Eq. 8)

$$J(\mathbf{p}) = tr(\mathbf{p}^t X X^t \mathbf{p}).$$

4. LDA–Latent variable model that maximizes

$$J_{LDA} = tr(\Sigma_w^{-1} \Sigma_b),$$

where Σ_w and Σ_b are given by (18) and (19), respectively.
5. OLPP–Orthogonal Locality Preserving Projection (OLPP) proposed in [9].

We state that OLPP is developed to address some of the problems associated with LPP (13). It has been shown that the eigenvectors resulting from optimizing (14) may not be orthogonal. OLPP addresses this problem by projecting the input examples onto the PCA subspace, from which it computes the solution to (14) so that orthogonality can be preserved. OLPP has been shown to perform better than LPP in a number of problems [9]. Therefore, we compare the proposed techniques P-Lpp and P-Lda against OLPP in the experiments.

5.2 Data Sets

Several data sets are used to demonstrate the generalization performance by each of the competing techniques. They are described below.

Fig. 1. Sample AR-face images, adapted from [30].

1. **AR-Face Image Data (ARFace).** This data set comes from the AR-face database [26]. A detailed description of the AR-face image data set is provided in [26]. For this data set, we randomly selected 50 different subjects (25 males and 25 females) from this AR-face database. All the face images used here were normalized to 85×60 pixel arrays of intensity values. Figure 1 shows some sample images from the AR-face data set. In the AR-face experiment we follow the setup of the Small Training Data set experiment detailed in [26]. When there are insufficient training examples per class, PCA has been shown to provide better performance than LDA [26]. Our goal here is to examine how well the proposed techniques P-Lpp and P-Lda perform against PCA in such a setting.

For this example, we selected the first seven images from each subject. This gives us a total of 350 face images. To emphasize the problems often associated with insufficient training examples, two instances from each subject were chosen as training examples, and the remaining five images were used as test examples. This gives rise to 21 different ways to split face images into training and testing. The results averaged over 21 runs are reported. Note that, as in [26], we apply PCA to transform the original face images of 85×60 pixels into vectors of 350 dimensions. These vectors are input to all the competing techniques examined here.

2. **MNIST Data (MNIST).** This dataset consists of handwritten digit images from the US National Institute of Standards and Technology (NIST)[1]. Each digit image is a array of 28 by 28 pixels of intensity values. Therefore, each example is a vector of 784 intensity values. 100 examples were randomly selected from each digit class in this experiment. Thus, The MNIST dataset has a total of 1000 examples. Sample MNIST digit images are shown in Fig. 2.

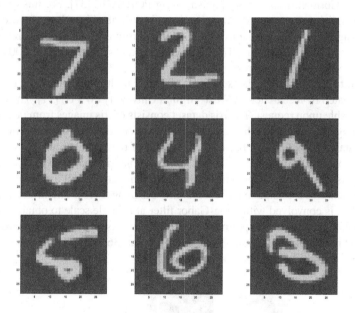

Fig. 2. Sample MNIST digit images.

3. **Cat and Dog data (CatDog).** The CatDog dataset consists of two hundred cat and dog face images. Each face image is an array of 64×64 pixels. These images have been normalized by aligning the eyes. Figure 3 shows some sample cat and dog face images.

4. **Multilingual Text (MText).** The MText dataset is a text data set consisting of multiple languages [2]. The data set is a collection of Reuters' RCV1 and RCV2. The text documents have six categories: (1) *Economics*, (2) *Equity Markets*,

---

[1] yann.lecun.com/exdb/mnist/.

Fig. 3. Sample images of the cat and dog face data, adapted from [30].

(3) *Government Social*, (4) *Corporate/Industrial*, (5) *Performance*, and (6) *Government Finance*. Each English document in the dataset has been translated into French, German, Italian and Spanish, using PORTAGE [37]. For this experiment, only English texts are used. Also, each text is described by a bag of words model, resulting in 21531 dimensions. 100 examples from each category were randomly selected for this experiment. Thus, the resulting dataset has a total of 600 examples described by 21531 features.

5. **Iris Data (Iris).** The Iris dataset is part of a large multimodal biometric data collection created by researchers at West Virginia University (WVU) [11]. The collection is available upon request. The Iris dataset consists of iris images from people of different age, gender, and ethnicity. A detailed description can be found in [11]. The Iris dataset is challenging because the quality of these images are low due to blur, occlusion, and noise. Figure 4 shows some sample iris images in the data set.

Each iris image is segmented into a 25×240 template [32]. It has been shown that Gabor features are suitable for representing iris images [13]. Therefore, each image template is convolved with a log-Gabor filter at a single scale to obtain a vector of 6000 features. For this experiment, a pair of subjects was randomly selected. One subject has 27 examples, and the other subject has 36 examples, resulting in a total of 63 examples described by 6000 features.

Fig. 4. Sample Iris images, adapted from [30].

6. **Fingerprint Data (Finger).** The Fingerprint dataset consists of fingerprint images of people of different age, gender, and ethnicity. Similar to the Iris dataset, it is part of a large multimodal biometric data collection created by researchers at WVU [11]. The fingerprint dataset is difficult because many examples are of low quality, as a result of blur, occlusion, and noise. Figure 5 shows sample fingerprint images used in this experiment.

Fig. 5. Sample fingerprint images, adapted from [30].

This dataset has a total of 124 fingerimages from randomly chosen pair of subjects. One of the subjects has 61 instances, and the other has 63. Ridge and bifurcation features are computed to represent the fingerprint images, using code that is publically available (sites.google.com/site/athisnarayanan/). As a result, each fingerprint image is represented by a feature vector of 7241 dimensions.

7. **Feret Face Data (FeretFace).** The FERET face image dataset has 400 facial images. There are 50 subjects of both males and females, selected randomly from the Feret face database [31]. There are 8 examples per subject. The images vary in terms of facial expressions and illumination. Each image has 150×130 pixels, resulting in an image vector of 19500 intensity values. Figure 6 shows the sample images used in this experiment.

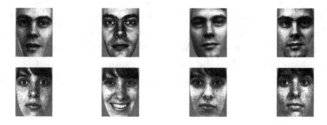

Fig. 6. Normalized Feret sample images, adapted from [30].

8. **Cooke City Hyperspectral Data (CookeCity).** The Cooke City data set consists of a hyperspectral image of Cooke City, Montana, a library of target spectral reflectances, and target (class) location information in the image (or regions of interest). Figure 7 shows a false color representation of the Cooke city scene. The self-test set of the Cooke City data set contains the ground truth information. Therefore, we only used the self-test set in this experiment. The Cooke city hyperspectral image contains 7 target classes, and the number of instances in each class varies from 9 to 34. Each instance is represented by 126 bands, resulting in a vector of 126 dimensions. The detailed information about the Cooke city hyperspectral image is provided in dirsapps.cis.rit.edu/blindtest/.

9. **Pavia University Hyperspectral Data(Pavia).** The Pavia University hyperspectral image data was captured by the ROSIS sensor during a flight over the Pavia University in northern Italy. There are 103 spectral bands, and the number of pixels is 610 by 610. The image has a resolution of 1.3 m. There are 9 target classes: Asphalt, Meadows, Gravel, Trees, Painted metal sheets, Bare soil, Bitumen, Self-Blocking

Fig. 7. False color representation of Cooke City.

bricks, and Shadows. Also, the data set has 42,776 examples, and the number of examples per target class varies from 947 to 18,649. Figure 8 shows a sample band image of the scene and the corresponding ground truth map.

10. **Indian Pines Hyperspectral Data (Pines).** This data set contains a hyperspectral image, covering the Indian Pines test site in north-western Indiana. The image is acquired by the AVIRIS sensor, and consists of 145 × 145 pixels. There are 224 spectral reflectance bands. In this experiment, there are only 200 bands after removing bands that cover the water absorption region: [104–108], [150–163], and 220. The data set has 10,249 examples and 16 target classes, which are not all mutually exclusive: Alfalfa, Corn-notill, Corn-mintill, Corn, Grass-pasture, Grass-trees, Grass-pasture-mowed, Hay-windrowed, Oats, Soybean-notill, Soybean-mintill, Soybean-clean, Wheat, Woods, Buildings-Grass-Trees-Drives, and Stone-Steel-Towers. And the number of examples per target class varies from 20 to 2,455. Figure 9 shows the image and the corresponding ground truth map.

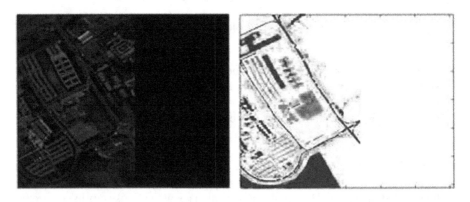

Fig. 8. Sample band representation of Pavia University scene in Northern Italy and the corresponding ground truth map.

Fig. 9. Sample band representation of the Indian Pines test site and the ground truth map.

Table 1. Average error rates obtained by the competing methods on the 10 diverse data sets.

	PCA	P-Lpp	P-Lda	LDA	OLPP
ARFace	0.307	0.245	0.245	0.394	0.314
MNIST	0.143	0.152	0.143	0.402	0.148
CatDog	0.492	0.216	0.210	0.457	0.286
MText	0.405	0.217	0.232	0.365	0.305
Iris	0.480	0.133	0.133	0.141	0.136
Finger	0.466	0.378	0.387	0.444	0.467
FeretFace	0.088	0.042	0.042	0.092	0.098
CookeCity	0.155	0.045	0.045	0.121	0.164
Pavia	0.224	0.248	0.180	0.220	0.214
Pines	0.408	0.395	0.436	0.405	0.400
Ave	0.317	0.207	0.205	0.304	0.253

5.3 Empirical Results

In this section, we report the empirical performance by each method. We have normalized all the training data to have zero mean and unit variance along each feature. We have also normalized all the test data using the corresponding training mean and variance. Since we want to highlight the techniques for learning latent variable models, we prefer simple methods for classification in latent space. Thus, we used the one nearest neighbor rule for classification in the resulting latent space. Note that all the procedural parameters such as the regularization constant λ and the kernel parameter η in the graph Laplacian (13) were selected through cross validation. Table 1 shows the 10-fold crossed validated error rates achieved by the five competing methods on the 10 data sets described above.

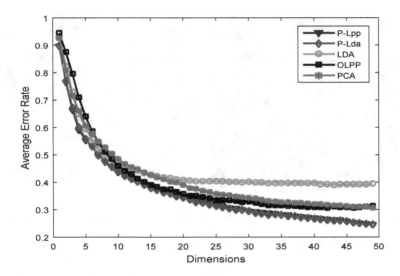

Fig. 10. Average error rates obtained by P-Lpp, P-Lda, LDA, OLPP, and PCA as a function of subspace dimensionality on the AR face data set (adapted from [30]).

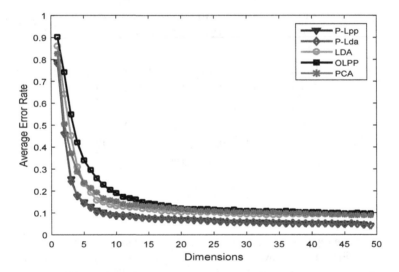

Fig. 11. Average error rates obtained by P-Lpp, P-Lda, LDA, OLPP, and PCA as a function of subspace dimensionality on the Feret face data.

The table shows that on average both P-Lpp and P-Lda performed well, compared to the competing methods for learning latent variable models. The table also shows that P-Lpp and P-Lda performed similarly on these datasets. The results show that performing classification in a latent space that is both information preserving and discriminant gives rise to better generalization than in either latent space alone.

Figure 10 shows the average error rates achieved by the competing techniques over 21 runs on the AR face dataset as a function of increasing dimensions. The plots show clearly that on average both P-Lpp and P-Lda performed better than PCA across the 49 subspaces, and consistently performed better than the remaining techniques. Also, the average error rates over the 21 runs in a subspace with 49 dimensions are shown in the first row in Table 1.

Figures 11, 12, 13, and 14 plot the 10-fold error rates computed by the competing methods on the Feret face, the Cooke City, Pavia University, and Indian Pines datasets with increasing subspace dimensionality, respectively. For the Feret face data, both P-Lpp and P-Lda consistently outperformed the competing methods across the 49 subspaces. P-Lda achieved consistently better performance in the hyperspectral datasets.

We can observe that overall the performance of P-Lpp correlates well with that of OLPP on the Indian Pines (Fig. 14). Likewise, the performance of P-Lda in general correlates well with that of LDA on the Cooke City and Pavia University data (Figs. 12 and 13). It is interesting to note that PCA performed competitively in these experiments. By placing constraints on latent variable positions, the proposed technique for learning latent variable models with discriminant regularization seems to provide better generalization.

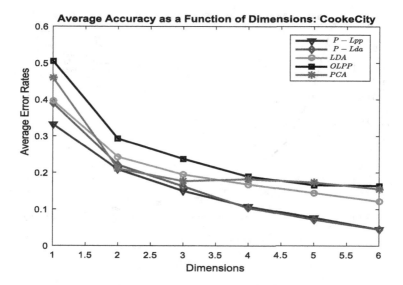

Fig. 12. Average error rates obtained by P-Lpp, P-Lda, LDA, OLPP, and PCA as a function of subspace dimensionality on the Cooke City hyperspectral data.

5.4 Performance Robustness

The empirical results show that P-Lpp and P-Lda achieved overall the best performance across the 10 diverse data sets, followed by OLPP. We ask the question of performance robustness. It is the question of how well a particular method m performs in problems

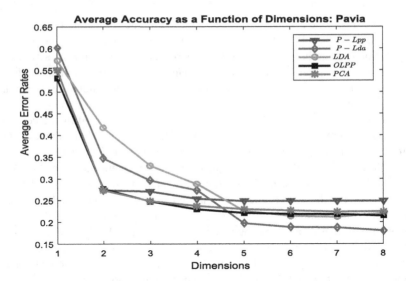

Fig. 13. Average error rates obtained by P-Lpp, P-Lda, LDA, OLPP, and PCA as a function of subspace dimensionality on the Pavia University hyperspectral data.

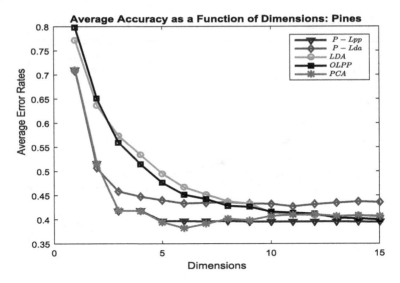

Fig. 14. Average error rates obtained by P-Lpp, P-Lda, LDA, OLPP, and PCA as a function of subspace dimensionality on the Indian Pines hyperspectral data.

that are most favorable to other methods. One possible measure of performance robustness can be described by computing the ratio r_m of the error rate err_m by method m to the smallest error rate over all methods in a particular problem. That is, we compute the following

$$r_m = err_m / \min_{1 \leq k \leq 5} err_k. \tag{21}$$

According to this measure, the best method m^* for the problem has $r_{m^*} = 1$. And for all other methods other than the best, their r_m values should be greater than one. Clearly, the larger the value of r_m, the worse the performance of method m is in relation to the best method for the problem. Therefore, the distribution of the r_m values for each method m over all the problems provides a good measurement for its performance robustness.

The distributions of the r_m values for each method over the 10 data sets are shown in Fig. 15. The boxed areas show the lower and upper quartiles of the distribution. They are separated by the median (red horizontal line). The entire range of values for each distribution is represented by the outer vertical lines.

Figure 15 shows that the performance of P-Lda was most robust over the 10 data sets. Tts error rates were the best (median = 1.0) in 7/10 of the data sets. It was no worse than 10.0% higher than the best error rate in the worst case. The next is P-Lpp. Its error rates were the best (median = 1.0) in 7/10 of the data sets. In 2/10 of the data sets, its error rates were no worse than 6% higher than the best error rate. Also, P-Lpp was no worse than 38.0% in the worst case.

Figure 15 also shows that PCA's worst error rate was 260.9% higher than the best error rate, which was worse than LDA's worst error rate (181.1% higher than the best error rate).

On the other hand, the median r_{PCA} value for PCA was 1.56. In contrast, the median r_{LDA} value for LDA was 1.645, which was worse than that of PCA. PCA achieved the best error rate on one of the data sets. LDA did not. Overall, PCA and LDA performed similarly, in terms of the distributions of the values of r_{PCA} and r_{LDA}.

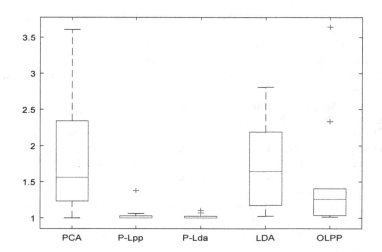

Fig. 15. Distributions of r_m (robustness) values for PCA, P-Lpp, P-Lda, LDA, and OLPP over the 10 data sets. (Color figure online)

6   Conclusion

A technique for learning latent variable models with discriminant regularization has been presented. By incorporating discriminant regularization into PCA, the proposed technique is capable of learning latent variable models that achieve better generalization. An empirical evaluation of the proposed technique against competing techniques using a variety of examples has been provided. The empirical results show that the proposed technique is competitive in the examples that have been experimented with.

References

1. Abolhasanzadeh, B.: Gaussian process latent variable model for dimensionality reduction in intrusion detection. In: 2015 23rd Iranian Conference on Electrical Engineering, pp. 674–678 (2015)
2. Amini, M., Usunier, N., Goutte, C.: Learning from multiple partially observed views-an application to multilingual text categorization. In: Advances in Neural Information Processing Systems, pp. 28–36 (2009)
3. Aved, A., Blasch, E., Peng, J.: Regularized difference criterion for computing discriminants for dimensionality reduction. IEEE Trans. Aerosp. Electron. Syst. **53**(5), 2372–2384 (2017)
4. Banerjee, B., Peng, J.: Efficient learning of multi-step best response. In: Proceedings of the Fourth International Joint Conference on Autonomous Agents and Multiagent Systems, AAMAS 2005, pp. 60–66. ACM, New York (2005)
5. Belhumeur, V., Hespanha, J., Kriegman, D.: Eigenfaces vs. Fisherfaces: recognition using class specific linear projection. IEEE Trans. Pattern Anal. Mach. Intell. **19**(7), 711–720 (1997)
6. Bellman, R.E.: Adaptive Control Processes: A Guided Tour. Princeton University Press, Princeton (1961)
7. Bourlard, H., Kamp, Y.: Auto-association by multilayer perceptrons and singular value decomposition. Biol. Cybern. **59**(4–5), 291–294 (1988)
8. Breiman, L., Friedman, J.H., Olshen, R.A., Stone, C.J.: Classification and Regression Trees. Wadsworth and Brooks, Monterey (1984)
9. Cai, D., He, X., Han, J., Zhang, H.: Orthogonal Laplacianfaces for face recognition. IEEE Trans. Image Process. **15**(11), 3608–3614 (2006)
10. Cai, L., Huang, L., Liu, C.: Age estimation based on improved discriminative Gaussian process latent variable model. Multimedia Tools Appl. **75**(19), 11977–11994 (2016)
11. Crihalmeanu, S., Ross, A., Schukers, S., Hornak, L.: A protocol for multibiometric data acquisition, storage and dissemination. Technical report, WVU, Lane Department of Computer Science and Electrical Engineering (2007)
12. Darnell, G., Georgiev, S., Mukherjee, S., Engelhardt, B.: Adaptive randomized dimension reduction on massive data. J. Mach. Learn. Res. **18**(140), 1–30 (2017)
13. Daugman, J.: How iris recognition works. IEEE Trans. Circ. Syst. Video Technol. **14**(21), 21–30 (2004)
14. Eleftheriadis, S., Rudovic, O., Pantic, M.: Discriminative shared Gaussian processes for multiview and view-invariant facial expression recognition. IEEE Trans. Image Process. **24**(1), 189–204 (2015)
15. Fukunaga, K.: Introduction to Statistical Pattern Recognition. Academic Press, San Diego (1990)

16. Gao, X., Wang, X., Tao, D., Li, X.: Supervised Gaussian process latent variable model for dimensionality reduction. IEEE Trans. Syst. Man Cybern. Part B Cybern. **41**(2), 425–434 (2011)
17. Harandi, M., Salzmann, M., Hartley, R.: Joint dimensionality reduction and metric learning: a geometric take. In: Precup, D., Teh, Y.W. (eds.) Proceedings of the 34th International Conference on Machine Learning, vol. 70, pp. 1404–1413. International Convention Centre, Sydney. PMLR (2017)
18. Hinton, G.E., Salakhutdinov, R.R.: Reducing the dimensionality of data with neural networks. Science **313**(5786), 504–507 (2006)
19. He, X., Niyogi, P.: Locality preserving projections. In: Proceedings of the 16th International Conference on Neural Information Processing Systems, NIPS 2003, pp. 153–160. MIT Press (2003)
20. Heisterkamp, D., Peng, J., Dai, H.: Feature relevance learning with query shifting for content-based image retrieval. In: Proceedings 15th International Conference on Pattern Recognition, ICPR 2000, vol. 4, pp. 250–253 (2000)
21. Howland, P., Park, H.: Generalizing discriminant analysis using the generalized singular Valuke decomposition. IEEE Trans. Pattern Anal. Mach. Intell. **26**(8), 995–1006 (2004)
22. Huo, X., et al.: Optimal reduced-rank quadratic classiers using the Fukunaga-Koontz transform, with applications to automated target recognition. In: Proceedings of SPIE Conference (2003)
23. Jiang, X., Gao, J., Wang, T., Zheng, L.: Supervised latent linear Gaussian process latent variable model for dimensionality reduction. IEEE Trans. Syst. Man Cybern. Part B Cybern. **42**(6), 1620–1632 (2012)
24. Kaluarachchi, A.C., et al.: Incorporating terminology evolution for query translation in text retrieval with association rules. In: Proceedings of the 19th ACM International Conference on Information and Knowledge Management, pp. 1789–1792 (2010)
25. Lawrence, N.: Probabilistic non-linear principal component analysis with Gaussian process latent variable models. J. Mach. Learn. Res. **6**, 1783–1816 (2005)
26. Martinez, A.M., Kak, A.: PCA versus LDA. IEEE Trans. Pattern Anal. Mach. Intell. **23**(2), 228–233 (2001)
27. Peng, J.: Efficient memory-based dynamic programming. In: Proceedings of the 12th International Conference on Machine Learning, pp. 438–446 (1995)
28. Peng, J., Zhang, P., Riedel, N.: Discriminant learning analysis. IEEE Trans. Syst. Man Cybern. Part B Cybern. **38**(6), 1614–1625 (2008)
29. Peng, J., Seetharaman, G., Fan, W., Varde, A.: Exploiting fisher and Fukunaga-Koontz transforms in chernoff dimensionality reduction. ACM Trans. Knowl. Disc. Data **7**(2), 8:1–8:25 (2013)
30. Peng, J., Aved, J.A.: Information preserving discriminant projections. In: Proceedings of the 12th International Conference on Agents and Artificial Intelligence (ICAART), pp. 162–171 (2020)
31. Phillips, P.J., et al.: The FERET database and evaluation procedure for face recognition algorithms. Image Vis. Comput. **16**(6), 295–306 (1998)
32. Pundlik, S., Woodard, D., Birchfield, S.: Non-ideal iris segmentation using graph cuts. In: IEEE Conference on Computer Vision and Pattern Recognition Workshops, pp. 1–6 (2008)
33. Rasmussen, C., Williams, C.: Gaussian Processes for Machine Learning (Adaptive Computation and Machine Learning). The MIT Press, Cambridge (2005)
34. Sarveniazi, A.: An actual survey of dimensionality reduction. Am. J. Comput. Math. **4**(2), 55–72 (2014)
35. Song, G., Wang, S., Huang, Q., Tian, Q.: Similarity Gaussian process latent variable model for multi-modal data analysis. In: 2015 IEEE International Conference on Computer Vision (ICCV), pp. 4050–4058 (2015)

36. Tipping, M., Bishop, C.: Probabilistic principal component analysis. J. Roy. Stat. Soc. Ser. B **61**(3), 611–622 (1999)
37. Ueffing, N., Simard, M., Larkin, S., Johnson, J.: NRC's PORTAGE system for WMT 2007. In: ACL-2007 Second Workshop on SMT, pp. 185–188 (2007)
38. Urtasun, R., Darrell, T.: Discriminative Gaussian process latent variable model for classification. In: Proceedings of the 24th International Conference on Machine Learning, ICML 2007, pp. 927–934. ACM, New York (2007)
39. Williams, R.J., Peng, J.: Function optimization using connectionist reinforcement learning algorithms. Connect. Sci. **3**(3), 241–268 (1991)
40. Xie, S., Fan, W., Peng, J., Verscheure, O., Ren, J.: Latent space domain transfer between high dimensional overlapping distributions. In: Proceedings of the 18th International Conference on World Wide Web, pp. 91–100 (2009)
41. Xie, P., et al.: Learning latent space models with angular constraints. In: Precup, D., Teh, Y.W. (eds.) Proceedings of the 34th International Conference on Machine Learning. Proceedings of Machine Learning Research, vol. 70, pp. 3799–3810. International Convention Centre, Sydney. PMLR (2017)
42. Yu, J., Tian, Q., Rui, T., Huang, T.S.: Integrating discriminant and descriptive information for dimension reduction and classification. IEEE Trans. Circ. Syst. Video Technol. **17**(3), 372–377 (2007)
43. Zhang, P., Peng, J., Domeniconi, C.: Kernel pooled local subspaces for classification. IEEE Trans. Syst. Man Cybern. Part B Cybern. **35**(3), 489–502 (2005)
44. Zhao, N., Mio, W., Liu, X.: A hybrid PCA-LDA model for dimension reduction. In: The 2011 International Joint Conference on Neural Networks, pp. 2184–2190 (2011)

Continuous Multi-agent Path Finding
via Satisfiability Modulo Theories (SMT)

Pavel Surynek[(✉)]

Faculty of Information Technology, Czech Technical University in Prague,
Thákurova 9, 160 00 Praha 6, Czech Republic
`pavel.surynek@fit.cvut.cz`

Abstract. We address multi-agent path finding (MAPF) with continuous movements and geometric agents, i.e. agents of various geometric shapes moving
smoothly between predefined positions. We analyze a new solving approach
based on satisfiability modulo theories (SMT) that is designed to obtain optimal
solutions with respect to common cumulative objectives. The standard MAPF is
a task of navigating agents in an undirected graph from given starting vertices
to given goal vertices so that agents do not collide with each other in vertices
or edges of the graph. In the continuous version (MAPF$^{\mathcal{R}}$), agents move in an
n-dimensional Euclidean space along straight lines that interconnect predefined
positions. Agents themselves are geometric objects of various shapes occupy-
ing certain volume of the space - circles, polygons, etc. We develop concepts
for circular omni-directional agents having constant velocities in the 2D plane
but a generalization for different shapes is possible. As agents can have different shapes/sizes and are moving smoothly along lines, a movement along certain
lines done with small agents can be non-colliding while the same movement may
result in a collision if performed with larger agents. Such a distinction rooted in
the geometric reasoning is not present in the standard MAPF. The SMT-based
approach for MAPF$^{\mathcal{R}}$ called SMT-CBS$^{\mathcal{R}}$ reformulates previous Conflict-based
Search (CBS) algorithm in terms of SMT. Lazy generation of constraints is the
key idea behind the previous algorithm SMT-CBS. Each time a new conflict is
discovered, the underlying encoding is extended with new to eliminate the conflict. SMT-CBS$^{\mathcal{R}}$ significantly extends this idea by generating also the decision
variables lazily. Generating variables on demand is needed because in the continuous case the number of possible decision variables is potentially uncountable
hence cannot be generated in advance as in the case of SMT-CBS. We compared
SMT-CBS$^{\mathcal{R}}$ and adaptations of CBS for the continuous variant of MAPF experimentally.

Keywords: Multi-agent path finding (MAPF) · Satisfiability modulo theory
(SMT) · Continuous time · Continuous space · Makespan optimal solutions ·
Sum-of-costs optimal solutions · Geometric agents

1 Introduction

Multi-agent path finding (MAPF) [13,21–23,25,28,33] is the task of navigating agents
from given starting positions to given individual goals. Usually MAPF is understood to

© Springer Nature Switzerland AG 2021
A. P. Rocha et al. (Eds.): ICAART 2020, LNAI 12613, pp. 399–420, 2021.
https://doi.org/10.1007/978-3-030-71158-0_19

be a discrete problem that takes place in undirected graph $G = (V, E)$ where agents from set $A = \{a_1, a_2, ..., a_k\}$ are placed in its vertices. The constraint that there is at most one agent per vertex is followed in the basic variant. The initial configuration of agents in vertices of the graph can be written as an assignment $\alpha_0 : A \rightarrow V$ and similarly the goal configuration as $\alpha_+ : A \rightarrow V$. The task of navigating agents can be formally expressed as a task of transforming the initial configuration of agents $\alpha_0 : A \rightarrow V$ into the goal configuration $\alpha_+ : A \rightarrow V$.

In the standard MAPF, movements are instantaneous and are possible into vacant neighbors assuming no other agent is entering the same target vertex[1]. We usually denote the configuration of agents at discrete time step t as $\alpha_t : A \rightarrow V$. Non-conflicting movements transform configuration α_t *instantaneously* into next configuration α_{t+1} so we do not consider what happens between t and $t + 1$.

To reflect various aspects of real-life applications variants of MAPF have been introduced such as those considering *kinematic constraints* [10], *large agents* [15], or *deadlines* [17] - see [16] for more variants.

This work focuses on an extension of MAPF introduced only recently [1,32] that considers continuous time and space and continuous movements of agents between predefined positions placed arbitrarily in the n-dimensional Euclidean space. The continuous version will be denoted as $MAPF^{\mathcal{R}}$. It is natural in $MAPF^{\mathcal{R}}$ to assume geometric agents of various shapes that occupy certain volume in the space - circles in the 2D space, polygons, spheres in the 3D space etc. In contrast to MAPF, where the collision is defined as the simultaneous occupation of a vertex by two agents, collisions are defined as any spatial overlap of agents' bodies in $MAPF^{\mathcal{R}}$ or a an occurrence that is too close to each other. Agents move along straight lines connecting predefined positions. Different shapes of agents' bodies play a role. Hence for example a movement along two distinct lines that is collision free when done with small agents may turn into a collision if performed with large agents.

The motivation behind introducing $MAPF^{\mathcal{R}}$ is the need to construct more realistic paths in many applications such as controlling fleets of robots or aerial drones [8,11] where continuous reasoning is closer to the reality than the standard MAPF.

1.1 Contribution

The contribution of this paper consists in showing how to apply satisfiability modulo theory (SMT) reasoning [6,18] in $MAPF^{\mathcal{R}}$ solving. This is an extension of the conference paper [30] where the usage of SMT paradigm for the makespan optimal solving of $MAPF^{\mathcal{R}}$ has been described. In this paper, we further improve the concept and adapt it for the sum-of-costs optimal solving.

The SMT paradigm constructs decision procedures for various complex logic theories by decomposing the decision problem into the propositional part having arbitrary Boolean structure and the theory part that is restricted on the conjunctive fragment. We introduce an SMT-based algorithm for finding makespan optimal solutions to $MAPF^{\mathcal{R}}$. Extending the algorithm by *nogood recording* enables finding solutions that are sum-of-costs optimal.

---

[1] Different versions of MAPF permit entering of a vertex being simultaneously vacated by another agent excluding the trivial case when agents swap their position across an edge.

1.2   Related Work and Organization

The original version of the SMT-based approach focuses on *makespan optimal* MAPF solving and builds on top of the Conflict-based Search (CBS) algorithm [22,24]. Makespan optimal solutions minimize the overall time needed to relocate all agents into their goals.

CBS tries to solve MAPF lazily by adding conflict elimination constraints on demand. It starts with the empty set of constraints. The set of constraints is iteratively refined with new conflict elimination constraints after conflicts are found in solutions for the incomplete set of constraints. Since conflict elimination constraints are disjunctive (they forbid occurrence of one or the other agent in a vertex at a time) the refinement in CBS is carried out by branching in the search process.

CBS can be adapted for MAPF$^\mathcal{R}$ by implementing conflict detection in continuous time and space while the high-level framework of the CBS algorithm remains the same as shown in [1]. In the SMT-based approach we are trying to build an *incomplete* propositional model so that if a given MAPF$^\mathcal{R}$ $\Sigma^\mathcal{R}$ has a solution of a specified makespan then the model is solvable (but the opposite implication generally does not hold). This is similar to the previous SAT-based [5] MAPF solving [27,31] where a *complete* propositional model has been constructed (that is, the given MAPF has a solution of a specified makespan if and only is the model is solvable).

The propositional model in the SMT-based approach in constructed *lazily* through conflict elimination refinements as done in CBS. The incompleteness of the model is inherited from CBS that adds constraints lazily. This is in contrast to SAT-based methods like MDD-SAT [31] where all constraints are added *eagerly* resulting in a complete model. We call our new algorithm SMT-CBS$^\mathcal{R}$. The major difference of SMT-CBS$^\mathcal{R}$ from CBS is that instead of branching the search we only add a disjunctive constraint to eliminate the conflict in SMT-CBS$^\mathcal{R}$. Hence, SMT-CBS$^\mathcal{R}$ does not branch the search at all at the high-level (the model is incrementally refined at the high-level instead).

Similarly as in the SAT-based MAPF solving we use decision propositional variables indexed by *agent* a, *vertex* v, and *time* t with the meaning that if the variable is $TRUE$ agent a appears in v at time t. However the major technical difficulty with the continuous version of MAPF is that we do not know all necessary decision variables in advance due to continuous time. After a conflict is discovered we may need new decision variables to avoid that conflict. For this reason we introduce a special decision variable generation algorithm.

The paper is organized as follows: we first introduce MAPF$^\mathcal{R}$ formally. Then we recall a variant of CBS for MAPF$^\mathcal{R}$. Details of the novel SMT-based solving algorithm SMT-CBS$^\mathcal{R}$ for finding *makespan optimal* solutions follow. Next, an experimental evaluation of SMT-CBS$^\mathcal{R}$ against the continuous version of CBS is shown. We also show a brief comparison with the standard MAPF. Finally we introduce nogood recording into the SMT-CBS$^\mathcal{R}$ to enable optimization with respect to the *sum-of-costs* objective.

1.3   MAPF with Continuous Time

We follow the definition of MAPF with continuous time denoted MAPF$^\mathcal{R}$ from [1] and [32]. MAPF$^\mathcal{R}$ shares several components with the standard MAPF: the underlying undirected graph $G = (V, E)$, set of agents $A = \{a_1, a_2, ..., a_k\}$, and the initial and goal configuration of agents: $\alpha_0 : A \to V$ and $\alpha_+ : A \to V$.

Definition 1. (MAPF$^\mathcal{R}$) *Multi-agent path finding with continuous time (MAPF$^\mathcal{R}$) is a 5-tuple $\Sigma^\mathcal{R} = (G = (V, E), A, \alpha_0, \alpha_+, \rho)$ where G, A, α_0, α_+ are from the standard MAPF and ρ determines continuous extensions as follows:*

- *$\rho.x(v), \rho.y(v)$ for $v \in V$ represent the position of vertex v in the 2D plane; to simplify notation we will use x_v for $\rho.x(v)$ and y_v for $\rho.x(v)$*
- *$\rho.velocity(a)$ for $a \in A$ determines constant velocity of agent a; simple notation $v_a = \rho.velocity(a)$*
- *$\rho.radius(a)$ for $a \in A$ determines the radius of agent a; we assume that agents are circular discs with omni-directional ability of movements; simple notation $r_a = \rho.radius(a)$*

Naturally we can define the distance between a pair of vertices u, v with $\{u, v\} \in E$ as $dist(u, v) = \sqrt{(x_v - x_u)^2 + (y_v - y_u)^2}$. Next we assume that agents have constant speed, that is, they instantly accelerate to v_a from an idle state. The major difference from the standard MAPF where agents move instantly between vertices is that in MAPF$^\mathcal{R}$ continuous movement of an agent between a pair of vertices (positions) along the straight line interconnecting them takes place. Hence we need to be aware of the presence of agents at some point in the 2D plane on the lines interconnecting vertices at any time.

Collisions may occur between agents due to their size which is another difference from the standard MAPF. In contrast to the standard MAPF, collisions in MAPF$^\mathcal{R}$ may occur not only in a single vertex or edge but also on pairs of edges (on pairs of lines interconnecting vertices). If for example two edges are too close to each other and simultaneously traversed by large agents then such a condition may result in a collision. Agents collide whenever their bodies overlap[2].

We can further extend the set of continuous properties by introducing the direction of agents and the need to rotate agents towards the target vertex before they start to move towards the target (agents are no more omni-directional). The speed of rotation in such a case starts to play a role. Also agents can be of various shapes not only circular discs [15]. For simplicity we elaborate our solving concepts for the above basic continuous extension of MAPF with circular agents only. We however note that all developed concepts can be adapted for MAPF with more continuous extensions like directional agents which only adds another dimension to indices of propositional variables.

A solution to given MAPF$^\mathcal{R}$ $\Sigma^\mathcal{R}$ is a collection of temporal plans for individual agents $\pi = [\pi(a_1), \pi(a_2), ..., \pi(a_k)]$ that are mutually collision-free. A temporal plan for agent $a \in A$ is a sequence $\pi(a) = [((\alpha_0(a), \alpha_1(a)), [t_0(a), t_1(a))); ((\alpha_1(a), \alpha_2(a)), [t_1(a), t_2(a))); ...; ((\alpha_{m(a)-1}(a), \alpha_{m(a)}(a)), (t_{m(a)-1}(a), t_{m(a)}(a)))]$ where $m(a)$ is the length of individual temporal plan and each pair $(\alpha_i(a), \alpha_{i+1}(a))$, $[t_i(a), t_{i+1}(a)))$ in the sequence corresponds to traversal event between a pair of vertices $\alpha_i(a)$ and $\alpha_{i+1}(a)$ starting at time $t_i(a)$ and finished at $t_{i+1}(a)$ (excluding).

---

[2] In our current implementation we followed a more cautious definition of the collision - it occurs even if agents appear too close to each other.

It holds that $t_i(a) < t_{i+1}(a)$ for $i = 0, 1, ..., m(a) - 1$. Moreover consecutive vertices must correspond to edge traversals or waiting actions, that is: $\{\alpha_i(a), \alpha_{i+1}(a)\} \in E$ or $\alpha_i(a) = \alpha_{i+1}(a)$; and times must reflect the speed of agents for non-wait actions, that is:

$$\alpha_i(a) \neq \alpha_{i+1}(a) \Rightarrow t_{i+1}(a) - t_i(a) = \frac{dist(\alpha_i(a), \alpha_{i+1}(a))}{v_a}.$$

In addition to this, agents must not collide with each other. One possible formal definition of a geometric collision is as follows:

Definition 2. (Collision) A collision *between individual temporal plans* $\pi(a) = [((\alpha_i(a), \alpha_{i+1}(a)), [t_i(a), t_{i+1}(a)))]_{i=0}^{m(a)}$ *and* $\pi(b) = [((\alpha_i(b), \alpha_{i+1}(a)), [t_i(b), t_{i+1}(b)))]_{i=0}^{m(b)}$ *occurs if the following condition holds:*

- $\exists i \in \{0, 1, ..., m(a)\}$ *and* $\exists j \in \{0, 1, ..., m(b)\}$ *such that:*
  - $dist([x_{\alpha_i(a)}, y_{\alpha_i(a)}; x_{\alpha_{i+1}(a)}, y_{\alpha_{i+1}(a)}]; [x_{\alpha_j(b)}, y_{\alpha_j(b)}; x_{\alpha_{j+1}(b)}, y_{\alpha_{j+1}(b)}])$ $< r_a + r_b$
  - $[t_i(a), t_{i+1}(a)) \cap [t_j(b), t_{j+1}(b)) \neq \emptyset$

(a vertex or an edge collision - two agents simultaneously occupy the same vertex or the same edge or traverse edges that are too close to each other).

The distance between two lines P and Q given by their endpoint coordinates $P = [x_1, y_1; x_2, y_2]$ and $Q = [x_1', y_1'; x_2', y_2']$ denoted $dist([x_1, y_1; x_2, y_2]; [x_1', y_1'; x_2', y_2'])$ is defined as the minimum distance between any pair of points $p \in P$ and $q \in Q$: $min\{dist(p, q) \mid p \in P \land q \in Q\}$. The definition covers degenerate cases where a line collapses into a single point. In such a case the definition of $dist$ normally works as the distance between points and between a point and a line.

The definition among other types of collisions covers also a case when an agent waits in vertex v and another agent passes through a line that is too close to v. We note that situations classified as collisions according to the above definition may not always result in actual collisions where agents' bodies overlap; the definition is overcautious in this sense.

Alternatively we can use more precise definition of collisions that reports collisions if and only if an actual overlap of agents' bodies occurs. This however requires more complex equations or simulations and cannot be written as simple as above. The presented algorithmic framework is however applicable for any kind of complex definition of collision as the definition enters the process as an external parameter.

The duration of individual temporal plan $\pi(a)$ is called an individual makespan; denoted $\mu(\pi(a)) = t_{m(a)}$. The overall makespan of MAPF$^{\mathcal{R}}$ solution $\pi = [\pi(a_1), \pi(a_2), ..., \pi(a_k)]$ is defined as $max_{i=1}^{k}(\mu(\pi(a_i)))$.

The **sum-of-costs** is another important objective used in the context of MAPF [23,32]. Calculated as the summation over all agents of times they spend moving before arriving to the goal. Due to its more complex calculation, the sum-of-costs objective is more challenging to be integrated in the SMT-based solving framework.

The individual makespan is sometimes called an *individual cost*. A *sum-of-cost* for given temporal plan $\pi(a)$ is defined as $\sum_{i=1}^{k} \mu(\pi(a_i))$.

An example of MAPF$^{\mathcal{R}}$ and makespan optimal solution is shown in Fig. 1. We note that the standard makespan optimal solution yields makespan suboptimal solution when interpreted as MAPF$^{\mathcal{R}}$.

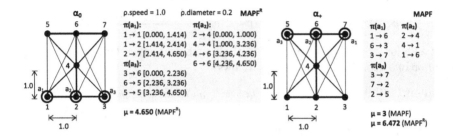

Fig. 1. An example of MAPF$^{\mathcal{R}}$ instance on a $[3, 1, 3]$-graph with three agents and its makespan optimal solution (an optimal solution of the corresponding standard MAPF is shown too) [30].

Through the straightforward reduction of MAPF to MAPF$^{\mathcal{R}}$ it can be observed that finding a makespan optimal solution with continuous time is an NP-hard problem [19,29,35].

2   Solving MAPF with Continuous Time

We will describe here how to find optimal solution of MAPF$^{\mathcal{R}}$ using the *conflict-based search* (CBS) [22]. CBS uses the idea of resolving conflicts lazily; that is, a solution of MAPF instance is not searched against the complete set of movement constraints. Instead of forbidding all possible collisions between agents we start with initially empty set of collision forbidding constraints that gradually grows as new conflicts appear. CBS originally developed for MAPF can be modified for MAPF$^{\mathcal{R}}$ as shown in [1]: let us call the modification CBS$^{\mathcal{R}}$.

2.1   Conflict-Based Search

CBS$^{\mathcal{R}}$ is shown using pseudo-code in Algorithm 1. The high-level of CBS$^{\mathcal{R}}$ searches a *constraint tree* (CT) using a priority queue (ordered according to the makespan or other cumulative cost) in the breadth first manner. CT is a binary tree where each node N contains a set of collision avoidance constraints $N.constraints$ - a set of triples $(a_i, \{u, v\}, [t_0, t_+))$ forbidding occurrence of agent a_i in edge $\{u, v\}$ (or in vertex u if $u = v$) at any time between $[t_0, t_+)$, a solution $N.\pi$ - a set of k individual temporal plans, and the makespan $N.\mu$ of the current solution.

The low-level process in CBS$^{\mathcal{R}}$ associated with node N searches temporal plan for individual agent with respect to set of constraints $N.constraints$. For given agent a_i, this is the standard single source shortest path search from $\alpha_0(a_i)$ to $\alpha_+(a_i)$ that at time t must avoid a set of edges (vertices) $\{\{u, v\} \in E \mid (a_i, \{u, v\}, [t_0, t_+)) \in$

Algorithm 1. Basic CBS$^{\mathcal{R}}$ algorithm for makespan optimal MAPF solving with continuous time, pseudo-code from [30].

```
 1  CBS^R_MAKE (Σ^R = (G = (V, E), A, α_0, α_+, ρ))
 2      R.constraints ← ∅
 3      R.π ← {shortest temporal plan from α_0(a_i) to α_+(a_i) | i = 1, 2, ..., k}
 4      R.μ ← max^k_{i=1} μ(N.π(a_i))
 5      OPEN ← ∅
 6      insert R into OPEN
 7      while OPEN ≠ ∅ do
 8          N ← min_μ(OPEN)
 9          remove-Min_μ(OPEN)
10          collisions ← validate-Plans(N.π)
11          if collisions = ∅ then
12              return N.π
13          let (a_i, {u, v}, [t_0, t_+)) × (a_j, {u', v'}, [t'_0, t'_+)) ∈ collisions
14          [τ_0, τ_+) ← [t_0, t_+) ∩ [t'_0, t'_+)
15          for each (a, {w, z}) ∈ {(a_i, {u, v}), (a_j, {u', v'})} do
16              N'.constraints ← N.constraints ∪ {(a, {w, z}, [τ_0, τ_+))}
17              N'.π ← N.π
18              update(a, N'.π, N'.conflicts)
19              N'.μ ← ∑^k_{i=1} μ(N'.π(a_i))
20              insert N' into OPEN
```

$N.constraints \wedge t \in [t_0, t_+)\}$. Various intelligent single source shortest path algorithms can be applied here such as A* [9].

CBS$^{\mathcal{R}}$ stores nodes of CT into priority queue OPEN sorted according to the ascending makespan. At each step CBS takes node N with the lowest makespan from OPEN and checks if $N.\pi$ represent non-colliding temporal plans. If there is no collision, the algorithms returns valid MAPF$^{\mathcal{R}}$ solution $N.\pi$. Otherwise the search branches by creating a new pair of nodes in CT - successors of N. Assume that a collision occurred between agents a_i and a_j when a_i traversed $\{u, v\}$ during $[t_0, t_+)$ and a_j traversed $\{u', v'\}$ during $[t'_0, t'_+)$. This collision can be avoided if either agent a_i or agent a_j does not occupy $\{u, v\}$ or $\{u', v'\}$ respectively during $[t_0, t_+) \cap [t'_0, t'_+) = [\tau_0, \tau_+)$. These two options correspond to new successor nodes of N: N_1 and N_2 that inherit set of conflicts from N as follows: $N_1.conflicts = N.conflicts \cup \{(a_i, \{u, v\}, [\tau_0, \tau_+))\}$ and $N_2.conflicts = N.conflicts \cup \{(a_j, \{u', v'\}, [\tau_0, \tau_+))\}$. $N_1.\pi$ and $N_1.\pi$ inherit plans from $N.\pi$ except those for agent a_i and a_j respectively that are recalculated with respect to the new sets of conflicts. After this N_1 and N_2 are inserted into OPEN.

Definition of collisions comes as a parameter to the algorithm though the implementation of validate-Plans procedure. We can switch to the less cautious definition of collisions that reports a collision after agents actually overlap their bodies. This can be done through changing the validate-Plans procedure while the rest of the algorithm remains the same.

2.2 A Satisfiability Modulo Theory (SMT) Approach

A close look at CBS reveals that it operates similarly as problem solving in *satisfiability modulo theories* (SMT) [6, 18]. The basic use of SMT divides a satisfiability problem in some complex theory T into an abstract propositional part that keeps the Boolean structure of the decision problem and a simplified decision procedure $DECIDE_T$ that decides fragment of T restricted on *conjunctive formulae*. A general T-formula Γ being decided for satisfiability is transformed to a *propositional skeleton* by replacing its atoms with propositional variables. The standard SAT-solving procedure then decides what variables should be assigned $TRUE$ in order to satisfy the skeleton - these variables tells what atoms hold in Γ. $DECIDE_T$ then checks if the conjunction of atoms assigned $TRUE$ is valid with respect to axioms of T. If so then satisfying assignment is returned and we are finished. Otherwise a conflict from $DECIDE_T$ (often called a *lemma*) is reported back to the SAT solver and the skeleton is extended with new constraints resolving the conflict. More generally not only new constraints are added to resolve a conflict but also new variables i.e. atoms can be added to Γ.

The above observation inspired us to the idea to rephrase CBS$^{\mathcal{R}}$ in terms of SMT. T will be represented by a theory with axioms describing movement rules of MAPF$^{\mathcal{R}}$; a theory we will denote $T_{MAPF^{\mathcal{R}}}$[3].

A plan validation procedure known from CBS will act as $DECIDE_{MAPF^{\mathcal{R}}}$ and will report back a set of conflicts found in the current solution. The propositional part working with the skeleton will be taken from existing propositional encodings of the standard MAPF such as the MDD-SAT [31] provided that constraints forbidding conflicts between agents will be omitted (at the beginning). In other words, we only preserve constraints ensuring that propositional assignments form proper paths for agents but each agent is treated as if it is alone in the instance.

2.3 Decision Variable Generation

MDD-SAT introduces decision variables $\mathcal{X}_v^t(a_i)$ and $\mathcal{E}_{u,v}^t(a_i)$ for discrete time-steps $t \in \{0, 1, 2, ...\}$ describing occurrence of agent a_i in v or the traversal of edge $\{u, v\}$ by a_i at time-step t. We refer the reader to [31] for the details of how to encode constraints of top of these variables. As an example we show here a constraint stating that if agent a_i appears in vertex u at time step t then it has to leave through exactly one edge connected to u or wait in u.

$$\mathcal{X}_u^t(a_i) \Rightarrow \bigvee_{v \mid \{u,v\} \in E} \mathcal{E}_{u,v}^t(a_i) \vee \mathcal{E}_{u,u}^t(a_i), \tag{1}$$

$$\sum_{v \mid \{u,v\} \in E} \mathcal{E}_{u,v}^t(a_i) + \mathcal{E}_{u,u}^t(a_i) \leq 1 \tag{2}$$

Vertex collisions expressed for example by the following constraint are omitted. The constraint says that in vertex v and time step t there is at most one agent.

---

[3] The formal details of the theory $T_{MAPF^{\mathcal{R}}}$ are not relevant from the algorithmic point of view. Nevertheless let us note that the signature of $T_{MAPF^{\mathcal{R}}}$ consists of non-logical symbols describing agents' positions at a time such as $at(a, u, t)$ - agent a at vertex u at time t.

Algorithm 2. Generation of decision variables in the SMT-based algorithm for MAPF$^\mathcal{R}$ solving, pseudo-code from [30].

---

1 **generate-Decisions** $(\Sigma^\mathcal{R} = (G = (V, E), A, \alpha_0, \alpha_+, \rho), a_i, conflicts, \mu_{max})$
2   VAR $\leftarrow \emptyset$
3   **for** *each* $a \in A$ **do**
4   OPEN $\leftarrow \emptyset$
5   insert $(\alpha_0(a), 0)$ into OPEN
6   VAR $\leftarrow$ VAR $\cup \{\mathcal{X}_{\alpha_0(a)}^{t_0}(a)\}$
7   **while** OPEN $\neq \emptyset$ **do**
8            $(u, t) \leftarrow \min_t(\text{OPEN})$
9   remove-Min$_t$(OPEN)
10   **if** $t \leq \mu_{max}$ **then**
11   **for** *each* v *such that* $\{u, v\} \in E$ **do**
12                $\Delta t \leftarrow dist(u, v)/v_a$
13   insert $(v, t + \Delta t)$ into OPEN
14   VAR $\leftarrow$ VAR $\cup \{\mathcal{E}_{u,v}^{t}(a), \mathcal{X}_{v}^{t+\Delta t}(a)\}$
15   **for** *each* v *such that* $\{u, v\} \in E \cup \{u, u\}$ **do**
16   **for** *each* $(a, \{u, v\}, [t_0, t_+)) \in conflicts$ **do**
17   **if** $t_+ > t$ **then**
18   insert (u, t_+) into OPEN
19   VAR $\leftarrow$ VAR $\cup \{\mathcal{X}_{u}^{t_+}(a)\}$

20   **return** VAR

$$\sum_{a_i \in A \mid v \in V} \mathcal{X}_v^t(a_i) \leq 1 \tag{3}$$

A significant difficulty in MAPF$^\mathcal{R}$ is that we need decision variables with respect to continuous time. Fortunately we do not need a variable for any possible time but only for important moments.

If for example the duration of a conflict in neighbor v of u is $[t_0, t_+)$ and agent a_i residing in u at $t \geq t_0$ wants to enter v then the earliest time a_i can do so is t_+ since before it would conflict in v (according to the above definition of collisions). On the other hand if a_i does not want to waste time (let us note that we search for a makespan optimal solution), then waiting longer than t_+ is not desirable. Hence we only need to introduce decision variable $\mathcal{E}_{u,v}^{t_+}(a_i)$ to reflect the situation.

Generally when having a set of conflicts we need to generate decision variables representing occurrence of agents in vertices and edges of the graph at important moments with respect to the set of conflicts. The process of decision variable generation is formally described as Algorithm 2. It performs breadth-first search (BFS) on G using two types of actions: *edge traversals* and *waiting*. The edge traversal is the standard operation from BFS. Waiting is performed for every relevant period of time with respect to the end-times in the set of conflicts of neighboring vertices.

As a result each conflict during variable generation through BFS is treated as both present and absent which in effect generates all possible important moments.

Procedure generate-Decision generates decision variables that correspond to actions started on or before specified limit μ_{max}. For example variables corresponding to edge traversal started at $t < \mu_{max}$ and finished as $t' > \mu_{max}$ are included (line 10). Variables corresponding to times greater than μ_{max} enable determining what should be the next relevant makespan limit to test (see the high-level algorithm for details). Assume having a decision node corresponding to vertex u at time t at hand. The procedure first adds decision variables corresponding to edge traversals from u to neighbors denoted v (lines 11–14). Then all possible relevant waiting actions in u with respect to its neighbors v are generated. Notice that waiting with respect to conflicts in u are treated as well.

2.4 Eliminating Branching in CBS by Disjunctive Refinements

The SMT-based algorithm itself is divided into two procedures: SMT-CBS$^{\mathcal{R}}$ representing the main loop and SMT-CBS-Fixed$^{\mathcal{R}}$ solving the input MAPF$^{\mathcal{R}}$ for a fixed maximum makespan μ. The major difference from the standard CBS is that there is no branching at the high-level. The set of conflicts is iteratively collected during the entire execution of the algorithm whenever a collision is detected.

Procedures *encode-Basic* and *augment-Basic* build formula $\mathcal{F}(\mu)$ over decision variables generated using the aforementioned procedure. The encoding is inspired by the MDD-SAT approach but ignores collisions between agents. That is, $\mathcal{F}(\mu)$ constitutes an *incomplete model* for a given input $\Sigma^{\mathcal{R}}$: $\Sigma^{\mathcal{R}}$ is solvable within makespan μ then $\mathcal{F}(\mu)$ is satisfiable.

Conflicts are resolved by adding disjunctive constraints (lines 13–15 in Algorithm 4). The collision is avoided in the same way as in the original CBS that is one of the colliding agent does not perform the action leading to the collision. Consider for example a collision on two edges between agents a_i and a_j as follows: a_i traversed $\{u, v\}$ during $[t_0, t_+)$ and a_j traversed $\{u', v'\}$ during $[t'_0, t'_+)$.

These two movements correspond to decision variables $\mathcal{E}^{t_0}_{u,v}(a_i)$ and $\mathcal{E}^{t'_0}_{u',v'}(a_j)$ hence elimination of the collision caused by these two movements can be expressed as the following disjunction: $\neg\mathcal{E}^{t_0}_{u,v}(a_i) \vee \neg\mathcal{E}^{t'_0}_{u',v'}(a_j)$. At level of the propositional formula there is no information about the semantics of a conflict happening in the continuous space; we only have information in the form of above disjunctive refinements. The disjunctive refinements are propagated at the propositional level from $DECIDE_{MAPF^{\mathcal{R}}}$ that verifies solutions of incomplete propositional models.

The set of pairs of collected disjunctive conflicts is propagated across entire execution of the algorithm (line 16 in Algorithm 4).

Algorithm 3 shows the main loop of SMT-CBS$^{\mathcal{R}}$. The algorithm checks if there is a solution for given MAPF$^{\mathcal{R}}$ $\Sigma^{\mathcal{R}}$ of makespan μ. The algorithm starts at the lower bound for μ that is obtained as the duration of the longest temporal plan from individual temporal plans ignoring other agents (lines 3–4).

Then μ is iteratively increased in the main loop (lines 5–9). The algorithm relies on the fact that the solvability of MAPF$^{\mathcal{R}}$ w.r.t. cumulative objective like the makespan behaves as a non decreasing monotonic function. Hence trying increasing makespans

Algorithm 3. High-level of the SMT-based MAPF$^{\mathcal{R}}$ solving - makespan optimal version [30].

```
 1  SMT-CBS$_{MAKE}^{\mathcal{R}}$ ($\Sigma^{\mathcal{R}} = (G = (V, E), A, \alpha_0, \alpha_+, \rho)$)
 2      conflicts ← ∅
 3      π ← {π*(a_i) a shortest temporal plan from α_0(a_i) to α_+(a_i) | i = 1, 2, ..., k}
 4      μ ← max_{i=1}^{k} μ(π(a_i))
 5      while TRUE do
 6          (π, conflicts, μ_{next}) ← SMT-CBS-Fixed$_{MAKE}^{\mathcal{R}}$(Σ^{\mathcal{R}}, conflicts, μ)
 7          if π ≠ UNSAT then
 8              return π
 9          μ ← μ_{next}
```

eventually leads to finding the optimal makespan provided we do not skip any relevant makespan μ. The next makespan to try will then be obtained by taking the current makespan plus the smallest duration of the continuing movement (line 19 of Algorithm 4). The iterative scheme for trying larger makespans follows MDD-SAT [31].

3   Evaluation of the Makespan Optimal Version

In this section we present results of the experimentation with SMT-CBS$^{\mathcal{R}}$ for makespan optimal MAPF$^{\mathcal{R}}$ solving. We implemented SMT-CBS$^{\mathcal{R}}$ in C++ to evaluate its performance[4]. SMT-CBS$^{\mathcal{R}}$ was implemented on top of Glucose 4 SAT solver [3] which ranks among the best SAT solvers according to recent SAT solver competitions [4]. The incremental mode of the SAT solver has been used - that is, when the formula has been modified the solver was not consulted from scratch but instead learned clauses are preserved from the previous run.

It turned out to be important to generate decision variables in a more advanced way than presented in Algorithm 2. We need to prune out decisions from that the goal vertex cannot be reached under given makespan bound μ_{max}. That is whenever we have a decision (u, t) such that $t + \Delta t > \mu_{max}$, where $\Delta t = dist_{estimate}(u, \alpha_+(a))/v_a$ and $dist_{estimate}$ is a lower bound estimate of the distance between a pair of vertices, we rule out that decision from further consideration. Moreover we apply a postprocessing step in which we iteratively remove decisions that have no successors. The propositional model is generated only after this preprocessing.

In addition to SMT-CBS$^{\mathcal{R}}$ we re-implemented in C++ CBS$^{\mathcal{R}}$, currently the only alternative solver for MAPF$^{\mathcal{R}}$ based on own dedicated search [1]. The distinguishing feature of CBS$^{\mathcal{R}}$ is that at the low-level it uses a more complex single source shortest path algorithm that searches for paths that avoid forbidden intervals, a so-called *safe-interval path planning* (SIPP) [34].

Our implementation of CBS$^{\mathcal{R}}$ used the standard heuristics to improve the performance such as the preference of resolving *cardinal conflicts* [7]. In the preliminary

---

[4] The complete source codes will be made available to enable reproducibility of presented results on the author's website: http://users.fit.cvut.cz/surynpav/research/icaart2020.

Algorithm 4. Low-level of the SMT-based MAPF$^{\mathcal{R}}$ solving, makespan optimal version [30]

---

1 **SMT-CBS-Fixed$^{\mathcal{R}}_{MAKE}$($\Sigma^{\mathcal{R}}$, $conflicts$, μ)**

2   VAR $\leftarrow$ generate-Decisions($\Sigma^{\mathcal{R}}$, $conflicts$, μ)

3      $\mathcal{F}(\mu) \leftarrow$ encode-Basic(VAR, $\Sigma^{\mathcal{R}}$, $conflicts$, μ)

4   **while** $TRUE$ **do**

5          $assignment \leftarrow$ consult-SAT-Solver($\mathcal{F}(\mu)$)

6   **if** $assignment \neq UNSAT$ **then**

7              $\pi \leftarrow$ extract-Solution($assignment$)

8              $collisions \leftarrow$ validate-Plans(π)   /* $DECIDE_{MAPF\mathcal{R}}$ */

9   **if** $collisions = \emptyset$ **then**

10   **return** $(\pi, \emptyset, UNDEF)$

11   **for** *each* $(a_i, \{u, v\}, [t_0, t_+)) \times (a_j, \{u', v; \}, [t'_0, t'_+)) \in collisions$ **do**

12                 $\mathcal{Y} \leftarrow (u = v)$? $\mathcal{X}^{t_0}_u(a_i) : \mathcal{E}^{t_0}_{u,v}(a_i)$

13                 $\mathcal{Z} \leftarrow (u' = v')$? $\mathcal{X}^{t'_0}_{u'}(a_j) : \mathcal{E}^{t'_0}_{u',v'}(a_j)$

14                 $\mathcal{F}(\mu) \leftarrow \mathcal{F}(\mu) \cup \{\neg\mathcal{Y} \vee \neg\mathcal{Z}\}$

15                 $[\tau_0, \tau_+) \leftarrow [t_0, t_+) \cap [t'_0, t'_+)$

16                 $conflicts \leftarrow$
                   $conflicts \cup \{(a_i, \{u, v\}, [\tau_0, \tau_+)), (a_j, \{u', v'\}, [\tau_0, \tau_+))\}$

17   VAR $\leftarrow$ generate-Decisions($\Sigma^{\mathcal{R}}$, $conflicts$, μ)

18             $\mathcal{F}(\mu) \leftarrow$ augment-Basic($\mathcal{F}(\mu)$, VAR, $\Sigma^{\mathcal{R}}$, $conflicts$, μ)

19   **else**

20             $\mu_{next} \leftarrow \min\{t \mid \mathcal{X}^t_u(a_i) \in$ VAR $\wedge t > \mu)\}$

21   **return** *(UNSAT, $conflicts$, μ_{next})*

---

tests with SMT-CBS$^{\mathcal{R}}$, we initially tried to resolve against single cardinal conflict too but eventually it turned out to be more efficient to resolve against all discovered conflicts (the presented pseudo-code shows this variant)[5, 6].

3.1   Benchmarks and Setup

SMT-CBS$^{\mathcal{R}}$ and CBS$^{\mathcal{R}}$ were tested on synthetic benchmarks consisting of *layered graphs*, *grids*, game maps [26]. The layered graph of height h denoted $[l_1, l_2, ..., l_h]$-graph consists of h layers of vertices placed horizontally above each other in the 2D plane (see Fig. 1 for $[3, 1, 3]$-graph). More precisely the i-th layer is placed horizontally at $y = i$. Layers are centered horizontally and the distance between consecutive points in the layer is 1.0. Size of all agents was 0.2 in radius.

We measured runtime and the number of decisions/iterations to compare the performance of SMT-CBS$^{\mathcal{R}}$ and CBS$^{\mathcal{R}}$. Small layered graphs consisting of 2 to 5 layers with

---

[5] All experiments were run on a system with Ryzen 7 3.0 GHz, 16 GB RAM, under Ubuntu Linux 18.

[6] To enable reproducibility of presented results we will provide complete source code of our solvers on author's web: http://users.fit.cvut.cz/surynpav/icaart2020.

Average **runtime** and **makespan** (μ) on selected layered graphs

Graph	CBS^R	SMT-CBS^R	μ MAPF^R	CBS	μ MAPF
[2,2]	2.78	**1.22**	2.41	0.01	2.00
[3,1,3]	17.91	**2.33**	3.65	0.02	2.75
[4,2,2,4]	19.34	**4.78**	3.80	0.02	2.67
[5,3,1,3,5]	57.23	**6.11**	6.78	0.03	3.15
[5,3,5,3,5]	-	**19.93**	5.39	0.03	3.75

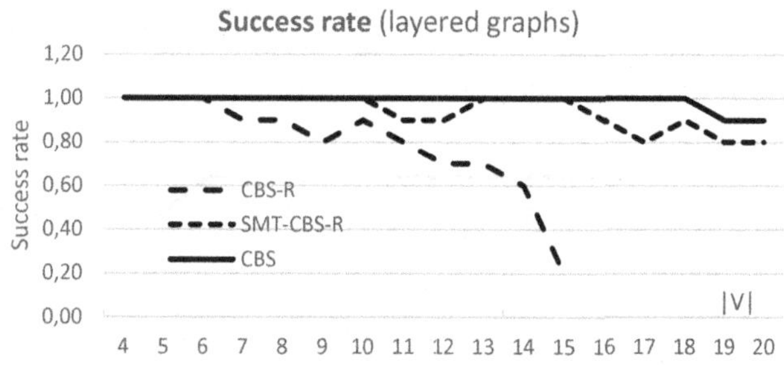

Fig. 2. Comparison of CBS^R and SMT-CBS^R in terms of average runtime, makespan, and success rate on layered graphs. The standard CBS on the corresponding standard MAPF is shown too (times are in seconds). Makespan is shown for the case when the instance is interpreted as the standard MAPF and as MAPF^R [30].

up to 5 vertices per layer were used in tests. Three consecutive layers are always fully interconnected by edges. There is not edge across more than three layers of the graphs. That is in graphs with more than 3 layers agents cannot go directly to the goal vertex.

In all tests agents started in the 1-st layer and finished in the last h-th layer. To obtain instances of various difficulties random permutations of agents in the starting and goal configurations were used (the 1-st layer and h-th layer were fully occupied in the starting and goal configuration respectively). If for instance agents are ordered identically in the starting and goal configuration with $h \leq 3$, then the instance is relatively easy as it is sufficient that all agents move simultaneously straight into their goals.

We also used grids of sizes 8×8 and 16×16 with no obstacles in our tests. Initial and goal configuration of agents have been generated randomly. In contrast to MAPF benchmarks where grids are 4-connected we used interconnection with all vertices in the neighborhood up to certain distance called 2^k-neighborhood in [1]. A similar setup has been used in game maps (Dragon Age). The difference here is that the game maps are larger and contain obstacles.

Ten random instances were generated for individual graph. The timeout for all tests has been set to 1 min in layered graphs and small grids and 10 min for game maps. Results from instances finished under this timeout were used to calculate average runtimes.

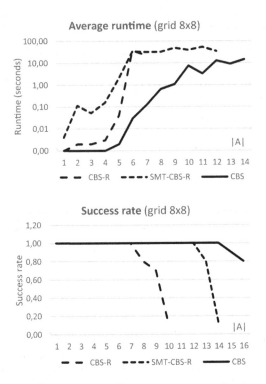

Fig. 3. Comparison of CBS$^{\mathcal{R}}$ and SMT-CBS$^{\mathcal{R}}$ on 8×8 grid with 2^k neighborhood ($k = 3$) [30].

3.2 Comparison of MAPF$^{\mathcal{R}}$ and MAPF Solving

Part of the results obtained in our experimentation with layered graphs is shown in Fig. 2. The general observation from our runtime evaluation is that MAPF$^{\mathcal{R}}$ is significantly harder than the standard MAPF. When continuity is ignored, makespan optimal solutions consist of fewer steps. But due to regarding all edges to be unit in MAPF, the standard makespan optimal solutions yield significantly worse continuous makespan (this effect would be further manifested if we use longer edges).

SMT-CBS$^{\mathcal{R}}$ outperforms CBS$^{\mathcal{R}}$ on tested instances significantly. CBS$^{\mathcal{R}}$ reached the timeout many more times than SMT-CBS$^{\mathcal{R}}$. In the absolute runtimes, SMT-CBS$^{\mathcal{R}}$ is faster by factor of 2 to 10 than CBS$^{\mathcal{R}}$.

In terms of the number of decisions, SMT-CBS$^{\mathcal{R}}$ generates order of magnitudes fewer iterations than CBS$^{\mathcal{R}}$. This is however expected as SMT-CBS$^{\mathcal{R}}$ shrinks the entire search tree into a single branch in fact. We note that branching within the search space in case of SMT-CBS$^{\mathcal{R}}$ is deferred into the SAT solver where even more branches may appear.

In case of small grids and large maps (Figs. 3, 4 and 5), the difference between CBS$^{\mathcal{R}}$ and SMT-CBS$^{\mathcal{R}}$ is generally smaller but still for harder instances SMT-CBS$^{\mathcal{R}}$ tends to have better runtime and success rate. We attribute the smaller difference

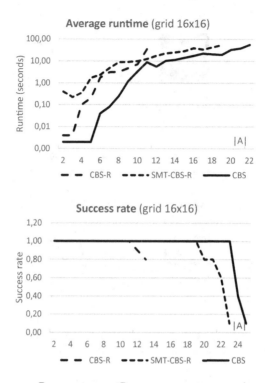

Fig. 4. Comparison of CBS$^\mathcal{R}$ and SMT-CBS$^\mathcal{R}$ on 16×16 grid with 2^k neighborhood ($k = 3$) [30].

between the two algorithms to higher regularity in grids compared to layered graphs that exhibit higher combinatorial difficulty.

4 Sum-of-Costs Bounds and Nogood Recording

We modified the SMT-based MAPF$^\mathcal{R}$ solving framework for the sum-of-costs objective. Again the SMT-based algorithm for the sum-of-costs variants is divided into two procedures: SMT-CBS$^\mathcal{R}_{SOC}$ representing the main loop (Algorithm 5) and SMT-CBS-Fixed$^\mathcal{R}_{SOC}$ solving the input MAPF$^\mathcal{R}$ for a fixed maximum makespan μ and sum-of-costs ξ (Algorithm 6).

Procedures *encode-Basic* and *augment-Basic* in Algorithm 6 build a formula according to given RDDs and the set of collected collision avoidance constraints. New collisions are resolved **lazily** by adding *mutexes* (disjunctive constraints). A collision is avoided in the same way as in the makespan optimal variant. Collision eliminations are tried until a valid solution is obtained or until a failure for current μ and ξ which means to try bigger makespan and sum-of-costs.

After resolving all collisions we check whether the sum-of-costs bound is satisfied by plan π. This can be done easily by checking if $\mathcal{X}^t_u(a_i)$ variables across all agents together yield higher cost than ξ or not. If cost bound ξ is exceeded then corresponding

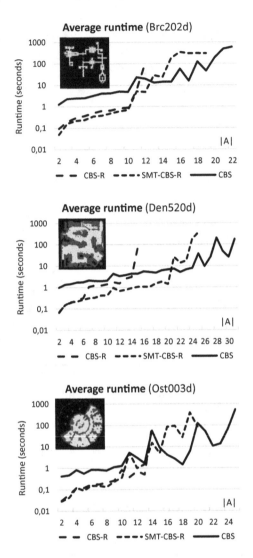

Fig. 5. Comparison of CBS$^{\mathcal{R}}$ and SMT-CBS$^{\mathcal{R}}$ on game maps (Dragon Age) with 2^k neighborhood ($k = 3$).

nogood is recorded and added to $\mathcal{F}(\mu)$ and the algorithm continues by searching for a new satisfying assignment to $\mathcal{F}(\mu)$ now taking all recorded *nogoods* into account. The nogood says that $\mathcal{X}_u^t(a_i)$ variables that jointly exceed ξ cannot be simultaneously set to *TRUE*.

Formally, the nogood constraint can be represented as a set of variables $\{\mathcal{X}_{u_1}^{t_1}(a_1),$ $\mathcal{X}_{u_2}^{t_2}(a_2), \ldots \mathcal{X}_{u_k}^{t_k}(a_k)\}$. We say the nogood to be *dominated* by another nogood $\{\mathcal{X}_{u_1}^{t_1'}(a_1), \mathcal{X}_{u_2}^{t_2'}(a_2), \ldots \mathcal{X}_{u_k}^{t_k'}(a_k)\}$ if and only if $t_i' \leq t_i$ for $i = 1, 2, \ldots k$ and $\exists i \in \{1, 2, \ldots, k\}$ such that $t_i' < t_i$. To make the nogood reasoning more efficient we do not

Algorithm 5. High-level of SMT-CBS$^{\mathcal{R}}$ for the sum-of-costs objective.

1 **SMT-CBS**$^{\mathcal{R}}_{SOC}$ $(\Sigma^{\mathcal{R}} = (G = (V, E), A, \alpha_0, \alpha_+, \rho))$
2      $constraints \leftarrow \emptyset$
3      $\pi \leftarrow \{\pi^*(a_i)$ a shortest temporal plan from $\alpha_0(a_i)$ to $\alpha_+(a_i) \mid i = 1, 2, ..., k\}$
4      $\mu \leftarrow \max^k_{i=1} \mu(\pi(a_i)); \xi \leftarrow \sum^k_{i=1} \mu(\pi(a_i))$
5   **while** $TRUE$ **do**
6          $(\pi, constraints, \mu_{next}, \xi_{next}) \leftarrow$ SMT-CBS-Fixed$^{\mathcal{R}}_{SOC}(\Sigma^{\mathcal{R}}, constraints, \mu,$
            $\xi)$
7   **if** $\pi \neq UNSAT$ **then**
8   **return** π
9          $\mu \leftarrow \mu_{next}; \xi \leftarrow \xi_{next}$

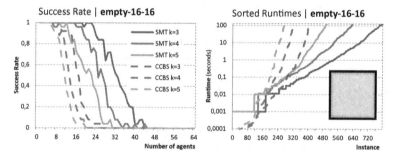

Fig. 6. Comparison of SMT-CBS$^{\mathcal{R}}$ and CCBS on empty-16-16. **Left:** Success rate (the ratio of solved instances out of 25 under 120 s), the higher plot is better. **Right:** and sorted runtimes where the lower plot is better are shown.

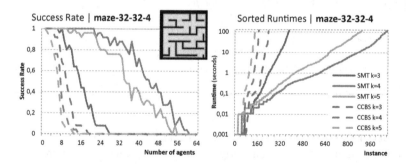

Fig. 7. Comparison of SMT-CBS$^{\mathcal{R}}$ and CCBS on maze-32-32-4. Surprisingly the best performance with SMT-CBS$^{\mathcal{R}}$ highly connected neighborhoods ($K = 4, 5$ is easier than $K = 3$.

need to store nogoods that are dominated by some previously discovered nogood. In such case however, the single nogood does not forbid one particular assignment but all assignments that could lead to dominated nogoods.

Algorithm 6. Low-level of SMT-CBS$^{\mathcal{R}}$

---

1 **SMT-CBS-Fixed**$^{\mathcal{R}}_{SOC}(\Sigma^{\mathcal{R}}, cons, \mu, \xi)$
2   RDD $\leftarrow$ build-RDDs($\Sigma^{\mathcal{R}}, cons, \mu$)
3     $\mathcal{F}(\mu) \leftarrow$ encode-Basic(RDD, $\Sigma^{\mathcal{R}}, cons, \mu$)
4   **while** $TRUE$ **do**
5        $assignment \leftarrow$ consult-SAT-Solver($\mathcal{F}(\mu)$)
6   **if** $assignment \neq UNSAT$ **then**
7           $\pi \leftarrow$ extract-Solution($assignment$)
8           $collisions \leftarrow$ validate-Plans(π)
9   **if** $collisions = \emptyset$ **then**
10   **while** $TRUE$ **do**
11                $nogoods \leftarrow$ validate-Cost(π, ξ)
12   **if** $nogoods = \emptyset$ **then**
13   **return** $(\pi, \emptyset, UNDEF, UNDEF)$
14                $\mathcal{F}(\mu) \leftarrow \mathcal{F}(\mu) \cup nogoods$
15                $assignment \leftarrow$ consult-SAT-Solver($\mathcal{F}(\mu)$)
16   **if** $assignment = UNSAT$ **then**
17                    $(\mu_{next}, \xi_{next}) \leftarrow$ calc-Next-Bounds($\mu, \xi, cons$, RDD)
18   **return** $(UNSAT, cons, \mu_{next}, \xi_{next})$
19                $\pi \leftarrow$ extract-Solution($assignment$)
20   **else**
21   **for** $each (m_i \times m_j) \in collisions$ $where$ $m_i = (a_i, (u_i, v_i), [t_i^0, t_i^+))$
               and $m_j = (a_j, (u_j, v_j), [t_j^0, t_j^+))$ **do**
22                $\mathcal{F}(\mu) \leftarrow \mathcal{F}(\mu) \wedge (\neg \mathcal{E}_{u_i, v_i}^{t_i^0, t_i^+}(a_i) \vee \neg \mathcal{E}_{u_j, v_j}^{t_j^0, t_j^+}(a_j))$
23                $([\tau_i^0, \tau_i^+); [\tau_j^0, \tau_j^+)) \leftarrow$ resolve-Collision(m_i, m_j)
24                $cons \leftarrow cons \cup \{[(a_i, (u_i, v_i), [\tau_i^0, \tau_i^+)); (a_j, (u_j, v_j), [\tau_j^0, \tau_j^+))]\}$
25   RDD $\leftarrow$ build-RDDs($\Sigma^{\mathcal{R}}, cons, \mu$)
26             $\mathcal{F}(\mu) \leftarrow$ augment-Basic(RDD, $\Sigma^{\mathcal{R}}, cons$)
27   **else**
28          $(\mu_{next}, \xi_{next}) \leftarrow$ calc-Next-Bounds($\mu, \xi, cons$, RDD)
29   **return** $(UNSAT, cons, \mu_{next}, \xi_{next})$

The set of pairs of collision avoidance constraints is propagated across entire execution of the algorithm. Constraints originating from a single collision are grouped in pairs so that it is possible to introduce mutexes for colliding movements discovered in previous steps.

Algorithm 3 shows the main loop of SMT-CBS$^{\mathcal{R}}$. The algorithm checks if there is a solution for $\Sigma^{\mathcal{R}}$ of makespan μ and sum-of-costs ξ. It starts at the lower bound for μ and ξ obtained as the duration of the longest from shortest individual temporal plans ignoring other agents and the sum of these lengths respectively.

Then μ and ξ are iteratively increased in the main loop following the style of SAT-Plan [12]. The algorithm relies on the fact that the solvability of MAPF$^{\mathcal{R}}$ w.r.t. cumulative objective like the sum-of-costs or makespan behaves as a non decreasing function. Hence trying increasing makespan and sum-of-costs eventually leads to finding the optimum provided we do not skip any relevant value.

We need to ensure important property in the makespan/sum-of-costs increasing scheme: any solution of sum-of-costs ξ has the makespan of at most μ. The next sum-of-costs to try is be obtained by taking the current sum-of-costs plus the smallest duration of the continuing movement (lines 17–27 of Algorithm 6).

The following proposition is a direct consequence of soundness of CCBS and soundness of the encoding (Proposition 1) and soundness of the makespan/sum-of-costs increasing scheme (proof omitted).

Proposition 1. *The SMT-CBS$^{\mathcal{R}}$ algorithm returns sum-of-costs optimal solution for any solvable MAPF$^{\mathcal{R}}$ instance $\Sigma^{\mathcal{R}}$.*

5 Evaluation of the Sum-of-Costs Optimal Variant

The sum-of-costs optimal version of SMT-CBS$^{\mathcal{R}}$ and CCBS were tested on benchmarks from the movingai.com collection [26]. We tested algorithms on three categories of benchmarks:

  (i) **small** empty grids (presented representative benchmark empty-16-16),
 (ii) **medium** sized grids with regular obstacles (presented maze-32-32-4),
(iii) **large** game maps (presented ost003d, a map from Dragon Age game).

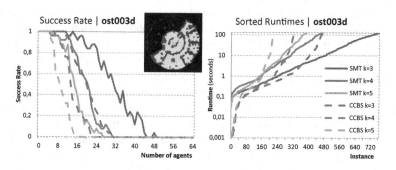

Fig. 8. Comparison of SMT-CBS$^{\mathcal{R}}$ and CCBS on ost003d. SMT-CBS$^{\mathcal{R}}$ is fastest for $K = 3$ but for higher K the performance decreases significantly.

In each benchmark, we interconnected cells using the 2^K-neighborhood [20] for $K = 3, 4, 5$ - the same style of generating benchmarks as used in [2] ($K = 2$ corresponds to MAPF hence not omitted). Instances consisting of k agents were generated by taking first k agents from random scenario files accompanying each benchmark on movingai.com. Having 25 scenarios for each benchmarks this yields to 25 instances per number of agents.

Part of the results obtained in our experimentation is presented in this section[7]. For each presented benchmark we show *success rate* as a function of the number of agents. That is, we calculate the ratio out of 25 instances per number of agents where the tested algorithm finished under the timeout of 120 s. In addition to this, we also show concrete runtimes sorted in the ascending order. Results for one selected representative benchmark from each category are shown in Figs. 6, 7 and 8.

The observable trend is that the difficulty of the problem increases with increasing size of the K−neighborhood with notable exception of maze-32-32-4 for $K = 4$ and $K = 5$ which turned out to be easier than $K = 3$ for SMT-CBS$^{\mathcal{R}}$.

Throughout all benchmarks SMT-CBS$^{\mathcal{R}}$ tends to outperform CCBS. The dominance of SMT-CBS$^{\mathcal{R}}$ is most visible in medium sized benchmarks. CCBS is, on the other hand, faster in instances containing few agents. The gap between SMT-CBS$^{\mathcal{R}}$ and CCBS is smallest in large maps where SMT-CBS$^{\mathcal{R}}$ struggles with relatively big overhead caused by the big size of the map (the encoding is proportionally big). Here SMT-CBS$^{\mathcal{R}}$ wins only in hard cases.

6   Discussion and Conclusion

We extended the approach based on *satisfiability modulo theories* (SMT) for solving MAPF$^{\mathcal{R}}$ from the makespan objective (described in the conference version of the paper [30]) towards the sum-of-costs objective. Our approach builds on the idea of treating constraints lazily as suggested in the CBS algorithm but instead of branching the search after encountering a conflict we refine the propositional model with the conflict elimination disjunctive constraint as it has been done in previous application of SMT in the standard MAPF. Bounding the sum-of-costs is done in similar lazy way through introducing nogoods incrementally. If it is detected that a conflict free solution exceeds given cost bound then decisions that jointly induce cost greater than given bound are forbidden via a nogood (that is, at least one of these decisions must not be taken). As nogoods storing all possible nogoods representing cases when the cost bound is exceeded could be inefficient, we introduce a concept of nogood dominance. It is sufficient to store important nogoods only while all dominated nogoods are enforced automatically.

SMT-CBS$^{\mathcal{R}}$ was compared with CCBS [2], currently the only alternative algorithm for MAPF$^{\mathcal{R}}$ that modifies the standard CBS algorithm, on a number of benchmarks. The outcome of our comparison is that SMT-CBS$^{\mathcal{R}}$ performs well against CCBS. The best results SMT-CBS$^{\mathcal{R}}$ are observable on medium sized benchmarks with regular obstacles. We attribute the better runtime results of SMT-CBS$^{\mathcal{R}}$ to more efficient handling of disjunctive conflicts in the underlying SAT solver through *propagation*, *clause learning*, and other mechanisms. On the other hand SMT-CBS$^{\mathcal{R}}$ is less efficient on large instances with few agents.

The important restriction which our concept rely on is that agents cannot move completely freely in the continuous space. We strongly assume that agents only move on the fixed embedding of finite graph $G = (V, E)$ into some continuous space where vertices are assigned points and edges are assigned curves on which the definition of

---

[7] All experiments were run on a system with Ryzen 7 3.0 GHz, 16 GB RAM, under Ubuntu Linux 18.

smooth movement is possible. Hence for example using curves other than straight lines for interconnecting vertices does not change the high-level SMT-CBS$^{\mathcal{R}}$.

We plan to extend the RDD generation scheme to directional agents where we need to add the third dimension in addition to space (vertices) and time: *direction* (angle). The work on MAPF$^{\mathcal{R}}$ could be further developed into multi-robot motion planning in continuous configuration spaces [14].

Acknowledgement. This work has been supported by GAČR - the Czech Science Foundation, grant registration number 19-17966S.

References

1. Andreychuk, A., Yakovlev, K., Atzmon, D., Stern, R.: Multi-agent pathfinding (MAPF) with continuous time CoRR ArXiv:abs/1901.05506 (2019). http://arxiv.org/abs/abs/1901.05506
2. Andreychuk, A., Yakovlev, K.S., Atzmon, D., Stern, R.: Multi-agent pathfinding with continuous time. In: Proceedings of IJCAI 2019, pp. 39–45 (2019)
3. Audemard, G., Simon, L.: Predicting learnt clauses quality in modern SAT solvers. In: IJCAI, pp. 399–404 (2009)
4. Balyo, T., Heule, M.J.H., Järvisalo, M.: SAT competition 2016: recent developments. In: AAAI 2017, pp. 5061–5063 (2017)
5. Biere, A., Heule, M., van Maaren, H., Walsh, T.: Handbook of Satisfiability. Frontiers in Artificial Intelligence and Applications, vol. 185, p. 980. IOS Press, The Netherlands (2009)
6. Bofill, M., Palahí, M., Suy, J., Villaret, M.: Solving constraint satisfaction problems with SAT modulo theories. Constraints **17**(3), 273–303 (2012). https://doi.org/10.1007/s10601-012-9123-1
7. Boyarski, E., et al.: ICBS: improved conflict-based search algorithm for multi-agent pathfinding. In: IJCAI, pp. 740–746 (2015)
8. Cáp, M., Novák, P., Vokrínek, J., Pechoucek, M.: Multi-agent RRT: sampling-based cooperative pathfinding. Proceedings of AAMAS 2013, pp. 1263–1264 (2013)
9. Hart, P.E., Nilsson, N.J., Raphael, B.: A formal basis for the heuristic determination of minimum cost paths. IEEE Trans. Syst. Sci. Cybern. (SSC) **4**(2), 100–107 (1968)
10. Hönig, W., et al.: Summary: multi-agent path finding with kinematic constraints. In: Proceedings of IJCAI 2017, pp. 4869–4873 (2017)
11. Janovsky, P., Cáp, M., Vokrínek, J.: Finding coordinated paths for multiple holonomic agents in 2-D polygonal environment. In: Proceedings of AAMAS 2014, pp. 1117–1124 (2014)
12. Kautz, H.A., Selman, B.: Unifying sat-based and graph-based planning. In: Proceedings of IJCAI 1999, pp. 318–325 (1999)
13. Kornhauser, D., Miller, G.L., Spirakis, P.G.: Coordinating pebble motion on graphs, the diameter of permutation groups, and applications. In: FOCS 1984, pp. 241–250 (1984)
14. LaValle, S.M.: Planning Algorithms. Cambridge University Press, Cambridge (2006)
15. Li, J., Surynek, P., Felner, A., Ma, H., Koenig, S.: Multi-agent path finding for large agents. In: Proceedings of AAAI 2019. AAAI Press (2019)
16. Ma, H., et al.: Overview: generalizations of multi-agent path finding to real-world scenarios CoRR ArXiv:abs/1702.05515 (2017). http://arxiv.org/abs/1702.05515
17. Ma, H., Wagner, G., Felner, A., Li, J., Kumar, T.K.S., Koenig, S.: Multi-agent path finding with deadlines. In: Proceedings of IJCAI 2018, pp. 417–423 (2018)
18. Nieuwenhuis, R.: SAT modulo theories: getting the best of SAT and global constraint filtering. In: Proceeding of CP 2010, pp. 1–2 (2010)

19. Ratner, D., Warmuth, M.K.: NxN puzzle and related relocation problem. J. Symb. Comput. **10**(2), 111–138 (1990)
20. Rivera, N., Hernández, C., Baier, J.A.: Grid pathfinding on the 2k neighborhoods. In: Proceedings of AAAI 2017, pp. 891–897 (2017)
21. Ryan, M.R.K.: Exploiting subgraph structure in multi-robot path planning. J. Artif. Intell. Res. (JAIR) **31**, 497–542 (2008)
22. Sharon, G., Stern, R., Felner, A., Sturtevant, N.: Conflict-based search for optimal multi-agent pathfinding. Artif. Intell. **219**, 40–66 (2015)
23. Sharon, G., Stern, R., Goldenberg, M., Felner, A.: The increasing cost tree search for optimal multi-agent pathfinding. Artif. Intell. **195**, 470–495 (2013)
24. Sharon, G., Stern, R., Felner, A., Sturtevant, N.R.: Conflict-based search for optimal multi-agent path finding. In: AAAI (2012)
25. Silver, D.: Cooperative pathfinding. In: AIIDE, pp. 117–122 (2005)
26. Sturtevant, N.R.: Benchmarks for grid-based pathfinding. Comput. Intell. AI Games **4**(2), 144–148 (2012)
27. Surynek, P.: Towards optimal cooperative path planning in hard setups through satisfiability solving. In: Anthony, P., Ishizuka, M., Lukose, D. (eds.) PRICAI 2012. LNCS, vol. 7458, pp. 564–576. Springer, Berlin, Heidelberg (2012). https://doi.org/10.1007/978-3-642-32695-0_50
28. Surynek, P.: A novel approach to path planning for multiple robots in bi-connected graphs. ICRA **2009**, 3613–3619 (2009)
29. Surynek, P.: An optimization variant of multi-robot path planning is intractable. In: AAAI 2010. AAAI Press (2010)
30. Surynek, P.: On satisfisfiability modulo theories in continuous multi-agent path finding: compilation-based and search-based approaches compared. In: Rocha, A.P., Steels, L., van den Herik, H.J. (eds.) ICAART 2020, vol. 2, pp. 182–193. SciTePress, Portugal (2020)
31. Surynek, P., Felner, A., Stern, R., Boyarski, E.: Efficient SAT approach to multi-agent path finding under the sum of costs objective. In: ECAI, pp. 810–818 (2016)
32. Walker, T.T., Sturtevant, N.R., Felner, A.: Extended increasing cost tree search for non-unit cost domains. In: Proceedings of IJCAI 2018, pp. 534–540 (2018)
33. Wang, K., Botea, A.: MAPP: a scalable multi-agent path planning algorithm with tractability and completeness guarantees. JAIR **42**, 55–90 (2011)
34. Yakovlev, K., Andreychuk, A.: Any-angle pathfinding for multiple agents based on SIPP algorithm. In: Proceedings of the Twenty-Seventh International Conference on Automated Planning and Scheduling, ICAPS 2017, Pittsburgh, Pennsylvania, USA, June 18–23, 2017, p. 586 (2017)
35. Yu, J., LaValle, S.M.: Optimal multi-robot path planning on graphs: structure and computational complexity. CoRR ArXiv:abs/1507.03289 (2015)

Unsupervised Feature Value Selection
Based on Explainability

Kilho Shin[1(⊠)], Kenta Okumoto[2], David Lawrence Shepard[3], Akira Kusaba[6],
Takako Hashimoto[4], Jorge Amari[1], Keisuke Murota[1], Junnosuke Takai[1],
Tetsuji Kuboyama[1], and Hiroaki Ohshima[5]

[1] Gakushuin University, Tokyo, Japan
yoshihiro.shin@gakushuin.ac.jp
[2] Japan Post Bank, Tokyo, Japan
[3] Evidental Health, California, CA, USA
[4] Chiba University of Commerce, Chiba, Japan
[5] University of Hyogo, Kobe, Japan
[6] Kyushu University, Fukuoka, Japan

Abstract. The problem of feature selection has been an area of considerable research in machine learning. Feature selection is known to be particularly difficult in unsupervised learning because different subgroups of features can yield useful insights into the same dataset. In other words, many theoretically-right answers may exist for the same problem. Furthermore, designing algorithms for unsupervised feature selection is technically harder than designing algorithms for supervised feature selection because unsupervised feature selection algorithms cannot be guided by class labels. As a result, previous work attempts to discover intrinsic structures of data with heavy computation such as matrix decomposition, and require significant time to find even a single solution. This paper proposes a novel algorithm, named Explainability-based Unsupervised Feature Value Selection (EUFVS), which enables a paradigm shift in feature selection, and solves all of these problems. EUFVS requires only a few tens of milliseconds for datasets with thousands of features and instances, allowing the generation of a large number of possible solutions and select the solution with the best fit. Another important advantage of EUFVS is that it selects feature values instead of features, which can better explain phenomena in data than features. EUFVS enables a paradigm shift in feature selection. This paper explains its theoretical advantage, and also shows its applications in real experiments. In our experiments with labeled datasets, EUFVS found feature value sets that explain labels, and also detected useful relationships between feature value sets not detectable from given class labels.

Keywords: Feature selection · Unsupervised learning · Clustering

1 Introduction

Feature selection is one of the classical problems of machine learning. While many methods have been developed for supervised learning because the problem is relatively

© Springer Nature Switzerland AG 2021
A. P. Rocha et al. (Eds.): ICAART 2020, LNAI 12613, pp. 421–444, 2021.
https://doi.org/10.1007/978-3-030-71158-0_20

easy given the presence of class labels, in unsupervised learning, no such labels are available and the problem is classically hard.

In supervising learning, a target phenomenon is predetermined and is described in a dataset through class labels associated with individual instances. Each instance of the dataset is a vector of values of the same dimensionality, and each dimension is referred to as a feature. The objective of feature selection in supervised learning is to select as few features as possible with high explanatory ability of the target phenomenon. Since it is theoretically evident that fewer features cannot have more explanatory ability, the objective of supervised feature selection is to find an optimal balance to this trade-off between the number of features and the explanatory ability that they bear. The explanatory ability of features, however, can be understood in multiple ways. One typical way is to define it through statistical or information-theoretic indices like correlation coefficients and mutual information. Another is to define it as the potential predictive power of the features, which can be measured by accuracy of prediction by classifiers, when the values of the features and the class labels of instances are input into the classifiers. Different definitions of explanatory ability may lead us to different conclusions to the question of what is the best result of feature selection. In fact, feature selection methods for obtaining high explanatory ability defined through statistical and information-theoretic indices are categorized as filter-type feature selection, while methods belonging to the wrapper-type and embedded-type feature selection aim to realize high predictive performance for particular classifiers. Nevertheless, it is common in any case that the target phenomenon is given and unchanging, and instances' class labels play a critical role in feature selection.

In contrast, unsupervised feature selection operates without a definite solution or source of truth, because a target phenomenon is not pre-defined. What counts as the "right" result in unsupervised feature selection is unclear. We refer to this as the *indefiniteness problem*. It is as if we were traveling without knowing our destination, and had to decide if we reached the right destination when we arrived.

One possible solution to the indefiniteness problem is using clustering to generate pseudo-labels for each instance. Clustering is the process of categorizing instances based on their similarity. For example, when instances are plotted as points in a Euclidean space, similarity between two instances can be defined as the Euclidean distance between the corresponding points. By assuming that clusters define class labels, we can reduce unsupervised feature selection to supervised feature selection. Eventually, some unsupervised feature selection algorithms proposed in the literature first determine pseudo-labels through clustering and then apply supervised feature selection to explain the pseudo-labels [8, 9, 12].

Using clustering to generate pseudo-class labels, however, does not solve the indefiniteness problem, because diverse definitions of similarity exist, and different definitions lead to different sets of selected features. For example, the L^∞ distance between $(x_1, \ldots, x_n)$ and $(y_1, \ldots, y_n)$ is identical to $\max\{|x_i - y_i| \mid i = 1, \ldots, n\}$ and evidently yields a totally different similarity measure than the Euclidean distance does. This issue also occurs for other methods known in the literature like methods to select features so as to preserve manifold structures [4, 7, 25] and data-specific structures [21, 22].

In principle, the indefiniteness problem cannot be solved, as shown by the following thought experiment. A DNA array of human beings determines a sequence of genes, and each gene corresponds to an individual biological function. Given a particular biological function, for example, a particular genetic disease, identifying the gene that causes the function is nothing more than supervised feature selection: each gene is a feature. Unsupervised feature selection for a DNA array requires to identify *some* gene without specifying a particular biological function, and we see that, in theory, a great number of right answers exists.

Thus, in this paper, we accept the indefiniteness problem as an inherent limitation of unsupervised feature selection and propose a new approach to address this issue. The key is the development of an unsupervised feature selection algorithm with the following properties:

- High time efficiency
- Hyperparameters for selecting different features

By leveraging such an algorithm, we can run many iterations of the algorithm with different hyperparameter values and can obtain many different answers (sets of features). From these results, we choose the most appropriate answer according to our purpose.

In fact, the main contribution of this paper is to propose a novel algorithm, namely, *Explainability-based Unsupervised Feature Value Selection* (EUFVS), which is both highly efficient and has hyperparameters for selecting different feature sets. In fact, EUFVS requires only a few tens of milliseconds to obtain a single answer for a dataset with thousands of features and thousands of instances. EUFVS is based on the algorithm presented in [19]. For example, EUFVS selects feature values instead of features. This idea was initially introduced in [19] and yields the advantages of more concrete and more efficient interpretation of selection results. On the other hand, EUFVS has two key differences:

- EUFVS is theoretically based on the novel concept of *explainability*;
- EUFVS takes two hyper-parameters rather than a single hyper-parameter, which change the search space of the algorithm in two independent directions, and as a result, can output a wider range of answers.

This paper is organized as follows. Section 2 introduces some mathematical notations and explains some mathematical concepts used in this paper. Section 3 compares supervised and unsupervised feature selection in more detail, and Sect. 4 explains the advantages of feature value selection over feature selection. In Sect. 5, we introduce the concept of explainability and our algorithm, EUFVS. Section 6 is devoted to reporting the results of our experiments to evaluate effectiveness of our algorithm.

2 Formalization and Notations

In this paper, a dataset D is a set of instances, and $\mathcal{F}$ denotes the entire set of the features that describe D. A feature $f \in \mathcal{F}$ is a function $f : D \to R(f)$, where $R(f)$ denotes the range of f, which is a finite set of values.

More formally, we canonically determine a probability space as follows and can view features as random variables. We define a sample space Ω as $\prod_{f \in \mathcal{F}} R(f)$ and a σ-algebra Σ as $\mathfrak{P}(\Omega)$, the power set of Ω. Then, the dataset D introduces an empirical probability measure $p : \mathfrak{P}(\Omega) \to [0, 1]$: For an element $v \in \Omega$, $p(\{v\})$ is determined by the ratio of the number of occurrences of v in D to the size of D, that is, $p(\{v\}) = \frac{|\{x \in D | x = v\}|}{|D|}$; For a set $S \in \mathfrak{P}(\Omega)$, we let $p(S) = \sum_{v \in S} p(\{v\})$. Evidently, the triplet (Ω, Σ, p) determines a probability space, which is also known as an *empirical probability space*. Furthermore, we identify a feature f with the projection $\pi_f : \Omega \to R(f)$, and hence, we can view f as a random variable. Thus, we can view f in two different ways, as a function $f : D \to R(f)$ and as a function $f : \prod_{f \in S} R(f) \to R(f)$. This is natural, however, because the support of a multiset D is a subset of Ω.

Moreover, we identify a finite set of features $\{f_1, \ldots, f_n\} \subseteq \mathcal{F}$ with the product of random variables $f_1 \times \cdots \times f_n : \Omega \to R(f_1) \times \cdots \times R(f_n)$. Under this definition, the probability distribution for a feature set is identical to the joint probability distribution of the random variables (features) involved.

By viewing feature sets, say S and T, as random variables, we can apply many useful information theoretical indices to S and T. Such indices include information entropy $H(S)$, mutual information $I(S; T)$, normalized mutual information $\mathrm{NMI}(S; T)$, Bayesian risk $\mathrm{Br}(S; T)$ and complementary Bayesian risk $\overline{\mathrm{Br}}(S; T)$. In general, these indices are defined as follows for arbitrary random variables X and Y:

$$H(X) = - \sum_{x \in R(X)} \Pr(X = x) \log_2 \Pr(X = x);$$

$$I(X; Y) = \sum_{(x,y) \in R(X) \times R(Y)} \left[\Pr(X = x, Y = y) \cdot \log_2 \frac{\Pr(X = x, Y = y)}{\Pr(X = x) \Pr(Y = y)} \right];$$

$$\mathrm{NMI}(X; Y) = \frac{2 \cdot I(X; Y)}{H(X) + H(Y)};$$

$$\mathrm{Br}(X; Y) = 1 - \sum_{x \in R(X)} \max_{y \in R(Y)} \Pr(X = x, Y = y);$$

$$\overline{\mathrm{Br}}(X; Y) = 1 - \mathrm{Br}(X; Y).$$

In the equations above, we assume that the range $R(X)$ and $R(Y)$ of random variables X and Y are finite, but however, these indices can be defined for more general settings: A random variable $X : \Omega \to R(X)$ is a measurable function from a probability space (Ω, Σ, p) to a measure space $(R(X), \mathcal{A}, \mu)$, and a Radon-Nikodym derivative of $p \circ X^{-1}$ (probability density function) $f : R(X) \to \mathbb{R}$, if present, satisfies $\Pr[X \in A] \triangleq p(X^{-1}(A)) = \int_A f d\mu$ for any $A \in \mathcal{A}$. Therefore, the information entropy $H(X)$ of X, for example, is defined by $H(X) = \int_{R(X)} -f \log_2 f d\mu$.

The Shannon information (or information content) of an event observing a value x for a random variable X is defined by $- \log_2 \Pr[X = x]$. It is interpreted as the quantity of information that the event carries, and the information entropy $H(X)$ is the mean across all the possible observables of X. Moreover, when we simultaneously observe

$X = x$ and $Y = y$, $-\log_2 \Pr[X = x] - \log_2 \Pr[Y = y] - (-\log_2 Pr[X = x, Y = y])$ quantifies the overlap of Shannon information between the events of $X = x$ and $Y = y$. The mutual information $I(X;Y)$ is the mean of the overlap, and therefore, quantifies overall correlational relation between observables of X and Y. In fact, we have:

- $I(X;Y) = 0$, if, and only if, X is independent of Y;
- $I(X;Y) = H(Y)$, if, and only if, Y is totally dependent on X, that is, $\Pr[Y = y \mid X = x]$ is either 0 or 1 for any x and y.

The normalized mutual information $\text{NMI}(X;Y)$, on the other hand, is defined by the harmonic mean of $\frac{I(X;Y)}{H(X)}$ and $\frac{I(X;Y)}{H(Y)}$, and hence, takes values in $[0,1]$. We have:

- $\text{NMI}(X;Y) = 0$, if, and only if, X is independent of Y;
- $\text{NMI}(X;Y) = 1$, if, and only if, X and Y are isomorphic as random variables.

Bayesian risk $\text{Br}(X;Y)$ also quantifies correlation of X to Y, which takes values in $\left[0, \frac{|R(Y)|-1}{|R(Y)|}\right]$. In contrast to mutual information, a smaller value of $\text{Br}(X;Y)$ indicates a tighter correlation. This is why we use $\overline{\text{Br}}(X;Y) = 1 - \text{Br}(X;Y)$ in some cases. In particular, we have:

- $\text{Br}(X;Y) = 0$, if, and only if, Y is totally dependent on X;
- $\overline{\text{Br}}(X;Y) = 1$, if, and only if, Y is totally dependent on X.

The inequality below describes the relationship between $I(X;Y)$ and $\overline{\text{Br}}(X;Y)$ [17]:

$$-\log_2 \overline{\text{Br}}(X;Y) \leq H(Y) - I(X;Y)$$

$$\leq -\overline{\text{Br}}(X;Y) \log_2 \overline{\text{Br}}(X;Y) + \text{Br}(X;Y) \log_2 \frac{\text{Br}(X;Y)}{|R(Y)| - 1}. \qquad (1)$$

In the remainder of this paper, we suppose that D is a dataset described by a feature set $\mathcal{F}$, which consists of only categorical features. Furthermore, unless otherwise noted, a feature f is supposed to be a member of $\mathcal{F}$, and a feature set S is a subset of $\mathcal{F}$.

3 Supervised Feature Selection Vs. Unsupervised Feature Selection

The most significant difference between feature selection in supervised learning and feature selection in unsupervised learning lies in whether class labels can be used as effective guides when selecting features. We will first review the literature on supervised feature selection.

The literature shows that the following four principles are commonly considered in designing supervised feature selection algorithms:

- Maintaining high class relevance;
- Reducing the number of selected features;
- Reducing the internal redundancy of selected features;
- Reducing the information entropy of selected features.

In the following illustration, we assume that S is a feature set selected by any feature selection algorithm from the entire feature set $\mathcal{F}$ that describes a dataset D. We also let C denote the random variable that yields class labels.

The class relevance of S represents the extent to which the features of S correlate to class labels and can typically be measured by the mutual information $I(S;C)$. In fact, $I(S;C)$ quantifies the part of the information content $H(C)$ of C that is also born by S. And hence, the class relevance $I(S;C)$ of S cannot exceed the entire information content $H(C)$ or the class relevance $I(\mathcal{F};C)$ of $\mathcal{F}$.

On the other hand, the purpose of feature selection is indeed to reduce the number of features to be used for explaining class labels. By its nature, the class relevance of selected features is a monotonically-increasing function with respect to the inclusion relation. In fact, for mutual information, we have $I(T;C) \leq I(S;C)$, if $T \subseteq S$. Therefore, the most fundamental problem of supervised feature detection can be stated as follows:

The fundamental problem of supervised feature selection.

Eliminate the maximum number of features while minimizing the resulting reduction of class relevance.

We have two important categories of features to eliminate or not to select.

Irrelevant features bear only a small amount of information content useful for explaining class labels. A feature f with small mutual information $I(f;C)$ is irrelevant.

Redundant features, on the other hand, bear content information that is mostly covered by the remaining features. For example, we suppose that S is a set of features selected tentatively. A redundant feature $f \in S$ makes $H(S) - H(S \setminus \{f\})$ sufficiently small. This implies that $I(S;C) - I(S \setminus \{f\};C)$ is also sufficiently small.

In the literature, the well-known feature selection algorithm MRMR (Minimum Redundancy and Maximum Relevance) [11] tries to eliminate irrelevant features and redundant features. To determine a feature f to add to the tentative solution S, it intends to evaluate the index of

$$b(f,S) = (I(S,f;C) - I(S;C)) - \frac{I(S;f)}{|S|},$$

which quantifies a balance between contribution to class relevance and increase of redundancy by adding f to S. Computing $b(f,S)$ is, however, costly, and MRMR uses the following approximation.

$$b(f,S) \approx b'(f,S) = I(f;C) - \frac{\sum_{f' \in S} I(f;f')}{|S|}. \tag{2}$$

Algorithm 1 describes MRMR. The asymptotic time complexity of MRMR is estimated by $O(k^2 |\mathcal{F}| |D|)$.

MRMR is one of the most well-known feature selection algorithms and in fact has been not only intensively studied but also used widely in practice [2,5,10,13,14,20,23, 23,26]. CFS [6] is another feature selection algorithm that is widely used in practice.

Algorithm 1. MRMR [11].

Require: A dataset D described by $\mathcal{F} \cup \{C\}$; and $k < |\mathcal{F}|$.
Ensure: A feature subset $S \subseteq \mathcal{F}$ with $|S| = k$.
 1: Let $S = \emptyset$.
 2: **while** $|S| < k$ **do**
 3:     Let $f \in \arg\max\{b'(f, S) \mid f \in \mathcal{F} \setminus S\}$.
 4:     Let $S = S \cup \{f\}$.
 5: **end while**
 6: Return S.

It is also based on the same principle as MRMR but uses a different formula than Eq. (2) to evaluate a balance of class relevance and interior redundancy.

These algorithms, however, encounter the problem of ignoring feature interaction [24]. We say that two or more features *mutually interact* when each individual feature has only low class relevance, but the group of these features has high class relevance. The aforementioned algorithms, which only evaluate the information entropy of individual features, cannot detect mutual feature interaction, and are likely to discard interacting features, which can result in a loss of class relevance.

Zhao et al. [24] pointed out the importance of this issue and proposed INTER-ACT, the first algorithm that evaluates feature interaction and realizes practical time-efficiency at the same time. INTERACT has led to the development of many algorithms including LCC [15, 16], which improve INTERACT in both accuracy (when used with classifiers) and time-efficiency. INTERACT and LCC use the complementary Bayesian risk $\overline{\mathrm{Br}}(S;C)$ to measure class relevance of S. Equation (1) describes the correlational relation between $\overline{\mathrm{Br}}(S;C)$ and $I(S;C)$. LCC takes a single hyper-parameter t, which specifies a lower limit of class relevance of the output feature set. Algorithm 2 describes the algorithm of LCC. Also, CWC [15, 18] is equivalent to LCC with $t = 1$.

Algorithm 2. LCC [15,16].

Require: A dataset D described by a feature set $\mathcal{F} \cup \{C\}$; and a threshold $t \in [0, 1]$.
Ensure: A minimal feature subset $S \subseteq \mathcal{F}$ with $\overline{\mathrm{Br}}(S;C) \geq t\overline{\mathrm{Br}}(\mathcal{F};C)$.
 1: Number the features of $\mathcal{F}$ so that $f_1, \ldots, f_{|\mathcal{F}|}$ are in a decreasing order of $\mathrm{NMI}(f_i;C)$.
 2: Let $S = \mathcal{F}$ and $i = n_{|\mathcal{F}|}$.
 3: **while** $i \geq 1$ **do**
 4:     Let $j = \arg\min\{j \mid j \in [1, i+1], \overline{\mathrm{Br}}(S \setminus \mathcal{F}[j, i]; C) \geq t\overline{\mathrm{Br}}(\mathcal{F};C)\}$.
 5:     Let $S = S \setminus \mathcal{F}[j, i]$ and $i = j - 2$.
 6: **end while**
 7: Return S.

Unlike MRMR, INTERACT and LCC evaluate class relevance of S by $\overline{\mathrm{Br}}(S;C)$ without using approximation based on evaluation of individual features. By this, they not only can eliminate irrelevant and redundant features but also can incorporate feature interaction into feature selection. Although computing $\overline{\mathrm{Br}}(S;C)$ is more costly than using the approximation, LCC drastically improves time efficiency by taking advantage of binary search when searching a feature f_j to select in Step 4 of Algorithm 2. Due to this, the asymptotic time complexity of Lcc is $O(|\mathcal{F}||D|\log|\mathcal{F}|)$, and its practical time efficiency is significantly high.

The principle of reducing information entropy is loosely related to the principle of reducing number of features, although they are not equivalent to each other. Explanation of phenomena using fewer features is more understandable for humans, while explanation using features with smaller entropy is more efficient from a information-theoretical point of view.

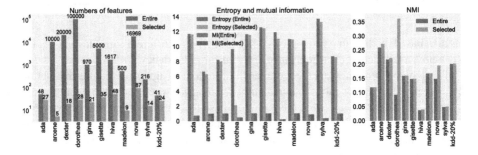

Fig. 1. Before and after of supervised feature selection.

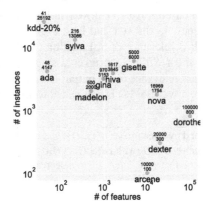

Fig. 2. Eleven datasets used in our experiment.

Figure 1 shows the results of feature selection by CWC when applied to the 11 datasets described in Fig. 2 and below. These datasets are relatively large and encompass a wide range in terms of the numbers of features and instances. They are taken from the literature: five from NIPS 2003 Feature Selection Challenge, five from WCCI 2006 Performance Prediction Challenge, and one from KDD-Cup Challenge. Since our interest in this paper lies in the selection of categorical features, the continuous features included in the datasets are categorized into five equally-long intervals before feature selection. The instances of all of the datasets are annotated with binary labels.

From the left chart of Fig. 1, we first notice that CWC has selected a reasonably small number of features for all the datasets. For example, while the dataset DOROTHEA originally includes 100,000 features, CWC has selected only 28 features.

The middle chart of Fig. 1 shows that the dataset except DOROTHEA and NOVA include many redundant features and only a few irrelevant features. In fact, we see only small losses of the information entropy between the entire features $\mathcal{F}$ (blue) and the selected features S (orange). In contrast, CWC eliminates many irrelevant features from DOROTHEA and NOVA: The gaps between the information entropy of $\mathcal{F}$ and S are large for these datasets. By the nature of CWC, there is no loss in mutual information. It is interesting to note that the normalized mutual information scores of S are better than $\mathcal{F}$ for some of the datasets (the right chart of Fig. 1). In particular, the extents of improvement for DOROTHEA and NOVA are significant. Since the normalized mutual information quantifies the extent of the identity between two random variables, the selected features S can explain class labels more confidently than the entire features $\mathcal{F}$. This emphasizes the importance of feature selection in addition to the advantages in model construction and the improved efficiency of post-feature-selection learning.

So far, we have shown the four most important guiding principles in designing supervised feature selection algorithms. Among them, the principle of maintaining high class relevance cannot be used in unsupervised feature selection, because we do not have class labels in unsupervised learning. The issue here lies in the fact that there is a trade-off between maintaining high class relevance and each of the last three principles, and supervised feature selection selects features that realize an appropriate balance between class relevance and the other indices. Without class relevance, the other three indices do not mutually constrain, and it turns out that selecting no features is always the optimal answer. Thus, the most important question for realizing successful unsupervised feature selection is how to find one or more principles that constrain the other three principles without leveraging class labels. We propose an answer for this question in Sect. 5.

4   Feature Value Selection Vs. Feature Selection

The advantages of feature value selection over feature selection are two-fold:

1. Feature value selection is likely to explain the same phenomena using factors with less information content. This means that the explanation is more efficient and more accurate.
2. We sometimes use the term *modeling* to indicate selecting of a small number of effective explanatory variables from a larger pool of possible variables to explain objective variables. Using feature values as explanatory variables improves the concreteness of the explanation.

4.1   More Efficient Explanation of Phenomena

For formalization, we first introduce a binarized feature and a binarized feature set. The purpose is to reduce feature value selection to feature selection by converting a feature value into a binary vector using one-hot encoding.

Definition 1. *For a value $v \in R(f)$, $v_{@f}$ denotes a binary feature such that for an instance $x \in D$, $v_{@f}(x) = 1$ if $f(x) = v$; otherwise, $v_{@f}(x) = 0$.*

Definition 2. *For a set S of features, we determine $S^b = \{v_{@f} \mid f \in S, v \in R(f)\}$.*

As explained in Sect. 2, a binarized feature $v_{@f} \in S^b$ is canonically viewed as a random variable defined over the sample space $\prod_{v_{@f} \in S^b} \mathbb{Z}_2$, where D determines an empirical probability measure. $\mathbb{Z}_2$ denotes $\{0, 1\}$. In particular, we can convert a dataset D into a new dataset D^b, which consists of the same instances but is described by $\mathcal{F}^b$. Thus, we can equate feature value selection on a dataset D to feature selection on D^b.

The entire features $\mathcal{F}$ of the dataset of the next example can explain class labels necessarily and sufficiently. We see that we can also select feature values $S \subset \mathcal{F}^b$ that completely explain the class labels as well. Although the cardinality of S is the same as that of $\mathcal{F}$, $H(S)$ is significantly smaller than $H(\mathcal{F})$.

Example 1. We consider n features $f_1, \ldots, f_n$, whose values are arbitrary b-dimensional binary vectors (b-bit-long natural numbers), that is, $R(f_i) = \mathbb{Z}_2^b$. For an instance $x \in D$, we determine its class label $C(x)$ by

$$C(x) = \left(\sum_{i=1}^{n} 2^{i-1} \cdot 0_{@f_i}(x) \right) \mod L,$$

where L is an odd number that determines the number of classes. To illustrate, we further assume that f_i is independent of any other f_j, and the associated probability distribution is uniform. Because the class labels of x rely on all of $f_1(x), \ldots, f_n(x)$, the answer of feature selection for this dataset is unique and must be $\{f_1, \ldots, f_n\}$. For the same reason, the answer of feature value selection must be $\{0_{@f_1}, \ldots, 0_{@f_n}\}$. While it is evident that

$$I(f_1, \ldots, f_n; C) = I(0_{@f_1}, \ldots, 0_{@f_n}; C) = H(C)$$

holds, the information entropy $H(f_1, \ldots, f_n) = nb$ is significantly greater than

$$H(0_{@f_1}, \ldots, 0_{@f_n}) = n \left(b2^{-b} - (1 - 2^{-b}) \log_2(1 - 2^{-b}) \right) \approx n(b+1)2^{-b},$$

when b is not small. This means that, $0_{@f_1}, \ldots, 0_{@f_n}$ can explain the class C with the same accuracy but significantly more efficiently than $f_1, \ldots, f_n$.

The following general mathematical results justify the result of Example 1.

Theorem 1. *For disjoint feature sets S and T in $\mathcal{F}$, $H(S, T) = H(S^b, T)$ holds.*

Proof. For $v \in R(S) = \prod_{f \in S} R(f)$, we determine $v^b \in R(S^b) = \prod_{v_{@f} \in S^b} \mathbb{Z}_2$ by $v_{@f}(v^b) = 1 \Leftrightarrow f(v) = v$. When we let $\mathcal{D} = \{v^b \mid v \in R(S)\} \subset R(S^b)$, we have the following for arbitrary $w \in R(S^b)$ and $u \in R(T)$:

$$\Pr[S^b = w, T = u] = \begin{cases} \Pr[S = v, T = u], & \text{if } w \in \mathcal{D}, \text{ that is, } \exists \left(v \in \prod_{f \in S} R(f)\right)[w = v^b]; \\ 0, & \text{if } w \notin \mathcal{D}. \end{cases}$$

Hence, the assertion follows:

$$\begin{aligned} H(S,T) &= \sum_{v \in R(S)} \sum_{u \in R(T)} -\Pr[S = v, T = u] \log_2 \Pr[S = v, T = u] \\ &= \sum_{w \in \mathcal{D}} \sum_{u \in R(T)} -\Pr[S^b = w, T = u] \log_2 \Pr[S^b = w, T = u] \\ &\quad + \sum_{w \in R(S^b) \setminus \mathcal{D}} \sum_{u \in R(T)} -\Pr[S^b = w, T = u] \log_2 \Pr[S^b = w, T = u] \\ &= H(S^b, T). \end{aligned}$$

$\square$

The following corollaries to Theorem 1 explain Example 1.

Corollary 1. *For $S \subseteq \mathcal{F}$, $H(S) = H(S^b)$ holds.*

Corollary 2. *For feature subsets S and T in $\mathcal{F}$, $I(S;T) = I(S^b;T)$ holds.*

Proof. Theorem 1 implies

$$I(S;T) = H(S) + H(T) - H(S,T) = H(S^b) + H(T) - H(S^b,T) = I(S^b;T). \square$$

By the monotonicity properties of information entropy and mutual information, if $S' \subset S^b$, we have $H(S') \leq H(S)$ and $I(S';T) \leq I(S;T)$. Example 1 is the case where $H(S') \ll H(S)$ holds, while $I(S';T) = I(S;T)$ holds, for $S = \{f_1, \ldots, f_n\}, S' = \{0_{@f_1}, \ldots, 0_{@f_n}\}$ and $T = \{C\}$.

4.2 More Concrete Modeling

Feature value selection explains how features contribute to the determination of class labels more clearly. Even if a feature f is selected through feature selection, not all of the possible values of f necessarily contribute to the determination equally. In particular, only a small portion of values may be useful for explaining class labels.

For example, an Intrusion Protection System (IPS) tries to detect a small portion of packets generated for malicious purposes out of the large volume of packets that are transmitted in networks. Based on the information of the detected malicious packets, IPS tries to take effective measures to protect a system. To a packet, multiple headers of protocols such as TCP, IP and IEEE 802.x are attached. The information born by these headers is the main source of information for IPS. For example, a TCP header includes a *Destination Port* field, and a value of this field usually specifies what application will receive this packet and will execute particular functions as a result of the reception. Since malicious attackers target particular vulnerable applications, knowing what potion numbers are correlated to malicious attacks will allow an IPS to take more accurate countermeasures than only knowing that values of the destination port field.

5 Fast Unsupervised Feature Selection

The basis of our proposed algorithm was presented in [19]. We now explain our improvements to this algorithm using explainability.

To review, [19] provides a useful basis for developing an efficient unsupervised feature value selection algorithm:

- It leverages the principle that every instance must be explained by at least one selected feature value. This principle constrains the minimization of the three remaining factors (feature value count, internal redundancy, and information entropy, as discussed in Sect. 3) and guarantees that at least one meaningful solution exists.
- It incorporates the algorithmic framework of LCC [16,18] by leveraging binary search, which gives it significantly high time efficiency;
- It contains one hyperparameter for excluding feature values below a threshold of information entropy;

We build on this algorithm by adding two features:

1. We introduce the concept of *explainability* as a substitute for the concept of class relevance that plays a central role in supervised feature selection.
2. We add two hyperparameters: the minimum of collective explainability across all selected feature values, and a minimum explainability for each individual feature value.

5.1 Explainability-Based Unsupervised Feature Selection

Supervised learning provides an effective guide for feature selection in the form of class relevance scores. There are several measures of class relevance: MRMR [26] and CFS [6] use mutual information $I(S;C)$ following [3], while INTERACT [24] and LCC [16] deploy the complementary Bayesian risk $\overline{\mathrm{Br}}(S;C)$.

On the other hand, unsupervised feature selection has no class labels to measure the relevance of features to class labels. As a substitute, then, we introduce *explainability*. In [19], the support of a set of feature values is defined as follows:

Definition 3. ([19]). *For $S \subseteq \mathcal{F}^b$, the support of S is defined by*

$$\mathrm{supp}_D(S) = \{x \in D \mid \exists (v_{@f} \in S)[f(x) = v]\}.$$

The support $\mathrm{supp}_D(S)$ consists of the instances that possess at least one feature value included in S, or, in other words, are explained by the feature values in S.

Definition 4. *The* explainability *of S is determined by*

$$\mathfrak{X}_D(S) = \frac{|\mathrm{supp}_D(S)|}{|D|}.$$

Having defined explainability, we can formally define ξ-*explainability-based unsupervised feature value selection* as follows.

ξ-Explainability-Based Unsupervised Feature Value Selection (ξ-EUFVS).

Given an unlabeled dataset D described by a feature set $\mathcal{F}$ and the lower limit ξ of explainability, find $S \subseteq \mathcal{F}^b$ that minimizes $H(S)$ or $|S|$, or both if possible, subject to the condition of $\mathfrak{X}_D(S) \geq \xi$.

As explained in Sect. 3, although the information entropy $H(S)$ and the size $|S|$ are loosely correlated, minimizing one does not necessarily mean minimizing the other. Also, $H(S)$ is important from an explanation efficiency point of view, while $|S|$ affects the understandability of the obtained model by humans. Thus, the aforementioned formalization leaves some ambiguity in terms of objective functions, but however, this does not significantly matter in practice, because finding exact solutions to the problem of ξ-EUFVS is likely to be computationally impossible. When solving it approximately, the aforementioned loose correlation between $H(S)$ and $|S|$ helps us reach a reasonable balance between them.

We see how explainability performs as a substitute for class relevance using Fig. 3. To illustrate, we assume that $\mathcal{F}^b$ consists of only four values v_1, v_2, v_3, v_4.

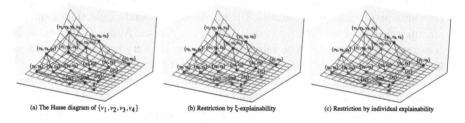

(a) The Hasse diagram of $\{v_1, v_2, v_3, v_4\}$ (b) Restriction by ξ-explainability   (c) Restriction by individual explainability

Fig. 3. Search space of EUFVS.

The chart (a) depicts the Hasse diagram of $\mathcal{F}^b$, which is a directed graph (V_H, E_H) such that V_H is the power set of $\mathcal{F}^b$, and $(S, T) \in V_H \times V_H$ is in E_H, if, and only if, $S \supset T$ and $|S| - |T| = 1$ hold. The height of a plot of $S \subseteq \mathcal{F}^b$ represents the magnitude of $H(S)$. We will start at the top node of $\mathcal{F}^b$ and will search the node that minimizes $H(S)$ and/or $|S|$ by following directed edges downward. If the search space is the entire Hasse diagram, it is evident that we can stop when we reach the bottom node that represents the empty set $\emptyset$. This solution is indeed trivial and meaningless. Thus, we need an appropriate restriction on the search space. For supervised feature selection, the principle of maintaining high class relevance narrows down the search space, because small feature sets can have only low class relevance (for example, $I(\emptyset; C) = 0$ holds), and such nodes are eliminated from the search space. As a result, we can reach a non-trivial meaningful node in the search space. The condition that the explainability $\mathfrak{X}_D(S)$ is no smaller than the predetermined threshold ξ has the same effect. Like mutual information, the explainability index is monotonous with respect to the inclusion relation of feature value sets: if $T \subseteq S \subseteq \mathcal{F}^b$, $\mathfrak{X}_D(T) \leq \mathfrak{X}_D(S)$ holds. This means that, if S is out of the search space, that is, $\mathfrak{X}_D(S) < \xi$ holds, any $T \subseteq S$ is out of the search space as well. In particular, $\mathrm{supp}_D(\emptyset) = \emptyset$ and $\mathfrak{X}_D(\emptyset) = 0$ hold. Chart (b) of Fig. 3 depicts this.

The sets $T \subseteq \mathcal{F}^b$ with $\mathfrak{X}_D(T) < \xi$ are displayed in red, and we see that there is more than one minimal selection S in the sense that $\mathfrak{X}_D(S) \geq \xi$ holds but $\mathfrak{X}_D(T) < \xi$ holds for arbitrary $T \subsetneq S$. All of these minimal nodes S comprise the set of candidate solutions to the ξ-EUFVS problem.

As the threshold ξ for the entire explainability $\mathfrak{X}_D(S)$ increases, the resulting search space becomes narrower, and the border has a higher altitude. In other words, the threshold ξ moves the border of the search space in the vertical direction.

In addition to the threshold ξ, we introduce a different threshold t for individual explainability $\mathfrak{X}_D(v)$ for individual feature value $v \in \mathcal{F}^b$. This threshold t constrains the search space so that a node in the space includes only feature values v whose individual explainability $\mathfrak{X}_D(v)$ is not smaller than t. In contrast to the threshold ξ to collective explainability, this threshold has the effect of moving the border of the search space in the horizontal direction. For example, in Fig. 3(c), we assume that $\mathfrak{X}_D(v_1) > \mathfrak{X}_D(v_2) > \mathfrak{X}_D(v_3) \geq t > \mathfrak{X}_D(v_4)$. Then, the subgraph displayed in blue is the search space determined in combination with ξ.

The introduction of this threshold t can be justified as follows.

- For example, if $\mathcal{F}$ includes a feature f, which yields a unique identifier for each instance of D, the support of any feature value $v_{@f}$ is a singleton, and hence, its individual explainability is positive but minimum. Evidently, selecting a unique identifier $v_{@f}$ is of no help for understanding the dataset. Although this example is extreme, in general, a feature value whose support is a very small set of instances lacks generality, and it is not desirable to include it in selection.
- As already explained, the threshold t for individual explainability moves the border of the search space in the horizontal direction, while the threshold ξ for entire explainability does in the vertical direction. By combining these two thresholds, we can move the border of the search space in both the vertical and horizontal directions, and hence, we will have multiplicative flexibility to define the range of solutions to the EUFVS problem.

At last of this subsection, we note the relation between $\mathfrak{X}_D(v)$ and $H(v)$. Since v is a feature value, and therefore, is binary as a random variable, we have

$$H(v) = -\mathfrak{X}_D(v) \log_2 \mathfrak{X}_D(v) - (1 - \mathfrak{X}_D(v)) \log_2(1 - \mathfrak{X}_D(v)).$$

Since the function $F(x) = -x \log_2 x - (1-x) \log_2(1-x)$ is an increasing function for $x \in [0, \frac{1}{2}]$, if $\mathfrak{X}_D(v) \leq \frac{1}{2}$, the threshold t on $\mathfrak{X}_D(v)$ is equivalent to the threshold $F(t)$ on $H(v)$. The algorithm presented in [19] takes a threshold to $H(v)$ as a hyperparameter. When we assume that $\mathfrak{X}_D(v) \leq \frac{1}{2}$, these two definitions of hyperparameters are equivalent to each other.

5.2   The Algorithm

Algorithm 3 describes the algorithm that we propose in this paper. Due to the monotonicity property of $\mathfrak{X}_D(S) \leq \mathfrak{X}_D(T)$ for $S \subseteq T$, we can take advantage of a binary search to find the next feature value to leave in S (Step 5). As a result, the algorithm is significantly fast as shown in Sect. 6.1.

Algorithm 3. Explainability-based Unsupervised Feature Value Selection (EUFVS).

Require: An unlabeled dataset D described by $\mathcal{F}$; a threshold $\xi \in \left[\frac{1}{2}, 1\right]$; a threshold $t \in \left[0, \frac{1}{2}\right]$.

Ensure: A minimal feature value set $S \subseteq \mathcal{F}^b$.

1: Let $\overline{S} = \mathcal{F}^b \setminus \{v_{@f} \in \mathcal{F}^b \mid \mathfrak{X}_D(v_{@f}) \leq t\}$.

2: Number the feature values of $\overline{S}$ so that $\overline{S} = \{v_1, \ldots, v_{|\overline{S}|}\}$ and $\mathfrak{X}_D(v_i) \geq \mathfrak{X}_D(v_j)$ for $i < j$.

3: Let $l = 0$ and $S = \overline{S}$.

4: **while** $l < |\overline{S}|$ **do**

5:     Let $k = \max\{j \mid \mathfrak{X}_D(S \setminus \overline{S}[l+1, j]) \geq \xi, j = l, \ldots, |\overline{S}|\}$ by binary search.

6:     Let $S = S \setminus \overline{S}[l+1, k]$ and $l = k+1$.

7: **end while**

8: **return** S.

The time complexity of Algorithm 3 can be estimated as follows: the complexity of computing $\mathfrak{X}_D(v_i)$ and $\mathfrak{X}_D(\mathcal{F}^b[i, |\mathcal{F}^b|])$ for all i is $O(|\mathcal{F}^b| \cdot |D|)$; By updating $\mathfrak{X}_D(S \cap \mathcal{F}^b[1, l])$ whenever we update l, $\mathfrak{X}_D(S \setminus \mathcal{F}^b[l+1, j]) \geq \xi$ can be investigated in $O(|D|)$-time, and the average complexity to execute the while loop is estimated by $O((\log_2 |\mathcal{F}^b|)^2 \cdot |D|)$.

6   Empirical Performance Evaluation

We conducted three experiments with EUFVS. The first assessed the basic performance of EUFVS, while the second and third applied EUFVS to real-world data, specifically tweets and electricity consumption.

6.1   Basic Performance Evaluation

To measure EUFVS's performance compared to other algorithms, we tried it on the 11 datasets from well-known machine learning challenges shown in Fig. 2. We used well-known datasets to ensure our results were comparable to other algorithms tested on these datasets. Our goal was to discover how accurately and quickly EUFVS could build feature value sets that explained these datasets' labels, with the labels removed.

In the experiment, we set the threshold on collective explainability to $\xi = 1$ and changed the threshold on individual explainability t on each iteration so that the maximum value would not exceed 5% of the total number of instances in each datsets.

Runtime Performance. Figure 4 describes the runtime of Algorithm 3 in milliseconds for three typical datasets: KDD-20% with significantly many instances, DOROTHEA with significantly many features, and GISETTE with both many instances and many features (Fig. 2). The scores include only the search time. The runtime was under 100 milliseconds for all datasets, except for when we used very small thresholds. The longest run was GISETTE with a threshold of $t = 0$, which took only 2,500 ms.

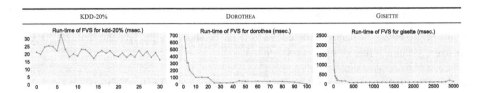

Fig. 4. Runtime in milliseconds for different t values (x-axis).

Selection Performance. Several affinities appear in the results of nine of these eleven datasets. We will describe these using the examples of GISETTE and SYLVA (The left and middle columns of Fig. 5).

1. All 11 datasets consisted of labelled data, which provided a ground truth to test against. Our goal was to see how well EUFVS could produce feature sets that explained the labels without the labels for guidance, so we removed the labels from the datasets.

   Even so, it found feature value sets that explain the labels well. In fact, $I(S;C)$ remains close to $I(\mathcal{F};C)$, until t exceeds a certain limit. This property is significant evidence that our algorithm has an excellent ability to select *appropriate feature values*, because the dataset labels are a *perfect summary* of the datasets.

2. When t exceeds the said limit, $I(S;C)$ rapidly decreases. In other words, the different selected feature value sets represent different views of the datasets.

3. As t increases, $I(S;C)$ and $H(S)$ synchronously decrease. This implies that our algorithm eliminates non-redundant and relevant feature values after it has eliminated all the redundant feature values.

4. $H(S)$ remains very close to its upper bound of $H(\mathcal{F})$ (the orange line) until t reaches the said limit. By contrast, the number of feature values selected decreases rapidly immediately when t increases. This may imply that an overwhelming majority of feature values v with small $H(v)$ are redundant.

5. The number of the selected feature values approaches the number of the features selected by CWC (the green line). This implies that approximately one value for each feature selected by CWC is truly relevant to class labels.

The evaluation result of KDD-20% are also interesting. KDD-20% is a dataset of network packet headers gathered by intrusion detection software. Each instance is labelled as either "normal" or "anomalous". Unlike in the other datasets, the score of $H(S)$ moves around half of $H(\mathcal{F})$, while $I(S;C)$ remains close to $I(\mathcal{F};C)$. In fact, KDD-20% and ADA are the only datasets that could exhibit higher NMI$(S;C)$ than NMI$(\mathcal{F};C)$. With high $I(S;C)$ and low $H(S)$, the feature values selected could have good classification capability when used with a classifier. Also, it is surprising that the number of feature values selected is smaller than 30, when they show the highest score of NMI$(S;C)$. The figure is significantly lower than the 225 feature values that CWC selects for this dataset, and hence, could provide a much more interpretable model.

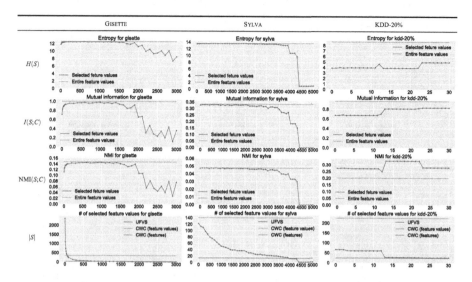

Fig. 5. Comparison in $H(S)$, $I(S;C)$, NMI$(C;S)$ and $|S|$ for typical three datasets.

Classification Performance. The experimental results on the (normalized) mutual information scores for the selection results of EUFVS imply that the selection results can accurately predict the dataset's class labels even though the inputs into EUFVS do not include them.

To investigate their potential classification performance, we ran experiments with the three typical classifiers: CART, Naïve Bayes (NB) and Supprt Vector Machine (C-SVM) classifiers. When we use the SVM classifier, we project instances to points in higher-dimensional spaces using the RBF kernel.

We evaluate classification performance using averaged accuracy scores obtained through five-fold cross-validation. Optimal hyperparameter values are determined using grid search based on five-fold cross-validation scores on training data, executed at each fold execution to compute a single accuracy score. For comparison, we also run the same experiments on feature value sets selected by MRMR [11].

Figure 6 describes the results for the three typical datasets of GISETTE, SYLVA and KDD-20%. From the charts, we can observe the following.

- For four deatasets including GISETTE, the accuracy scores for EUFVS encompass a relatively wide range, and some of them are compatible with the results of MRMR.
- For six datasets including SYLVA, the accuracy scores for the selection results of EUFVS varies within a relatively narrow range, and are sometimes better and sometimes worse than those for MRMR. Overall, their classification performance appear to be compatible with the selection results of MRMR.
- The results for KDD-20% is surprising, since the accuracy scores significantly better than MRMR. To be precise, for all classifiers and all feature value sets selected by MRMR, the accuracy scores fall within the range between 0.5 and 0.6. This will make us conclude that the selection results of MRMR are not useful for the purpose of classification. In contrast, the accuracy scores for EUFVS distributes in a narrow range around the value of 0.9.

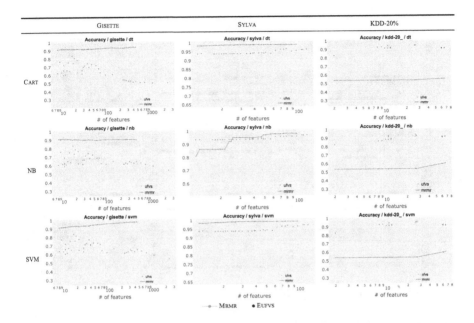

Fig. 6. Comparison in accuracy by CART, NB and SVM classifiers for typical three datasets.

Phase Transition by Change of Threshold. For the experiments using the 11 labeled datasets, we investigate the differences between the feature value sets selected by EUFVS for different threshold values t. For this purpose, we leverage the distance derived from the Jaccard coefficient and the k-means algorithm, a distance-based clustering algorithm.

The Jaccard index between two sets S and T is defined by $J(S,T) = \frac{|S \cap T|}{|S \cup T|}$. It is known that $J(S,T)$ is positive definite, and hence, $d_J(S,T) = \sqrt{2 - 2J(S,T)}$ is identical to the Euclid distance in some Euclidean space (reproducing kernel Hilbert space) between the projections of S and T in the space. This is derived from the well-known cosine formula. In particular, when a finite number of sets $S_1, \ldots, S_n$ are given, they can be projected into a common n-dimensional Euclidean space, and their coordinates in the space is computed as follows. We let $J = [J(S_i, S_j)]_{i,j}$ be the Gram matrix. Since the Jaccard index is positive definite, the Schur decomposition of J is as follows with $\lambda_i \geq 0$:

$$J = U^{\mathsf{T}} \mathrm{diag}(\lambda_1, \ldots, \lambda_n) U.$$

When we let $[v_1, \ldots, v_n] = \mathrm{diag}(\sqrt{\lambda_1}, \ldots, \sqrt{\lambda_n})U$, v_i gives a coordinate of S_i in an n-dimensional space.

Here, we let $S_1, \ldots, S_n$ be the feature value sets selected by EUFVS for n different thresholds. Because we can concretely project them into an n-dimensional space, we can apply the k-means clustering algorithms to the projections in plural times for different cluster count k.

The upper row of Fig. 7 shows the transition of the silhouette coefficient and the Davies Bouldin index as k increases, and based on it, we determine the optimal k for each dataset. Note that a greater silhouette coefficient and a smaller Davies Bouldin index indicate better clustering. At the same time, We also prefer to use the smallest possible k. With these constraints, we determine $k = 15$ for GISETTE, $k = 7$ for SYLVA and $k = 11$ for KDD-20% as optimal cluster counts.

With these values of k determined individually for the three datasets, the charts in the lower row of Fig. 7 depict the distributions of plots of the feature value sets in a three-dimensional space after reducing the dimensionality by MDS. For SYLVA and KDD-20%, we see that clustering has performed well, and clusters correspond exactly to consecutive intervals of thresholds. This implies that changing threshold parameter values results in a continuous change of viewpoint over these datasets. For GISETTE, no clear correspondence between clusters and thresholds was found.

6.2   Experiments on Analysis of Twitter Data

This experiment shows an example of applying EUFVS to the analysis of real Twitter data.

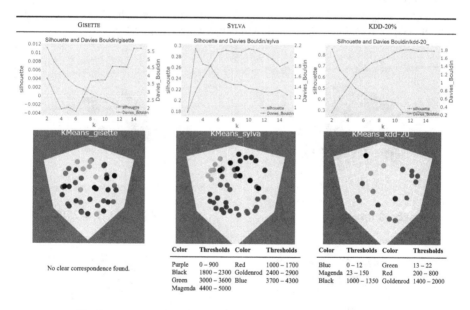

Fig. 7. Clustering of selected feature sets based on the jaccard index.

The data used in this experiment include 24,142 tweets posted on March 1, 2020 from 9:00 PM to 9:30 PM. This dataset is a set of tweets sent by users during the time who were tweeting about the COVID-19 pandemic. All of the users tweeted at least once about COVID-19, but not all of the tweets in the data set were about COVID-19. We extracted keywords from each tweets using the MeCab morphological analyzer, resulting in a matrix of 24,142 tweets (instances) × 49,342 unique words (features) as a feature table.

We performed feature selection using EUFVS multiple times with different parameter settings. Then, the UFVS results were compressed into two dimensions by TSNE (Manhattan distance) and were clustered by DBSCAN. Figure 8 shows the clustering results with different parameter settings: (a) $\xi = 1.0, t = 0$; (b) $\xi = 0.95, t = 20$; (c) $\xi = 0.9, t = 40$; and (d) $\xi = 0.95, t = 80$.

Figure 8(a) shows the clustering result with $\xi = 1.0$ and $t = 0$. After EUFVS, 3154 features remained. Several relatively large clusters can be seen. We have observed some clusters that represent COVID-19-related topics.

Figure 8(b) shows the clustering result with $\xi = 0.95$ and $t = 20$. After EUFVS, 2519 features remained. The set of Tweets was clearly divided into right and left sides. They may represent the characteristics of some Tweets groups. In fact, coronavirus-related clusters can be observed on the right side.

Figure 8(c) (1173 features, $\xi = 0.90$, $t = 40$) is also divided into two major groups, showing a trend similar to that of Fig. 8(b). On the other hand, Fig. 8(d) (486 features, $\xi = 0.95$, $t = 80$) shows a pattern similar to Fig. 8(a). In addition, the ring-shaped Tweet set can be seen in Figs. 8(a) and (d). The significance of these clusters will be a subject of future research.

Changing the parameter settings of EUFVS allows us to view the set of tweets from different perspectives. Our future work will explore these applications.

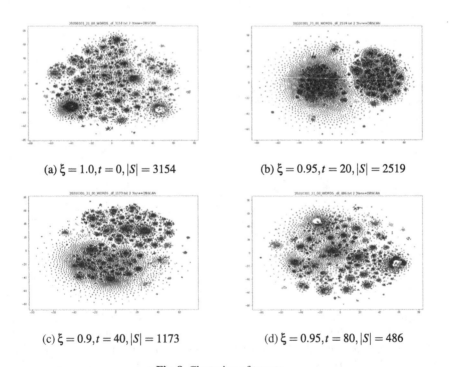

(a) $\xi = 1.0, t = 0, |S| = 3154$

(b) $\xi = 0.95, t = 20, |S| = 2519$

(c) $\xi = 0.9, t = 40, |S| = 1173$

(d) $\xi = 0.95, t = 80, |S| = 486$

Fig. 8. Clustering of tweets.

6.3 Experiments on Analysis of Electricity Consumption Data

In this experiment, we apply EUFVS to analyzing power consumption in university classrooms. The on/off binary data of electricity consumption in each classroom is recorded in 30-min. time slots over one semester of 15 weeks. By concatenating daily slices (9 am to 6 pm) of this data, we obtain a table where one instance is one classroom on one day, and each feature is a one-hour time slot from 9 am to 6 pm. The data size is 3782 instances and 19 features.

We performed a number of feature selection trials using EUFVS with varying parameter settings of ξ and t. Here, we show two examples. Figures 9 includes 3D visualizations of the data after feature selection by EUFVS. For a dimensionality reduction algorithm, we used UMAP with the Euclidean distance. Figure 9(a) shows the results of EUFVS with the parameter settings of $\xi = 1.0$ and $t = 1660$. Thirteen features remained in this parameter setting. There are two dense clusters on the right and center of the figure, and a spreading, string-like cluster on the left side of the figure. The present data include classrooms in two buildings. Classrooms in the same building tend to cluster together, which reflects different power consumption patterns in different buildings.

Figure 9(b) shows the results of EUFVS with $\xi = 0.95$ and $t = 2000$. Five features remain in this parameter setting. Two dense clusters similar to those in Fig. 9(a) can be found, but the spreading, string-like cluster disappears. On the other hand, the structures of the two dense clusters of Fig. 9(b) are easily visible.

Figure 10 shows an enlarged view of the two dense clusters. These clusters also have a string-like structure. Furthermore, the structure is found to be sequentially linked from the first week to the 15th week. The instances are plotted in different colors for each day of the week, and the same color appears periodically, which is a manifestation of that.

As described above, by changing the parameter settings, we can obtain the visualizations suitable for the spreading, string-like cluster and suitable for the dense clusters. This is due to the design of EUFVS, which allows us to check a large number of various solutions through lightweight calculations.

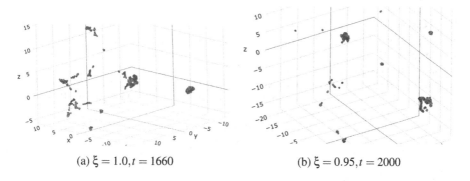

(a) $\xi = 1.0, t = 1660$ (b) $\xi = 0.95, t = 2000$

Fig. 9. UMAP 3D view.

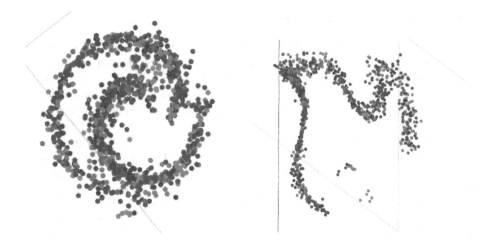

Fig. 10. Enlarged views of two dense clusters in Fig.9.

7   Conclusion

The intractability of unsupervised feature selection is caused by the indefiniteness prob-lem: any dataset can contain multiple theoretically-correct solutions, but there is no metric for picking the best one. Instead of attempting to find a metric, EUFVS accepts the indefiniteness problem and works around it by speeding up the feature selection process. Because EUFVS is a fast, tunable algorithm, it empowers a human being to select the best result from many options.

Acknowledgements. This work was partially supported by the Grant-in-Aid for Scientific Research (JSPS KAKENHI Grant Numbers 16K12491 and 17H00762) from the Japan Society for the Promotion of Science.

References

1. Almuallim, H., Dietterich, T.G.: Learning boolean concepts in the presence of many irrele-vant features. Artif. Intell. **69**(1–2), 279–305 (1994)
2. Angulo, A.P., Shin, K.: mRMR+ and CFS+ feature selection algorithms for high-dimensional data. Appl. Intell. **49**(5), 1954–1967 (2019). https://doi.org/10.1007/s10489-018-1381-1. https://doi.org/10.1007/s10489-018-1381-1
3. Battiti, R.: Using mutual information for selecting features in supervised neural net learning. IEEE Trans. Neural Netw. **5**(4), 537–550 (1994)

4. Cai, D., Zhang, C., He, X.: Unsupervised feature selection for multi-cluster data. In: Proceedings of the 16th ACM SIGKDD International Conference on Knowledge Discovery and Data Mining (KDD 2010), pp. 333–342 (2010)

5. Ding, C., Peng, H.: Minimum redundancy feature selection from microarray gene expression data. In: Proceedings of the 2003 IEEE Bioinformatics Conference. CSB2003, pp. 523–528 (2003)

6. Hall, M.A.: Correlation-based feature selection for discrete and numeric class machine learning. In: ICML 2000 (2000)

7. He, X., Cai, D., Niyogi, P.: Laplacian score for feature selection. In: Advances in Neural Information Processing Systems (NIPS 2005), pp. 507–514 (2005)

8. Li, Z., Liu, J., Yang, Y., Zhou, X., Liu, H.: Clustering-guided sparse structural learning for unsupervised feature selection. IEEE Trans. Knowl. Data Eng. 26(9), 2138–2150 (2014)

9. Liu, H., Shao, M., Fu, Y.: Consensus guided unsupervised feature selection. In: Proceedings of the 28th AAAI Conference on Artificial Intelligence (AAAI 2016), pp. 1874–1880 (2016)

10. Mohamed, N.S., Zainudin, S., Othman, Z.A.: Metaheuristic approach for an enhanced MRMR filter method for classification using drug response microarray data. Expert Syst. Appl. $\mathbf{90}$, 224–231 (2017). https://doi.org/10.1016/j.eswa.2017.08.026. http://www.sciencedirect.com/science/article/pii/S0957417417305638

11. Peng, H., Long, F., Ding, C.: Feature selection based on mutual information: criteria of max-dependency, max-relevance and min-redundancy. IEEE Trans. Pattern Anal. Mach. Intell. $\mathbf{27}$(8), 1226–1238 (2005)

12. Qian, M., Zhai, C.: Robust unsupervised feature selection. In: Proceedings of 23rd International Joint Conference on Artificial Intelligence (IJCAI 2013), pp. 1621–1627 (2013)

13. Radovic, M., Ghalwash, M., Filipovic, N., Obradovic, Z.: Minimum redundancy maximum relevance feature selection approach for temporal gene expression data. BMC Bioinform. $\mathbf{18}$(1), 9 (2017). https://doi.org/10.1186/s12859-016-1423-9

14. Senawi, A., Wei, H., Billings, S.A.: A new maximum relevance-minimum multicollinearity (mrmmc) method for feature selection and ranking. Pattern Recognit. $\mathbf{67}$, 47–61 (2017). https://doi.org/10.1016/j.patcog.2017.01.026

15. Shin, K., Fernandes, D., Miyazaki, S.: Consistency measures for feature selection: a formal definition, relative sensitivity comparison, and a fast algorithm. In: 22nd International Joint Conference on Artificial Intelligence (IJCAI 2011). pp. 1491–1497 (2011)

16. Shin, K., Kuboyama, T., Hashimoto, T., Shepard, D.: sCWC/sLCC: highly scalable feature selection algorithms. Information $\mathbf{8}$(4), 159 (2017)

17. Shin, K., Xu, X.: Consistency-based feature selection. In: 13th International Conference on Knowledge-Based and Intelligent Information & Engineering System (2009)

18. Shin, K., Kuboyama, T., Hashimoto, T., Shepard, D.: Super-CWC and super-LCC: super fast feature selection algorithms. Big Data $\mathbf{2015}$, 61–67 (2015)

19. Shin, K., Okumoto, K., Shepard, D., Kuboyama, T., Hashimoto, T., Ohshima, H.: A fast algorithm for unsupervised feature value selection. In: 12th International Conference on Agents and Artificial Intelligence (ICAART 2020), pp. 203–213 (2020). https://doi.org/10.5220/0008981702030213

20. Vinh, L.T., Thang, N.D., Lee, Y.K.: An improved maximum relevance and minimum redundancy feature selection algorithm based on normalized mutual information. In: 2010 10th IEEE/IPSJ International Symposium on Applications and the Internet, July 2010. https://doi.org/10.1109/saint.2010.50. http://dx.doi.org/10.1109/SAINT.2010.50

21. Wei, X., Cao, B., Yu, P.S.: Unsupervised feature selection on networks: a generative view. In: Proceedings of the 28th AAAI Conference on Artificial Intelligence (AAAI 2016), pp. 2215–2221 (2016)

22. Wei, X., Cao, B., Yu, P.S.: Multi-view unsupervised feature selection by cross-diffused matrix alignment. In: Proceedings of 2017 International Joint Conference on Neural Networks (IJCNN 2017), pp. 494–501 (2017)
23. Zhang, Y., Ding, C., Li, T.: Gene selection algorithm by combining reliefF and mRMR. BCM Genomics **9**(2), 1–10 (2008)
24. Zhao, Z., Liu, H.: Searching for interacting features. In: Proceedings of International Joint Conference on Artificial Intelligence (IJCAI 2007), pp. 1156–1161 (2007)
25. Zhao, Z., Liu, H.: Spectral feature selection for supervised and unsupervised learning. In: Proceedings of the 24th International Conference on Machine Learning (ICML 2007), pp. 1151–1157 (2007)
26. Zhao, Z., Anand, R., Wang, M.: Maximum relevance and minimum redundancy feature selection methods for a marketing machine learning platform, August 2019

Reducing the Need for Manual Annotated Datasets in Aspect Sentiment Classification by Transfer Learning and Weak-Supervision

Ermelinda Oro[1,2]([envelope]) [ID], Massimo Ruffolo[1,2] [ID], and Francesco Visalli[2] [ID]

[1] High Performance Computing and Networking Institute of the National Research Council (ICAR-CNR), Via Pietro Bucci 8/9C, 87036 Rende, CS, Italy
{ermelinda.oro,massimo.ruffolo}@icar.cnr.it
[2] altilia.ai, Piazza Vermicelli, Technest, University of Calabria,
87036 Rende, CS, Italy
{ermelinda.oro,massimo.ruffolo,francesco.visalli}@altiliagroup.com

Abstract. Users' opinions can be greatly beneficial in developing and providing products and services and improving marketing techniques for customer recommendation and retention. For this reason, sentiment analysis algorithms that automatically extract sentiment information from customers' reviews are receiving growing attention from the computer science community. Aspect-based sentiment analysis (ABSA) allows for a more detailed understanding of customer opinions because it enables extracting sentiment polarities along with the sentiment target from sentences. ABSA consists of two steps: Aspect Extraction (AE) that allows recognizing the target sentiment; Aspect Sentiment Classification (ASC) that enables to classify the sentiment polarity. Currently, most diffused sentiment analysis algorithms are based on deep learning. Such algorithms require large labeled datasets that are extremely expensive and time consuming to build. In this paper, we present two approaches based on transfer learning and weak supervision, respectively. Both have the goal of reducing the manual effort needed to build annotated datasets for the ASC problem. In the paper, we describe the two approaches and experimentally compare them.

Keywords: Deep learning · Aspect sentiment classification · Aspect based sentiment analysis · Sentiment analysis · Natural language processing · Transfer learning · Post-trained language model · Fine-tuning · Post-training · Transformers · BERT · Weak-supervision · Data programming

This work was supported by Horizon 2020 - Asse I – PON I&C 2014–2020 FESR - Fondo per la Crescita Sostenibile - Sportello Fabbrica Intelligente DM 05/03/2018 – DD 20/11/2018. "Validated Question Answering" Project.

A. P. Rocha et al. (Eds.): ICAART 2020, LNAI 12613, pp. 445–464, 2021.
https://doi.org/10.1007/978-3-030-71158-0_21

1   Introduction

The volume of social Web content is rapidly growing. Social media, e-commerce websites, and booking platforms enable users and customers to share their comments, opinions and preferences about products and services with the rest of the world. Opinions influence single and group of Web users, which potentially are customers for products and services providers. Users' opinions can be of great help in developing and providing new products and services [66], modifying existing ones [39], as well as improving marketing techniques for recommending their products to customers [34,35]. The enormous amount of available reviews posted on the Web is attracting both the research community and business companies. Many applications can exploit sentiment analysis for obtaining insights from reviews [19].

Sentiment analysis concerns the development of algorithms that can automatically extract sentiment information from a set of reviews. It operates at the intersection of information retrieval, natural language processing, and artificial intelligence [39]. Because sentiment is related to the human emotions communicated by natural language expressions, it can be hard to write, measure, and quantify. For these reasons, most sentiment analysis approaches have the objective of classifying the sentiment polarity of a text, such as *positive, negative, neutral*. As discussed in [25], sentiment analysis has been studied mainly at three levels of classification: document level, sentence level, or target level. Document and sentiment levels are useful if we assume that the text taken as input expresses sentiment about only one topic. More interesting is the case that considers the target of the sentiment. In general, sentiment analysis can be formally defined as finding the quadruple (s, g, h, t) where s represents the sentiment, g represents the *target* object for which the sentiment is expressed, h represents the holder (i.e., the one expressing the sentiment), and t represents the time at which the sentiment was expressed. Most approaches focus on finding only the pair (s, g) [25]. The target can have different granularities: (i) The whole entity considered in the review (e.g., a laptop, a restaurant). (ii) An aspect of the entity, i.e., a characteristic or property of an entity (e.g., battery, food).

Aspect-based sentiment analysis (ABSA) aims to find sentiment-target (s, g) pairs in a given text where targets are aspects of the reviewed entity. It allows for a more detailed analysis that utilizes more of the information provided by the textual review. We use the two following sentences to explain some further details: *"The **battery** gets so <u>hot</u> it is scary"* and *"All the **food** was <u>hot</u> tasty"*. These sentences are related to the laptops and restaurants domains respectively. ABSA can be split down into two major problem sets [45]:

(i) Aspect Extraction (AE), or aspect detection, has the objective to recognize the target object g in sentences. For instance, considering our previous sentences, **battery** and **food** respectively. Given a review, sentences can be easily extracted from reviews with a sentence splitter. Whereas, there exist different approaches to retrieve aspects [15,42].

(ii) Aspect Sentiment Classification (ASC) has the objective of recognizing and classifying the sentiment polarity of terms related to aspects and expressing a sentiment/opinion. The sentiment can depend on the knowledge domain. For instance, in both previous sentences, the sentiment is associated to the word _**hot**_, but in the laptop domain such word is related to the aspect *battery* and takes a *negative* meaning, whereas in the second restaurant the same word is referred to the aspect food and takes a *positive* connotation. In fact, a battery that gets hot is not desirable, while a hot tasty food is good. ASC is a challenging problem because it is difficult to model the semantic relatedness of a target with its surrounding context words. It is necessary to understand semantic connections between the target word and the context words, which influence the sentiment polarity (e.g., the adjective related to an aspect).

Recently, and particularly since the introduction of BERT [11], deep transfer-learning methods have been applied successfully to a myriad of Natural Language Processing (NLP) tasks, including ABSA [54,76]. Deep learning automates the feature engineering process typical of classical machine learning approaches.

However, deep learning, in particular when applied to unstructured data, needs very large training sets to learn and generalize the parameters, and avoid overfitting [50]. But, building large labeled datasets is an extremely expensive and time-consuming task that often requires domain expertise [36]. To deal with this problem, different approaches that reduce the need for labeled data, such as transfer learning [59] and weak supervision [52], have been presented in the literature. Transfer learning methods like [70,79] rely on the fact that a model trained on a specific source domain can be exploited to do the same task in another target domain, thus reducing the need for labeled data in the target domain. Recently, transfer learning exploits pre-trained language models (PTMs), which can learn accurate general language representation from huge unlabeled corpora. One of the most important works of semi-supervised learning is BERT [11]. PTMs can be fine-tuned in a supervised way to learn various down-stream NLP tasks. The idea behind fine-tuning is that most of the features are already learned and represented in the PTM. Then, the model just needs to be specialized for the specific NLP task. For instance, BERT can be fine-tuned on the ASC problem requiring less annotated data than learning the entire task from scratch. Instead, weak supervision simplifies the annotation process to make it more automatic and scalable, even less accurate and noisier. Weak supervised methods rely on several different data annotation techniques such as heuristics, distant learning, pattern matching, weak classifiers, etc. Recently, [52] proposed data programming as a paradigm for semi-automatic datasets labeling, and Snorkel [51] the system that implements it. Data programming is based on the concept of Labeling Functions (LFs), where LFs are procedures that automatically assign labels to data on the base of domain knowledge embedded in the form of annotation rules. At Google, Batch et al. [3] extended Snorkel in order to achieve better scalability and knowledge base re-usability for enterprise-grade training sets labeling.

In this paper, we define and compare a transfer learning approach with a weakly-supervised approach [60] for ASC task, assuming that aspects have already been recognized in the input text.

The main contributions of this work are:

- We present a brief overview of sentiment analysis research. In particular, first, we indicate recent related surveys and datasets. Then, we provide a short review with a categorization of the existing literature related to deep learning, transfer learning, and weak supervision methods for sentiment analysis.
- We define two approaches, respectively based on cross-domain transfer learning and weak supervision, aimed at reducing the need for manually annotated datasets for ASC in a specific domain. In particular, the weak supervision method we propose is grounded on the paper [60].
- We provide the experimental evaluation of the two presented approaches for solving the ASC task considering two disjoint domains, laptops, and restaurants. In particular we used the datasets of SemEval task 4 subtask 2 [45].

The rest of this paper is organized as follows. Section 2 briefly reviews related work of sentiment analysis classifying it by adopted approaches and objectives. Section 3 describes our transfer learning approach and our weak-supervision method for ASC. In Sect. 4, we experimentally compare the two presented approaches used to reduce the need for annotated training sets in the target domain to perform ASC. Finally, Sect. 5 concludes the work.

2   Related Work

In recent years, many papers related to sentiment analysis have been presented. There exists different surveys that address various characteristics of the sentiment analysis [2,4,8,20,31,46,53,62,81]. In addition, many datasets have been created for sentiment analysis, for instance Amazon product reviews [6,22], tweets [1,16,18,56,80], IMDB movie review [29,37,38,40], news [10,74], Stanford Sentiment Treebank [61], Yelp dataset[1], SemEval Aspect-Based sentiment analysis dataset [43–45].

In this section, we briefly review related work classifying in different categories: (i) Methods based on different architectures of deep neural networks for ASC, opinion expression extraction, and sentiment classification. (ii) Recent papers exploit transformers with transfer learning techniques to perform ABSA, in particular, BERT-based approaches. (iii) Papers that apply weak-supervision methods to perform ABSA.

2.1   Deep Neural Network for ABSA

Aspect Sentiment Classification. Many deep learning architectures and techniques have been defined for aspect-level sentiment analysis before transformers. To the best of our knowledge, there were no dominating techniques in the literature. Dong et al. [12] present an adaptive recursive neural network (AdaRNN). They apply their method to perform a target-dependent sentiment analysis of

---

[1] https://www.yelp.com/dataset/challenge.

tweets. Vo and Zhang [69] use rich automatic features to perform aspect-based Twitter sentiment classification. The authors prove that rich sources of feature information help achieve better performance considering multiple embeddings, multiple pooling functions, and sentiment lexicons. Zhang et al. [82] present two-gated neural networks. Tang et al. [63] extend LSTM to consider the target of sentiment defining target-dependent LSTM (TD-LSTM) and target-connection LSTM (TC-LSTM). In these models, the target is given as feature and it is concatenated with the context features. Ruder et al. [58] use hierarchical and bidirectional LSTM model. They consider both intra- and inter-sentence relations. Wang et al. [73] present an attention-based LSTM method with target embedding (ATAE-LSTM). Yang et al. [78] present a two attention-based bidirectional LSTMs. Liu and Zhang [26] extend the attention modeling considering different attention to the left and right context of the given target. Tang et al. [64] use an end-to-end memory network for aspect-level sentiment classification, adding attention mechanisms. The method is able to understand the importance of each context word for the sentiment. Lei et al. [23] use a neural network method to extract pieces of input text as rationales (reasons) for review ratings. Li et al. [24] present an end-to-end approach. Ma et al. [28] present an interactive attention network (IAN) that considers attention on target and context. Chen et al. [9] use recurrent/dynamic attention network. Tay et al. [65] present a dyadic memory network (DyMemNN) that models dyadic interactions between aspect and context.

Opinion Expression Extraction. Different deep neural networks have also been introduced to addresses the problem of extracting opinion expressions. Yang and Cardie [77] use traditional shallow RNNs Irsoy and Cardie [21] use deep bi-RNN that outperformed [77]. Liu et al. [27] defined a model based on RNNs and word embedding. Wang et al. [71] combine RecNNs and CRF to extract aspect and opinion terms. Successively, Wang et al. [72] defined the CMLA method.

Sentiment Classification. To understand the polarity of the sentiment, it is often necessary to combine textual expressions with individually different polarities that influence each other. In addition, the polarity of terms can be dependent on the specific context and domain. Socher et al. [61] defined a Tree-based neural network based on RecNNs. Irsoy and Cardie [21] use deep RecNNs. Zhu et al. [83] present a neural network to combine compositional and non-compositional sentiment.

2.2   Transfer Learning for ABSA

With BERT [11], which obtained outstanding performances in multiple NLP tasks, pre-training with fine-tuning has become one of the most effective and used methods to solve NLP related problems. Compared to the word-level vectors (e.g. Word2Vec [32] released in 2013 and still quite popular, Glove [41], and FastText [7]) BERT trains sentence-level vectors and gets more information from context. BERT uses a bi-directional Transformer. Transformers were introduced from

Vaswani et at. [67]. After introducing BERT, many approaches based on it have been proposed by the natural language processing and understanding community [55].

Pre-trained language models (PTMs) can learn a good general representation from huge unlabeled corpora. Transfer learning enables for adapting the knowledge from a source task (or domain) to a target task (or domain) [57].

Xu et al. [76] propose a review reading comprehension (RRC) task and investigate the use of reviews for answering questions about sentiments of aspects, perform AE, and ASC. They adopt BERT as a base model and propose a joint post-training and fine-tuning approach to add both domain and task knowledge.

Rietzler et al. [54] extend the work by Xu et al. by further investigating the behavior of BERT models with post-training and fine-tuning in and cross domains, focusing on the ASC problem and considering the SemEval 2014 datasets [45].

In this paper, we follow the approaches presented in [54,76] and compare two approaches, transfer learning and weak-supervision, for addressing the ASC task.

2.3   Weak-Supervision for ABSA

Many papers have been presented to address the ABSA problem. To the best of our knowledge, few of these papers exploit weak-supervision methods.

García Pablos et al. [13] use some variations of [48] and [49] to perform AE and ASC. In particular, they use a double-propagation approach, and they model the obtained terms and their relations as a graph. Then, they apply the PageRank algorithm to score the obtained terms.

After, García Pablos et al. [14] perform AE task by bootstrapping a list of candidate domain aspect terms and using them to annotate the reviews of the same domain. The polarity detection is performed using a polarity lexicon exploiting the Word2Vec model [33] for each domain[2].

Then, García Pablos et al. [15] present a fully "almost unsupervised" ABSA system. Starting from a customer reviews dataset and a few words list of aspects they extract a list of words per aspect and two lists of positive and negative words for every selected aspect. It is based on a topic modeling approach combined with continuous word embeddings and a Maximum Entropy classifier.

Purpura et al. [47] perform the AE phase with a topic modeling technique called Non-negative Matrix Factorization. It allows the user to embed a list of seed words to guide the algorithm towards a more significant topic definition. The ASC is done by using a list of positive and negative words, with a few sentiment terms for each topic. This list is then extended with the Word2Vec model [33].

In [42], aspect and opinion lexicons are extracted from an unsupervised dataset belonging to the same domain as the target domain. The process is

---

[2] In [14] the addressed task is a bit different from ASC: the authors classify *entity-attribute* pair, where *entity* and *attribute* belong to predefined lists, e.g. food, price, location for *entity* and food-price, food-quality for *attribute*.

initialized with a seed lexicon of generic opinion terms. New aspect and opinion terms are extracted by using the dependency rules proposed in [49]. The opinion lexicon is then filtered and scored while the aspect lexicon can be modified by hand in a weakly supervised manner. ASC is performed on a target domain by detecting a direct or second-order dependency relation of any type between aspect-opinion pairs.

Unlike previous works, the proposed weak-supervision approach [60] simplifies and automates the sentiment terminology annotation making the ASC approach easily applicable in multiple domains. In addition, it enables the use of any discriminative and deep learning models.

3   Transfer Learning and Weak-Supervision Approaches for ASC

Insufficient supervised training data significantly limits the performance of the ASC task. To reduce the cost of human annotation in creating training sets, transfer learning exploits the knowledge obtained in other domains to avoid training parameters of deep learning algorithms from scratch, while weak-supervision provides semi-automatic data labeling methods to lower the manual effort. In this section, we present two approaches based on transfer learning and weak-supervision, respectively.

ASC aims to classify the sentiment polarity (*positive*, *negative*, or *neural*) related to an aspect from a review. The input in a couple $\langle d, g \rangle$ where d is a sentence and g is an aspect mentioned in d, The output is the polarity of the sentiment associated to the aspect g.

Our approach is based on BERT [11] and follows the pipeline defined in [76] and [54] for ASC. We define a standard training procedure as follows:

$$D_{post\text{-}training} \rightarrow D_{fine\text{-}tuning} \rightarrow D_{testing} \tag{1}$$

where $D_{post\text{-}training}$, $D_{fine\text{-}tuning}$, and $D_{testing}$ are three consecutive steps:

 (i) **post-training**, the BERT pre-trained language model is post-trained on the specific domain dataset $D_{post\text{-}training}$ to obtain a language model with knowledge obtained from the considered dataset.
 (ii) **fine-tuning**, the obtained model is fine-tuned on the specific labeled training dataset $D_{fine\text{-}tuning}$ to add task knowledge.
(iii) **testing**, the model is tested on the target test dataset $D_{testing}$.

BERT is a deep learning architecture built on Transformers [68] and it provides a language model pre-trained on a non-review knowledge, i.e., on Wikipedia and BooksCorpus dataset [84]. Post-training enables injecting into BERT the missing domain knowledge training the language model on an unsupervised corpus (i.e., without any manual annotations). BERT learns needed information from data and produces a new, more domain-related, language model. Xu et al. [76] show that post-training the model on a specific domain contributes to performance improvement.

The model resulting from the post-training is fine-tuned for the down-stream task to inject the task knowledge into the model. In fact, the idea behind BERT is to provide a pre-trained language model that can be further fine-tuned requiring almost no specific architecture for each end task. In our case, as describe and like in [76], we obtain a language model further post-trained on an additional unsupervised corpus. BERT learns needed information from data. To fine-tune BERT on the specific ASC end-task we just extend BERT with one extra task-specific layer, detailed in the following.

Let $x = ([CLS], g_1, \ldots, g_m, [SEP], d_1, \ldots, d_n, [SEP])$, where $, g_1, \ldots, g_m$ is the aspect (goal of our ABSA) having m tokens, and $d_1, \ldots, d_n$ is our document taken as input, which correspond to a review sentence containing that aspect g. Tokens of the input sentence and aspect are tokenized by the WordPiece algorithm [75]. [CLS] and [SEP] are two special tokens. The [SEP] token is used to separate two different inputs. Applying BERT, we obtain $h =BERT(x)$. [CLS] is used for classification problem and $h_{[CLS]}$ is the aspect-aware representation of the whole input through BERT [11]. The distribution of polarity is predicted with the added task-specific layer as $l = softmax(W \cdot h_{[CLS]} + b)$, where $W \in \mathbb{R}^{3*r_h}$ and $b \in \mathbb{R}^3$, with 3 the number of polarities (*positive*, *negative*, or *neural*). Softmax is applied along the dimension of labels on [CLS] : $l \in [0, 1]^3$.

The training of loss function is the cross-entropy on the polarities. Formula (2) is the cross-entropy function used to measures the discrepancy between a true distribution p and an estimated one q output of a classifier.

$$H(p,q) = - \sum_{x \in X} p(x) \log q(x) \tag{2}$$

It is noteworthy that, depending on the nature of the training set, the true distribution p can be a one-hot vector when we know the correct class as input or a probabilistic vector. In general, machine learning/deep learning methods use a human-annotated dataset. Therefore we are in the first case where the true distribution is a one-hot vector having the bit set to one to the correct class of the training example. Instead, as described in the following, for the weak-supervision approach, we will have a probability distribution over the classes as input.

3.1   Transfer Learning for ASC

A standard evaluation of machine learning models exploits train set and test set in the same domain, i.e., *in-domain*, and in particular standard approach uses the same distribution of the sets. In order to evaluate the capabilities and robustness of transfer learning approaches, models can be evaluated *cross-domain*. Thus, we apply cross-domain transfer learning for ASC and we use BERT language model fine-tuning, according to [54].

Following the standard training procedure defined in (1), unlike the in-domain case, in cross-domain settings we have $D_{fine-tuning}$ and $D_{testing}$ belonging to different domains. A special case of cross-domain is when post-training and testing are in the same domain (for instance, both on Laptops or both on Restaurants). This case is named cross-domain adaptation.

3.2 Weak Supervision for ASC

Our proposed weak-supervision method [60], specifically designed for the ASC task of the ABSA problem, is grounded on data programming [52] that is a weak-supervised paradigm based on the concept of Labeling Functions (LFs). LFs are procedures, designed by data scientists and/or subject matter experts, that automatically assign labels to data based on domain knowledge embedded in the form of annotation rules.

More in detail, our method consists of a set of predefined, easy-to-use, and flexible LFs capable of automatically assigning sentiment to sentence-aspect pairs. The method is based on the ideas that: (i) it must require minimum NLP knowledge to the user, and (ii) it must be reusable in multiple domains with minimal effort for domain adaptation.

One of the most important characteristics of data programming is that LFs are noisy (e.g., different LFs may label the same data in different ways, LFs can label false positive examples). In this paper, to deal with the ASC task of ABSA problems by data programming, we use the Snorkel system [51] that enables handling the entire life-cycle of data programming tasks. Once LFs have been written, Snorkel applies them to data and automatically learns a generative model over these LFs, which estimates their accuracy and correlations, with no ground-truth data needed. It is noteworthy that Snorkel applies LFs as a generative process, which automatically de-noises the resulting dataset by learning the accuracy of the LFs along with their correlation structure. Thus, this process's output is a training set composed of probabilistic labels that can be used as input for deep learning algorithms that have to use a noise-aware loss function.

In our weak-supervised method LFs take as input pairs having the form $\langle d, g \rangle$ where d is a sentence and g is an aspect, and return triples having the form $\langle d, g, s \rangle$ where d and g are the sentence and the aspect respectively, and $s \in \{Positive, Negative, Neutral\} \cup \{Abstain\}$ is the sentiment obtained in output. A LF can choose to abstain if it doesn't have sufficient information to label a sentiment.

The proposed method recognizes and exploits chunks in the input text, in particular noun phrase (*NP*) verb phrase (*VP*). To recognize chunks the Stanford CoreNLP Parser [30] is used. The aspects g are recognized and assigned to chunks. To compute sentiment polarity s of chunks, external sentiment analyzers are exploited, such as Stanford CoreNLP [30], TextBlob[3], NLTK [5], and Pattern[4]. To assign s to the pair $\langle d, g \rangle$ two different simple and intuitive strategies are applied. The first computes the polarity of every single chunk. For instance, if all chunks have the same polarity, the method returns the corresponding label. If chunks have mixed *Positive* and *Negative* polarity the method returns the

---

[3] https://textblob.readthedocs.io/.

[4] https://www.clips.uantwerpen.be/pages/pattern-en/.

Abstain label. When there are *Neutral* chunks mixed with at least one *Positive* chunk the method returns the *Positive* label, and the same happens for mixed *Neutral* and *Negative* chunks. The second strategy computes the global polarity of the resulting text string. Considering the two different strategies and the four exploited sentiment analyzers, the approach includes a total of 8 LFs. For more details, refer to [60]. It is noteworthy that created labeling function templates are simple and powerful. They enable to reuse of existing knowledge embedded in already available NLP tools to create new training sets.

Table 1 and Table 2 show statistics about the LFs when applied to laptops and restaurants datasets, respectively. In particular, columns of the tables represent coverage, overlaps, conflicts, and empirical accuracy of LFs when they are executed to a small number (150 in our case) of manually labeled examples called dev set. Rows in the tables correspond to the eight LFs we defined by using NLP tools and strategies described above, where each row of the tables contains values computed for a specific labeling function.

Table 1. LFs application stats on laptops domain. Source [60].

LF srategy	Coverage	Overlaps	Conflicts	Emp. Acc.
LF(StanfordCoreNLP, FirstStrategy)	0.7667	0.7667	0.5267	0.5478
LF(StanfordCoreNLP, SecondStrategy)	0.7933	0.7933	0.5333	0.5042
LF(TextBlob, FirstStrategy)	0.7400	0.7400	0.4867	0.4775
LF(TextBlob, SecondStrategy)	0.7933	0.7933	0.5333	0.5042
LF(NLTK, FirstStrategy)	0.7533	0.7533	0.4933	0.4956
LF(NLTK, SecondStrategy)	0.7933	0.7933	0.5333	0.4874
LF(Pattern.en, FirstStrategy)	0.7467	0.7467	0.4933	0.4821
LF(Pattern.en, SecondStrategy)	0.7933	0.7933	0.5333	0.4790

Experiments on laptops in Table 1 show that LFs have about 77% of coverage and 50% of empirical accuracy, while Table 2 shows that restaurants have a

Table 2. LFs application stats on restaurants domain. Source [60].

LF strategy	Coverage	Overlaps	Conflicts	Emp. Acc.
LF(StanfordCoreNLP, FirstStrategy)	0.6200	0.6200	0.3867	0.4946
LF(StanfordCoreNLP, SecondStrategy)	0.6800	0.6800	0.4200	0.5882
LF(TextBlob, FirstStrategy)	0.6667	0.6667	0.4067	0.5100
LF(TextBlob, SecondStrategy)	0.6800	0.6800	0.4200	0.5098
LF(NLTK, FirstStrategy)	0.6667	0.6667	0.4133	0.5000
LF(NLTK, SecondStrategy)	0.6800	0.6800	0.4200	0.5098
LF(Pattern.en, FirstStrategy)	0.6667	0.6667	0.4067	0.5100
LF(Pattern.en, SecondStrategy)	0.6800	0.6800	0.4200	0.5000

coverage of about 69% and empirical accuracy of 52%. Results on coverage and empirical accuracy suggest that defined LFs work properly and can be used to annotate the two datasets.

The result of the labeling process is a matrix of labels $\Lambda \in (\{Positive, Negative, Neutral\} \cup \{Abstain\})^{m \times n}$, where m is the cardinality of the training set and n is the number of LFs. This matrix is the input of the Snorkel generative model [51]. Such model produces a list of probabilistic training labels $\tilde{Y} = (\tilde{y}_1, \ldots, \tilde{y}_m)$, where each $\tilde{y}_i \in \mathbb{R}^3$ is a probability distribution over the classes $\{Positive, Negative, Neutral\}$.

This probabilistic dataset is the input of discriminative models that use noise-aware loss functions described in Formula (2), where p is a probability distribution for a training example over the classes obtained as output from the Snorkel generative model.

4 Experiments

In this section, we compare the two presented approaches, i.e., transfer learning and weak-supervision, used to reduce the need for annotated training sets in the target domain to perform aspect sentiment classification (ASC). In particular, we describe the used datasets, the applied parameters, and the performed experiments for ASC task.

4.1 Dataset

For domain knowledge post-training, we used those presented in [76] consisting of around 1 Million of examples derived from Amazon laptop reviews [17], and around 2.5 Million of examples derived from 700K Yelp Dataset Challenge reviews[5].

To perform fine-tuning, we use two disjoint domains, laptops and restaurants, of SemEval task 4 subtask two datasets [45], which we simply call SemEval from now. Each dataset is already split into training, development, and test set. Statistics with the number of examples for each set are shown in Table 3. Each partition was hand-labeled by subject matter experts with labels within the set $\{Positive, Negative, Neutral\}$.

Table 3. Number of examples for each dataset. Source [60].

Domain	Train set	Dev set	Test set
Laptops	2163	150	638
Restaurants	3452	150	1120

---

[5] https://www.yelp.com/dataset.

In transfer learning experiments, we use ground truth labels, i.e., human-annotated labels of training and test set provided by SemEval. Instead, we replace original annotations in the training sets with probability distributions computed by Snorkel generative models in weak-supervision experiments. We use the dev set for tuning the LFs and the hyper-parameters of the generative models. We calculate metrics on the test set.

4.2   Experimental Settings

Cross-domain Transfer Learning Models. In our experiments we consider the two domains *laptops* and *restaurants*, and we test the different combination of our procedure $D_{post-training} \rightarrow D_{fine-tuning} \rightarrow D_{testing}$, defined in (1). So, for instance, *laptops* $\rightarrow$ *laptops* $\rightarrow$ *restaurants* is a model post-trained and fine-tuned on the laptops domain and tested on the restaurants domain. The best results can be obtained when in-domain or joint-domains [54]. In this paper, because the purpose is to reuse data on different domains, we have tried all possible cross-domain combinations (i.e., *laptops* $\rightarrow$ *laptops* $\rightarrow$ *restaurants*, *laptops* $\rightarrow$ *restaurants* $\rightarrow$ *laptops*, *restaurants* $\rightarrow$ *restaurants* $\rightarrow$ *laptops*, and *restaurants* $\rightarrow$ *laptops* $\rightarrow$ *restaurants*).

The backbone architecture for the post-training step is uncased BERT-base [11]. Models were post-trained by using the following settings: the maximum length of an example is 320, batch size 16 for each type of knowledge, the learning rate set to $3e-5$ leveraging the Adam optimizer, the number of post-training steps were 70.000 and 140.000 for the laptops and restaurants domains respectively, which corresponds about an epoch for each domain.

Generative Model. The hyperparameters of the generative model for the weak-supervision approach are searched through a grid search. A search configuration can be formally defined as a triple $\langle e, lr, o \rangle$ where $e \in \{100, 200, 500, 1000, 2000\}$ is the number of epochs, $lr \in \{0.01, 0.001, 0.0001\}$ is the learning rate, and $o \in \{sgd, adam, adamax\}$ is the optimizer. To tune the hyperparameters, we use the dev sets of SemEval.

The best configuration for laptops domain we found is $\langle 100, 0.01, adamax \rangle$. With these settings, the generative model applied to SemEval produced a dataset of 1702 probabilistic examples on laptops. The best configuration for restaurants domain we obtained is $\langle 100, 0.001, adamax \rangle$. The cardinality of the probabilistic dataset produced by Snorkel on restaurants is 2471.

Table 4 shows for each considered training set the number of examples obtained by Snorkel classified in *Positive*, *Negative* or *Neutral* labels. Because the labels are probabilistic, we consider for each training example the class with highest probability.

Table 4. Number of (the most probable) examples for each label. Source [60].

Train set	Positive	Negative	Neutral
Laptops	627	448	627
Restaurants	1371	301	792
Sampled restaurants	700	301	700

The restaurants' training set obtained by Snorkel is unbalanced. Therefore, we limit the number of *Positive* and *Neutral* examples to 700. The results discussed discussed in the next section are computed by averaging the metrics of 10 models trained with *Positive* and *Neutral* examples obtained by different sampling strategies.

During the fine-tuning step of both considered approaches, like in [76], we trained a simple softmax classifier whose output belongs to $\mathbb{R}^3$, where 3 is the number of polarities, on top of BERT post-trained models. We fine-tuned the discriminative models for 4 epochs using a batch size of 32 and the Adam optimizer with a learning rate of 3e-5. Results are obtained by averaging 10 runs sampling the mini-batches differently.

4.3   Results and Discussion

Table 5 shows results of transfer learning (Subsect. 3.1) with focus on cross-domain adaptation case considering laptops and restaurants SemEval dataset.

Table 5. Results of the experiments on laptops and restaurants using transfer learning methodology.

Test Set	Laptops		Restaurants	
Training Set for fine-tuning	Restaurants		Laptops	
	Accuracy	Macro F1	Accuracy	Macro F1
Xu_post-training Laptops	73.31	67.34	78.73	71.00
Xu_post-training Restaurants	73.95	70.74	81.00	71.79

In particular, in Table 5, accuracy and Macro F1 are computed for cross-domain configurations and considering both language models fine-tuned on the target or different domain. The cells with gray background correspond to the case of a cross-domain adaptation, where the language model is post-trained on the same target domain. Xu_post-training Laptops and Xu_post-training Restaurants are models post-trained with unsupervised data on laptops and restaurants respectively. So, for instance, the model post-trained on the laptops, then fine-tuned on the restaurants, and finally tested on the laptops, i.e., *laptops* → *restaurants* → *laptops*, obtains accuracy 73.31 and Macro F1 67.34. It is noteworthy that for *laptops* domain, we obtain better results performing post-training and fine-tuning on the different domain *restaurants* wrt using the same dataset for pre-training *laptops*. This is explainable by considering that *restaurants* is a wider dataset, and it seems to be sufficient to learn language model that generalizes well cross-domain.

Table 6 shows results of accuracy and macro F1 on laptops and restaurants domains with the weak-supervision approach (Subsect. 3.2) compared with the approach proposed in [76] but limiting the size of the datasets used for fine-tuning.

Table 6. Results of the experiments on laptops and restaurants respectively, by using weak-supervision methodology.

Model type	Laptops		Restaurants	
	Accuracy	Macro F1	Accuracy	Macro F1
Xu_150	57.77	52.60	48.62	39.15
Xu_300	71.59	68.00	69.49	60.79
Xu_450	—	—	77.93	67.57
Xu_Weak	69.36	65.37	75.39	67.33

More in detail, Xu_Weak, shown in Table 6, is the model trained with probabilistic labels computed by our weak-supervision method. The weak-supervision approach uses 150 examples belonging to SemEval dev sets in order to fine-tune the Snorkel generative model. Xu_150, Xu_300, Xu_450 are the models obtained by fine-tuning [76] with a different number of hand-labeled examples (150, 300, and 450 respectively) belonging to the in-domain SemEval training set. To obtain balanced datasets, examples are randomly extracted. In particular, we sampled the train set 10 times averaging the results. The weak-supervision approach reaches better results in the restaurants domain. It could be due to the availability of more examples obtained in post-trained for the restaurant domain.

Summarizing, as shown in these experiments, when different domains with commons features are available, it is convenient to use cross-domain transfer learning. In fact, a lot of syntactic features, structural information, and semantic language relationships can be learned and exploited cross-domains. Instead, weak-supervision remains a useful way to deal with real-world use cases where hand-labeled training sets with specific knowledge are needed and may become a bottleneck for implementing deep learning models. The main advantage of discriminative models for automatically label probabilistic examples is the easy capability to scale the number of labeled examples needed to get better performances.

5   Conclusions

In this paper, we described two approaches, based on transfer learning and weak supervision, both having the goal to reduce the manual effort needed to build an annotated dataset for the ASC problem. We adopted a general transfer learning approach that exploits the knowledge obtained in other domains to avoid training parameters of deep learning algorithms from scratch. At the same time, we presented a weak-supervision approach, specifically designed for the ASC task of the ABSA problem, that provides semi-automatic data labeling methods to lower the manual effort. To test effectiveness and applicability, we extensively tested proposed approaches on the laptops and restaurants dataset of SemEval task 4 subtask 2. Experiments have shown that when different domains with commons features are available, it is convenient to use cross-domain transfer learning. In fact, a lot of syntactic features, structural information, and semantic language relationships can be learned and exploited cross-domains. Instead, weak-supervision remains a useful way to deal with real-world use cases where hand-labeled training sets with specific knowledge are needed and may become a bottleneck for implementing deep learning models.

References

1. Abdul-Mageed, M., Ungar, L.: EmoNet: fine-grained emotion detection with gated recurrent neural networks. In: Proceedings of the 55th Annual Meeting of the Association for Computational Linguistics: Volume 1, Long Papers, vol. 1, pp. 718–728 (2017)
2. Al-Moslmi, T., Omar, N., Abdullah, S., Albared, M.: Approaches to cross-domain sentiment analysis: a systematic literature review. IEEE Access **5**, 16173–16192 (2017)
3. Bach, S.H., et al.: Snorkel drybell: a case study in deploying weak supervision at industrial scale. In: Proceedings of the 2019 International Conference on Management of Data, pp. 362–375. ACM (2019)
4. Balazs, J.A., Velásquez, J.D.: Opinion mining and information fusion: a survey. Inf. Fusion **27**, 95–110 (2016)
5. Bird, S.: NLTK: the natural language toolkit. In: Proceedings of the COLING/ACL on Interactive presentation sessions, pp. 69–72. Association for Computational Linguistics (2006)
6. Blitzer, J., Dredze, M., Pereira, F.: Biographies, bollywood, boom-boxes and blenders: Domain adaptation for sentiment classification. In: Proceedings of the 45th Annual Meeting of the Association of Computational Linguistics, pp. 440–447 (2007)
7. Bojanowski, P., Grave, E., Joulin, A., Mikolov, T.: Enriching word vectors with subword information. Trans. Assoc. Comput. Linguist. **5**, 135–146 (2017)
8. Borele, P., Borikar, D.A.: A survey on evaluating sentiments by using artificial neural network (2016)
9. Chen, P., Sun, Z., Bing, L., Yang, W.: Recurrent attention network on memory for aspect sentiment analysis. In: Proceedings of the 2017 Conference on Empirical Methods in Natural Language Processing, pp. 452–461 (2017)
10. Deng, L., Wiebe, J.: MPQA 3.0: an entity/event-level sentiment corpus. In: HLT-NAACL, pp. 1323–1328 (2015)
11. Devlin, J., Chang, M.W., Lee, K., Toutanova, K.: BERT: pre-training of deep bidirectional transformers for language understanding. In: NAACL-HLT (2019)

12. Dong, L., Wei, F., Tan, C., Tang, D., Zhou, M., Xu, K.: Adaptive recursive neural network for target-dependent twitter sentiment classification. In: Proceedings of the 52nd Annual Meeting of the Association for Computational Linguistics: Volume 2, Short Papers, vol. 2, pp. 49–54 (2014)
13. García-Pablos, A., Cuadros, M., Rigau, G.: V3: unsupervised generation of domain aspect terms for aspect based sentiment analysis. In: Proceedings of the 8th International Workshop on Semantic Evaluation (SemEval 2014), pp. 833–837 (2014)
14. Garcia-Pablos, A., Cuadros, M., Rigau, G.: V3: unsupervised aspect based sentiment analysis for SemEval2015 task 12. In: Proceedings of the 9th International Workshop on Semantic Evaluation (SemEval 2015), pp. 714–718 (2015)
15. García-Pablos, A., Cuadros, M., Rigau, G.: W2VLDA: almost unsupervised system for aspect based sentiment analysis. Expert Syst. Appl. **91**, 127–137 (2018)
16. Go, A., Bhayani, R., Huang, L.: Twitter sentiment classification using distant supervision. CS224N Project Report, Stanford 1(12) (2009)
17. He, R., McAuley, J.: Ups and downs: modeling the visual evolution of fashion trends with one-class collaborative filtering. In: Proceedings of the 25th International Conference on World Wide Web, pp. 507–517 (2016)
18. Hltcoe, J.: SemEval-2013 task 2: sentiment analysis in twitter, Atlanta, Georgia, USA, p. 312 (2013)
19. Hu, M., Liu, B.: Mining and summarizing customer reviews. In: Proceedings of the tenth ACM SIGKDD International Conference on Knowledge Discovery and Data Mining, pp. 168–177. ACM (2004)
20. Hussein, D.M.E.D.M.: A survey on sentiment analysis challenges. J. King Saud Univ. Eng. Sci. **30**(4), 330–338 (2016)
21. Irsoy, O., Cardie, C.: Deep recursive neural networks for compositionality in language. In: Advances in Neural Information Processing Systems, pp. 2096–2104 (2014)
22. Jo, Y., Oh, A.H.: Aspect and sentiment unification model for online review analysis. In: Proceedings of the Fourth ACM International Conference on Web Search and Data Mining, pp. 815–824. ACM (2011)
23. Lei, T., Barzilay, R., Jaakkola, T.: Rationalizing neural predictions. arXiv preprint arXiv:1606.04155 (2016)
24. Li, C., Guo, X., Mei, Q.: Deep memory networks for attitude identification. In: Proceedings of the Tenth ACM International Conference on Web Search and Data Mining, pp. 671–680. ACM (2017)
25. Liu, B.: Sentiment analysis and opinion mining. Synth. Lect. Hum. Lang. Technol. **5**(1), 1–167 (2012)
26. Liu, J., Zhang, Y.: Attention modeling for targeted sentiment. In: Proceedings of the 15th Conference of the European Chapter of the Association for Computational Linguistics: Volume 2, Short Papers, vol. 2, pp. 572–577 (2017)
27. Liu, P., Joty, S., Meng, H.: Fine-grained opinion mining with recurrent neural networks and word embeddings. In: Proceedings of the 2015 Conference on Empirical Methods in Natural Language Processing, pp. 1433–1443 (2015)
28. Ma, D., Li, S., Zhang, X., Wang, H.: Interactive attention networks for aspect-level sentiment classification. arXiv preprint arXiv:1709.00893 (2017)
29. Maas, A.L., Daly, R.E., Pham, P.T., Huang, D., Ng, A.Y., Potts, C.: Learning word vectors for sentiment analysis. In: Proceedings of the 49th Annual Meeting of the Association for Computational Linguistics: Human Language Technologies, vol. 1, pp. 142–150. Association for Computational Linguistics (2011)

30. Manning, C., Surdeanu, M., Bauer, J., Finkel, J., Bethard, S., McClosky, D.: The stanford CoreNLP natural language processing toolkit. In: Proceedings of 52nd Annual Meeting of the Association for Computational Linguistics: System Demonstrations, pp. 55–60 (2014)
31. Medhat, W., Hassan, A., Korashy, H.: Sentiment analysis algorithms and applications: a survey. Ain Shams Eng. J. **5**(4), 1093–1113 (2014)
32. Mikolov, T., Chen, K., Corrado, G., Dean, J.: Efficient estimation of word representations in vector space. arXiv preprint arXiv:1301.3781 (2013)
33. Mikolov, T., Sutskever, I., Chen, K., Corrado, G.S., Dean, J.: Distributed representations of words and phrases and their compositionality. In: Advances in Neural Information Processing Systems, pp. 3111–3119 (2013)
34. Oro, E., Pizzuti, C., Procopio, N., Ruffolo, M.: Detecting topic authoritative social media users: a multilayer network approach. IEEE Trans. Multimedia **20**(5), 1195–1208 (2017)
35. Oro, E., Pizzuti, C., Ruffolo, M.: A methodology for identifying influencers and their products perception on twitter. In: ICEIS (2018)
36. Oro, E., Ruffolo, M., Pupo, F.: A cognitive automation approach for a smart lending and early warning application. In: Poulovassilis, A., et al. (eds.) Proceedings of the Workshops of the EDBT/ICDT 2020 Joint Conference, Copenhagen, Denmark, March 30, 2020. CEUR Workshop Proceedings, vol. 2578. CEUR-WS.org (2020). http://ceur-ws.org/Vol-2578/DARLIAP6.pdf
37. Pang, B., Lee, L.: A sentimental education: sentiment analysis using subjectivity summarization based on minimum cuts. In: Proceedings of the 42nd Annual Meeting on Association for Computational Linguistics, p. 271. Association for Computational Linguistics (2004)
38. Pang, B., Lee, L.: Seeing stars: exploiting class relationships for sentiment categorization with respect to rating scales. In: Proceedings of the 43rd Annual Meeting on Association for Computational Linguistics, pp. 115–124. Association for Computational Linguistics (2005)
39. Pang, B., Lee, L.: Opinion mining and sentiment analysis. Found. Trends Inf. Retrieval **2**(1–2), 1–135 (2008)
40. Pang, B., Lee, L., Vaithyanathan, S.: Thumbs up? Sentiment classification using machine learning techniques. In: Proceedings of the ACL-02 conference on Empirical Methods in Natural Language Processing-Volume 10, pp. 79–86. Association for Computational Linguistics (2002)
41. Pennington, J., Socher, R., Manning, C.D.: Glove: global vectors for word representation. EMNLP **14**, 1532–1543 (2014)
42. Pereg, O., Korat, D., Wasserblat, M., Mamou, J., Dagan, I.: ABSApp: a portable weakly-supervised aspect-based sentiment extraction system. arXiv preprint arXiv:1909.05608 (2019)
43. Pontiki, M., et al.: SemEval-2016 task 5: aspect based sentiment analysis. In: Proceedings of the 10th International Workshop on Semantic Evaluation (SemEval-2016), pp. 19–30 (2016)
44. Pontiki, M., Galanis, D., Papageorgiou, H., Manandhar, S., Androutsopoulos, I.: SemEval-2015 task 12: aaspect based sentiment analysis. In: Proceedings of the 9th International Workshop on Semantic Evaluation (SemEval 2015), pp. 486–495 (2015)

45. Pontiki, M., Galanis, D., Pavlopoulos, J., Papageorgiou, H., Androutsopoulos, I., Manandhar, S.: SemEval-2014 task 4: aspect based sentiment analysis. In: Proceedings of the 8th International Workshop on Semantic Evaluation (SemEval 2014), pp. 27–35. Association for Computational Linguistics, Dublin, Ireland (2014). https://doi.org/10.3115/v1/S14-2004
46. Poria, S., Hazarika, D., Majumder, N., Mihalcea, R.: Beneath the tip of the iceberg: Current challenges and new directions in sentiment analysis research. arXiv preprint arXiv:2005.00357 (2020)
47. Purpura, A., Masiero, C., Susto, G.A.: WS4ABSA: an NMF-based weakly-supervised approach for aspect-based sentiment analysis with application to online reviews. In: Soldatova, L., Vanschoren, J., Papadopoulos, G., Ceci, M. (eds.) Discovery Science. Lecture Notes in Computer Science, vol. 11198, pp. 386–401. Springer, Cham (2018). https://doi.org/10.1007/978-3-030-01771-2_25
48. Qiu, G., Liu, B., Bu, J., Chen, C.: Expanding domain sentiment lexicon through double propagation. In: Twenty-First International Joint Conference on Artificial Intelligence (2009)
49. Qiu, G., Liu, B., Bu, J., Chen, C.: Opinion word expansion and target extraction through double propagation. Comput. Linguist. **37**(1), 9–27 (2011)
50. Rajpurkar, P., Zhang, J., Lopyrev, K., Liang, P.: Squad: 100, 000+ questions for machine comprehension of text. In: EMNLP (2016)
51. Ratner, A., Bach, S.H., Ehrenberg, H., Fries, J., Wu, S., Ré, C.: Snorkel: rapid training data creation with weak supervision. Proc. VLDB Endow. **11**(3), 269–282 (2017)
52. Ratner, A.J., De Sa, C.M., Wu, S., Selsam, D., Ré, C.: Data programming: creating large training sets, quickly. In: Advances in Neural Information Processing Systems, pp. 3567–3575 (2016)
53. Ravi, K., Ravi, V.: A survey on opinion mining and sentiment analysis: tasks, approaches and applications. Knowl.-Based Syst. **89**, 14–46 (2015)
54. Rietzler, A., Stabinger, S., Opitz, P., Engl, S.: Adapt or get left behind: domain adaptation through bert language model finetuning for aspect-target sentiment classification. arXiv preprint arXiv:1908.11860 (2019)
55. Rogers, A., Kovaleva, O., Rumshisky, A.: A primer in bertology: what we know about how bert works. arXiv preprint arXiv:2002.12327 (2020)
56. Rosenthal, S., Farra, N., Nakov, P.: SemEval-2017 task 4: sentiment analysis in twitter. In: Proceedings of the 11th International Workshop on Semantic Evaluation (SemEval-2017), pp. 502–518 (2017)
57. Ruder, S.: Neural transfer learning for natural language processing. Ph.D. thesis, NUI Galway (2019)
58. Ruder, S., Ghaffari, P., Breslin, J.G.: A hierarchical model of reviews for aspect-based sentiment analysis. arXiv preprint arXiv:1609.02745 (2016)
59. Ruder, S., Peters, M.E., Swayamdipta, S., Wolf, T.: Transfer learning in natural language processing. In: Proceedings of the 2019 Conference of the North American Chapter of the Association for Computational Linguistics: Tutorials, pp. 15–18 (2019)
60. Ruffolo, M., Visalli, F.: A weak-supervision method for automating training set creation in multi-domain aspect sentiment classification. In: ICAART (2020)
61. Socher, R., et al.: Recursive deep models for semantic compositionality over a sentiment treebank. In: Proceedings of the conference on empirical methods in natural language processing (EMNLP), vol. 1631, p. 1642. Citeseer (2013)
62. Soleymani, M., Garcia, D., Jou, B., Schuller, B., Chang, S.F., Pantic, M.: A survey of multimodal sentiment analysis. Image Vis. Comput. **65**, 3–14 (2017)

63. Tang, D., Qin, B., Feng, X., Liu, T.: Effective lstms for target-dependent sentiment classification. arXiv preprint arXiv:1512.01100 (2015)
64. Tang, D., Qin, B., Liu, T.: Aspect level sentiment classification with deep memory network. arXiv preprint arXiv:1605.08900 (2016)
65. Tay, Y., Tuan, L.A., Hui, S.C.: Dyadic memory networks for aspect-based sentiment analysis. In: Proceedings of the 2017 ACM on Conference on Information and Knowledge Management, pp. 107–116. ACM (2017)
66. Van Kleef, E., Van Trijp, H.C., Luning, P.: Consumer research in the early stages of new product development: a critical review of methods and techniques. Food Qual. Prefer. **16**(3), 181–201 (2005)
67. Vaswani, A.,et al.: Attention is all you need. In: NIPS (2017)
68. Vaswani, A., et al.: Attention is all you need. In: Advances in Neural Information Processing Systems, pp. 5998–6008 (2017)
69. Vo, D.T., Zhang, Y.: Target-dependent twitter sentiment classification with rich automatic features. In: IJCAI, pp. 1347–1353 (2015)
70. Wang, W., Pan, S.J.: Recursive neural structural correspondence network for cross-domain aspect and opinion co-extraction. In: Proceedings of the 56th Annual Meeting of the Association for Computational Linguistics: Volume 1, Long Papers, pp. 2171–2181 (2018)
71. Wang, W., Pan, S.J., Dahlmeier, D., Xiao, X.: Recursive neural conditional random fields for aspect-based sentiment analysis. arXiv preprint arXiv:1603.06679 (2016)
72. Wang, W., Pan, S.J., Dahlmeier, D., Xiao, X.: Coupled multi-layer attentions for co-extraction of aspect and opinion terms. In: AAAI, pp. 3316–3322 (2017)
73. Wang, Y., Huang, M., Zhao, L., et al.: Attention-based lstm for aspect-level sentiment classification. In: Proceedings of the 2016 Conference on Empirical Methods in Natural Language Processing, pp. 606–615 (2016)
74. Wiebe, J., Wilson, T., Cardie, C.: Annotating expressions of opinions and emotions in language. Lang. Resour. Eval. **39**(2), 165–210 (2005)
75. Wu, Y., et al.: Google's neural machine translation system: bridging the gap between human and machine translation. arXiv preprint arXiv:1609.08144 (2016)
76. Xu, H., Liu, B., Shu, L., Yu, P.S.: Bert post-training for review reading comprehension and aspect-based sentiment analysis. arXiv preprint arXiv:1904.02232 (2019)
77. Yang, B., Cardie, C.: Extracting opinion expressions with semi-markov conditional random fields. In: Proceedings of the 2012 Joint Conference on Empirical Methods in Natural Language Processing and Computational Natural Language Learning, pp. 1335–1345. Association for Computational Linguistics (2012)
78. Yang, M., Tu, W., Wang, J., Xu, F., Chen, X.: Attention based LSTM for target dependent sentiment classification. In: AAAI, pp. 5013–5014 (2017)
79. Ying, D., Yu, J., Jiang, J.: Recurrent neural networks with auxiliary labels for cross-domain opinion target extraction (2017)
80. Zagibalov, T., Carroll, J.: Automatic seed word selection for unsupervised sentiment classification of Chinese text. In: Proceedings of the 22nd International Conference on Computational Linguistics, vol. 1, pp. 1073–1080. Association for Computational Linguistics (2008)
81. Zhang, L., Wang, S., Liu, B.: Deep learning for sentiment analysis: a survey. Data Mining and Knowledge Discovery. Wiley Interdisciplinary Reviews. Wiley, Hoboken, New Jersey (2018)
82. Zhang, M., Zhang, Y., Vo, D.T.: Neural networks for open domain targeted sentiment. In: Proceedings of the 2015 Conference on Empirical Methods in Natural Language Processing, pp. 612–621 (2015)

83. Zhu, X., Guo, H., Sobhani, P.: Neural networks for integrating compositional and non-compositional sentiment in sentiment composition. In: Proceedings of the Fourth Joint Conference on Lexical and Computational Semantics, pp. 1–9 (2015)

84. Zhu, Y., Kiros, R., Zemel, R., Salakhutdinov, R., Urtasun, R., Torralba, A., Fidler, S.: Aligning books and movies: towards story-like visual explanations by watching movies and reading books. In: Proceedings of the IEEE International Conference on Computer Vision, pp. 19–27 (2015)

Quantifying Gaze-Based Strategic Patterns in Physics Vector Field Divergence

Saleh Mozaffari[1,2,3(✉)], Pascal Klein[4], Mohammad Al-Naser[1,2], Stefan Küchemann[1], Jochen Kuhn[1], Thomas Widmann[3], and Andreas Dengel[1,2]

[1] Technische Universität Kaiserslautern, Kaiserslautern, Germany
[2] German Research Center for Artificial Intelligence (DFKI GmbH), Kaiserslautern, Germany
[3] WidasConcepts GmbH, Wimsheim, Germany
saleh.mozafari@widas.de
[4] Georg-August-Universität Göttingen, Göttingen, Germany

Abstract. We instructed a group of 20 undergraduate physics students with an instruction to visually interpret divergence of vector field with integral and differential strategies. We designed two distinct sets of 10 tasks and recorded the students' eye gaze while they completed the task. In this study, we first developed Attentive Region Clustering (ARC), a novel unsupervised approach to analyze and evaluate the fixations and saccadic movements of the participants. Secondly, a linear Support Vector Machine model was used to classify the two problem-solving strategies in the vector field domain. The results revealed the implication of vector flow orientation in the eye movement patterns. We achieved an accuracy 10-$fold$ cross-validation, we achieved 81.2% (11%) accuracy by evaluating a linear Support Vector Machine model to classify which strategy was applied by the student to comprehend the divergence of a vector field problem. The outcome of this work is useful to monitor the student visual performance on similar tasks. Besides, advances in Human-Computer Interaction empower students by getting objective feedback on their progress by visual clues in a vector field problems.

Keywords: Physics education · Eye-tracking · Gaze-pattern · Problem-solving · Classification

1 Introduction

The interpretation of graphical representations plays a significant role in physics education and is also essential in several related fields. The development of this skill for students is considered a gateway to their future employment and life opportunities [15]. With the recent advances in Artificial Intelligence (AI) and Human-Computer Interaction (HCI), Physics Education aims to provide an effective system to enhance learning quality. Such a system needs to investigate how the students explore, perceive, process, and interpret different kinds of information. The visual system plays a crucial role in exploring and extracting information from different sorts of graphical representations to interpret physics concepts. Many problems in upper-division physics and

© Springer Nature Switzerland AG 2021
A. P. Rocha et al. (Eds.): ICAART 2020, LNAI 12613, pp. 465–481, 2021.
https://doi.org/10.1007/978-3-030-71158-0_22

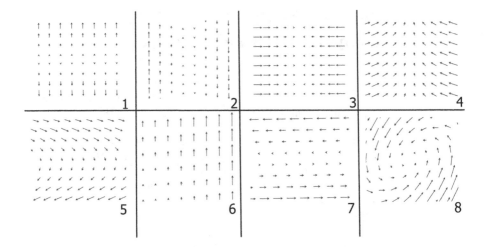

Fig. 1. Vector field plot representations used in this study [15].

other scientific disciplines require students to relate abstract concepts to multiple external representations, including diagrams, equations, graphics, or data tables. Substantially, from an educational perspective, it is well known that multiple representations of abstract concepts have the potential to promote learning [14]. However, the acquisition of this skill requires instructional support, especially concepts that become more sophisticated. A great deal of uncertainty rises when the eyes scan the representations for visually informative clues. This uncertainty roots in many factors, including individual differences, educational background, ethnicity, culture, environment, and many more. Also, in many physics concepts, the myriad ways of visual strategies are available for interacting with the different types of representations [16–18]. However, some physics domains have distinct visual strategy rules. One example of such a domain, consists of the visual interpretation of two-dimensional vector field plots according to divergence [2,7,10,11,13]. When students engage with multiple representations, eye tracking offers unique possibilities for tracking their processing of context, including text, tables, equations, and diagrams. It allows analyzing and computationally modeling the eye-gaze data to evaluate the students' visual cognitive performance objectively. Consequently, such an objective evaluation helps to improve the quality of learning in that particular physics domain. Furthermore, Eye-Tracking provides educators to assess the students' non-verbal cognitive performance, and besides, the students benefit from the feedback on their gaze-driven approach. Despite the vast attention paid by the eye-tracking research community to the data analysis, fewer studies address the classification of eye-movements patterns in education [6]. Therefore, the modeling of the strategic-based eye movement behavior sounds promising to increase the learning quality in the physics domain. This research investigated the student's visual understanding of vector field plots indicated in Fig. 1, which are fundamental for learning theoretical physics. This concept occurs in the introductory and upper-division university physics curricula [11]. Prior research has shown that most students and even graduates fail to connect the concept of divergence to graphical vector field representations [2,20].

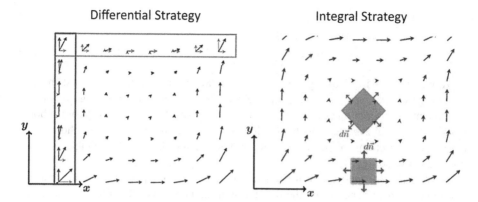

Fig. 2. Graphical representation of a two-dimensional vector field. The left panel displays the procedure of the differential strategy. To judge whether y-component of the vector field (red arrows) changes in y-direction, the students need to focus on the red box. Similarly, to judge whether x-component of the vector field (yellow arrows) changes in x-direction, the students only need to focus on the yellow box. Combining both information, the students can conclude on the divergence of the vector field. The right panel shows the procedure of the integration strategy. To determine the divergence, the students need to quantify the arrows entering and exiting certain areas (here red squares) [15].

Briefly, There are two similar but yet different approaches to this problem, requiring different visual strategies; integral and differential approaches, which are presented in Fig. 2. This paper's contribution is three-fold: Firstly, it explores context-related eye-tracking features and investigates on feature engineering of eye movement transitions. Secondly, it introduces a novel unsupervised method to cluster the attentive regions on the vector field representations. Thirdly, it presents and evaluates a supervised model of the two approaches upon the derived features.

2   Subject Background

2.1   Vector Field Divergence

A vector field is a structure that a vector is assigned to every point in a subset of space. Divergence is a mathematical concept that applies to vector fields. Divergence can be interpreted locally (sources/sinks at specific points) or globally (net flow outwards of an area or volume). This intuition is made precise by the divergence theorem of Gauss. The divergence concept can be expressed in many different representations [1], but most often expressed in a graphical representation. Both interpretations of divergence mentioned above can be applied qualitatively to a vector field representation. We refer to them as the Differential Strategy (DS) and the Integral Strategy (IS), and illustrate them in Fig. 2 for a simple but useful case for teaching.

Differential Strategy (DS)

$$\text{div}\,\mathbf{F} = \frac{\partial F_x}{\partial x} + \frac{\partial F_y}{\partial y} \tag{1}$$

Integral Strategy (IS):

$$\mathrm{div} \boldsymbol{F} = \lim_{V \to 0} \frac{1}{V} \int_{\partial V} \boldsymbol{F} \cdot d\boldsymbol{n}. \tag{2}$$

Application of Eq. 1 to a graphical vector field plot means that one must inspect the change of the x-component of the field in the x-direction and change of the y-component in y-direction (see Fig. 2 center). Vividly speaking, we must perform horizontal and vertical eye movements to judge the change of the vector field in horizontal and vertical directions, respectively, making this visual task perfectly suitable for eye-tracking methodology.

In contrast, the application of Eq. 1 to a graphical vector field plot means that we determine the divergence using the flux through the boundary ∂V of a test volume V in the field (or test areas in the two-dimensional case), see Fig. 2 right. For instance, qualitative reasoning is simple if the outer surface normal $d\boldsymbol{n}$ is either parallel or perpendicular to the field vector $\boldsymbol{F}$ (e.g., cuboids or spheres in 3D and rectangles or circles in 2D). When students use this strategy, we expect a higher number of fixations, longer fixation duration and shorter saccade lengths compared to the application of Eq. 1 to the field [11].

2.2 Eye-Tracking

Eye-Tracking is a non-intrusive tool for acquiring and quantifying visual attention and cognitive processing.

Eye-Tracking Metrics. Eye-Tracking metrics is fundamentally comprised of two components gathered from raw gaze points: fixations and saccadic.

Fixation is a relatively long period event usually lasting between 100 ms to 600 ms (fixation duration), in which the eye is almost still. Technically, it is a cluster of raw gaze points close in the specific spatio-temporal range. The most often used eye-tracking features are derived from fixations.

Saccades are the rapid eye shifts between fixations with velocities as high as 500° per second.

According to the theory of long-term working memory, the information-reduction hypothesis, and the holistic model of image perception, fixation duration, number of fixations, and saccadic length are associated with information processing, selective attention allocation, and visual span, respectively [5]. Even though these measures are fundamental to general eye-tracking methodology, they are not enough to evaluate attention. In the Methodology section, the more sophisticated eye-tracking features introduced.

3 Data Collection

This section demonstrates the data collection phase. The participants, the study design, as well as the experiment's procedure, are presented here.

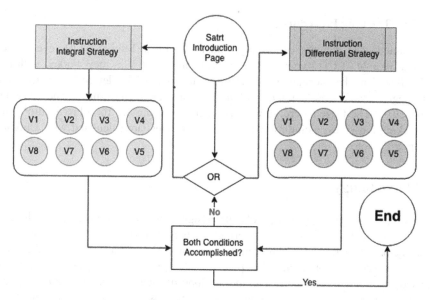

Fig. 3. The procedure of the experiment. The students started with an introduction about the concept of Vector Divergence Problem displayed on a computer screen. Then, students started with the DS strategy (see Fig. 2 left panel) or with the IS strategy (see Fig. 2 right panel). Both instructions, DS and IS, covered 250 words and included a step-by-step description with visual cues about the application. In each instruction period, students applied the prevailing strategy to eight vector fields (V1—V8) Fig. 1 which were presented one after another [15].

3.1 Participants

Twenty major physics students of Technische Universität Kaiserslautern (15 male, 5 female) aged 19–24 (average 20.6 years) took part in the experiment. All participants were about to attend an introductory electromagnetism course and had completed two mechanics lectures (calculus-based mechanics and experimental physics). Divergence has been introduced in both mechanics lectures and has also been recapitulated in the electromagnetism course before the experiment was conducted. Participation was voluntary, took 30 min in total (survey and experiment), and was compensated with 10$.

3.2 Study Design and Material

The students started with an introduction to the concept of vector field divergence displayed on a computer screen. The sequence of the experiment is illustrated in Fig. 3. All students started with strategy 1 (Fig. 2 left); the derivative strategy, DS) or strategy 2 (Fig. 2 right; the integral strategy, IS). Both instructions, DS and IS; covered 250 words (1 textbook page), respectively, and included a detailed description with visual cues about the application (worked-out example). In each instruction period, students applied the prevailing strategy to eight vector fields shown in Fig. 1, which were presented one after another. Figure 1 presents the vector fields used in the study. Students did not receive any feedback after completing a VDP and were unable to revisit the instruction page.

3.3   Eye-Tracking Procedures

We obtained gaze data for all twenty students using a Tobii X3-120[1] eye-tracker installed on a 24″ LCD screen with an aspect ratio of 16:9 as they worked with the VDP. All students had normal or correct-to-normal vision. The device has an accuracy of 0.4 degrees[2] and allows a relatively high freedom of head movement. The sampling frequency 120 Hz. Gaze recording was accomplished using the Tobii Pro Studio[3]. The eye-tracking measures, including fixations and saccades, are calculated with a library written in Python.

4   Methodology

As mentioned in Sect. 2, in order to solve the assignments, students need to scan the presented vector fields according to the informed strategy. This strategy contains which part of the vector field and in which order must be scanned. Due to the spatio-temporal characteristics of recorded data, traditional position based metrics, i.e., fixation duration, are not adequate as it demands more of temporal supportive features. In this section, we first introduce the investigated eye-tracking features. Also, we introduce a novel attention-based clustering for clustering the gaze on the Area of Interest (AOI) (Fig. 4).

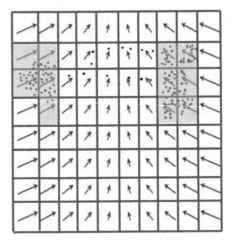

Fig. 4. Illustration of the identification of tiles (yellow) which are regions within the 10 × 10 grid which received more fixations (black dots) then the threshold (here 3 fixations) [15]. (Color figure online)

---

[1] https://www.tobiipro.com/product-listing/tobii-pro-x3-120/.

[2] Reported by the manufacturer.

[3] https://www.tobiipro.com/product-listing/tobii-pro-studio/.

4.1   Attentive Region Clustering

It is inevitable having noise and outliers in an eye-tracking experiment. Besides, depending on experiment design, not all of the collected gaze patterns are relevant to the research. For instance, in this study, we ignored the fixations outside of the desired Area of Interest (AOI), which is the area of the vector field (see Fig. 1). Furthermore, in particular, this algorithm tends to find attentive region(s) in the vector fields 1–8 for both DS and IS. The inattentive regions could bias the dispersion-based features. Hence, we propose a novel approach, here termed Attentive Region Clustering Algorithm (ARCA), to cluster the attentive region(s) inside the vector field. The Attentive Region Clustering Algorithm is presented in Algorithm 1. The ARCA (Algorithm 1) provides the fixations during problem-solving, whereas inattentive fixations are mostly scattered broadly inside the vector representation. Using the filtered fixations, in the next section, we propose a similarity measure to evaluate the divergence of the vector field representations.

Algorithm 1. Attentive Region Clustering.

Result: Write here the result
calculate $fixations$ from raw gaze samples ;
define AOI in the stimuli as the representative region for the vector field area;
omit the fixations out of the AOI box;
$threshold = 3 fixations$;
for $strategies : (DS, IS)$ **do**
   for $participants : [1 : 20]$ **do**
      for $stimulus : [V1 : V8]$ **do**
         M = split AOI into $10x10$ grid;
         create attention map: calculate the fixation population on M $tiles$;
         for $tile : M[1 : 10, 1 : 10]$ **do**
            if $|tile| < threshold$ **then**
               discard $tile$;
         end
         label-connected tiles: finding islands in M;
         intersect fixations of AOI area with M;
      end
   end
end

4.2   Saccadic Codifications

The visual strategies indicated in Fig. 2 offer either axis-wise evaluation in the differential problem or observing the vector flow through an arbitrary rectangle inside the vector field. Hence, eye movement directions during the problem-solving task reveal the quality of visual approaches made by the students based on the instructions. Selection of the axis side left or right, and up or down is optional to solve differential (DS) problems. It is somehow similar to integral (IS) tasks' visual strategy where the position of the rectangle with any rotation inside the vector field representation is flexible. Hence, we group the saccades into X for the x-axis, Y for the y-axis, M for diagonal, and N for anti-diagonal directions. To group saccades into X, Y, M, and N, the *absolute saccadic angularity* is used for the labeling. In this sense, as Fig. 5 presents, all saccades within in the angular range of 337.5°–22.5° combined with those from 157.5°–202.5° are labeled as **X**, the ones from 22.5°–67.5° combined with those from 202.5°–247.5° are labeled as **N**, the ones from 67.5°–112.5° combined with those from 253.5°–297.5° are labeled as **Y** and the ones from 22.5°–67.5° combined with those from 202.5°–247.5° are labeled as **M**.

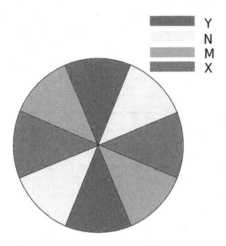

Fig. 5. Illustration of saccadic codification.

4.3   Transition Matrix

The sequence of saccades constructs a string for each trial. The elements of the string are associated with the corresponding saccadic labels. Consequently, $N = 320$ sequences from $20 \times 8 \times 2$ trials were constructed (20 participants processed 8 vector fields for two trials, IS and DS). These sequences are essential for calculating the corresponding transition matrices.

A transition matrix is 4×4 2-D array as an alternative representation of the sequence. For instance, Table 1 presents an exemplary transition matrix for the sequence **"XXXXMYYYNYX"**.

Table 1. An exemplary transition matrix for the sequence "XXXMYYYNYX". For example, $X \longrightarrow X$ transition two times happened in the beginning of the sequence.

	X	Y	M	N
X	3	0	1	0
Y	1	2	0	1
M	0	1	0	0
N	0	1	0	0

4.4 Feature Extraction

Appropriate feature selection is a highly vital stage to construct a robust machine learning model. Both dispersion-based and sequential-based features are necessary to build a robust model for the classification of the visual strategies defined in Sect. 2. In this study, we calculated the following features for each trial ($N = 320$) to build up our model:

Stationary Entropy (H_s). *Entropy* is a measure in information theory to describe the information in a variable in terms of ordering. This measure is called Shannon entropy and it is defined as:

$$H_s = - \sum_i p(r_i) \log_2(r_i), r_i > 0 \tag{3}$$

where H_s is the stationary entropy in bits and $p(r_i)$ is the proportion of saccadic label r_i. r_i replaced with 1e-9 in case $r_i = 0$. We normalized the stationary entropy by dividing the result with the maximum possible entropy. In our case, four labels construct the sequence. Therefore, $\sum_{i=1}^{4} \frac{1}{4} \log_2(\frac{1}{4}) = 2.0$, is the maximum possible bits. Hence, all stationary entropy results divided by 2.0.

Transition Entropy (H_t). The entropy can be calculated for a transition matrix [12, 17]. The lowest possible value is zero when there is no uncertainty about what type of transition will occur. The maximum value for entropy is when all the cells in the transition matrix carry different values. As a measure of uncertainty, we investigated Jensen-Shannon divergence(JSD) in the transition matrices. JSD is a Shannon Entropy-based method to measure the similarity between two probability distributions [6]. It is an extended version of Kullback-Leibler divergence (KLD). As KLD fails to fulfill the triangle inequality, which leads to asymmetric results, we preferred to apply the JSD [6] for our purpose. The JSD results range in $[0..1]$ intervals, where the higher value indicates, the more the divergence. The Kullback-Leibler divergence and Jensen-Shannon divergence are defined as following:

$$KLD(p\|q) = \sum_X p(x) \log_2(\frac{p(x)}{q(x)}) \tag{4}$$

$$JSD(p(x)\|q(x)) = \frac{KLD(p(x)\|\frac{p(x)+q(x)}{2}) + KLD(q(x)\|\frac{p(x)+q(x)}{2})}{2} \tag{5}$$

Input data—$p(x)$ and $q(x)$—have the form of probability density functions, i. e., the normalized transition matrices.

Separated for both IS and DS strategies, for all we calculated the normalized transition matrix of each participant. Then for each group (IS and DS), the JSD similarity measure applied.

Relative Saccade Angularity (A_r). The average of relative saccade angles shows the students' tendency to drive their visual attention in the same direction. Relative saccade angularity is defined as the angle between a saccade, and the previous saccade[4].

Fixation Duration (F_d). Fixation duration [6] is a classical metric in eye-tracking research. It is a dispersion-based measure indicating the density of visual attention.

Attention Score (F_s). We calculate the attention score (F_s) by dividing the number of fixations in the attentive region calculated with ARCA (Algorithm 1) by all the fixations in the AOI. This measure approximates the focus on the instructed strategy.

Direction Rank Entropy (H_d). According to Sect. 2, in the vector field representation, there is a freedom of landing on the visual targets and drawing attention towards the arbitrary directions. However, tracing one direction, e.g. moving the visual attention simply up and down yield the same saccadic code (Y). Discriminating IS, and DS visual strategies requires information about opposite direction movements. The procedure to calculate H_d is the following:

1. In each sequence, directions to the left, down, down-left, and down-right weighted with -1 and the rest with $+1$. For instance, label X in the left directions becomes $-X$ and $+X$ Vice versa.
2. Then we add all the labels and get the absolute weight for each label. For example, $-2X$, $-4Y$, and 2M yields [2, 4, 2, 0].
3. Divide the weighted vector with the length of the sequence.
4. Normalize the weighted vector with the *l1* norm.
5. Replace zero values with 1e−9.
6. Calculate entropy of the weighted vector using Eq. 3.

Attentive Cluster Numbers (C_r). The attentive region acquired by ARCA could distinguish the visual strategies. To elaborate more, students may like to assume multiple rectangles in the vector field area to solve the integration (IS) problem. Therefore, in the IS, the number of attentive regions is relatively higher $(mean = 2.65, std = 0.36)$ compared to the axis-based strategy for DS $(mean = 1.71, std = 0.23)$.

4.5   Classification

To classify two visual strategies in the vector fields (IS and DS), in this stage of the research, the Support Vector Machine (SVM) was employed to build up the binary classifier. By using 10-fold cross-validation, 65% of data was selected randomly for training, and the rest was used for testing. Also, the best-tuned parameters $(C, \gamma,$ and $kernel)$ were selected by performing a grid search accompanied by the cross-validation. The model trained with the feature vector presented in Sect. 4.4. The investigation of other machine learning models left for future work.

---

[4] Absolute saccade angularity defines as the angle between the saccade and horizon.

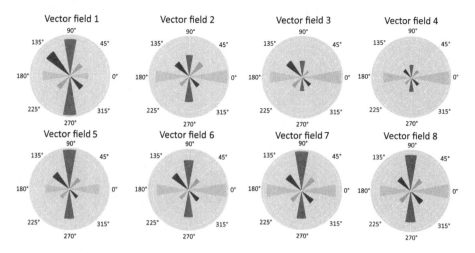

Fig. 6. The saccadic direction when students applying the DS to judge whether a vector field has zero or non-zero divergence. The colors indicate the angular interval labeled with X (light red) indicating horizontal saccades, Y (green) meaning vertical saccades, M (yellow) diagonal saccades and N (blue) anti-diagonal saccades. Horizontal (X) and vertical eye-movements are more pronounced in this approach compared to the IS [15]. (Color figure online)

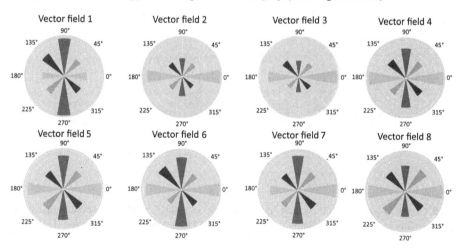

Fig. 7. The saccadic direction when students applying the IS to judge whether a vector field has zero or non-zero divergence. The colors indicate the angular interval labeled with X (light red) indicating horizontal saccades, Y (green) meaning vertical saccades, M (yellow) diagonal saccades and N (blue) anti-diagonal saccades. Exploring diagonally and anti-diagonally is more evident in this approach compared to DS [15]. (Color figure online)

5   Results

By looking at Fig. 8, it is clear that students have relatively more attention on the integration task (IS) in all of the vector fields compare to differentiation (DS) tasks. On the other hand, as Fig. 9 suggests the higher score of uncertainty in students for solving

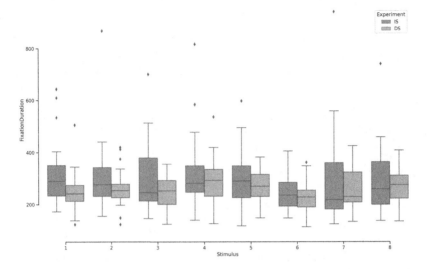

Fig. 8. Comparing fixation duration of two tasks IS and DS. Students showed relatively denser attentions on the integration task (IS) in all of the vector fields compare to differentiation (DS) task.

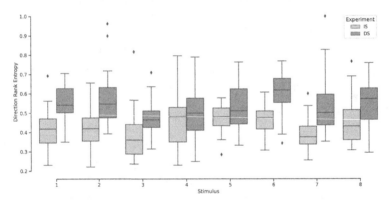

Fig. 9. Comparing Direction Rank Entropy of two tasks IS and DS. Students showed higher score of uncertainty in students for solving differentiation (DS) trial compare to integration (IS) trials.

differentiation (DS) trial compare to integration (IS) trials considering Direction Rank Entropy Sect. 4.4. It suggests, even though fixation duration is higher on IS task, participants performed their tasks in a more straight forward fashion.

Figures 6 and 7 show the saccadic directions preferred by students in integral and differential approaches, respectively. The axis-wise scanning tendency is higher in the DS. However, horizontal or vertical movements are varied in different movements. The similarity measure based on the Jensen-Shannon divergence for the vector flows presented in Fig. 10 and Fig. 11.

The results suggest in some vector field—but not all— that there is a tendency to choose various options of selecting the area or saccadic direction, implying that students dynamically fitting the strategy to the vector flows to get the right answer.

Classification Results. According to the Table 2, the best model selected by grid search and cross validation is an SVM with linear kernel, $C = 10$, and $\gamma = 0.001$ for the vectors presented in Sect. 4.4.

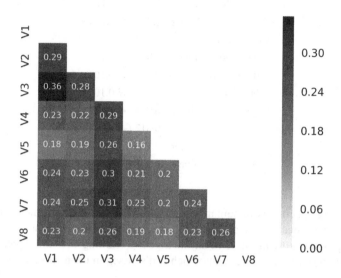

Fig. 10. The Jensen-Shannon divergence in vector field representations for IS.

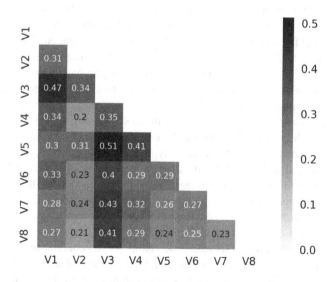

Fig. 11. The Jensen-Shannon divergence in vector field representations for DS.

Table 3 indicates the precision and recall of the model on the testing set. The linear SVM model has achieved an accuracy of 81.2% (0.11%).

Table 2. The best model selected by grid search and cross validation is an SVM with linear kernel, $C = 10$, and $\gamma = 0.001$.

C	gamma	kernel	accuracy
1	0.001	linear	0.774 (+/-0.129)
10	0.001	linear	0.817 (+/-0.111)
10	0.0001	linear	0.793 (+/-0.182)
100	0.001	linear	0.808 (+/-0.107)
100	0.0001	linear	0.808 (+/-0.107)
1000	0.001	linear	0.808 (+/-0.107)
1	-	linear	0.774 (+/-0.129)
10	-	linear	0.817 (+/-0.111)
100	-	linear	0.793 (+/-0.182)
1000	-	linear	0.808 (+/-0.107)

Considering uncertainty in human behavior, particularly eye movements, the results of the binary classification are promising to model expert gaze patterns to evaluate the real-world problem-solving tasks in an intelligent e-learning user interface. However, there is much room for improvement, which is discussed in the next section.

6   Discussion and Future Work

Considering the Dreyfus model of skill acquisition perspective [1,3,4], this work's contribution is twofold: First, it helps to offer the novice learners by providing appropriate instruction needed for conceptual learning. The awareness of students' visual behavior by monitoring a particular problem-solving strategy might be highly beneficial for them. Although not all of the physics problems are based on graphical representations such as the divergence of a vector field plot, it opens the door for an investigation of how to address certain missed instructions. Thus, the second contribution is from another point of view: "How to detect non-verbal patterns of the skilled persons and transfer it heuristically to the novices?". Fortunately, with the rising of deep learning in recent years, those associated visual patterns for solving and comprehending the related problem can be exploited and encoded with modern technologies [9]. According to these concerns, we start to use a simple linear model to have proof for the future investigations of more sophisticated machine-learning techniques. The classification score indicates the right path to pursue, although there are some constraints on data in both terms of quality and quantity. Jenson-Shanon Divergence (JSD) score is intentionally used in this research because of its role in designing an autoencoder for learning transfer purpose. An autoencoder is an unsupervised type of artificial neural network used to learn efficient data codings. Autoencoders aim to minimize the degree of uncertainty, e.g., JSD, to hold an efficient representation of data. Hence, to give a picture for further research, a similarity measure was performed to evaluate the difference between the JSD score means of two independent groups, which are DS and IS. The classification results are promising to develop gaze-based pattern, classification models.

Table 3. The score of the linear SVM model with $C = 10$ and $\gamma = 0.001$.

	Precision	Recall	f1-score	Support
DS	0.89	0.70	0.78	59
IS	0.73	0.91	0.81	53
Avg/total	0.81	0.81	0.79	112

In this study, we trained a linear SVM model for our purpose. However, other machine learning techniques can be investigated. For instance, Recurrent Neural Networks are highly suitable for sequential-based gaze data. The problem of deep networks is to have an adequate training set. Such an amount of data is very cumbersome to collect in the eye-tracking studies. By the rising interest in using generative models, the main idea of future work is to create a generative model from recorded data. Synthetic domain-specific eye movement data then can be used and evaluated with an appropriate deep network architecture [19].

The results also showed the effect of vector flow to form the strategy. Deeper data analysis in this regard leads to develop a more generic model in VDP. For instance, the correlation of the direction of the vector in the vector field plot with saccadic direction is worthy of exploring. Conducting a none-instruction-based experiment with the same vector field stimuli is in our agenda of research. Evaluating and quantifying the performance of students' task-related gaze behavior (IS and DS) with the model has been achieved in this study. Furthermore, investigation of gaze-patterns in reading—reading speed, regression rate, and reading depth—and find the relations to the comprehensibility of the problem-solving technique is another area of future work. The methods and ideas used in this research are plausible to apply in other domains of eye-tracking research. Finally, the concept idea of this paper connects machine learning and human-computer interaction [7,8] to develop an intelligent user interface to advance education in fundamental science such as physics and mathematics.

7   Conclusion

In this paper, we explored the eye-movement pattern of 20 students in instruction-based problem solving for integral and differential approaches in the domain of vector field divergence in physics. The results show that the vectors' flow orientations influence students' attention areas in the vector field representation and on the pursuit of different saccadic directions. Using a 10-fold cross-validation and grid search parameter, we tune the Support Vector Machine to classify the visual strategies (DS and IS), a linear kernel SVM with $C = 10$, and $\gamma = 0.001$ has achieved an accuracy of 81.2% (0.11%). The result shows that besides significant individual variations in eye-gaze patterns among students, the algorithm can classify strategic gaze-patterns in a specific problem domain. On the one hand, the results help improve the quality of learning and teaching since they provide a valid and detailed feedback for teachers on the effectiveness of their instructions to teach a defined strategy from monitoring the student's non-verbal performance. On the other hand, the algorithm may provide students with immediate objective feedback on their progress of learning.

References

1. Benner, P.: Using the dreyfus model of skill acquisition to describe and interpret skill acquisition and clinical judgment in nursing practice and education. Bull. Sci. Tech. Soc. **24**(3), 188–199 (2004)
2. Bollen, L., van Kampen, P., Baily, C., De Cock, M.: Qualitative investigation into students' use of divergence and curl in electromagnetism. Phys. Rev. Phys. Educ. Res. **12**(2), 020134 (2016)
3. Dreyfus, S.E.: The five-stage model of adult skill acquisition. Bull. Sci. Tech. Soc. **24**(3), 177–181 (2004)
4. Dreyfus, S.E., Dreyfus, H.L.: A Five-stage Model of the Mental Activities Involved in Directed Skill Acquisition. California University Berkeley Operations Research Center, Technical report (1980)
5. Gegenfurtner, A., Lehtinen, E., Säljö, R.: Expertise differences in the comprehension of visualizations: a meta-analysis of eye-tracking research in professional domains. Educ. Psychol. Rev. **23**(4), 523–552 (2011)
6. Holmqvist, K., Nyström, M., Andersson, R., Dewhurst, R., Jarodzka, H., Van de Weijer, J.: Eye Tracking: A Comprehensive Guide to Methods and Measures. OUP Oxford (2011)
7. Ishimaru, S., Bukhari, S.S., Heisel, C., Kuhn, J., Dengel, A.: Towards an intelligent textbook: eye gaze based attention extraction on materials for learning and instruction in physics. In: Proceedings of the 2016 ACM International Joint Conference on Pervasive and Ubiquitous Computing: Adjunct, pp. 1041–1045. ACM (2016)
8. Ishimaru, S., et al.: Hypermind builder: Pervasive user interface to create intelligent interactive documents. In: Proceedings of the 2018 ACM International Joint Conference and 2018 International Symposium on Pervasive and Ubiquitous Computing and Wearable Computers, pp. 357–360. ACM (2018)
9. Kise, K., et al.: Quantified reading and learning for sharing experiences. In: Proceedings of the 2017 ACM International Joint Conference on Pervasive and Ubiquitous Computing and Proceedings of the 2017 ACM International Symposium on Wearable Computers, pp. 724–731. ACM (2017)
10. Klein, P., et al.: Visual attention while solving the test of understanding graphs in kinematics: an eye-tracking analysis. Euro. J. Phys. **41**(2), 025701 (2020)
11. Klein, P., Viiri, J., Mozaffari, S., Dengel, A., Kuhn, J.: Instruction-based clinical eye-tracking study on the visual interpretation of divergence: How do students look at vector field plots? Phys. Rev. Phys. Educ. Res. **14**(1), 010116 (2018)
12. Krejtz, K., Szmidt, T., Duchowski, A.T., Krejtz, I.: Entropy-based statistical analysis of eye movement transitions. In: Proceedings of the Symposium on Eye Tracking Research and Applications, pp. 159–166. ACM (2014)
13. Maries, A., Singh, C.: Exploring one aspect of pedagogical content knowledge of teaching assistants using the test of understanding graphs in kinematics. Phys. Rev. Spec. Top.-Phys. Educ. Res. **9**(2), 020120 (2013)
14. Meltzer, D.E.: Relation between students' problem-solving performance and representational format. Am. J. Phys. **73**(5), 463–478 (2005)
15. Mozafari, S., et al.: Classification of visual strategies in physics vector field problem-solving. In: Proceedings of the 12th International Conference on Agents and Artificial Intelligence - Volume 2: ICAART, pp. 257–267. SciTePress (2020). ISBN 978-989-758-395-7. https://doi.org/10.5220/0009173902570267

16. Mozaffari, S., Klein, P., Al-Naser, M., Bukhari, S.S., Kuhn, J., Dengel, A.: A study on representational competence in physics using mobile eye tracking systems. In: Proceedings of the 18th International Conference on Human-Computer Interaction with Mobile Devices and Services Adjunct, pp. 1029–1032. ACM (2016)
17. Mozaffari, S., Klein, P., Bukhari, S.S., Kuhn, J., Dengel, A.: Entropy based transition analysis of eye movement on physics representational competence. In: Proceedings of the 2016 ACM International Joint Conference on Pervasive and Ubiquitous Computing: Adjunct, pp. 1027–1034. ACM (2016)
18. Mozaffari, S., Klein, P., Viiri, J., Ahmed, S., Kuhn, J., Dengel, A.: Evaluating similarity measures for gaze patterns in the context of representational competence in physics education. In: Proceedings of the 2018 ACM Symposium on Eye Tracking Research & Applications, p. 51. ACM (2018)
19. Mozaffari, S.S., Raue, F., Hassanzadeh, S.D., Agne, S., Bukhari, S.S., Dengel, A.: Reading type classification based on generative models and bidirectional long short-term memory (2018)
20. Pepper, R.E., Chasteen, S.V., Pollock, S.J., Perkins, K.K.: Observations on student difficulties with mathematics in upper-division electricity and magnetism. Phys. Rev. Spec. Top.-Phys. Educ. Res. 8(1), 010111 (2012)

Economic and Food Safety: Optimized Inspection Routes Generation

Telmo Barros[1](✉), Alexandra Oliveira[1,2] (iD), Henrique Lopes Cardoso[1] (iD),
Luís Paulo Reis[1] (iD), Cristina Caldeira[3], and João Pedro Machado[3]

[1] Laboratório de Inteligência Artificial e Ciência de Computadores (LIACC),
Faculdade de Engenharia da Universidade do Porto,
Rua Dr. Roberto Frias, s/n, 4200-465 Porto, Portugal
{up201405840,aao,hlc,lpreis}@fe.up.pt
[2] Escola Superior de Saúde do Instituto Politécnico do Porto (ESS-IPP),
Rua Dr. António Bernardino de Almeida, 400, 4200-072 Porto, Portugal
[3] Autoridade de Segurança Alimentar e Económica (ASAE),
Rua Rodrigo da Fonseca, 73, 1269-274 Lisbon, Portugal
{accaldeira,jpmachado}@asae.pt

Abstract. Data-driven decision support systems rely on increasing amounts of information that needs to be converted into actionable knowledge in business intelligence processes. The latter have been applied to diverse business areas, including governmental organizations, where they can be used effectively. The Portuguese Food and Economic Safety Authority (ASAE) is one example of such organizations. Over its years of operation, a rich dataset has been collected which can be used to improve their activity regarding prevention in the areas of food safety and economic enforcement. ASAE needs to inspect Economic Operators all over the country, and the efficient and effective generation of optimized and flexible inspection routes is a major concern. The focus of this paper is, thus, the generation of optimized inspection routes, which can then be flexibly adapted towards their operational accomplishment. Each Economic Operator is assigned an inspection utility – an indication of the risk it poses to public health and food safety, to business practices and intellectual property as well as to security and environment. Optimal inspection routes are then generated typically by seeking to maximize the utility gained from inspecting the chosen Economic Operators. The need of incorporating constraints such as Economic Operators' opening hours and multiple departure/arrival spots has led to model the problem as a Multi-Depot Periodic Vehicle Routing Problem with Time Windows. Exact and meta-heuristic methods were implemented to solve the problem and the Genetic Algorithm showed a high performance with realistic solutions to be used by ASAE inspectors. The hybrid approach that combined the Genetic Algorithm with the Hill Climbing also showed to be a good manner of enhancing the solution quality.

Keywords: Planning · Scheduling · Optimization · Decision support · Vehicle routing problem

© Springer Nature Switzerland AG 2021
A. P. Rocha et al. (Eds.): ICAART 2020, LNAI 12613, pp. 482–503, 2021.
https://doi.org/10.1007/978-3-030-71158-0_23

1 Introduction

Business Intelligence refers to the set of techniques and processes used by companies or organizations to convert their information into actionable knowledge which, when allied with Artificial Intelligence (AI) and Machine Learning (ML) techniques, can result in powerful decision support systems. This is the case of some governmental administrative institutions, which are currently optimizing their complex operational processes by exploiting useful knowledge extracted from a vast amount of data.

Some of these organizations have as mission the close supervision and constant assessment of a large amount and geographically sparse of other entities. In order to efficiently inspect the maximum possible entities an accurate and flexible route plan must be built taking into account several constraints inherent to the type of entities to be inspected in each operation.

In Portugal exists the Portuguese Food and Economic Safety Authority (ASAE), responsible for supervising and preventing non-compliance with the National and European legislation regarding the food and non-food sectors. Some of their duties lies in the report of detected hazards in the food chain, risk assessment and inspections to selected Economic Operators, either planned or unplanned. It is a reference entity in consumer protection, public health, safeguarding market rules and free competition by providing a public service of excellence.

ASAE's internal information system has a large dataset of portuguese Economic Operators and historic complaints. This information can be used to determine the inspection utility through the definition of risk matrices and the number and type of complaints per Economic Operator. Their data can also be used alongside external sources, using as much information as possible and enhancing, this way, the solutions and the selection of Economic Operators to be inspected.

Given an inspection utility function, the inspection routes must be generated such as to maximize the number of inspections to Economic Operators with the maximum utility. The routes that are part of the solution should be adaptable upon suggestions by the user, reflecting the nature of the work of the human inspectors. Previous research has shown that vehicle routing optimization can promote significant economic savings [10,17,26].

This problem was addressed in previous work [4] as a Multi-Depot Periodic Vehicle Routing Problem with Time Windows, and approached it using both exact and meta-heuristic methods. Although this was an operative solution, some details need to be added as the inclusion of distinct departure and arrival points, real opening hours of Economic Operators or dynamic inspection times. Hybrid approaches that combined the Genetic Algorithm with the Hill Climbing and Simulated Annealing were also implemented and put to the test.

The inclusion of these constrains turn the problem into a complex problem of generation and optimization of inspection routes to assess the set of selected Economic Operators. The developed models were then embedded in an Web Application that allows ASAE's collaborators to visualize geographically the Economic Operators, assign utilities and generate inspections routes.

The proposed methodologies to solve a problem that has existed for several years are an considerable advantage. Although the paper focus on the application to a specific food and economic safety context, the constraints can be easily applied in other situations without significantly changing the analyzed behavior of the algorithms.

The rest of the paper is structured as follows. Section 2, discusses the currently processes in use and data size. The formulation of the routing problem in hands and related work are given in Sect. 3. Section. 4 explains the main choices regarding the algorithms implementation and new additions from the previous version [4]. Recent results and algorithms execution comparison appear in Sect. 5. Section 6 shows the applicability of the methods by giving an overview of the developed web application. In Sect. 7 we present the conclusions and pointed some directions for future work.

2   ASAE's Data Dimension and Key Procedures

There exist more than 3,500,000 Economic Operators currently registered in ASAE's internal database. Every year, the number of customer complaints against Economic Operators, received via the complaint book or ASAE's website, surpass the 200,000. This number, which include the infractions implied by the complaints themselves and the type of targeted economic activity, will determine the utility of inspection. Consequently, complaint-targeted Economic Operators should be more likely to be included in inspection operations.

The information system in use relies on multiple data sources and platforms which, allied with the aforementioned numbers, make it difficult to automate some processes such as:

  i. the prioritization of Economic Operators that need to be supervised;
 ii. the assignment of these Economic Operators to brigades of inspectors; and
iii. the determination of optimal inspection routes taking into account the minimization of travel distances or time.

The ASAE's organic structure covers mainland Portugal and is divided into three regional units. On a lower level there are a total of twelve operational units with a specific number of inspectors and vehicles at their disposal. The allocation and management of these resources occur at multiple levels but the ones addressed here are the:

Operational – which focuses on the generation of the brigades inspection plans, through the selection of specific Economic Operators to be inspected and the definition of starting and finishing points for each brigade; and the

Brigade – which is responsible for making minor changes in the inspection plan in real-time, due to unexpected reasons (such as the closure of an Economic Operator).

The inspections planning and the visualization of georeferenced information (Economic Operators) are two areas that can be improved. It is possible to enhance the selection of Economic Operators that maximize the usefulness of being inspected in the inspections planning and also the generation of flexible routes for the inspectors while minimizing the spent resources.

3   Routing Problem

The three processes listed in Sect. 2 can be interpreted and solved as a single problem that falls into the family of Vehicle Routing Problems (VRP). This problem is part of the logistics operations in almost any supply chain. The approach to solve this complex combinatorial optimization problem lies in finding the set of routes with overall minimum route cost which service all the demands given: a fleet of vehicles with uniform capacity, a common depot, and several costumer demands [22,25]. One of the first problems modeled as a VRP was the *Truck Dispatching Problem* [14], which may be seen as a generalization of the *Traveling Salesman Problem* (TSP) [16,19].

A VRP is usually modeled as a weighted graph

$$\mathcal{G} = (\mathcal{V}, \mathcal{A}, \mathcal{C})$$

where: $\mathcal{V} = \{v_0, v_1, ..., v_n\}$ is a set of vertices composed by the depot (vertex v_0) and various cities or customers to visit (vertex subset $\{v_1, ..., v_n\}$); $\mathcal{A}$ is the set of arcs joining these vertices. Each arc (v_i, v_j), for $i \neq j$, has a non-negative distance c_{ij} associated with, and represented in the matrix $\mathcal{C}$. In some cases, these distances may be interpreted as travel costs or travel times. There is also a set $\mathcal{K}$ of vehicles available at the depot. The problem's purpose is to determine the lowest cost vehicle route set, subject to the following restrictions [20]:

i. each city (v_i) is visited exactly once by exactly one vehicle (k); and
ii. all vehicle routes start and end at the depot (v_0).

A VRP also comprises four equations that model the objective function and its restrictions [8,26]. Let x_{ijk} be a binary decision variable taking the value of 1 if vehicle k traverses the arc (v_i, v_j), and 0 otherwise and c_{ij} defined as above, the minimum sum of costs of all the arcs is given by Eq. 1:

$$min \sum_{k=1}^{m} \sum_{i=0}^{n} \sum_{j=0}^{n} c_{ij} x_{ijk} \tag{1}$$

With the constraint from Eq. 2 of a vertex being visited only once, with the exception of the depot [4]:

$$\sum_{i=0}^{n} \sum_{k=1}^{m} x_{ijk} = 1, \forall\, j > 0 \tag{2}$$

Equation 3 ensures that the number of the vehicles arriving at every customer and entering the depot is equal to the number of the vehicles leaving [4]:

$$\sum_{j=0}^{n} x_{ijk} = \sum_{j=0}^{n} x_{jik}, \forall\, i \geq 0,\, i \neq j,\, \forall\, k = 1, ..., m \tag{3}$$

Equation 4 ensures that all vehicle depart from the depot [4]:

$$\sum_{j=1}^{n}\sum_{k=1}^{m} x_{0jk} = |K| \tag{4}$$

Even though the classical VRP may provide very useful solutions in some real life problems, the ASAE's inspections routing problem have some constraints that are not satisfied by the definition above, namely:

- Inspections can only take place during opening hours of the Economic Operators;
- The inspections plans may have a multiple days duration;
- The departure and arrival points of each brigade vehicle can be two distinct points, since each operational unit has more than one parking spaces.
- An inspection plan is targeted to a specific economic activity or a set of economic activities, which directly affects the Economic Operators selection for inspection;
- Each operational unit is associated with a set of municipalities that make up the geographical boundary on which the its brigades can operate. This limit is well defined and must be respected without exception;

Many authors have already proposed several extensions and generalizations by adding or removing constraints leading to different route design process [6,27]. The most relevant variations to the problem in hands are:

i. the **Multi-Depot** (MDVRP) that considers more than one depot/place where the vehicles may start and arrive [18,23];
ii. the **Periodic** (PVRP) which assumes a multi-day planning with the capability to choose when to visit an Economic Operator [7]; and
iii. the **Time Windows** (VRPTW) that takes into account a list of visiting schedules when each Economic Operator can be visited [9,28].

Combining them leads to a Multi-Depot Periodic Vehicle Routing Problem with Time Windows (MDPVRPTW) [11]. In Fig. 1 is possible to see a solution of MDPVRPTW in a geographical representation. The solution has four complete inspection routes (set of green arrows) from three operational units (orange circles) and eleven (out of thirteen) Economic Operators inspected (blue circles).

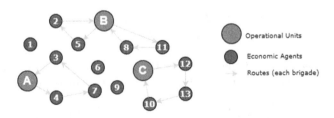

Fig. 1. MDPVRPTW representation [4]. (Color figure online)

Finally considering the problem in hands, $\mathcal{V} = \mathcal{EO} \cup \mathcal{D}$ is a set of nodes. composed of depots $d \in \mathcal{D}$ and Economic Operators $eo \in \mathcal{EO}$. $\mathcal{A} = \{(v_i, v_j)\}, i \neq j$ is the set of arcs that connect these nodes excluding the arcs that connect two depots and the matrix $\mathcal{C}$ has the arcs travel times. There is also a set of brigades $\mathcal{B}$ which will perform the inspections. Each brigade $b \in \mathcal{B}$ is a combination of a vehicle w (from a set $\mathcal{W}$ of all available vehicles) and a set of inspectors I_b (a subset of $\mathcal{I}$ of all inspectors) where $|I_b| \geq 2, \forall b \in \mathcal{B}$.

Each brigade $b \in \mathcal{B}$ has also an associated work shift $[SS_b, ES_b]$, where SS and ES are starting and ending of the work shift time, respectively, similar to Cordeau et al. [12] proposal.

Each Economic Operator eo has opening hours associated OH_{eo}. This is a set of time windows where they can be inspected. $OH_{eo} = \{[ot_j, ct_j]_{eo} : j = 1, \ldots\}$ where ot_j and ct_j are the opening and closing times of consecutive working periods j in a day, respectively. Thus, if the arrival time at eo is not between any pair of $[ot_j, ct_j] \in OH_{eo}$, the brigade has to wait.

Every eo has also an expected time of inspection, represented by ti_{eo}, defined according to the type of their economic activity [4].

Additionally, another key factor that must be taken into consideration is the utility of inspecting a determined Economic Operator eo and can be defined as $u_{eo} \in [0, 1]$. This utility function is also known as the demand level at each node, as the importance of the node in the network, etc. [1,2].

In this paper, the problem solving objectives are either the maximization of the global utility (defined in Eq. 5) or the maximization of the number of inspected Economic Operators in each day of inspection planning (defined in Eq. 6). The solution must satisfy the constraints for the classical VRP with Multi-Depot within the geographical limits of an operational unit, the time window of each Economic Operator and the brigade's work shift:

$$max \sum_{b \in \mathcal{B}} \sum_{i \in \mathcal{V}} \sum_{j \in \mathcal{EO}} u_j x_{ijb} \tag{5}$$

$$max \sum_{b \in \mathcal{B}} \sum_{i \in \mathcal{V}} \sum_{j \in \mathcal{EO}} x_{ijb} \tag{6}$$

Although the study of such methods is not a recent topic, the discussion on how to achieve optimal solutions in less iterations/time is something that still remains today. The reason behind that is that the TSP, the VRP and its variant problems are NP-hard since they are not solved in polynomial time [9]. Due to their complexity, many heuristics and meta-heuristic approaches have been used to solve them as they can return solutions close to the optimum and present lower (and often adjustable) execution times, even for large data sets. Despite the problems' difficulty, exact approaches have been developed like the branch and cut algorithm [21], but because they require a high computational power they are only feasible in small data sets. The difference between these two categories is related to the behaviour of algorithms when determining the solution [20]. To the best of our knowledge, a Tabu Search heuristic is the most explored technique to solve the Periodic Vehicle Routing Problem with Time Windows

(PVRPTW) and the Multi-Depot Vehicle Routing Problem with Time Windows (MDVRPTW) separately [13].

4   Flexible Routes Generation

The methodologies implemented to solve the problem involved one exact method, three meta-heuristic methods and hybrid approaches that combined the Genetic Algorithm with two meta-heuristics to achieve the best results. The concept of inspection utility and its determination are presented in Sect. 4.1, while in Sect. 4.2 the representation of the solution is described. Then, the details of the implemented algorithms are included in Sects. 4.3 and 4.4.

4.1   Inspection Utility

The inspection utility function u_{eo} is the basis for determining optimal inspection routes. u_{eo} must be interpreted as the gain of inspecting an Economic Operator eo. The summed utilities of the inspected eo set is the component intended to be maximized when solving the routing problem. The definition of u_{eo} appears in Eq. 7 as a weighted sum of n functions $f(eo)$ defined based on some problem context criteria and taking into consideration the eo.

$$u_{eo} = \sum_{i=1}^{n} w_i f_i(eo) \tag{7}$$

So, for a given eo, u_{eo} retrieve a value in the interval $[0, 1]$ corresponding to the gain of inspecting that eo. This gain would be higher to eo operating in certain economic activities that pose higher risk in any of the scope inspected by ASAE. Highlighted criteria taken into account include the following eo attributes:

  i. the number and severity of **pending complaints**;
 ii. previous inspections results (its **inspections historic**); and
iii. the operator's **economic activity**.

Focusing only on the first criteria, each eo can have a number of pending complaints received by ASAE and that have not yet been investigated or inspected. These pending complaints have associated an estimated infraction severity based on the complaint's description. This evaluation is currently being inserted manually by a collaborator but progresses have been made in the areas of automatic complaint analysis and classification of the infraction severity [3,15]. The three severity types are shown in Table 1, and their respective weights are used to determine the severity score S assigned to each eo, represented in Eq. 8, where SC is the set of severity classes, NC the number of complaints and SW the severity weight.

$$S_{eo} = \sum_{sc \in SC} NC_{sc,eo} \, SW_{sc} \tag{8}$$

Table 1. Infraction severity classes and their weights.

Infraction severity - sc	Weight - sw
Crime	4
Administrative infringement	2
Other	1

The determination of this first criterion's function was done by allying the empirical knowledge and experience from ASAE members with the analysis of the distribution of the severity scores per Economic Operator, graphically visible in Fig. 2 (the vertical axis is in logarithmic scale). In the figure there are only represented 99% of the targeted Economic Operators which corresponds to a maximum severity score of 32. The green bars show the absolute number of Economic Operators with a given Severity Score and the orange line show the cumulative percentage.

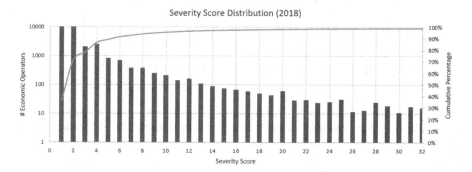

Fig. 2. Severity Scores distribution for received complaints in the year 2018. (Color figure online)

Equation 9 is an exponential function to define a higher rate of change for smaller SS. The rate of growth was defined with the ASAE field experts.

$$f_1(eo) = -1.3^{-S_{eo}} + 1 \tag{9}$$

4.2 Representation

The implemented methodologies described in the following sections are able to solve the optimization problem in hands but require, among other data structures, a form of representation to hold the solution routes (inspection plan). With regards to the inspection plan representation for $|\mathcal{B}|$ brigades, a set of $|\mathcal{B}| + 1$ lists is used. The first $|\mathcal{B}|$ lists include the actual inspection routes, while the last list contains a set of Economic Operators that will not be inspected in this plan. This form of representation allows us to deal with the periodic nature of the VRP, by planning daily and not requiring all Economic Operators to be visited in one day. The Economic Operators are stored by inspection order in the $|\mathcal{B}|$ generated routes. Figure 3 shows an inspection plan geographically representation in detail by the example in Fig. 1, with four routes/brigades and thirteen Economic Operators.

This representation is used by all with the exception of the genetic algorithm, which, due to the crossover and mutation operations, requires another form of representation. This adaptation is achieved by converting the multidimensional list into a linearized single-dimensional one. For the specific representation illustrated in Fig. 3, the individual in the genetic algorithm would be [4, 7, 3, 5, 2, 11, 8, 12, 13, 10, 1, 6, 9]. To decode the individual back into the routes, each *eo* is inserted sequentially in the routes until no more *eo* fit the brigade's work shift duration [28].

Representation		
[4,7,3], [5,2], [11,8], [12,13,10], [1,6,9]		
Brigades		Uninspected eo
$4 \rightarrow 7 \rightarrow 3$	$5 \rightarrow 2$	1, 6, 9
$11 \rightarrow 8$	$12 \rightarrow 13 \rightarrow 10$	

Fig. 3. Inspection plan representation and its meaning.

The information about the departing and arriving depots does not appear in this inspection plan representation because it is kept in the brigades data structure alongside with other information such as work shift duration and departure time.

4.3   Exact Approach

Exact methods are capable of determining the optimal solution but are well known to require more computational effort than heuristic approaches. For the problem in hands there are some real case scenarios where route generation is targeting a small set of pre-filtered Economic Operators and brigades and which allow exact methods to be employed.

The Branch and Bound algorithm is an exact methodology capable of solving optimization problems as the Vehicle Routing Problem. For this specific problem, a branching strategy that allows to traverse the whole solution space consists of adding each possible Economic Operator to each brigade at a time. The bounding occurs when the generated solution disrespects the work shift duration of any brigade.

The application of the method to the specific problem is shown in Fig. 4. The example includes three Economic Operators [1, 2, 3] with utilities of 0.05, 0.40 and 0.10, respectively, and two brigades. In the first node, every economic agent is in the set of agents not inspected by any brigade, so the utility of the solution is 0. At each layer, an agent is removed from the last array and inserted into one of the brigades.

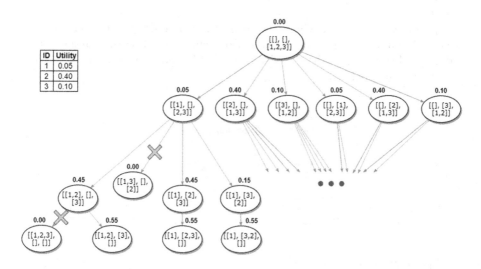

Fig. 4. Branch and Bound applied to the routing problem [4].

4.4 Meta-heuristic Approaches

Regarding meta-heuristic approaches, three different methods were developed:

i. **Hill Climbing,**
ii. **Simulated Annealing** and
iii. **Genetic Algorithm.**

The main details are described in this section and these approaches allowed to obtain a sufficiently good solution in a short execution time, when compared to the Branch and Bound algorithm, for instance.

All the three meta-heuristic implementations require at least one initial solution to start. The initial solution is always valid, although it may not have a high utility. It is generated by randomly allocating Economic Operators to each brigade, ensuring that travel times and inspection durations fit in the brigade's work shift. The remaining Economic Operators are kept in the last list, as shown in Fig. 3.

From this solution, Hill Climbing and Simulated Annealing approaches proceed to find the optimal solution out of all possible solutions (the search space). The neighborhood function for the two methodologies is based on two equiprobable operators (Fig. 5):

- *Swapping* consists of exchanging the order of two Economic Operators; swapping can occur between two operators of the same brigade, from different brigades or from one brigade and the list of uninspected Economic Operators.
- *Repositioning* consists of changing the position of an Economic Operator; just as with swapping, repositioning can also occur within the same brigade, to a different brigade or to the list of uninspected Economic Operators (removing it from being visited).

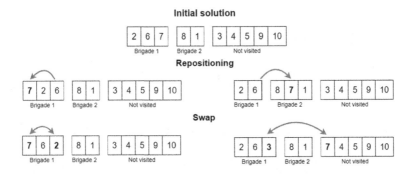

Fig. 5. Neighborhood generation operations.

The implementation of Simulated Annealing has the specificity of probabilistically accepting solutions with lower utility than the current solution. Equation 10 shows the temperature update function determined by the current iteration and total number of steps. Equation 11 shows the acceptance probability formula in this specific application of the method.

$$temperature = 1 - \left(\frac{\text{iteration}}{\text{n of steps}} \right)^{\frac{1}{100}} \tag{10}$$

$$p = e^{\frac{\text{new utility} - \text{best utility}}{\text{temperature}}} \tag{11}$$

The probability of accepting solutions with lower utility is thus related with the differences in utility and the number of iterations already performed (which directly determines the temperature).

The Genetic Algorithm implementation followed the selection process suggested by Zhu [28] – tournament selection. The implication in this selection scheme is to give priority in mating to genetically superior chromosomes, while allowing less good entities to be selected.

Two crossover processes were implemented: PMX and heuristic crossover. The application of general-purpose crossover operations unavoidably produces invalid offspring that have duplicated genes in one string.

With Heuristic crossover, an arbitrary cut is made on both chromosomes and one of the genes immediately following the cut position is chosen to be maintained. The not selected gene is replaced or deleted to avoid duplication in the following iterations. After this decision, an iterative process begins that traverses the chromosomes and compares, in each iteration i, the distance between the gene at position i and position $i + 1$ of both progenitor chromosomes. The $i + 1$ position gene presenting lower distance to the previous gene is selected to be part of the descending chromosome. The gene that was not selected is either deleted or swapped with the selected gene. Figure 6 portraits the process with two chromossomes of size 5. c_{ij} is the distance from gene i to gene j. Two offsprings are generated, one from repositioning and the other from deletion.

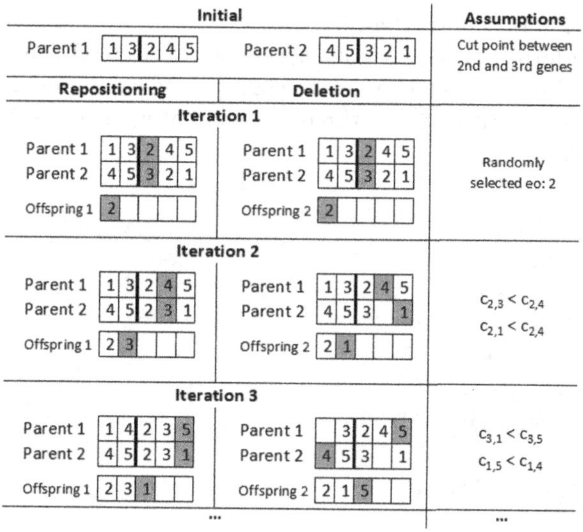

Fig. 6. Heuristic crossover example (3 iterations).

PMX is a slightly different and not so complex process as it does not take into account the distance between the Economic Operators. It starts by selecting two arbitrary points, then swapping the portions of the chromosomes between these points. In order to remove duplicate Economic Operators, a series of gene swappings are performed within each chromosome. This crossover operation originates two descending chromosomes [28].

Following the crossover process, there is a low probability of the descending chromosomes being mutated. The genetic approach encompasses four types of mutations, equally likely to occur:

– *Gene Repositioning:* a gene (Economic Operator) is randomly selected and repositioned at a random position inside the chromosome.

– *Gene swap*: two genes (Economic Operators) are randomly selected and their positions are swapped.
– *Sequence Repositioning:* a set of randomly selected consecutive genes is repositioned at a random position inside the chromosome (keeping their original sequence).
– *Sequence Swap:* a set of randomly selected consecutive genes swap their position with a gene (keeping their original sequence).

5 Results

The evaluation of the implemented methods was performed under a simulated environment using multiple tests and experiments and allowed to collect relevant information regarding the performance and solution quality of the four algorithms and hybrid approaches.

Test were performed using a set of 500 randomly selected Economic Operators from northern Portugal. The test set geographic distribution is displayed in Fig. 7. In the figure are also visible three depots, that work as points of departure and arrival of the brigades.

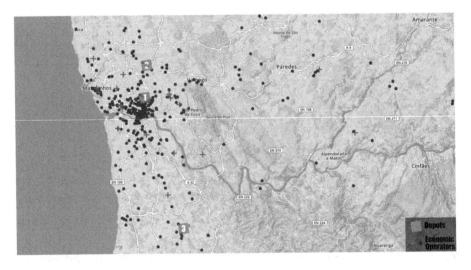

Fig. 7. Test set geographic distribution. (Color figure online)

From the 500 Economic Operators, a smaller subset of 20 operators (red crosses on the map) was randomly selected to allow the comparison of the metaheuristic solutions with the Branch and Bound method. As such, two test cases were setup.

Some considerations about every algorithm execution:

– Brigades always start their route at the same hour and their work shift have the same duration of 8 consecutive hours.

- Economic Operators real utility or opening hours were not used; they were assigned a random utility instead and are assumed to be always open.
- Inspection time was fixed on 1 h for each Economic Operator.
- The values shown for meta-heuristic methods are always the average of 10 executions.
- For the Genetic Algorithm, executions were performed using a population of 100 individuals, with crossover probability, mutation probability and recovery percentage of 85%, 5% and 4% respectively.

Varying parameters were:

- *Objective Function*: Maximize the total utility of inspected agents, or maximize the number of Economic Operators to be inspected.
- *Brigades*: Number of brigades and departure/arrival points.
- *Stopping Criterion*: Maximum number of iterations or maximum execution time.

Varying the objective function and the number of brigades allowed us to analyze the direct effect of these variables in the algorithms performance.

The results for the referred subsets are shown in Tables 2 and 3. The test set results from Table 2 are related to the execution of the four approaches applied to the subset of 20 Economic Operators and 1 brigade that starts and finishes its shift in Depot 1. Table 3 presents the results for the algorithms execution given the full test set of 500 Economic Operators and 27 brigades. The brigades set is evenly distributed by the depots, that is, there are 3 brigades assigned to each pair of departure and arrival depot.

Each results table is split into four sections corresponding to different test cases with the number of iterations and execution times used as stop criteria. The results for the two objective functions appear in two columns: maximization of the global inspection utility ($max\ u_{eo}$) and maximization of the number of inspected Economic Operators ($max\ inspected\ eo$). Columns u_{eo} and eo contain the average of obtained inspection utilities and number of inspected Economic Operators, respectively. The total number of iterations executed by the methods appear in column i, while column $best\ i$ shows the iteration where the best solution was found. The average execution times are displayed in column t.

Each row stands for one algorithm execution: Branch and Bound (BB), Hill Climbing (HC), Simulated Annealing (SA), Genetic Algorithm with PMX crossover ($GA(P)$) and Heuristic crossover($GA(H)$). The Genetic Algorithm was also combined with Hill Climbing and Simulated Annealing into a hybrid approach. Using the solution obtained from the Genetic Algorithm, the two meta-heuristics are applied (both executed with a stopping criterion of 100 iterations without evolution) to verify if it significantly increase the previous solution utility.

Table 2. Results for 20 eos and 1 brigade.

Algo.	max u_{eo}				max inspected eo			
	u_{eo}	best i	i	t	eo	best i	i	t
BB	5,6181	–	–	–	7,0	–	–	–
Max. i: 10000								
HC	5,6181	574	10000	0,3922	6,4	2882	10000	0,3892
SA	5,6181	624	10000	0,3983	6,2	1258	10000	0,3986
GA(P)	5,6181	7	100	1,1358	7,0	21	100	1,1557
GA(H)	5,4826	64	100	1,6443	7,0	2	100	1,6350
Max. i: 100000								
HC	5,6181	634	100000	3,8581	7,0	16283	100000	3,9408
SA	5,6181	583	100000	3,9795	7,0	19628	100000	4,0257
GA(P)	5,6181	13	1000	11,3204	7,0	43	1000	11,6694
GA(H)	5,6181	255	1000	16,6012	7,0	4	1000	16,2462
Max. t: 1s								
HC	5,6181	626	25343	–	6,8	4982	25170	–
SA	5,6181	423	24727	–	6,9	10626	24414	–
GA(P)	5,6012	11	89	–	7,0	30	86	–
GA(P)+HC	5,6181	98	198	–	7,0	30	186	–
GA(P)+SA	5,6181	90	189	–	7,0	30	186	–
GA(H)	5,5037	32	61	–	7,0	2	61	–
GA(H)+HC	5,5097	75	175	–	7,0	2	161	–
GA(H)+SA	5,5093	71	171	–	7,0	2	161	–
Max. t: 2s								
HC	5,6181	390	51267	–	6,8	10075	50451	–
SA	5,6181	652	48941	–	6,9	10344	47745	–
GA(P)	5,6181	21	176	–	7,0	31	174	–
GA(P)+HC	5,6181	21	276	–	7,0	31	274	–
GA(P)+SA	5,6181	21	276	–	7,0	31	274	–
GA(H)	5,6091	49	123	–	7,0	2	123	–
GA(H)+HC	5,6121	132	232	–	7,0	2	223	–
GA(H)+SA	5,6091	125	225	–	7,0	2	223	–

Through the global analysis of the obtained results, it is possible to conclude that they are satisfactory with multiple approaches achieving close solutions with approximately equal utilities as the exact method. The results also led to conclude that, when a lower number of iterations was given, the HC and SA could not achieve the optimal solution for the *max inspected eo* and the GA(H) for the *max u_{eo}*. By increasing the iterations limit, all of the metaheuristic approaches were capable of determining a solution with equal utility as the solution found by the Branch and Bound method.

When the algorithms were tested under the same execution time limit, HC and SA performed well in the maximization of the inspection utility. They also enhanced the solution quality obtained by the GA. For the maximization of the number of inspected Economic Operators, GA(P) and GA(H) were able to consistently find optimal solutions and the fastest one was the heuristic crossover with an average of 2 iterations. Considering the total number of steps and the time to execute them the HC and the SA methods were the fastest to execute each iteration with very similar times, followed by the GA(P) and the GA(H).

Table 3. Results for 500 eos and 27 brigades.

Algo.	max u_{eo}				max inspected eo			
	u_{eo}	best i	i	t	eo	best i	i	t
Max. i: 10000								
HC	98,7232	9881	10000	5,5247	149,4	9119	10000	6,0015
SA	97,6994	9903	10000	5,5530	148,4	8990	10000	5,9492
GA(P)	94,9479	84	100	21,4769	151,5	49	100	22,8349
GA(P)+HC	95,9764	386	486	21,7019	151,5	49	200	22,8958
GA(P)+SA	95,6239	251	351	21,6159	151,5	49	200	22,8978
GA(H)	96,7180	69	100	84,3511	178,3	62	100	89,6848
GA(H)+HC	96,9691	219	319	84,4806	178,3	62	200	89,7489
GA(H)+SA	97,3835	235	335	84,4901	178,3	62	200	89,7475
Max. i: 100000								
HC	129,5417	98925	100000	55,0777	169,5	82586	100000	59,0404
SA	130,2098	98684	100000	54,6503	168,4	85063	100000	59,0773
GA(P)	106,4061	952	1000	216,7616	154,7	742	1000	228,8047
GA(P)+HC	106,6261	1142	1242	216,9005	154,7	742	1100	228,8688
GA(P)+SA	106,6185	1109	1209	216,8819	154,8	1005	1105	228,8688
GA(H)	102,4479	862	1000	877,2816	181,3	339	1000	845,2185
GA(H)+HC	102,9940	1178	1278	877,4526	181,3	339	1100	845,2795
GA(H)+SA	102,7018	1101	1201	877,4051	181,3	339	1100	845,2810
Max. t: 1s								
HC	72,0507	1706	1755	–	128,7	1445	1647	–
SA	71,6273	1698	1750	–	127,2	1397	1653	–
GA(P)	71,9183	4	5	–	135,7	2	4	–
GA(P)+HC	73,9384	354	454	–	136,1	24	124	–
GA(P)+SA	73,4790	235	335	–	135,9	10	110	–
GA(H)	83,0392	0	1	–	157,7	0	1	–
GA(H)+HC	83,9257	206	306	—	157,7	1	101	–
GA(H)+SA	83,6991	134	234	—	157,7	1	101	–
Max. t: 2s								
HC	80,9007	3493	3578	–	135,3	3163	3373	–
SA	82,6057	3487	3580	–	134,0	3105	3348	–
GA(P)	76,8735	8	10	–	140,4	8	9	–
GA(P)+HC	78,1521	229	329	–	140,5	12	112	–
GA(P)+SA	78,0103	200	300	–	140,5	17	117	–
GA(H)	86,1844	2	3	–	164,2	1	3	–
GA(H)+HC	86,8208	197	297	–	164,2	3	103	–
GA(H)+SA	87,4639	209	309	–	164,2	3	103	–

As expected and against to what happened in the first experiment, the methods utilities solutions obtained for the larger dataset were more scattered.

Table 3 shows that regarding inspection utility maximization, all methods were still improving their solution quality when the stopping criterion was met. HC and SA presented similar utilities and were able to always slightly improve the solution obtained by the GA. The solutions obtained by both crossovers in GA were very similar, but the Heuristic one can generally find a better solution in a earlier iteration than the PMX crossover.

Regarding the maximization of inspected Economic Operators, results followed almost the same pattern from Table 2. In general, GA(P) and GA(H) were able to find solutions with more Economic Operators inspected and almost never taking advantage of the HC/SA complementary layer. Heuristic crossover was again able to find a solution with higher utility than the other methods.

The time to perform each iteration kept the same distribution from the first test case, with HC and the SA methods executing faster, followed by GA(P) and GA(H).

6   Applicability

A crucial factor for being successful in solving sophisticated vehicle routing problems (VRP) is to offer reliable and flexible solutions [24]. Taking this into account, a Web application was designed [4,5]. It is the entry point to the visualization and interaction with the routing algorithms. The application has two main views or pages:

i. the *Inspection Planning Form*, shown in Fig. 8, which can be used to customize route generation, and
ii. the *Inspection Planning Overview*, shown in Fig. 9, where it is possible to see the solution and its details, also enabling editing and storing operations.

The *Inspection Planning Form* allows to input the custom conditions for a new inspection plan generation. The input variables are directly correlated with the ones specified in Sect. 3 and are the following:

- *Objective Function:* It is either the maximization of u_{eo} or the maximization of agents to be inspected;
- *Starting Date:* Starting date and time for the inspections route;
- *Meal Break:* Time interval where a 1 h break may occur;
- *Economic Activities:* List of economic activities to include in the solution (may be empty to consider all registered Economic Operators);
- *Brigade:* List of brigades composed by:
  - *Vehicle:* Vehicle to be used;
  - *Duration:* Maximum amount of time to be spent on the field preforming the inspections;
  - *Inspectors:* List of inspectors (minimum of 2 per brigade);
  - *Starting/Finishing Points:* Geographic location of the starting and finishing points (the operational unit headquarter is used by default).

Fig. 8. Input conditions page (multiple views).

The *Inspection Planning Overview*, portrayed in Fig. 9, presents the solutions found from a geographical and chronological point of view. The routes are outlined in the map and can be selected or toggled from the left sidebar. This sidebar also contains main information about each brigade and global details of the solution. It is also possible to generate a new solution by clicking on the button "New Route". In the bottom part there is a chronological view of the events of the selected brigade on left sidebar.

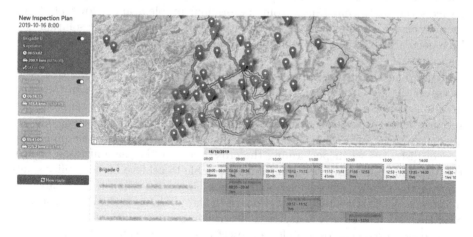

Fig. 9. Web application overview.

The developed system can work as a decision support system for inspectors by creating a daily plan for one or more brigades of inspectors and promote, this way, a maximum number of inspections in a day or the maximization of the utility of inspected agents with an efficient use of resources. The inspection plan can be consulted by any worker and the routes are manageable by workers who suggest the additions/removals of Economic Operators. The inserted suggestions affect directly the defined utility of each Economic Operator and force the previous solution to be recalculated and presented.

7   Conclusions and Future Work

In this paper, we presented the modeling and resolution of a complex combinatorial optimization problem related with the inspections planning process of ASAE. The generation and optimization of routes is not a novel problem and the solutions presented always aim at determining the most effective route for a fleet of vehicles to visit a set of points. The constraints of the problem at hands led to classify it as an MDPVRPTW. To solve it, four base strategies were implemented: one exact, three meta-heuristic methodologies and hybrid approaches combining Genetic Algorithm with the Hill Climbing and Simulated Annealing.

Another key factor was the determination of an utility function capable of determining the inspection utility of an Economic Operator based on the number and severity of pending complaints, inspections historic and economic activity area among others.

This work is integrated in an interactive platform capable of generating flexible inspection routes targeted to support the decision of the ASAE's personnel and enhance current processes of Economic Operators selection for inspection and inspections routing. It offers functionalities that facilitate the whole process of selecting and assigning Economic Operators to the multiple brigades, respects the main constraints from the original problem and allows platform users to customize the desired inspection plan before and after the solution has been generated, through the addition and removal of Economic Operators to be inspected.

Regarding the methodologies performance, despite the fact that Heuristic crossover (in the Genetic Algorithm approach) has a higher execution time per iteration than the PMX option it was able to consistently find better solutions specially with the larger dataset and the maximization of the inspected eo. This phenomenon can be explained because it takes into consideration the minimization of distances when performing the crossover. For the maximization of $u_e o$ Hill Climbing and Simulated Annealing were able to achieve higher utility solutions in the smaller dataset case and with a bigger execution time/number of iterations. With time limited executions in the larger dataset, Genetic Algorithm with Heuristic crossover was faster to determine greater solutions.

The development prospects for a project of this nature and scope are varied. There are at least one feature missing and more testing is necessary, specially on the field:

- Inclusion of break-time periods for inspectors and supervisors during the inspection route. The fact that this period is flexible, relative to each brigade and can be different according to the start time of the inspection actions makes it difficult to add to the methods currently implemented, but should be taken into account in a next version of the system since it may compromise the use of the routes in a real context.

- Test the whole system in the field with ASAE's collaboration, to extract metrics from algorithms in a real context and detect gaps that are not visible in a simulated environment without professionals in the area.

Within respect to the break time periods some progresses have been made but the work is still not complete. Regarding the second item a model was developed to track the brigades and compare their real routes with the predicted by the system to support the field-tests.

Within the scope of the project as a whole, there are development prospects that will directly and indirectly affect the module of the generation of flexible routes, such as:

- Implementation of risk matrices that will allow a determination of a more accurate inspection utility.
- The new pending complaints are already being taken into account automatically but the extraction of other new information from the ASAE system may also improve the utility definition of specific Economic Operators.
- Development of a system in constant learning of visiting times to establishments. The quality of the obtained solutions will increase by replacing the manually inserted inspection times with the categorization of average control times by economic operator's area of activity.

Acknowledgements. This work is supported by project IA.SAE, funded by Fundação para a Ciência e a Tecnologia (FCT) through program INCoDe.2030. This research was partially supported by LIACC (FCT/UID/CEC/0027/2020).

References

1. Allahviranloo, M., Chow, J., Recker, W.: Selective vehicle routing problems under uncertainty without recourse. Transportation Research Part E Logistics and Transportation Review (2013). https://doi.org/10.1016/j.tre.2013.12.004
2. Bansal, S., Goel, R.: Multi Objective Vehicle Routing Problem: A Survey. Asian Journal of Computer Science and Technology pp. 1–6 (2018)
3. Barbosa, L., et al.: Automatic identification of economic activities in complaints. In: Martín-Vide, C., Purver, M., Pollak, S. (eds.) SLSP 2019. LNCS (LNAI), vol. 11816, pp. 249–260. Springer, Cham (2019). https://doi.org/10.1007/978-3-030-31372-2_21
4. Barros, T., Oliveira, A., Lopes Cardoso, H., Reis, L.P., Caldeira, C., Machado, J.P.: Generation and Optimization of Inspection Routes for Economic and Food Safety. In: Proceedings of the 12th International Conference on Agents and Artificial Intelligence - Volume 2: ICAART, pp. 268–278. SciTePress (2020). DOI: 10.5220/0009182002680278, backup Publisher: INSTICC

5. Barros, T., et al.: Interactive Inspection Routes Application for Economic and Food Safety. In: Rocha, Á., Adeli, H., Reis, L.P., Costanzo, S., Orovic, I., Moreira, F. (eds.) WorldCIST 2020. AISC, vol. 1159, pp. 640–649. Springer, Cham (2020). https://doi.org/10.1007/978-3-030-45688-7_64

6. Braekers, K., Ramaekers, K., Nieuwenhuyse, I.V.: The vehicle routing problem: State of the art classification and review. Computers & Industrial Engineering **99**, 300–313 (2016). https://doi.org/10.1016/j.cie.2015.12.007

7. Campbell, A.M., Wilson, J.H.: Forty years of periodic vehicle routing. Networks **63**(1), 2–15 (2014)

8. Cardoso, S.R.d.S.N.: Optimização de rotas e da frota associada. Master's thesis, Universidade Técnica de Lisboa, Instituto Superior Técnico, Lisbon (2009)

9. Caric, T., Gold, H.: Vehicle routing problem. In-Teh, Vienna, Austria (2008)

10. Cattaruzza, D., Absi, N., Feillet, D., González-Feliu, J.: Vehicle routing problems for city logistics. EURO Journal on Transportation and Logistics **6**(1), 51–79 (2015). https://doi.org/10.1007/s13676-014-0074-0

11. Cordeau, J.F., Gendreau, M., Laporte, G., Potvin, J.Y., Semet, F.: A guide to vehicle routing heuristics. Journal of the Operational Research society **53**(5), 512–522 (2002)

12. Cordeau, J.F., Gendreau, M., Laporte, G.: A Tabu Search heuristic for periodic and multi-depot vehicle routing problems. Networks **30**, 105–119 (1997). https://doi.org/10.1002/(SICI)1097-0037(199709)30:23.3.CO;2-N

13. Cordeau, J.F., Laporte, G., Mercier, A.: A unified tabu search heuristic for vehicle routing problems with time windows. Journal of the Operational Research Society **52**, 928–936 (2001)

14. Dantzig, G.B., Ramser, J.H.: The truck dispatching problem. Management science **6**(1), 80–91 (1959)

15. Filgueiras, J., Barbosa, L., Rocha, G., Lopes Cardoso, H., Reis, L.P., Machado, J.P., Oliveira, A.M.: Complaint Analysis and Classification for Economic and Food Safety. In: Proceedings of the Second Workshop on Economics and Natural Language Processing. pp. 51–60. Association for Computational Linguistics, Hong Kong (Nov 2019). 10.18653/v1/D19-5107

16. Flood, M.M.: The traveling-salesman problem. Operations research **4**(1), 61–75 (1956)

17. Hasle, G., Lie, K.A., Quak, E.: Geometric modelling, numerical simulation, and optimization. Springer (2007)

18. Ho, W., Ho, G.T., Ji, P., Lau, H.C.: A hybrid genetic algorithm for the multi-depot vehicle routing problem. Engineering Applications of Artificial Intelligence **21**(4), 548–557 (2008). https://doi.org/10.1016/j.engappai.2007.06.001

19. Kruskal, J.B.: On the Shortest Spanning Subtree of a Graph and the Traveling Salesman Problem. Proceedings of the American Mathematical Society **7**(1), 48 (Feb 1956). https://doi.org/10.2307/2033241

20. Laporte, G.: The vehicle routing problem: An overview of exact and approximate algorithms. European journal of operational research **59**(3), 345–358 (1992)

21. Letchford, A.N., Lysgaard, J., Eglese, R.W.: A branch-and-cut algorithm for the capacitated open vehicle routing problem. Journal of the Operational Research Society **58**(12), 1642–1651 (2007). https://doi.org/10.1057/palgrave.jors.2602345

22. Machado, P., Tavares, J., Pereira, F.B., Costa, E.: Vehicle routing problem: Doing it the evolutionary way. In: Proceedings of the 4th Annual Conference on Genetic and Evolutionary Computation. pp. 690–690. Morgan Kaufmann Publishers Inc. (2002)

23. Montoya-Torres, J.R., López Franco, J., Nieto Isaza, S., Felizzola Jiménez, H., Herazo-Padilla, N.: A literature review on the vehicle routing problem with multiple depots. Computers & Industrial Engineering **79**, 115–129 (2015). https://doi.org/10.1016/j.cie.2014.10.029
24. Ritzinger, U., Puchinger, J., Hartl, R.F.: A survey on dynamic and stochastic vehicle routing problems. International Journal of Production Research **54**(1), 215–231 (2016)
25. Ruiz, E., Soto-Mendoza, V., Barbosa, A.E.R., Reyes, R.: Solving the open vehicle routing problem with capacity and distance constraints with a biased random key genetic algorithm. Computers & Industrial Engineering **133**, 207–219 (2019). https://doi.org/10.1016/j.cie.2019.05.002
26. Toth, P., Vigo, D. (eds.): The Vehicle Routing Problem. Society for Industrial and Applied Mathematics (2002). DOI: 10.1137/1.9780898718515
27. Weise, T., Podlich, A., Gorldt, C.: Solving real-world vehicle routing problems with evolutionary algorithms. In: Natural intelligence for scheduling, planning and packing problems, pp. 29–53. Springer (2009)
28. Zhu, K.Q.: A new genetic algorithm for VRPTW. In: Proceedings of the international conference on artificial intelligence. Citeseer (2000)

Author Index